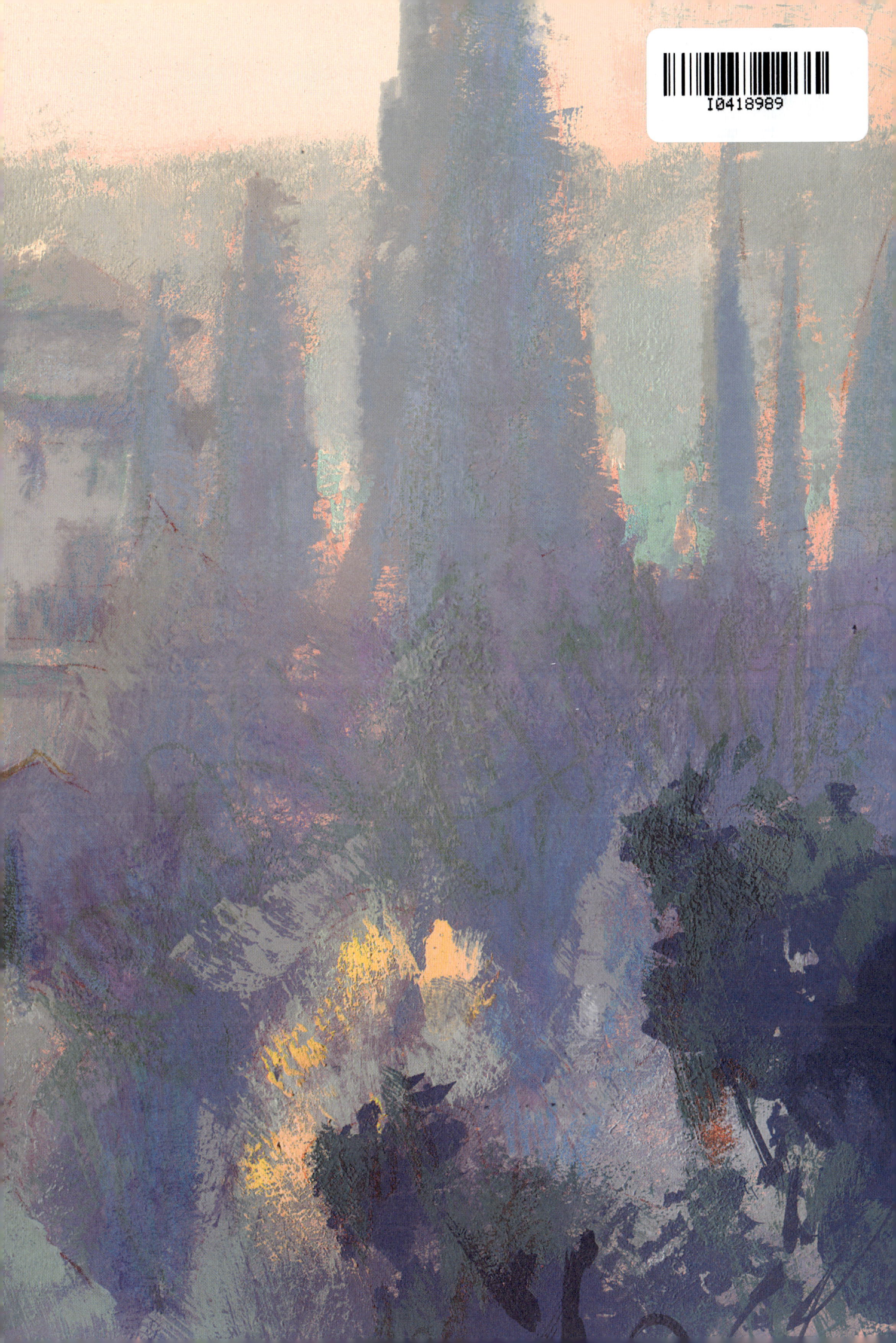

ARTISTS' MASTER SERIES

COLOR & LIGHT

3dtotal Publishing

3dtotalPublishing

Correspondence: publishing@3dtotal.com
Website: store.3dtotal.com

Every effort has been made to ensure the credits and contact information listed are present and correct. In the case of any errors that have occurred, the publisher respectfully directs readers to store.3dtotal.com/pages/information for any updated information and/or corrections.

First published in the United Kingdom, 2021, by 3dtotal Publishing.

Address: 3dtotal.com Ltd,
6 Sansome Street, Worcester,
WR1 1UH, United Kingdom.

Reprinted in 2025 by 3dtotal Publishing

Hard cover ISBN: 978-1-912843-41-1
Printed and bound in China by
C&C Offset Printing Co., Ltd
www.candcprinting.com

Visit store.3dtotal.com for a complete list of available book titles.

Managing Director: Tom Greenway
Studio Manager: Simon Morse
Lead Designer: Fiona Tarbet
Lead Editor: Samantha Rigby
Editor: Marisa Lewis
Designer: Matthew Lewis

Front cover image © Nathan Fowkes
Back cover image © Guweiz
End papers images © Nathan Fowkes

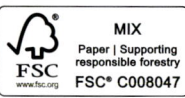

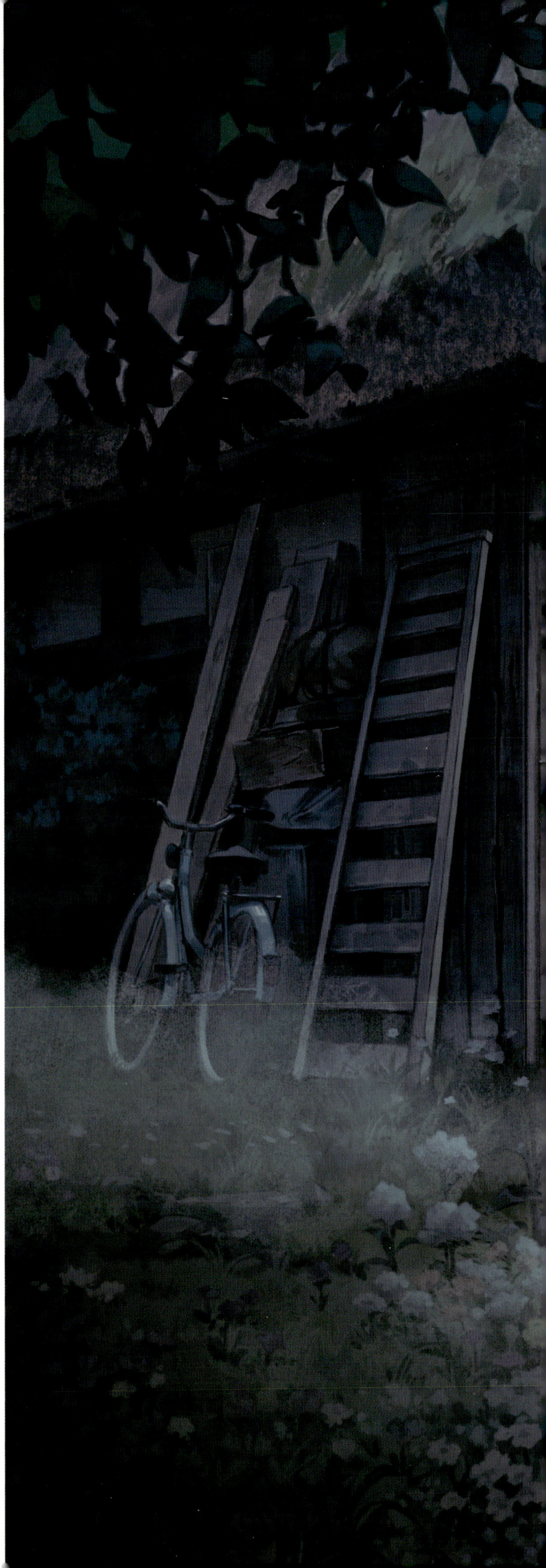

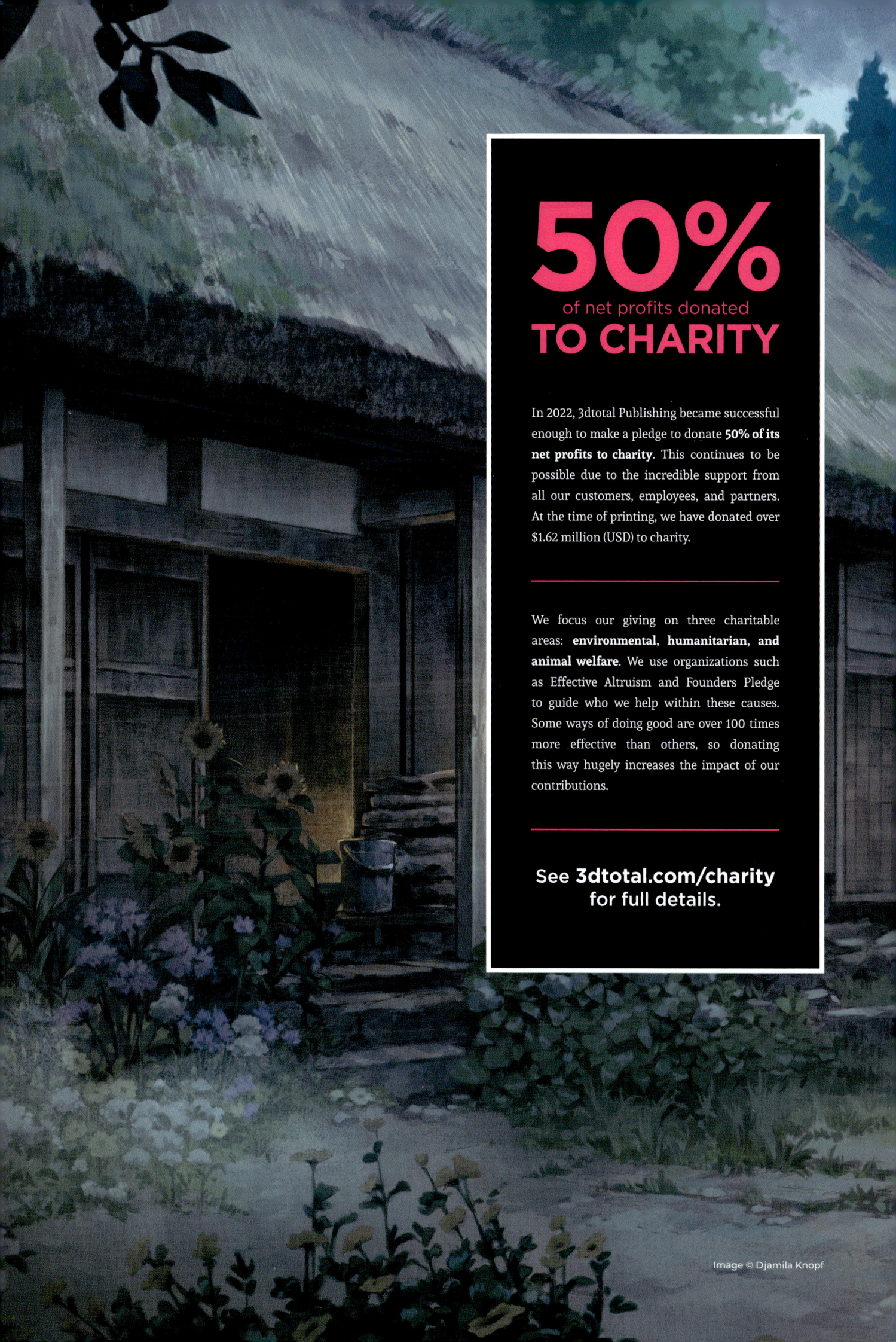

Image © Djamila Knopf

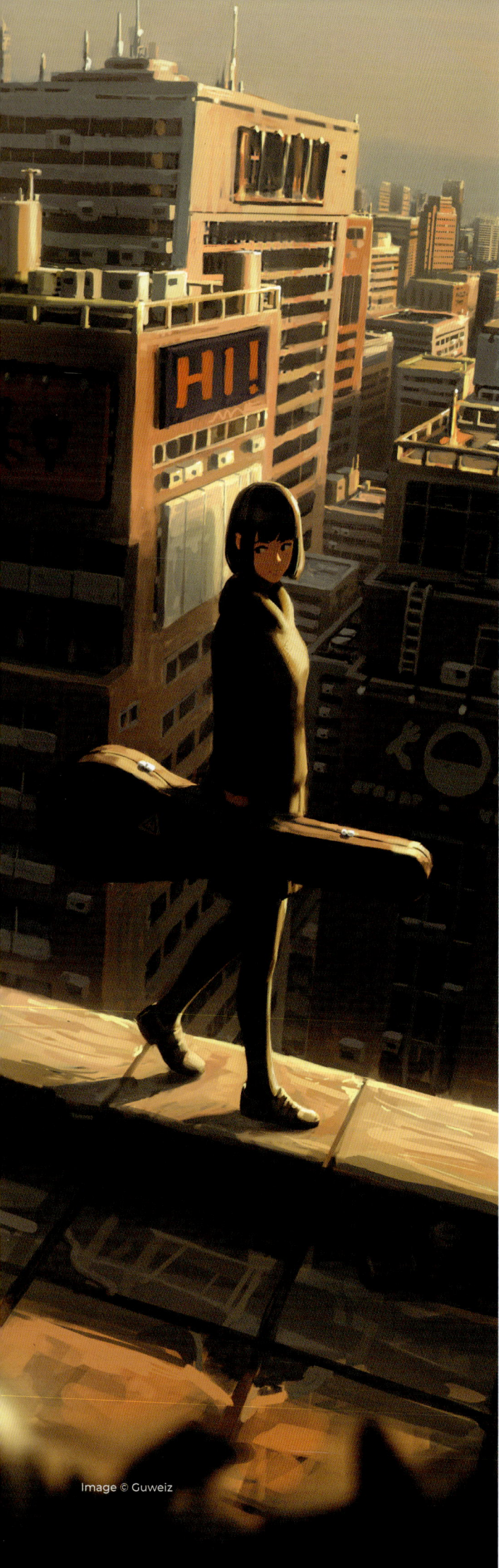

Image © Guweiz

CONTENTS

HOW TO USE THIS BOOK

Welcome to *Artists' Master Series: Color & Light*. The majority of this book can be considered as two main parts: the theory chapters and the tutorials.

The subjects of color and light are closely intertwined, forming two sides of the coin of art. We highly recommend studying Charlie Pickard's **Color** (page 8) and **Light** (page 60) chapters in order to intuitively build up your knowledge of color terminology, color theory, lighting types, and how different types of light and material interact.

These chapters will teach you not only how to understand and control the hue, value, and chroma that create color, but how to create shape, form, and texture with skillful modeling of light and shadow. Studying these chapters closely, and practicing the techniques and exercises inside, will give you the knowledge needed to improve your digital or traditional renditions of any subject.

The three **tutorial** chapters that follow, by Djamila Knopf (page 208), Guweiz (page 260), and Nathan Fowkes (page 302), can be treated as completely standalone projects, but will benefit from the knowledge and terminology set up earlier in the book. Each tutorial is by an artist with a different style and creative background, each tackling scenes with very different focuses and atmospheres. Follow along with these to see how three unique professionals apply their knowledge of color and light in practice.

Finally, the **Gallery** (page 336) walks you through the portfolios of our three tutorial artists and seven inspiring guests, each sharing some insights into the use of color and lighting in their personal images.

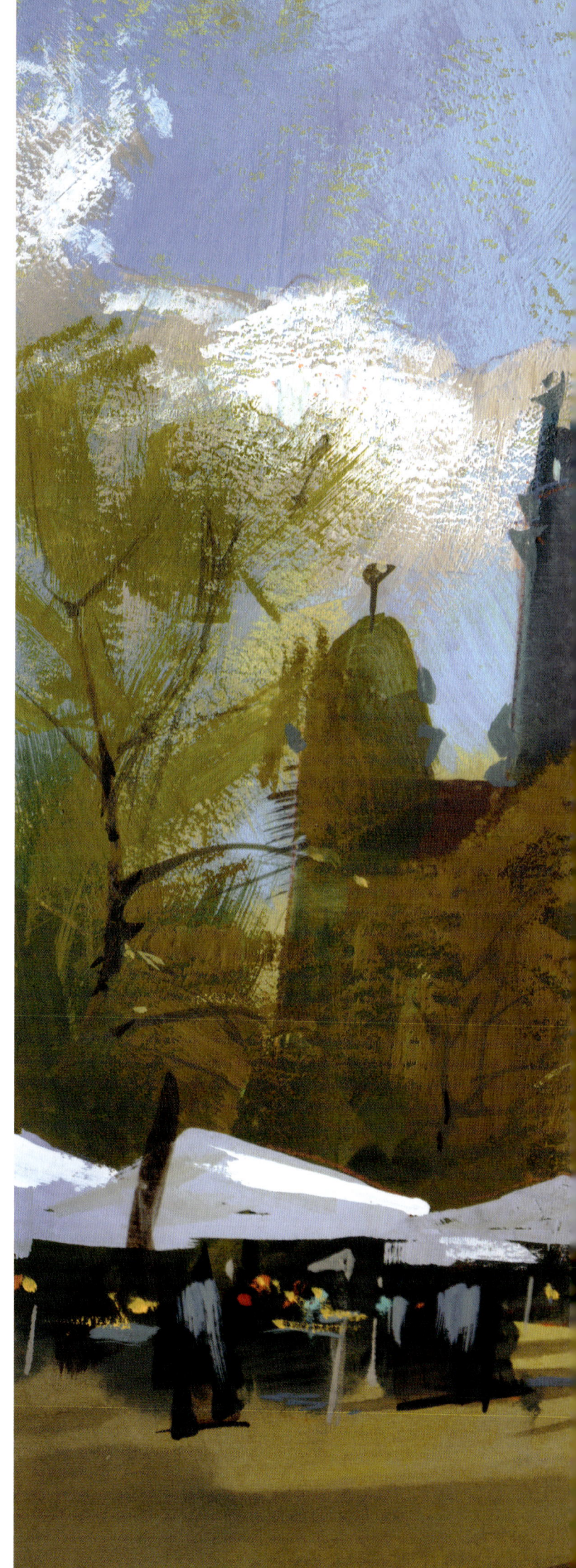

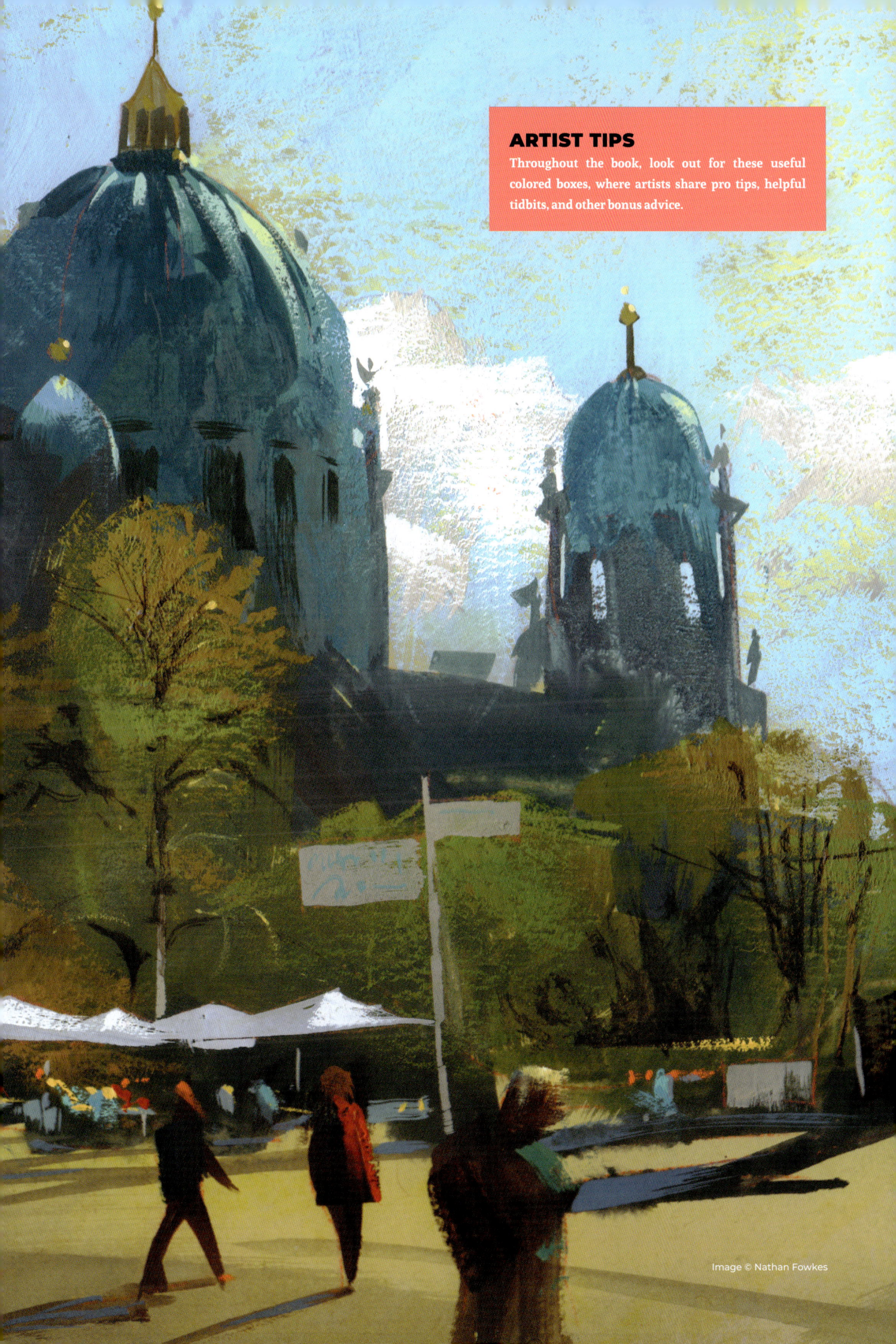

Image © Nathan Fowkes

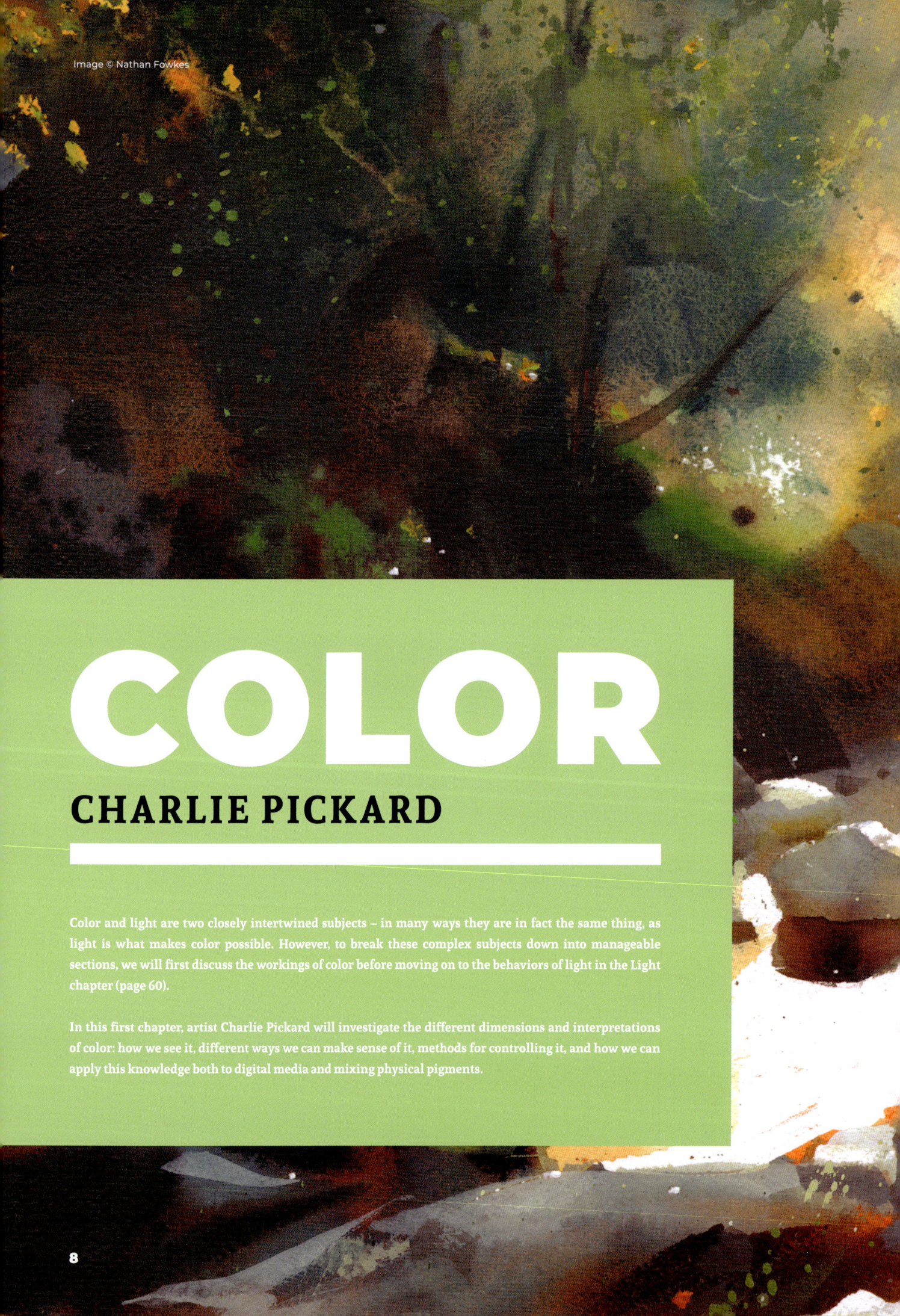

Image © Nathan Fowkes

COLOR

CHARLIE PICKARD

Color and light are two closely intertwined subjects – in many ways they are in fact the same thing, as light is what makes color possible. However, to break these complex subjects down into manageable sections, we will first discuss the workings of color before moving on to the behaviors of light in the Light chapter (page 60).

In this first chapter, artist Charlie Pickard will investigate the different dimensions and interpretations of color: how we see it, different ways we can make sense of it, methods for controlling it, and how we can apply this knowledge both to digital media and mixing physical pigments.

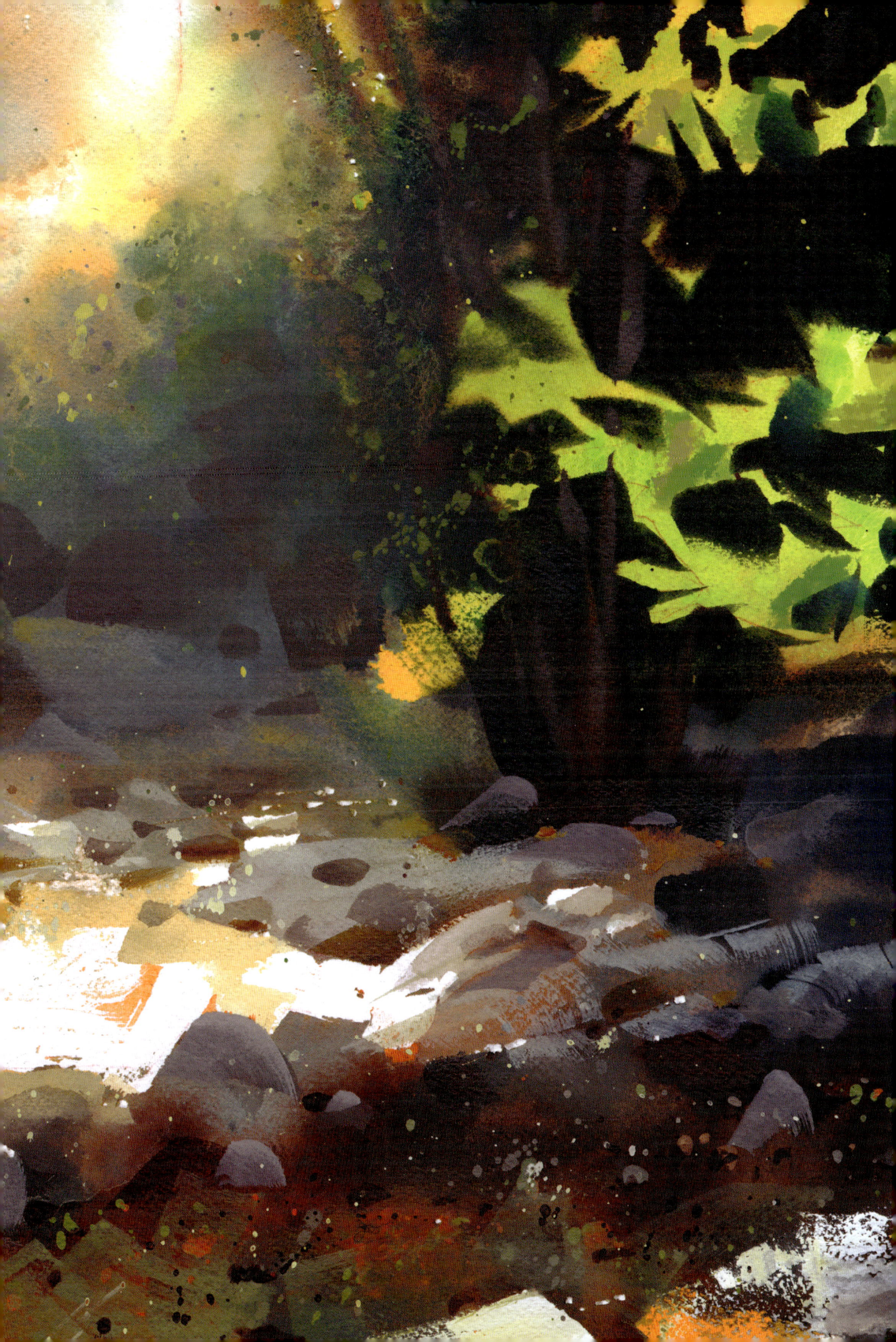

VISION IS SUBJECTIVE

We all start out with the notion that our vision is objective – that the way we see things is fundamentally how they are. We imagine that our eyes collect visual facts that we only need to transfer to our canvas. But this is fundamentally not true. Vision, at all levels, is subjective by nature.

We don't perceive things "as they are" but rather "as they are *compared to their surroundings*." All that our eye can perceive is raw data – patches of light – and anything that we actually understand about what we see takes place in the brain. We learned how to interpret this data as children, so don't remember that it didn't always make sense. Many things that we understand about what we see are not present in the raw data our eyes receive.

You know that a pillow is soft and a wall is hard without touching them, but there is nothing in the light given off by those objects that tells you this. It is learned through experience in your youth – for example, hitting something hard and comforting yourself with something soft.

We know that distant mountains are still large because our brains compare them to smaller things in the environment, correct for the distance, and arrive at an understanding of their relative size **(01)**. Things are not objectively large, small, bright, or dark – they become so when our brain makes comparisons. Everything we observe or communicate to our viewer is based on relationships and past experiences.

You might understandably be skeptical. You may feel that your eyes have never failed you in navigating the world. How could they be subjective?

The illusion on the right might help convince you **(02)**. It might be hard to believe, but

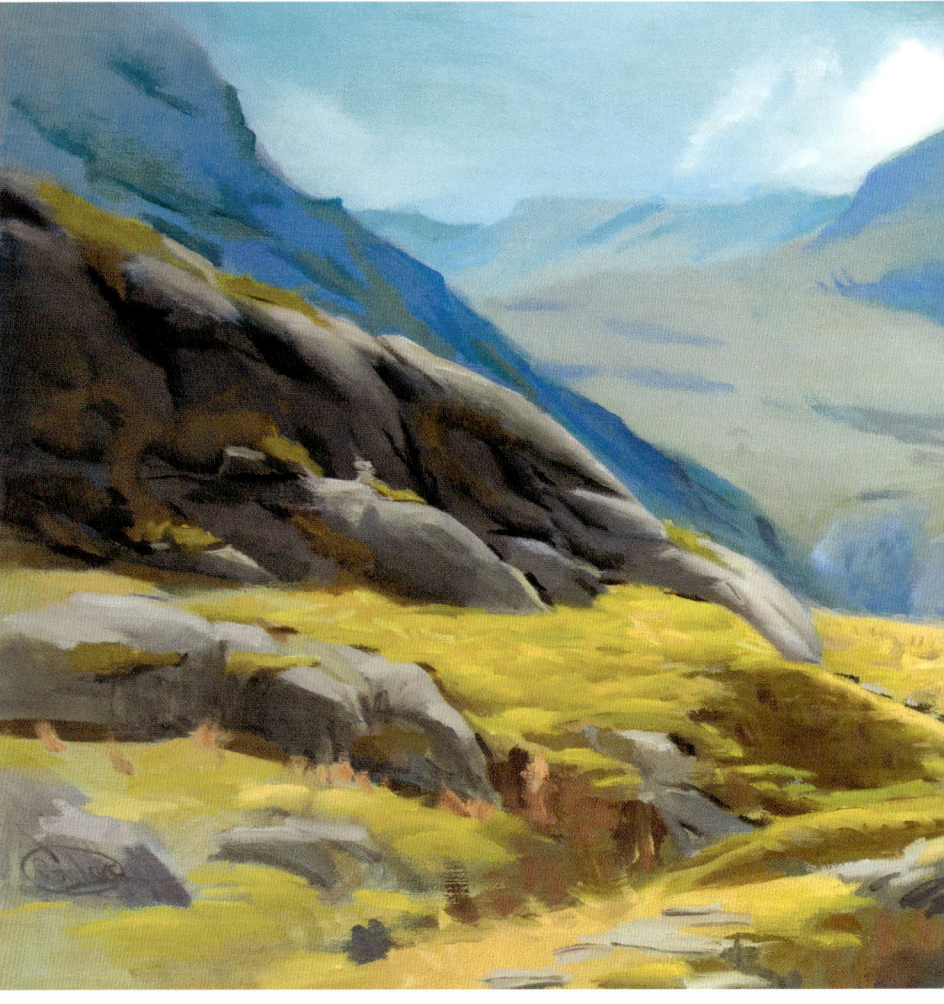

01 The distant mountains are objectively the same height as the trees closer to us, but we do not perceive them that way.

both blue dots are exactly the same size. Get a ruler and check if you don't believe it! One only appears larger by virtue of being surrounded by smaller dots. This illusion is obviously more applicable to shape than color, but I chose it because shape is an area we often feel is the most objective. This chapter will explore many similar illusions to show the ways that different relationships affect our perception.

As artists, we are visual communicators. We often work within limited means and strive to create grand effects. Our goal is not to reproduce exactly what we see, as this is often impossible and only gives us the most superficial results. We should aim to heighten what we care about in the subject, and understanding the subjectivity of our vision can help us use it to our advantage for a greater clarity of purpose in our work.

But if everything is subjective, how do we organize ourselves and ground our artwork? There are many ways – each artwork sets its own rules and can only be judged against those. You are the creator and you can make the artwork obey any rules you wish. It must, however, be consistent in its own rules in order for the viewer to understand it.

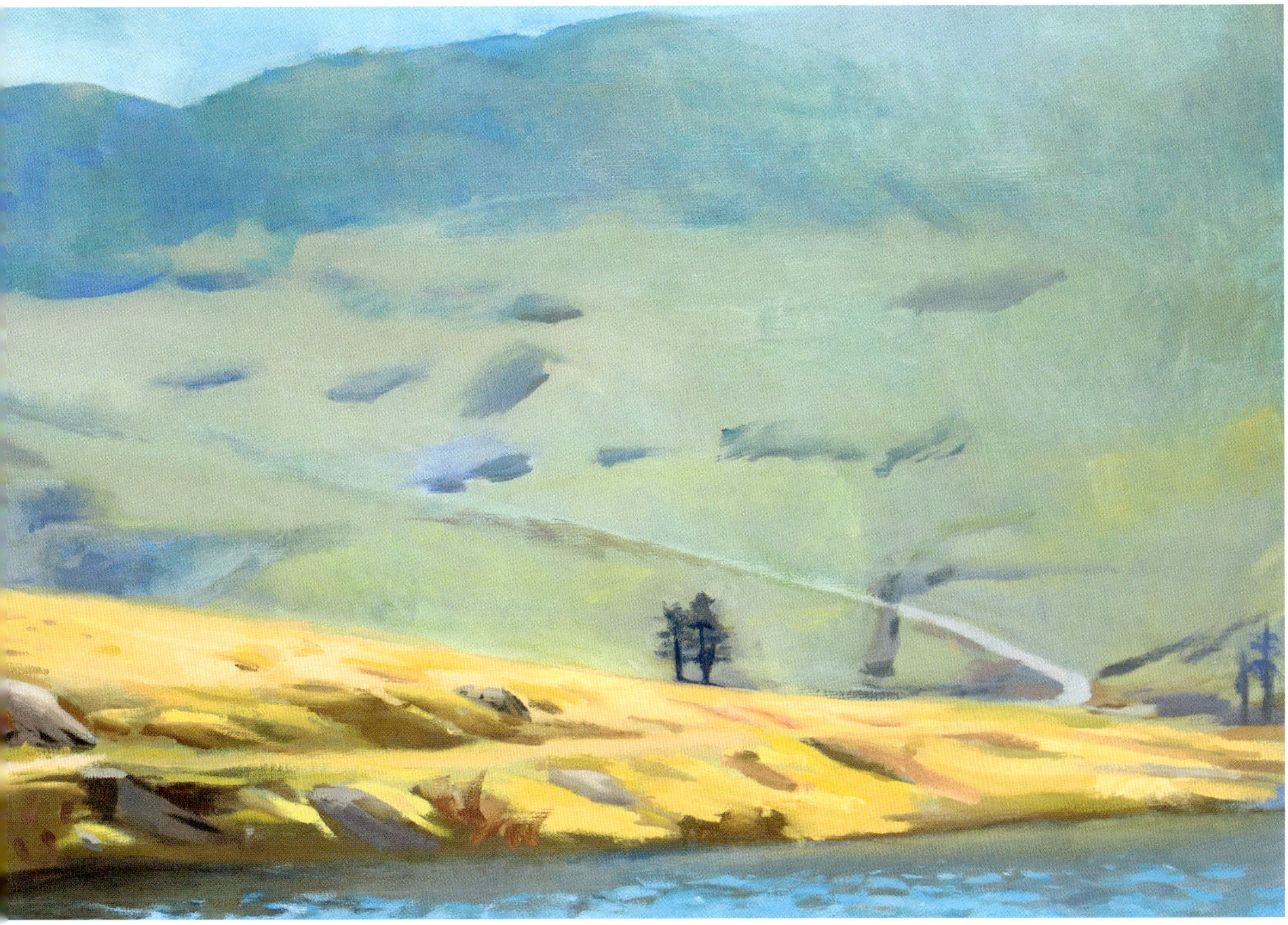

We all experience the same physical world with the same physical rules, so studying how light and color work in reality will ground our art for the viewer. This mindset will form the basis of our approach to studying color and light in this book. First, however, we must discuss one idea that is common to every viewer and artist: the idea of contrast and harmony.

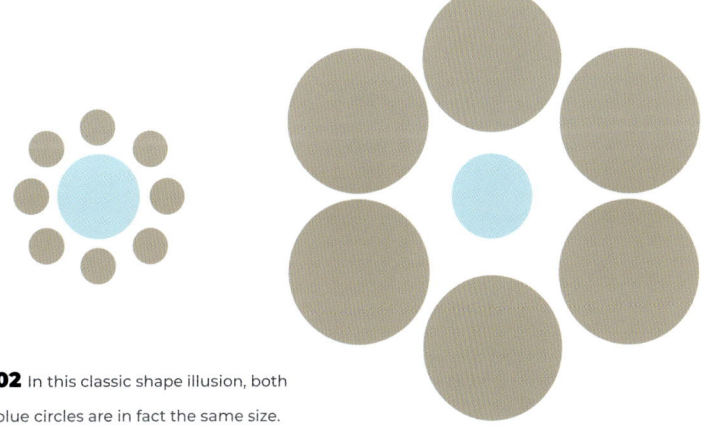

02 In this classic shape illusion, both blue circles are in fact the same size.

CONTRAST AND HARMONY

This dichotomy goes by many names – unity and variety, order and chaos – but they all refer to harmonizing the elements that are similar and contrasting the elements that are different. To clarify this concept, here's a series of simple abstractions (03).

A. This gray has perfect harmony. It is simple, ordered, and even boring, with no variation to look at.

B. Changing values adds contrast. Splitting gray into black and white is a common beginner's approach to creating contrast.

C. Varying the sizes of each value increases contrast further.

D. Breaking up the two-shape setup creates even more contrast.

E, F, G. Contrast can be increased infinitely: changing the angles and types of shapes, adding colors, and so on.

There is a fundamental balancing act here – perfectly harmonious elements are ordered but boring to our eye, while perfectly contrasting elements are more interesting but chaotic and difficult to look at. Contrast is the fundamental driver of interest and is a powerful tool to direct the viewer's eye through an artwork. As we move through the rest of this book, keep these concepts in mind for every element: Do they harmonize or contrast?

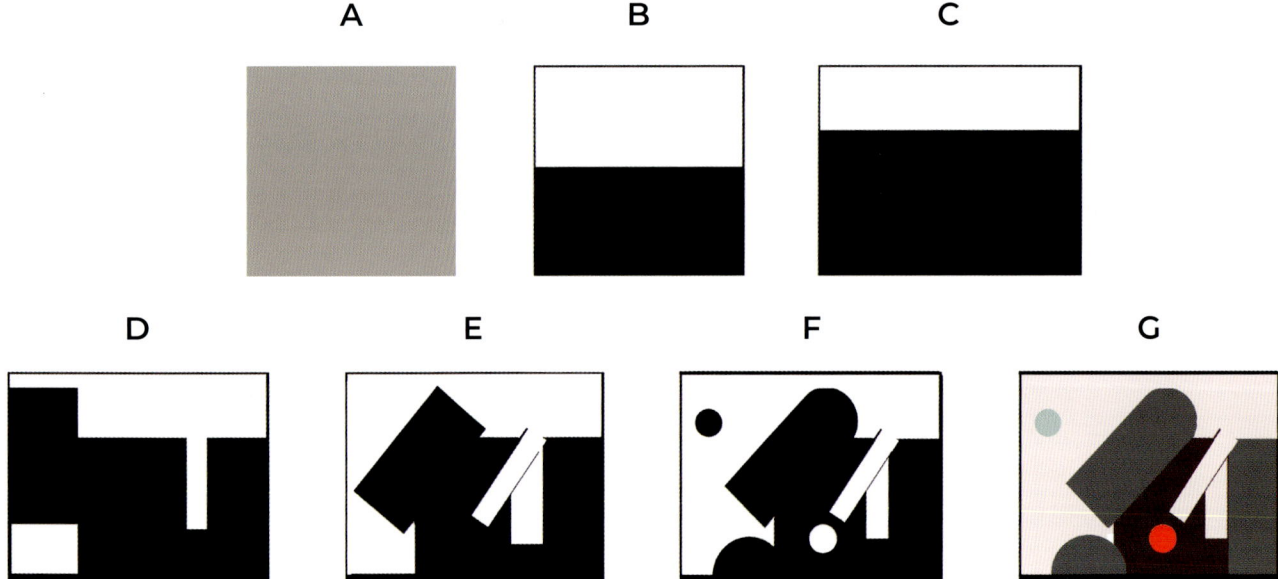

03 Examples of creating contrast with shapes and proportions of value.

CONTRAST AND HARMONY IDEAS

Exploring ways to balance contrast and harmony is a lifelong journey, forming the core of how we create work, consciously or not. The more we can be aware of this, the more thoughtfully and deliberately we can explore.

One great habit is to keep a list in your sketchbook of every way you can think to contrast and harmonize an artwork. The more unique ways you can come up with, the more unique your aesthetic will become.

MUNSELL COLOR THEORY

The fascinating, complex world of color can be overwhelming to a newcomer. Even the simple act of mixing two colors can seem an insurmountable challenge. Before we embark on this journey, it helps to equip ourselves with clear, precise language.

The most helpful guide to use is the system created by the nineteenth-century artist and color theorist Albert Henry Munsell. Munsell conceptualized color as a physical shape consisting of three dimensions: hue, value, and chroma **(04)**.

Hue is the dimension the layman thinks of as "color." It is essentially the position of the color on a rainbow or color spectrum – for example, whether it's red or green.

Value is a dimension familiar to artists. It is essentially a color's brightness or darkness level, measured from black to white.

Chroma is the dimension most likely to be a new concept to beginners. It is a color's intensity or purity level, measured from a neutral gray.

MUNSELL'S COLOR TREE

Munsell visualized these three dimensions together as a great "tree of color" with its central trunk being ten steps of value from black to white. This trunk expands out in every direction in "branches" of hue (ten steps) and chroma (fourteen steps).

The tree makes it possible to identify individual colors numerically by their position on the trunk and branches **(05a–c)**.

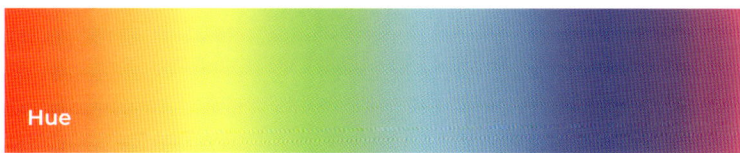

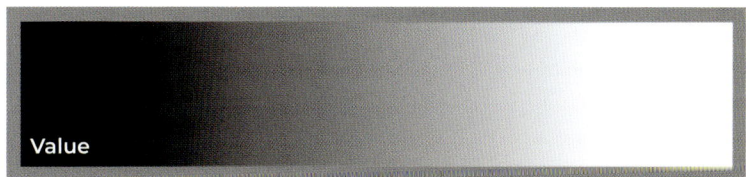

04 Munsell's three dimensions of color: hue, value, and chroma.

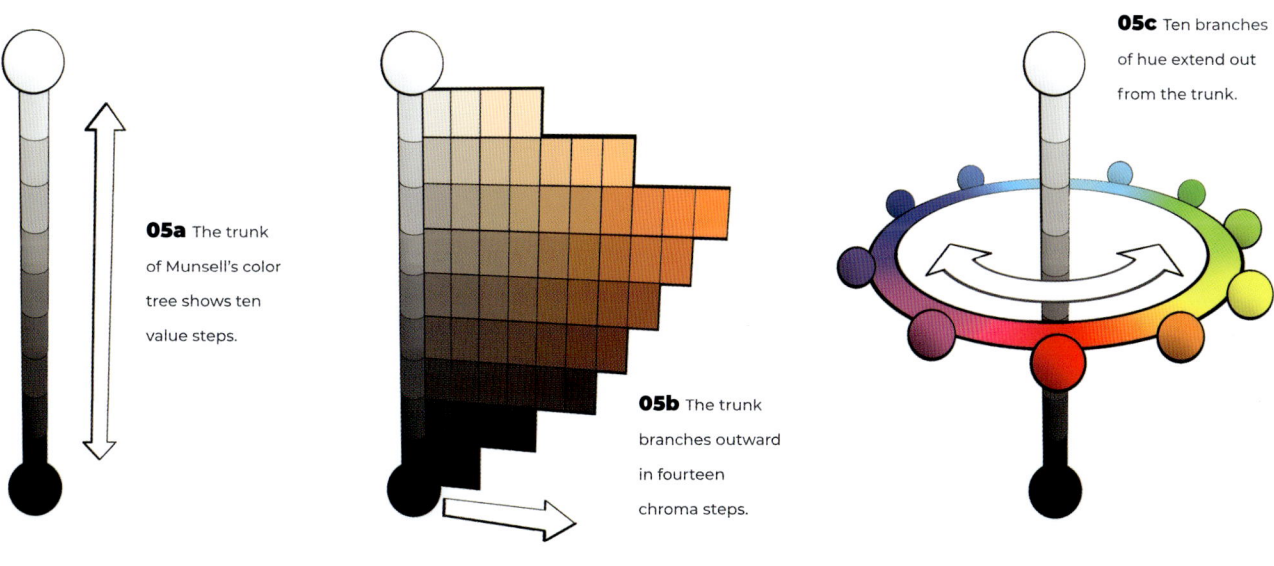

05a The trunk of Munsell's color tree shows ten value steps.

05b The trunk branches outward in fourteen chroma steps.

05c Ten branches of hue extend out from the trunk.

13

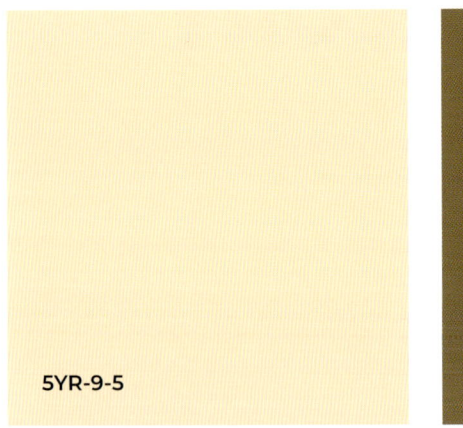

5YR-9-5

5YR-4-8

06 Using the Munsell system to notate light and dark skin tones.

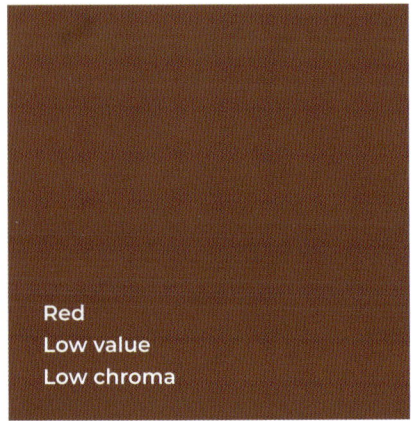

Red
Low value
Low chroma

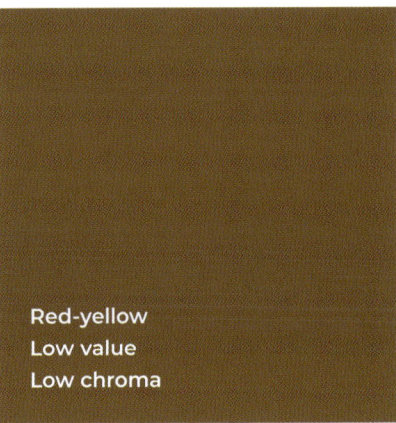

Red-yellow
Low value
Low chroma

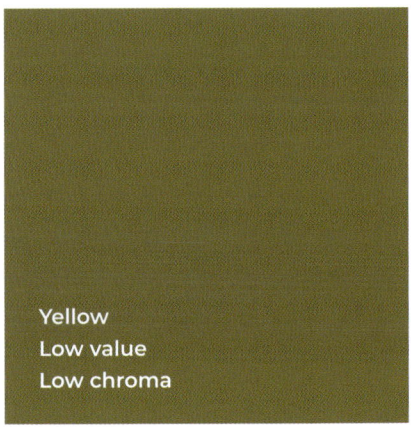

Yellow
Low value
Low chroma

07 See if you can notate these colors yourself using Munsell's system.

MUNSELL COLOR NOTATION

Munsell conceived of five fundamental hues: yellow, red, green, blue, and purple. Each of these colors has ten steps in between. When notated, the colors would be indicated in this order: hue, then value, then chroma.

For example, a light skin tone might be notated as 5YR-9-5, meaning it's directly between red and yellow (the fifth step between them), is extremely high in value (ninth step), and is low in chroma (fifth step). A darker skin tone might be notated as 5YR-4-8, indicating that it's also a middle red-yellow, while being lower in value (fourth step), and higher chroma (eighth step) **(06)**.

When it comes to describing color, there is a lot of vague language in everyday use. Paint manufacturers may call a color "sea-foam green" or "sky blue," but these terms can mean different things to different people. A system such as Munsell's enables us to be highly specific and avoid vagueness when describing what we see.

For example, the three colors in **07** are quite different, but could all reasonably be described as "brown." Comparing them, we can clearly see that such language falls short! Through the lens of Munsell's color tree, however, we can see that while they are all low in value and chroma, they vary hugely in hue.

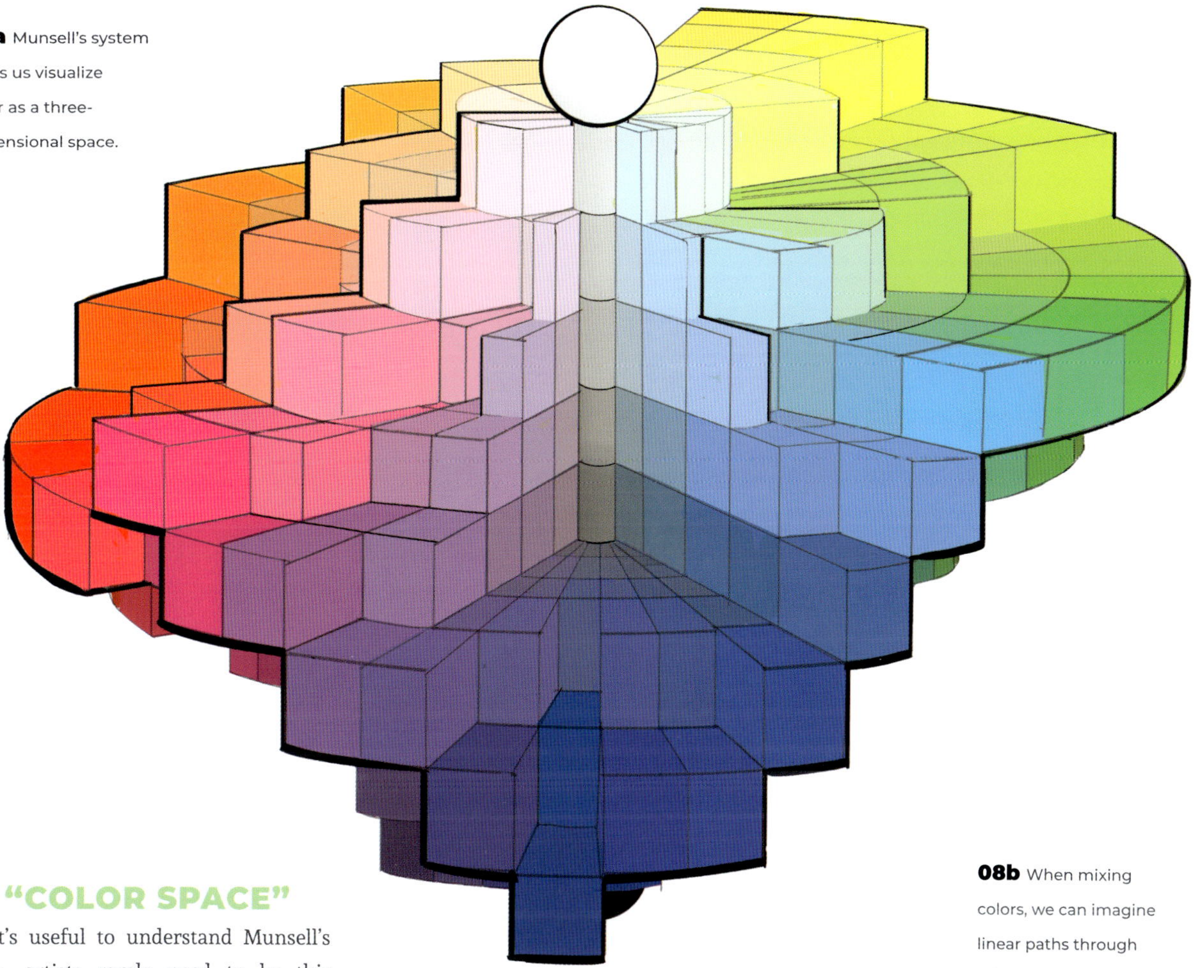

08a Munsell's system helps us visualize color as a three-dimensional space.

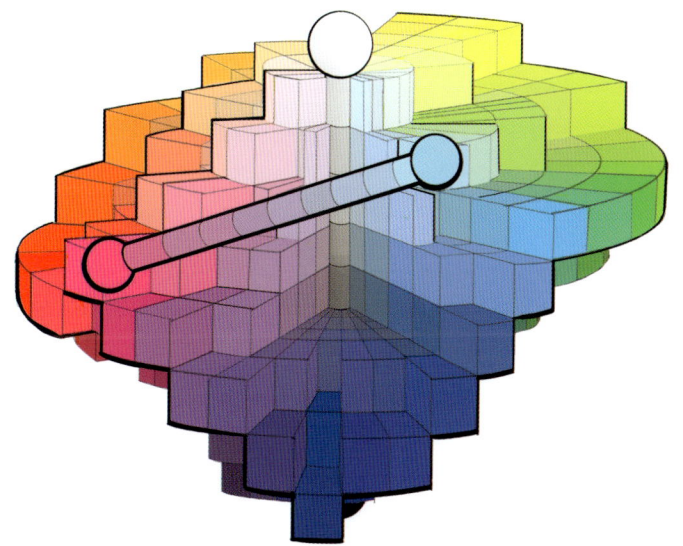

THE "COLOR SPACE"

While it's useful to understand Munsell's notation, artists rarely need to be this specific. This level of accuracy might be necessary in other design fields, such as printing, but the core concepts suffice for us.

Most importantly, Munsell's system enables us to think of each color as a point in three-dimensional space **(08a–b)**. For traditional artists, this space would be our physical pigments. For digital artists, the concept is incredibly easy to grasp, as it's built into most graphics programs in the form of "Hue/Saturation/Brightness" sliders.

When we mix our colors, we can think of them traveling in a straight line through this space, giving us an easy way to predict the path of color mixtures. This may seem complex at first, but it will quickly become intuitive as you practice using it.

08b When mixing colors, we can imagine linear paths through this color space.

COLOR HIERARCHY

The different qualities of color, for our artistic purposes, are not created equally – there is a hierarchy of importance that is essential for our work. Having this hierarchy of importance clear in our heads gives us a useful structure when planning our study and creating art, and will always be relevant to any artwork we create (09).

VALUE

Value is at the top of this hierarchy. It is the first and most important consideration for every artwork. The extent of this can be seen below (10). With the values isolated, only a small amount of information is lost, but when we remove the value information, the image almost entirely breaks.

The parts of our visual system that evolved to interpret value (the rod cells, which we'll explore later on page 30) are actually the oldest, and all of our ideas of form arise from this part of our vision.

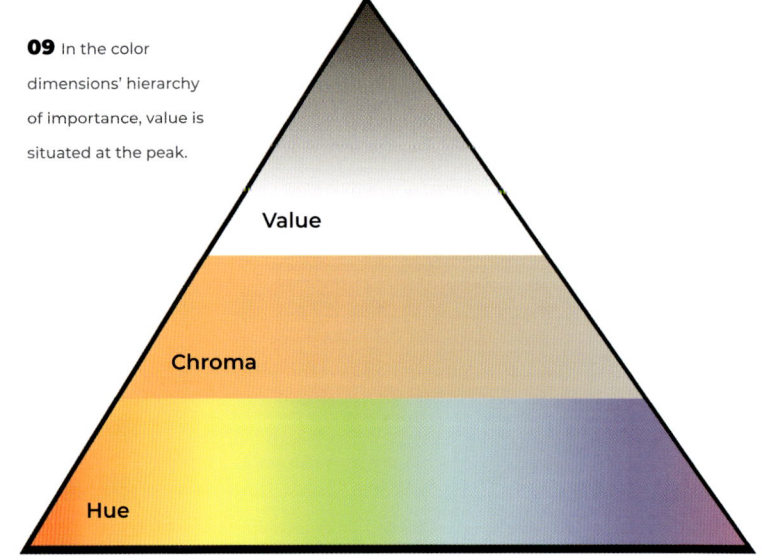

09 In the color dimensions' hierarchy of importance, value is situated at the peak.

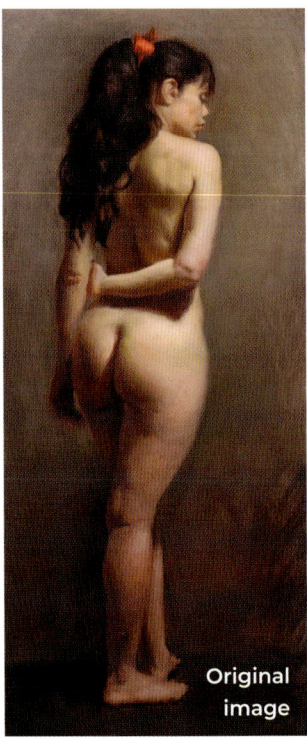

Original image

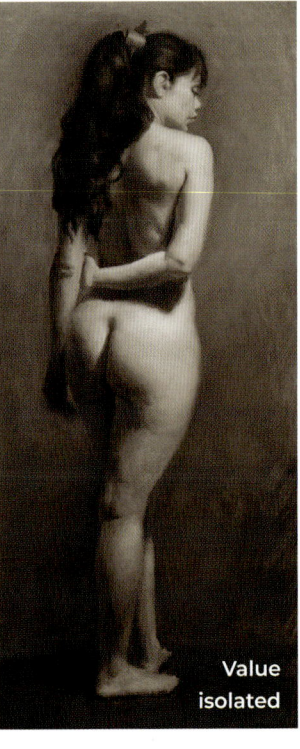

Value isolated

Hue and chroma isolated

10 Without value, the forms of an image become impossible to interpret.

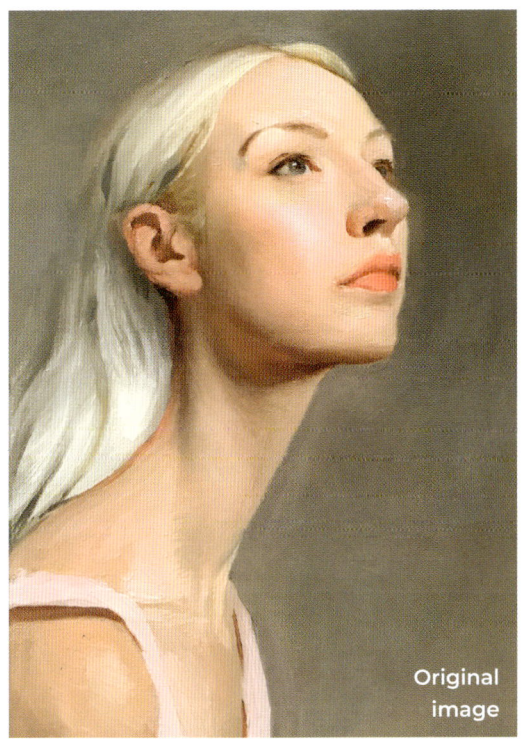

Original image

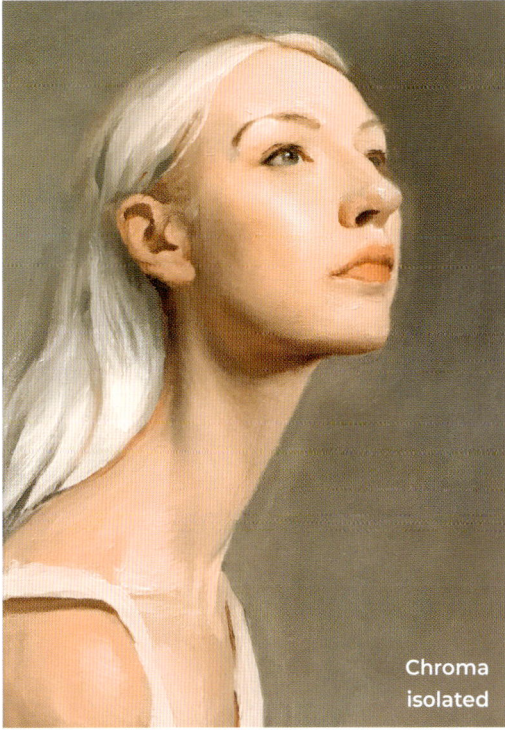

Chroma isolated

11 Even with the hue range heavily limited, and subtle hue changes removed, the value and chroma remain completely readable.

CHROMA

Chroma is next in the hierarchy and is the quality most undervalued by students. It is more responsible for our experience of color than we realize. If we purposely limit our image to one hue, limiting it to only chromatic relationships, a surprising amount of color is retained **(11)**. We lose some of the subtler shifts in the skin and hair, but the color is still fully believable.

HUE

Hue is lowest in importance, which may be surprising to many students. It is often overvalued for its impact on the emotive experience that artwork gives us, but when our pure goal is representing a subject, it's largely unimportant. If the previous two qualities are properly understood in our work, the hues are more of an expressive choice than a requirement for realism. The strawberries in image **12** are represented entirely without their natural red hue, having been wildly adjusted to cyan, but our eye still manages to read them as red! Hues are simply the spice and flavor of the image.

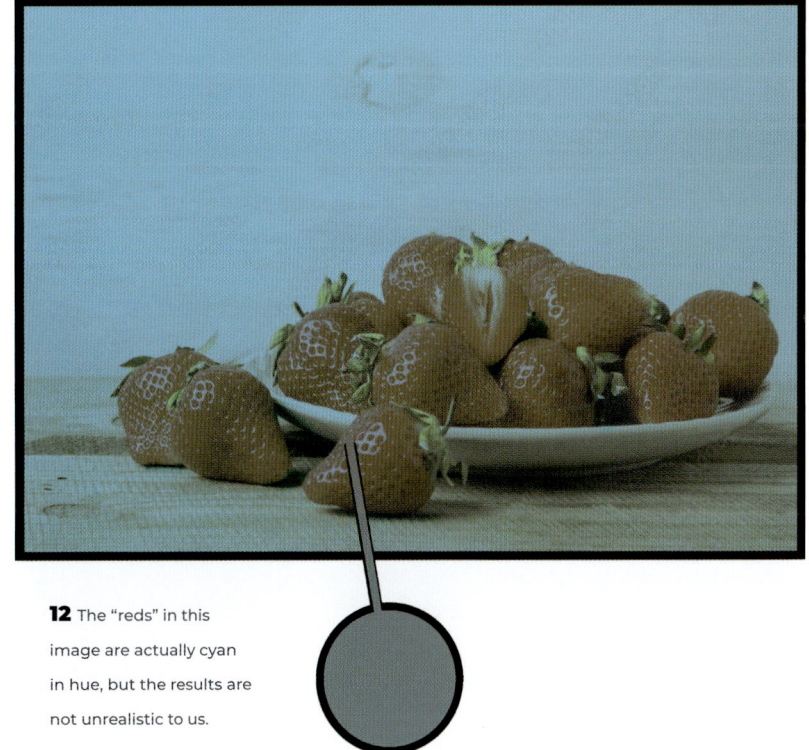

12 The "reds" in this image are actually cyan in hue, but the results are not unrealistic to us.

Image 12 photo © Svetlana Lukienko (via Adobe Stock)

LIMITED PALETTES

A fantastic way to introduce ourselves to color, in a manner that reinforces the color hierarchy, is through limited palettes. There are as many ways to limit our palette as there are ways to express ourselves, and this approach can be an important tool for exploring your personal artistic expression. Here are three common, academic approaches that can help reinforce this idea of color hierarchy.

Grisaille. Grisaille (gray) or monochrome palettes are often the first palettes used to introduce students to working with paint and color in academic settings. These types of paintings allow us to fully isolate value as a color quality and focus on how to use it to communicate form. These would traditionally be painted with one color plus white – in this example, Titanium White and Mars Black **(13)**. Digital artists can create monochrome images by limiting themselves to only adjusting the Value slider.

Limited temperature. Palettes limited by temperature can be a fantastic introduction to color. Here we limit ourselves to only the chroma relationships of color, giving us an excellent way to fully understand this color quality **(14)**. Traditional artists would paint these with one color mixed with black and white to neutralize it – in this case, Titanium White, Ivory Black, and Cadmium Orange. With digital software, we can limit ourselves to only adjusting the Value and Saturation sliders.

Limited hue. Limited-hue palettes are a great way to introduce ourselves to a selection of hues that is easier to control. We can use any hue range we like, but the most popular is the Zorn palette **(15)**, named after the Swedish painter Anders Zorn, which consists of red, yellow, and orange hues. These would use two colors of different hues, with black and white to neutralize them – in this case, Titanium White, Cadmium Red, Yellow Ochre, and Ivory Black. Working digitally, we can limit hues by picking the two we want to use and only adjusting the Value and Saturation sliders.

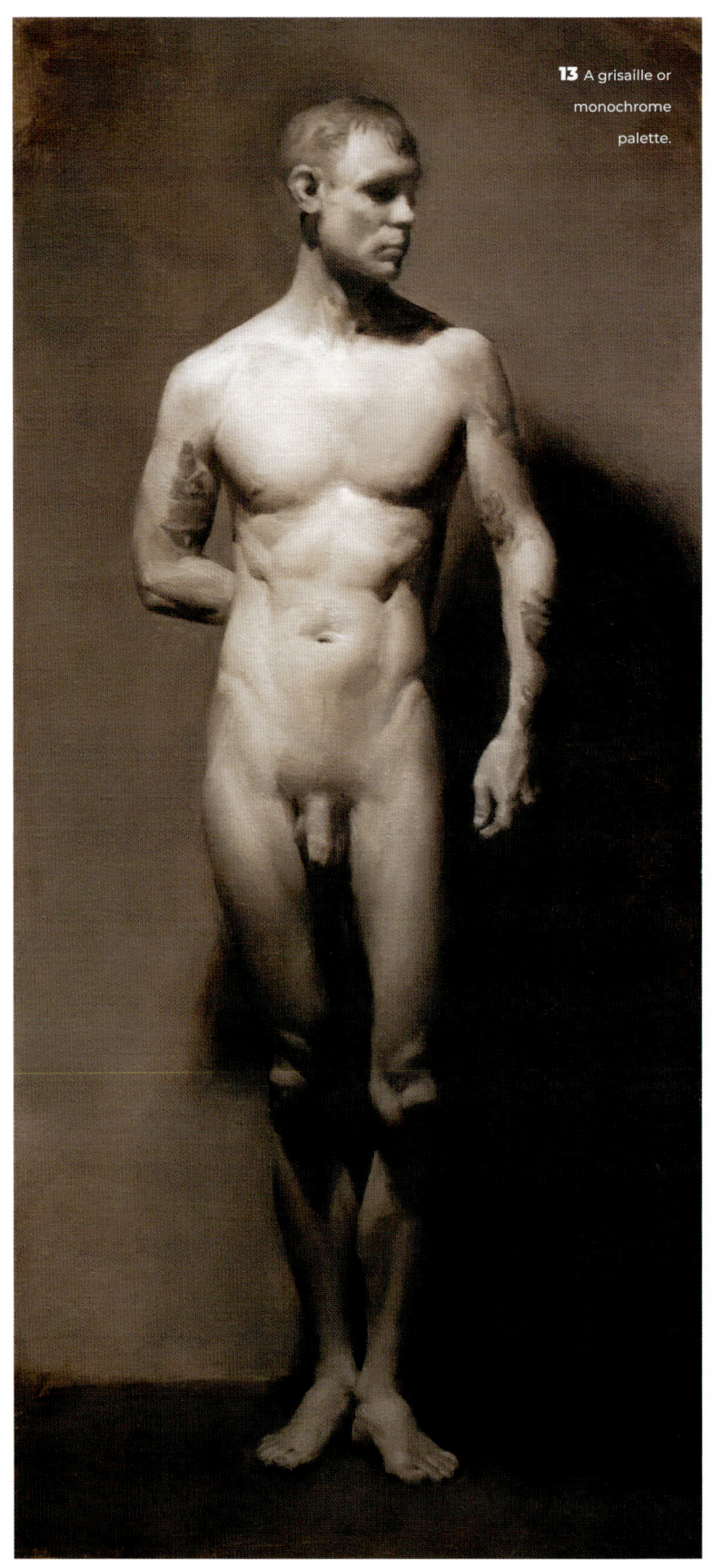

13 A grisaille or monochrome palette.

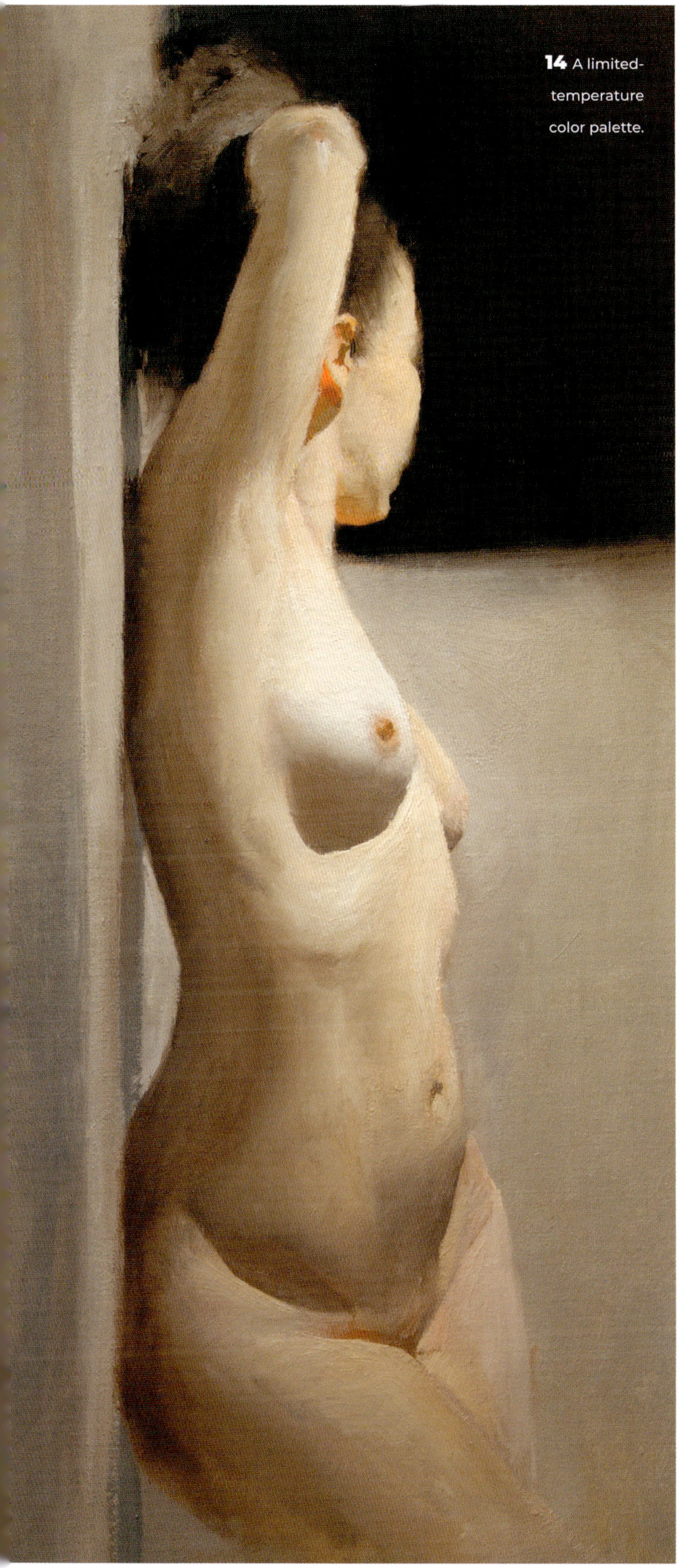

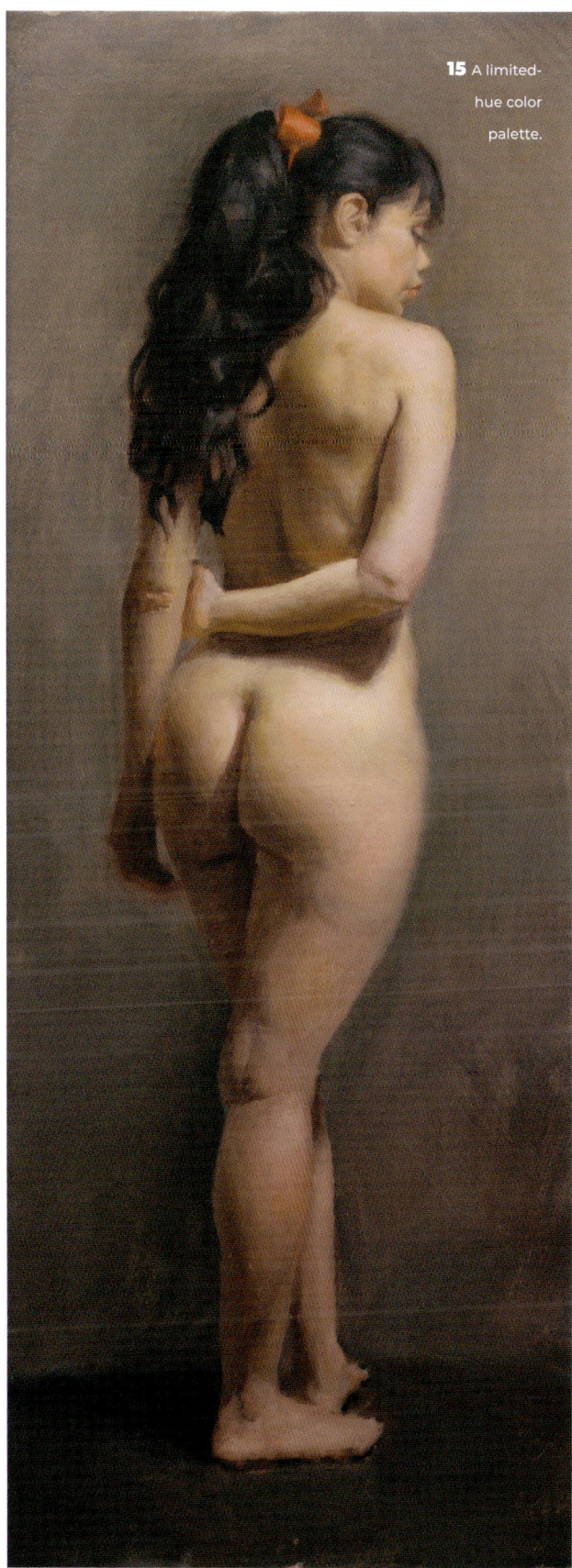

14 A limited-temperature color palette.

15 A limited-hue color palette.

COLOR CONSTANCY, PART 1: VALUE

As we begin to look at value, I first want to reinforce that vision is subjective by taking a quick look at another illusion. On the right is a famous checkerboard pattern illusion, first devised by the neuroscientist Edward Adelson, that will give us some insight here.

The two selected squares on the checkerboard pattern, under different lighting, are both represented using *exactly the same value* **(16)**. You might wonder how this can be possible, as they appear so different! It is due to an effect called "color constancy."

This effect occurs because our brains are strongly adapted to perceive an object as having the same color despite the many different lighting situations that we might encounter throughout the day. Thus a white ball always appears white, whether seen in a dim indoor light, bright sunlight, or even in shadow. If our brains could not do this, you can only imagine how disorienting the world would be – objects would be constantly changing color in front of us!

However, while this correction works extremely well for us in our everyday lives, it wreaks havoc on our ability to judge and paint values accurately. We need to keep it in mind when we work and find solutions for dealing with it in our art.

We can understand the basic mechanics behind Adelson's illusion if we look at these simpler abstractions **(17)**. Again, each smaller square is exactly the same value. As the background square surrounding this value gets darker, each center square takes on the appearance of a brighter value. This leads us to an important truth: Colors will take on some of the value opposing their surroundings.

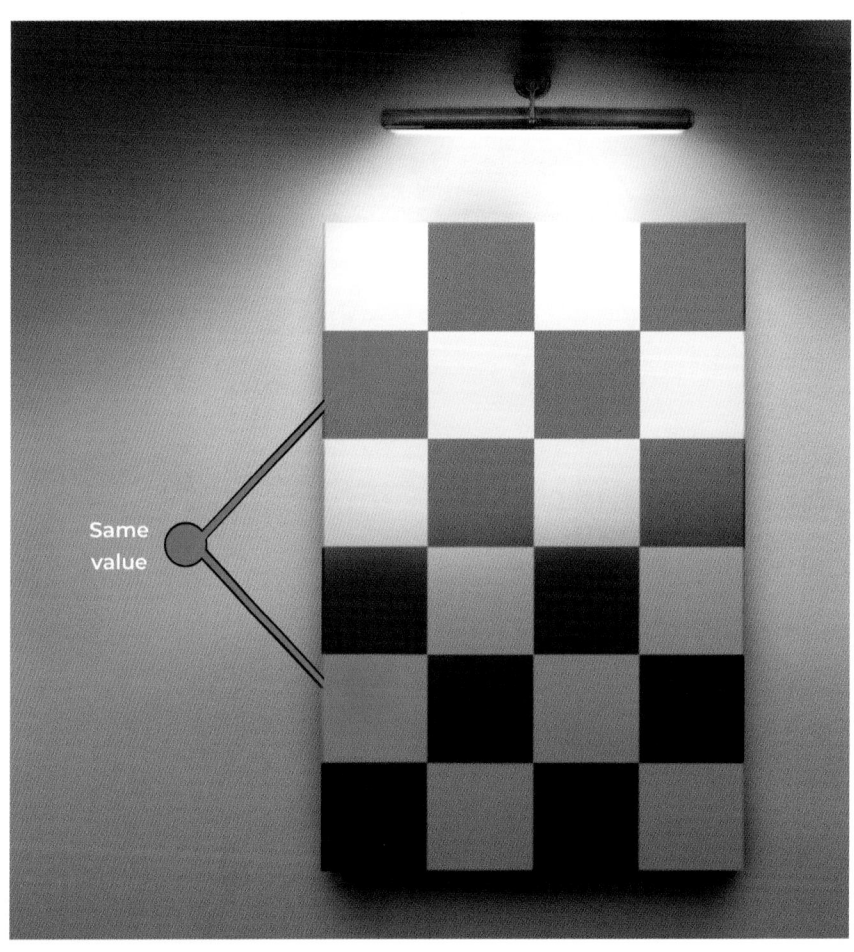

16 These two squares are the same value, but our eyes perceive them differently.

Since the dark square in the checkerboard pattern above is surrounded by bright squares, it appears darker to our eyes. Since the light square is surrounded by dark squares, it appears brighter. In effect, contrast between two values is exaggerated when they sit side by side.

This is not only limited to value, but occurs for every dimension of color that we have discussed, and we will examine the effects of this later.

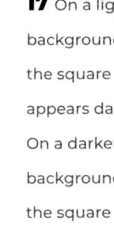
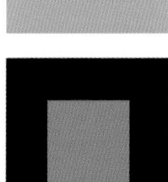

17 On a lighter background, the square appears darker. On a darker background, the square appears lighter.

VALUE GROUPING

How can we depict values if we don't see them properly and can't trust our vision? This is a problem that anyone who has tried to paint has experienced first-hand. However, while our eyes are not good at making objective statements about value, they are extremely good at working out subtle distinctions in their proper context.

Our first goal, whenever we work, should be to establish the large value context of our work as soon as possible. The secret to doing this lies in simplifying our approach. Instead of focusing on depicting every different value presented to us in nature, it's helpful to deliberately restrict ourselves to only three: lights, midtones, and darks **(18)**.

In images **19a–b**, you can see how much can be communicated with just these simple values. This idea is called "value grouping" and it presents us with a powerful utility for effective communication. If you are ever confused by which group to put a value in, try squinting to simplify your vision.

This stage is rarely where a painting will finish, though some artists do finish here. However, you can see that by the time we expand the range to five values, we have all of the information we need. Beyond that, all of the modeling present in the final painting can just be viewed as transitions between these broader value groups.

Once these groups have been established, it's vital to keep them absolutely separate. We can subtly vary the values within them to add modeling, but none of the values in the highlights can ever drop to the values of the midtones, and so on. This results in "overmodeling," which is an extremely common mistake in student work and makes images confusing to look at **(20)**.

 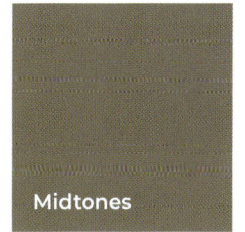 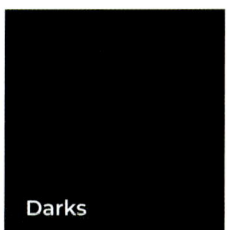

Lights | Midtones | Darks

18 It is helpful to group values into these three categories.

Start with three values | Expand to five values – more are not needed

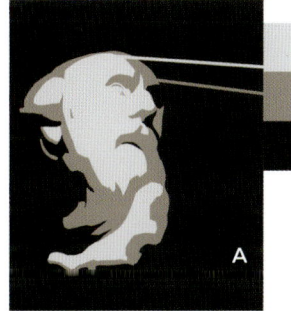 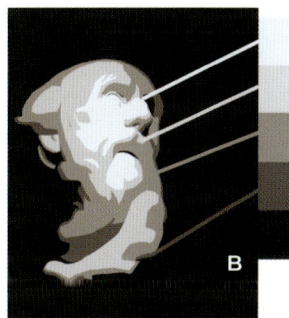

A | B

19a–b Start with three values and build up the transition between them.

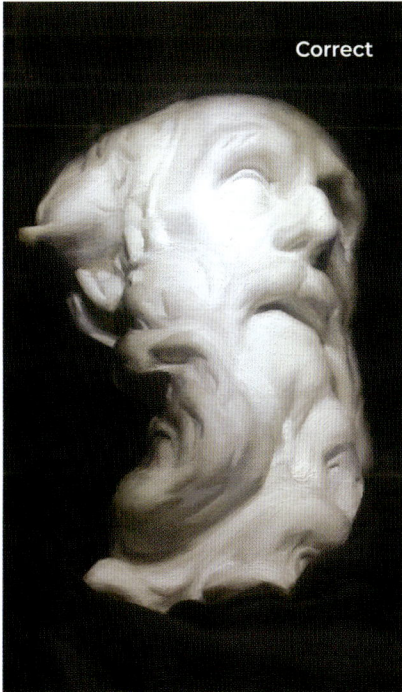 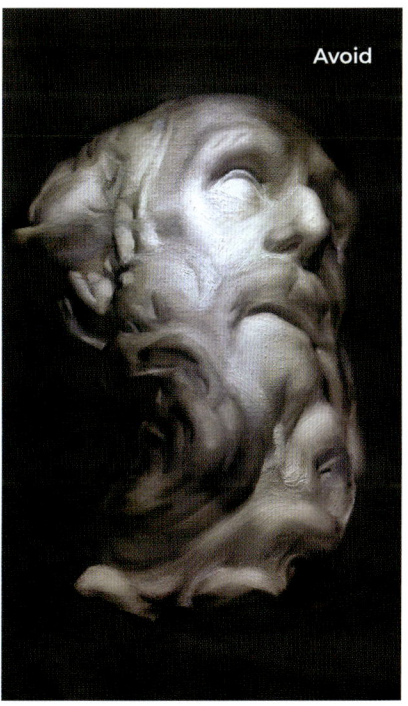

Correct | Avoid

20 Add modeling by exploring transitions between the value groups, but be careful – the effect becomes broken up when the groups are allowed to mix.

While the previous example shows a simple subject, the principles of value grouping stay true regardless of the complexity of the scene we are representing. In this illustration by Guweiz **(21a)**, we can see that even for this more complex scene, careful consideration has been paid to maintain the separation of the lights, midtones, and darks.

See just how much of the image's message is retained when we strip it back to just three fundamental values **(21b)**. Thinking in this simplified language when we plan our images is a key skill for visual communication and will always lie at the core of good composition.

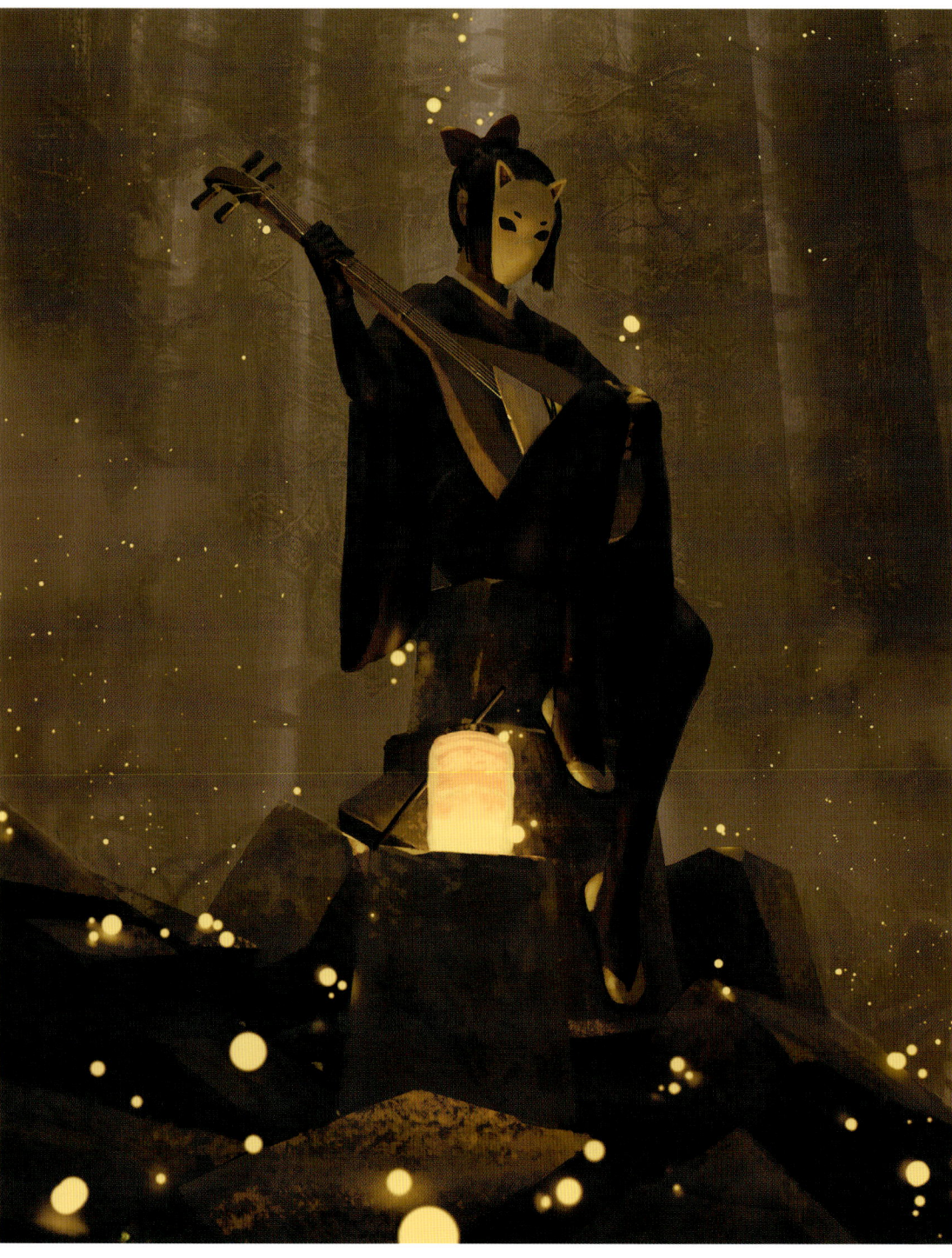

21a This scene achieves clarity in a dark atmosphere by paying close attention to the separation of value.

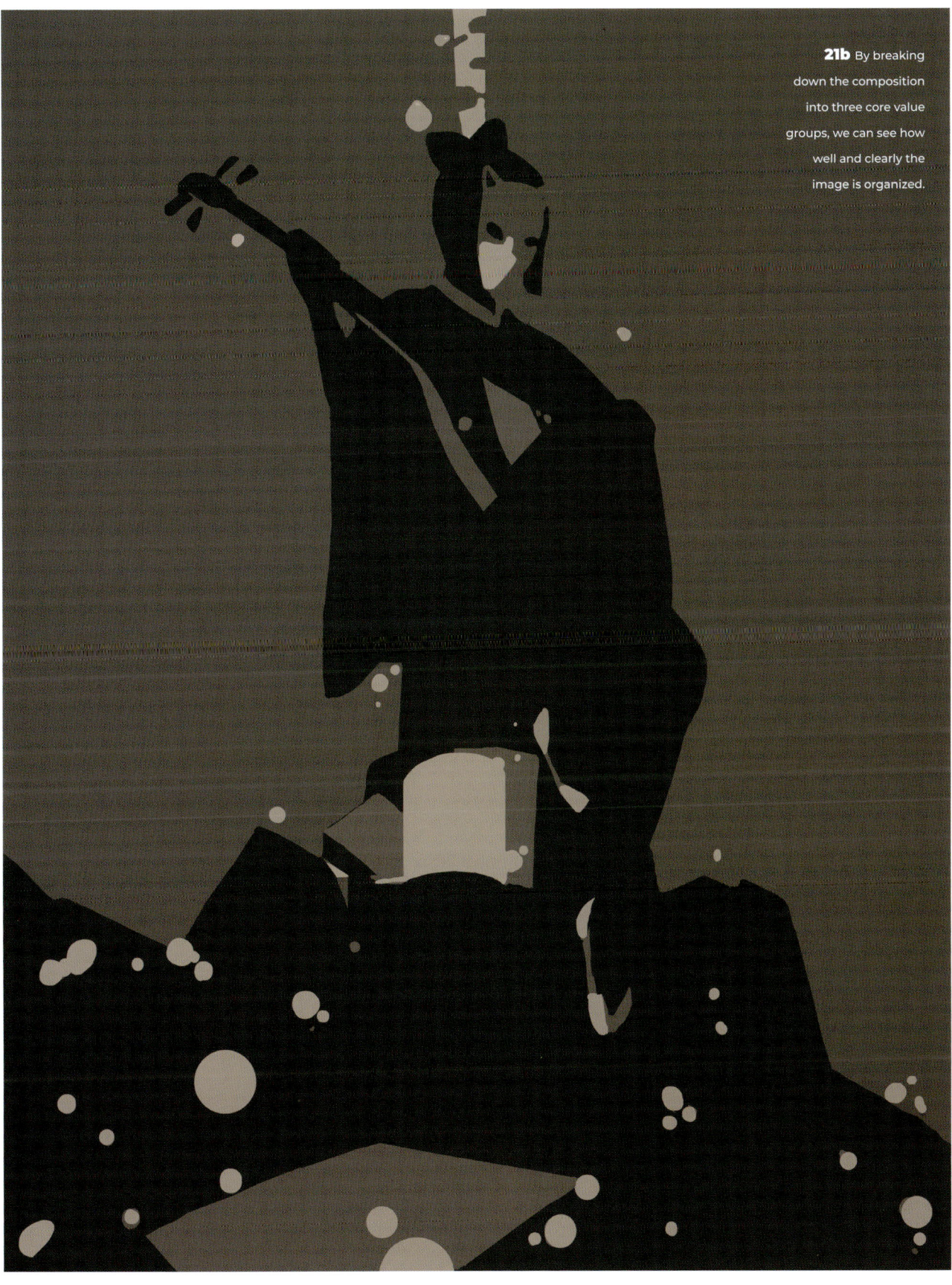

21b By breaking down the composition into three core value groups, we can see how well and clearly the image is organized.

EXPOSURE AND US

As artists, we are always working with extremely limited materials. Regardless of medium, we can only access a small fraction of the values available in nature. White paint may seem bright, but it can't begin to compare to the brightness of the sun. Black paint will always reflect some light, so can never be darker than the depths of space.

In fact, not even our eyes can match the immense range of nature. Most light sources are so bright that they are painful for us to look at directly. If light levels are too low, we can't see anything. We could never create paint that comes close to these extremes.

We can visualize this in image **22**. The first scale is purely symbolic, as nature's range is so broad that we could never truly represent it in print, but this simplification will help us visualize some of the solutions to this fundamental problem of painting.

VALUE CLIPPING

We can see one important effect of this if we borrow a concept from the world of photography: exposure. While it may be hard to believe, the two photographs below were taken at the same time and location, though they look wildly different **(23a–b)**.

The first image contains a lot of information in the sky but less in the ground, which is very dark, sometimes black. The reverse is true of the second image, where the ground contains a lot of information but much of the sky is just white.

This effect is called "clipping," where the camera moves its limited range of values to different parts of nature's range in order to better capture it. It then interprets everything above this range as just white, and everything below as just black.

Your eyes actively do the same thing as you look around you. Imagine being in a bright room and turning the lights off – you're unable to see anything for a moment until your eyes adjust (or re-expose). This happens constantly, in every environment.

22 Our tools can only capture a fraction of the values found in nature.

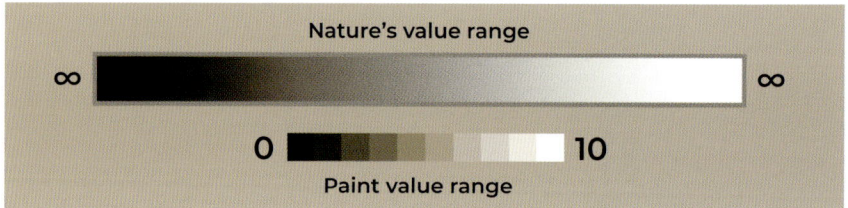

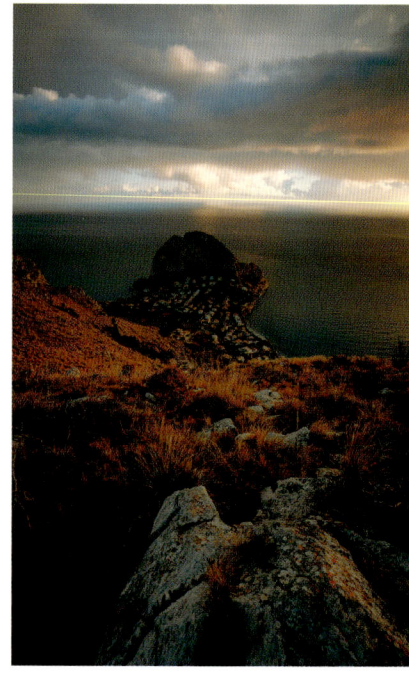

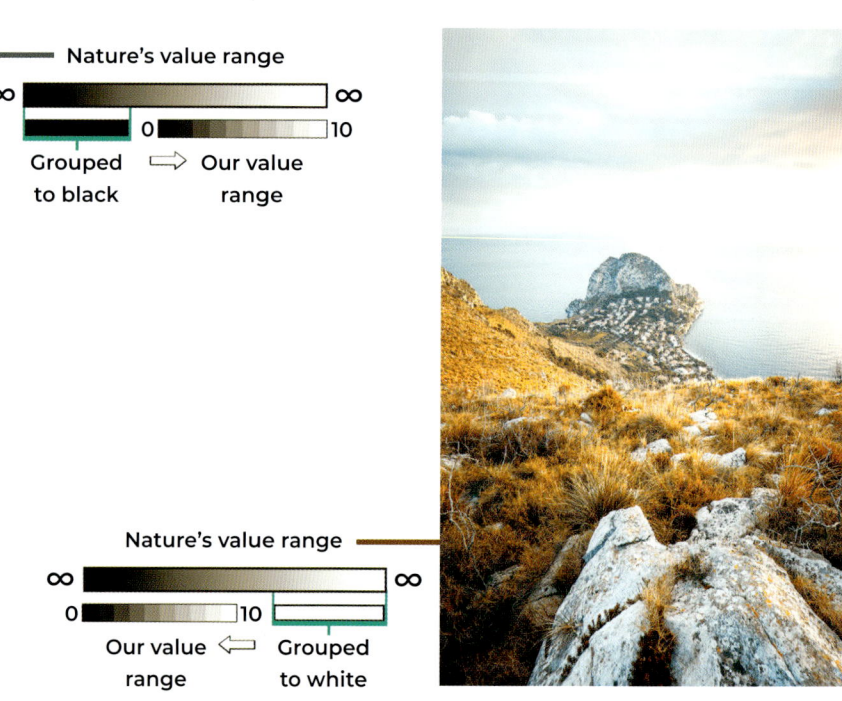

23a Exposing for the lights, with everything below the chosen range clipping to black.

23b Exposing for the darks, with everything above the chosen range clipping to white.

Based on analysis and principles developed by Devin Korwin for his eBook Creative Fundamentals.
Image 23 photos © Creative Travel Projects/Shutterstock.com

VALUE KEYING

Many students will try to simply copy the values of a scene as they see them, but as we have learned when trying to capture nature, this approach does not work. We have to make a choice about what part of our subject we want the painting to focus on, using the limited range available to us.

The three-value grouping introduced on page 21 is extremely helpful to us here. The simplest approach is to decide at the beginning which of the three values will contain the most information. Then, when we expand our value range from three to five values, we know to place the most variety within the value we have chosen to expose for. When we want to expose for the lights, we expand the light value group, and vice versa (24a–b). This process of choosing our value range and the areas of the subject it represents is called "keying" the painting, and is an important consideration for every image we create.

To give you an example of what these two types of exposure look like in a painting, below are two of my pieces (25a–b). For each of them, I made a conscious decision to fully omit the lights and darks respectively, to increase the strength of the information in the areas I chose.

Value keying should be a conscious choice in our work, as it enables us to be as effective as possible in expressing our subjects. There are multiple reasons why you might choose to use your value groups differently depending on the goal of the painting, and we will discuss a few other ways of manipulating them as we move further through the book. For now, just keep in mind that your use of values is a creative choice, and is not dictated by the values of the subject.

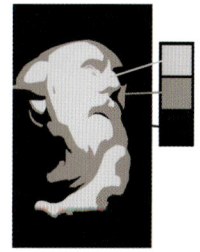
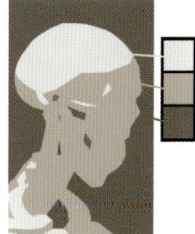
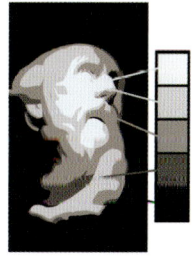
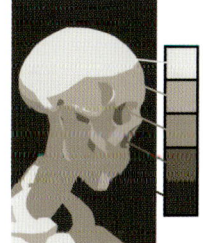
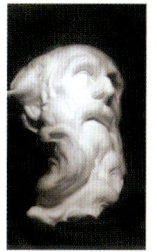
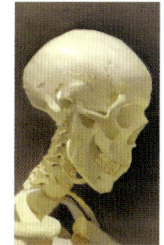

24a Expanding the value range to include more lights.

24b Expanding the value range to include more darks.

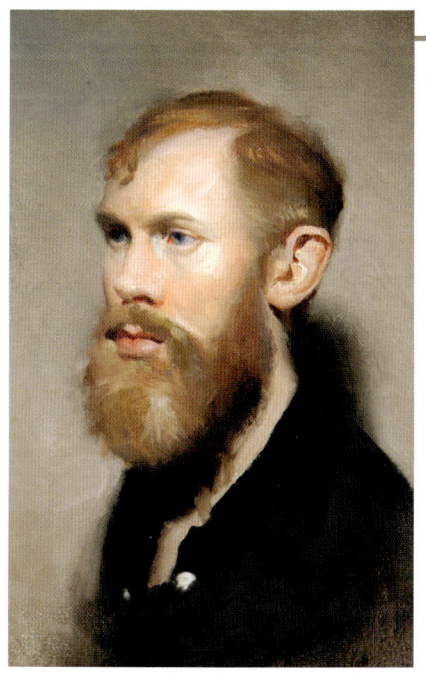

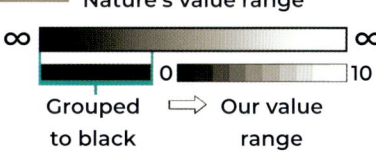

Nature's value range

∞ ────────────── ∞

0 ──── 10

Grouped to black ⇨ Our value range

25a Exposing for the lights, grouping the remaining values to dark.

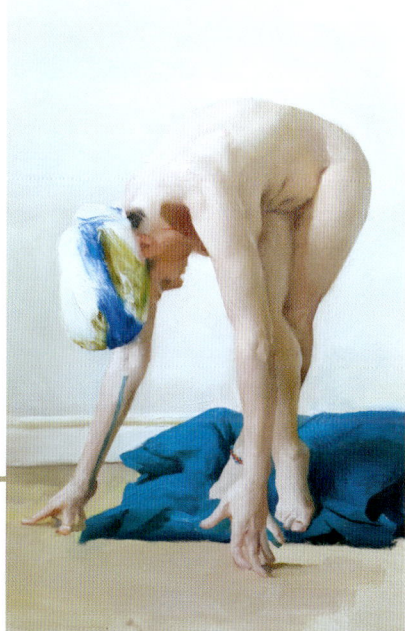

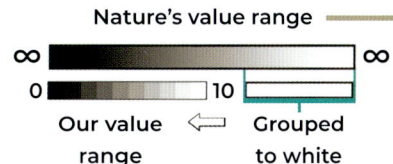

Nature's value range

∞ ────────────── ∞

0 ──── 10

Our value range ⇦ Grouped to white

25b Exposing for the darks, grouping the remaining values to white.

VALUE SCALES

The need to simplify values and maintain clear value groups is often taught as purely a lesson in design. While this is certainly true, and a simple, tonal design will always create a clearer, stronger image, many people do not realize that value grouping is also fundamentally a consequence of how we experience value.

It is often our instinct to consider value as linear. Often, one of the first exercises at art school is taking a student through a ten-value scale. This is a great way to begin to hone our understanding of value and intuitive sense of where it exists on a scale. However, while this linear scale will always be how we experience and judge value, *light does not follow this linear scale*. This is because our vision has evolved to be more sensitive to changes on the darker end of the value scale. In fact, light has what is called an "exponential drop-off." We will cover light in detail later, but for now, let's explore this topic as it relates to the dimension of value.

EXPONENTIAL DROP-OFF

It sounds like a complicated term, but all "exponential drop-off" means is that the loss of value accelerates the closer it gets to black. In image **26** you can see what this looks like in graph form, with our observed value scale along the horizontal axis and the real light values, measured with a light meter, on the vertical axis. The value scales include Photoshop value numbers so you can recreate the effect for yourself.

Seeing values this way and hearing terms like "exponential" may seem daunting, but you can simply imagine that same curve as a hill **(27)**. Imagine how a ball would speed up as it rolls downhill, moving faster as the curve gets steeper. The same is true of light.

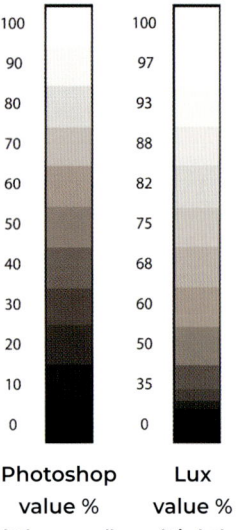
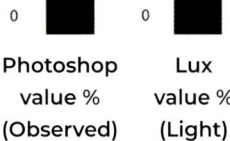

Photoshop value % (Observed) Lux value % (Light)

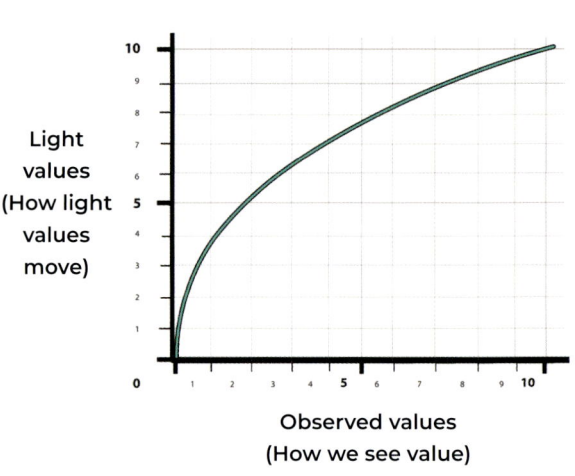

Light values (How light values move)

Observed values (How we see value)

26 The exponential drop-off of light, with corresponding Photoshop values on the side.

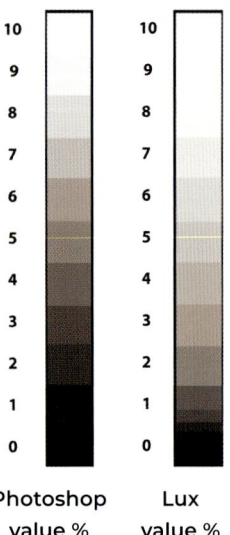

Photoshop value % (Observed) Lux value % (Light)

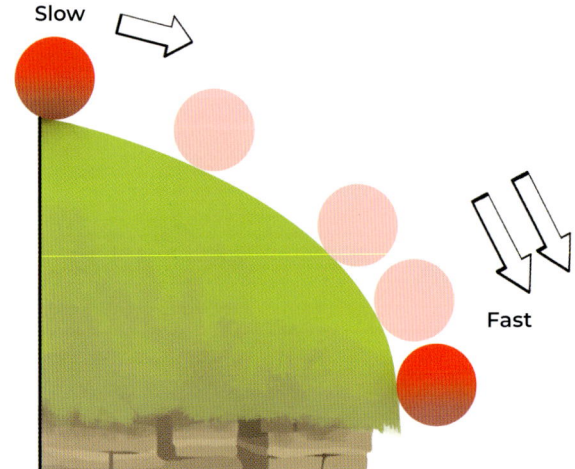

Slow

Fast

27 Think of exponential drop-off like a ball gaining speed down a hill.

EXPONENTIAL VERSUS LINEAR SCALES

It is easy to see the benefit of switching to this more accurate exponential light scale when we superimpose both scales onto a simple white sphere. Even without warping the scales to fit the form of the sphere, the exponential light scale matches the values in the lights almost perfectly. The linear scale, however, gets too dark far too quickly (28).

We can see this effect more clearly when we compare two spheres (29) – one painted with this exponential value drop-off (left) and the other painted with the linear scale (right). Understanding this scale and how it applies to modeling light in an artwork is the key to varying the modeling in our lights while avoiding the pitfalls of overmodeling.

Of course, we don't want to whip out our calculators every time we want to model a form in our paintings! We need an intuitive way of working with these scales. The easiest way to do this is to first mix a series of our observed values, starting with one halfway between black and white, then halfway between that value and white, and then one more halfway between that and white.

We can then set up our scale as seen in image **30**. For the in-between values, we can rely on our eye to judge. The main idea is to maintain a feeling of the value change accelerating as we go down the scale.

The same method can be used to create exponential scales between any two values (31). Since we will be working with these scales often as we move into modeling form, it is extremely helpful to get familiar with them before moving on to more complex concerns. Try to mix up as many value scales as you can with any medium you can get hold of.

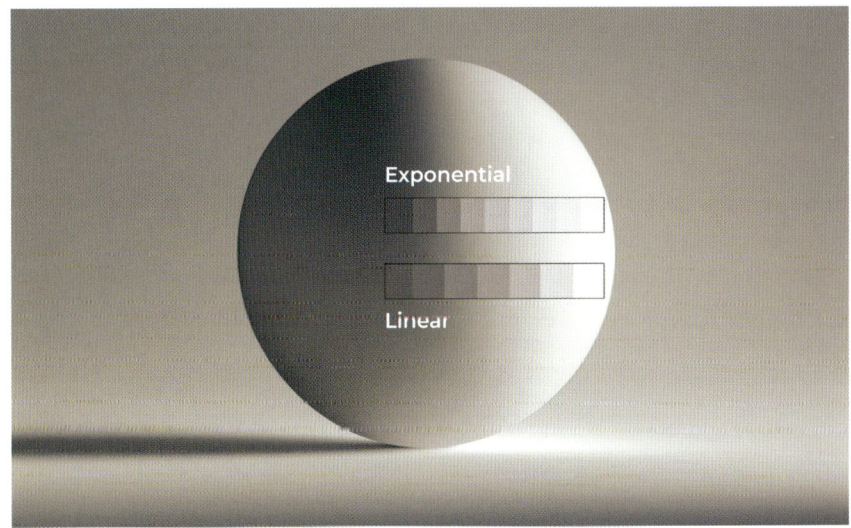

28 An exponential lighting drop-off follows a more realistic pattern than a linear one.

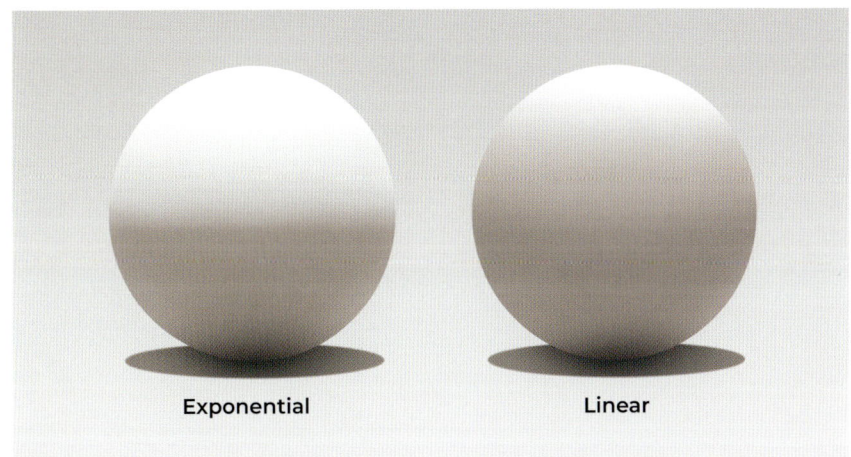

29 A sphere with an exponential lighting drop-off versus one with a linear drop-off.

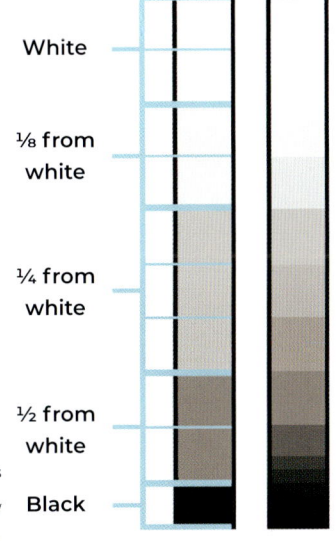

30 A range of values accelerating exponentially down the scale.

White

⅛ from white

¼ from white

½ from white

Black

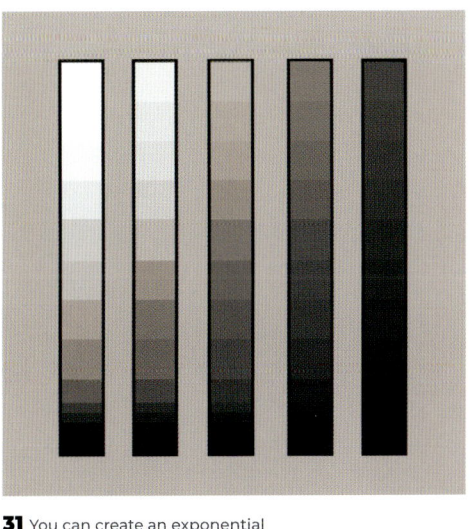

31 You can create an exponential scale between any two values.

SHAPES AND EDGES

When we first begin to draw, it's common to represent what we see using lines. However, in nature, lines don't exist. Everything that we see is, in reality, simply varying shapes of color. Once we realize this simple truth, we run into a problem. Shapes on their own appear two-dimensional, but when we look at the world we perceive three-dimensional forms. How can we express these forms?

Many students will try to express form by adding more and more value shapes, often resulting in broken-up, overmodeled artworks. However, we now know that the simpler our values, the stronger our artwork. To express form without breaking up our simple value structure, the key is to pay attention not to the shapes themselves, but to their boundaries. We can call these their "edges" and think of them as existing on a spectrum from perfectly distinct "sharp" edges to perfectly indistinct "soft" edges (often called "gradients").

While there is an infinite level of variety between these two extremes, we can think of a midpoint between the two as a "firm" edge. We can use these as our three main categories of edge, similar to how we use three value groups (lights, midtones, and darks) **(32)**.

CREATING SHAPE WITH VALUE EDGES

Think of these three types of edge as the levels of distinctness of a shape. The more perfectly clear it is, the more "sharp" it is, and the less clear it is, the more "soft." This seems like stating the obvious, but this simple relationship of shapes is often misunderstood, and the degree to which it relates to the appearance of reality cannot be overstated.

Students often consider the softening and play of edges as merely "blending" colors, performed toward the end of a work as a finishing touch. However, it is much deeper than this, and should be considered carefully at all stages of a painting.

Image **33** shows how fundamentally the play of different edge varieties creates form. All that has been done between steps B and C is surrounding the soft and firm edges with a hard edge, which immediately creates

a palpable sense of form and finish. The simplest way that we can think about form is merely as soft edges surrounded by sharp ones. Our exploration of form will become more complex later, but in its simplest state, this is how to create the entire sensation of it. With this fundamental concept, we can achieve a clear form very quickly.

This doesn't mean that the concept of edges replaces drawing lines – just that shape should also be a part of drawing. We do not need to separate "modeling" from drawing, as they are one and the same. Image **34** took ten minutes to draw, but you can see the level of volume that can be achieved just by applying this concept.

The idea of contrast also applies to edges. Soft edges appear softer next to sharp edges, and vice versa. We can use this to our advantage by starting with soft, blurry marks, then cutting into them with sharper accents, but this is by no means the only approach. Try as many ways as you can think of! But what actually causes this effect of edge variation? We can organize this topic around three main causes.

Sharp edge (perfectly defined)	Firm edge (somewhat defined)	Soft edge (perfectly undefined)

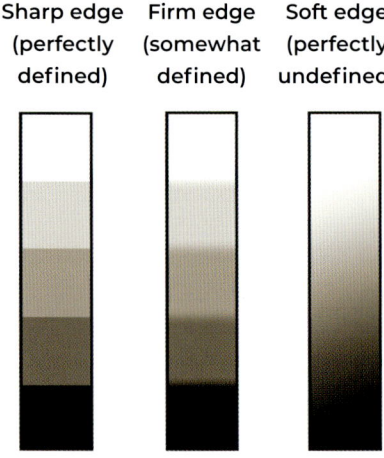

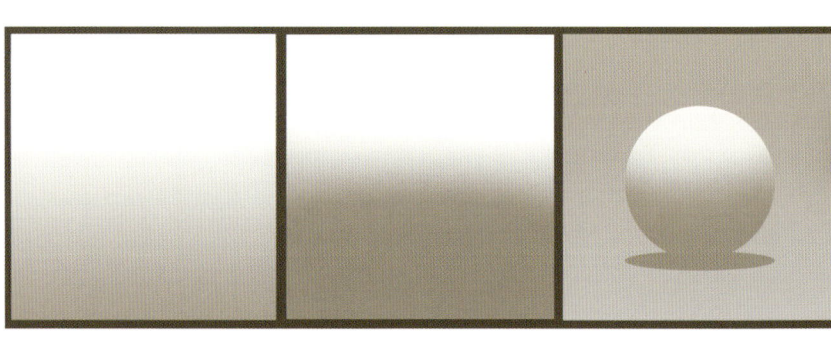

A) Create soft-edged gradient

B) Add a firm edge

C) Surround soft edges with sharp ones to create form

32 Three types of edge that we can use to create form in our work.

33 A minimal number of well-chosen edges can describe a form instantly.

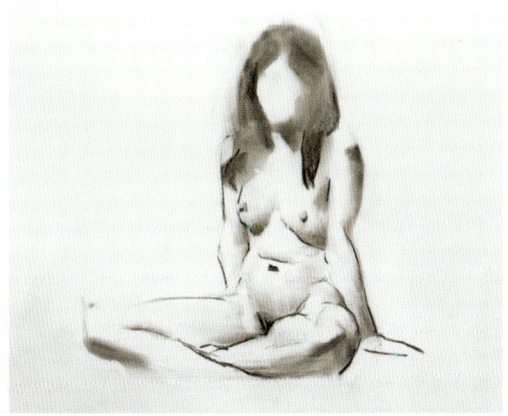

34 Two-value drawings exploring the concept of softs versus sharps are an efficient and fun way to approach sketching.

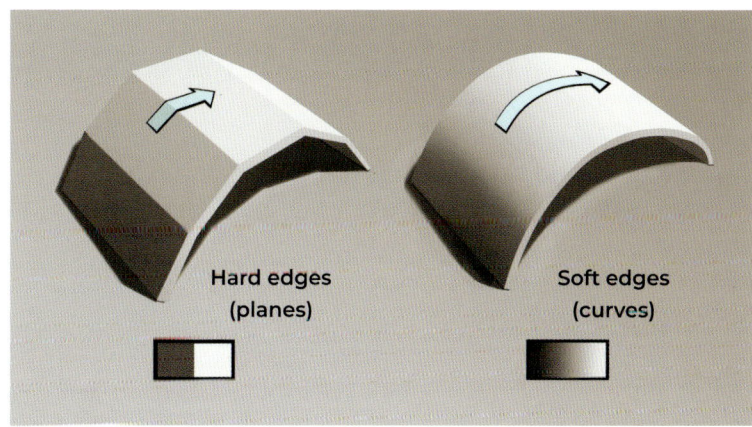

Hard edges (planes)

Soft edges (curves)

35 Creating blocky versus rounded planes using hard and soft edges respectively.

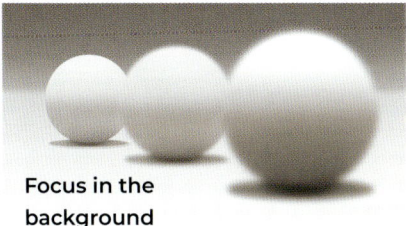

Focus in the background

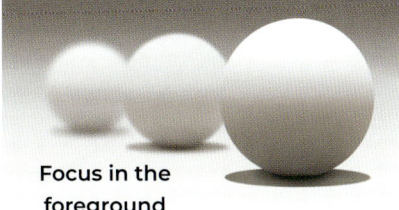

Focus in the foreground

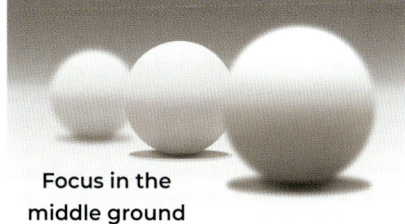

Focus in the middle ground

36 The human eye can only be fully focused at one level of depth, so choose your depth of field according to your desired focal point.

CHANGES IN FORM

Here, rounder forms are modeled with softer edges, and planar, blocky forms with sharper edges (35). This is often the first way that students think about softening edges. We will talk more specifically about how to plan this modeling on page 76, but for now we can just think of this round/blocky binary. It is simple to understand, but is the area that can have the most depth of variety and complexity.

DEPTH OF FIELD

The human eye is a lens, and like all lenses, it has a depth of focus and only one depth at which it is one hundred percent focused. Due to this, objects closer or farther away than this focal depth will appear more blurry. We can use this to our advantage when communicating distance. Simply pick your focal point and make sure that subjects closer or farther away are a level softer (36).

CENTER OF FOCUS

Our eye also only has a narrow range for its center of focus. We don't often realize this, but only about 15 degrees of our vision can be in focus at the same time. Due to this, levels of sharp, distinct detail will draw the eye most (37). One of the strongest ways to draw the viewer's attention is to sharpen the focal point of an image and soften the areas that you want to have less focus. In image 38, I wanted to place the focus on the model's head and hand, and achieved this by softening the edges of his legs and the box he was leaning against.

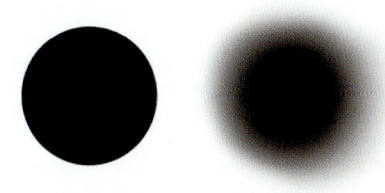

37 Which of these two dots is your eye drawn to?

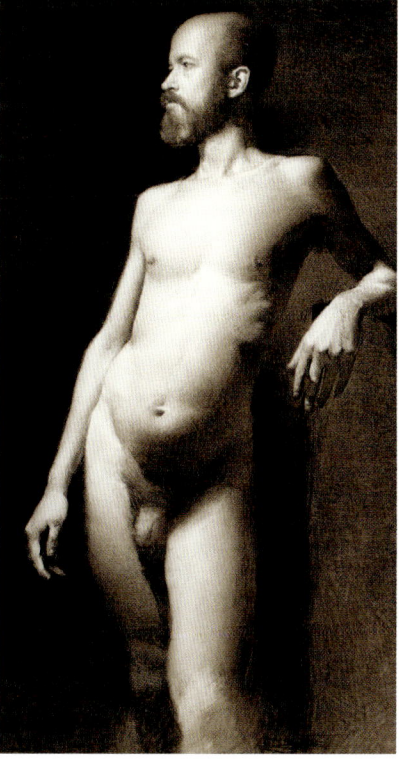

38 In this life study, I deliberately softened some edges to de-emphasize them.

COLOR PRIMARIES

Before we move forward in our discussion of hue and chroma, it's useful to know how colors actually arise in our perception. It is important to recognize that the color qualities of value are fundamentally separate from the other two dimensions of chroma and hue. The reason for this is actually biological in nature.

We perceive these qualities through signals we receive from cells at the back of our eye, called "rods" and "cones" **(39)**. We don't need to go deep into exactly how they work – it is enough for us to simply recognize that these cells constitute two different systems. The rods handle our perception of value and the cones handle hue and chroma. There are three different types of cone, generally referred to as red, blue, and green cones.

PRIMARY COLORS

We will discuss the more complex aspects of cones later (page 48), but for now we can think of them in simpler terms. Due to the three-cone nature of our color perception, we see three "primary colors." This is a vital concept to understand when we approach mixing color. The definition of "primary colors" that we will be working with is: Primary colors, when mixed, are able to mix the widest possible range of colors.

Due to each of these cones being responsible for detecting red, green, and blue, these three colors are our primaries in light. With these, we can mix functionally any color we want. In fact, this is the most common concept used for modern screens – if you have ever used an LED screen, these "RGB" primaries are responsible for every color you see on it.

As we discuss these primary colors, remember that they are the *primaries of light*. Therefore, the way they mix works differently to the way that colors mix in the physical materials we often use as artists.

Cones

Rods

39 Our eyes perceive hue, chroma, and value through rod and cone cells. The red, blue, and green cones perceive those respective colors in light.

40 Digital artists can try mixing colors in Screen mode to see additive mixing in action.

Light mixes *additively*, meaning colors become brighter as we add them together – unlike a physical material such as paint, which mixes *subtractively* and becomes darker. This additive nature makes white the most complete or "full of color" that light can be. When we add together the red, green, and blue primaries, we get white light **(40)**.

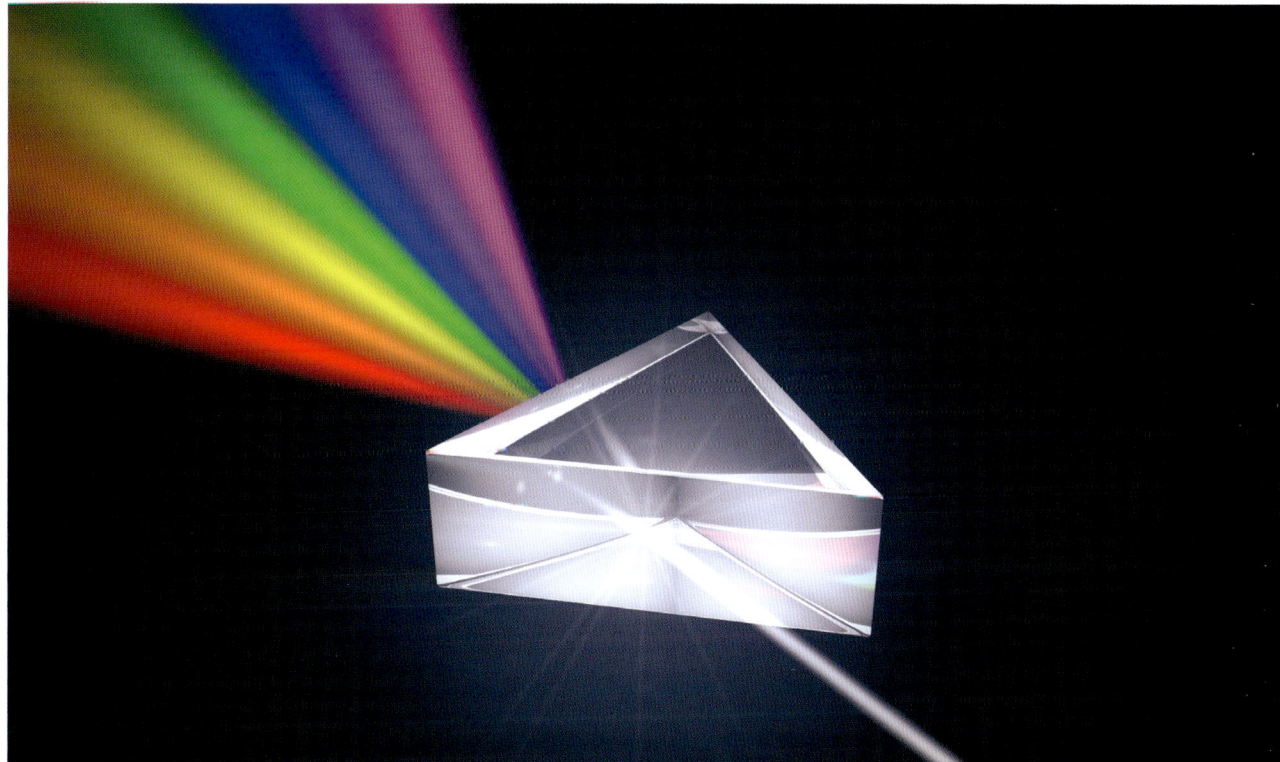

41 White light, when diffracted through a prism, is revealed to consist of a spectrum of colors.

THE COLOR SPECTRUM

The additive nature of light was originally discovered by Isaac Newton, the mathematician and physicist. He conducted a series of experiments in which he "diffracted" (bent) light through prisms to deconstruct it into its fundamental components. When we do this, we can see that the white light becomes a field of strongly chromatic colors that are its component parts **(41)**. This is called the color spectrum, which most of us will be familiar with seeing in rainbows.

Since this is a spectrum, remember that any points on it that we choose to call specific "colors" are invented by us, according to their usefulness to us. For our purposes, let's say there are six useful colors on this spectrum, all equally spaced: the red, blue, and green primary colors, and three "secondary" colors (meaning colors that are an even mix of two primaries), yellow, cyan, and magenta **(42)**.

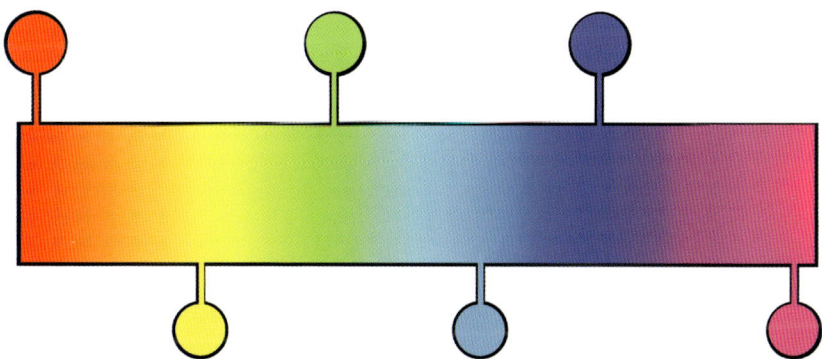

42 We can define six equally spaced colors on the spectrum: three primary (red, green, and blue) and three secondary (yellow, cyan, and magenta).

SUBTRACTIVE PRIMARIES

As artists, nearly all of our materials mix subtractively, meaning the colors become darker and mix into black rather than becoming white. In fact, the only medium capable of additive mixing is digital. Regardless of our tools, we need to have a good understanding of subtractive mixing.

Subtractive and additive mixing may seem so different that they must surely be irrelevant to each other, but the truth is that they follow exactly the same logic – subtractive mixing just has an additional interaction. Ultimately, everything we see is light and these mixing theories are unified.

In order to understand subtractive mixing, it's useful to know the mechanism behind why we see an object's color. If we take a red ball and shine white light on it, the green and blue light within the white light are absorbed into the object. Only the red light is reflected into our eye, which is why we see the object as red **(43)**. The color we see is the opposite of the light interaction happening within the object – the visible red is the light that the object has rejected.

We see the colors of our paints due to the same interaction: The absorbed color of the paint (invisible to us) is the opposite of the reflected colors that we see. When we mix our paints, these invisible, absorbed colors still mix additively, but we only see the rejected light. If the invisible, absorbed colors mix into white, it means all light is absorbed – and so we see black paint!

Just as the three additive primaries are red, blue, and green, we can use our knowledge of absorbed light to find the three subtractive primaries: cyan, yellow, and magenta **(44)**. These colors mix to black instead of white, which is the basic idea that governs all traditional paint-mixing. Digital artists have the option to work within either of these systems of color. To mix subtractively in

Photoshop, simply switch to the Multiply blending mode **(45)**.

Note that while these are the ideal primaries *in theory*, we don't have perfect options for these colors in practice. While this is the widest color space we can access with three colors, chroma and value will be lost whenever we mix any colors subtractively. We will explore the effects this has on our color choices and palettes next.

White light (all colors) enters object

Red is reflected into our eye

Blue and green are absorbed

43 The colors we perceive are actually the light rejected and reflected by objects.

White light enters object

Cyan (green and blue) reflects

Red is absorbed

44 The reflected light colors mix to create the subtractive primaries.

White light enters object

Magenta (red and blue) reflects

Green is absorbed

White light enters object

Yellow (red and green) reflects

Blue is absorbed

45 Digital artists can use Multiply mode to perform subtractive mixing.

CMY VERSUS RBY

You were likely already familiar with the concept of primary colors, as many of us were taught about them in school. However, you probably learned that the primaries were red, blue, and yellow, and are now wondering why this book says they are red, green, and blue for light, and cyan, magenta, and yellow for paint!

This topic can inspire heated discussions among artists. Proponents of CMY will decry the RBY color system as a lie told to us before were smart enough to know the truth, while those who prefer RBY will retort that all of the great masters of the past used RBY color. Others reject the discussion altogether, believing that paint and light should be studied entirely separately – that artists don't paint with light, so the study of light should be left to engineers **(46)**.

The reasons for this conflict are both historical and practical. The CMY color model is relatively recent, coming into mainstream commercial use in the 1950s. RBY is much older, going back to some of the earliest texts we have on color – as early as the fifteenth century. However, many of these texts were written long before we had any knowledge of how vision worked.

Many early color-mixing theories were also written before we even had access to any good pigments to represent the CMY model. The pigment Prussian Blue (created with ferrocyanide, where "cyan" gets its name) was only synthesized in the early eighteenth century. Many historical magenta pigments were not lightfast, so they faded over time. Even the best magentas we have today are very transparent compared to the red pigments available.

So the truth lies somewhere between the two extremes: RBY was developed by people who didn't have the full picture either

theoretically or practically, but there are practical reasons why CMY hasn't been ideal, both in the past and the modern day.

However, paint is not special as a material, and absolutely follows the logic discussed on the previous page. CMY offers the "ideal" mixing primaries, as they can mix the widest range of hues from just three colors. In image **47**, I mixed some in-between steps of hue to show the maximum chroma we can access with these two systems of color-mixing.

If we look at the resulting colors, the strengths and limitations of the RBY and CMY systems become clear. The RBY violets and greens are especially low-chroma and pale in comparison with their CMY equivalents. The oranges are actually stronger in RBY, but the overall CMY palette is more balanced and chromatic. So what's going on here? Shouldn't the "primaries" mix every color? This leads us to the next important aspect of traditional mixing: warm and cool primaries.

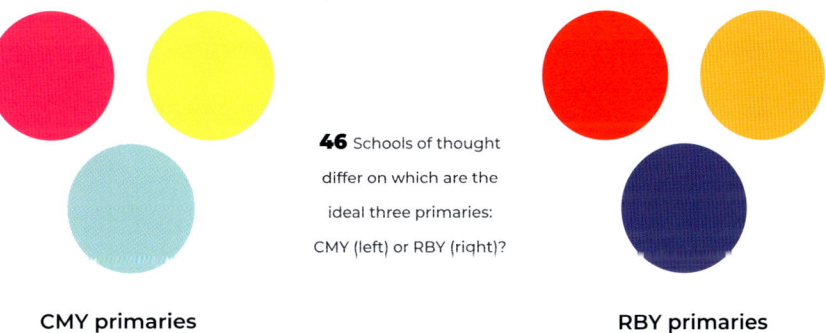

46 Schools of thought differ on which are the ideal three primaries: CMY (left) or RBY (right)?

CMY primaries

RBY primaries

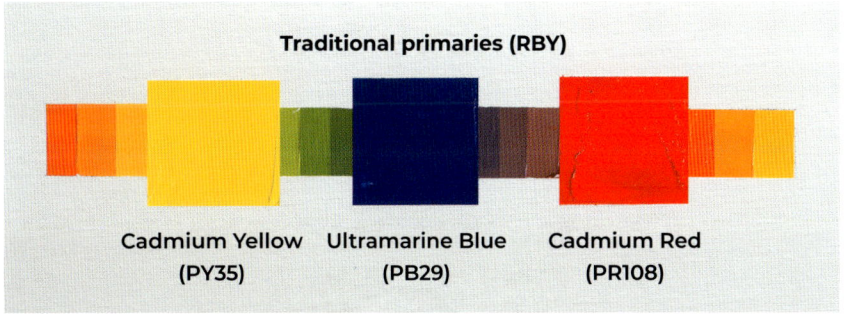

Traditional primaries (RBY)

Cadmium Yellow (PY35) Ultramarine Blue (PB29) Cadmium Red (PR108)

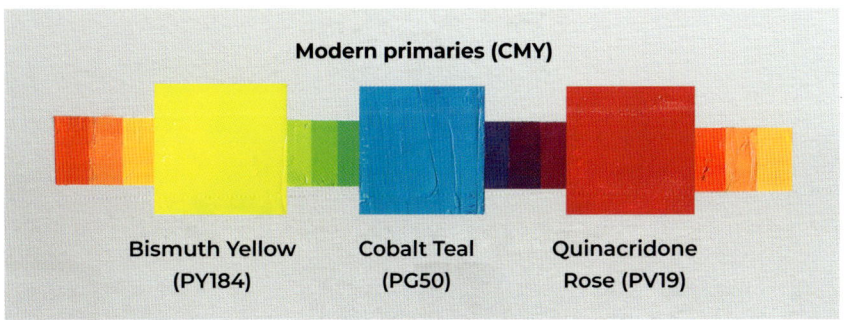

Modern primaries (CMY)

Bismuth Yellow (PY184) Cobalt Teal (PG50) Quinacridone Rose (PV19)

47 A comparison of the RBY and CMY primaries, mixed using six pigments with white added to equalize their values.

WARM VERSUS COOL PRIMARIES

The reason the RBY palette manages to outperform our "ideal" CMY palette is due to this fundamental fact of subtractive mixing: All mixtures of two or more pigments will lose chroma and lightness. In order to see how this works, let's map these pigments on a section of a color wheel. If we visualize our resulting mixes as straight lines along this color space **(48)**, we can see the results of the different mixtures.

Since the cold yellow and magenta of CMY are farther away from our target hue of orange than the warm red and yellow of RBY, more chroma and lightness are lost in the mix. We can also see that, even with the better performance of our warm red and yellow **(49)**, the resulting orange mix does not come close to the chromatic strength of a pure pigment (Cadmium Orange, PO20, in this case).

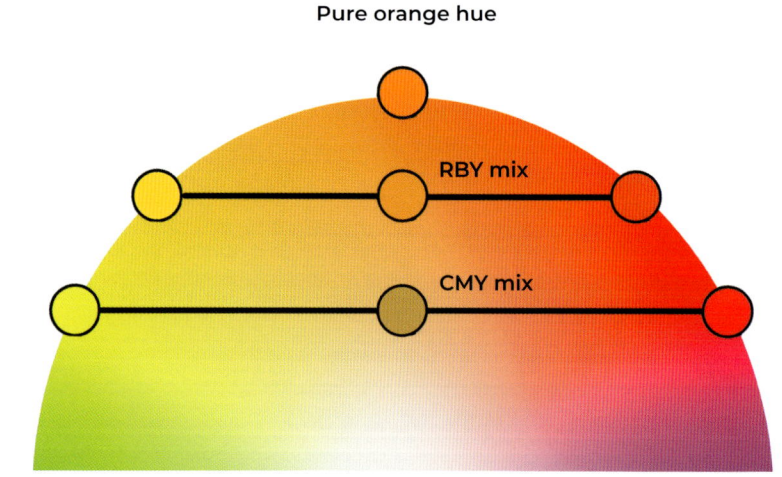

Pure orange hue

48 Depending on the pigments we mix, more or less chromatic strength can be lost.

This will always be the case for every part of the color space with subtractive media. In order to achieve strong chromatic color, it is important to limit the number of pigments present in a mix, as they will all contribute to this loss of chroma and brightness. The typical academic advice is to try to keep your mixes to no more than three pigments.

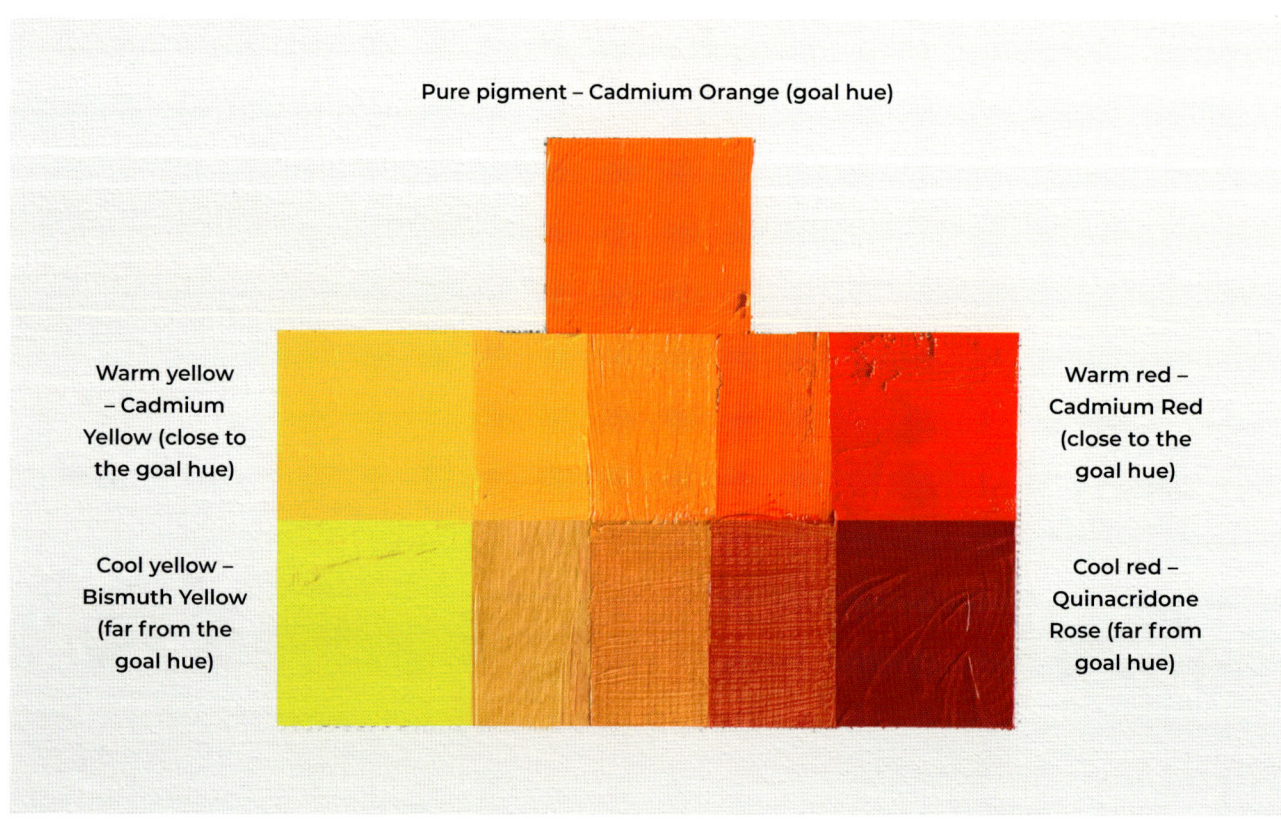

Pure pigment – Cadmium Orange (goal hue)

Warm yellow – Cadmium Yellow (close to the goal hue)

Warm red – Cadmium Red (close to the goal hue)

Cool yellow – Bismuth Yellow (far from the goal hue)

Cool red – Quinacridone Rose (far from goal hue)

49 Though some hues are closer than others, subtractive mixtures will always be darker and less chromatic than a pure pigment.

THE SPLIT-PRIMARY PALETTE

One way that many artists resolve these inherent problems with the two color systems is by viewing them as two sides of the same coin, choosing to see them as the "warm" (RBY) and "cool" (CMY) primaries (**50**). This can be an extremely useful way to plug the holes in both systems, giving us an impressive range of colors to use in our paintings. This is called a split-primary palette and many painters use it as their basic palette (**51**).

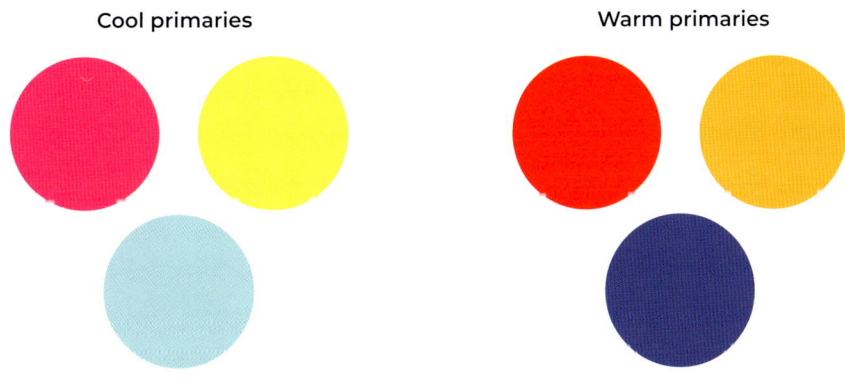

Cool primaries

Warm primaries

50 We can instead view the CMY and RBY primaries as warm and cool primaries.

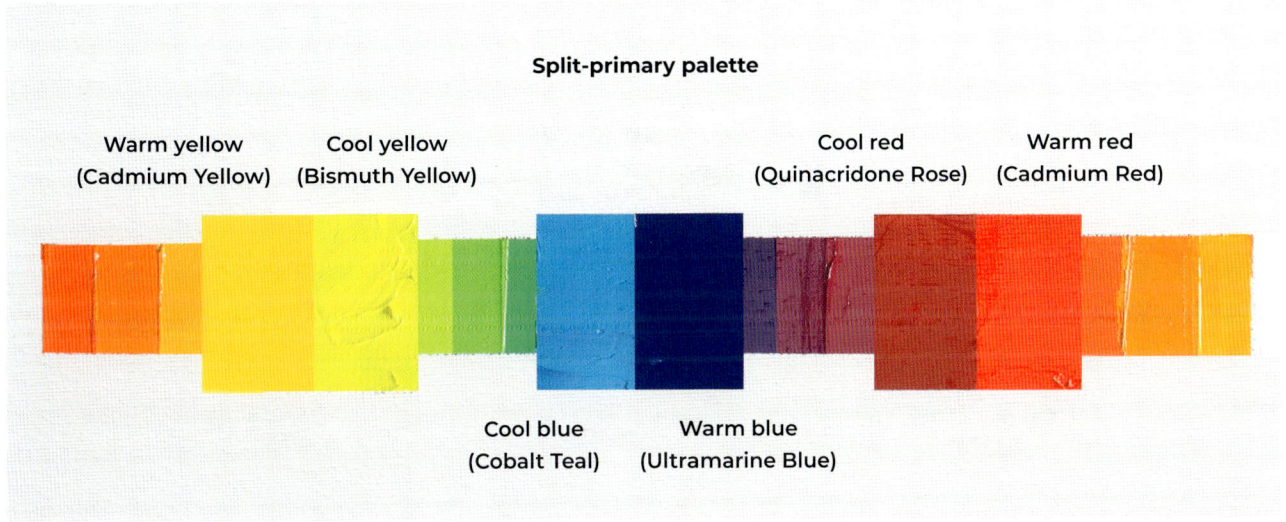

Split-primary palette

Warm yellow
(Cadmium Yellow)

Cool yellow
(Bismuth Yellow)

Cool red
(Quinacridone Rose)

Warm red
(Cadmium Red)

Cool blue
(Cobalt Teal)

Warm blue
(Ultramarine Blue)

51 By using a warm and cool of each primary, we can mix the most optimal in-between hues throughout the color spectrum.

As you can see in image **52**, there are only a few areas of the color wheel cut off in this approach. This loss of chroma will always be a factor when we desire a maximum chromatic note in a specific range. No mix will quite reach the level of pure pigment, though we can get close.

Due to this, when we compositionally want one of these extreme chromatic notes, it is useful to be flexible in swapping different colors in and out of our palette. While these concepts are aimed at providing the most chromatic versions of the widest range of hues, it is important to also recognize that it is only rarely that we will need the absolute

maximum chroma available in paintings. For most paintings, this loss of chroma will not be a problem we need to worry about.

PIGMENT NUMBERS

The numbers beside the paints' names are called pigment numbers – these are the most useful thing to keep track of when buying paint from different manufacturers, as the names will vary a lot, but these numbers will be consistent.

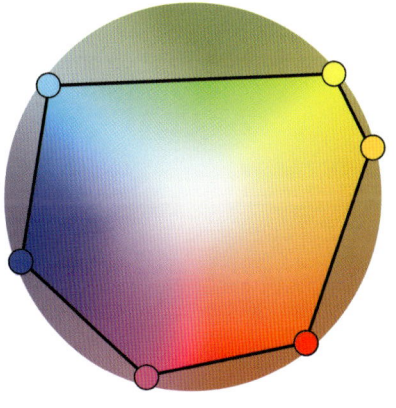

52 The majority of the color wheel can be accessed using a split-primary palette.

TRADITIONAL CHROMA MIXING

Now that we have solidified the basic mixing and palette-building principles in our heads, let's delve deeper into that second key color quality: chroma. Our first practical concern is how we can approach mixing and varying this quality. Most of the mixing discussed on the previous pages was concerned with how to access the most chromatic versions of colors, but how do we more generally explore chroma? Within traditional paint-mixing, there are three main methods for influencing chroma.

ADDING GRAY

The simplest, easiest way to control chroma is by mixing our color with a lower-chroma, "gray" version of the same color. The most obvious way to do this is by mixing a neutral gray of the same value as our starting color, usually using black and white. This can then be added to a new mixture with the original color, varying the proportions depending on how gray we want the final mix to be **(53)**.

A student's instinct will often be to attempt these adjustments with direct mixtures of tubed paints. This is an intuitive approach, but it's also more difficult to predict exactly how these colors will affect a mixture. As a beginner, it's good practice to first match the value of both mixtures before adjusting chroma. This way, you can approach each of Munsell's color qualities one at a time.

A great way to get to grips with controlling chroma is by creating a Munsell color slice **(54)**. This exercise involves "stringing out" the chroma of one hue at various values. As we learned, there is always some value loss when we mix two colors together. However, with this method, the colors aren't too far away from each other in the color space, so the value loss is minimal. You can simply lighten with white when darkening occurs.

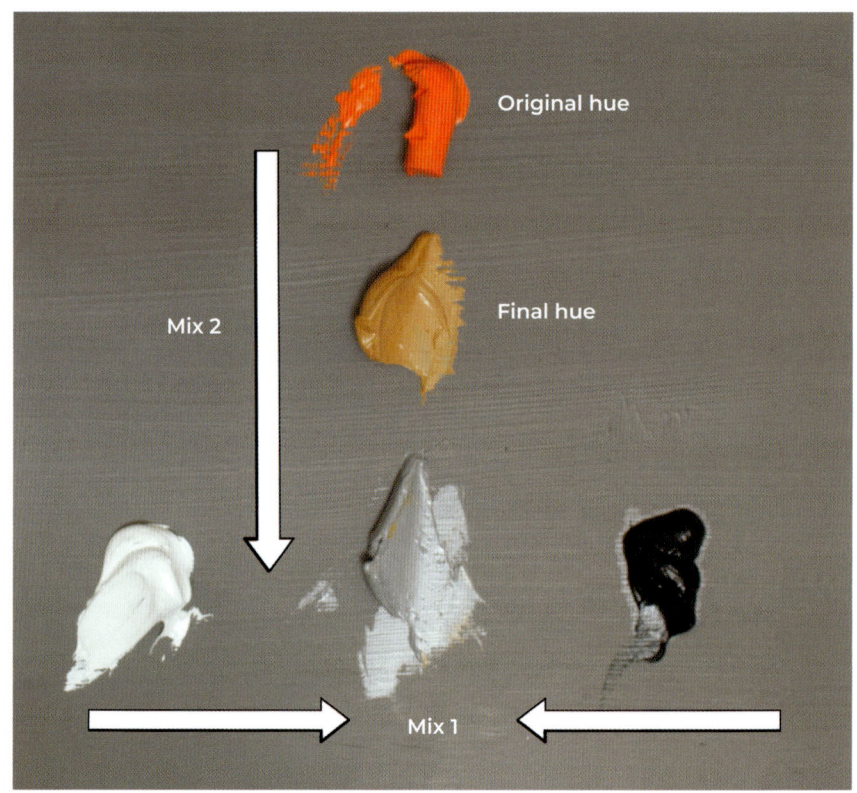

53 Mix a neutral gray of the same value as the color you wish to neutralize, then mix the original color with the new gray until you achieve the desired final color.

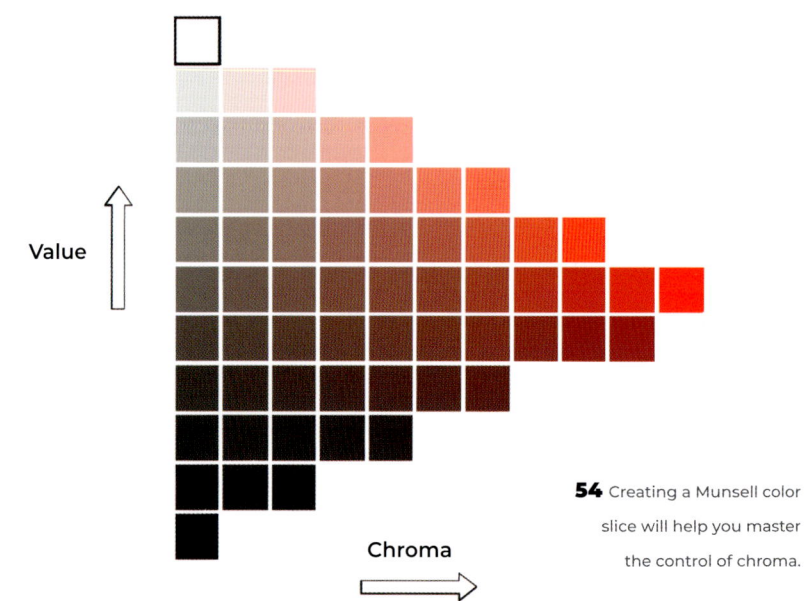

54 Creating a Munsell color slice will help you master the control of chroma.

MIXING COMPLEMENTS

The most common and versatile method for "graying" our colors in traditional mediums is through the mixing of complementary colors. First, let's define exactly what complementary means here and clear up a common misunderstanding of the term.

Many people, upon first hearing the term, assume that it means "complimentary" – as in to pay a compliment **(55a)**. This is a fair assumption to make, as complementary colors play off each other extremely well, and people commonly use them as the basis of their color choices. However, in relation to color-mixing, we are using a slightly different term: "complementary" as in "to complete" **(55b)**.

For example, when we talk about light, the most "complete" color is white, as we saw on page 30. So when we talk about colors being complementary, what we mean is:

- Complementary colors, when added together in light (additive), complete to neutral white.

- Complementary colors, when added together in paint (subtractive), complete to neutral black.

Since we only have three primaries, all the primaries add up to white, and the secondary colors are two of the primaries mixed together. These secondary colors form the complement of the "missing" primary. In image **56**, cyan is the complement of red, because cyan is the secondary mix of the blue and green primaries, and red is the leftover (complementary) primary.

Compl-i-mentary colors

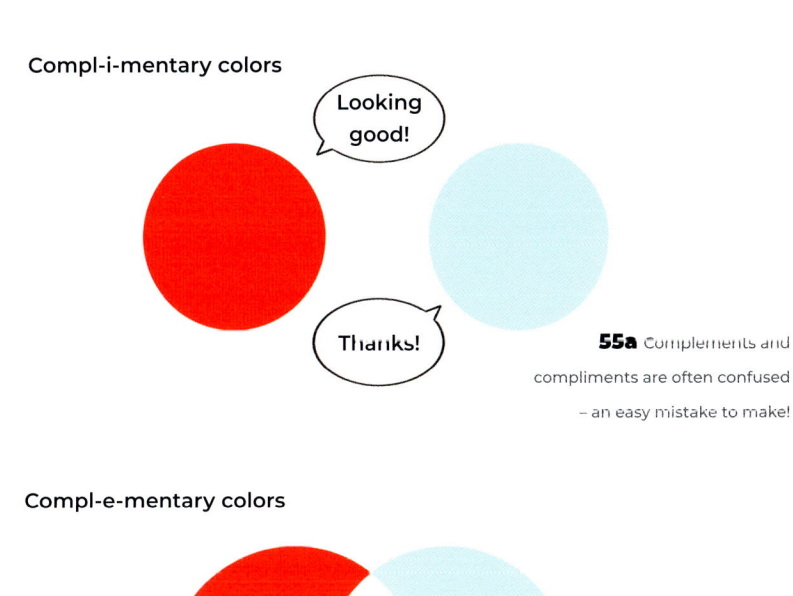

55a Complements and compliments are often confused – an easy mistake to make!

Compl-e-mentary colors

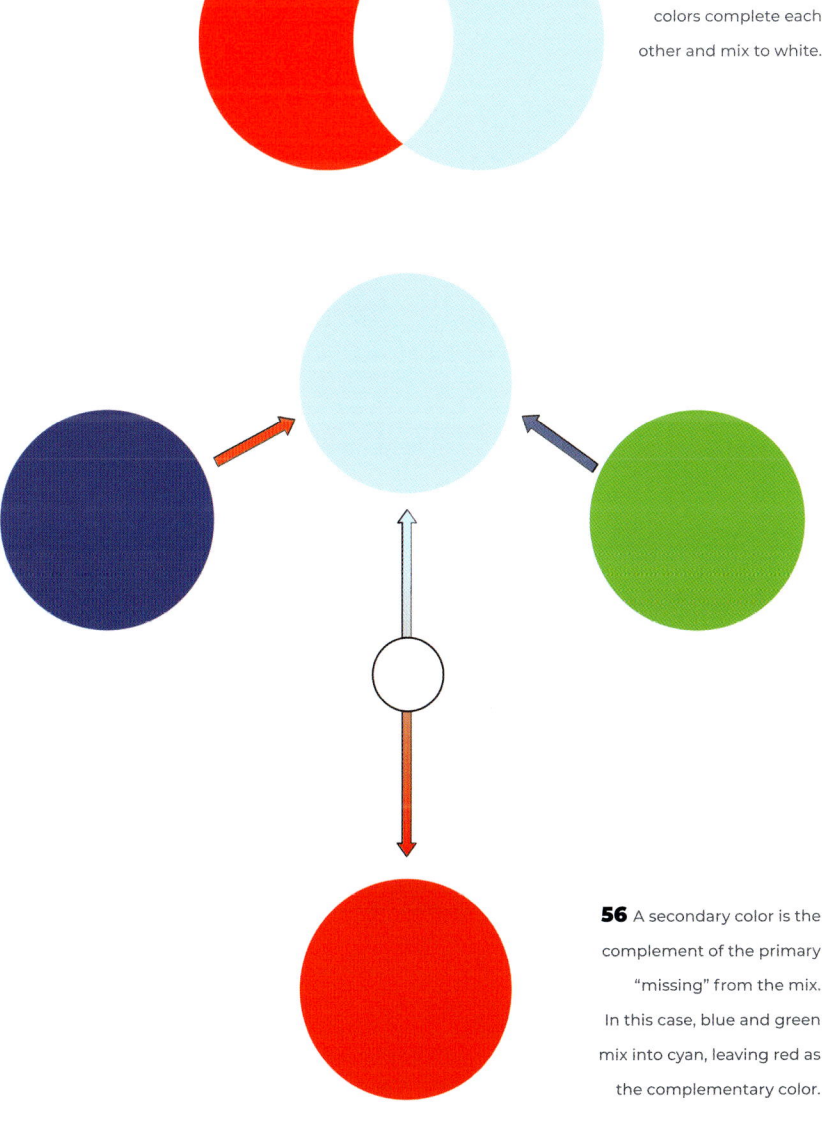

55b Complementary colors complete each other and mix to white.

56 A secondary color is the complement of the primary "missing" from the mix. In this case, blue and green mix into cyan, leaving red as the complementary color.

BROKEN COLOR

The final way that we can approach mixing grays in our paintings is through the use of "broken" color. The basic idea of broken color is that, instead of subtractively mixing our pigments together, we can instead "break" the gray into its component colors. By using these component colors next to each other at the same value, they will mix additively in our eyes as light, creating the sensation of the gray without mixing it directly.

This idea was most notably utilized by the Impressionists and Pointillists of the late nineteenth and early twentieth centuries, such as Georges Seurat and his contemporaries **(57)**. These painters limited themselves to a palette consisting of only the colors of the spectrum and white, placing their colors as purely as they could.

If these pure colors are made small enough, the eye becomes unable to distinguish between them, creating the illusion of a continuous color. In image **58**, we can see how broken colors are applied in smaller and smaller shapes until they resolve into a homogenous color. This form of mixing is how most screens work: Using only the three primary-colored, highly chromatic lights, the sensation of every color can be evoked.

COLOR WHEEL

Now that we understand the concept of complementary colors, we need a practical way to keep track of them. Luckily, we have the extremely useful concept of the artist's color wheel. The wheel shown in image **59a** is based on this modern theory of color, with six primary and secondary colors of light and paint.

The modern color theory wheel has a few key differences from the more traditional RBY wheel **(59b)**, and we can use the idea of complements to test out the accuracy of these two wheels.

On the modern wheel, red is complementary to cyan, while on the traditional wheel, red is complementary to green. Since the

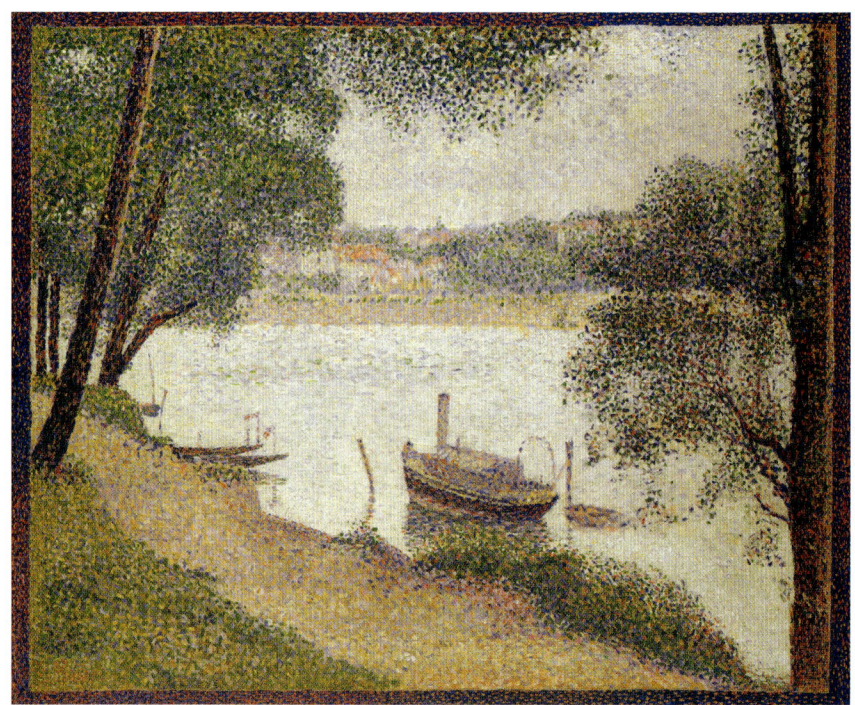

57 Pointillism in *Gray Weather, Grande Jatte* by Georges Seurat (ca. 1886–88).

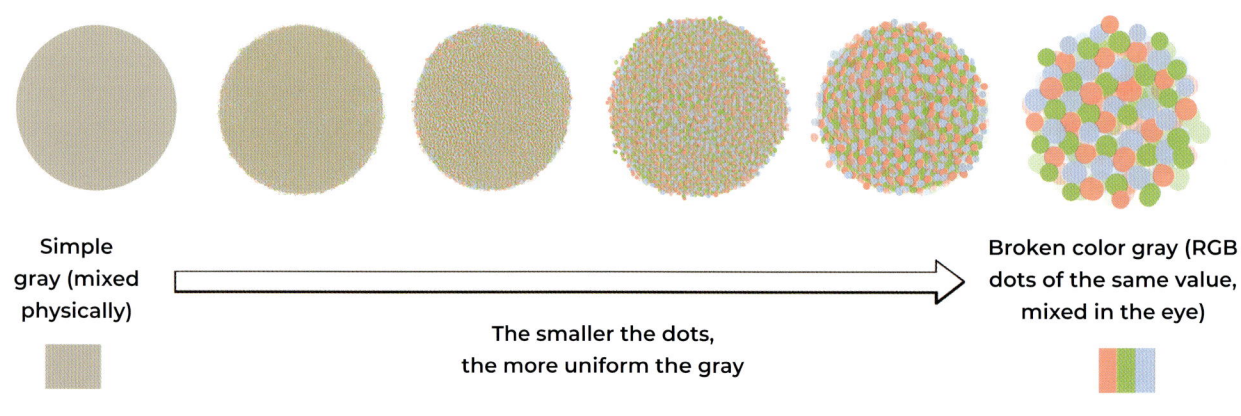

Simple gray (mixed physically)

The smaller the dots, the more uniform the gray

Broken color gray (RGB dots of the same value, mixed in the eye)

58 When spots of different colors become small enough, we perceive them as one hue.

definition of complementary is quite easy to test – the colors should mix to a neutral – we can carry out a simple test to compare these two color systems.

Image **60** shows the results of this test in pigments, starting with Cadmium Red at the top. The first column shows red's traditional complement of green (Cadmium Green here). The second shows red's modern complement of cyan (Cobalt Teal). When we mix them together, we can see that red and cyan mix to a much more neutral gray, while red and green mix to a yellow-brown. You can try this for yourself at home!

Modern color wheel

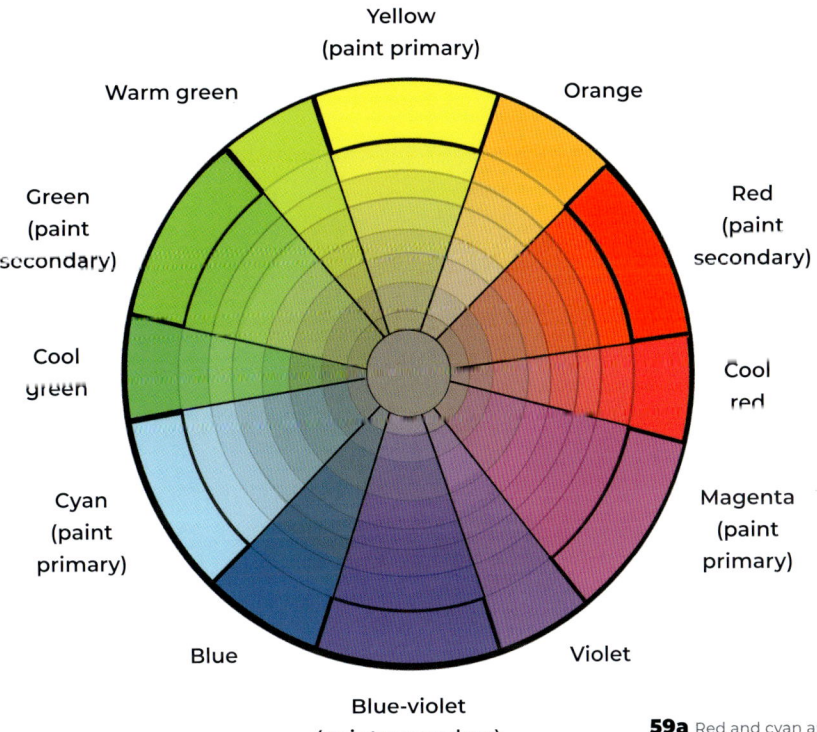

59a Red and cyan are complementary colors on the modern color wheel.

59b Red and green are complementary colors on a traditional color wheel.

Traditional color wheel

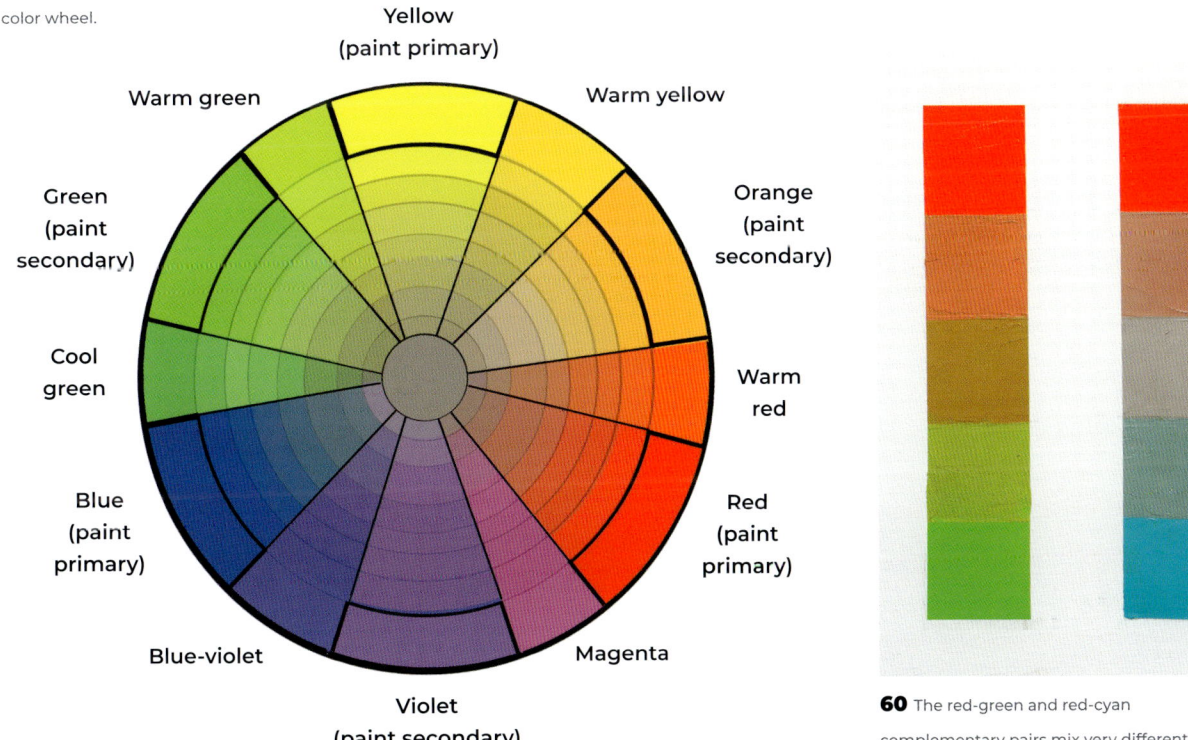

60 The red-green and red-cyan complementary pairs mix very differently.

CHROMA AND SATURATION

When we move into controlling chroma in digital media, all of these mixing principles work in the same way. Instead of mixing pigments, however, most artists elect to use the "Hue, Saturation, and Brightness" (HSB) sliders in their software – a fantastic way to easily control these qualities.

However, when we begin to use these sliders, there is one important misconception to dispel: Chroma is not the same thing as saturation. This is an extremely common misconception and you will often hear artists use them interchangeably. The difference between the two is subtle but important for us to understand, as it has certain implications for how we manipulate color in traditional and digital media.

Chroma is the raw intensity of a color – its distance from a neutral gray of the same value. You could think of it as the "purity" of a color. Since we must add low-chroma white or black to change a color's value, there can only ever be one value of a color with maximum chroma (**61**).

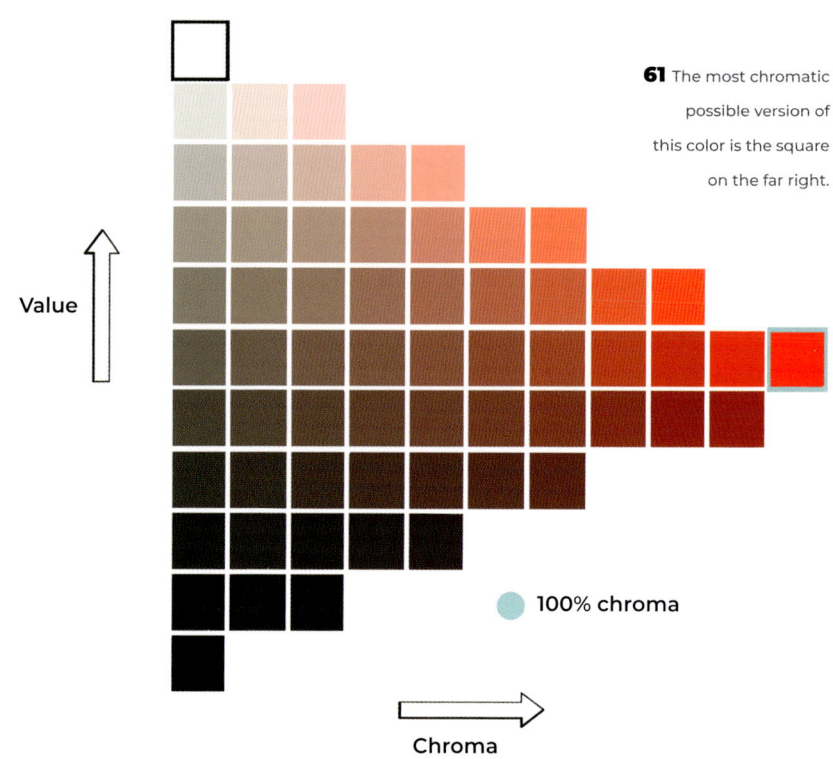

61 The most chromatic possible version of this color is the square on the far right.

100% chroma

Value

Chroma

SATURATION VERSUS CHROMA

At face value, saturation and chroma are quite similar. After all, when we increase saturation, we do get a more intense color. However, to see the difference between saturation and chroma, let's take a look at a ten-value step of a 100% saturated red (**62**). Immediately we see a key difference: There can be multiple values of maximum saturation.

The way that Photoshop creates these saturation paths is clear if we examine the RGB content of this set of colors. We can see in image **62** that in each of these colors, the red is the only RGB value turned on, while green and blue remain at zero. This persists from its maximum value down to black,

and holds true for every color taken down a saturation path. In effect, saturation is the path of a colored light brightening or darkening. Saturation is the path a color takes to black.

Let's compare chroma and saturation directly, starting from the same darker value (**63**). Here we can see a clear relationship that is going to be important for us when we work: Saturation paths increase in chroma as they increase in value. This is true of all colors in light and is always an important relationship to keep in mind.

We can see how saturation would be mapped on the "chroma page" for red in image **64**. Chroma is the horizontal axis and value is vertical. Saturation is a path diagonally out from neutral black, increasing equally in chroma and value.

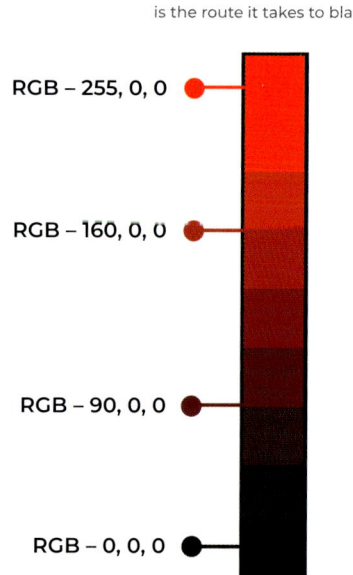

62 A color's saturation path is the route it takes to black.

RGB – 255, 0, 0

RGB – 160, 0, 0

RGB – 90, 0, 0

RGB – 0, 0, 0

Same chroma Same saturation

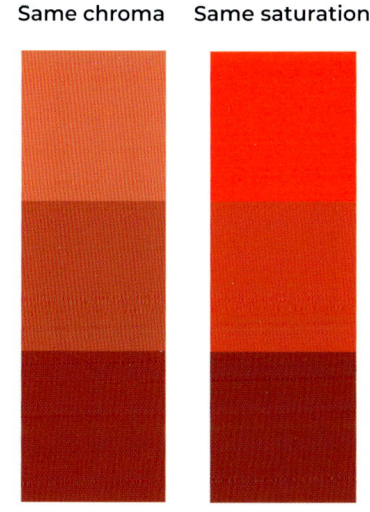

63 Comparing chroma and saturation as values increase.

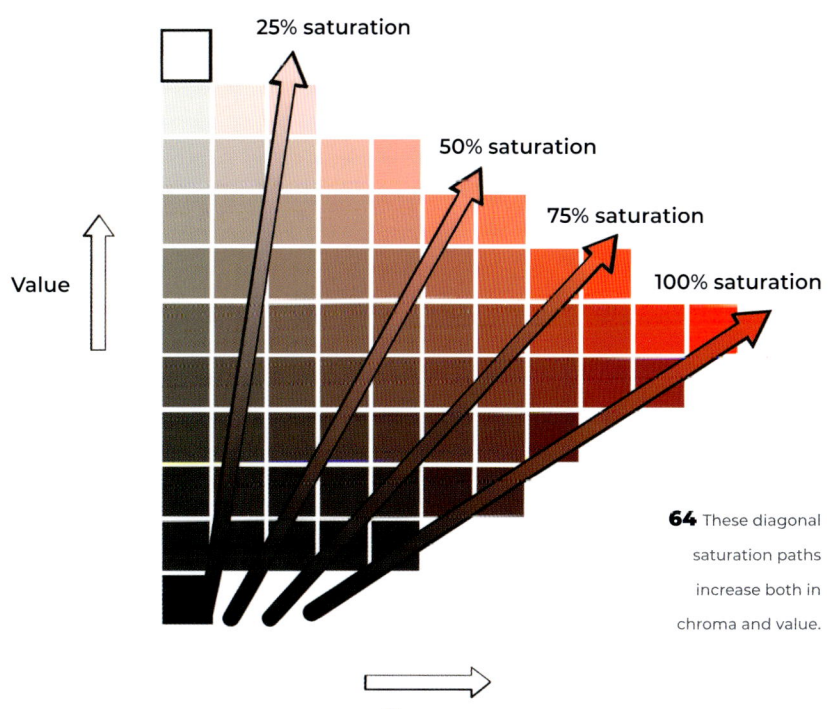

25% saturation

50% saturation

75% saturation

100% saturation

Value

Chroma

64 These diagonal saturation paths increase both in chroma and value.

CHROMA AND VALUE

In a way, we can think of all possible colors as having a common origin in neutral black (65). After all, with no light, there can be no color, so as colors darken they must also lose chroma. This relationship is commonly missed by students, but it is absolutely fundamental to how all colors behave as they brighten in value. However, when mixing traditionally, this theoretical neutral black is far darker than our paints will ever be.

Many students will try to use black to darken their paints. However, since our physical pigments cannot come close to absolute black, this will instead gray our mix far too much to maintain a saturation path. Image **66** compares the same color being darkened with black versus being darkened with the darkest version of itself in pigment. The latter clearly keeps us much closer to the color's true saturation path. Due to this, we will always need to do more than simply add black when darkening.

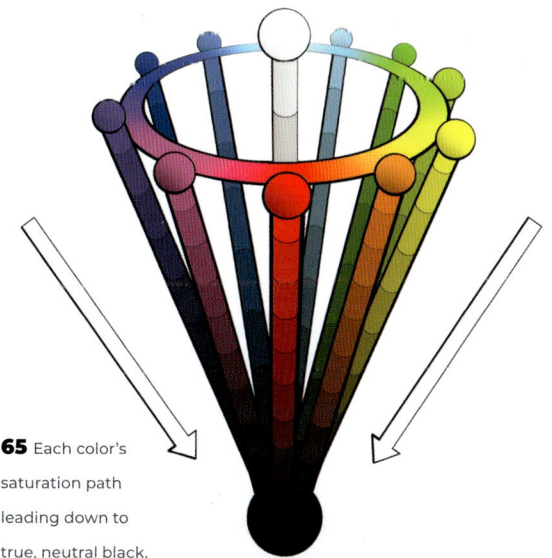

65 Each color's saturation path leading down to true, neutral black.

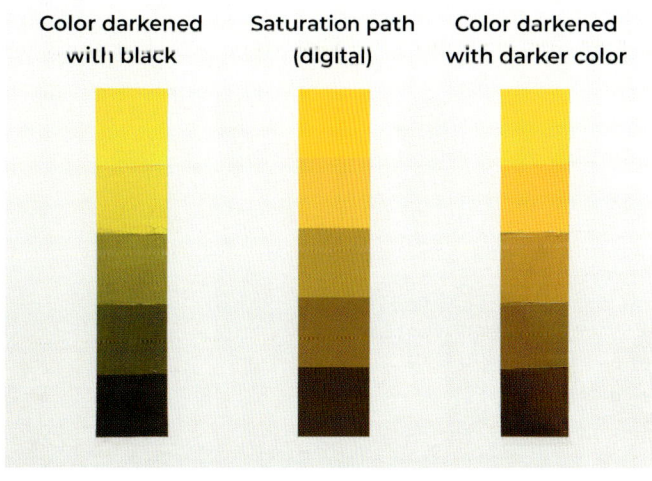

Color darkened with black

Saturation path (digital)

Color darkened with darker color

66 On the left is Cadmium Yellow Deep darkened with Mars Black; on the right is Cadmium Yellow Deep darkened with Transparent Oxide Yellow.

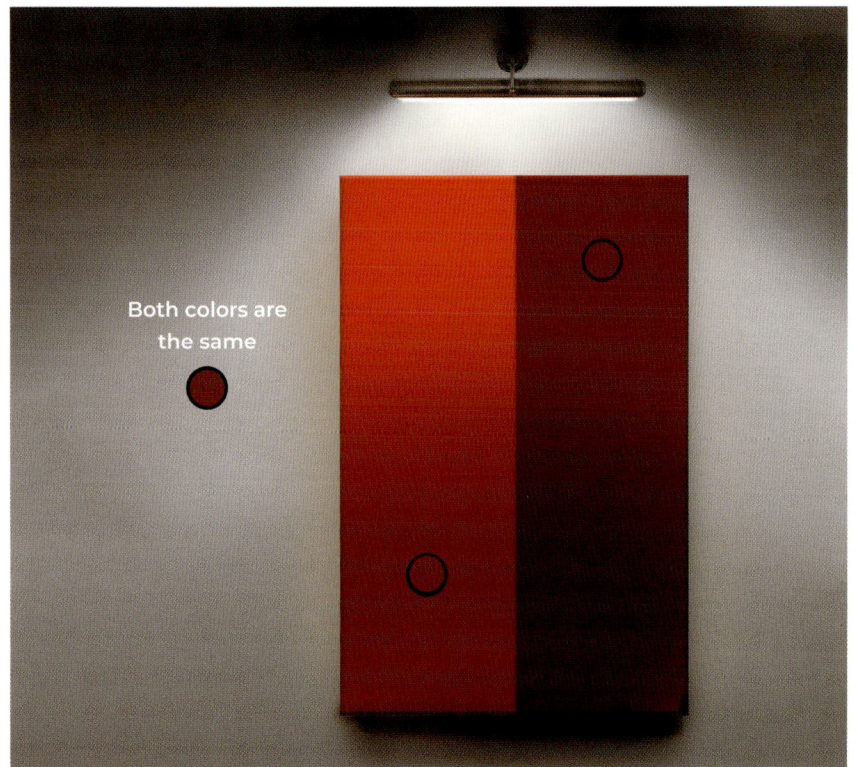

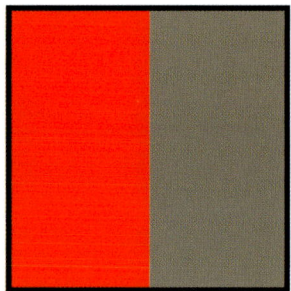

100% saturation red

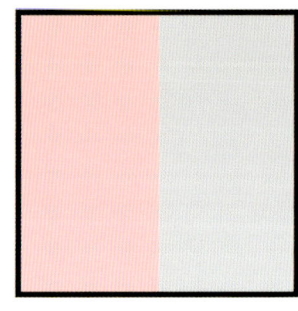

20% saturation red

67 These colors are the same despite appearing very different.

68 Desaturating a color also changes its value. See how much brighter in value the red becomes when we lower its saturation.

In image **67**, the two red circles are exactly the same color, but since one is surrounded by darker values, it appears brighter and more chromatic. When painting, this illusion will always affect us, so we need to judge color mixtures and relationships in context. Dark colors will always be slightly less chromatic than they appear in the reference. In fact, many traditional painters will deliberately gray their darks for this reason.

This matters for a digital painter because when we lower the saturation of a color, we might assume that its value remains consistent. However, this is not true. If we look at the two colors in image **68** and turn off the color information, we can see that the lower-saturation color is far brighter. This means that just lowering the Brightness slider or turning down an image's saturation doesn't help us accurately judge values in our work. This is a problem, as value is the most important quality in a painting!

Lab color

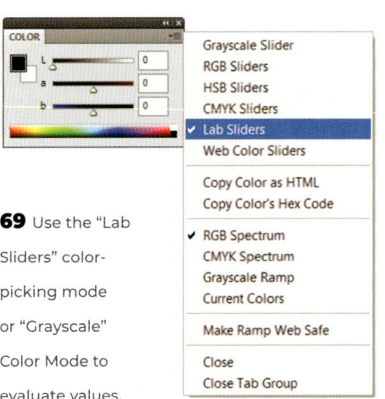

Grayscale

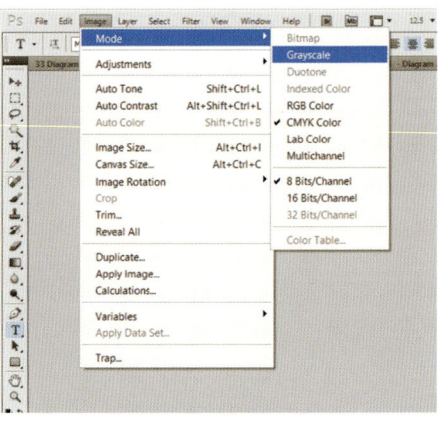

69 Use the "Lab Sliders" color-picking mode or "Grayscale" Color Mode to evaluate values.

Instead, if we want a reliable way to check our values in Photoshop, we can swap the image's color selection mode to "Lab Sliders" **(69)**. In this mode, the L value (lightness) will stay at a reliable and consistent level when color-picking. If we want to check the values of a painting as a whole, we can go to Image > Mode and convert to "Grayscale" color mode, or convert to "Lab color" before turning off the color information.

TINTS, SHADES, AND TONES

To organize and streamline how we think about color mixtures, it helps to make a separation in how we think of mixing colors. Using our most chromatic spectrum colors as a starting point, there are three ways that we can manipulate their chroma: by making tints, shades, or tones.

TINTS

"Tints" are the spectrum colors mixed up to white (70). As discussed on page 30, white is the most complete color in light, composed of all wavelengths. In a way, when we mix colors with white ("tinting" them), we are lowering the chroma by making the color more complete. These colors, often known as "pastel" colors, were favorites of the Impressionists (71). In terms of design, these colors tend to be associated with positive emotions, and images built around them can feel joyful and take on an "airy" atmosphere.

In traditional media, we can mix tints by mixing the pure pigment with white. Since this is the only way for us to access these colors traditionally, building images around them requires careful control of how many pigments are in our mixtures. In digital media, we can access these colors by keeping our Brightness slider high and lowering the Saturation slider instead.

SHADES

"Shades" are the spectrum colors mixed down to black (72). As discussed on page 41, these colors follow a saturation path down to black, like a colored light dimming down to total darkness. We create shades by taking away light. Traditional painters can create shades by mixing dark colors with the pure pigments. Digital artists can achieve the same effects by lowering the Brightness slider in their software.

While tints can make images feel light and airy, shades feel grounded and add a strong

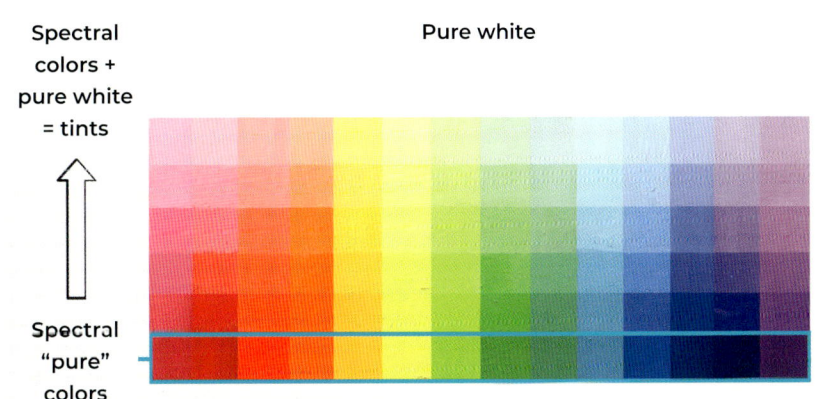

Spectral colors + pure white = tints

Pure white

Spectral "pure" colors

70 Tints are created by mixing the pure spectral colors with degrees of white.

71 Pastel colors are "tints" – colors mixed with white.

Spectral "pure" colors

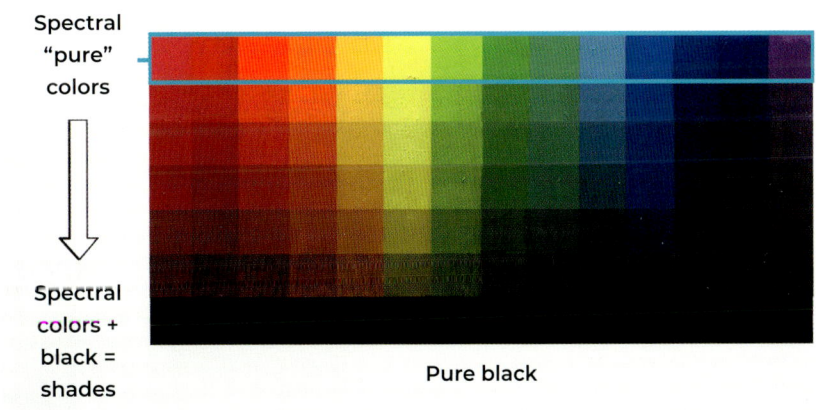

Spectral colors + black = shades

Pure black

72 Shades are the spectral colors mixed down to neutral black.

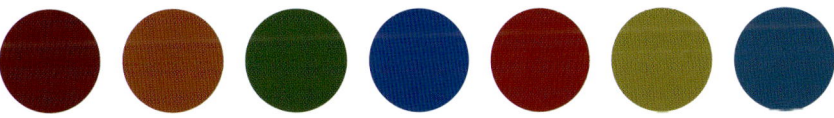

73 Examples of "shades" created by mixing colors with black.

sense of weight (73). For example, warm colors taken into shades become earthy browns. While both tints and shades lower the chroma of our mixtures, they have extremely different emotive qualities to consider when we design our imagery.

TONES

The final way that we can mix our colors are the "tones." Tones are created when both tinting (adding white) and shading (adding black) are applied to a color at the same time. Most paintings are built largely around tones. They require less mixing discipline, as they are achievable regardless of how much white and black is in a mixture. As you can see in image **74**, the deeper we get into tones, the closer we get to neutral gray, and the wider our range of available values.

PAINTING FOR VALUE VERSUS PAINTING FOR COLOR

This leads us to an important design choice we need to consider whenever we choose colors: How deep into the tones do we want to go? Just like the values on page 24, our available range of chroma is far more limited than the range visible in nature, so we need to make a conscious decision on what we want our paintings to convey.

· To access a wider range of values, we must limit the chroma in our image.

· To represent a full range of color, we must limit the range of values.

Students often believe that we can simply copy colors exactly as we see them, but this balancing act of limited ranges is always at play. It is often a surprise how much artists manipulate these qualities toward their chosen effect.

The examples in image **75** show what designing our work with these factors in mind looks like. Both paintings were created in the same lighting situation. In the top image, the chromatic range has been limited to allow a full range of value, while the bottom image shows the reverse design choice, limiting value but accessing a greater chromatic range.

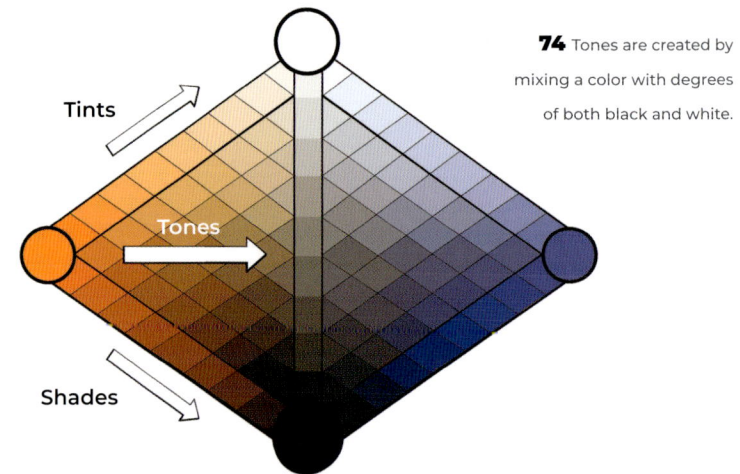

74 Tones are created by mixing a color with degrees of both black and white.

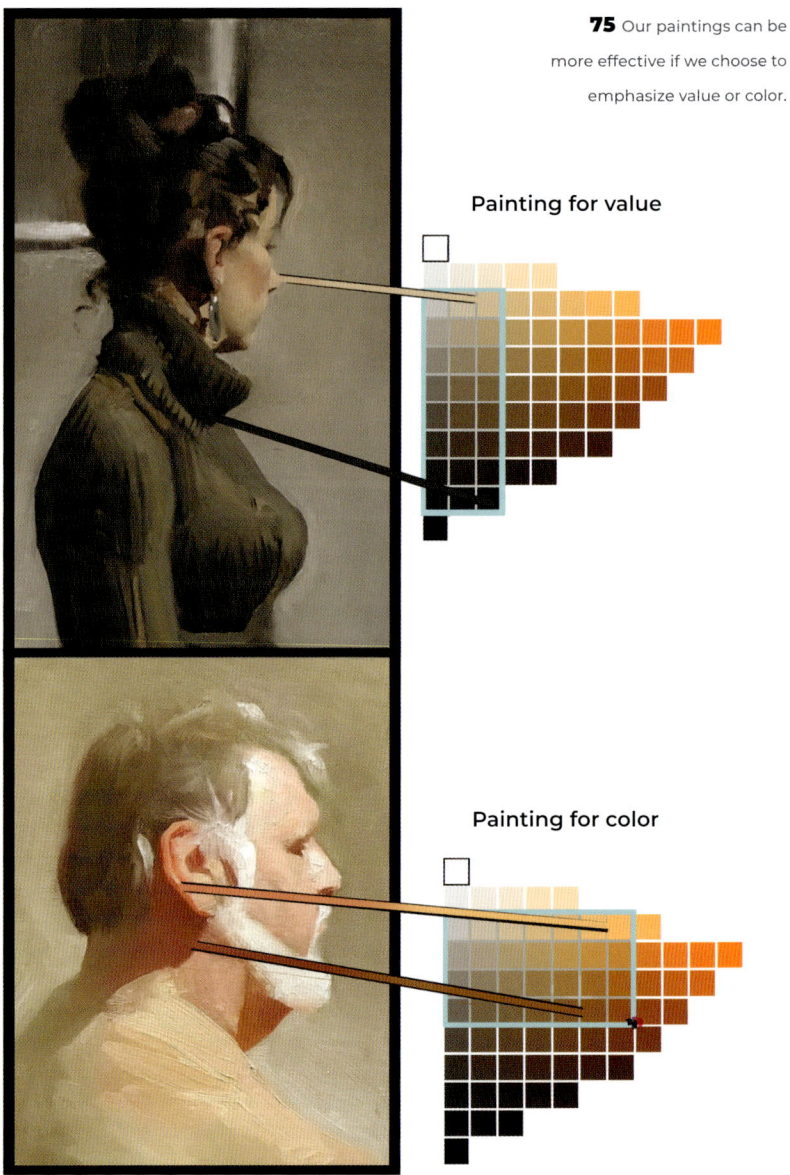

75 Our paintings can be more effective if we choose to emphasize value or color.

Painting for value

Painting for color

COLOR TEMPERATURE

However, even with the three Munsell qualities of hue, value, and chroma clearly set in our minds, the act of realistically representing our subject in full color can still be a challenge. Juggling various hues, chromas, and values can be confusing and it is easy to get overwhelmed. Luckily for us, there is a helpful simplification we can use to organize the varying color sensations: the concept of color temperature.

Through this concept, each color can be seen on a scale from "warm" colors (typically thought of as the oranges, yellows, and reds) to the "cool" colors (typically the blues). This is often the most fundamental question that we can ask ourselves when trying to judge a color relationship **(76)**.

Keep in mind that color temperature is highly subjective. It's difficult to make

absolute statements about exactly how cool or warm individual colors are. People tend to agree on the separation of the cool blues from the warmer red-yellow range, but where exactly the "most" cool or warm color is varies greatly with individual perception. Interestingly, this lines up with our knowledge of the color spectrum, with warm colors having low-energy wavelengths and cool colors being higher-energy **(77)**.

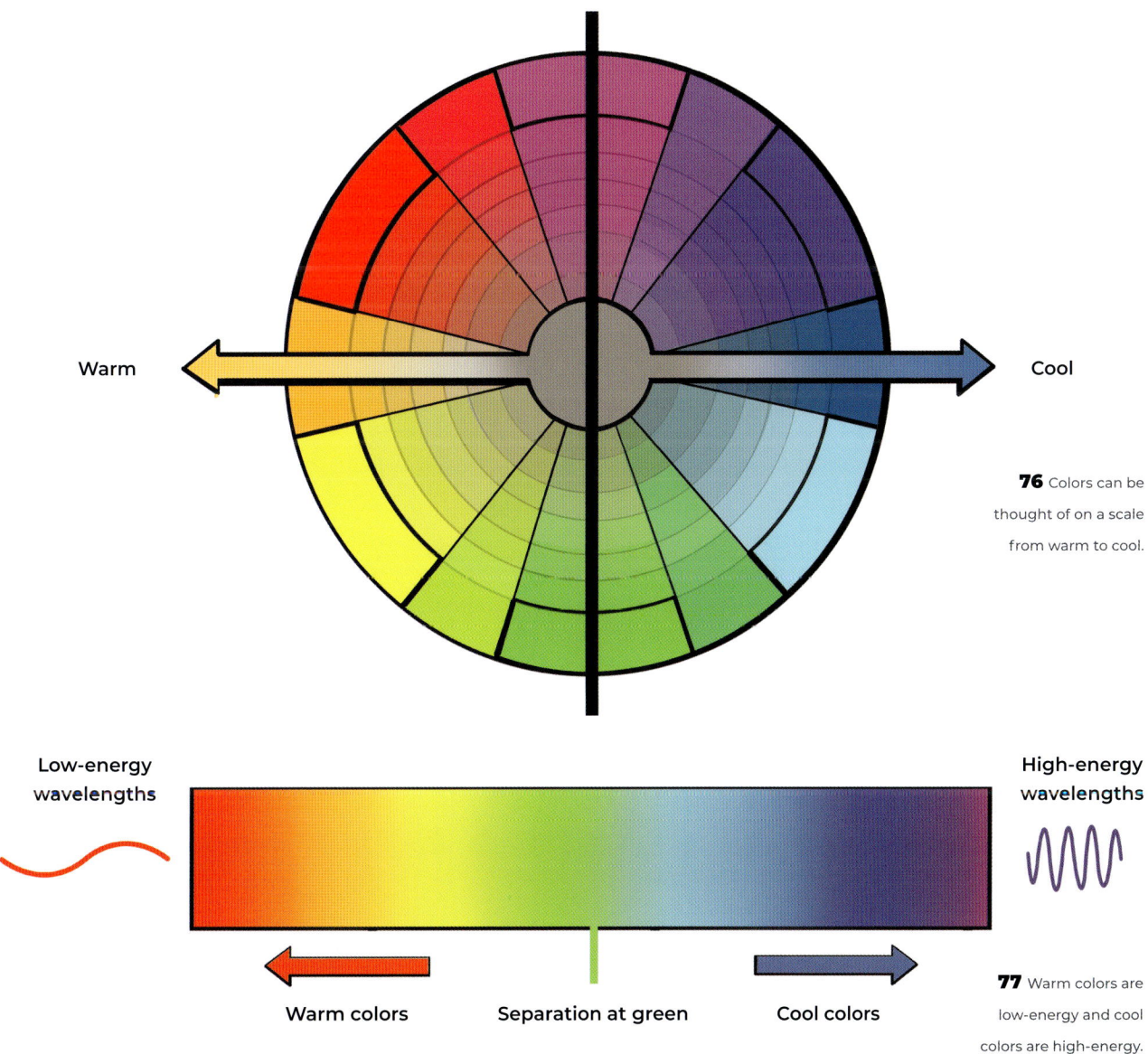

Warm

Cool

76 Colors can be thought of on a scale from warm to cool.

Low-energy wavelengths

High-energy wavelengths

Warm colors   Separation at green   Cool colors

77 Warm colors are low-energy and cool colors are high-energy.

WHY ARE COLOR TEMPERATURES USEFUL?

There is often disagreement among painters as to which colors are warm or cool in the absolute. Many artists will disagree about whether yellow is warmer or cooler than red, or whether cyan or violet-blue are the coldest colors. There are some theories that can explain how this is organized, which we will discuss on page 48, but for now we will simply focus on the broad separation of warm and cool (**78a–b**).

Attempting to assign an absolute temperature to colors is largely unimportant to our work as artists. Instead, the concept of temperature is most useful as a way to describe and judge the subtle relationship between two or more colors. In image **79**, we could say that the left square is a warm red, the middle square is a neutral red, and the right is a cool red. Even though they are all technically in the warm color range, we can examine this relationship between them and describe them in this way. We can do this for any two or more colors, and it will be the main question we ask ourselves when trying to judge the accuracy of our mixtures.

Just like with value, our eye will also exaggerate the contrast between a color's temperature and its surrounding context. Due to this visual exaggeration, the same color can be seen as both warm or cool depending on its surroundings, as you can see with the central gray squares in image **80**. Using the concept of temperature to judge colors allows us to get to the core of the relationships between colors. It grants us massive utility in making subtle adjustments, making it much easier to judge accurate color, as well as granting us a huge creative utility.

If we can make sure to represent these temperature relationships properly, we can take our paintings into any color field that we like and they will be believable. Color temperature allows us to move beyond simply copying the exact colors that we observe, freeing us up to design our colors in ways that bring out expression and storytelling.

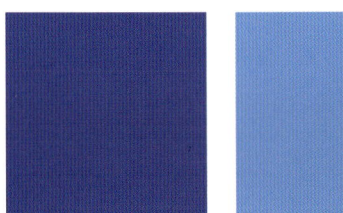

78a Which of these blues is the coldest to you?

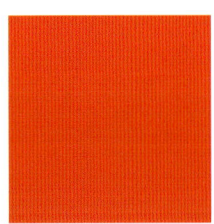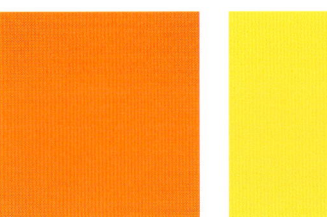

78b Which of these colors is the warmest?

79 Red can be thought of as a warm color, but even within it we can find temperature variations.

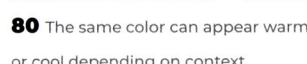

80 The same color can appear warm or cool depending on context.

TEMPERATURE AND LIGHT

The concept of high-energy and low-energy wavelengths and color temperatures will be revisited on pages 116–125, where you'll learn how different color temperatures of light are made and measured, and how different times of day can influence the temperature of the daylight we see. For now, just keep in mind what we've learned about the varying energy levels of the color spectrum, and that a color can change appearance depending on its surroundings.

THE VALUE OF HUES

As we move on to the third and final color dimension, hue, the first thing to discuss is that every pure hue on the spectrum has an inherent value. This is something often not initially realized, and it is often a beginner's instinct to ignore this and try to treat each color on its own. However, inherent values have a huge effect on how we approach mixing.

To understand this better, let's have a look at a spectrum simplified to our three primary hues, with two secondary colors in between, and convert it to black and white values **(81)**. When you initially look at this, you may be tempted to assume that this is a completely random set of values and it may be hard to work out any useful patterns. However, there are a few useful things that we can say here. First, we can see that the darkest of all of our hues is our light primary, blue, and the brightest of these values is our secondary yellow.

We can observe another pattern here if we group the hues into pure primaries and secondaries of light **(82)**. If we group the colors this way, we can see that the primary colors are generally darker than each secondary color, and the hues become higher in value as they move into the secondary colors. This is easily explainable via the primary color theory that we learned about on page 30: Since two of the cones in our eyes are activated when we observe a secondary color, and they mix additively, it makes sense that these in-between colors would be brighter.

If we place our three primaries directly next to each other, we can see a clear value difference between them, with blue being the darkest and green the brightest **(83)**. While we can easily observe this, it is not as easily explained by what we have discussed so far. What causes this value differential?

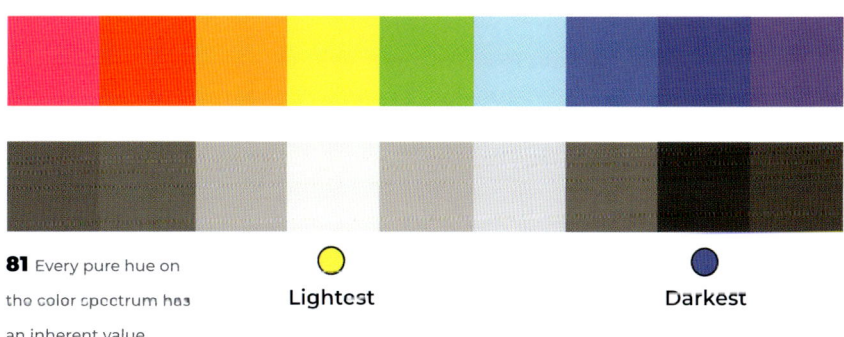

81 Every pure hue on the color spectrum has an inherent value.

Lightest   Darkest

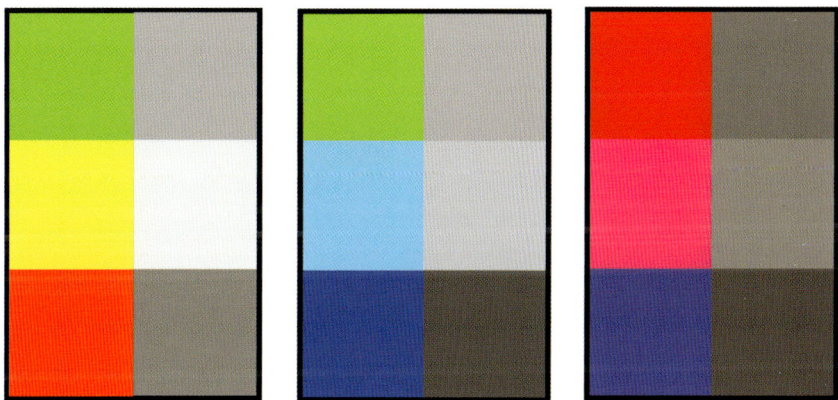

82 When mixing additively, the resulting colors (middle row) will have a lighter value.

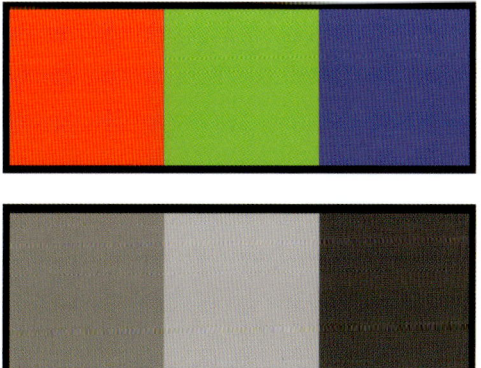

83 The primary colors have an obvious difference in value.

CONE SENSITIVITY

In order to explain this value difference between hues, it will be useful to get more accurate in how we conceptualize color. While it can sometimes be useful to think of color as something that physically exists in the world and is picked up by our eyes, this is not strictly true. The only objective aspect of color is that it is electromagnetic radiation of varying energies and wavelengths **(84)**. However, the colors in visible light do not actually "exist" physically on the spectrum or in the world.

We don't need to understand the entire spectrum in-depth, as visible light is the only section that matters to us as artists. All colors are invented in our brains as a way to organize these wavelengths of radiation and make sense of the world.

When the cone cells in our eyes were introduced on page 30, they were described as red, green, and blue cones. While it's true that we have these three different cones, it would be more accurate to call them short, medium, and long cones. These three cone types are actually sensitive to a range of wavelengths – they overlap in sensitivity and any single wavelength of light will activate at least two cone types **(85)**. Whenever a wavelength of light enters our eye, our brain compares the response levels of these different cones to work out what we are looking at.

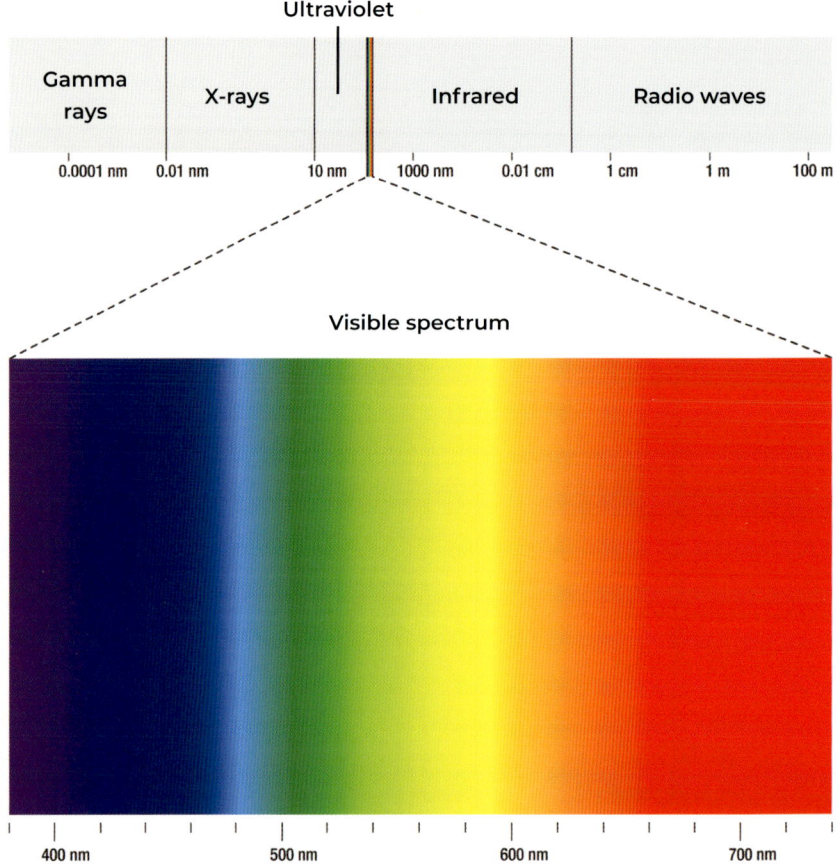

84 Only a small segment of the electromagnetic spectrum is visible to us as color.

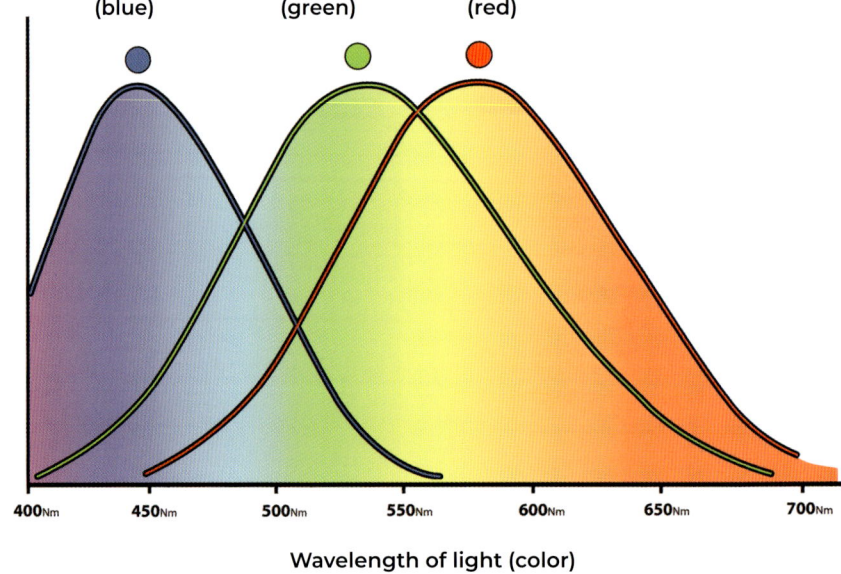

85 The three cones in our eye actually overlap in color sensitivity.

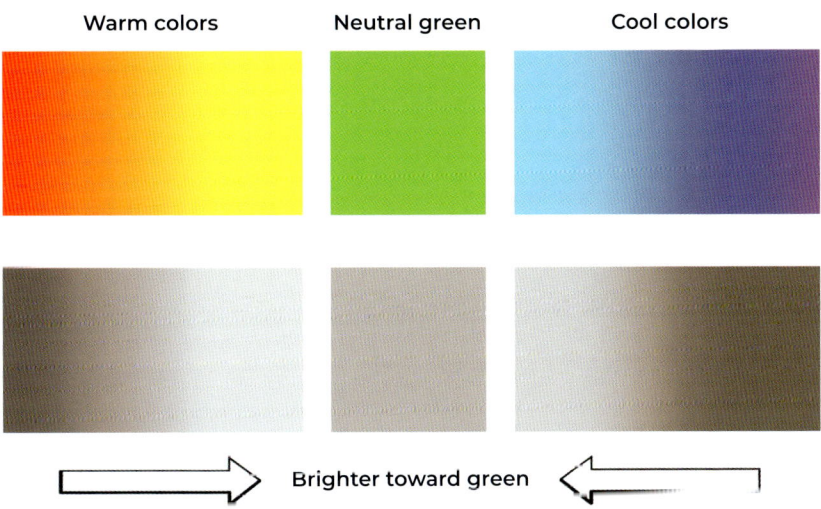

Warm colors   Neutral green   Cool colors

Brighter toward green

86 The cool and warm ends of the spectrum meet in the middle at green.

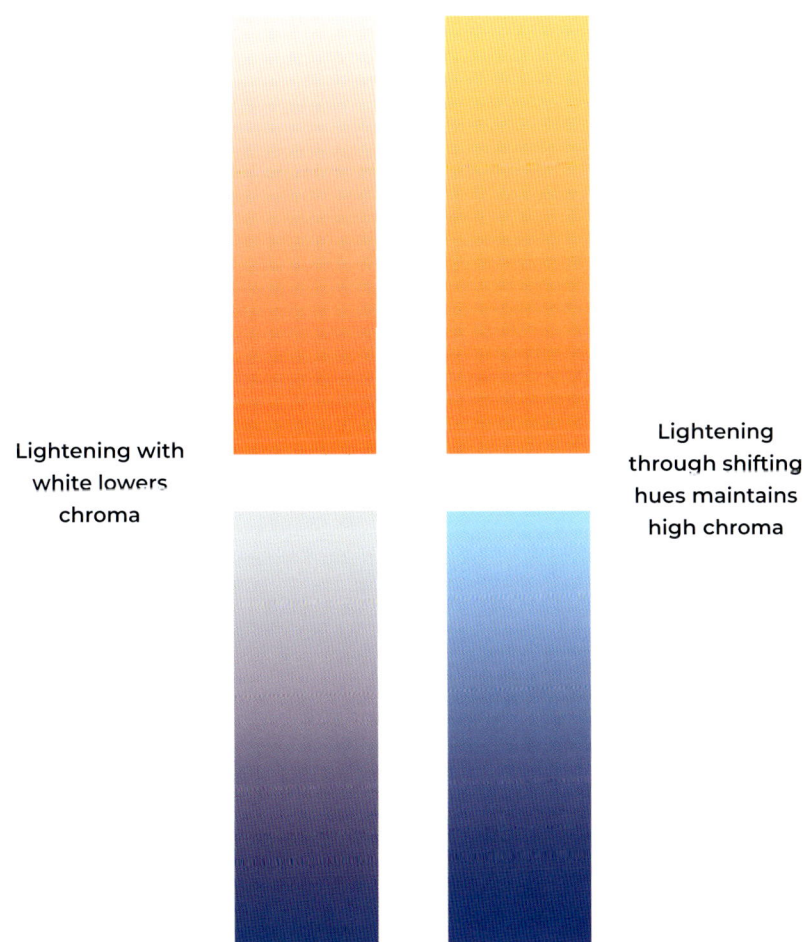

Lightening with white lowers chroma

Lightening through shifting hues maintains high chroma

87 We can achieve more vibrant mixes by using lighter-valued hues rather than white to brighten our colors.

One of the most interesting things that we learn by looking at the cones this way is that, while the blue (short) and green (medium) cones peak in sensitivity in their named colors, the red (long) cone doesn't peak in the red section of the spectrum. It actually peaks in the yellow/green section.

It's this varying sensitivity that explains the variation in the values of our primaries. As you can see in image **85**, when seeing blue, both the short and medium cones are activated. However, the medium cone is only activated weakly, so blue appears dark in value to us. When seeing red, the medium and long cones are weakly activated, but to fairly equal levels, so red appears dark but lighter than blue.

When seeing green, all three cones overlap and are activated, with the long and medium cones strongly activated. This makes green appear brighter. In the brightest color, yellow, both the long and medium cones are near their peak sensitivity, so we see yellow as the brightest color.

But how are these changing hue values helpful to our artistic practice? It is useful to return to the idea of warm and cool color temperatures here. As we learned previously, for this concept we can view green as the neutral between the two worlds of warm and cool colors **(86)**. If we take these two worlds, we can see a clear gradation from dark to light toward our central green.

This is useful for us in our practice because when we want to raise the value of a color mixture, it may feel like our only option is to add white, either with physical paint or through desaturation in digital work. However, being aware of inherent values opens up new options for mixing while maintaining maximal chroma. If we compare brightening our mixture by adding white versus adding a color with lighter inherent value, we can see how much more vibrant our mixtures can be **(87)**.

EXTRA-SPECTRAL COLORS

While this three-cone idea of color explains color-mixing extremely well, it leaves a few gaps in our understanding of how we psychologically experience color. As mentioned before, color is just a way for our brains to organize the various wavelengths we are always experiencing. There is another way we can organize these sensations, which will give us some new insight, but first let's examine some of those gaps in the three-cones theory.

WHAT ABOUT YELLOW?

The first of these gaps becomes clear when we look closer at the steps between our primaries **(88)**. If we look at the colors between red and blue, and green and blue, each step can be described in terms of the two primaries that make it up – for example, greenish blue or reddish purple. Each step feels like a combination of the two primaries in varying ratios.

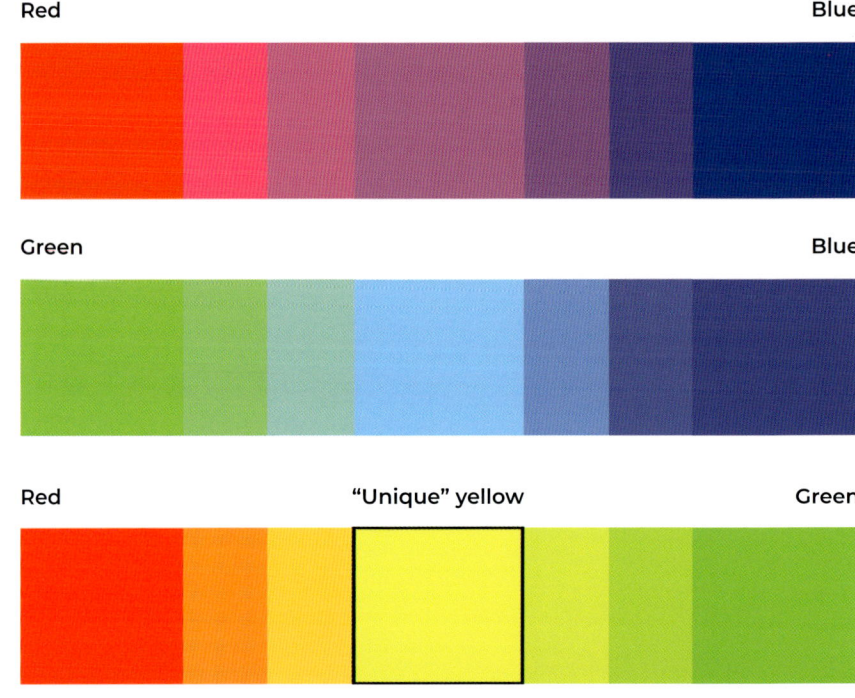

88 How is yellow made from the primaries we know?

However, when we look at the steps between red and green, a new "unique" hue appears: yellow. "Unique" means this color can't be described in the terms of the two other primaries. The colors next to this yellow cannot be described by the opposing primaries, but can be by this new, unique yellow. For example, we see yellowish green and yellowish orange – not reddish green or greenish red! This indicates a gap in our three-cones theory. Where does this new yellow come from?

LIMITS OF THE LINEAR SPECTRUM

For the second gap in the three-cone theory of color, let's take another look at the color spectrum. If we observe the blue end of the spectrum, we can see that the closer we get to the end, the more our blue "feels red," ending in violet. There is a clear psychological link between these colors.

However, if we consider these colors purely as a linear spectrum, this doesn't make sense – these colors are the farthest away from each other that two colors can be! If color is something "real" in the world and we are just detecting it, these should feel the furthest apart of any two colors, yet they feel similar **(89)**. Colors don't exist in a circle but our brain psychologically connects these two opposite ends of the spectrum.

EXTRA-SPECTRAL COLORS

The third problem you might already have noticed is that purple, magenta, and the colder red colors don't actually exist on the spectrum **(90)**. In fact, there is no single wavelength associated with any of these colors, yet we still see them. Our brain actually invents them when colors from both ends of the spectrum are added together. It's important to understand that this doesn't

make these colors any less "real." As we have already said, all colors are an invention of the brain, so these "extra-spectral" colors are as real as any others. They simply do not exist on our linear color spectrum.

These added colors seem to be the reason why a color wheel appeals to our sensation of color so well, even though the wheel does not conform to the physical reality of wavelengths. So where do these colors come from, and how can we understand them?

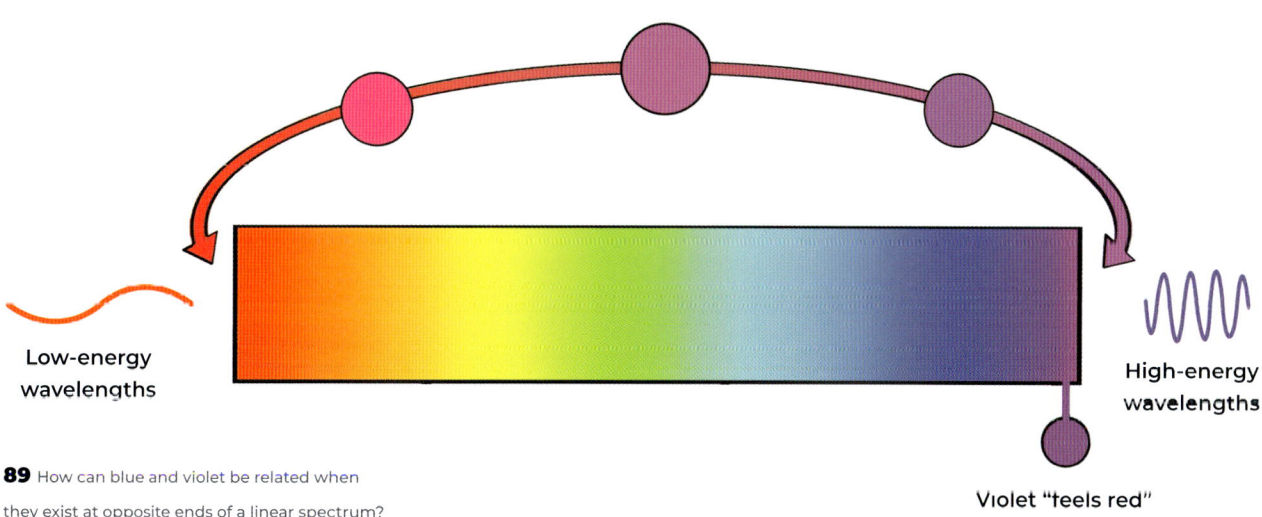

Low-energy
wavelengths

High-energy
wavelengths

Violet "feels red"

89 How can blue and violet be related when
they exist at opposite ends of a linear spectrum?

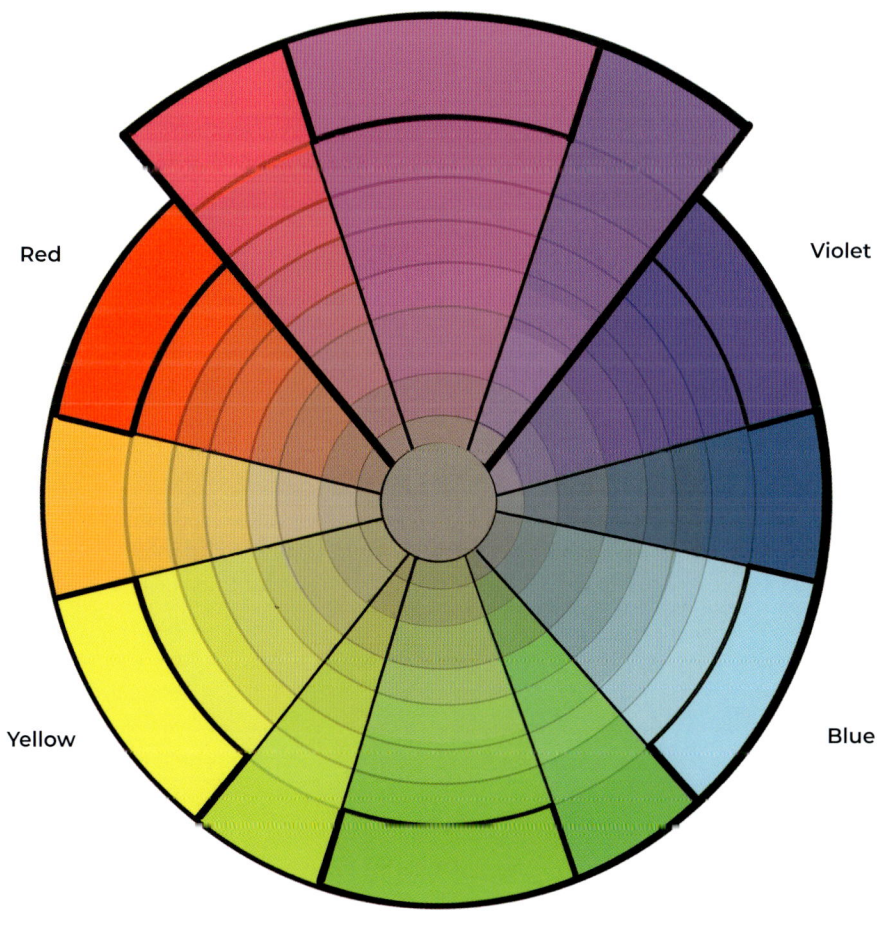

Red

Violet

Yellow

Blue

Green

90 "Extra-spectral" colors like purple and
magenta have no home on the linear spectrum.

COLOR OPPONENCY

Now that we have seen some of the gaps in our theory so far, we can introduce a new idea that will help us address these problems: color opponency. The basic idea of this theory is that all our sensations of color can result from just three sets of paired "opponent" colors. These opponent pairs are green versus red, blue versus yellow, and black versus white.

What we mean when we call these colors "opponent" is that they are all "unique" colors that cannot be described in terms of each other. There are no greenish reds, bluish yellows, or blackish whites. We conceive of them weakening into a neutral gray that connects them **(91)**. All other colors can be described in terms of these colors, which we can call the "psychological" primaries, as opposed to the "physical" mixing primaries we have discussed previously.

It is generally understood that color opponency is the way that our brain organizes the raw data we gain through our three different cones. Our cones don't receive the exact position a wave exists on the spectrum, but rather its raw output, so our brains need this additional level of organization to deal with the multiple ways that a color sensation can be created.

It is important to understand that these primaries do not properly describe what happens when we mix colors – instead, they are primarily important in understanding how we perceive and organize color **(92)**.

You may have noticed that these opponent colors appear to have a warm/cool relationship – red and yellow being warm, and green and blue being cool. In fact, color opponency can be helpful for us in understanding this warm/cool temperature sensation. On page 49, we learned that we are able to make quite an objective

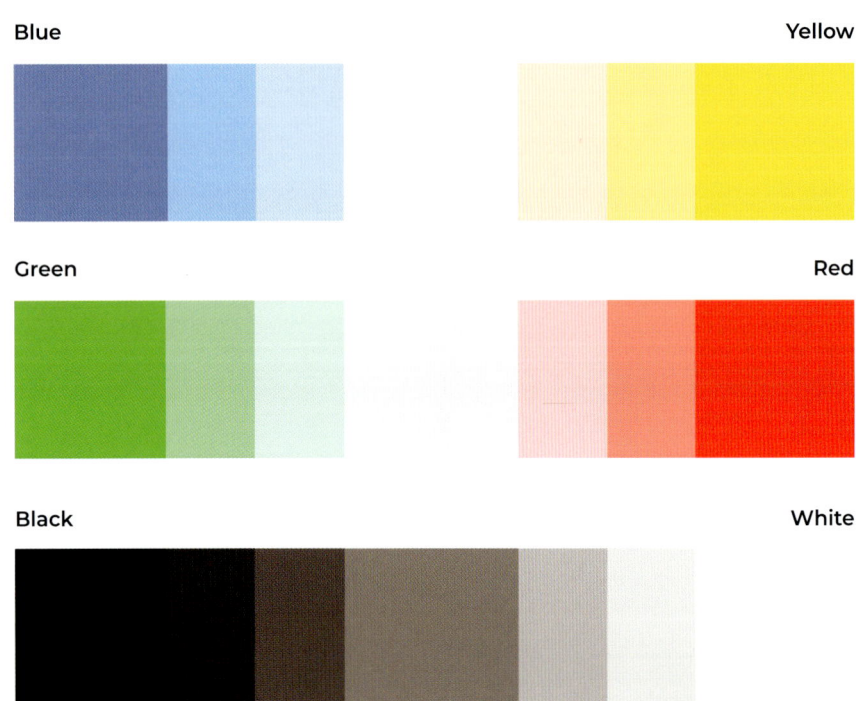

Blue · Yellow · Green · Red · Black · White

91 "Opponent" colors are complete opposites that cannot be described in terms of each other.

separation between warm and cool colors on either side of a neutral green. On either side of that neutral green are the yellow-blue opponent colors.

However, we have also learned that the warmth or coolness of specific colors is more subjective. Some would say that the warmest and coolest are the results of these psychological primaries mixed together: red-orange and cyan **(93)**. However, there is still room for variation here and not everyone will agree. What do you think?

We can see this color relationship clearly if we return to the spectrum **(94)**. Here we can also see the relationship between red and green. If we add in our extra-spectral colors (purple, magenta), then we can actually think of the sensation of red more as a distance from neutral green. In this way, both ends

of the spectrum are equally distant from our middle green, thus connecting them and explaining the "red" sensation we experience on both ends of the spectrum.

This linking of both ends of the spectrum explains why we instinctively favor a circular color model. We can see this concept illustrated on a color wheel in image **95**, with a separation of warms and cools with a central axis through green. If we want to explore this color space digitally, we can use the "Lab" color mode in Photoshop.

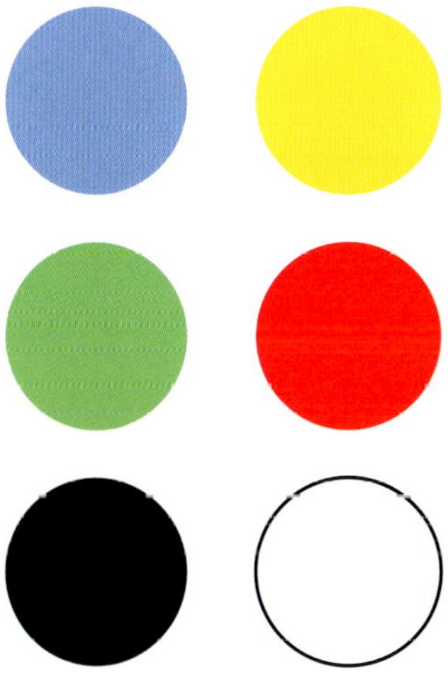

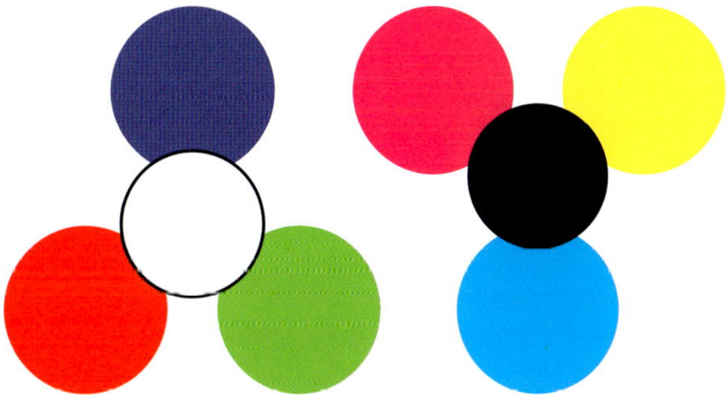

Psychological primaries

Mixing primaries

Additive   Subtractive

92 As well as our additive and subtractive mixing primaries, we can consider these opponent colors as a set of "psychological" primaries.

Red + yellow = warmest

Warm   Cool

Green + blue = coolest

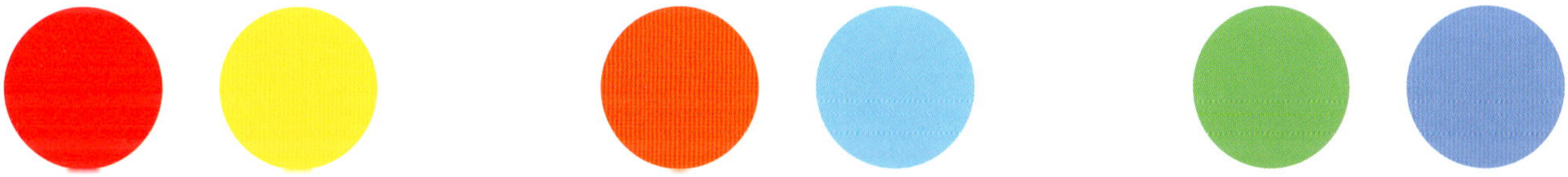

93 If we mix the warm and cool opponent pairs, we can find the two potentially warmest and coolest possible hues.

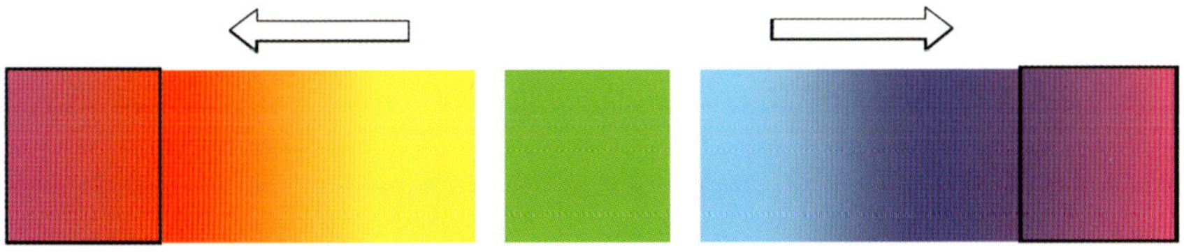

Warm colors   Neutral green   Cool colors

Yellow versus blue / Warm versus cool

94 The extra-spectral colors could be considered as equally distant from green.

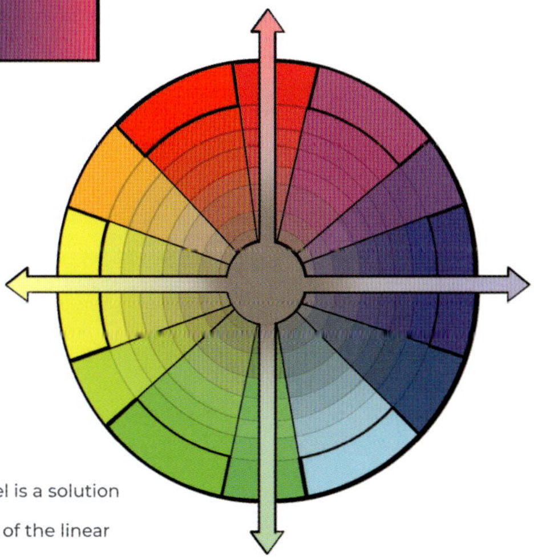

Red

Yellow   Blue

Green

95 The color wheel is a solution that joins the ends of the linear spectrum and feels natural to us.

COLOR CONSTANCY, PART 2: HUE

As you will have realized by now, one of the most important things to know about hue as a color quality is just how subjective it is. As we discussed on page 17, hue is just the spice of the image and is more responsible for a work's expression than it is for achieving realism.

It's common to think of the hue of an object as being contained within the object – something that is inherent and unchanging. However, the reality is that we move through many different-colored light sources throughout the day. The absolute color that we observe from an object is changing all the time and our eye is incredibly effective at correcting these changes. Just like with our other color dimensions, this is the illusion of color constancy.

As we now know, our eyes exaggerate the contrast between any two colors. If we look at the two squares in image **96**, we can see this effect in action. Both central squares are the same neutral gray. However, a blue background lends a warm tinge to the gray, while an orange background makes the gray appear slightly cooler.

This effect is seen even more clearly if we take it into a more realistic context. In image **97**, there are four paintings of a cube with multiple hues: yellow, blue, red, and green. By manipulating the surrounding context, we can make the same neutral gray take on the appearance of any one of these four hues. Even when this is clearly indicated to us, it's difficult to break the illusion.

This should be enough to convince you that we can really use any hues that we like within our images. This awareness will free us up to focus on the more important expressive messages of our artwork.

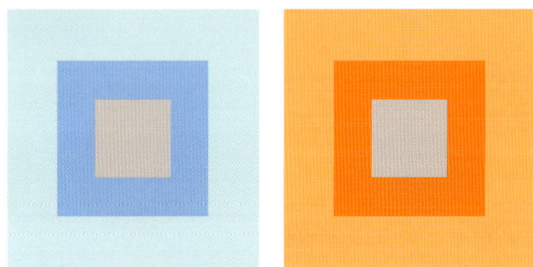
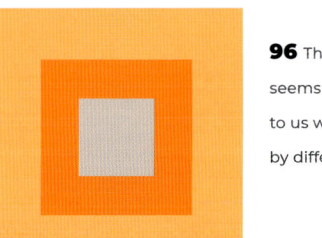

96 The same neutral gray seems completely different to us when surrounded by different hues.

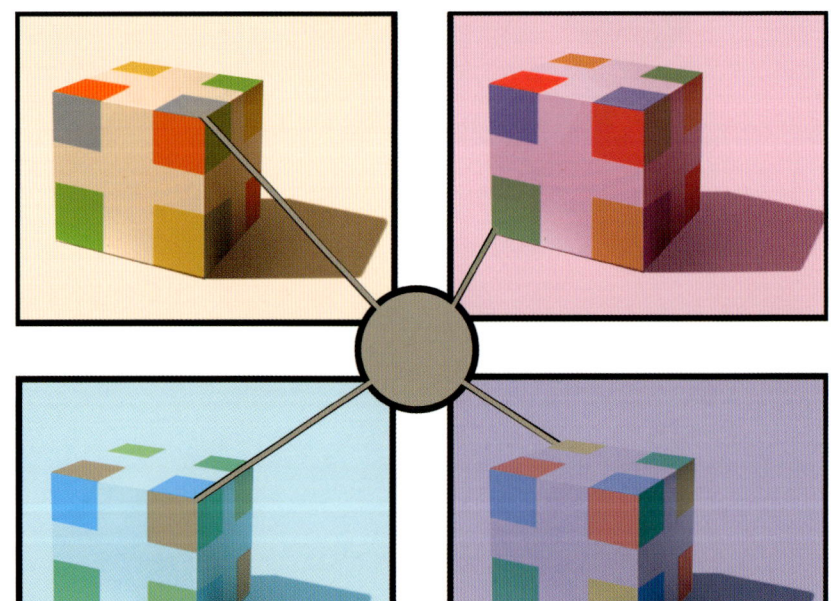

97 The same neutral gray appears radically different in the context of each painting.

COLOR GAMUTS

Now that we know the creative possibilities available to us, how do we actually go about controlling them in an image? A useful concept for us here is the idea of color gamuts. A color gamut is the range of colors available within a color space.

In image **98**, we have a representation of the shape of the full range of colors available to the human eye. However, note that many of these colors are not available to us on RGB screens, and even fewer in CMY printing. Since this book is printed, too, this shape can only ever be an artist's representation of this color space!

When we work, we will always be working within a limited gamut. Learning to define and deliberately work within a chosen gamut is the main skill we need to acquire in order to control the mood of our work. The examples in image **99** show the color illusion from above alongside the

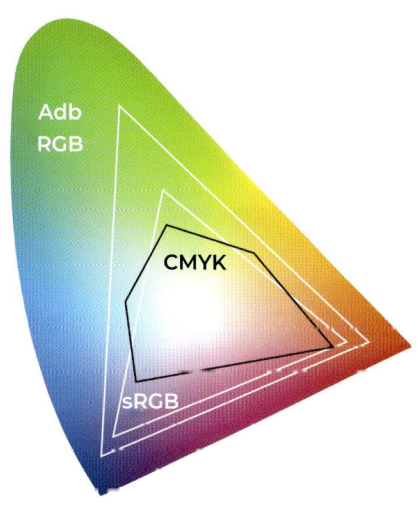

98 The visible color spectrum with the Adobe RGB color gamut, standard RGB (sRGB) gamut, and CMYK gamut inside it.

Blue gamut

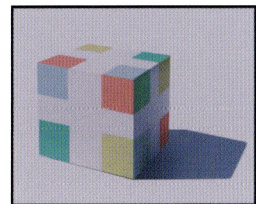 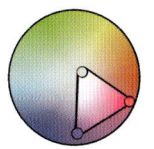

Cyan gamut

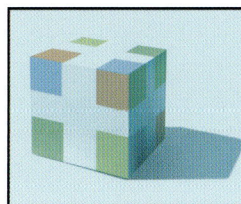 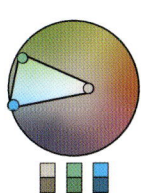

Magenta gamut

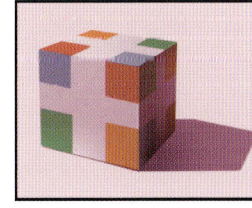 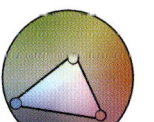

Yellow gamut

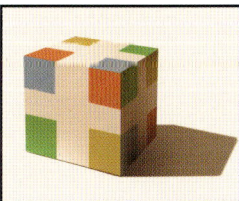 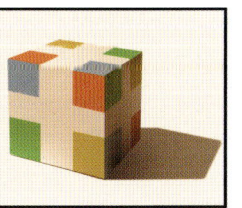 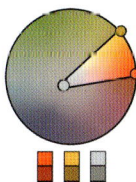

99 Limiting ourselves to color gamuts can help create very different effects. Below each wheel are samples of the light, midtone, and dark values for each primary.

Light
Midtone
Dark

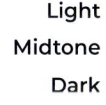 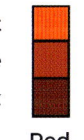 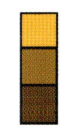 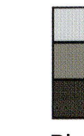

Red   Yellow   Blue

gamuts used to make them. To achieve this particular illusion, we start by defining each hue as a neutral gray, then shift the other two primaries in the same direction to build our gamut. It is useful to premix the limits of our desired color gamut, represented here as points on the color wheel, before we start our painting. Once we have a gamut mixed, it's a lot easier to work purposefully within our chosen limitations. While those limitations are represented here as a simple wheel, they need to be considered at each level of the value scale.

When working traditionally, we are forced to be much more deliberate when deciding on a gamut, since we are much more limited in the ways that we can color-correct an image. Digital work offers more flexibility to adjust colors later using sliders and adjustment layers, but when learning about color gamuts, it is helpful to try to use these tools as deliberately as possible.

Image **100** shows one way of organizing traditional gamut mixtures – mixing our chosen gamut at three value stages, so there are light, midtone, and dark options available for each. Many artists spend as

Light ⟵⟶ Dark

Warm

Cool

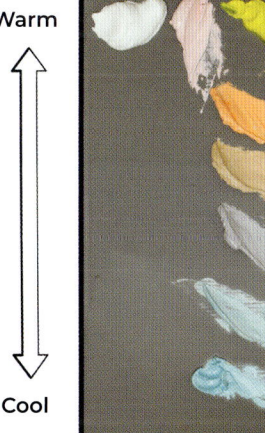 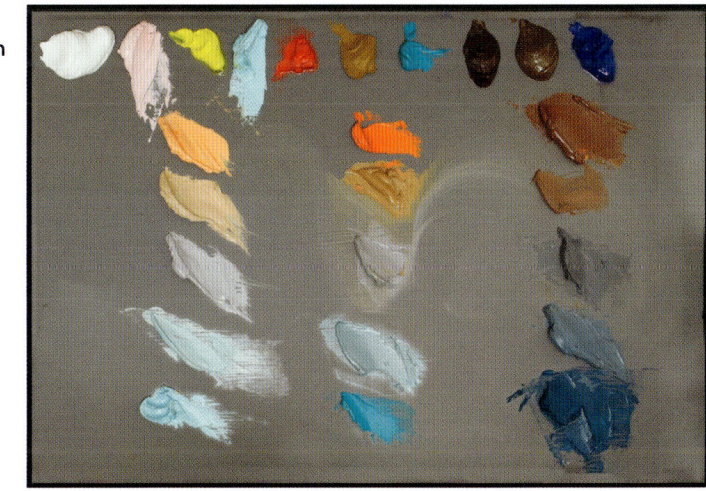

100 Establish a strong palette by mixing a range of lights, midtones, and darks in different color temperatures for your chosen color gamut.

much time considering and choosing these initial colors as they do creating the actual painting! Planning our color gamut is a vital step, and the more carefully we consider these initial color choices, the stronger our work will be.

EXPOSURE IN COLOR

As we delve into deciding color gamuts for an image, we need to understand how the concept of exposure applies when discussing color. As introduced on page 24, this concept, borrowed from photography, can be hugely helpful to us when we create our images.

Some of you may be familiar with the terms "overexposed" and "underexposed." Many of you may already understand that an overexposed image is too bright and an underexposed image is too dark. It will be useful for us to define these terms more precisely, and explore how they apply to our work as painters.

OVEREXPOSURE

As you may remember from our previous discussion on page 24, information is lost (or "clipped" out) when we try to capture the vast range of nature through a medium such as photography or paint. Since we work with limited materials, this will always be happening somewhat in any image we make.

Overexposure is when this clipping effect interacts with the value limitations of color. In the light areas of image **101**, we can see that the blue of the sea and sky, the gray of the rocks, and the orange of the grass are represented with bleached, barely distinct colors, even though they are extremely different in reality.

As mentioned on page 43, the only way to lighten colors past a certain point is to tint them with white. Adding white gradually brings our colors closer together, making them less distinct. If we go too high into these tints, overexposure is the result.

UNDEREXPOSURE

Underexposure, by contrast, is the reverse effect. Instead of the lights being too indistinct, losing information into the tints, an underexposed image occurs when the darks are taken too far down the value scale, leaving them indistinct.

As we learned on page 41, all colors darken to an imagined perfectly neutral black, losing chroma along their saturation paths as they darken and move deeper into the shades. In image **102**, we can see an example of this in the distant rocks and water, the orange shadows in the mountains, and the darker blues of the sky, which all look more or less the same.

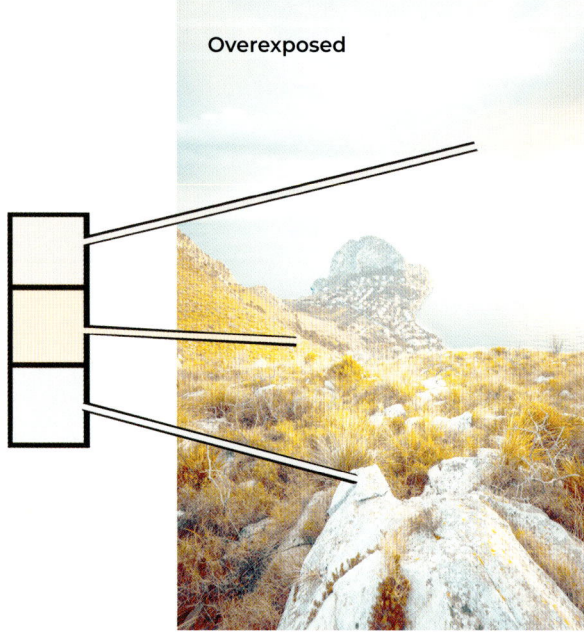

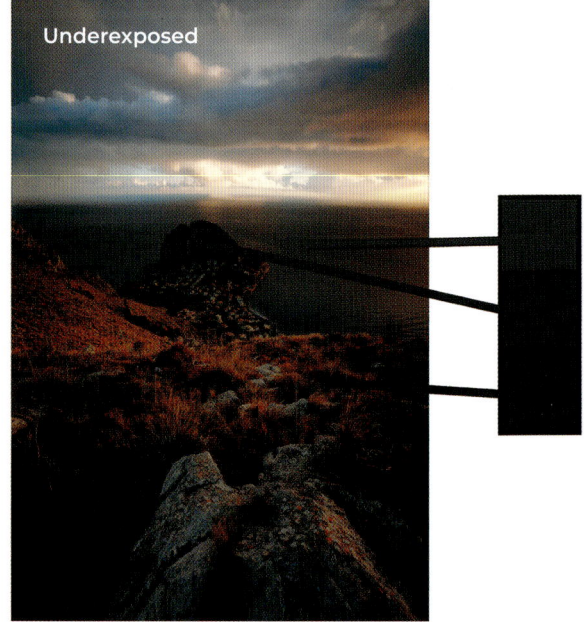

101 In an overexposed image, the lights are grouped too close to white, so colors in the lights become indistinct.

102 In an underexposed image, the darks are grouped too close to black, so colors in the darks become indistinct.

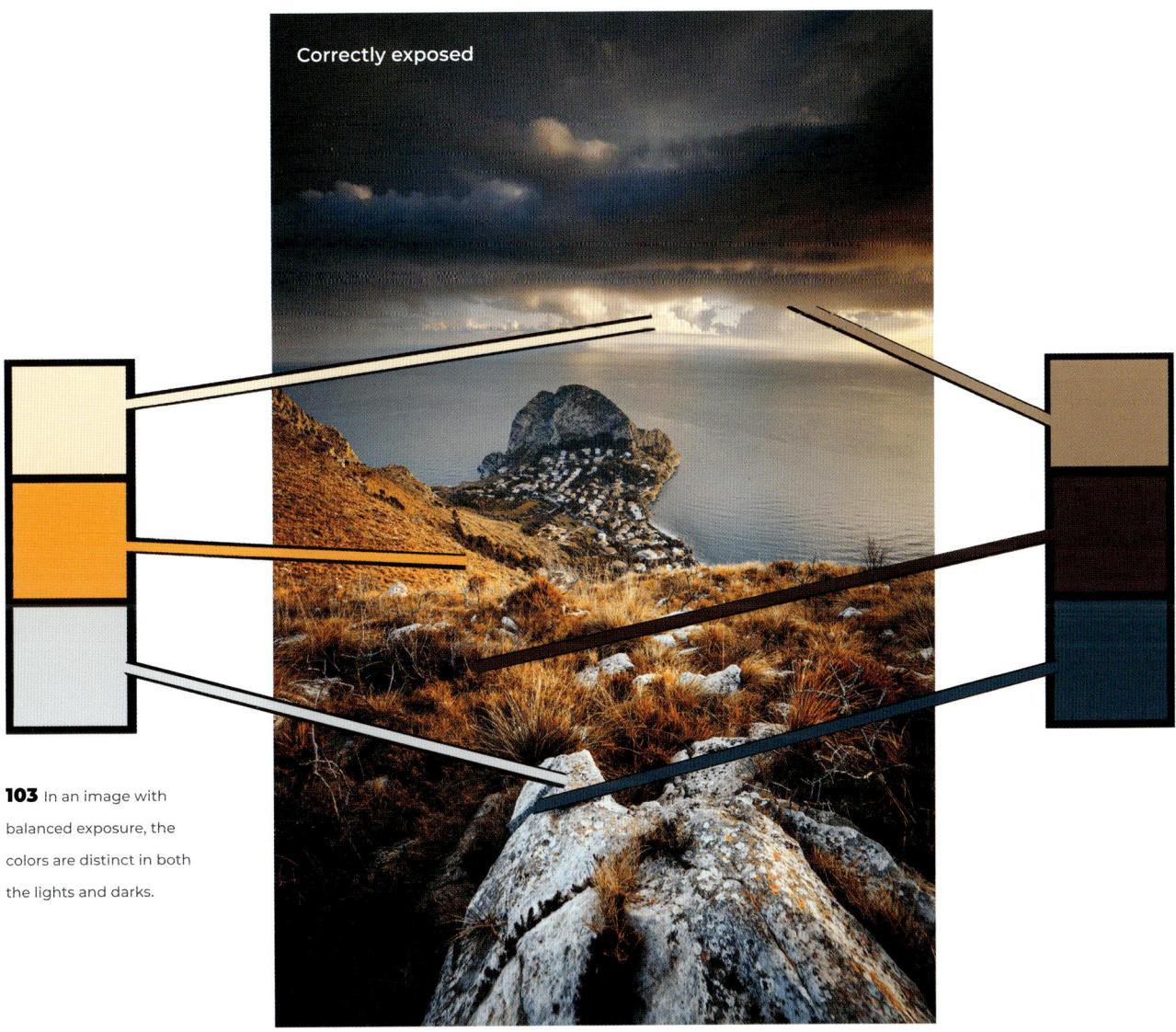

Correctly exposed

103 In an image with balanced exposure, the colors are distinct in both the lights and darks.

CORRECT EXPOSURE

So if we want our images to feel correctly exposed, we must aim for clear, distinctly separate colors all the way throughout the values of our images, as shown in image **103**. In this correctly exposed version of the scene, the full range of the sky is visible, the water is clearly blue, the foreground rocks are light-colored but still detailed, and we can properly see the range of light and shade in the orange grass.

Achieving correct exposure will often require us to deliberately limit how bright we go in our lights and how dark we go in our darks. Becoming sensitive to this quality in our work is an extremely important skill for us to develop.

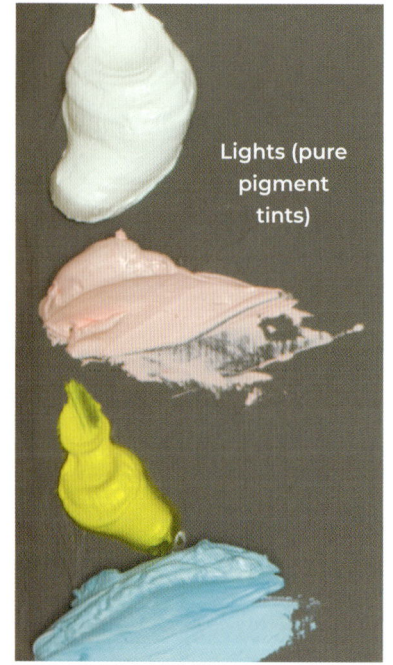

Lights (pure pigment tints)

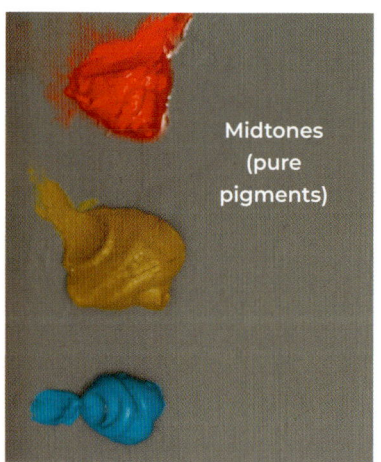

Midtones (pure pigments)

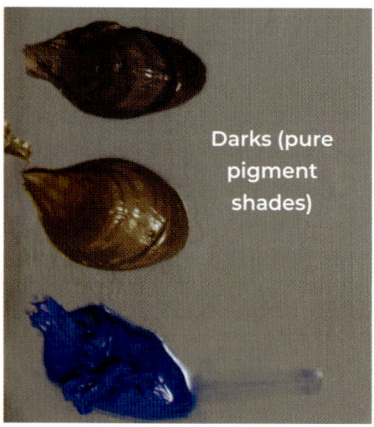

Darks (pure pigment shades)

COLOR SOLUTIONS TO EXPOSURE

You might now be asking, "How do we actually, practically avoid these problems of over- and underexposure in our imagery?" We now know that it is extremely useful to define a color gamut before we begin a painting. But how do we set this up in a way that will help us with exposure?

One extremely useful and practical way to control this aspect of our paintings is the practice of "stringing out" our colors before we begin painting. This practice involves mixing our chosen pure colors into lights, midtones, and darks in the purest way that we can. If we do this before creating any mixtures for our final painting, we can see how distinct our colors can be at their maximum chroma for our chosen value range **(104)**.

If we are disciplined in deciding and sticking to this in our work, we can avoid running into exposure problems by mistake. However, when approaching a painting, we may not be sure of exactly how wide we want our value range to be, and how this exposure effect will actually look in context. Due to this, it can be useful for us to keep

our options as open and flexible as possible. One way to do this, shown in image **105**, is to start an image low in contrast, staying as close to the middle of the value scale as possible for the early stages of the painting. As the painting develops, we can then work our way toward the higher-contrast values.

Since many of the pure colors fall among these middle values, working in this way keeps us relatively safe from accidentally over- or underexposing our image. This method was used by many great artists of the past and can be an extremely effective way of working.

COLOR ASSIMILATION

Of course, we are not obligated to fully follow these rules in every image, and many image designs may require us to over- or underexpose for expressive effect. In fact, purposefully breaking exposure rules can often open the way to some of the stronger effects available to us.

One illusion that we can use to our advantage when we want to overexpose is "color assimilation" **(106)**. This is the tendency for the color next to a neutral color to seemingly "bleed" into the neutral color. If we place an

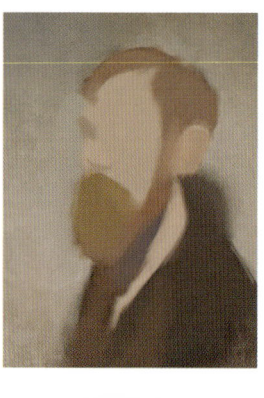

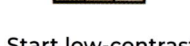

Start low-contrast

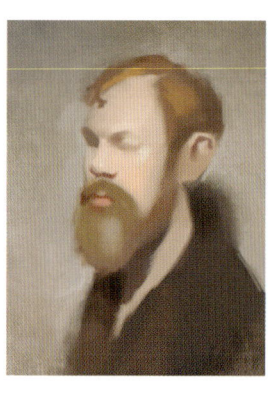

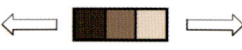

Expand contrast

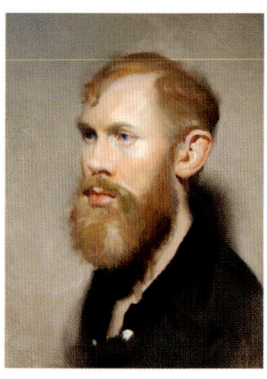

End high-contrast

104 Practice "stringing out" your colors before beginning a traditional painting – mixing the purest tints and shades that you can.

105 Try starting an image with mid-value grays, then gradually expanding both ends of the range until you achieve the full range of the final image.

extremely high-chroma color directly next to pure white, we can create the sensation of the white actually being an extremely bright version of that color.

The technique is used to wonderful effect in the scene below by Nathan Fowkes **(107)**. In an image like this one, where the forceful brightness of the sunlight is the desired effect, deliberately overexposing the lights and painting their colors up to a pure white can be advantageous. Juxtaposing pure white with extremely high-chroma yellows and oranges believably creates the effect of powerful sunshine.

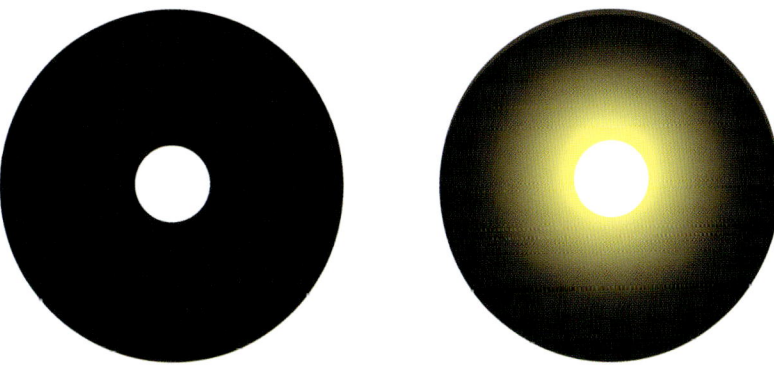

106 Color assimilation juxtaposes a high-chroma color with pure white to create the impression of extreme brightness.

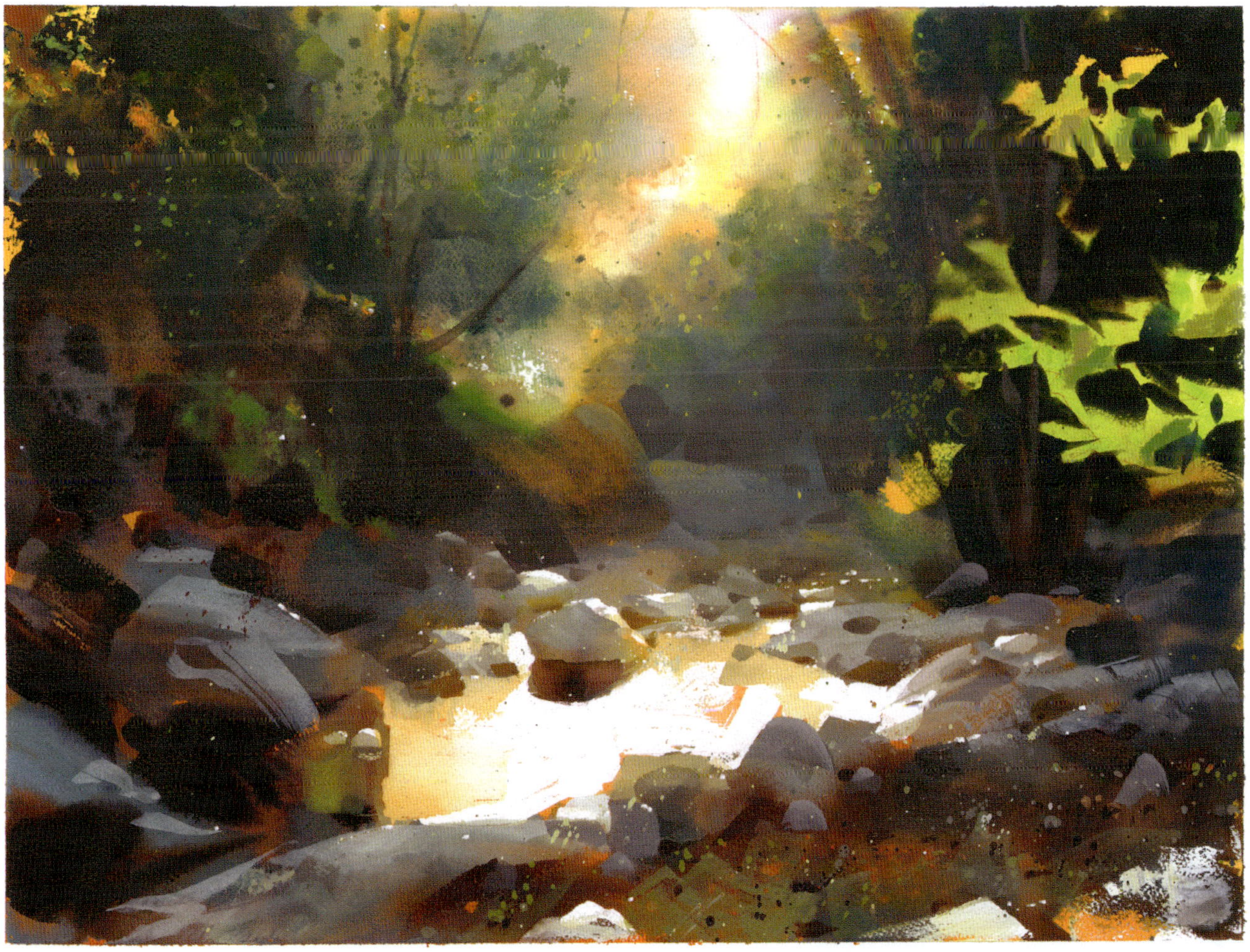

107 The effect of color assimilation can be seen in this painting's very bright sunlight and water.

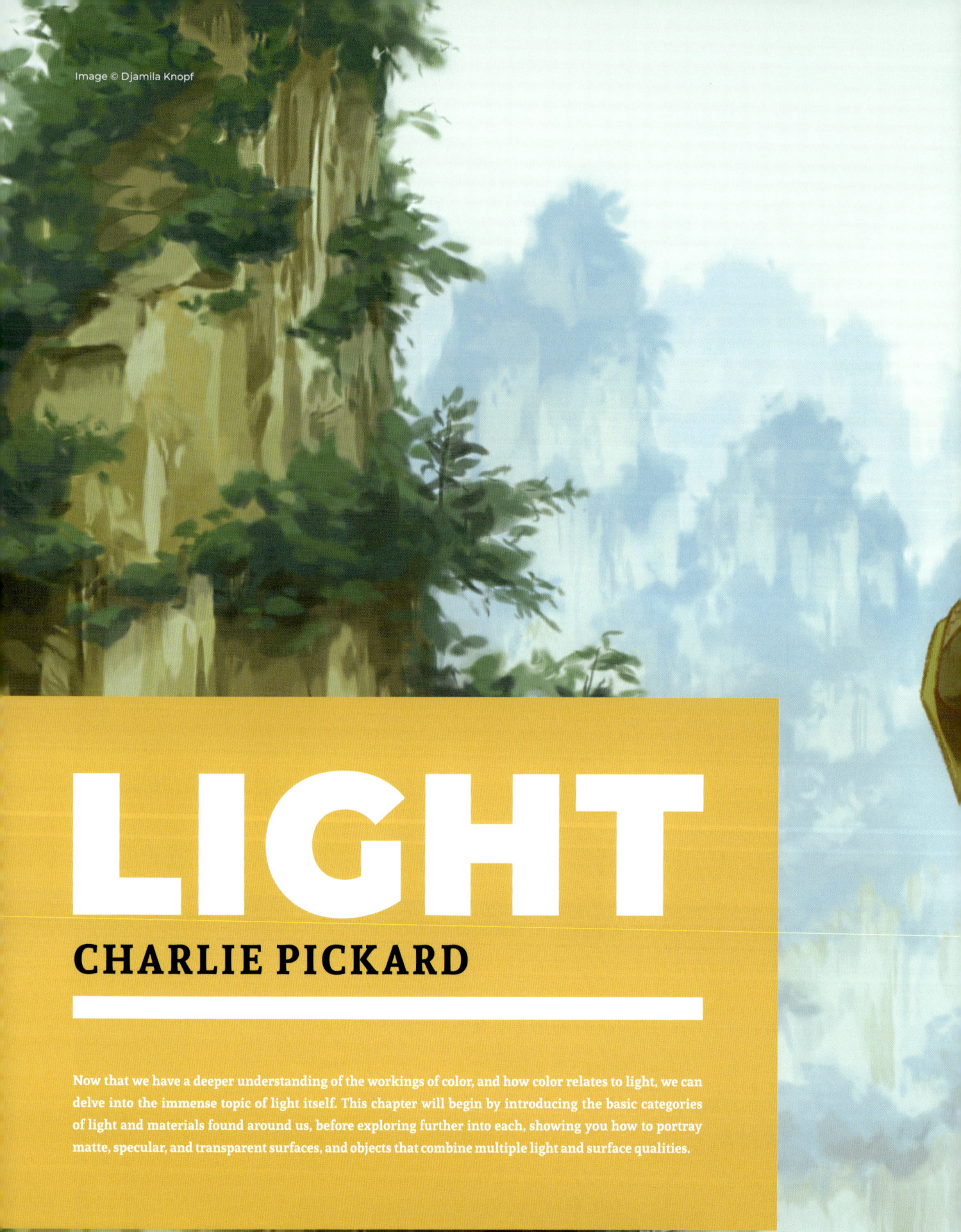

LIGHT

CHARLIE PICKARD

Now that we have a deeper understanding of the workings of color, and how color relates to light, we can delve into the immense topic of light itself. This chapter will begin by introducing the basic categories of light and materials found around us, before exploring further into each, showing you how to portray matte, specular, and transparent surfaces, and objects that combine multiple light and surface qualities.

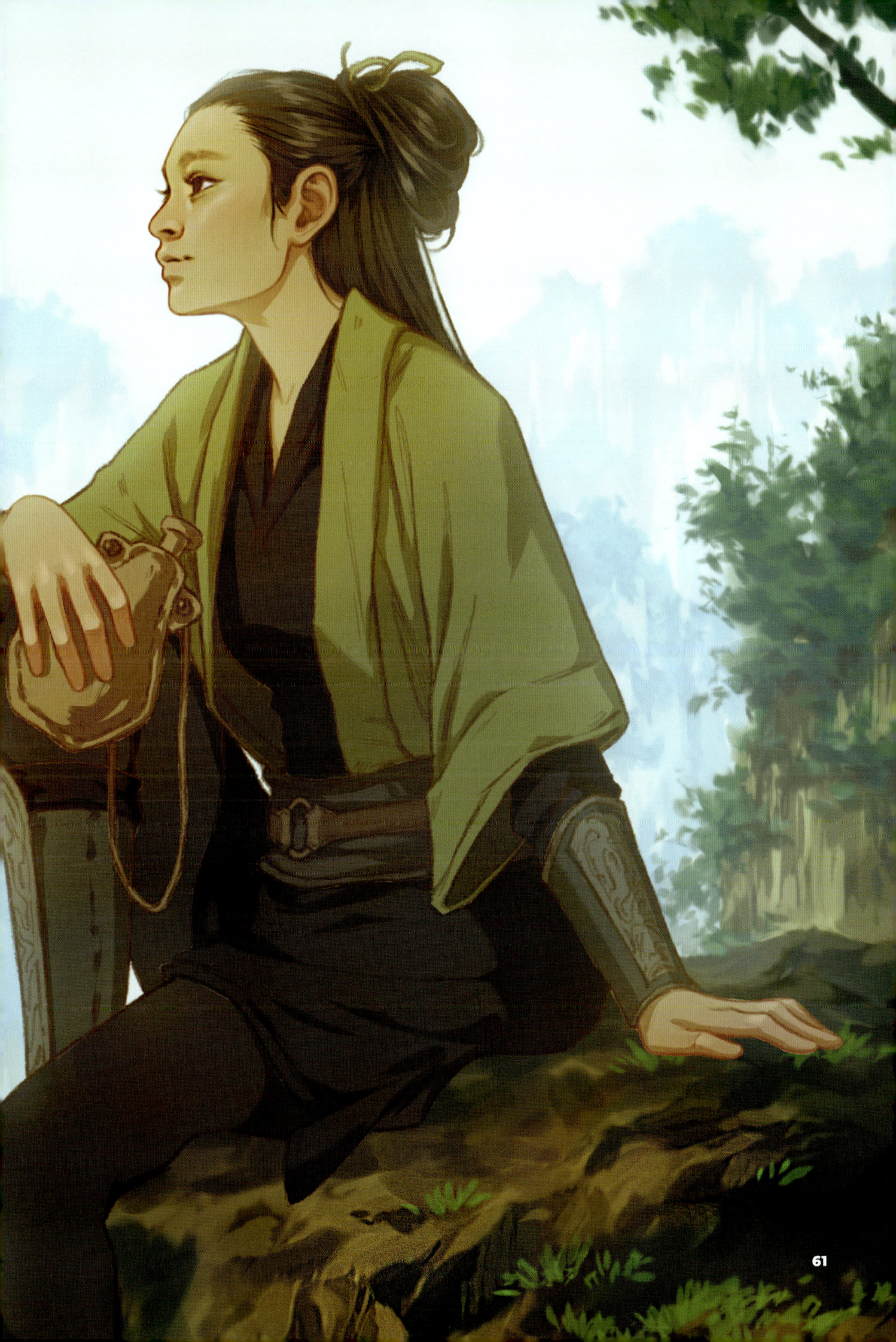

LIGHT:
MATTE

The first aspect of light that we'll be diving into is lighting matte surfaces. Matte surface shading is present on almost every object that we see every day. A strong understanding of how light interacts with matte surfaces – its logic and limits, and its effect on value, shape, and color – is foundational to our successful use of light and color.

MATERIAL QUALITIES

When we are confronted with the myriad different materials in nature, and try to represent their interactions with light in our artwork, it is important to understand the fundamental light interactions that materials can display. Let's look at those first of all.

LIGHT CATEGORIES

There are only four fundamentally different ways that materials can interact with light. The visual appearance of all objects is the result of different proportions of these four interactions occurring in a material. Emission is a special case that is rare in nature, but the other three all occur to greater or lesser degrees within all materials, even at the same time **(01)**.

Emission. Objects can emit light and be a primary light source – a bulb being the obvious example. This is rare in nature, as it typically requires some input of energy to achieve – for example, heat or electricity.

Reflection. In this interaction, light is reflected off surfaces, either in a direct or diffuse manner.

Refraction. Light can enter an object (such as clear glass), be transmitted through it, and then exit it at a different point.

Absorption. Light can also be absorbed by a material, losing energy as it passes into it.

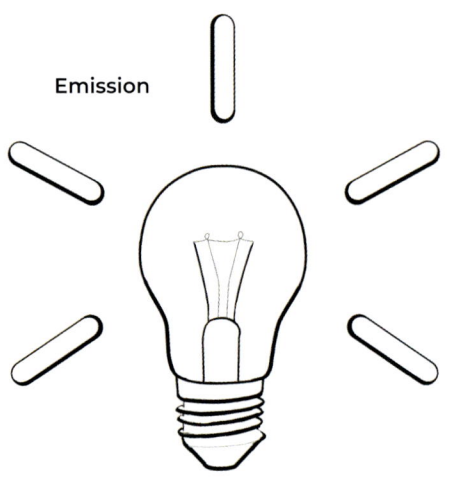

Emission

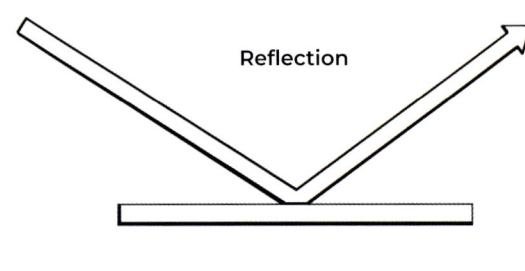

Reflection

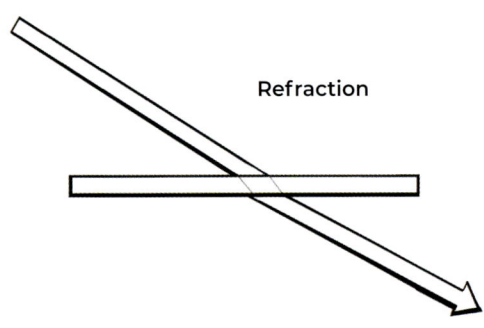

Refraction

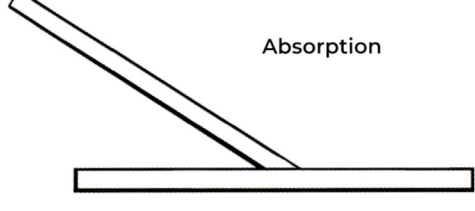

Absorption

01 The four fundamental light interactions an object can have.

MATERIAL CATEGORIES

We can also consider all materials as existing in five categories **(02)**. Throughout the Light chapters, we will examine these different effects and strategies for dealing with different interactions.

Specular reflectors. These are perfect reflectors of light, such as a mirror.

Shiny materials. These are imperfect specular reflectors.

Matte materials. These materials exhibit a combination of reflection, transmission, and absorption. They are the most common type of material that we deal with when broadly talking about shading and modeling, and will be the focus of this chapter.

Translucent materials. These are imperfect transmitters of light, with a degree of transparency.

Transparent materials. These are perfect transmitters of light, such as clear glass.

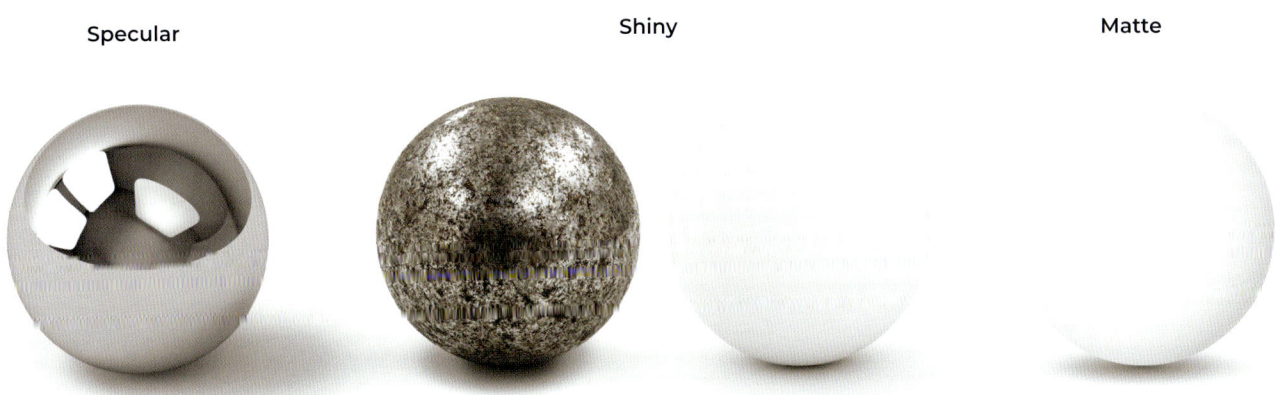

Specular   Shiny   Matte

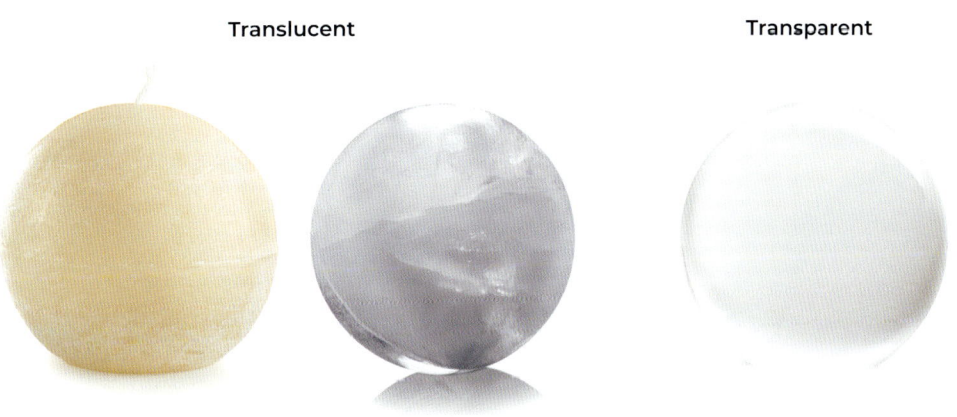

Translucent   Transparent

02 Like light, materials can be divided into specific categories.

FUNDAMENTAL FORMS

One of the oldest and most profound ideas in classical art is that of the fundamental forms. This is the idea that every object seen in nature can be considered as some combination of the four fundamental forms: the cube, sphere, cylinder, and pyramid (or cone).

Humanmade, artificial objects exhibit this quality especially clearly, as it is often how they are intentionally constructed. Organic, natural subjects can often appear more complex, but it is always possible to reduce them to these simple forms **(03)**.

FORM CATEGORIES

The cube. This is the most fundamental of all the forms and is often the simplest to help us initially understand lighting. A perfect cube has edges equal in width and height, connected by flat planes.

The sphere. The sphere is one continuous, perfectly round plane – the most fundamental curved form. It is able to give us the highest concentration of useful lighting information, and so is a very commonly used form for planning lighting.

The cylinder. This form combines the cube and sphere, being curved in one dimension and cube-like (planar) in the other.

The pyramid or cone. This form is a transformation of a cube or cylinder, where one end of the shape has been reduced from a plane to a point.

Learning these forms is an excellent tool for introducing ourselves to certain rules and strategies for representing lighting on all materials. They will form the bedrock of our study of materials: they should be the first thing a student tests their knowledge on, and we will return to them whenever we discuss strategies for lighting different materials.

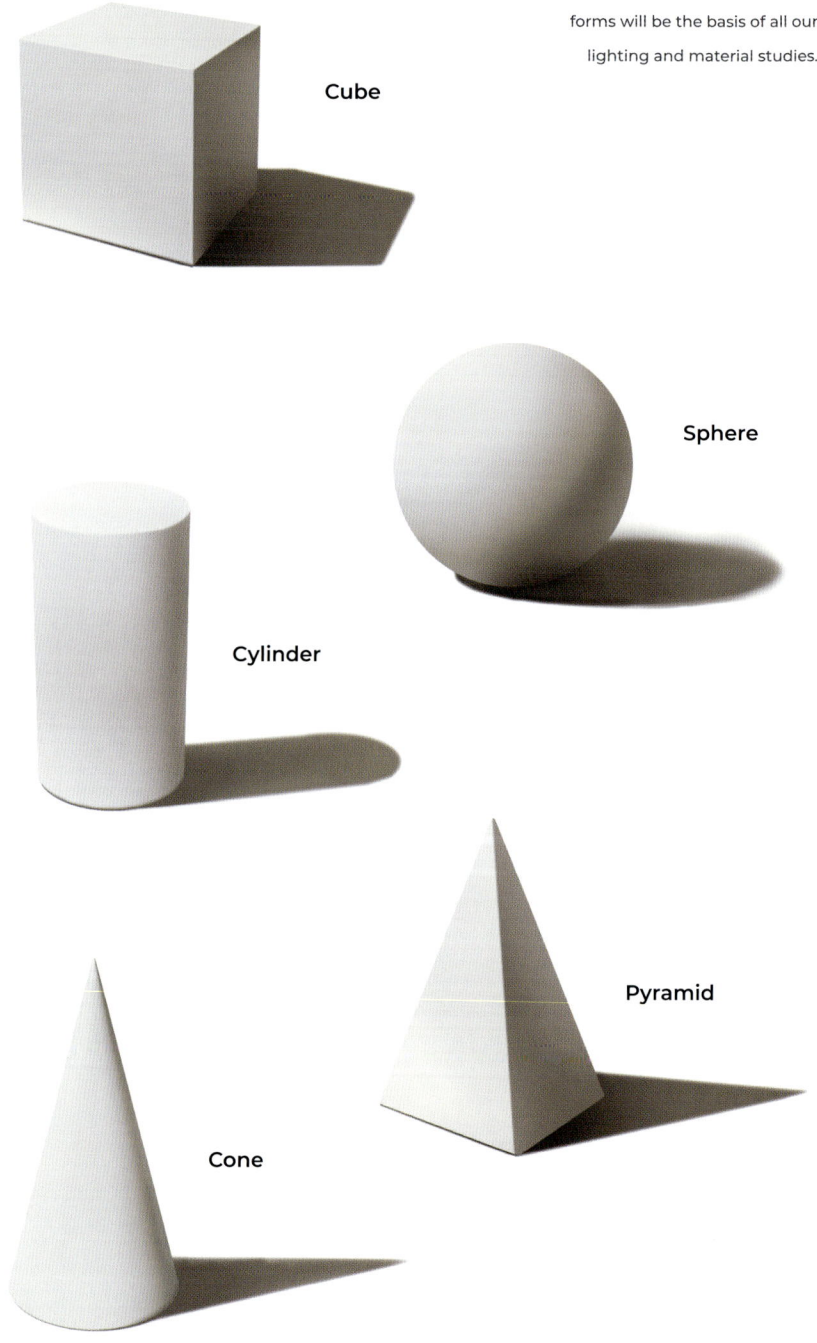

03 These basic geometric forms will be the basis of all our lighting and material studies.

Cube

Sphere

Cylinder

Pyramid

Cone

In images **04** and **05**, you can see how artificial and natural objects – even complex ones – can be constructed out of these forms.

04 Most inorganic object designs can be very easily simplified into fundamental geometric forms.

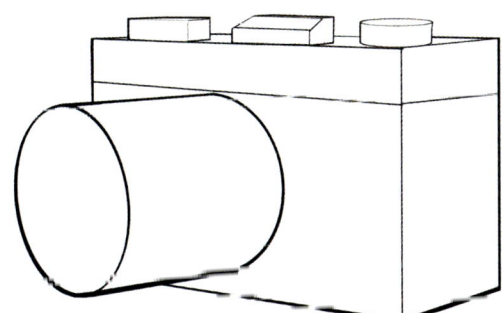
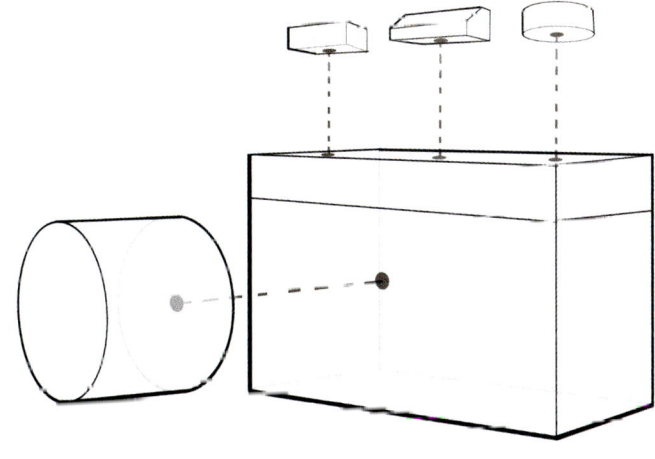

05 Even something as complex as the human body can be represented by fundamental forms.

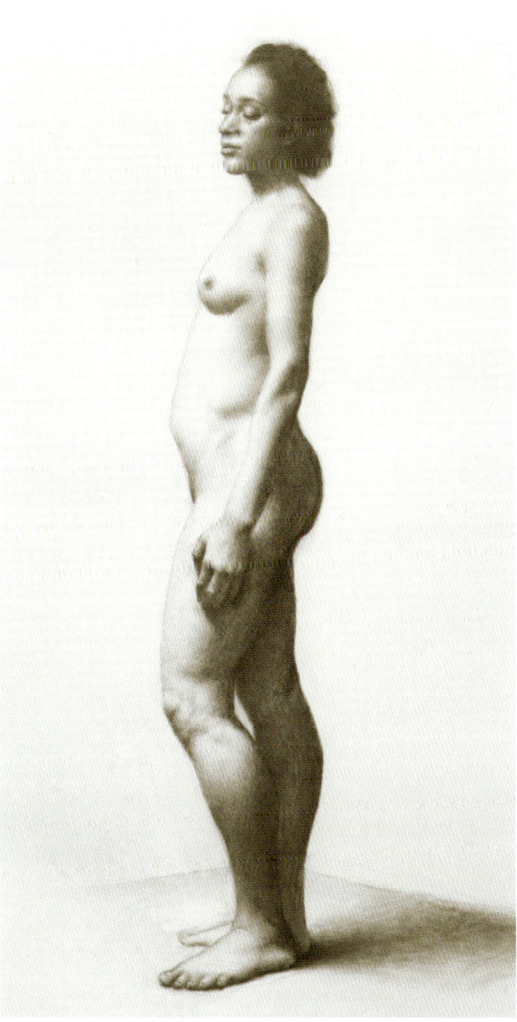

PLANES

Another fundamental idea we will continue to return to throughout our explanation of materials is the concept of planes. Planes can be thought of as the cube-like aspect of an object – the flattened facets of a surface. They are instrumental in understanding lighting on more complex forms.

An organic, curved surface will often be too complex and difficult to tackle directly, but considering simple forms and planes first is instrumental in knowing how to render a surface. In fact, by using enough small planes, the illusion of gradations can be created, which you may not feel the need to smooth out – many artists prefer not to **(06)**.

One of the most well-explored forms of this study in art is the planar human figure **(07)**. Understanding and memorizing the planes of the body is an important step toward controlling lighting on the human form. By learning to vary the lighting on a simplified planar human, we can unlock powerful, creative uses of lighting in our figure drawings **(08)**.

Planes will recur throughout the Light chapters as we learn about different lighting scenarios and interactions.

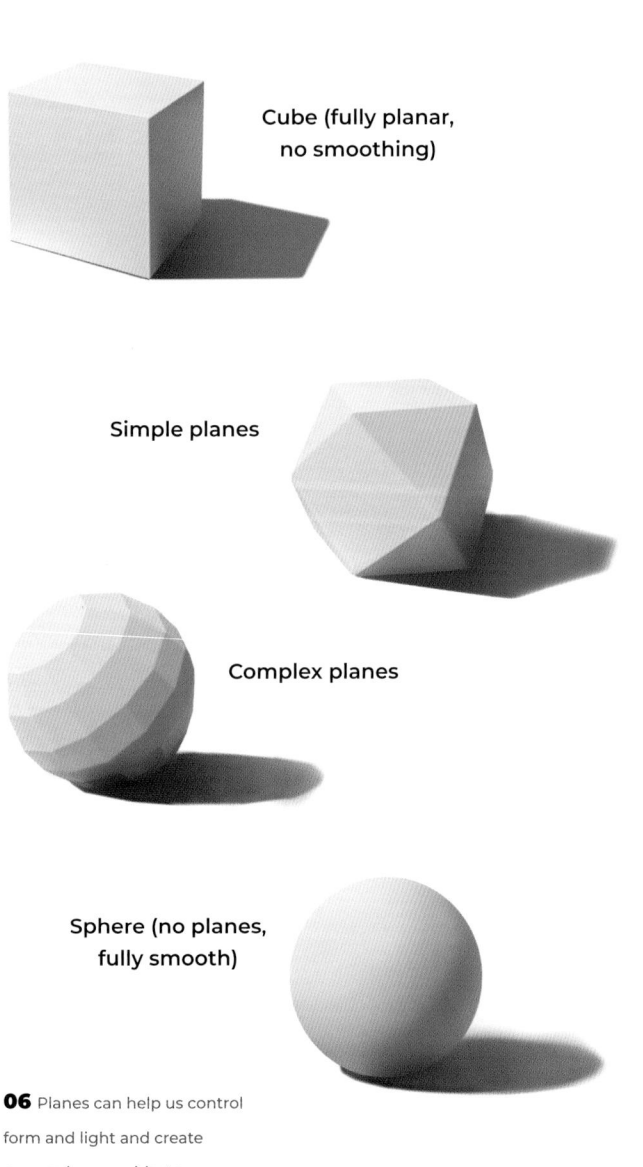

Cube (fully planar, no smoothing)

Simple planes

Complex planes

Sphere (no planes, fully smooth)

06 Planes can help us control form and light and create nuance in our subjects.

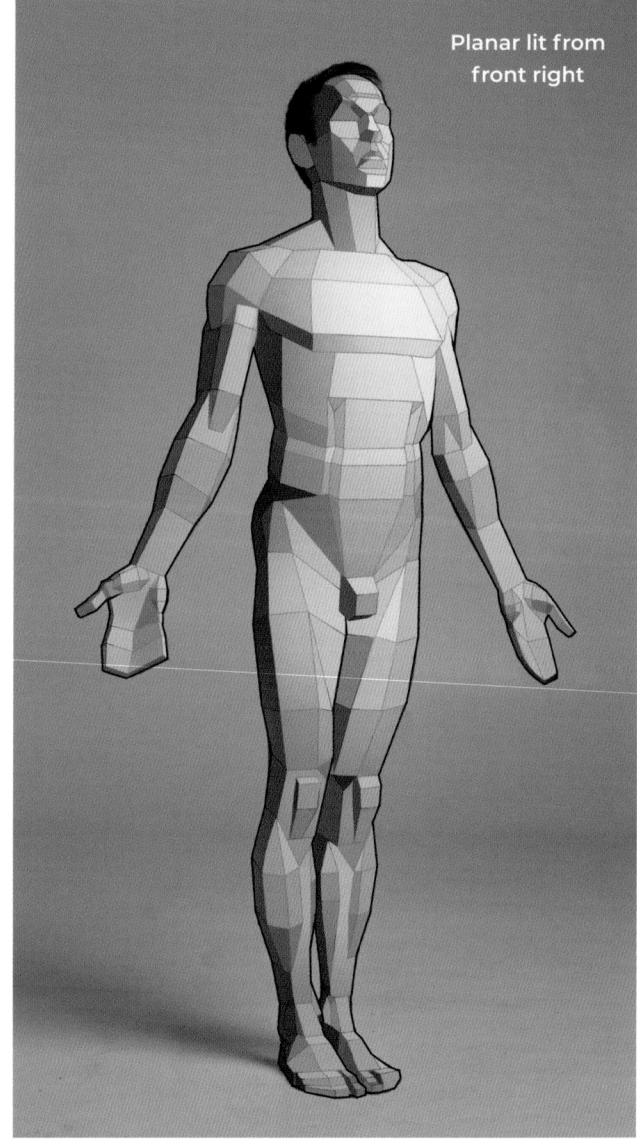

Planar lit from front right

07 Understanding planes can help us light the complex human figure.

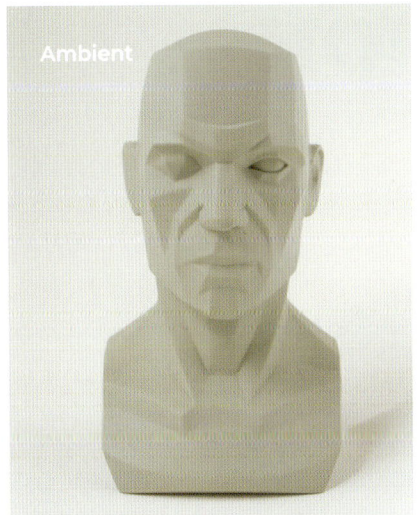

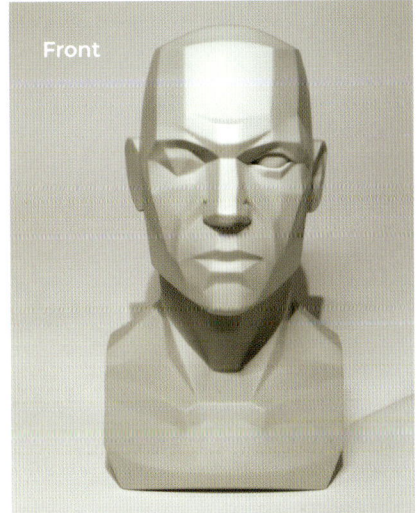

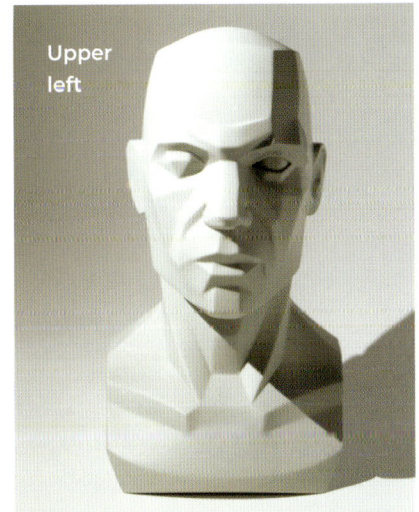

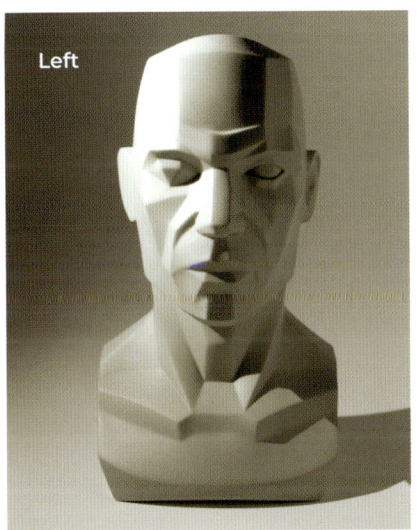

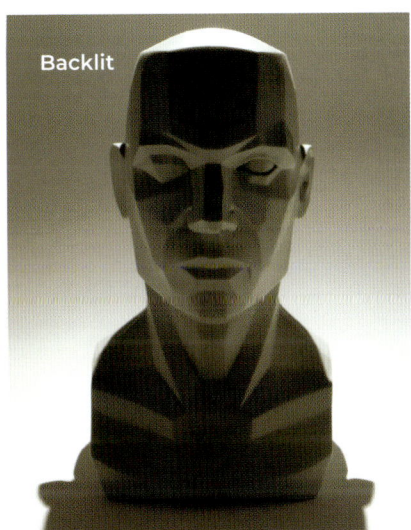

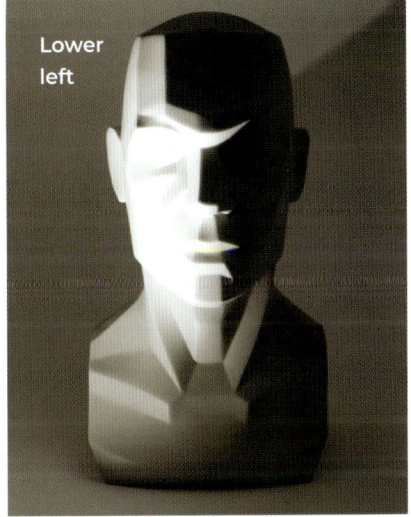

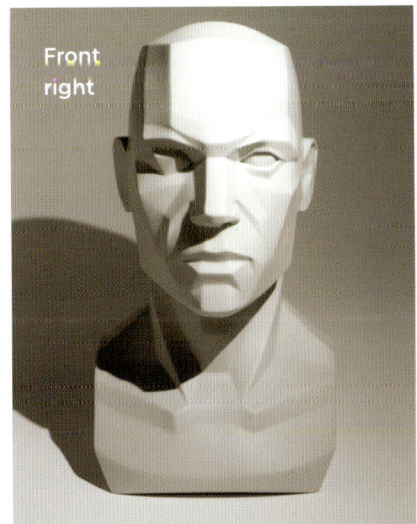

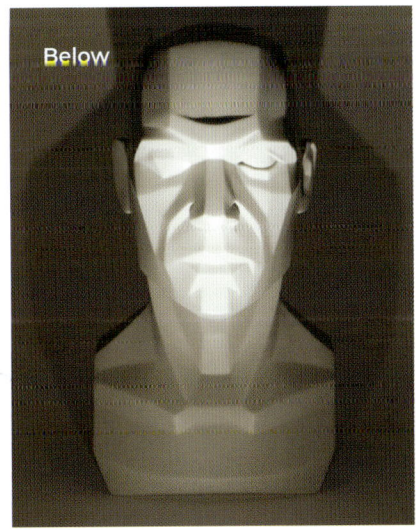

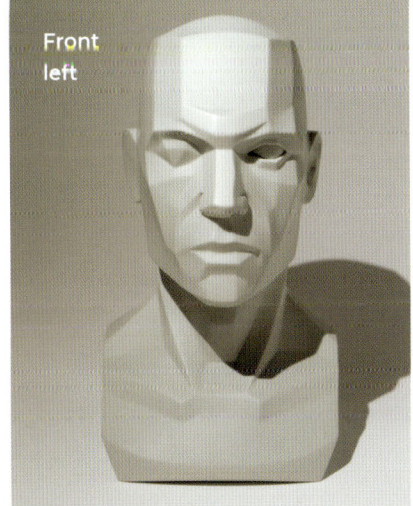

08 Studying different lighting scenarios on a simplified

planar model can be a powerful learning tool.

SPECULAR REFLECTION

Though this chapter will be focused on matte lighting, before we progress any further, we must briefly introduce its essential counterpart: specular reflection. We will be exploring the subject in depth in the Specular chapter (page 126), but knowing the basics will help contextualize our understanding of matte lighting.

Fundamentally, this effect is very simple. If we consider a single light ray striking a plane and then entering our eye, the light ray would be reflected from the surface at the same angle that it struck the surface

(09). This basic idea governs the entirety of specular reflection. A few key terms to understand here are:

The normal angle. A perpendicular line projected from the plane being struck.

The angle of incidence. The angle between the normal angle and the light ray striking the form.

The angle of reflection. The angle between the normal angle and the light ray leaving the plane.

The angle of incidence and angle of reflection are always equal. Due to the simplicity of this interaction with light, this type of material interaction in its most pure form is highly predictable. Most of us will be familiar with it, for example, as the flat plane of a mirror **(10)**.

The result of the interaction is simply an image of the surrounding environment wrapped and warped around whatever form our object takes. This image will also change depending on the position of the observer. If you are ever unsure of whether you are

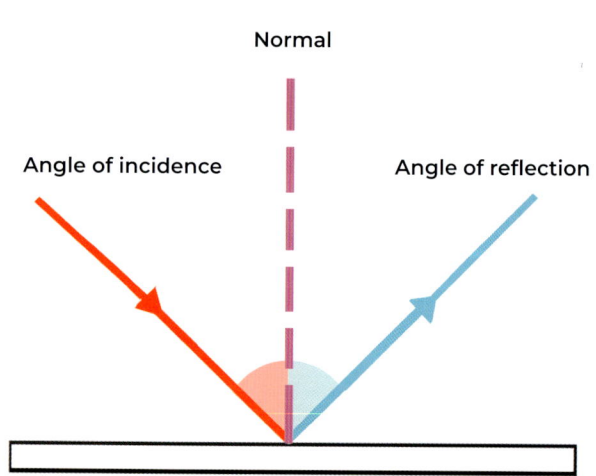

Normal

Angle of incidence

Angle of reflection

Angles always equal

09 In a specular reflection, the light reflects off a surface at an angle equal to its approach.

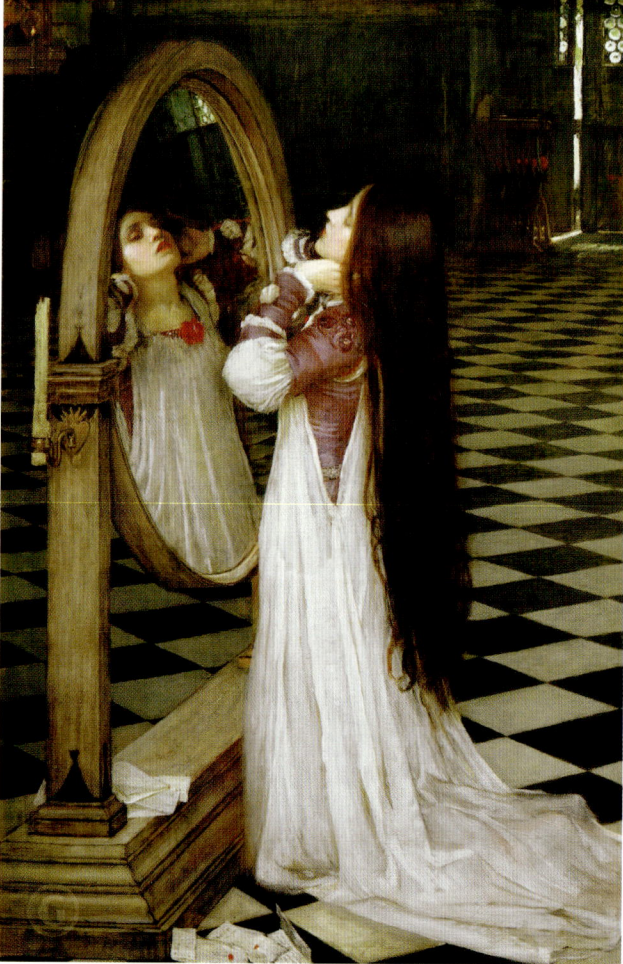

10 An example of specular reflection in John William Waterhouse's *Mariana in the South* (1897).

observing this type of reflection, the easiest way to check is simply to move around the object and see if the image shifts with your position. If it does, it is a specular reflection. Purely specular objects do not have any inherent color, so the observed colors and

rendering of the reflective surface will be entirely decided by the environment **(11)**.

Keep in mind that there are no perfect reflectors in nature, so there will also always be some level of loss of light when depicting

a natural specular reflection – the image represented will be slightly darker and less chromatic than what it is reflecting. This loss of light becomes stronger the less perfect the reflector, which is why many people think of metals as being gray objects.

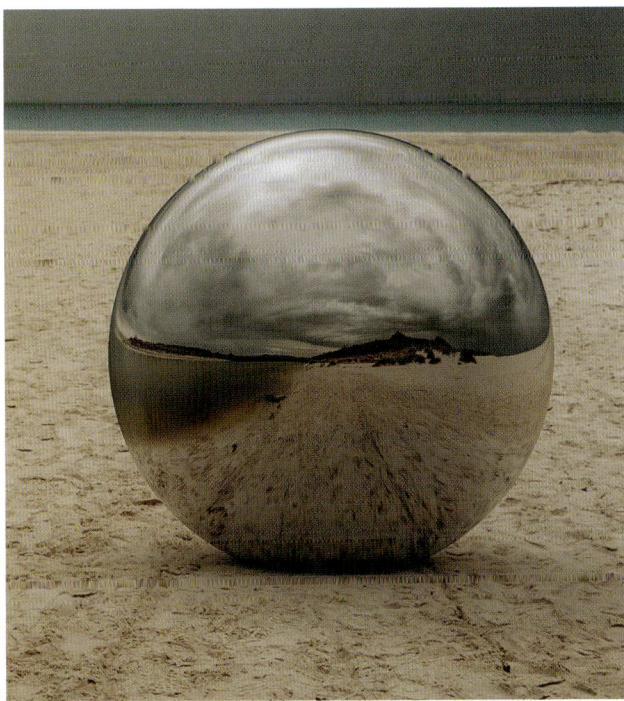

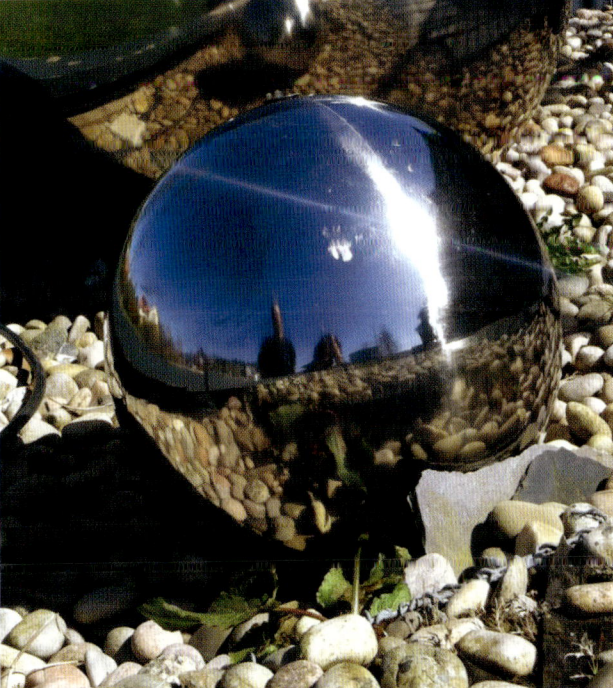

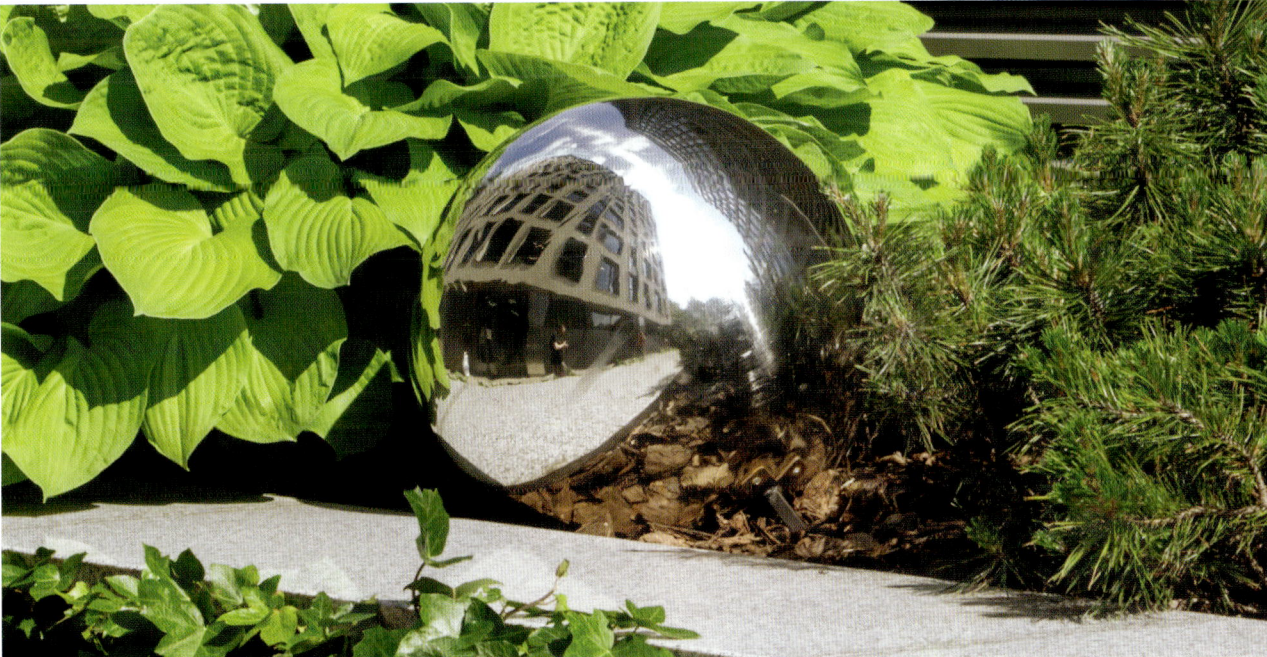

11 Purely specular objects take on the colors of their environment.

Image 11 spheres (top to bottom, left to right) © Sergio Eschini, Lorna Davidson, and Jakub (via Adobe Stock)

DIFFUSE REFLECTION

Diffuse reflection, responsible for all the effects of matte surface shading, is the most common light interaction that we as artists will observe and represent on a daily basis. It is also the interaction we will spend the most time with in this book, so we will acquaint ourselves with it here before continuing our analysis of form.

The way diffuse reflection is typically explained is as an extension of specular reflection, which in many ways it is. In general it will always be true that the angle of incidence will equal the angle of reflection. However, it is important that we think of this type of reflection as distinct, as it behaves quite differently.

One way to explain this distinction is that if a perfect specular reflection is one with a perfectly smooth surface, a diffuse reflection is one where the surface is imperfect or rough **(12)**. The path of light becomes more random and unpredictable, softening the reflected image and making it difficult for our eye to discern. We can observe this effect quite clearly if we sand the surface of a chrome ball.

However, no matter how much we might roughen up a specular surface and diffuse its reflections, it will not become a *matte* surface. The effect we observe will still fundamentally be a reflected image of the surrounding environment, just appearing more or less blurred as the paths of the bouncing light rays become more difficult for our eye to predict.

WHAT MAKES A SURFACE MATTE?

For simplicity, we tend to think of light rays as only interacting with the surface of a volume, but this is not strictly true. All objects have some level of transparency. What matte surfaces require are multiple layers of the roughed-up interaction shown below. Since each layer is then somewhat hard to predict, the layering of these interactions makes the original path of the light impossible to predict by your eye **(13)**.

Due to the randomness created by these layered interactions, all that our eyes are able to discern is the general amount of light reflected off a surface and projected in all directions. The resulting effect is therefore the same regardless of the observer's position, which is useful to us as artists. We know that the more light is striking the surface, the more light will be reflected and observed. All the effects of artistic modeling arise from this basic principle.

For each successive layer of material interacted with, the light rays have more chance of being selectively absorbed by the material, which is another key effect to consider. We can think of this simply as "the longer the light travels inside the object, the more of the object's local color the light rays will adopt" **(14, 15)**.

Specular

Diffuse

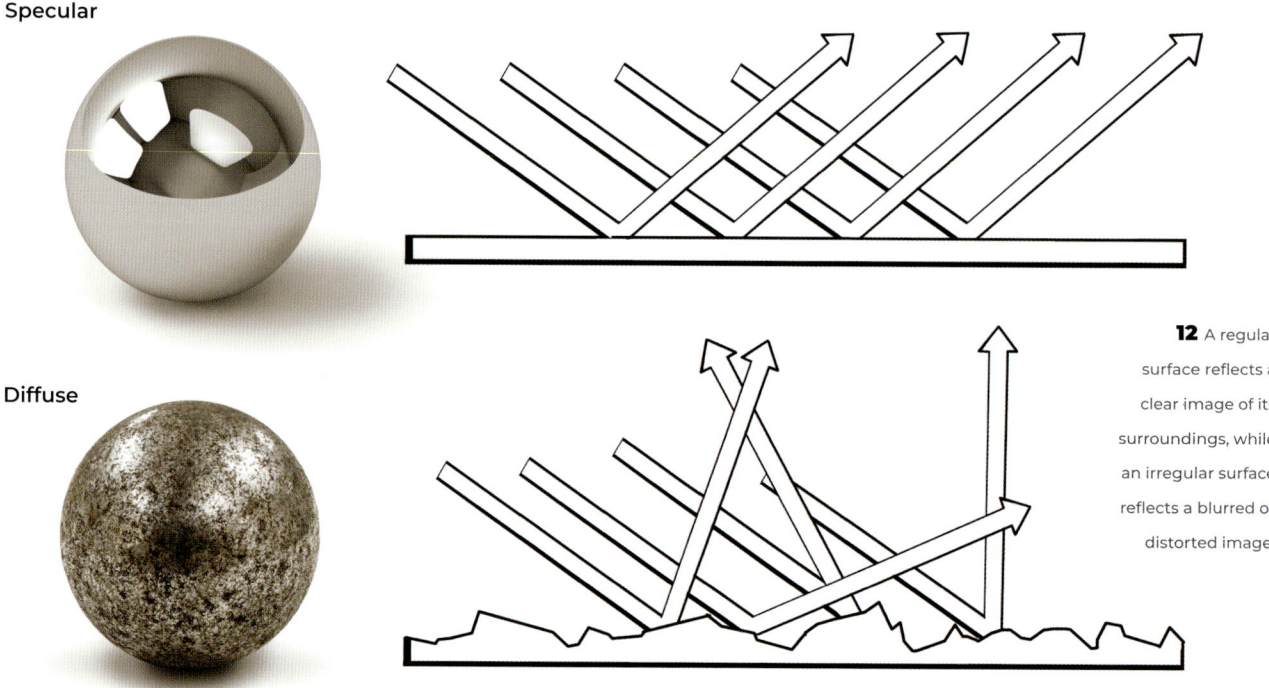

12 A regular surface reflects a clear image of its surroundings, while an irregular surface reflects a blurred or distorted image.

While we will study the different strategies to represent both specular and diffuse effects, it is important to realize that these two types of reflection will generally both be occurring at the same time in the vast majority of materials we represent – an object hardly ever exhibits just one or the other. We can generally think of diffuse reflection as occurring "below" the specular image of the object. If we are creating an image digitally, we can even set up our image file's layers to reflect this.

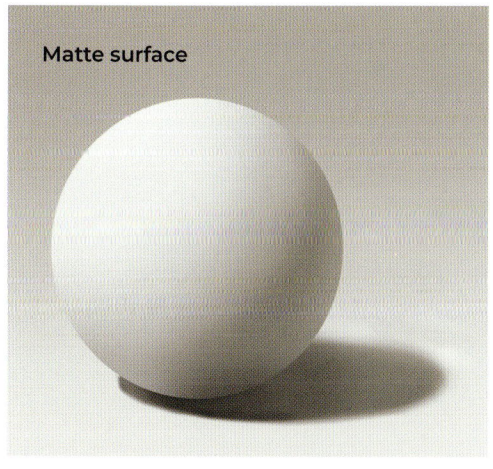

Matte surface

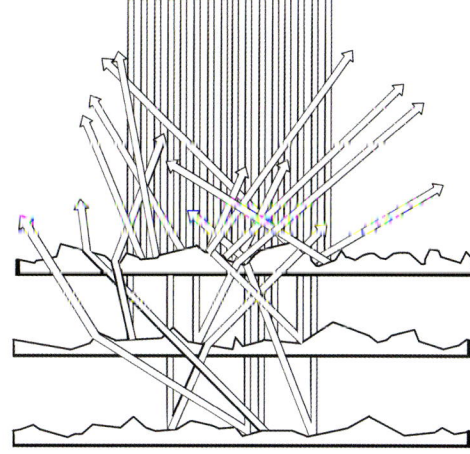

13 Unlike a specular surface, a matte surface is so irregular that our eye cannot see its reflections at all. Some of the light passes through multiple layers of material, becoming truly random and fully losing the surface image.

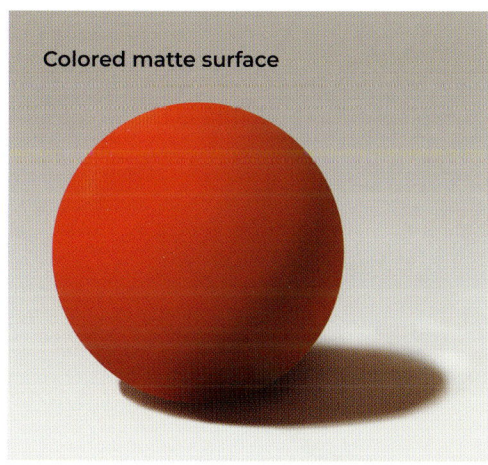

Colored matte surface

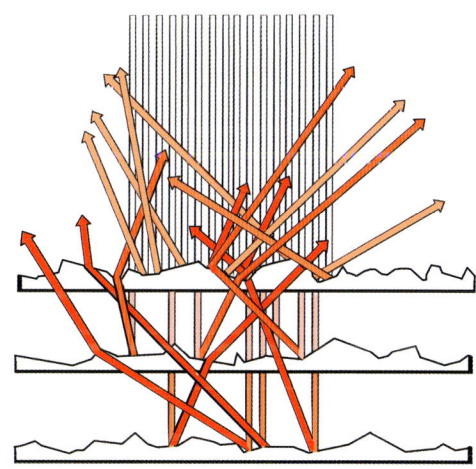

14 With a colored matte surface, each layer of material interaction edits the light toward the local color (in this case, red).

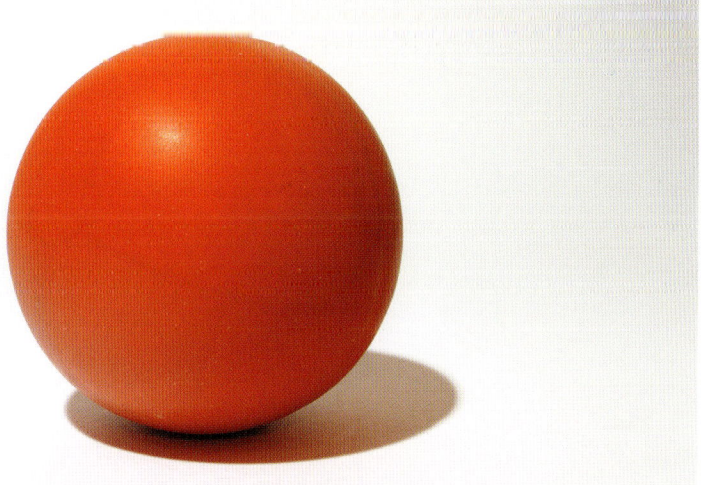

15 This sphere exhibits a red local color, matte material, and specular highlight. Matte and specular effects coexist and are rarely found in isolation, as we will learn on page 102.

DIRECTIONALITY OF LIGHT

Before we return to discussing form, the most important fact to understand about light is that it is directional in nature. The direction from which your light is influencing your subject is the first thing that we learn to consider when lighting our artworks, either from life or from our imaginations.

Due to this fundamental directional nature of light, when dealing with a single, direct light source, not every plane can be struck by the light rays emanating from that source. If we picture a sphere being struck by parallel light rays from above, as in image **16**, we can see the cause of this effect quite clearly: As the planes of the object turn away from the light, the rays miss them. This creates the most profound grouping of light in art: the separation of light and shadow. It is from this baseline that we can begin to consider lighting and its effects on form. On the right, you can see the essential features created by directional light, which are:

Light shape. The planes of a form directly struck by light rays. This is where the majority of artistic "modeling" occurs – the rendering of the forms, textures, and details that make our subject legible.

Form shadow. The shadow created by the light rays missing the planes of the form.

Shadow terminator. The in-between point where the light ends and the shadow begins.

Cast shadow. The shadow created by the object blocking the light from reaching the next surface (in this case, the ground).

In a perfect vacuum, such as when we look at the moon, this form shadow would have no light striking its surface whatsoever, thus appearing perfectly black. However, we never see such a perfect black shadow in the

natural world, because everything that we see is itself a light source, and so shadows are always affected by the ambient light in a scene – we'll learn more about the nuances of reflected light later, on page 110.

However, this simple separation of shadows from lights will always be present within

any scene, no matter how subtle. In fact, it holds massive potential for communicating with our audience, and many artists choose to use it as their sole communicative tool in many mediums (most prominently in ink work). It is important to think of the two worlds of tone and color as separate, and to maintain that separation.

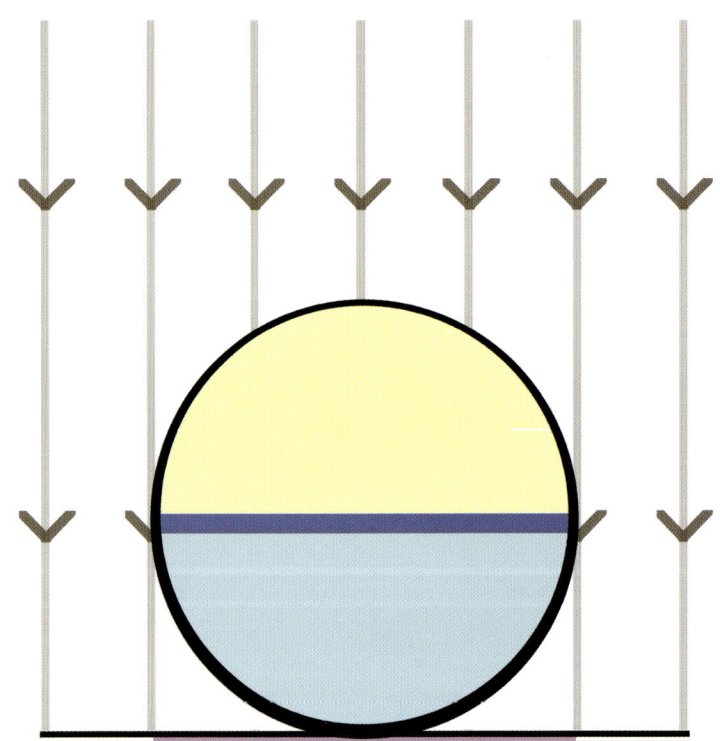

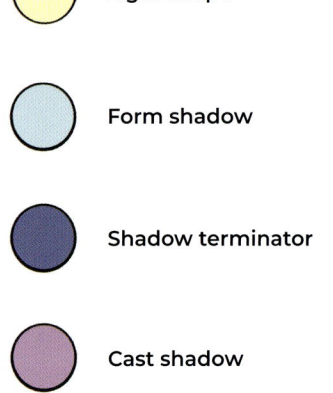

Light shape

Form shadow

Shadow terminator

Cast shadow

16 Shadows are formed where light rays fail to make contact with the object's planes.

THE SHADOW CONTOUR

One concept not commonly recognized by students is that the terminator of a shadow is actually the shadow's contour from the perspective of the light source. So for the example on the previous page, the shadow terminator would appear as a circular contour from the bird's-eye perspective of the light source **(17)**.

Similarly, the cast shadow is that same contour projected onto the next surface as the object blocks the light's path. Due to this, the cast shadow will always be related to the form shadow by a line that represents the direction of the light rays. This can often be an extremely useful way to identify or establish the direction of a light source **(18)**. We will learn more about how to project cast shadows later in this chapter, on page 90.

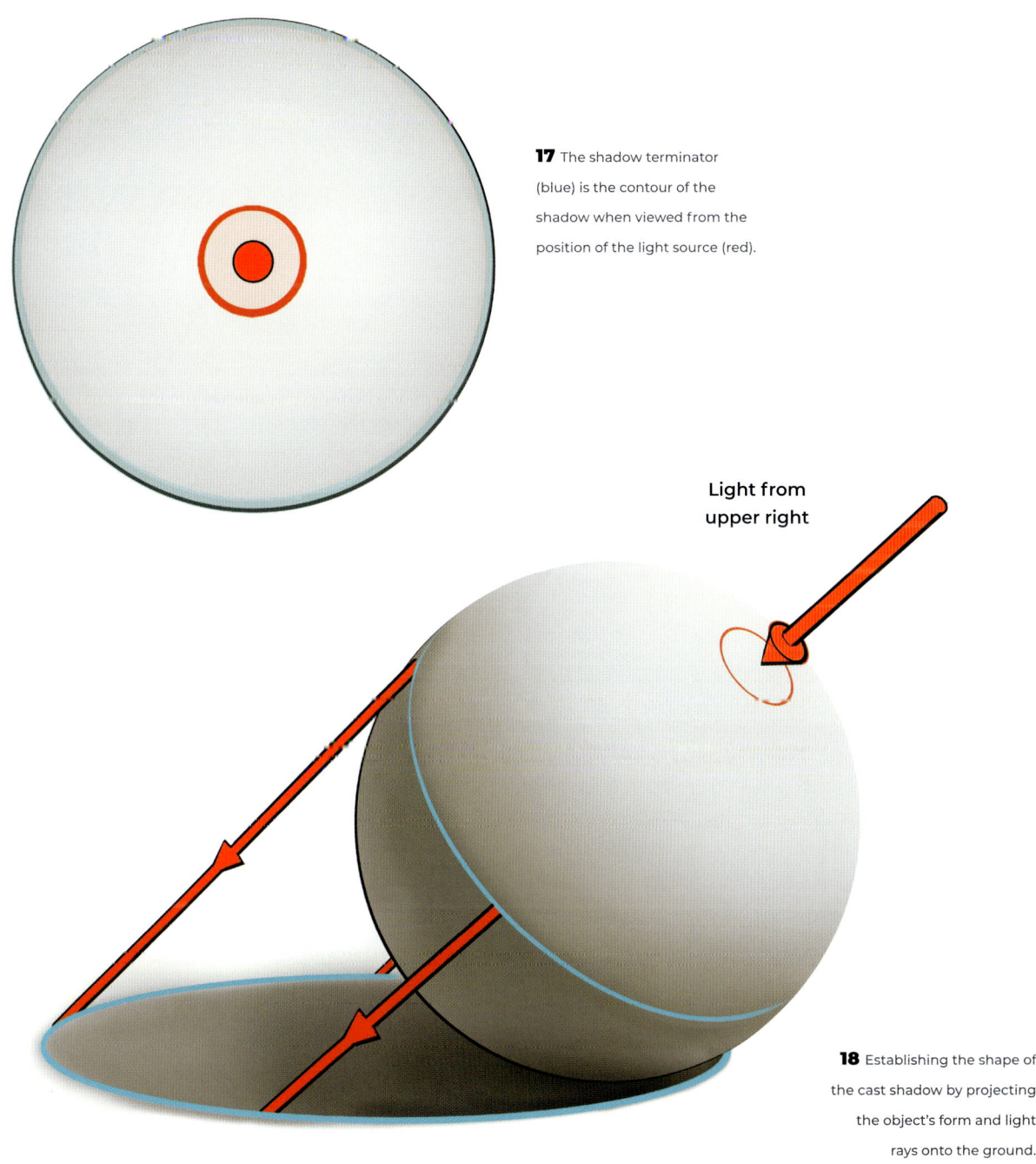

17 The shadow terminator (blue) is the contour of the shadow when viewed from the position of the light source (red).

Light from upper right

18 Establishing the shape of the cast shadow by projecting the object's form and light rays onto the ground.

FORM CHANGE = VALUE CHANGE

When we discuss the modeling of forms and light shapes in diffuse reflection, there is an extremely simple principle at work: Planes, as they turn away from the light source, will reflect progressively less light until the shadow begins.

We can see the cause of this quite clearly if we simplify the problem. In image **19**, we are following the progression of one plane on its path away from a light source. The number of photons striking the plane is simplified into four groups representing 25%, 50%, 75%, and 100% light.

As you can see, as the plane turns, it becomes foreshortened in relation to the light source. With less surface area to strike, the photons are more thinly spread, and less light is available to be reflected. This gives us an important rule for understanding light on form: form change = value change. A plane has a lighter value as it turns toward the light, and a darker value as it turns toward the shadow.

THE RETURN OF EXPONENTIAL DROP-OFF

Most people would assume, looking at the diagram, that the 45 degree (halfway) shift would see a 50% drop-off in value – but looking more closely, we can see that this is not true. In fact, a 45 degree change in value only sees a 25% drop-off in value. To reach a 50% drop-off, we have to turn 60 degrees (two-thirds) down. A 75% drop-off in value isn't seen until the form shifts to the last 10 degrees. This is because value drop-off is exponential, becoming greater as it moves toward shadow, rather than occurring in equal steps.

We can pair this with the idea of light gradients discussed on page 26, where we learned that our vision also perceives value differences exponentially. We perceive an incredibly strong grouping of values in light, with very little value shift within the groups, of which there are four: the light halftone, halftone, dark halftone, and shadow line **(20)**. These groups are our main tool for constructing believable lighting as we move forward. If you're curious, you can replicate the effect in real life by making folds in a strip of card and shining a light on it **(21)**.

19 As the plane turns away from the light, the fewer photons are able to strike it.

25% 50% 75% 100%

Form highlight, 100% (Direct to light)

Light halftone, 75% (45 degrees)

Halftone, 50% (60 degrees)

Dark halftone, 25% (80 degrees)

Shadow, 0% (90 degrees)

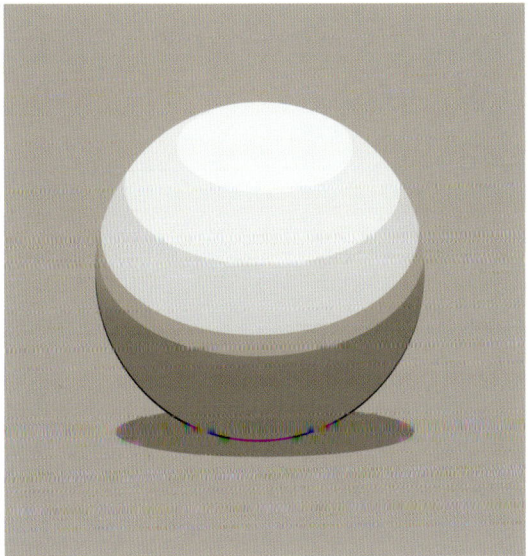
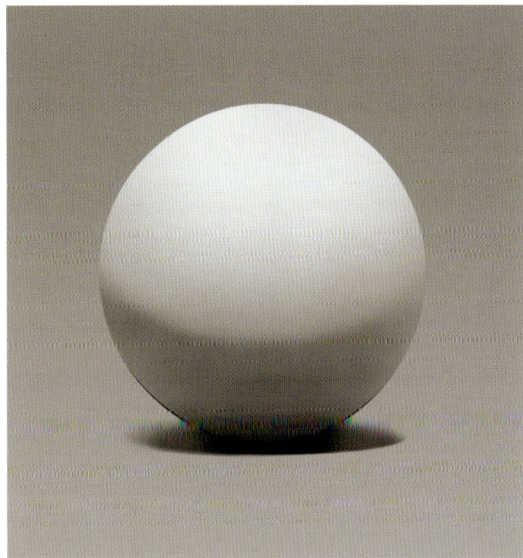

20 Above the shadow, we can see four values of light: the light halftone, halftone, dark halftone, and shadow line, which can help us construct form when light is able to strike it.

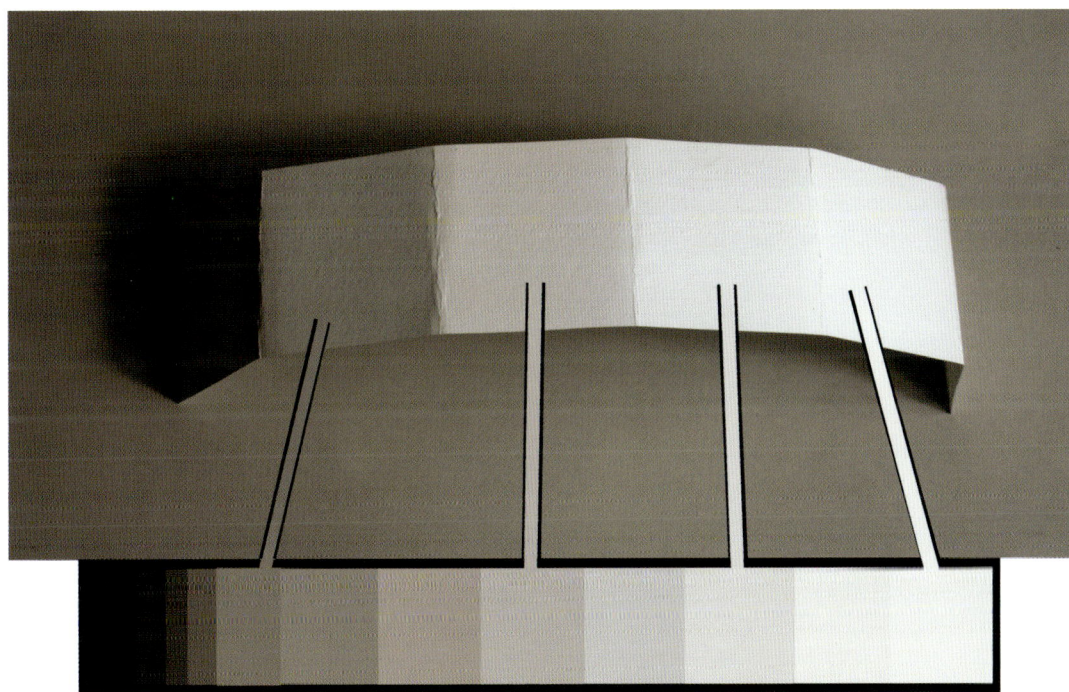

21 You can observe these groupings in real life by shining a light on folded card. We would refer to the exponential light value scale discussed on page 26 of the Color chapter for comparison.

CREATIVE SIMPLICITY IN LIGHT

Think of lighting groups as a creative tool and remember that you don't need all of them for every artwork. While the introductory chapters of this book aim to help you make your lighting as realistic as possible, many artists simplify these lighting groups to suit their needs. For example, a common way of simplifying light while keeping a strong level of solidity is to just use the values of the light, the shadow, and the dark halftone. This is called a three-value read – the minimum number of values needed to communicate form – and is commonly used by artists when efficiency is required.

LOCAL COLOR

Another effect that we have to be aware of whenever we deal with matte surface shading is the concept of local color. This is the aspect of an object that most people think of when they refer to the "color" of an object – for example, if someone is holding a "red" ball, the ball's local color is red. The local color of an object is its color when seen in a perfectly balanced white light.

The most perfectly white light that we have access to is the light seen on an overcast day through white clouds. When people refer to local color, this is often the lighting situation that they are visualizing. Objects rarely exhibit their true local color perfectly. As discussed on page 54, our eyes are extremely effective at correcting for the various lighting colors that we are confronted with in daily life, and we must be aware of this if we want to represent different lighting effects in our art **(22)**.

Objects have different local colors due to varying levels of efficiency in absorbing or reflecting different wavelengths of light. An object with a perfectly white local color is the most efficient reflector of light **(23)**, while an object with a perfectly black local color is the most efficient absorber **(24)**.

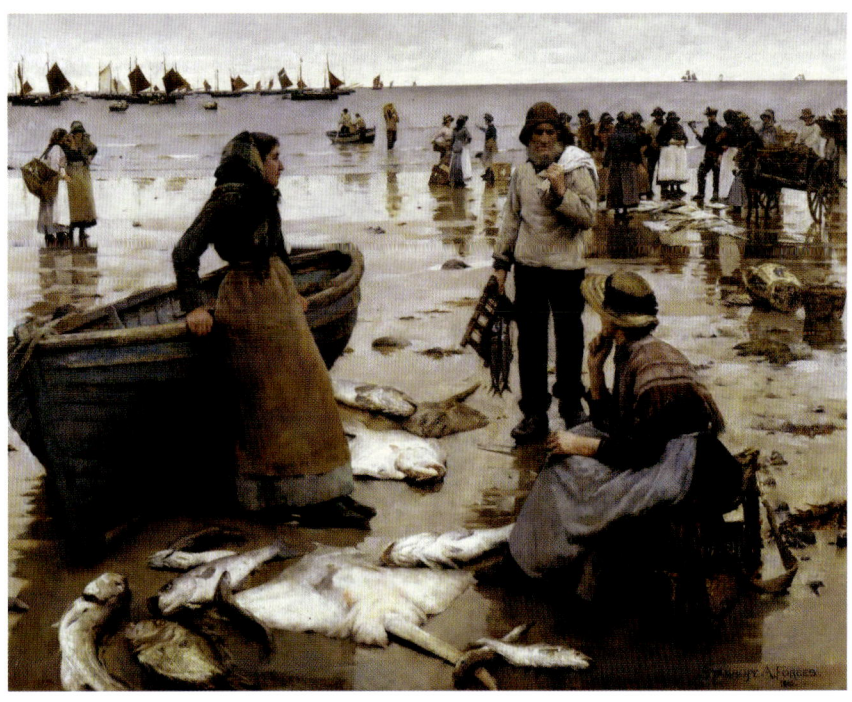

22 Local colors are most clearly demonstrated in overcast lighting, as shown in Stanhope Forbes' *A Fish Sale on a Cornish Beach* (1884–85).

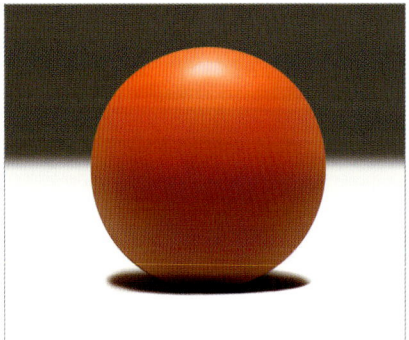
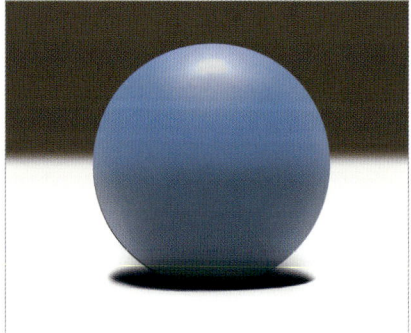

23 When people describe a ball as red or blue, they are referring to the object's local color.

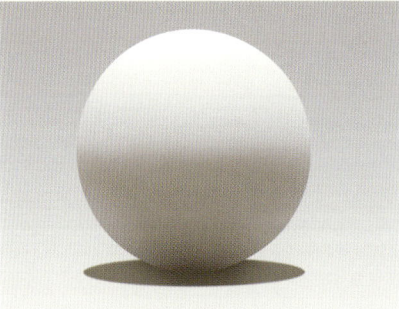
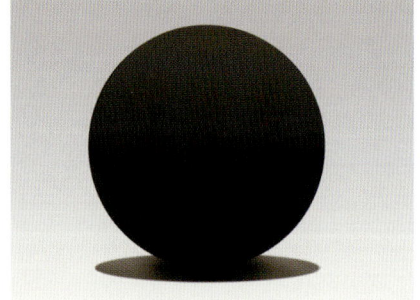

24 A white local color efficiently reflects light, with minimal light absorbed. A black local color is an extremely inefficient reflector of light, with maximal light absorbed.

LOCAL VALUE

The local color of an object, as with all color properties, can be split into the three dimensions of value, hue, and chroma that we learned about on page 16. However, the scenes we depict will rarely consist of objects with only one local color and value. How can we handle differing local values and ensure our subjects look believable and consistent?

When juggling multiple local values in a single object or image, we can follow a "halfway to black" rule to help maintain consistent shadows. For example, on a ten-step value scale, if a white sphere's local value is 0, the shadow value halfway down the scale would be 5 **(25)**.

As the sphere's local value moves down the value scale, the darkest value moves down with it, staying halfway between the lightest value and black. This works all the way down the value scale, from pure white to the darkest gray. The local value and shadow of the sphere darken believably while the lighting scenario remains consistent. This is a great rule of thumb when working with local color, though when an object is in a differently lit environment, as we will explore on page 105, it is no longer entirely accurate. For now, it serves extremely well for this initial demonstration.

Local colors may vary from object to object, or within a single object. However, if we maintain this simple value relationship throughout our image, we can represent all of these changes convincingly without losing any definition **(26)**.

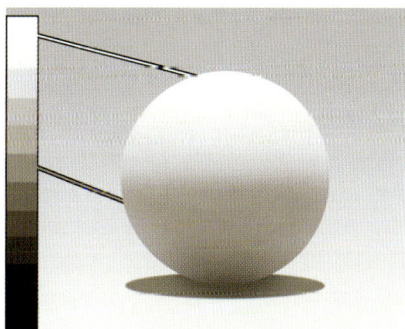
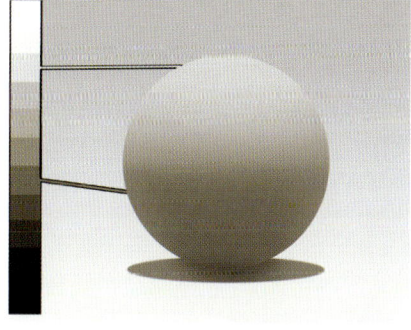
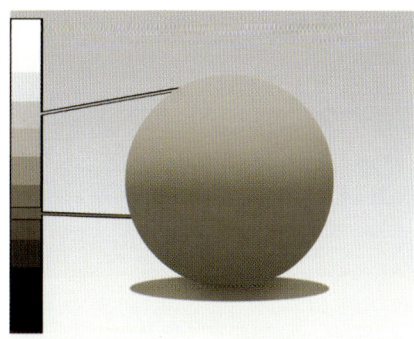
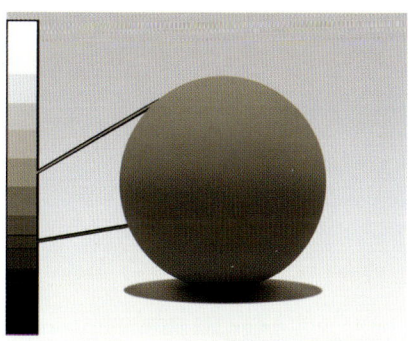
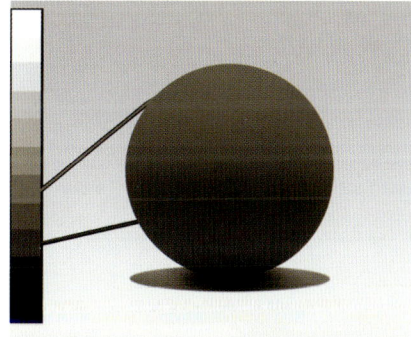
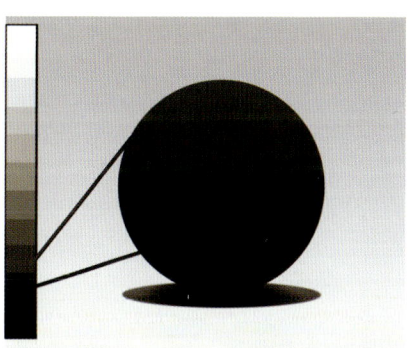

25 A value scale can help you match objects with different local values to the same neutral lighting scenario. In these examples, each shadow value is halfway between the local value and black.

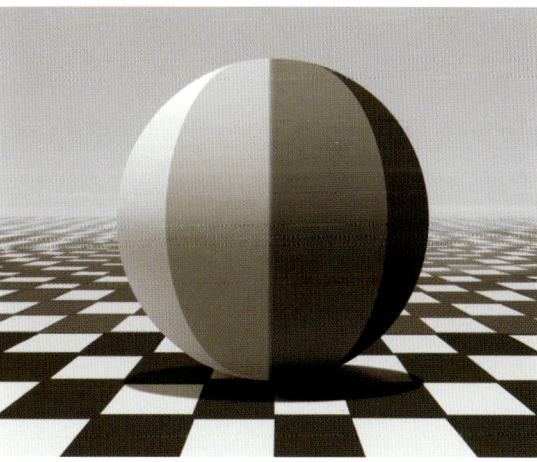

26 This multi-value sphere's local values are clearly distinct from the ambient lighting values, thanks to the scaling trick above.

CONSTRUCTING FUNDAMENTAL FORMS

Let's see how we can actually use this newly acquired knowledge of local value on a subject. We will first discuss how to apply basic light and shadow modeling on the fundamental forms covered on page 66 – the sphere, cube, cylinder, and cone – and then expand on how we can transform and combine this lighting into more complex forms. First, let's examine one idea about how values interact with our two most fundamental forms: cube (planar) forms and sphere (rounded) forms.

LIGHTING A PLANAR SPHERE

When we observe how values orient themselves on a planar form, we can see that while the values of the planes are determined by our light source, the shape and orientation of the value changes are determined largely by the planar object's form. On a simple planar object, like a cube, the results are clean and simple, but an object such as a planar sphere becomes far more complex to light **(27)**.

However, if we angle our planar sphere toward our light source, organized strips of simple values appear, all oriented to the light source **(28)**. Rounded forms can be said to be oriented in all directions at once, and we can observe this same effect even on a planar sphere. This idea can be of huge utility to us, since we can light our rounded subject by simply placing one strip of value at a time.

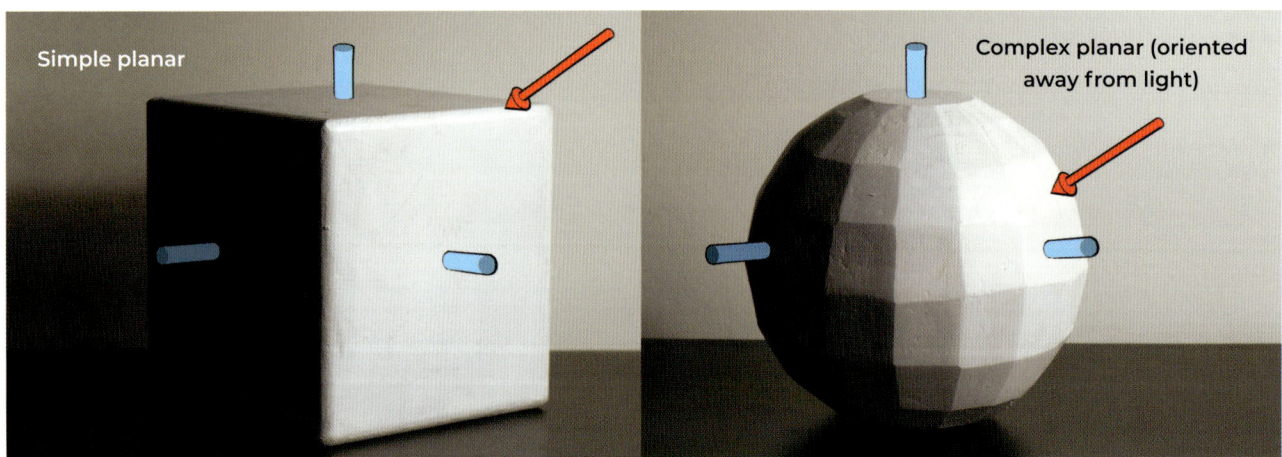

27 On a simple planar object, value shapes are decided by the planes' orientation to the light. The same is true of a complex shape, simply with more planes.

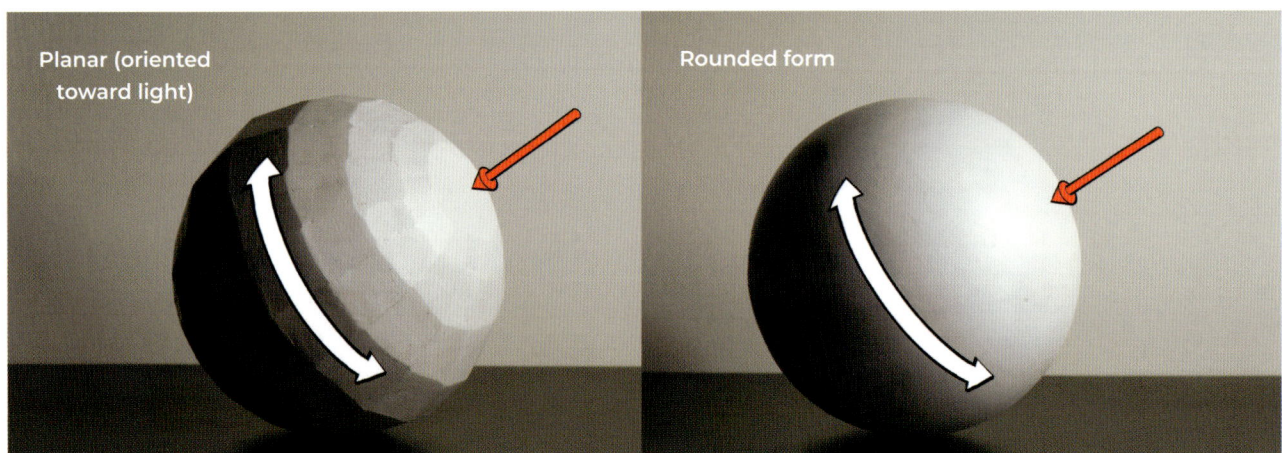

28 If the planar form is oriented to the light, the values gradate in groups up toward the light source. The same value relationships are true on a rounded form, but smoother.

LIGHTING A SPHERE

Using this logic, we can deduce that constructing a directly lit sphere requires placing our four value groups in concentric rings around the sphere. We can do this using the following steps. We can use this basic method to construct a sphere and its lighting from any angle **(29a–f)**. Our understanding of this sphere will inform everything we do moving forward, so try constructing some spheres of your own, lit from every angle you can think of! **(30)**

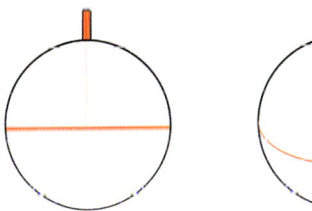

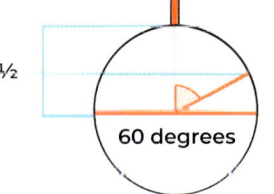

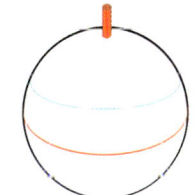

29a Decide on a light direction. Place an elliptical loop around the shadow terminator, where the light rays strike parallel to the form and the shadow begins. This is usually halfway down the sphere, and will always be placed at 90 degrees to the light direction.

29b Place another ellipse for the halftone, halfway along the central axis between the terminator and the top of the sphere.

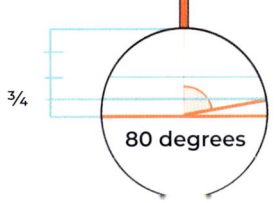

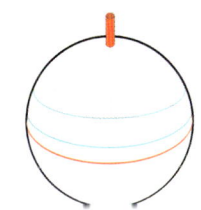

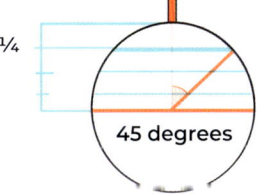

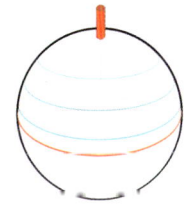

29c Place an ellipse for the dark halftone three-quarters of the way down the central axis, halfway between the terminator and the halftone lines.

29d Place an ellipse for the light halftone a quarter of the way down the central axis, halfway between the halftone line and the top of the sphere.

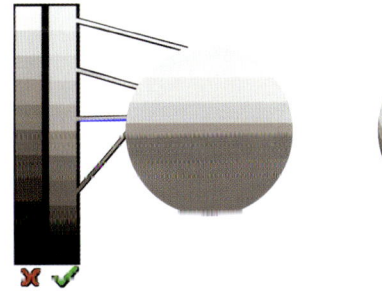

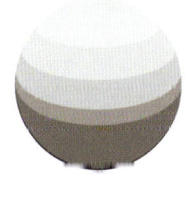

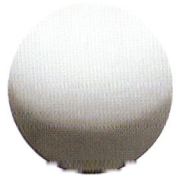

29e Decide your object's local value and assign values to each ellipse group. Remember that we are modeling with light now, not mixing a palette, so the light scale we use needs to be exponential.

29f Soften the edges between the planar value groups to achieve the round form of the final sphere.

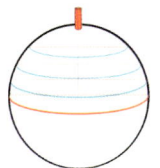
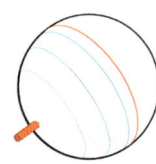
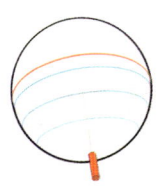
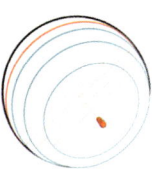
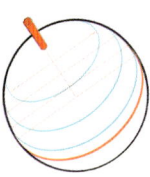
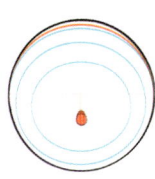

30 Practice the process by lighting spheres from different angles.

LIGHTING A CUBE

Our next form, the cube, introduces us to a new fundamental skill: identifying the relative angle of a plane to the light source. This will be required for all subsequent lighting and so is essential to master.

Luckily for us, when it comes to a cube or box, there is a simple construction process that will give us these orientations in relation to our form **(31a–f)**. This planar lighting process, using a dummy sphere to locate values, helps us maintain a consistent light

direction across an entire collection of cubes **(32)**. Use it to try lighting a cube from any angle! This ability to maintain consistent lighting is a key skill for all realistic artwork and is a worthy one to master.

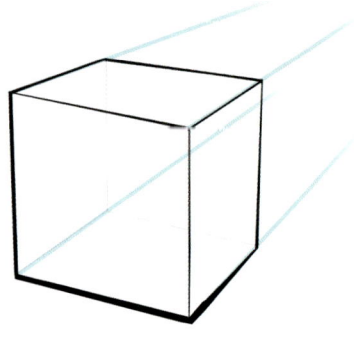

31a Draw a cube. You can create simple perspective by making sure the parallel edges of your cube converge together.

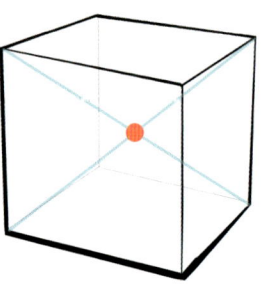

31b Identify the cube's center by drawing a cross from its four opposing corners and marking where the lines intersect.

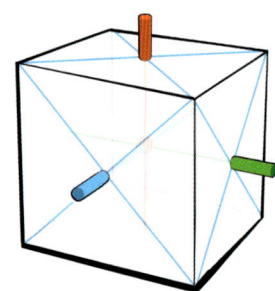

31c Identify the centers of each of the cube's six planes, draw an axis through each, and thicken these XYZ axes into cylinders so their orientation is clearer.

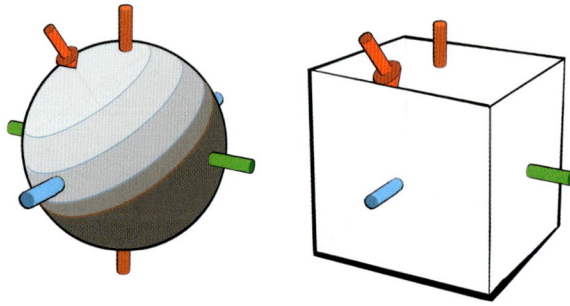

31d To find the planes' angles in relation to the light source, plot the light values out on a sphere oriented on the same axes as the cube.

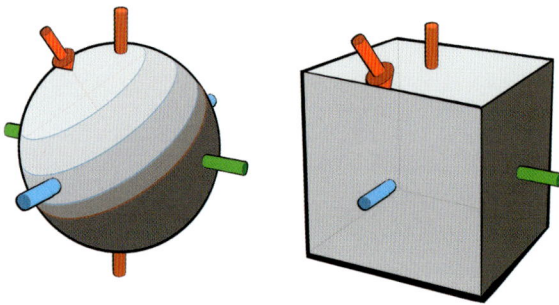

31e Each of the sphere's axis cylinders will mark a different value, which you can simply transfer directly to the cube's planes. In this case, the green axis falls within the shadow value, and the blue axis marks the halftone.

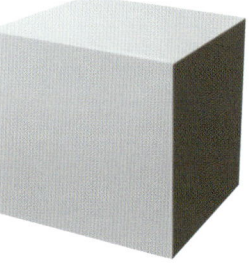

31f The resulting cube has consistent, convincing lighting. This method is a simple solution to a problem that can be very difficult in isolation, and can be applied to any planar surface!

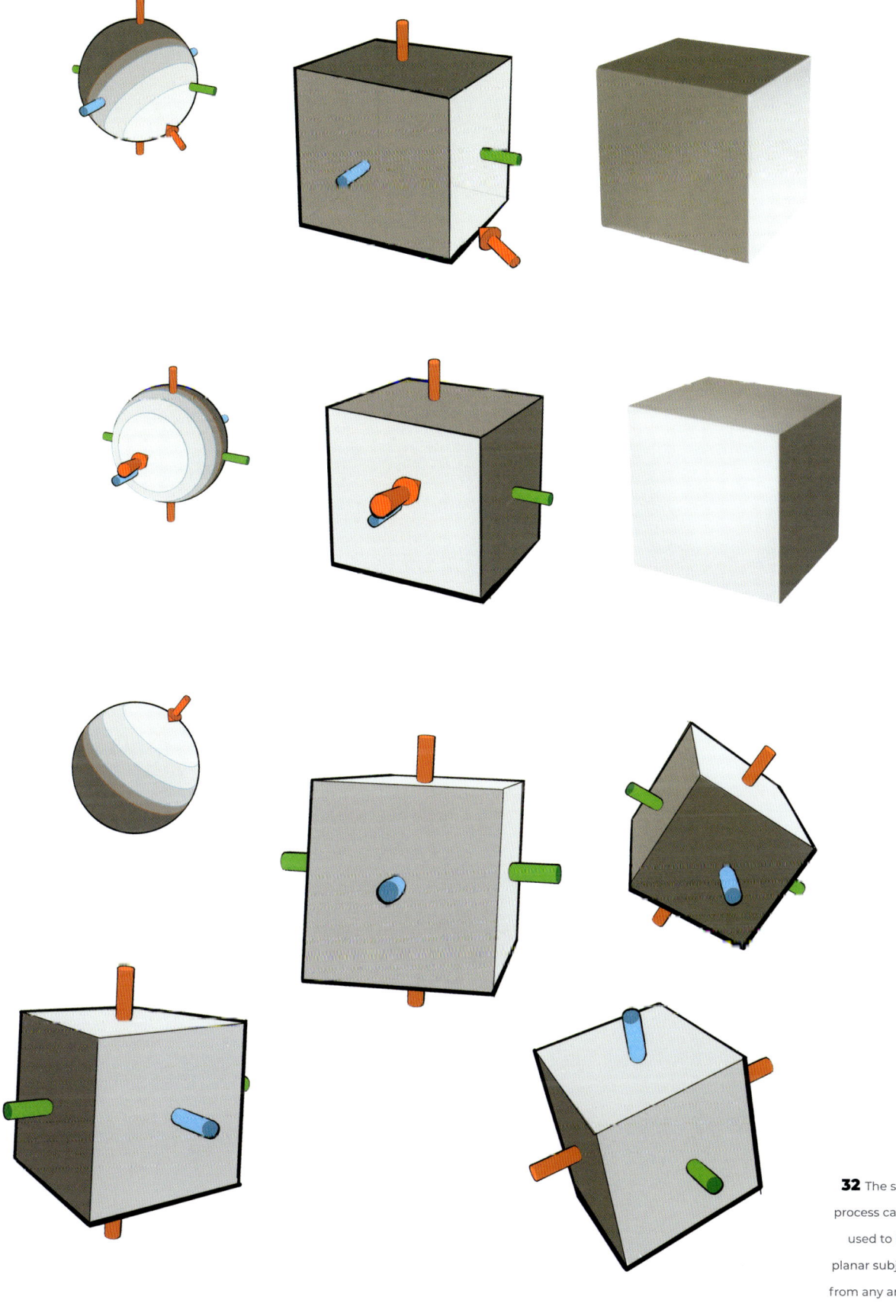

32 The same process can be used to light planar subjects from any angle.

LIGHTING A CYLINDER

Now that we have thoroughly discussed the two most fundamental forms, let's examine the secondary fundamental forms: the cylinder and the cone/pyramid. Both of these forms are fundamentally combinations and transformations of the cube and sphere. Our first form, the cylinder, is rounded in one dimension and planar in the other two **(33)**. The approach to lighting it requires is a combination of the two techniques discussed on the previous pages **(34a–g)**.

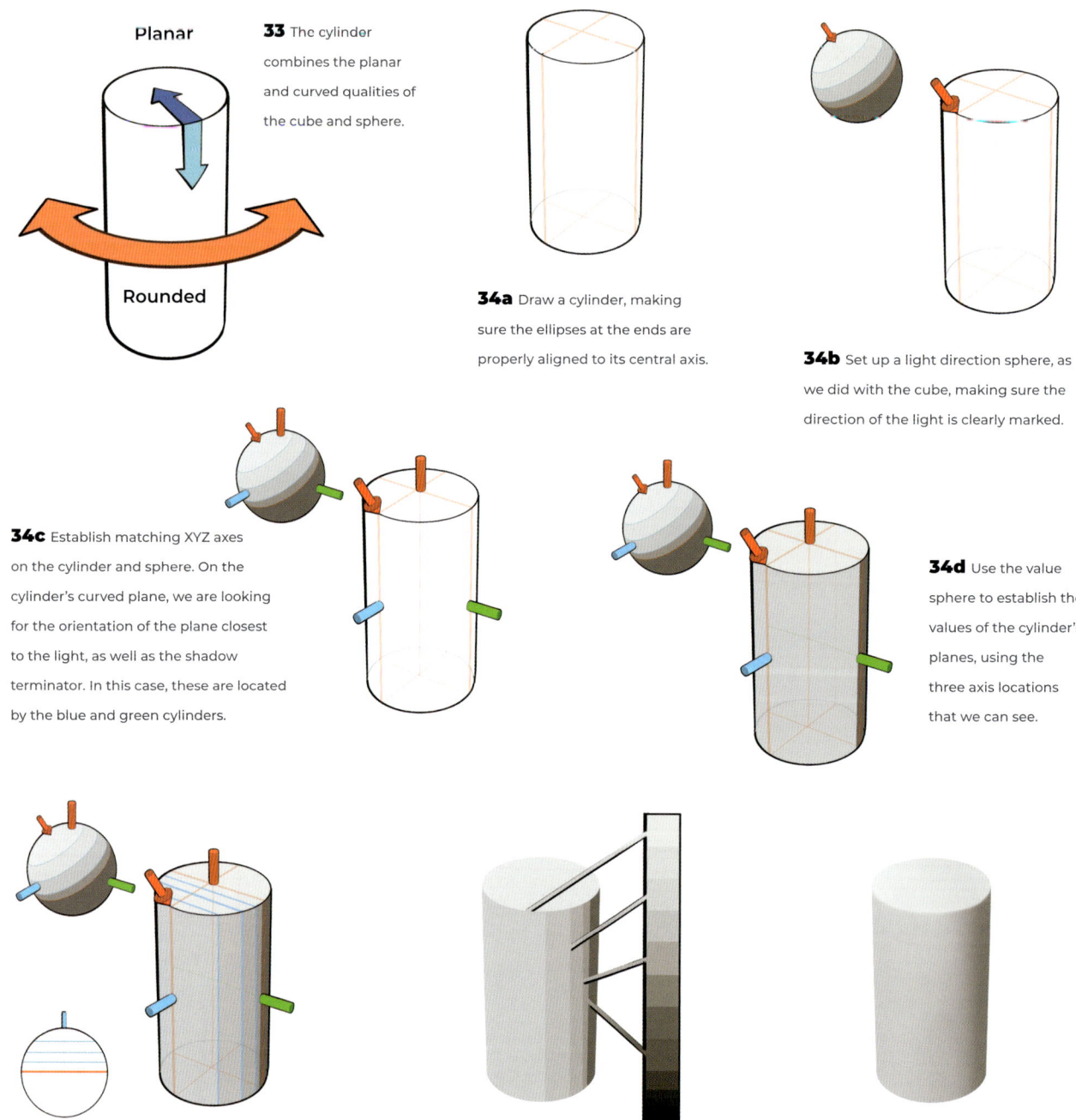

33 The cylinder combines the planar and curved qualities of the cube and sphere.

34a Draw a cylinder, making sure the ellipses at the ends are properly aligned to its central axis.

34b Set up a light direction sphere, as we did with the cube, making sure the direction of the light is clearly marked.

34c Establish matching XYZ axes on the cylinder and sphere. On the cylinder's curved plane, we are looking for the orientation of the plane closest to the light, as well as the shadow terminator. In this case, these are located by the blue and green cylinders.

34d Use the value sphere to establish the values of the cylinder's planes, using the three axis locations that we can see.

34e Without the axes, break down the curved plane using the same construction we used for the sphere – splitting the light in half and then into four.

34f Create a light gradient using the exponential value range, starting from the lightest curved plane, to achieve the correct drop-off.

34g Soften each value step on the curved planes to achieve the final rounded form. The planar surface at the end remains a single value, like the planes of a cube.

LIGHTING A CONE/ PYRAMID

Now let's look at the closely related forms of the pyramid and cone. These forms are simple transformations of the cube and cylinder respectively. To create a pyramid, all we need to do is squeeze the top or bottom plane of a cube into a point; to create a cone, we do the same to a cylinder (35).

The more familiar you get with these constructions, the more you will understand all light sources. Again, try to draw as many cones (36a–d) and pyramids (37a–d) as you can imagine, and try to light them from different angles until you feel comfortable with the method.

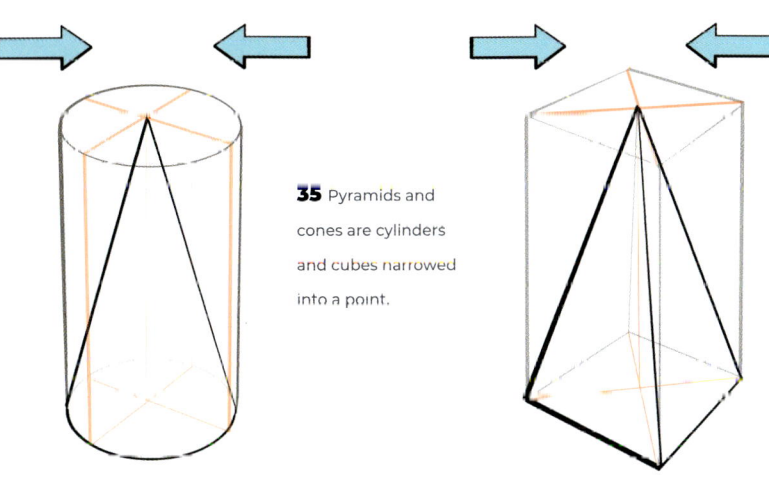

35 Pyramids and cones are cylinders and cubes narrowed into a point.

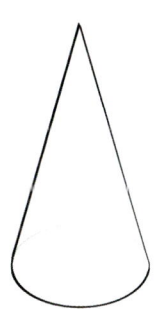
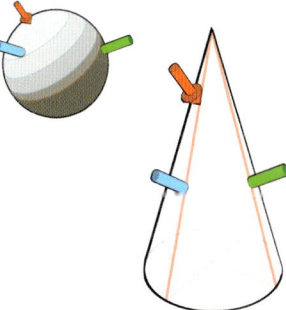
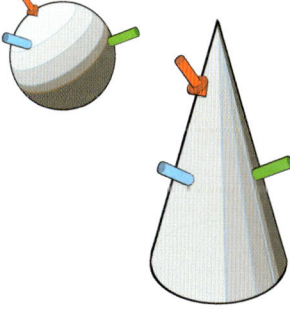
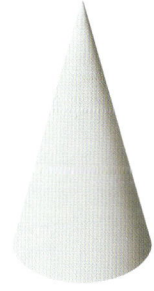

36a Draw a cone by starting with a cylinder and pinching one end into the center.

36b Set up the light direction sphere, then the plane orientations and axis cylinders. Note that on a cone, these axes won't align with XYZ.

36c Slice the sphere's light area into four segments, as we did for the cylinder, and assign these values to the cone.

36d Soften the value for each step to achieve a rounded form. This gradation gets tighter toward the tip of the cone.

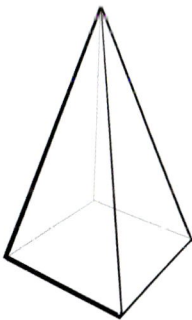
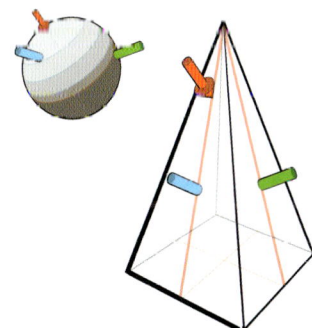
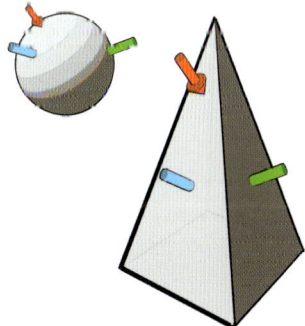
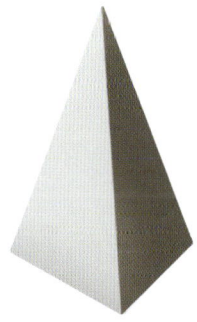

37a Draw a pyramid by starting with a cube and pinching one end into the center.

37b Set up the light sphere and mark the light direction as we did before. Mark the center of each plane to establish its orientation. Like the cone, these won't align with the regular XYZ axes.

37c Assign the sphere's values to the pyramid's planes.

37d Erase the construction lines for the final rendering.

FORM TRANSFORMATIONS

Moving beyond these specific fundamental forms and into more complex ones, the same logic will always apply. However, it can be helpful to understand a couple of fundamental transformations we can apply to our basic forms.

CUTTING

Cutting is taking a planar slice out of our fundamental form **(38)**. We can do this from any fundamental form, at any angle, and light the resulting shape using our sphere value assignment method.

Note that the value of the new plane will not always be a simple mix of the two values of the adjacent planes. In this case, the new

plane is more light-facing than either of the others, so it becomes the brightest plane.

The reverse effect of a cut can be created by adding an extra plane inside the angle of two existing planes, as shown in image **39**.

BEVELING

Beveling is the rounding of two planes into each other. It's just an extension of cutting, with more steps between the two planes, which we then soften to create our final curved form.

Beveling can be done as a broad curve **(40)** or tighter curve **(41)**, on the outside or inside of a shape **(42)**.

Again, it is important to note that the values for these in-between planes will not always be a straight mix of the two original planes – they may sometimes house the brightest planes. This is a good reason not to simply blend when we paint from life or imagination, but to try to establish the correct values for ourselves.

It is also important to note that every cube in real life is at least a little bit beveled at the edges, so these in-between values should be considered whenever we want to model believable planar surfaces.

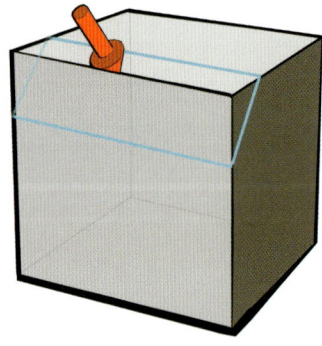 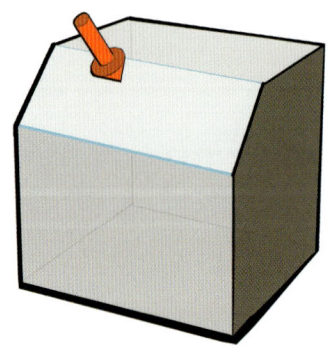 

38 Cutting a planar slice off a cube to create a more complex form.

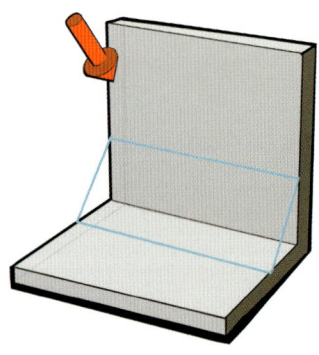 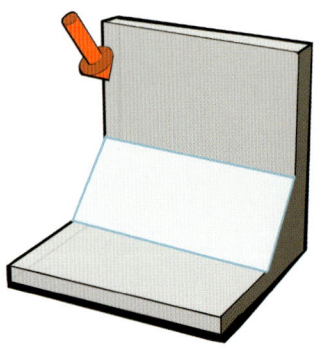 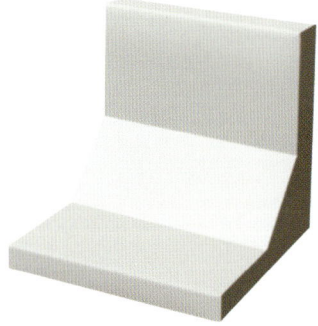

39 Adding a planar segment between two planes – the reverse effect of a cut.

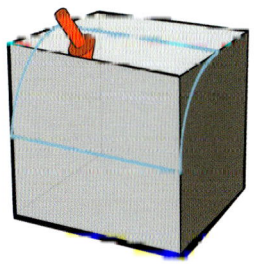 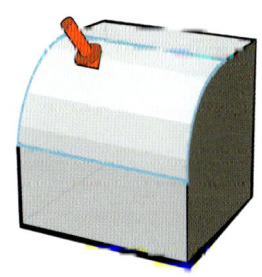 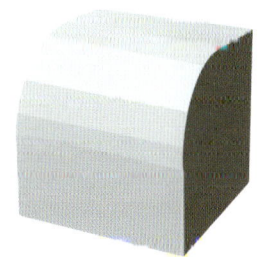 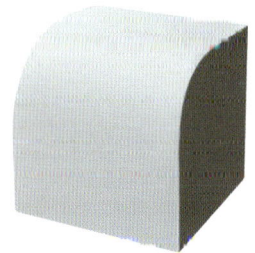

40 Applying a gently curved bevel to soften the edge of a cube.

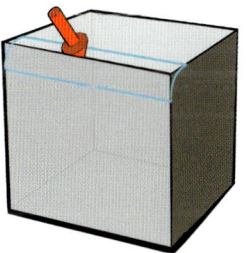 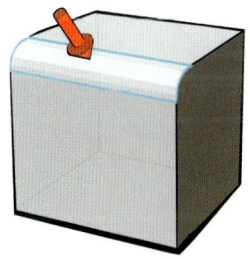  

41 Using a more tightly curved bevel on the edge of a cube.

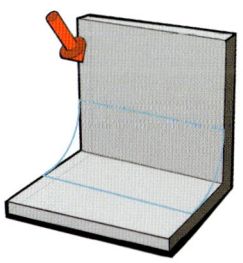 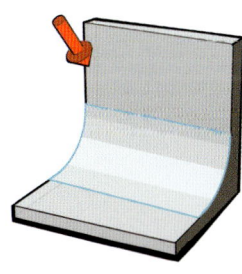 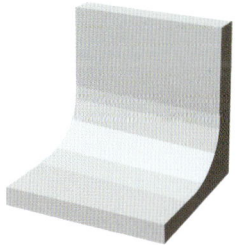 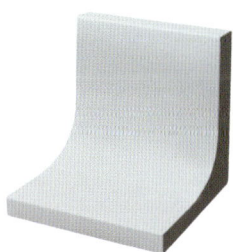

42 Applying a bevel to the inside angle of two planes.

EXERCISES FOR INTUITIVE LIGHTING

At this point in the book, we have gone a long way in describing the logic that will be consistently useful to us in lighting any form. However, whenever we try to really understand the technical mechanisms that build up the real world, we can tend to get mechanical and overly involved in the science and calculations of lighting our drawings. This analytical approach can be incredibly useful in truly understanding what we are doing and how to do it in the most "perfect" way.

However, when we want to work on more creative projects, this technical perfection can sometimes serve as a barrier to our work rather than a help. It's important to develop an intuitive understanding of how to apply this technical knowledge in a flexible and creative way, to forms that are less precise and perfect.

LIGHTING A PLANAR DOODLE FORM

Let's explore a few small exercises you can practice to build this more intuitive understanding of direct lighting, starting with a roughly doodled planar form (43a–e).

LIGHTING A ROUNDED DOODLE FORM

The process for lighting a rounded form is similar to the planar process, taking what we learned from lighting geometry such as spheres and cylinders. It just takes a little more time to plot out the orientation of the forms (44a–d).

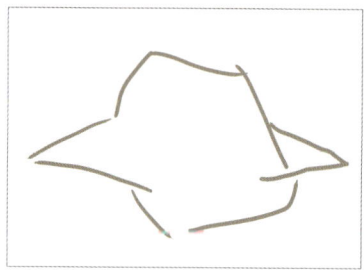

43a Draw a doodle. This can be any shape you want – there are no wrong answers here!

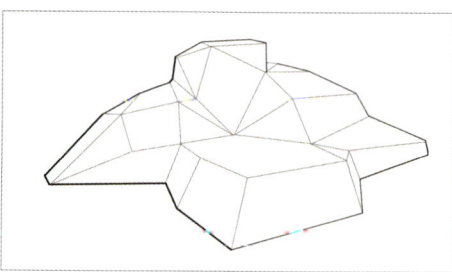

43b Add some planar structure to the doodle. Use a bit of perspective to add planes and depth to your shape.

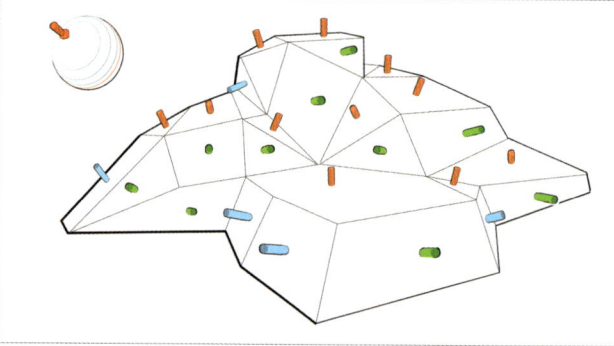

43c Decide on the orientation of your light and planes. Locate the central orientation of each plane and draw your lighting sphere.

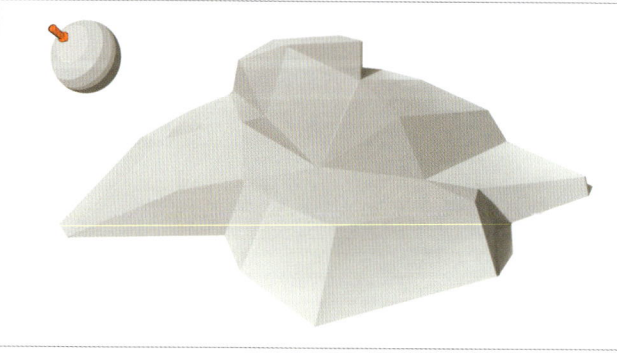

43d Assign values from the lighting sphere to the planes, aiming to properly communicate each plane with your values.

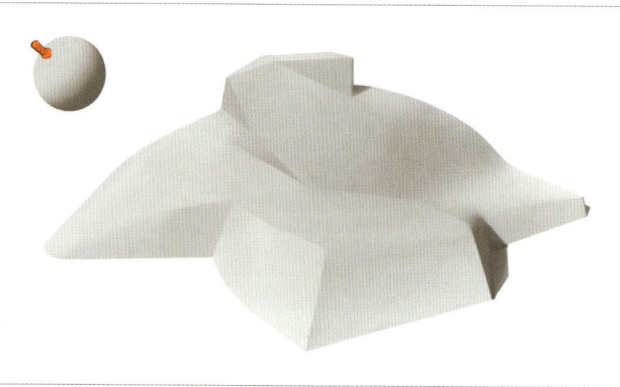

43e Smoothing some of the planar transitions creates more rounded forms, adding variety to the object. But what if an object is entirely rounded? We'll explore that next.

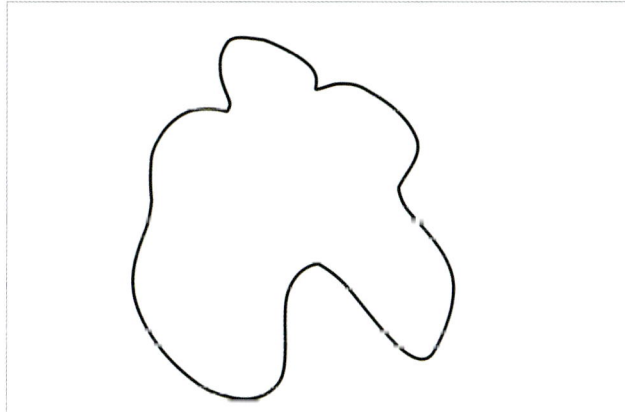

44a Draw a doodle. Again, it can be any shape, but try to use only rounded contours this time.

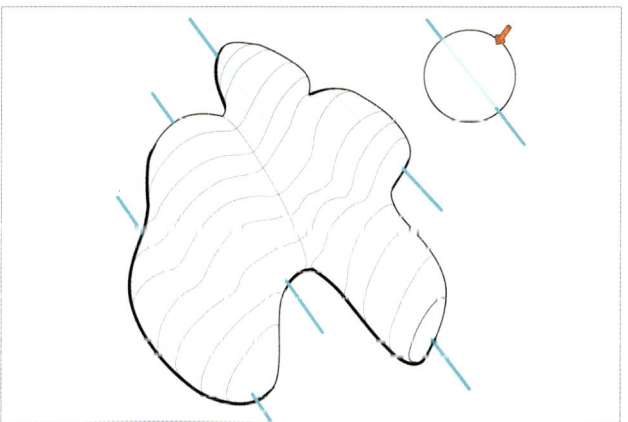

44b Add some rounded structure to the doodle, using cross-sections to add depth. Deciding on your light direction at the same time can be helpful for aligning your cross-sections with the light.

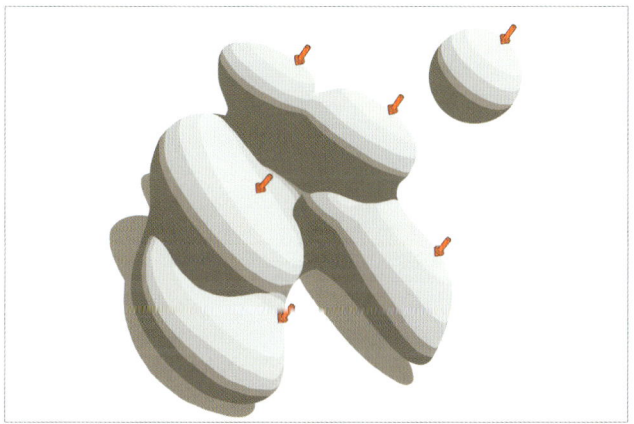

44c Assign the shadow, light, and three halftones from your lighting sphere to the doodle form. Here you can see how I've marked the planes directly facing the light.

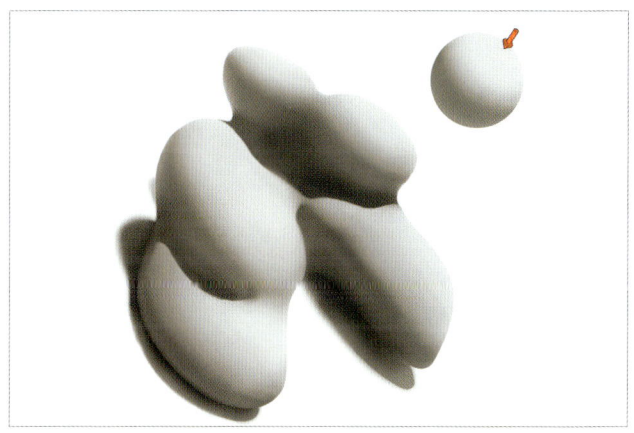

44d Round out the forms by softening the edges between the value groups. Make sure all of these groups are gradated clearly from shadow to light.

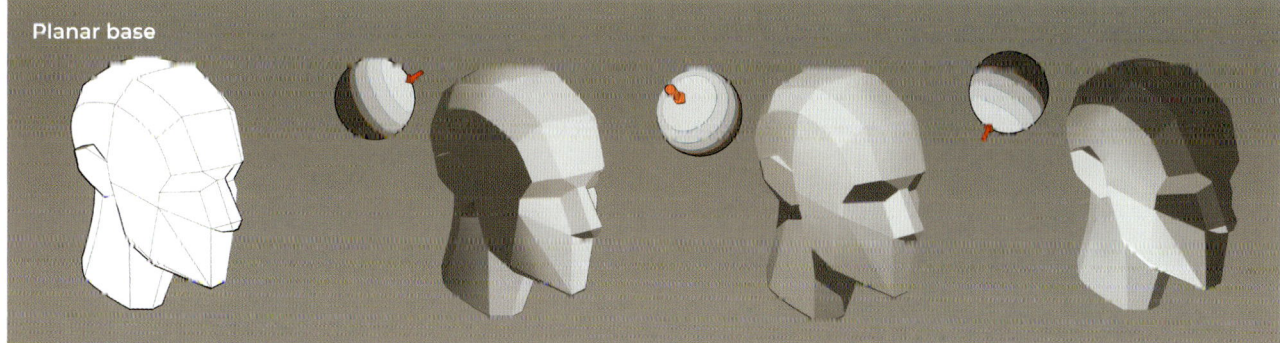

Planar base

45 Try simplifying a familiar subject into a planar form and lighting it from different angles.

VARYING LIGHTING ON ONE SUBJECT

Another great exercise is to take a known form and isolate the planes and their various orientations, such as this planar head. Once you have that drawing, you can relight the reference from any angle you like, using the basic logic that we have discussed.

You can experiment with varying the light direction and even the local color. Try to find as many different lighting scenarios as possible and have fun with it! **(45)**

CAST SHADOW CONSTRUCTION

So far in our discussion of light, we have been working with a very simplified scenario, free of environmental elements. Of course, this is never the case in life – any representation that aims to be realistic has to consider the environment. The first way we can approach this is by exploring the construction of cast shadows.

PROJECTING A BASIC CAST SHADOW

As discussed on page 74, cast shadows are the hard-edged shadows created by an object blocking the light. They work by the simple logic that light will always move in straight lines, casting shadows with highly predictable shapes.

The first thing we need to learn to construct a cast shadow is how to project it onto a flat ground plane. This is the simplest form of cast shadow we can construct, using the following process (46a–d).

This simple construction will always remain true in directional light, and reverse-engineering it is often the easiest and most reliable way to identify the light direction in a real-life reference. If you are ever confused when working from life or a photo reference, refer to the relationship between similar points, from the form shadow terminator to the cast shadow, to work out a reliable, consistent direction (47).

When dealing with more complex shapes, we may not have such a direct path to the ground plane to find our intersecting lines. However, there is a simple solution that will work in most scenarios. Simply project a vertical line straight down to the ground plane – imagine it as a piece of scaffolding holding up the points of the shape (48).

Once we have oriented our points to the ground plane, projecting the cast shadow runs along the same lines as in our last example. Simply project the light's path along the ground plane and place points where the lines meet. These points define the shape of the cast shadow.

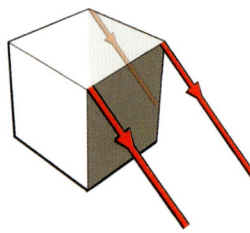

46a Draw the form that will cast the shadow (in this case, a simple cube). Decide the direction of the light (red) and indicate where it passes around the form.

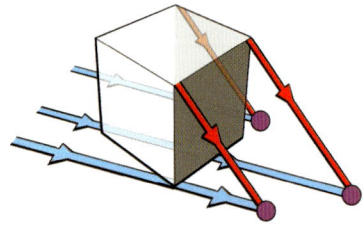

46b Normalize the light direction onto the ground plane (blue) using the procedure on the opposite page. Note the points where these lines intersect (purple).

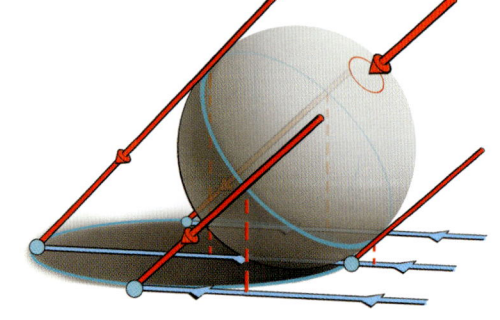

47 Regardless of the form, you can use the same principles to identify the light direction and cast shadow shape.

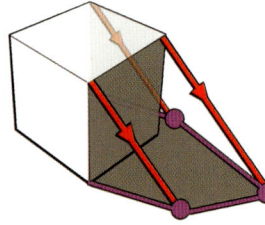

46c Connect the intersecting points to create the cast shadow shape.

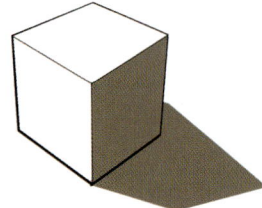

46d Erase the construction lines for the final cast shadow.

48 With some minor tweaks, the method works for objects that are not touching the ground plane.

NORMALIZING METHOD

We can generally imagine where the light source is coming from in our scene, but it can be harder to translate this from the air to the ground plane. Having a clear method for this is invaluable for working out how the light will hit the ground or other surfaces in a scene. Let's quickly cover how to "normalize" the light direction to the ground plane, so we can cast accurate shadows (**49a–f**).

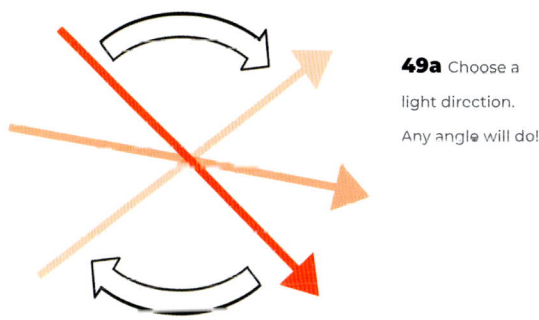

49a Choose a light direction. Any angle will do!

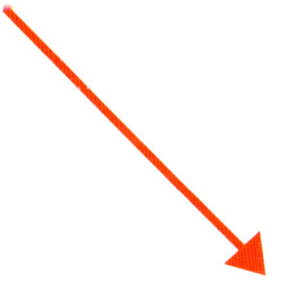

49b Let's go with this angle. However, this flat arrow lacks a third dimension. We can see the light is shining from left to right, but we don't know whether it's going toward or away from us in space. In order to add a third dimension, we need...

49c ...a cylinder. This is the easiest way to add dimension and direction to our arrow. Remember, the wider we make the elliptical end of the cylinder, the more the cylinder (our light source) faces toward us.

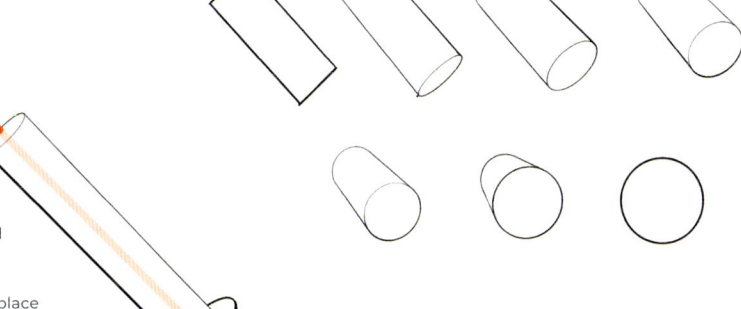

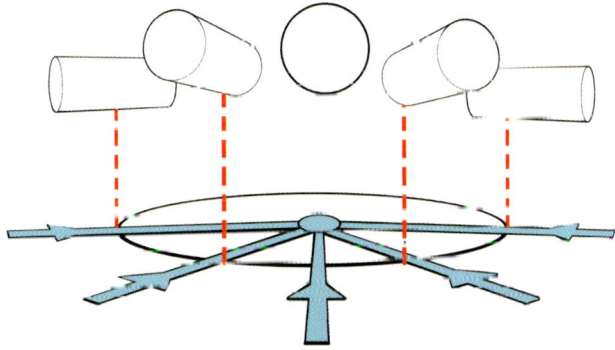

49d Expanding the arrow to a three-dimensional cylinder helps show our chosen light direction. However, it's still just floating in space. In order to place accurate shadow shapes on the ground, we need to find this direction on the ground plane as well.

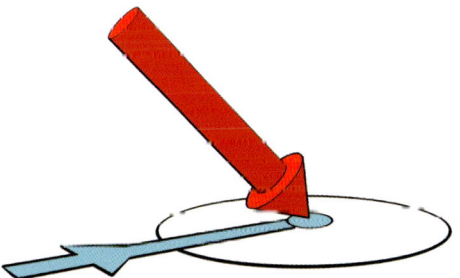

49e The ellipse is our friend for finding angles and placing shapes in perspective, as we will learn in more depth on page 133. By placing an ellipse on the ground, segmented like a clock face, we can match our floating cylinder to it and determine the direction of our light source along the ground plane. The narrower the angle, the closer the cylinder is to a perfect horizontal.

49f The ground plane direction can now be matched with our light source, making it clear at what angle the light hits the ground. We now have a full understanding of our light direction and can use this information to light as many forms in the scene as we like.

COMPLEX CAST SHADOWS

So far we have been studying cast shadows on a basic flat plane, but forms will rarely be that simple! Objects in more fleshed-out scenes will cast shadows on all sorts of elevated planes, and even onto each other.

In order to tackle these more complex problems, we must learn to expand our ground plane's line of direction into a cross-section of the form. This is quite straightforward when looking at two simple forms, with one casting shadow across the ground onto another, as demonstrated below **(50a–d)**. The same method can be used to cast a shadow across multiple objects **(51)**.

However, a complication arises when a complex form cast shadows onto itself. This can largely be solved through our normal procedures, but sometimes presents us with a new problem, as shown in the bridge form in images **52a–f**: An object can potentially cast a shadow onto another shadow.

The challenge here is that it's not obvious where the form would stop casting a shadow on itself and start casting a shadow onto the ground plane. In order to find this point, we can draw through the form and cast both of the shadows as they would sit on the ground plane. Once we have the two cast shadows mapped out, we can observe where they overlap (marked in red in **52d**).

We can then reverse-engineer the direction of the light back onto our original form – in this case, the wall – thus giving us all the points required to accurately draw our full cast shadow.

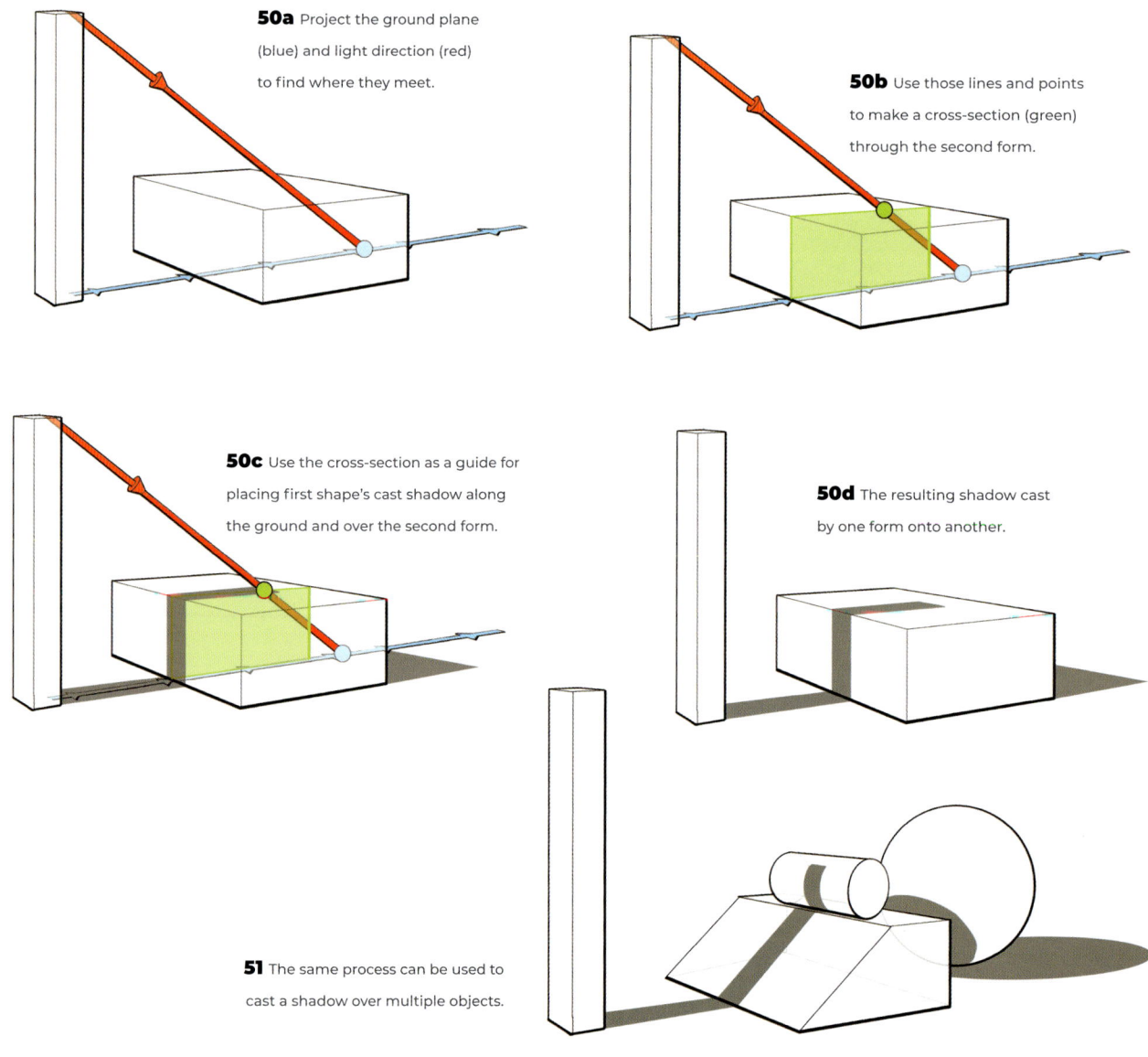

50a Project the ground plane (blue) and light direction (red) to find where they meet.

50b Use those lines and points to make a cross-section (green) through the second form.

50c Use the cross-section as a guide for placing first shape's cast shadow along the ground and over the second form.

50d The resulting shadow cast by one form onto another.

51 The same process can be used to cast a shadow over multiple objects.

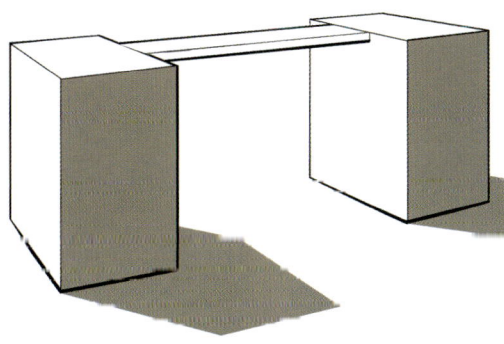

52a How can we project the cast shadow of the bridge section of this shape?

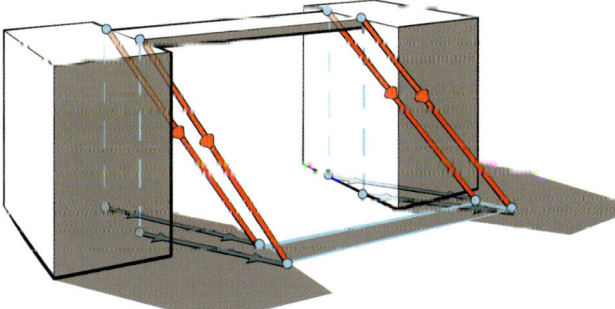

52b As we learned on page 90, scaffold the floating section down to the ground plane and project its shadow shape according to the light direction.

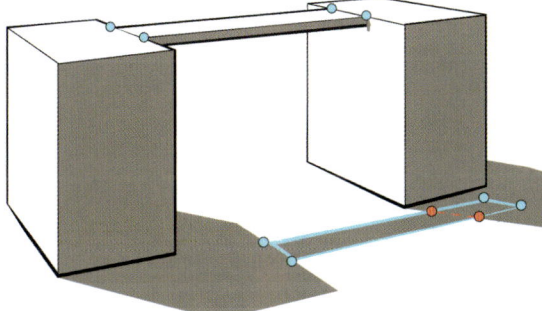

52c Note the area where the projected cast shadows of the two shapes would overlap.

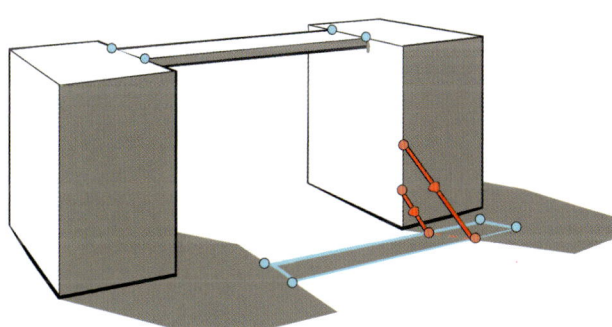

52d Reverse-engineer the light direction back onto the original form – in this case, the wall part of the shape – by drawing back along the light direction until you reach the surface.

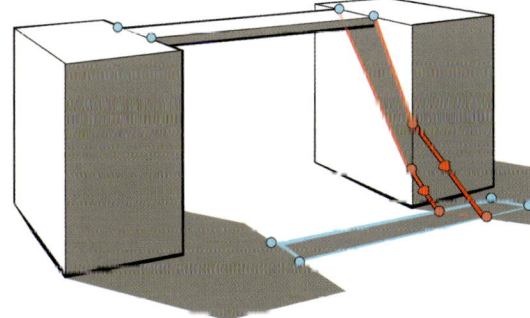

52e From these new points, connect the cast shadow of the bridge shape

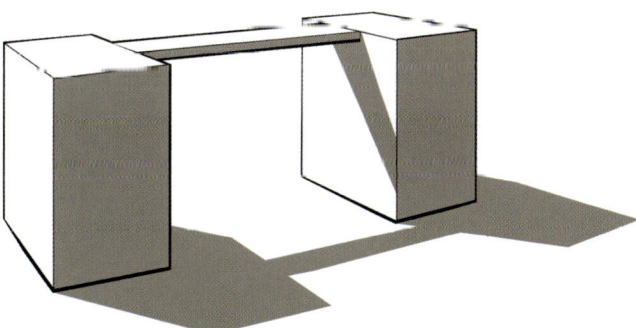

52f The resulting full cast shadow.

SOFTNESS OF LIGHT

So far we have been purely dealing with point light sources and parallel light directions. The results of these are generally referred to as "hard" light, due to the simple direction of the path of these kinds of light sources, where we can generally observe strong light shapes and dark shadow shapes.

While this type of rather stark lighting is incredibly useful to us for an initial study of modeling, it's extremely rare in nature and would hardly ever be seen in its purest form **(53)**. Instead, most light sources we encounter have a width and thickness that influence the character of the light and how it affects form.

In order to understand how this variation affects our modeling, let's double our point light sources **(54)**. As we can see, this functions along the same rules that we have discussed so far: The form appears brightest where it faces the light most, and gradually darkens as it turns away to shadow. The only change is that each of our value groups adds

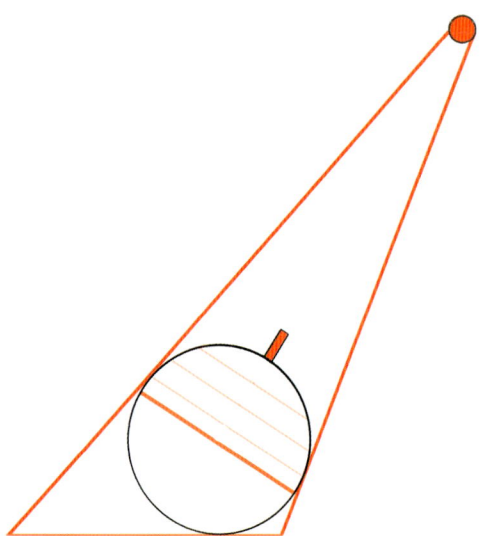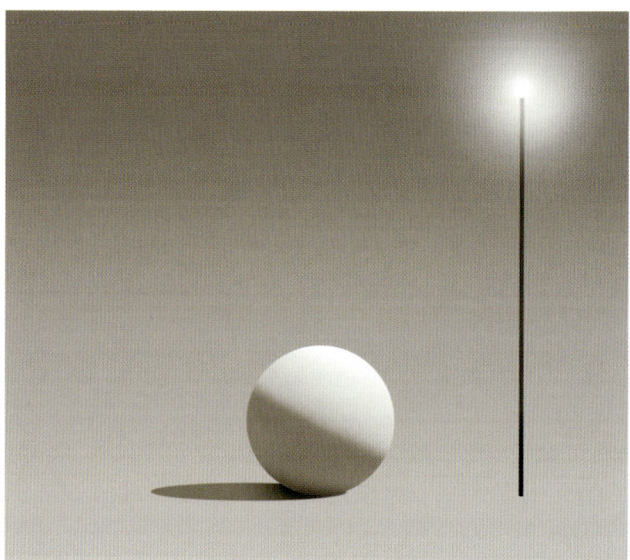

53 A single point light source (hard light) is useful for study but rarely found in real life.

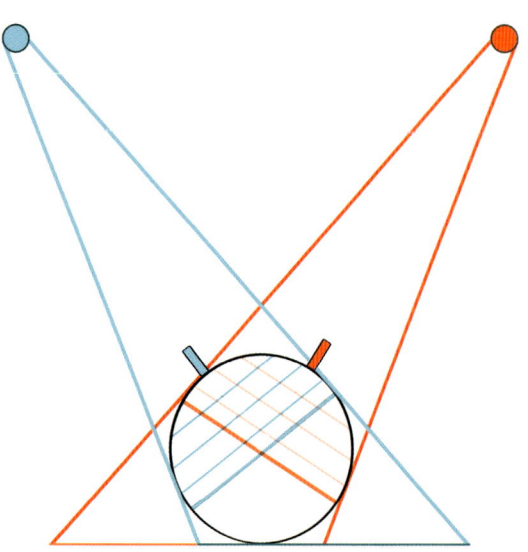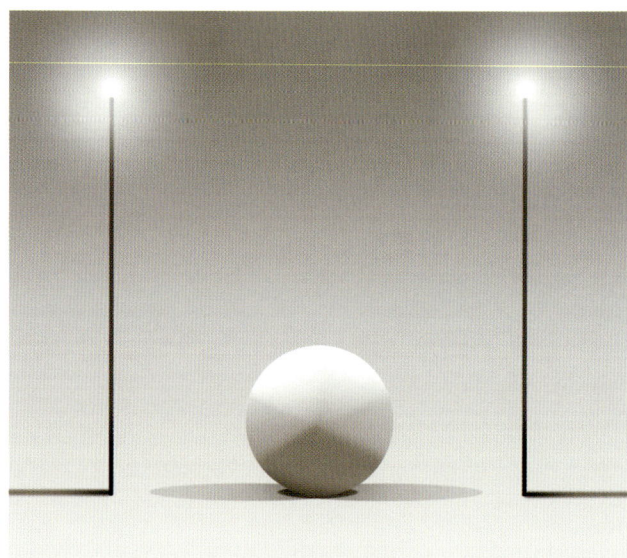

54 Two single point light sources (hard lights added together) create a penumbra.

together. If we assume the light given off by our object can't go over 100% brightness, we will see a larger light value group and an additive combination of the other value groups.

We can also see the secondary light striking the opposing light's cast shadow, creating a new effect called the "penumbra." The penumbra's size will increase with relative distance, both from the light source and from the plane the shadow is cast upon **(55)**.

If we connect the two light sources into one continuous light, like an indoor strip light, we can observe our first "soft" light source **(56)**. We can think of a continuous light source as an infinite series of point light sources. Its effect on our form is a softened version of our double light-source setup, softened in the dimension we have widened. This leads us to our next important idea about light: As the width of the light source increases, so does the softness of the light.

If we widen this light source in the third dimension, as if it's an LED panel or a window, this softening effect expands all over our form and cast shadow **(57)**. Many photographers achieve this effect through the use of a softbox or reflector. Since every light source will have some width, we must always consider this level of softness and how it's directly proportional to the width of the light source.

If we expand the light source infinitely in every direction, we can see it softened to its most extreme degree **(58)**. The closest we have to this in the natural world is the light coming from the sky. In this case, all sense of a shadow shape and usual value groups are lost. The only value change we can see is a general darkening as the form moves away from the light source. This extreme form of soft light is generally referred to as ambient or environmental light, which we'll explore on the next page.

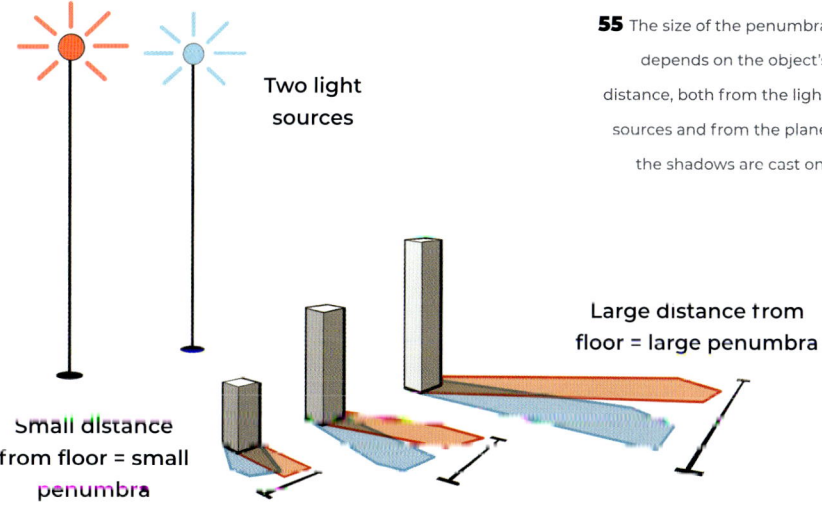

Two light sources

Small distance from floor = small penumbra

Large distance from floor = large penumbra

55 The size of the penumbra depends on the object's distance, both from the light sources and from the plane the shadows are cast on.

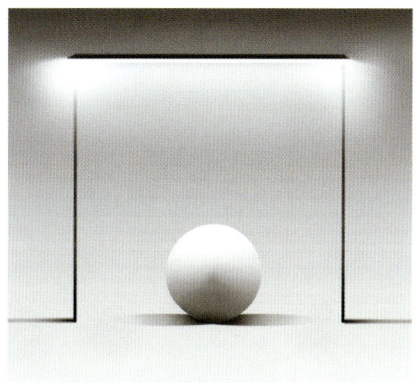

56 Lengthening the light softens its effects in the dimension we have widened.

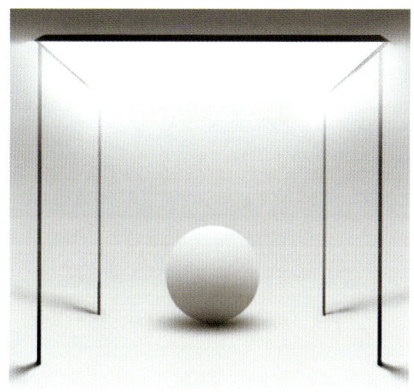

57 Expanding the light source in another dimension softens its effects on the form and shadows even further.

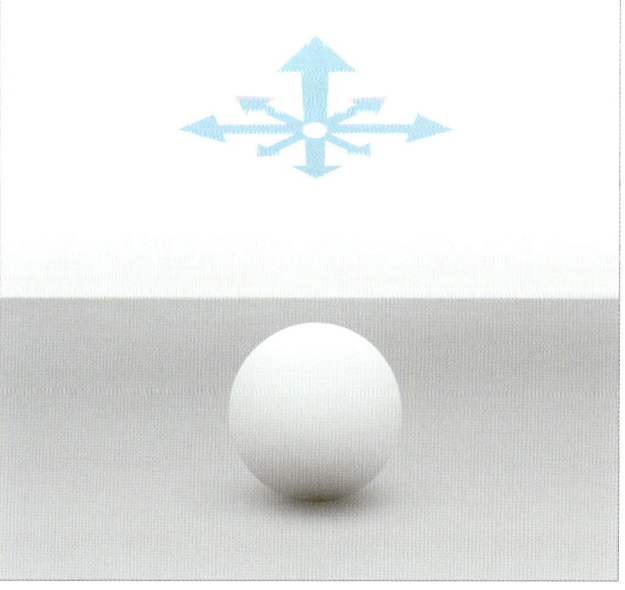

58 Expanding the light source infinitely in all directions creates the softest effect, like the ambient natural light from the sky.

AMBIENT LIGHT AND OCCLUSION

Ambient light is an essential type of light to understand, and we need to consider it separately from the direct light sources in any given scene. Everything that we see must be considered as a light source in itself – every matte surface projects light out in every direction and the ambient light in a scene can be thought of as an accumulation of this light. It is present in every environment and is the reason that not every shadow is completely black.

Due to this, the environmental ambient light is the primary driver behind all of the modeling and colors within the shadows of any subject. Since this light will be striking our forms from every direction equally, we cannot rely on our old principle of the lightest form being the one that faces the light most. If we can't use this logic to model our planes, how can we conceptualize modeling them? The answer lies in how the objects cast shadows upon themselves. As objects come closer and closer together, they eventually reach a point where no light can strike the surface from any direction. This leads us to another rule: As objects get closer together, the ambient light they present will decrease, showing a darker value.

This is called "ambient occlusion," an effect that is always occurring whenever a shadow is not pure black. It's an extremely subtle effect that is drowned out in direct light. It is the result of very soft light, so the darkening should also be represented as a very soft effect **(59)**. Many artists create images isolating this effect, especially in 3D.

A great amount of depth can be communicated purely through these "ambient occlusion passes." Some digital painters apply ambient occlusion using a Multiply layer over the local colors of an

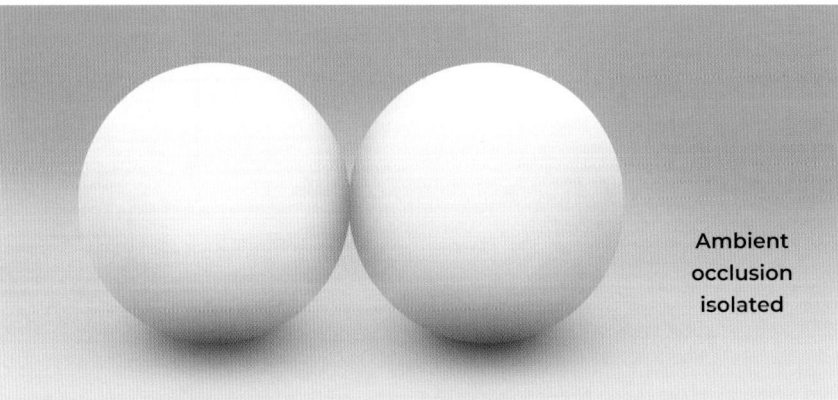

Ambient occlusion isolated

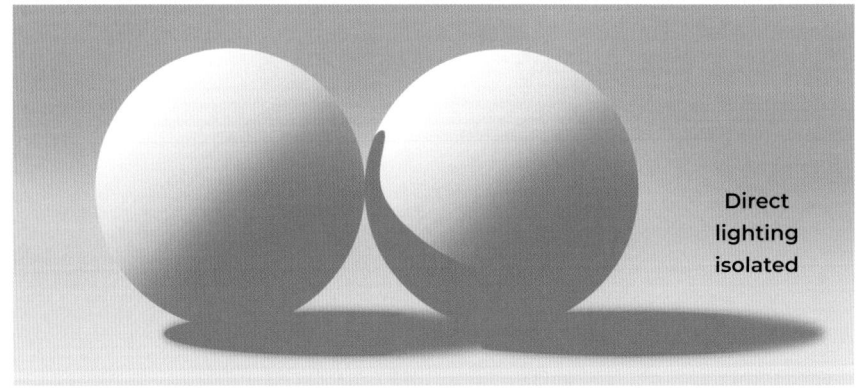

Direct lighting isolated

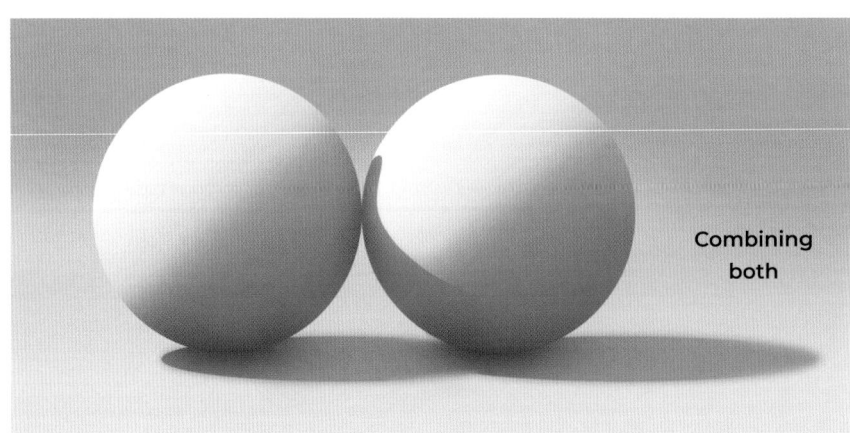

Combining both

59 Ambient occlusion is a darkening that occurs as forms get closer together. Combining them with direct lighting adds more depth to the forms.

image. When an image requires modeling in the shadows, ambient occlusion must be relied upon purely for the representation of form, as shown in image **60**. Note how softly the forms of the back have been modeled, while maintaining a realistic sense of form.

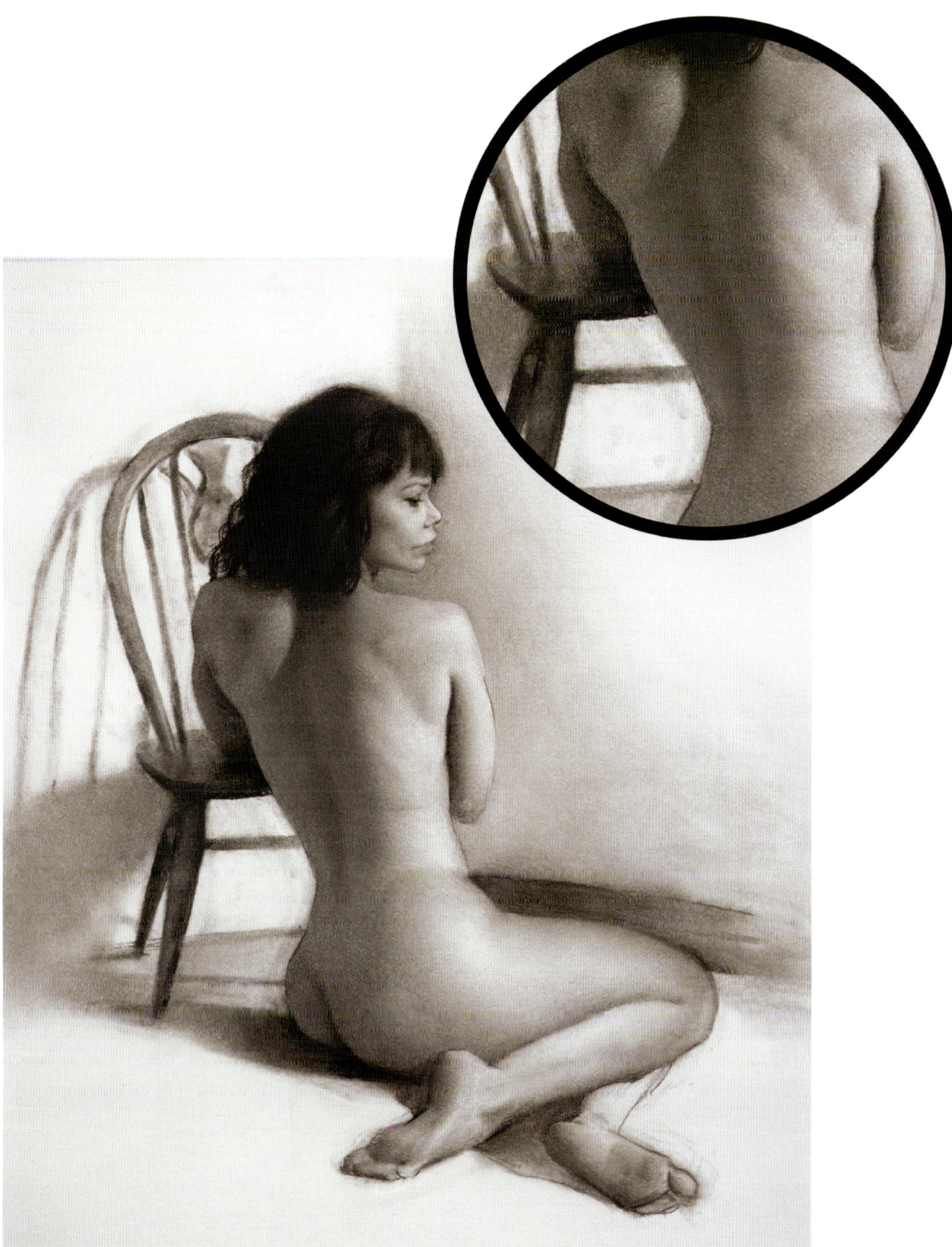

60 Ambient occlusion at work in a life study.

NATURAL VERSUS LOCAL LIGHT

In all our examples up to this point, we have been making one key assumption: that all of our light rays are traveling parallel to each other. This is a useful simplification that helps us understand the theory behind what we observe in nature. However, in practice this is commonly not the case, and most of the light sources that we observe in daily life are point light sources: lights that originate from one point and project out in all directions.

All light sources must start somewhere. All the artificial light sources that we deal with on a daily basis work by this principle. Even the sun does, but it exists at such an incredible distance from us that any difference in the angle of the light rays, by the time they reach us, is negligible for our purposes. Therefore, the only common example of parallel light rays that we can observe is the natural light from the sun **(61)**.

STRATEGIES FOR LOCAL LIGHT

As we are extremely unlikely to encounter parallel light rays in most other situations, we can make a broad separation between "natural" and "local" light sources **(62)**. Luckily, all of the logic that we have already studied still holds true, with just a few small adjustments to account for the limitations of local light.

The first of these adjustments is that, for our local light sources, it is important to place the light source within our scene. Once we have a light source placed, we can use it to project cast shadows consistently in relationship to the light, as we can see in image **63** and as we learned on page 90.

This adjustment also applies to the cross-sections we used for plotting more difficult

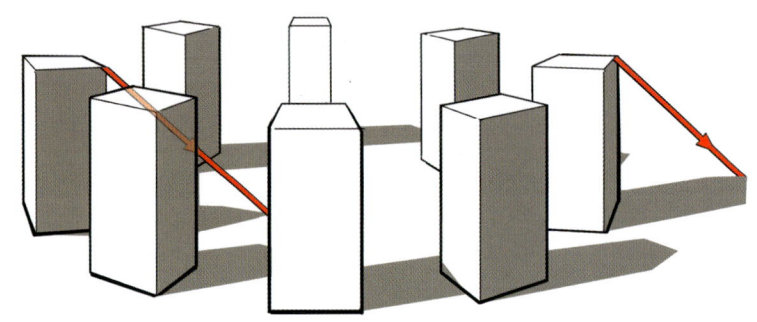

Natural light source

61 Parallel light rays cast by the huge natural light source of the sun.

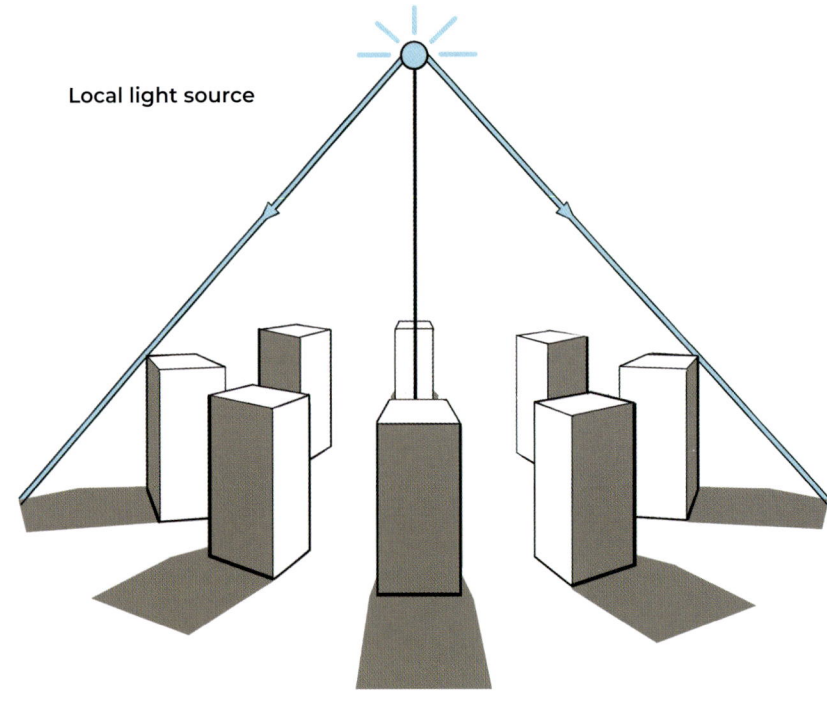

Local light source

62 With local light, the rays spread out from a point source.

cast shadows. We can no longer assume that a shadow will cover exactly half of a sphere's form – instead, the shadow coverage depends on the proximity of the light **(64)**.

Since the angles will now also vary considerably depending on a plane's position in our scene, it becomes more complex to calculate our values. We can still reliably use a sphere as a way to calculate these values, as it's still the simplest form for us to light. However, it's now important to place a few spheres around the scene at key points, so we can use them to find our initial planar values and ensure we get those right **(65)**.

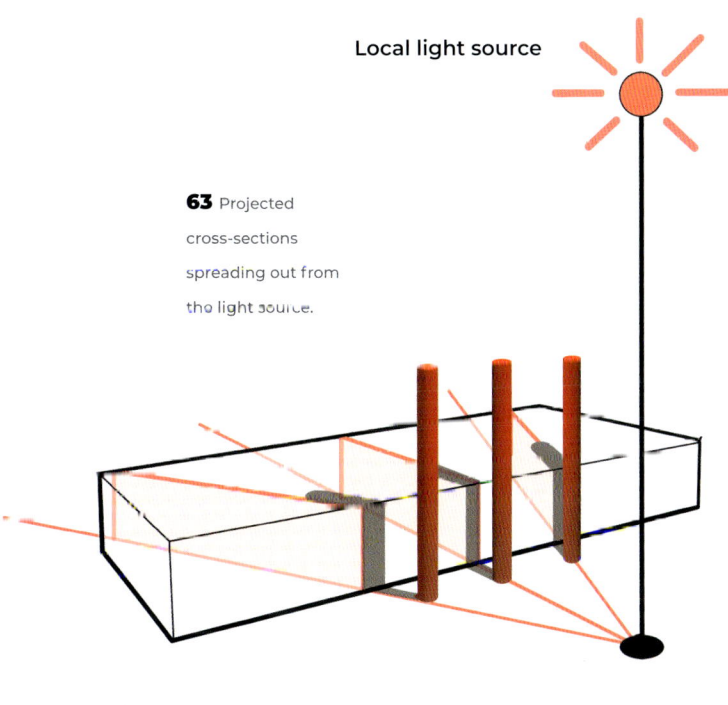

Local light source

63 Projected cross-sections spreading out from the light source.

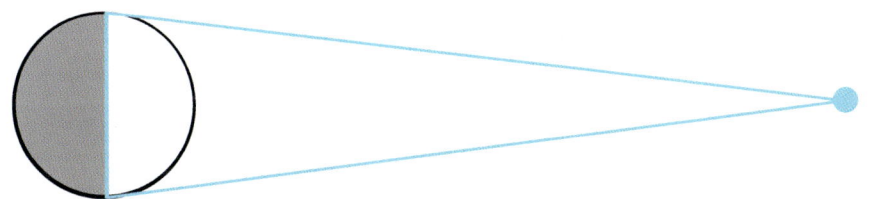

Closer light source = larger form shadow

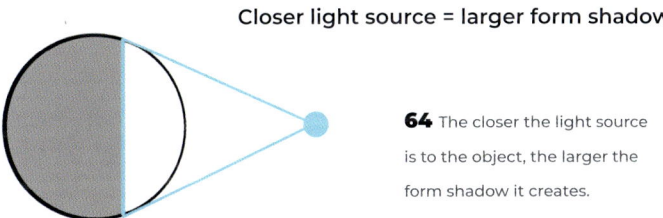

64 The closer the light source is to the object, the larger the form shadow it creates.

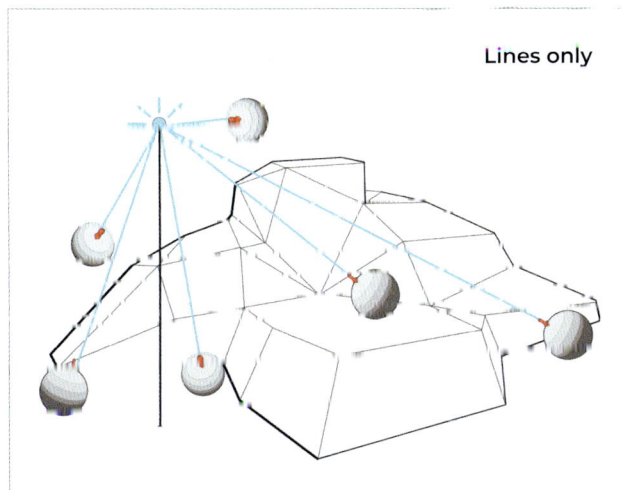

Lines only

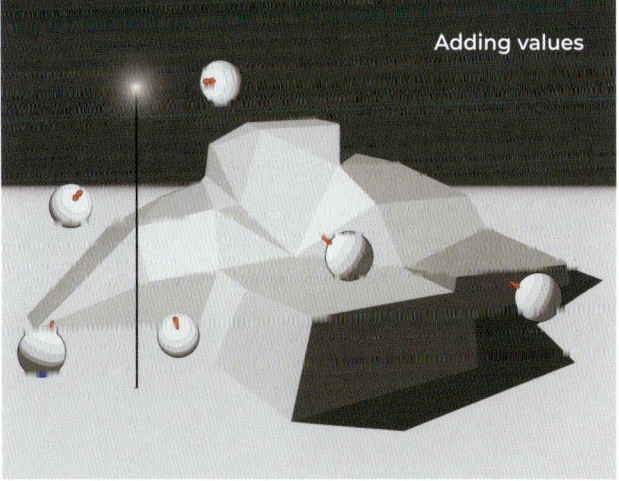

Adding values

65 Try lighting more complex planar subjects or environments using the value-mapping techniques we've covered so far.

LIGHT FALLOFF

Once we begin to consider local light sources, we must grapple with the idea of light falloff. Like the drop-off introduced on page 26, this is the idea that there will be an observed loss of brightness as forms and planes recede from a local light source.

This is most clearly seen when we compare two cubes **(66)**. The first has been lit by a natural light source from a window and the second by a local light source. The locally lit cube shows a pronounced loss of light over a single plane, while the naturally lit cube has no such shift.

This is because the angle between each plane and the local light source becomes shallower, causing a plane to lose value as it moves away from the light. Therefore, there is always this loss (falloff) of light with local light sources. Values will always move from dark to light toward the direction of our light source, on every plane in an image. If we apply these gradations to our planar rendering **(67)**, we can see just how much this adds to the believability of our scene.

When representing local light falloff in our artwork, we can use the darker values of adjacent planes as a hard limit on how dark

Natural light

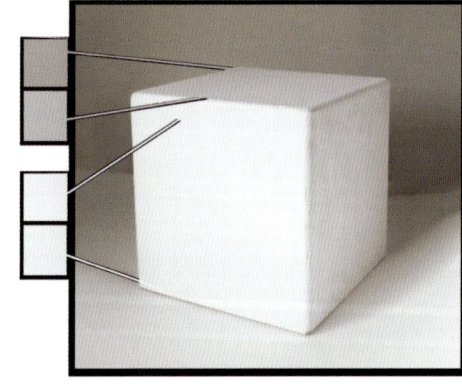

Parallel light rays hit all angles on a plane equally

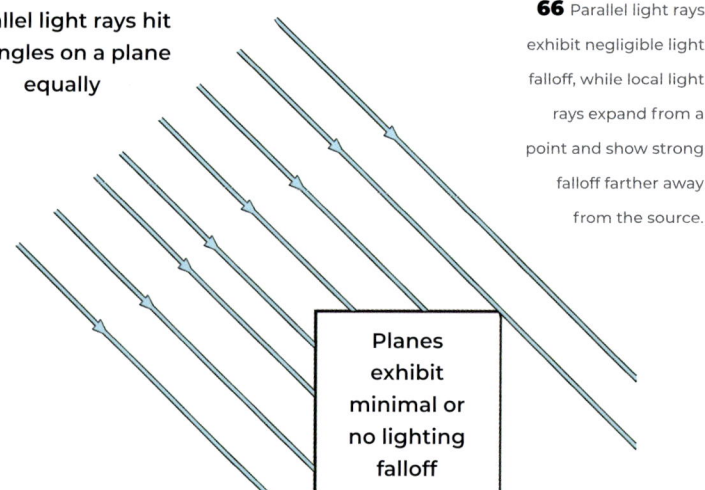

Planes exhibit minimal or no lighting falloff

66 Parallel light rays exhibit negligible light falloff, while local light rays expand from a point and show strong falloff farther away from the source.

Local light

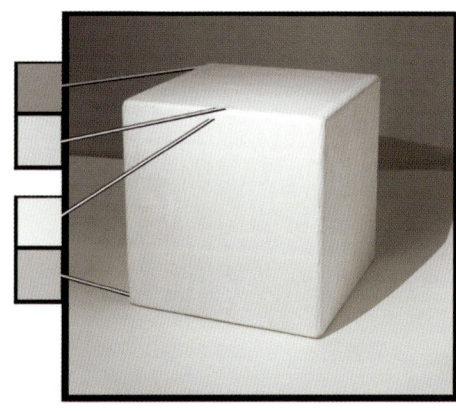

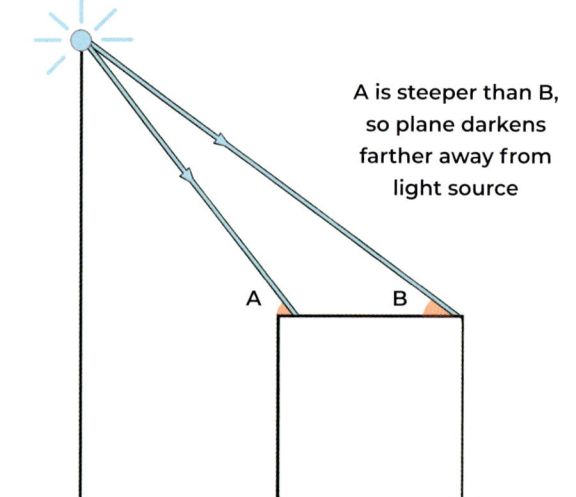

A is steeper than B, so plane darkens farther away from light source

A   B

we can gradate our current plane. Different planes would never have the exact same darkening of values! When creating these gradients, you must pay careful attention that you don't go too dark and make the plane appear curved **(67)**.

This steepening of the light's angle is not the only cause for this loss of light. Light sources simply diminish in intensity as we move farther away from them, due to the light rays spreading out as they move away from their source. This loss of light is exponential, obeying something called the "inverse square law." This law states that as the distance increases, the light decreases by the square of the distance. Basically, if our distance from a light source doubles, the intensity of the light diminishes by four. We don't need to calculate these value changes exactly, but it is helpful for us to remember that they are exponential in nature.

The amount of light lost in this way is dependent both on the intensity of the light source and the relative distances appearing in the scene. This is an effect that can be manipulated for artistic purposes, and can be an extremely useful tool for creating atmosphere **(68)**.

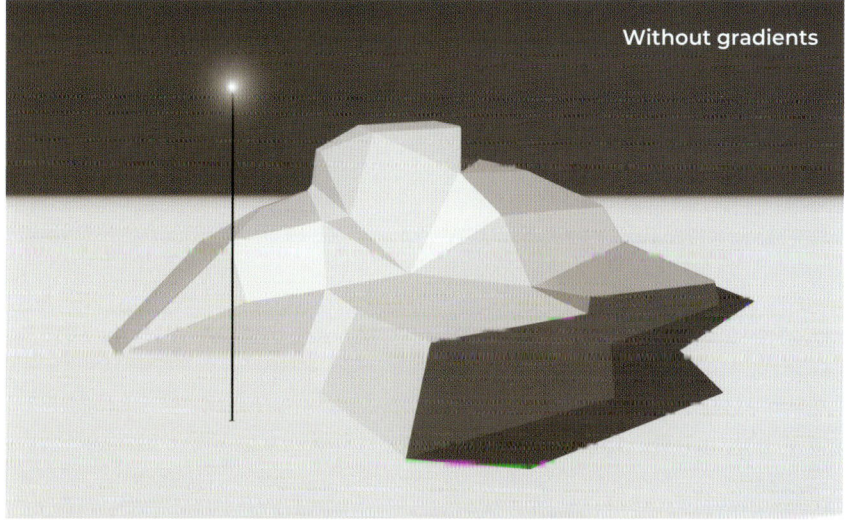

Without gradients

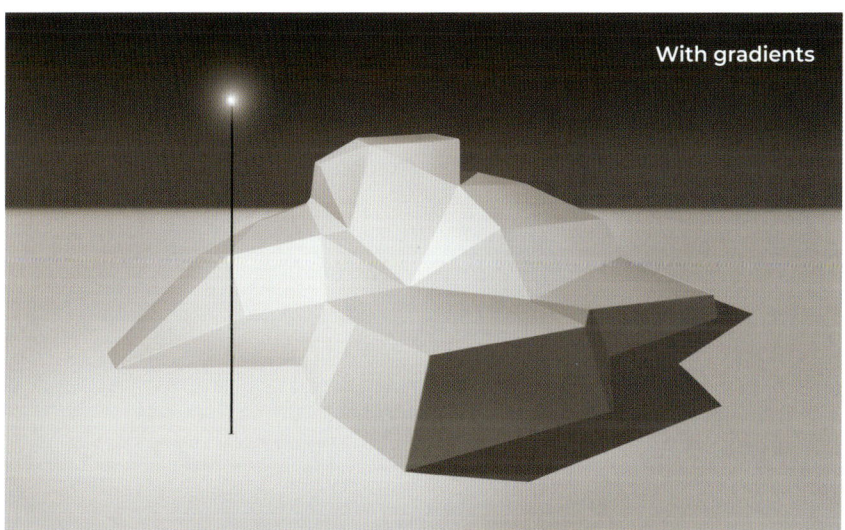

With gradients

67 Adding gradients to planar surfaces creates a more believable feeling of light falloff.

ATMOSPHERIC PERSPECTIVE

If the sun's rays are consistently strong and illuminate everything equally, you may be wondering why the things you see outdoors seem to become fainter and weaker in the distance. This phenomenon, called "atmospheric perspective," is actually due to the properties of the air – we'll be exploring the subject in more detail on page 164 of the Transparency chapter.

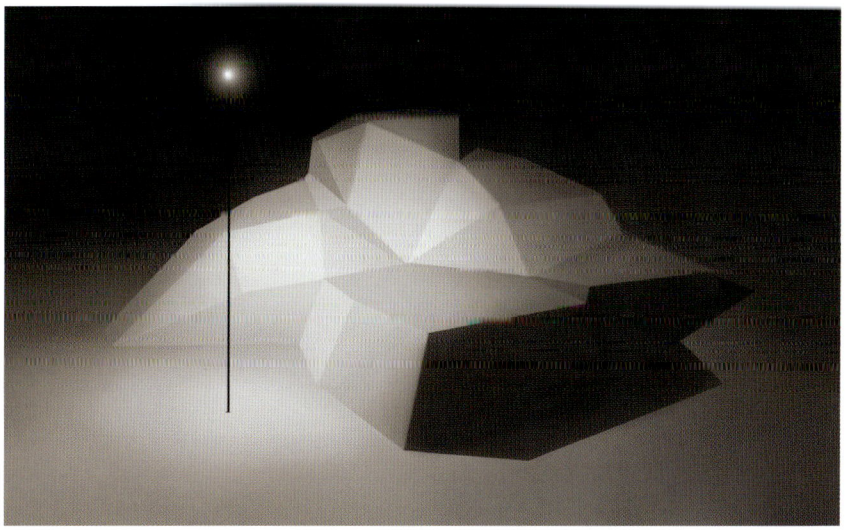

68 Light falloff can be used to create atmospheric lighting effects in your images.

COLOR MODELING AND COLORED LIGHT

At this point we have extensively discussed what happens to values in matte surface shading. But what happens to the two other color dimensions, hue and chroma? There can be a lot of confusion here, but the principles are simple.

Let's initially take the case of a white light source. As we learned on page 32, when white light enters an object, some wavelengths are absorbed and others are expelled. The proportion of the different wavelengths absorbed or reflected will decide the color that the object appears to be. The purer the wavelength, the more chromatic the observed color **(69)**.

The proportion of the wavelengths absorbed remains consistent regardless of the amount of light that enters the material, so the object's hue remains constant in simple matte surface shading in white light. We can think of the object's hue as a colored light dimming throughout the form.

As covered on page 41, lights follow a saturation path down to absolute black.

On this path, chroma simply diminishes in proportion to value. So, our general rule to follow when painting matte surfaces will be: Planes are most chromatic as the form faces the light, and lose chroma as they approach shadow **(70–71)**.

In digital media, this relationship is extremely easy to maintain, as most programs have Saturation sliders. However, when working traditionally, this is often the most important relationship to learn how to maintain within an image. It can be an excellent place to start your studies.

SEPARATING MATTE AND SPECULAR INFO

Students are often initially confused by the above relationship, as it's often not what we observe in nature. As we'll discuss later, no object is purely matte in the real world, and most will display a significant amount of specular reflectivity. This sits on top of the simple matte surface modeling and follows different rules. Students will often observe these reflections and, not thinking of them as separate, will paint chromatic halftones

with the least chroma at the brightest point. This is something to be avoided **(72)**.

If you turn the next page to image **73**, you can see I have used polarising filters to isolate these two separate forms of shading so we can observe this effect in action.

When the matte shading is isolated, you can see the clearly diminishing chroma on the areas that go into shadow. When the specular shading is isolated, you can see that it's a separate lighting effect influencing its own area. These bright areas are where the modeling deviates from the matte saturation paths in the original photograph.

While humanmade objects generally have clear separations between local colors, organic objects will change more gradually, as we can see in the apple in image **74**. If we want to represent these objects well, we need to understand what the various different local colors are in isolation.

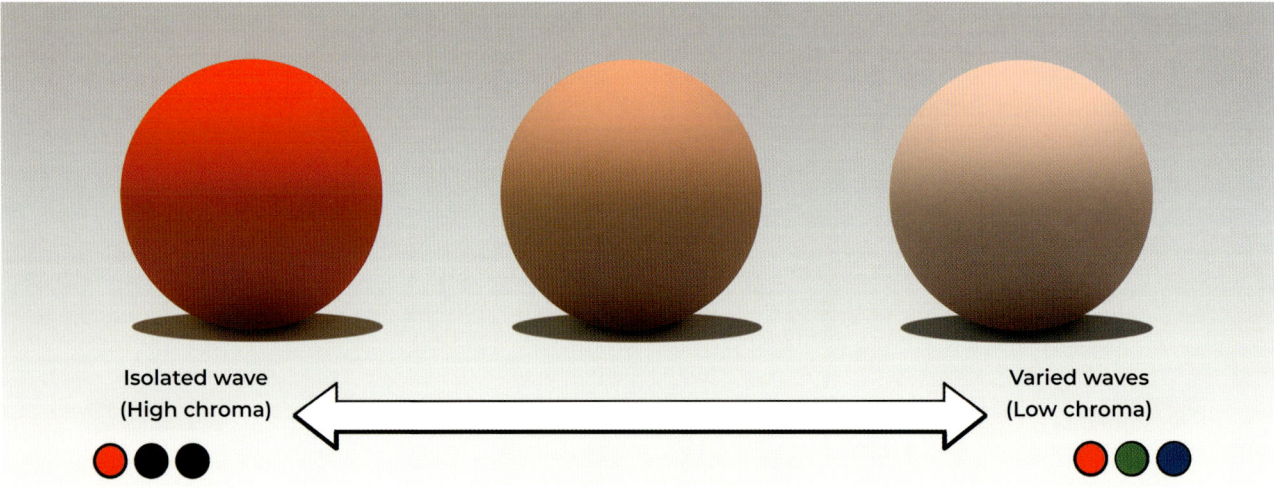

Isolated wave (High chroma) ⟷ Varied waves (Low chroma)

69 Highly chromatic colors, like the intense red on the left, are the result of purer, strongly isolated wavelengths.

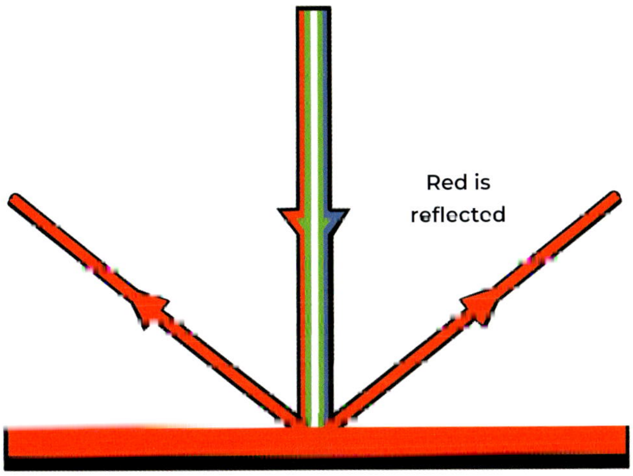

White light enters object

70 Here the light enters the surface at a direct angle and is reflected evenly. However, that won't be the case when dealing with a form that has any kind of complexity. What happens to the local color in such a case?

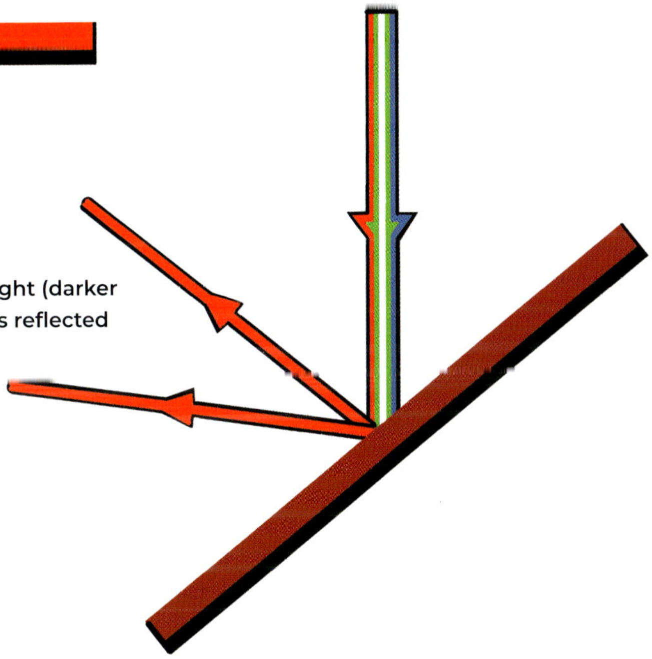

Red is reflected

White light enters object

Less light (darker red) is reflected

71 Though the ratio of reflected wavelengths stays the same, less light is reflected when the surface is at a different angle. This causes its color to darken along its saturation path.

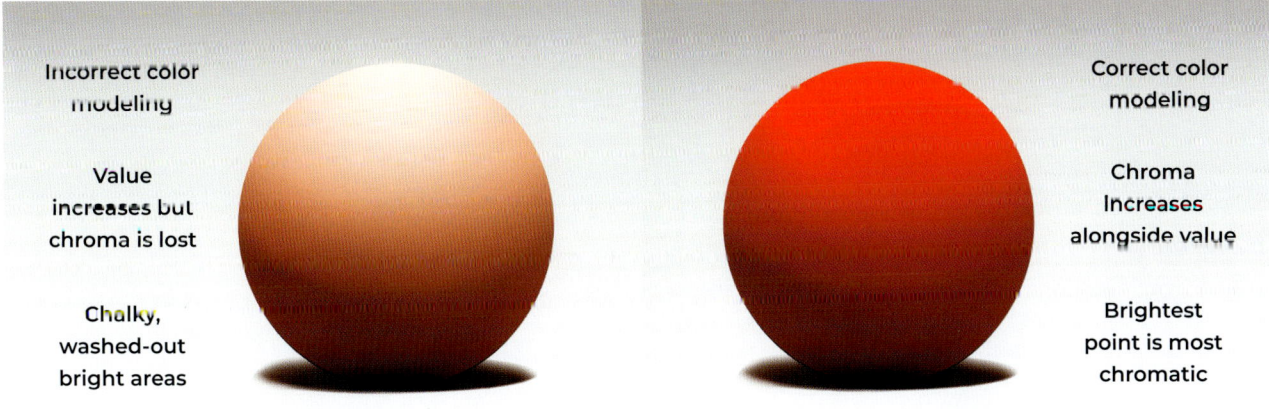

Incorrect color modeling

Value increases but chroma is lost

Chalky, washed-out bright areas

Correct color modeling

Chroma increases alongside value

Brightest point is most chromatic

72 Examples of correct and incorrect color modeling.

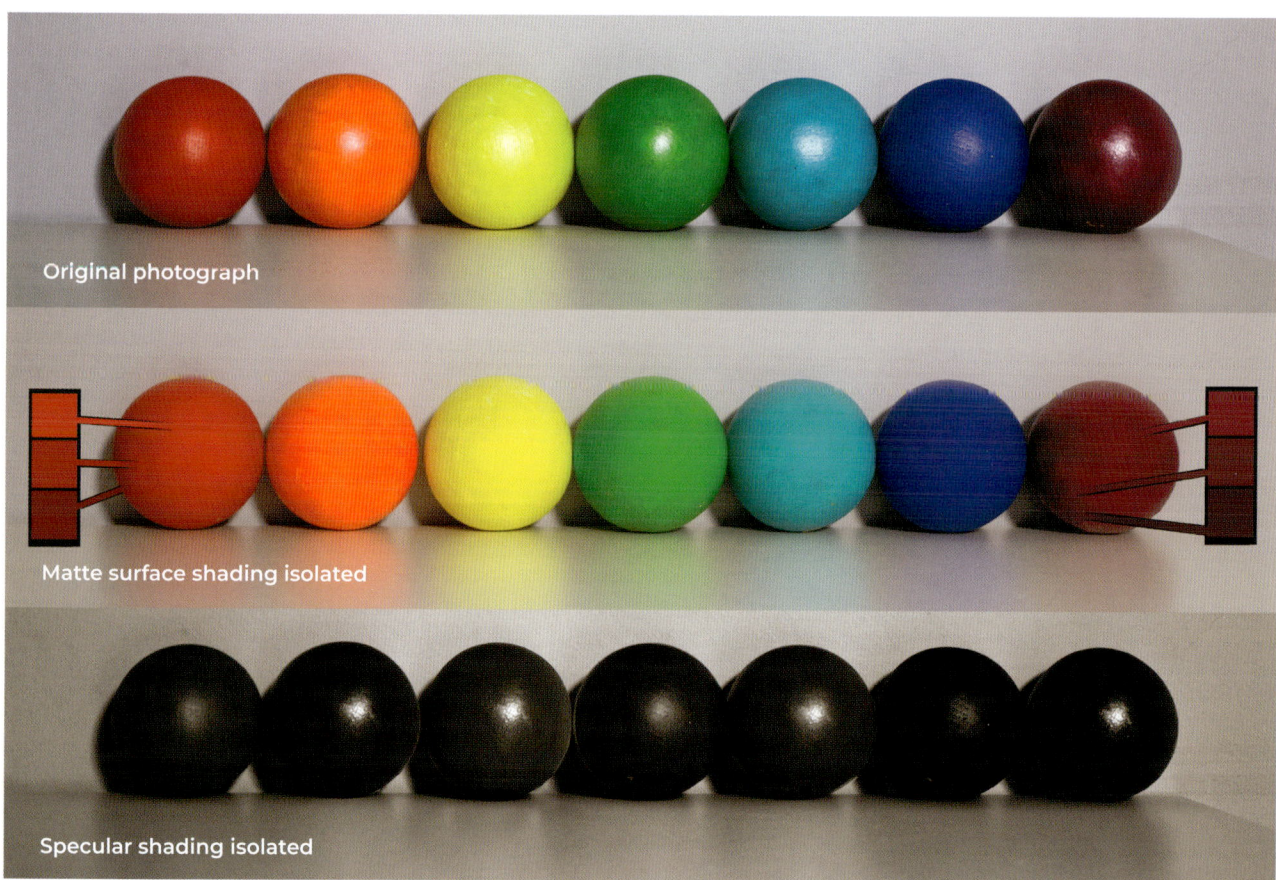

Original photograph

Matte surface shading isolated

Specular shading isolated

73 It's easier to see the clearly diminishing chroma of the objects' local color when the specular shading is filtered out.

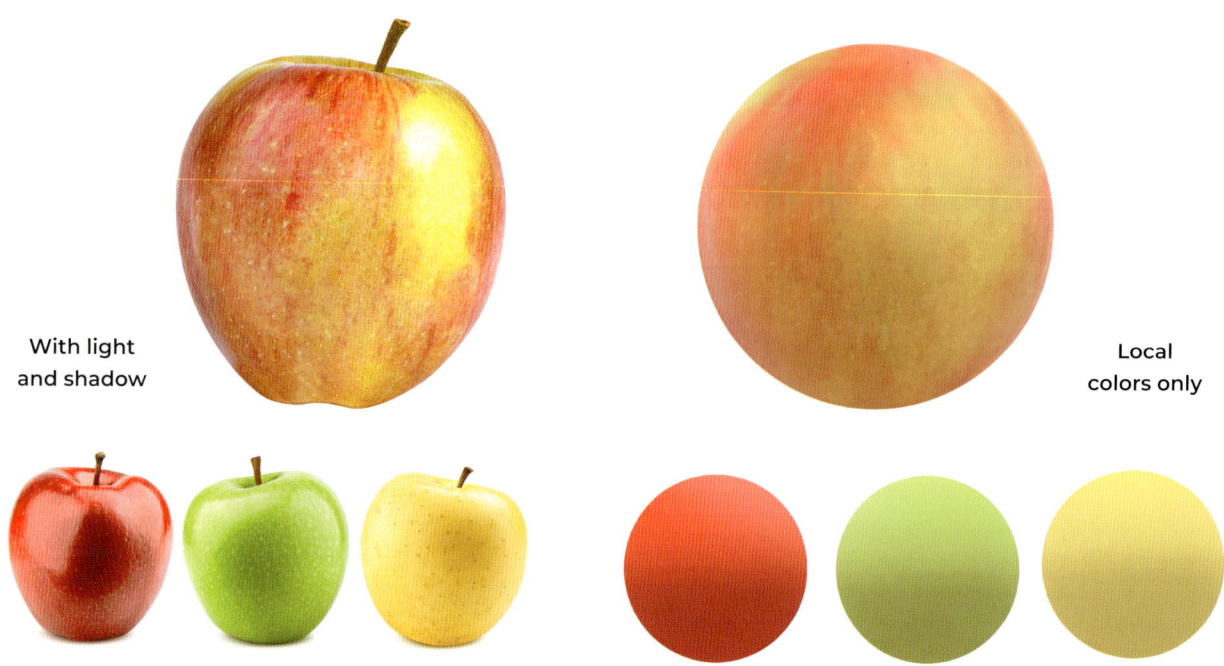

With light
and shadow

Local
colors only

74 The local colors of an organic object are much more nuanced, but can still be isolated in the same way.

Image 74 apples (top to bottom) © ilietus and grey (via Adobe Stock)

PRIMARY-COLORED LIGHT SOURCES

Hue and chroma are easy to see under white light sources, but we'll rarely have perfectly balanced light. The most perfect white light comes from natural sources, and even then, only during certain weather conditions and times of day. Colored light presents new effects on both the observed chroma and hue of local colors. Below are each of the primary and secondary local colors under white, red, green, and blue LED light sources **(75)**. We can see that the environment's saturation and hue remain constant – just with only one hue and saturation depicted. Under each colored light, the other two primaries are unable to reflect any light, appearing as a perfectly black local color. This leads us to our first rule of colored light: The local color of an object will mix subtractively with the color of a colored light source.

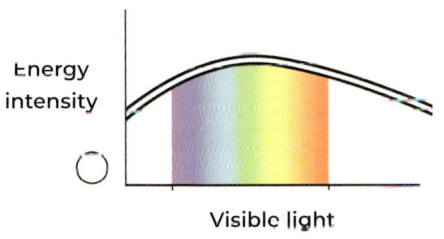
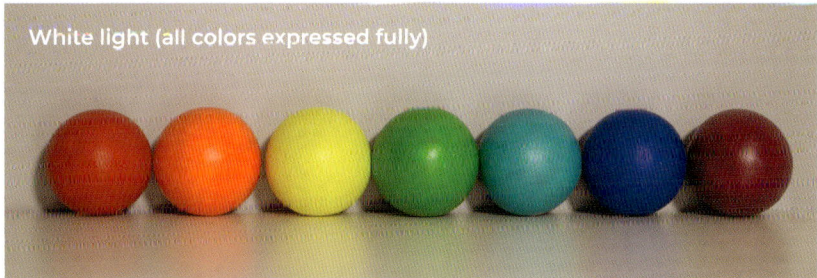
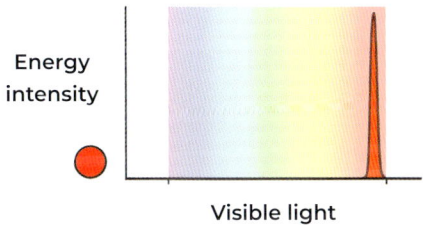
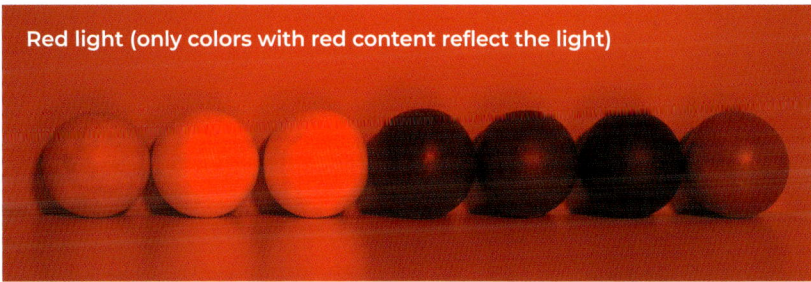
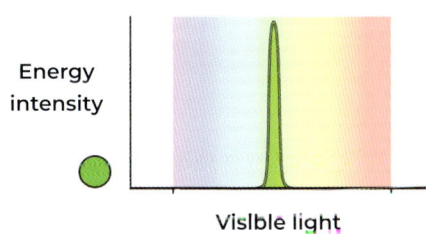
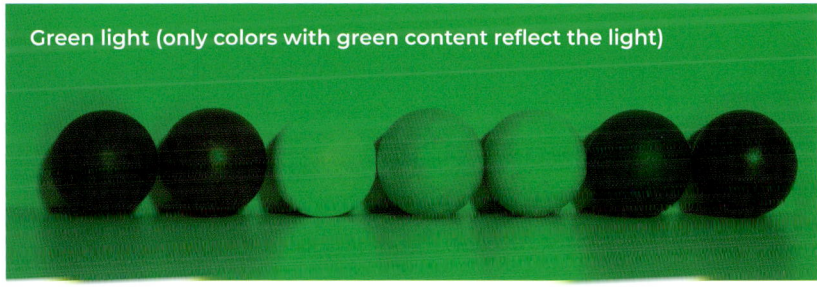
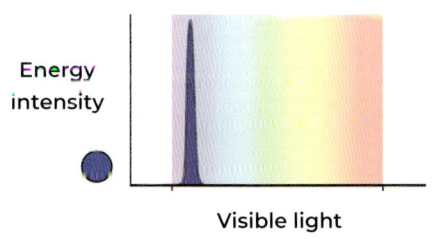
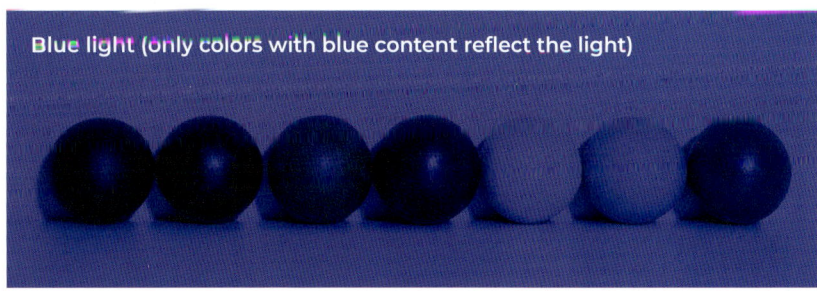

75 Only colors with content matching the light source color are reflected. All the other colors appear black.

SECONDARY-COLORED LIGHT SOURCES

If we add another simple wavelength to our light, we can learn some useful new facts. We can see that even though there are only two wavelengths present in the light, we can observe a third color (**76**). This shows us that we don't need to have every wavelength present in our light in order to perceive different colors. This leads us to a second useful rule that can simplify how we think about colored light: We only need to worry about the RGB proportion of our light. The other colors will resolve in our eye.

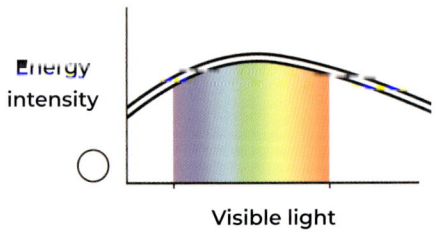
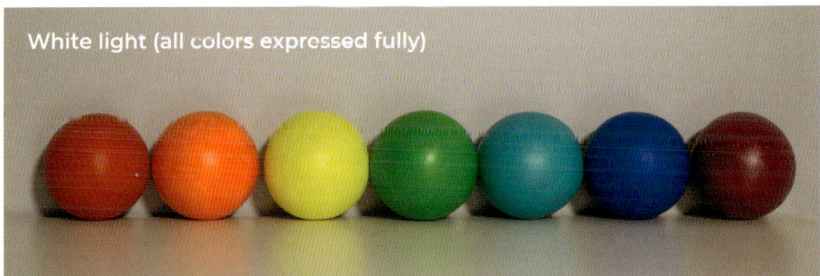

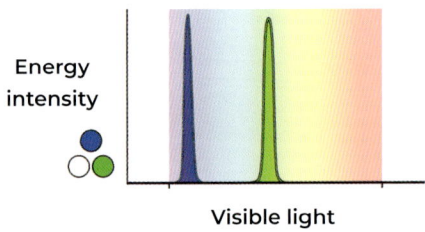
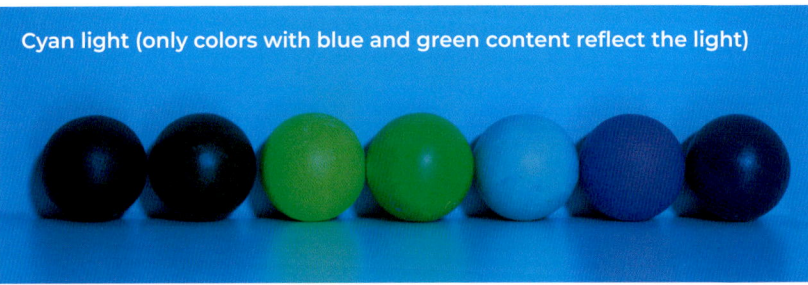

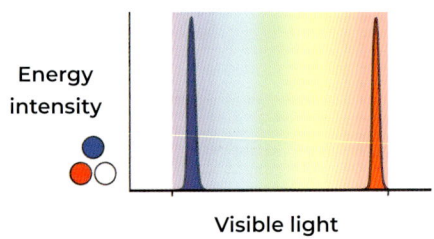
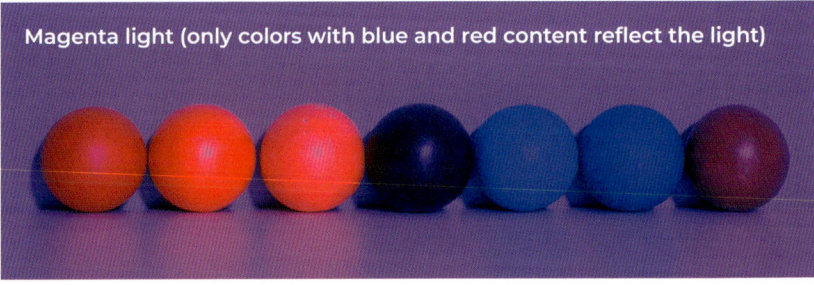

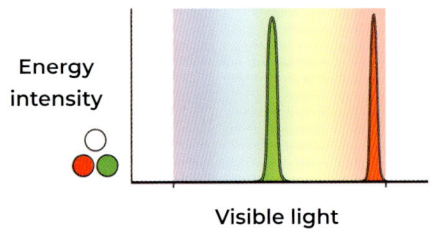
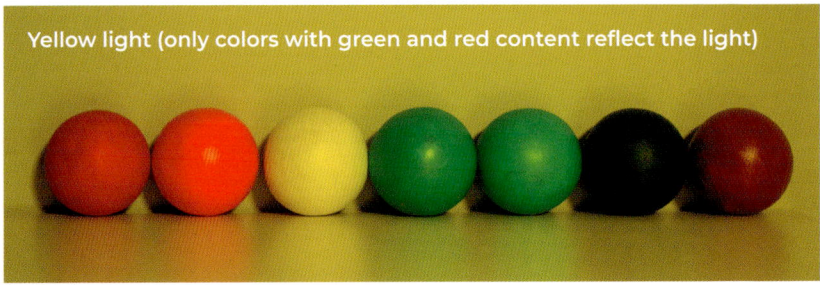

76 Adding a second wavelength of color allows us to perceive a much wider range of local colors.

WARM AND COOL LIGHTS

Now we move into more balanced light sources, the type that we will most often deal with in everyday life. Here, different color temperatures are generally labeled according to the heat (in kelvin) that an incandescent light source would need to reach in order to produce that color. We will explore light source temperatures further on page 116, but for now, we can split these broadly into warm and cool lights (**77a–c**).

These light sources create less extreme versions of the one- or two-color light effects we observed previously. In cool light, the cold colors that are usually less chromatic become more chromatic, while warm colors appear darker and less chromatic. The reverse effect is true for warm light.

Green can be seen as our neutral color between the warm and cool colors here. It is interesting to note that these light sources will shift from warm to cool, as in the color spectrum, but will skip green light. This is an inherent property of blackbody radiation – a thermal radiation given off by heat-emitting objects – so green-tinted lights are extremely rare and are something we won't often observe in the real world. We will revisit the concept of blackbody radiators on page 118.

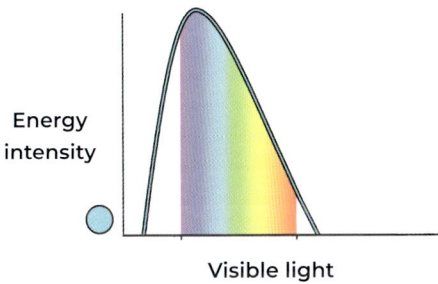
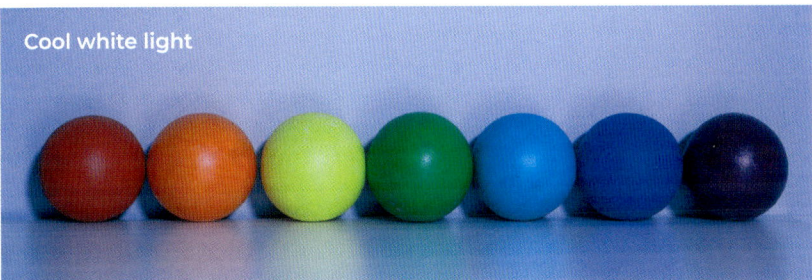

77a All colors are expressed, but warm colors have lower chroma while cool colors have higher chroma.

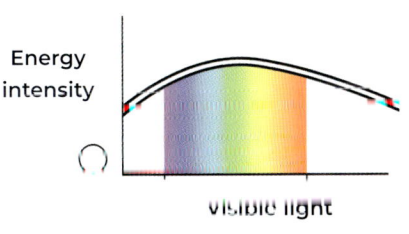
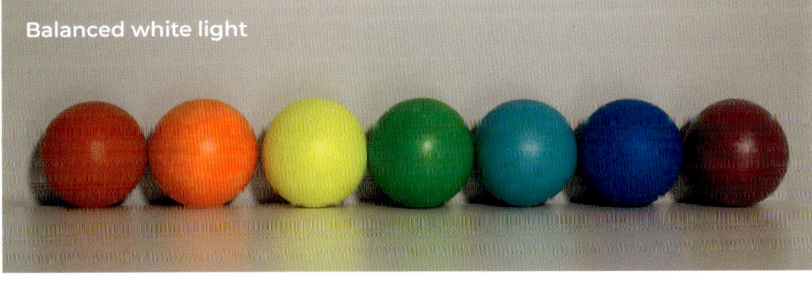

77b Under a balanced white light source, all the local colors are expressed equally.

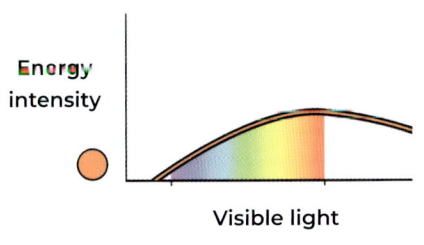
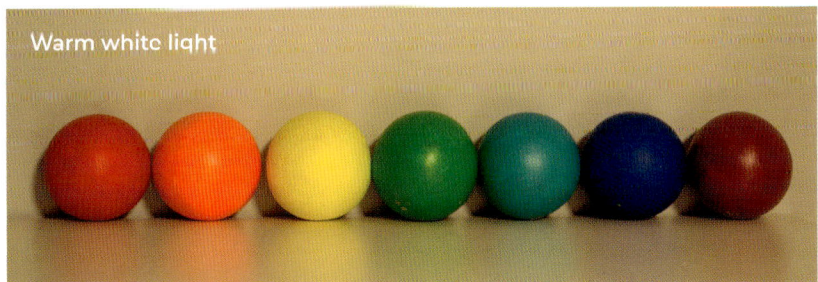

77c All colors are expressed, but cool colors have lower chroma while warm colors have higher chroma.

AMBIENT SHADOWS

Now that we have been introduced to the concept of ambient light, we need to learn about its effect on the presented values of our shadows. Many of the examples in this book so far have followed the "50% to black" rule shown on page 79, where the ambient light is white and the relative shadow value is a medium gray, halfway down the scale to black. This is a great generic rule to start with for white ambient light, but the way shadows work is somewhat more complex.

The most important thing to know is that the value of a shadow is not really a property of the object itself. In fact, absent of atmospheric light, there would be no value to the shadows of any local-colored object. They would all be black! Shadows only gain value and become visible to us as a result of ambient light. They are a negotiation between the ambient light and the local color of the object.

Since light sources will always lose light when they strike objects, the shadow will always be darker than the ambient light. Some photographers break this rule with external light sources, but in general this will be true. So whenever we design any scene, we should first consider the average value of our scene, as it indicates to us the general level of ambient light.

The "50% to black" rule is a good one to use when dealing with a white, high-value background. We also know from the moon that an absolute black background leads to absolute black shadows. We can treat each level of ambience as being between these two extremes. So, if a white background has shadows 50% of the way to black, a 50% mid-gray background will have shadows 75% of the way to black, and a black background will have shadows 100% of the way to black **(78)**. In this way, we can work out a ratio between our lights and shadows. As

long as we maintain this level of shadow within all the objects in our scene, we can paint any colored object believably in any environment **(79)**.

Keep in mind that this rule will not be absolute and there are many external factors that can potentially break it. Cameras can expose the shadows to any value they like and artists will often make creative adjustments for different expressive effects. What will always remain true, however, is the overall relationship. Rules like these can only ever serve us as a starting point, but the relationship of the shadows to the background must be consistent throughout an image. If we pay careful attention to our various shadows' relationships with black, we can create and maintain a strong believability in our images.

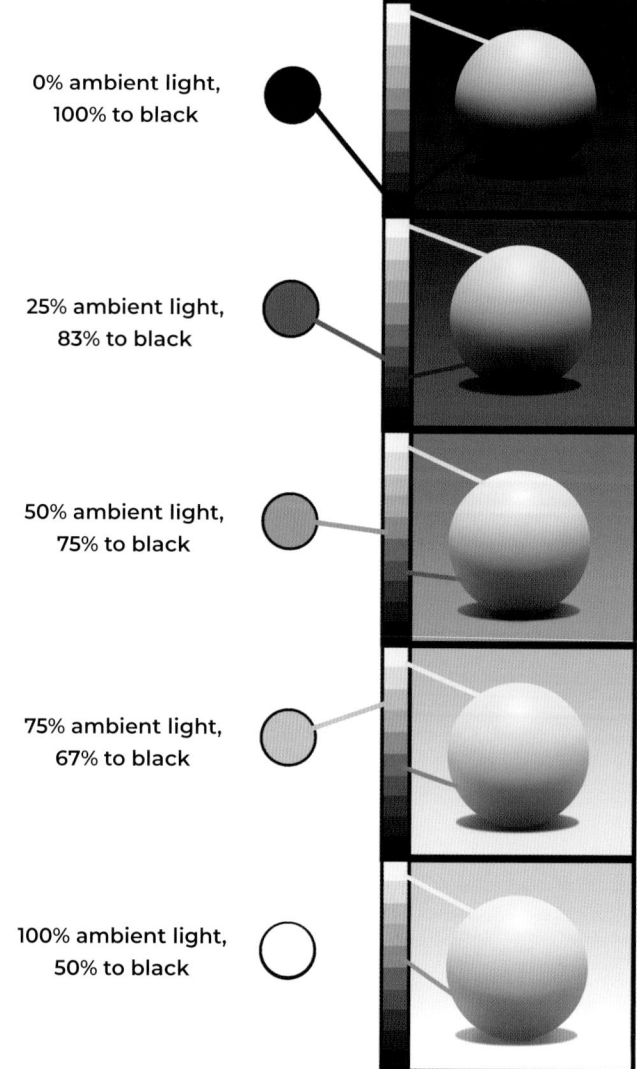

78 Following a consistent ratio of light to shadow will help you maintain believable lighting and shadow in your scene.

0% ambient light, 100% to black

25% ambient light, 83% to black

50% ambient light, 75% to black

75% ambient light, 67% to black

100% ambient light, 50% to black

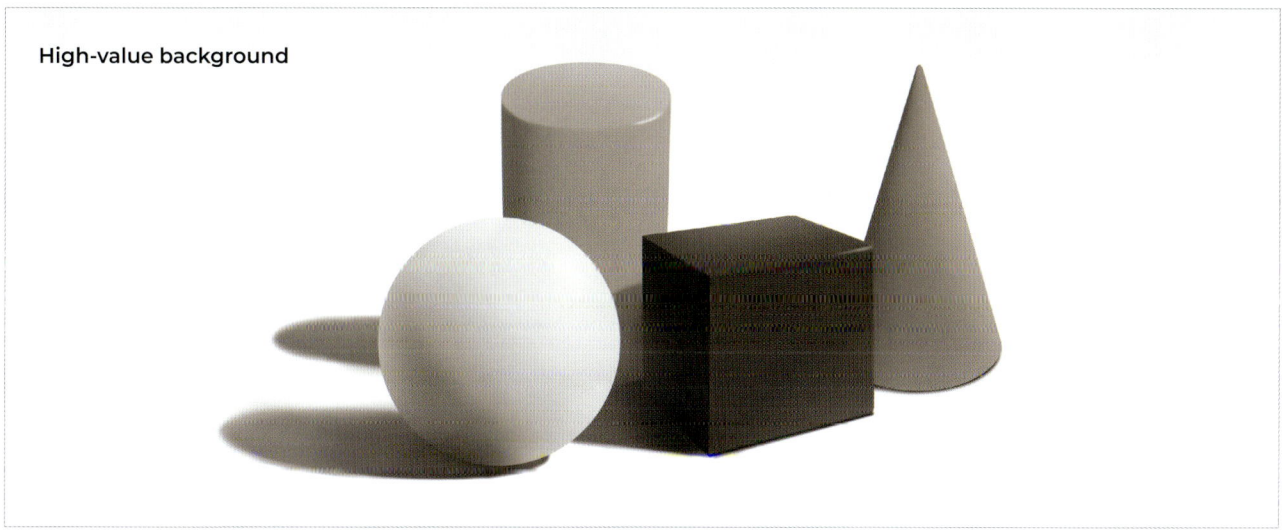

High-value background

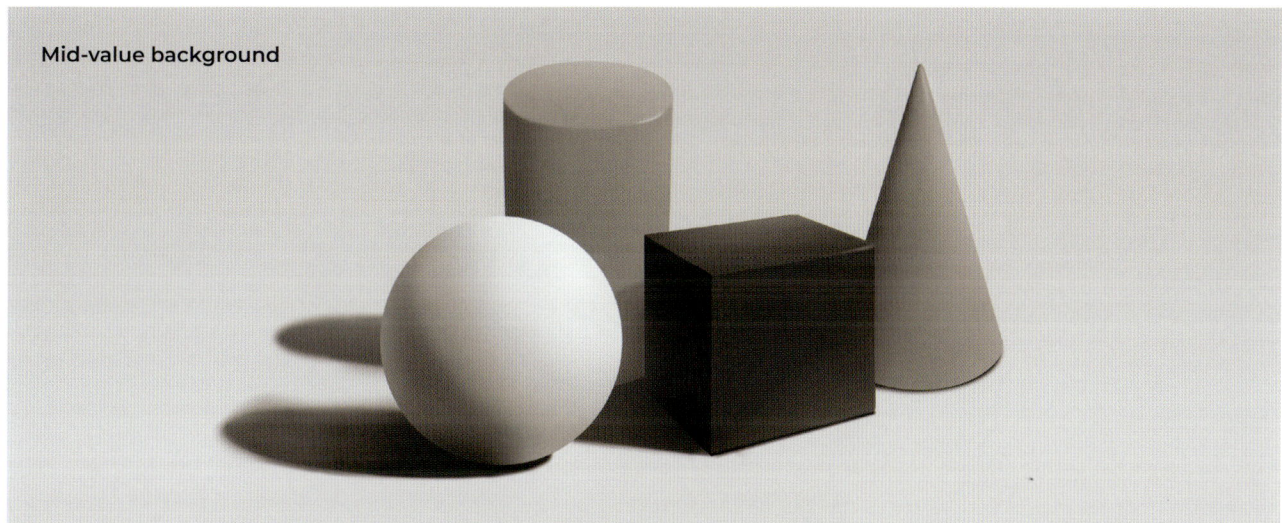

Mid-value background

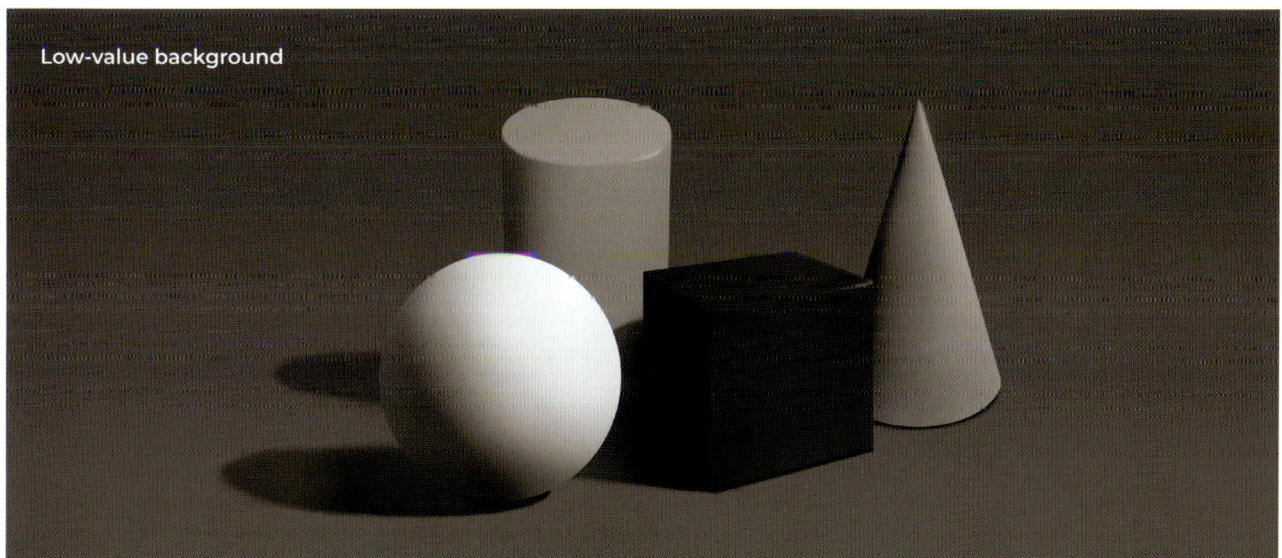

Low-value background

79 By maintaining a consistent proportion of light to shadow, you can paint any color of object on a background of any value.

REFLECTED LIGHT

One final effect to explore in our discussion of matte surface shading is the effect of reflected light (also known as bounce light). This is what we call light that is reflected off the surrounding environment and bounces back onto our form. This light is thought of separately from the general ambient light, as it behaves in a much more direct way.

The most important fact to remember about reflected light is that, by its nature, it is only secondhand light. Even if the reflected light is bouncing off a surface with the brightest possible local color, it can never reach the brightness of the primary light source. While a main light source is often so bright it's difficult to look at directly, no surface will generally reach that level of brightness.

When we think of direct light, we must remember that it is a local light source. As discussed on page 101, this means that it's subject to the "inverse square law" and will drop off exponentially. As these are extremely weak light sources compared to natural sunlight, their effects will fall off into general ambience very quickly. So, like our previously discussed ambient occlusion, we can think of reflected light in terms of its relative closeness to our forms. It will only be strongly observable when our form is close to the light-reflecting surface **(80)**.

While reflected light can be an extremely effective and beautiful way to communicate form in the shadows of our work, it is important to not overstate its effect. Due to the simultaneous contrasts shown on page 104, reflected light is one of the most common causes of trouble in students' work. It is often depicted as impossibly bright – a common error that destroys unified value groups and wreaks havoc on light effects. Remember that reflected light is subtle and must always remain within the limits of the shadow value group.

In image **81**, you can see how much confusion is created and atmosphere is lost when the reflected lights are too bright – they are brighter than the shadow group, and even brighter than the light areas. One way to avoid this problem is by starting the image in a higher key, with slightly brighter shadows than we intend to end with,

and then gradually deepening the values around the reflected light instead of adding brightness to achieve the effect **(82)**. As this method is simply adding darkness, it's impossible for the reflected light values to exit the values of the shadow group. It is an extremely effective and practical approach, commonly used by painters.

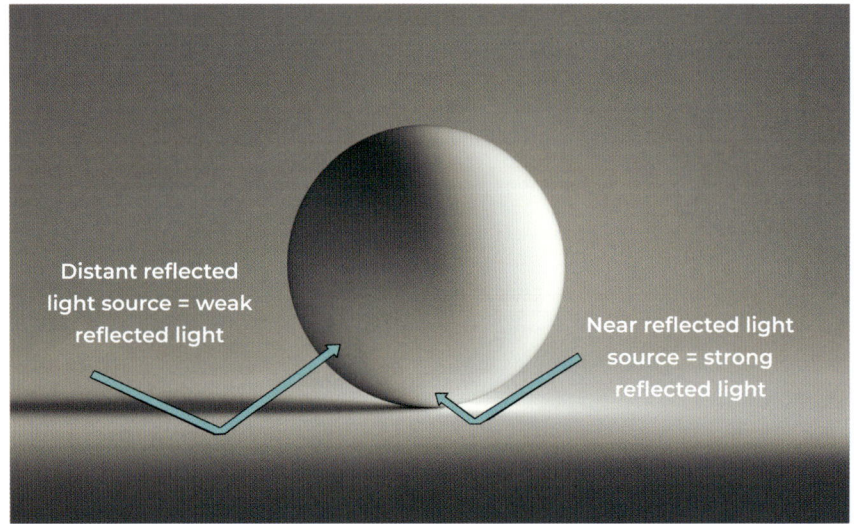

80 Reflected light is most visible when the reflecting surface is near the target object.

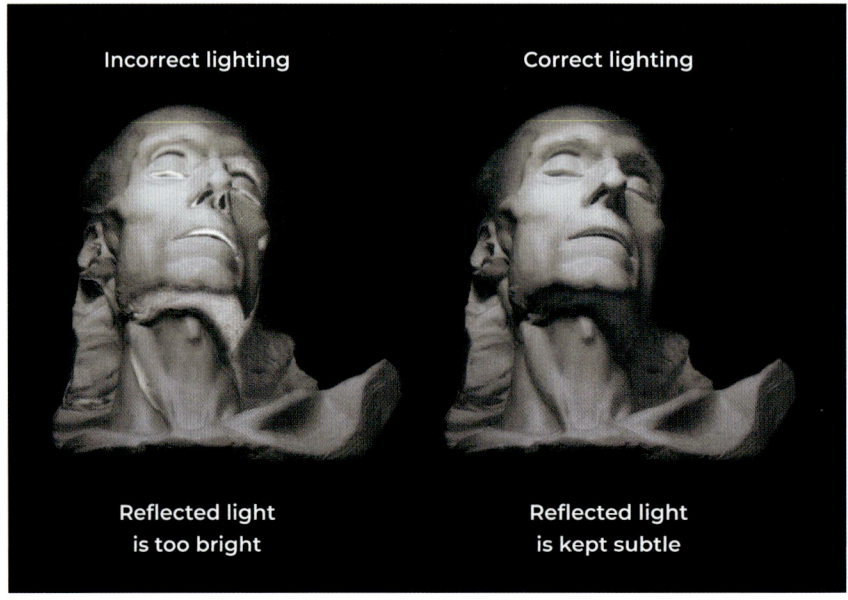

81 When the reflected lights are too bright, they could be mistaken for main lights, creating confusing values. When they are kept subtle, the value groups stay separate and believable.

Starting low-contrast

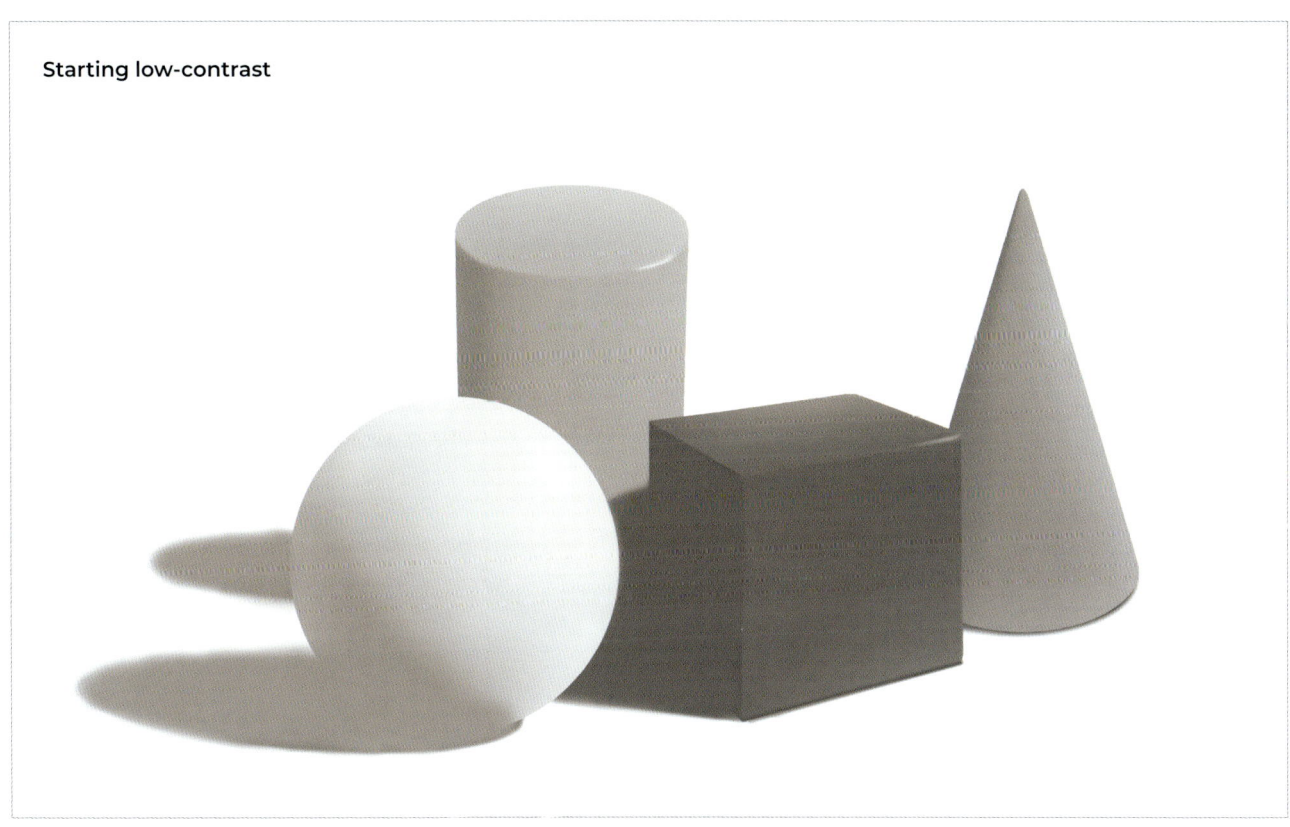

Finishing high-contrast

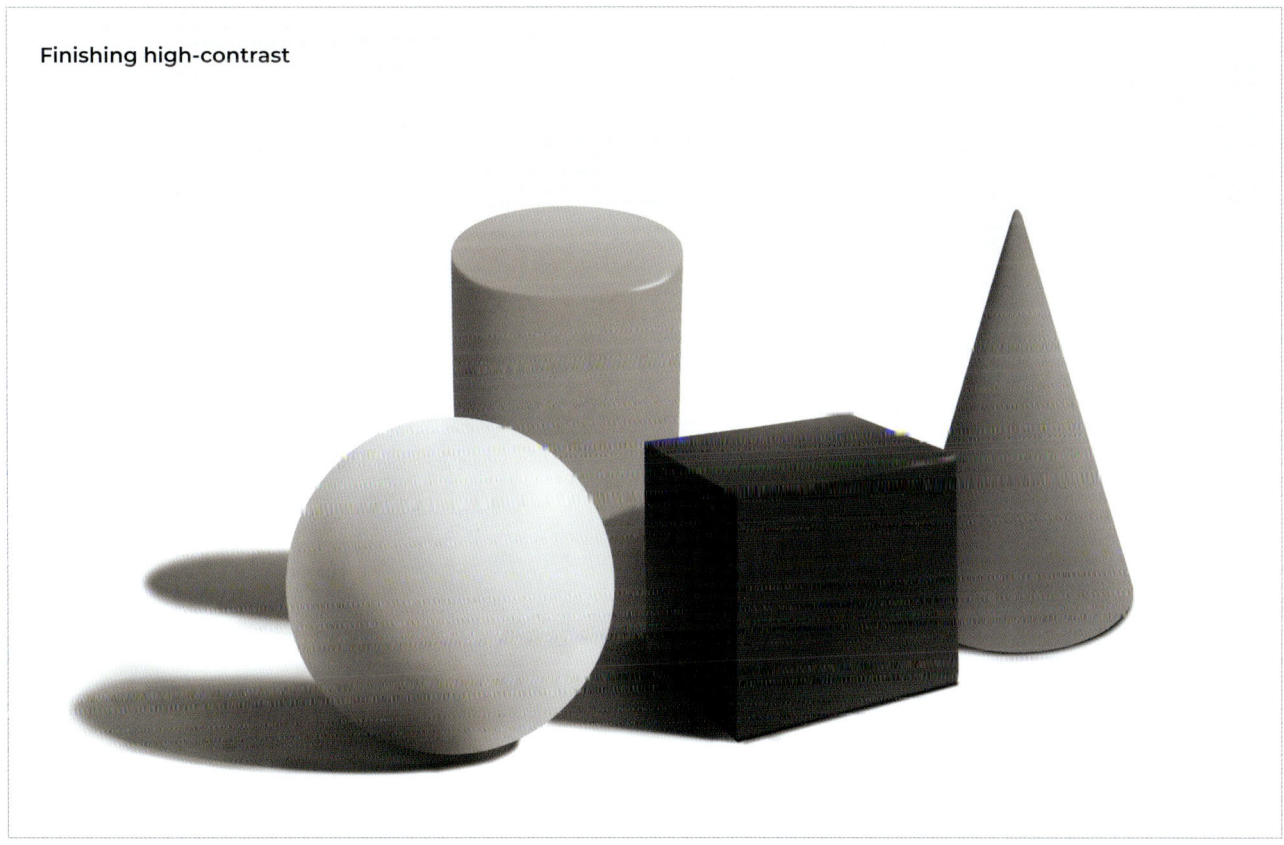

82 Try starting with brighter shadows and darkening them to the desired level, rather than adding light back in.

THE COLOR OF SHADOWS

Now that we have discussed how color operates in matte surface shading, we can explore the colors of shadows and what causes them. One commonly held idea among artists is that "warm light = cool shadows, cool light = warm shadows." This idea is useful for certain subjects and designs, but it's not entirely accurate to how shadows actually work.

In image **83**, you can see the same object lit by the same warm light source in three different environments, including one blue (cool) and one orange (warm). The shadows' color changes entirely with the color of the environment. The blue example follows the "warm light = cool shadows" rule, but the orange example flips this entirely, with a warm light and even warmer shadows.

Since this "warm = cool" rule is often not going to work for us, we need a more accurate guide to work with. As we have already discussed, shadows are defined by not being struck by the direct light source, and will only be lit by the environmental ambient light. So, our new general rule will be: The color of the shadow will be the color of the environment's ambient light.

The "warm light = cool shadows" formula seems to have risen from painters who primarily painted outdoors, and as a rule for landscapes it works very well. Outdoor shadows often appear extremely blue against the warm light of the sun, but it's important to understand the real reason behind this: The blue sky emits a strong, chromatic blue ambient light that will always be felt on the environment's upward-facing planes. We can see this in image **84**, where the blue light of the sky and reflected green light of the grass are clearly visible on the upward- and downward-facing planes of a white ball.

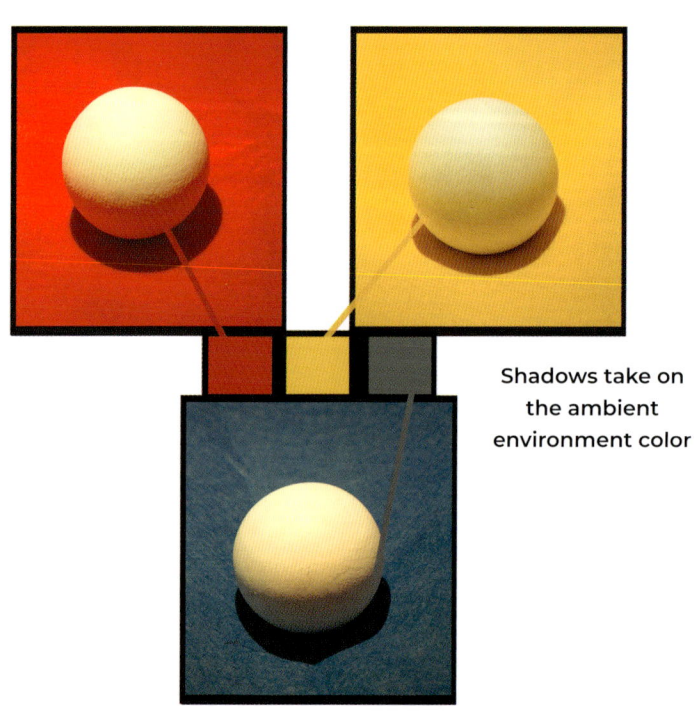

Warm light = cool shadows

Warm light = cool shadows (obeys rule)

Warm light = warmer shadows (breaks rule)

Shadows take on the ambient environment color

83 The color of the environment decides the color of the shadows.

So, the shadow will always be a result of multiple light sources of varying brightness and chromatic intensity. As a result, shadows are often the most varied, colorful areas of a scene and can provide us with tremendous opportunities for color.

We can see this effect in action in this wonderful painting by Joaquín Sorolla (85). Note that all of the planes facing up toward the blue sky carry cool colors. All of the planes facing more toward the ground carry warmer colors as a result of the warmer local colors of the ground plane.

Now we have a general method for working out our shadow colors: Start with the average ambient color of the scene and then visualize yourself looking out from the viewpoint of the shadow plane. What would you see? A blue sky? Sunlit grass? The colors you can "see" from this perspective will be the main colors affecting the shadow plane.

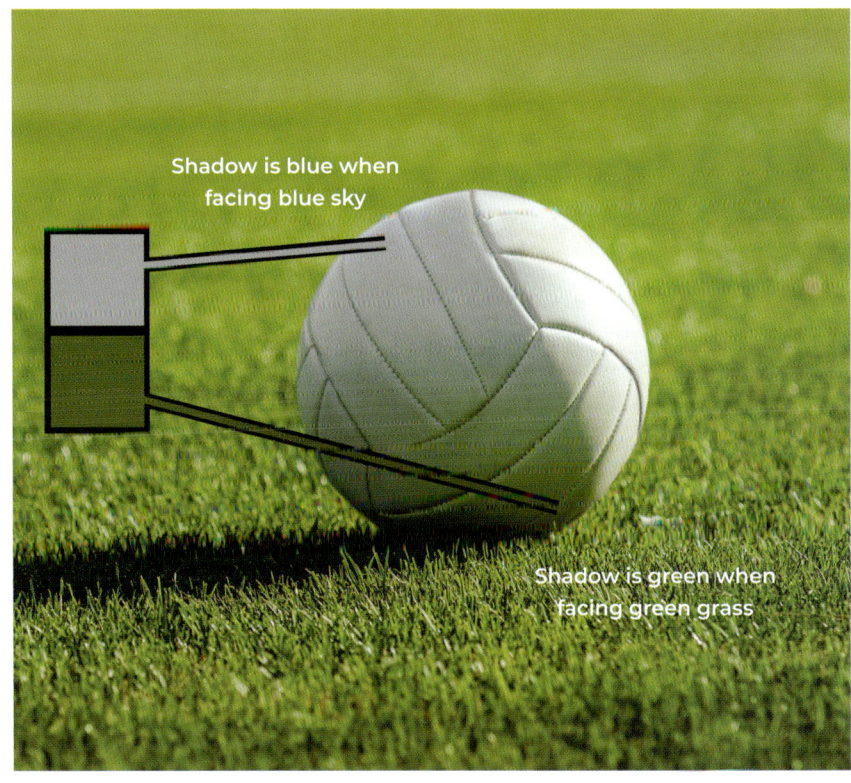

Shadow is blue when facing blue sky

Shadow is green when facing green grass

84 Shadows take on the ambient color of the surface they are facing.

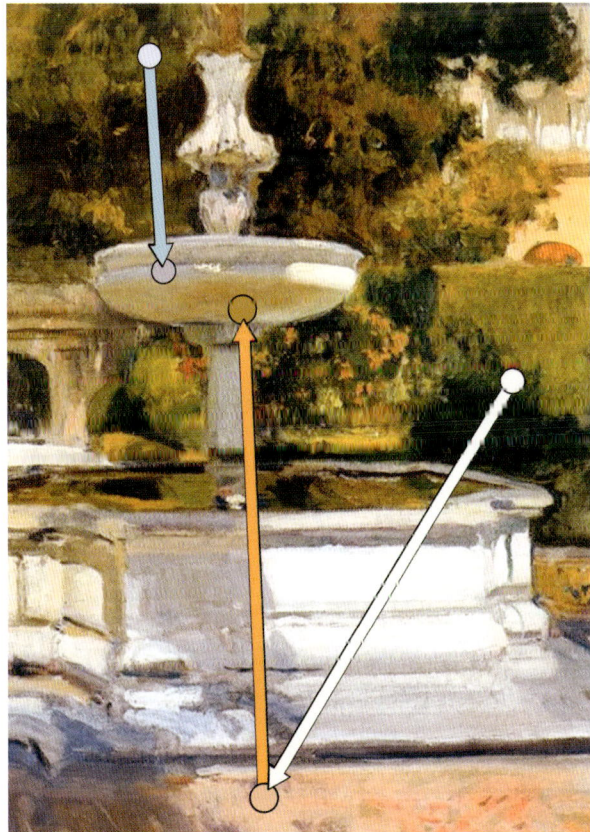

● Planes facing down to warm ground

● Planes facing up to cool blue sky

○ Sunlight direction

85 In Joaquín Sorolla's *Surtidor* (1899) the downward planes take on the warm color bounced up from the ground, while upward planes take on the coolness of the sky.

GLOBAL ILLUMINATION

This idea of considering every surface in the scene as its own light source, emitting light of its own local color, is called "global illumination" in 3D programs. This concept can add a huge amount of realism to the scene, as you can see in image 86.

This effect is generally weak in intensity, because, as we spoke about previously, all of this reflected light is secondhand by nature and so can never compete with the intensity of the primary light source. Due to this, the effect will primarily be noticeable in the

shadows, but it's always at play in all parts of the scene to some degree, and should always be considered when we paint. Paying close attention to global illumination can make our artwork feel full of light.

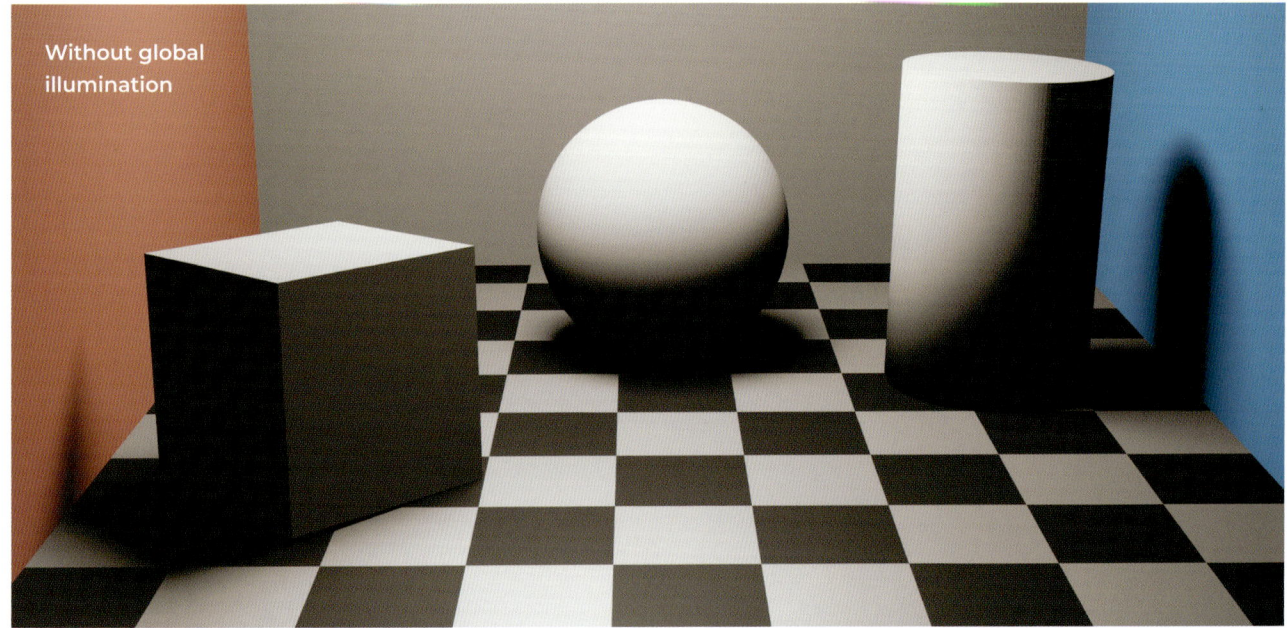

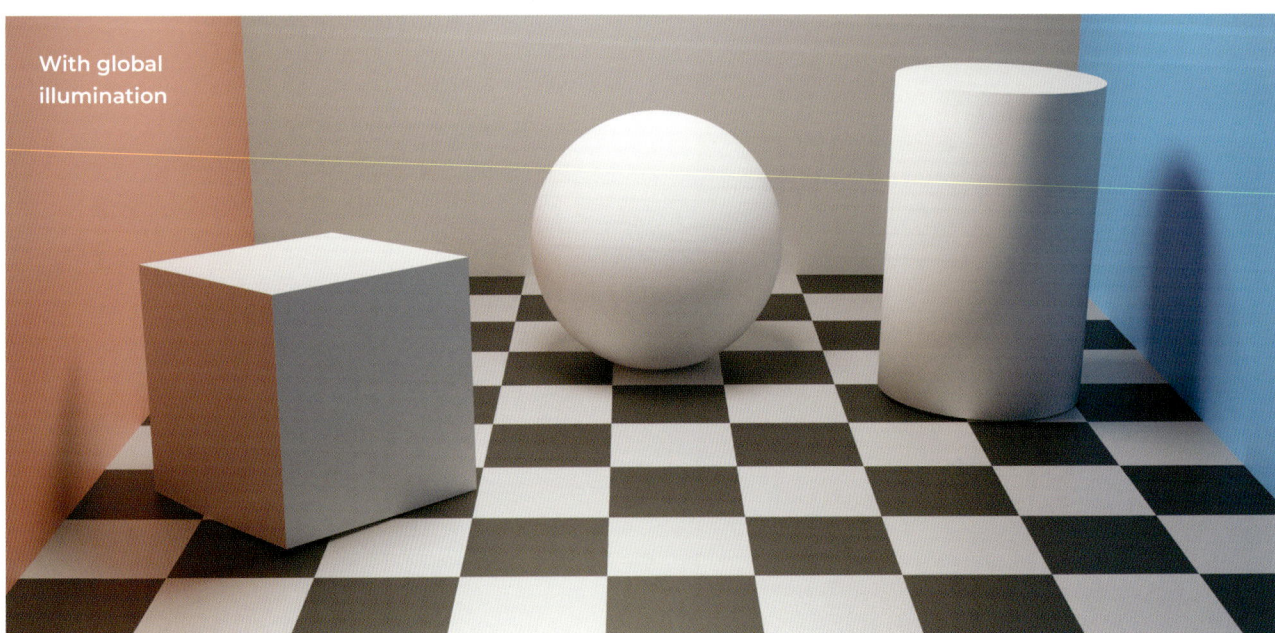

86 Comparing a scene before and after taking global illumination into account.

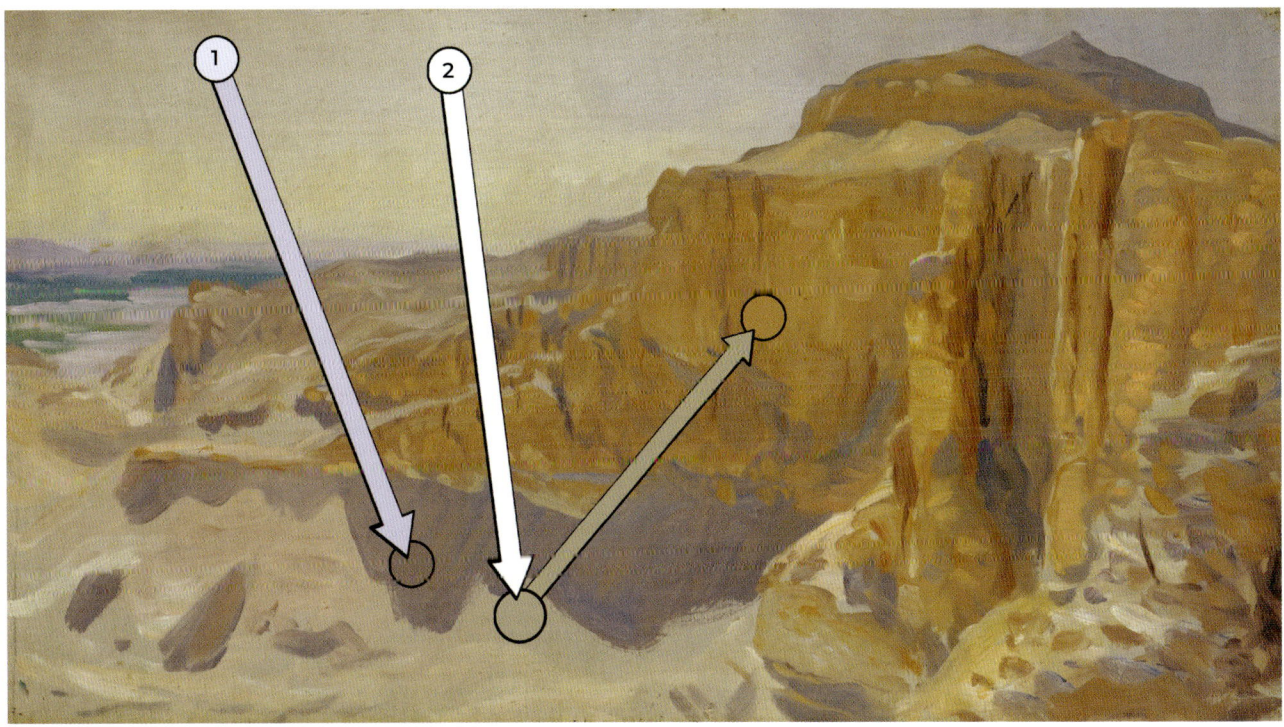

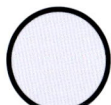 Cool white skylight comes in

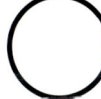 Warm white light comes in

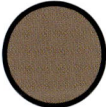 Warm gray surface absorbs more cool light than warm

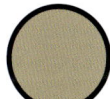 Warm gray surface absorbs more cool light than warm

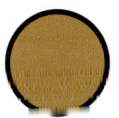 Resulting warm light is reflected onto warm gray again

87 In John Singer Sargent's *Cliffs at Deir el Bahri, Egypt* (1890–91), cool ambient light from the sky creates cool shadows on the warm gray ground, while warm white sunlight bounces off the ground and warms the cliffside.

ILLUMINATING OUR SHADOWS

It is also important for us to consider how these colored lights will interact in our shadows. Many people think of the light rays striking a surface and "picking up" the color of that surface, then carrying that color into the shadow. While this idea will generally work, it is important to recognize that these bounced colors will mix in a fundamentally subtractive way. Light is most complete as white, and with each material interaction,

more and more colors will be absorbed out of this complete white. As we learned on page 105, the more chromatic the color that we see, the more isolated the wavelength of the light. This subtractive nature affects how the resulting colors mix.

Notably, low-chroma colors reflecting into similar-hued, low-chroma shadows will intensify in chroma significantly. This is because, throughout both interactions, the light's colder colors are edited out of the

light, as you can see in image **87**. Since we get twice as much editing out of the colder colors, we get twice as much chroma in the warmer colors.

However, if a cold color is reflected onto a warm surface, the shadow color will darken significantly. This is because while the same amount of cool light is being absorbed, there is less red light to be reflected, resulting in a darker color.

LIGHT SOURCE TEMPERATURE

One challenge in understanding how light sources work, both when we buy lighting equipment and create paintings, is knowing how the concept of color temperature relates to light sources. Luckily for us, most light sources are not too complex in color, existing on a predictable spectrum of warm reds to cool blues, with balanced whites in the middle. These light temperatures are measured in kelvin.

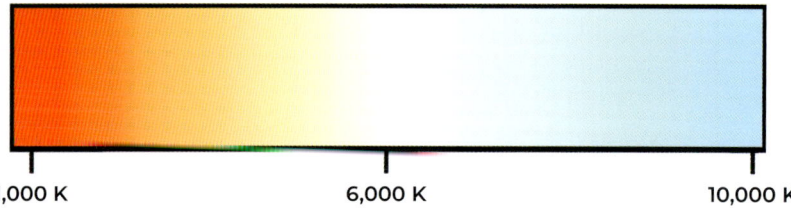

88 As you may have seen on light bulbs in real life, the color temperature of a light is measured in kelvin. The lower the kelvin value, the warmer the color.

Kelvin measurements are represented by the letter K, with low values indicating warmer orange colors and high values being the colder blue colors. On this spectrum, candlelight falls below 2,000 K, daylight is around 5,000–6,000 K, and blue skylight is 10,000 K or higher **(88)**.

You may be surprised that this measurement sounds counterintuitive – that as the temperature of the light source goes up, the colors appear cooler and bluer. This can sometimes be confusing, but the easiest way to remember it is to look at a flame – a light source that conforms to this scale. A low-temperature flame such as a candle has colors in the low, orange range, and as the temperature rises, such as to a gas stove's more powerful flame, it moves into the blue range **(89)**.

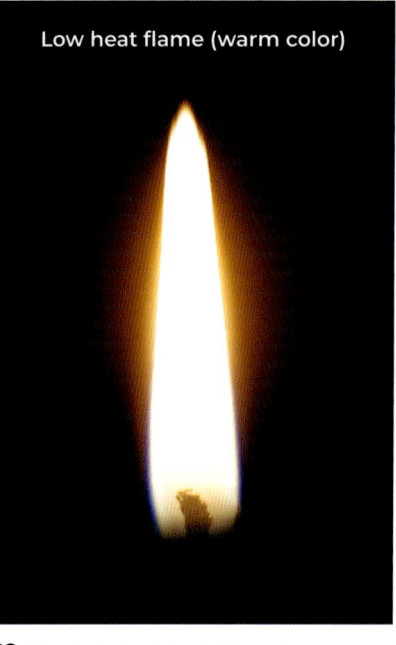
Low heat flame (warm color)

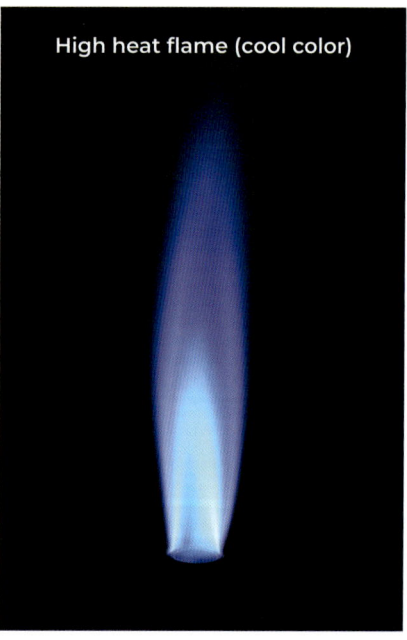
High heat flame (cool color)

89 A low-heat candle flame has a warm orange color, while a high-heat gas flame has a cool blue color.

The types of lights that conform to this set of colors are called "blackbody radiators" – types of object that emit light when heated – and are the most common types of light source that we will see in both natural and artificial light.

In image **90**, we can see this progression of color mapped onto the full gamut of visible color. If we compare the full extent of the spectrum (the blue line, measured in nanometers) to the color temperature spectrum (the red line, measured in kelvin), we can see that the latter peaks in the central white instead of the chromatic greens. Hence we wouldn't typically see a hot flame glowing green!

We can learn some interesting facts by comparing these two spectrums. We can see that they broadly follow in the same direction from warmer oranges to cooler blues, but with two key differences. The first difference is that there are no green or violet colors – violet is simply omitted, while green is replaced by a balanced white, as mentioned. The second is that the colors gradually lose chroma as they move toward this central white.

These omissions are extremely useful to us, as they mean we don't generally need to worry about green or violet lights when dealing with most natural or everyday light sources. We can simply limit our concerns to warm or cool light sources, save for special

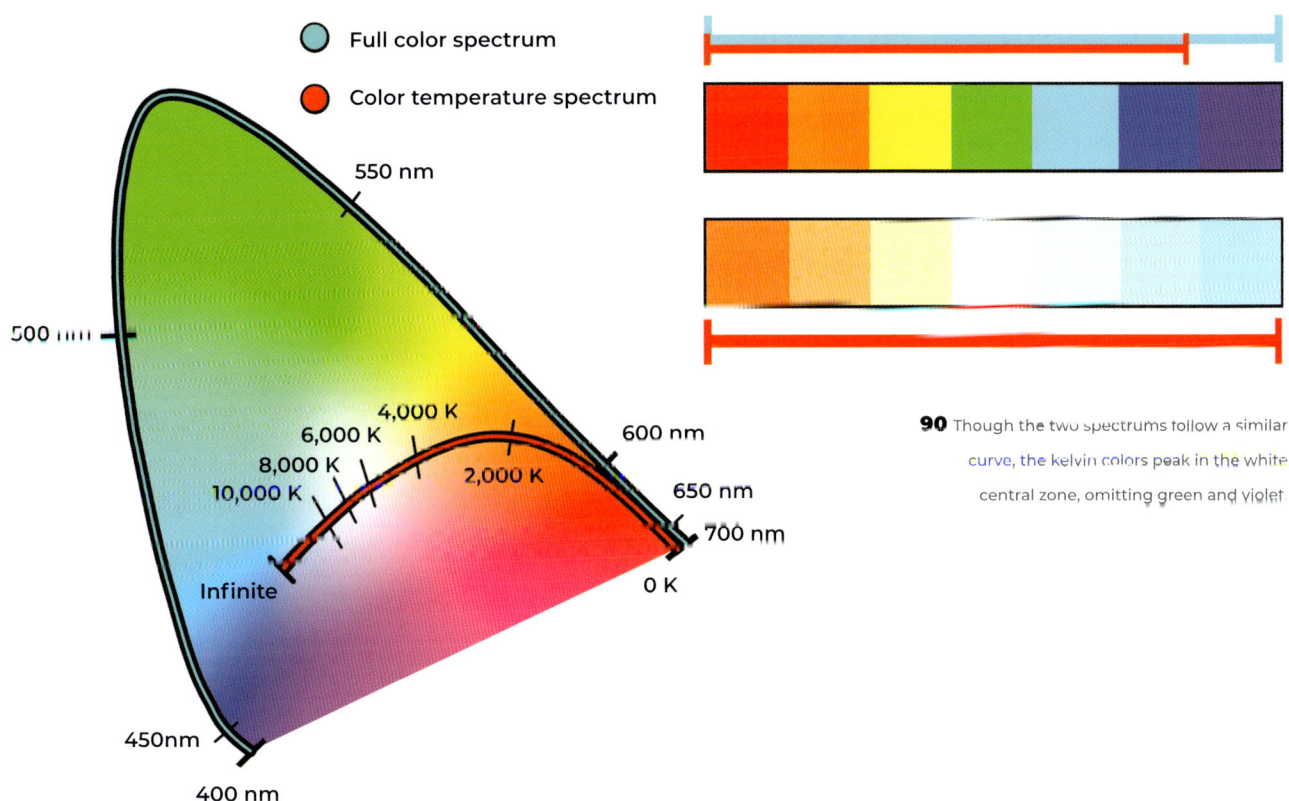

90 Though the two spectrums follow a similar curve, the kelvin colors peak in the white central zone, omitting green and violet.

circumstances, such as artificial colored bulbs. However, this does leave us with questions. Why does this happen? What turns the green into white? Why do we not see violet lights?

In order to explain this, we will need to know a little about the physics of what is happening. Primarily, the new idea that we must now remember is that all light is actually radiation. As you may remember from page 48, the section of radiation that we can actually see is an extremely narrow band of the full range of wavelengths. There are many other wavelengths of radiation, such as ultraviolet and infrared light, which are below and above the range of nanometers (nm) our eyes can see **(91)**.

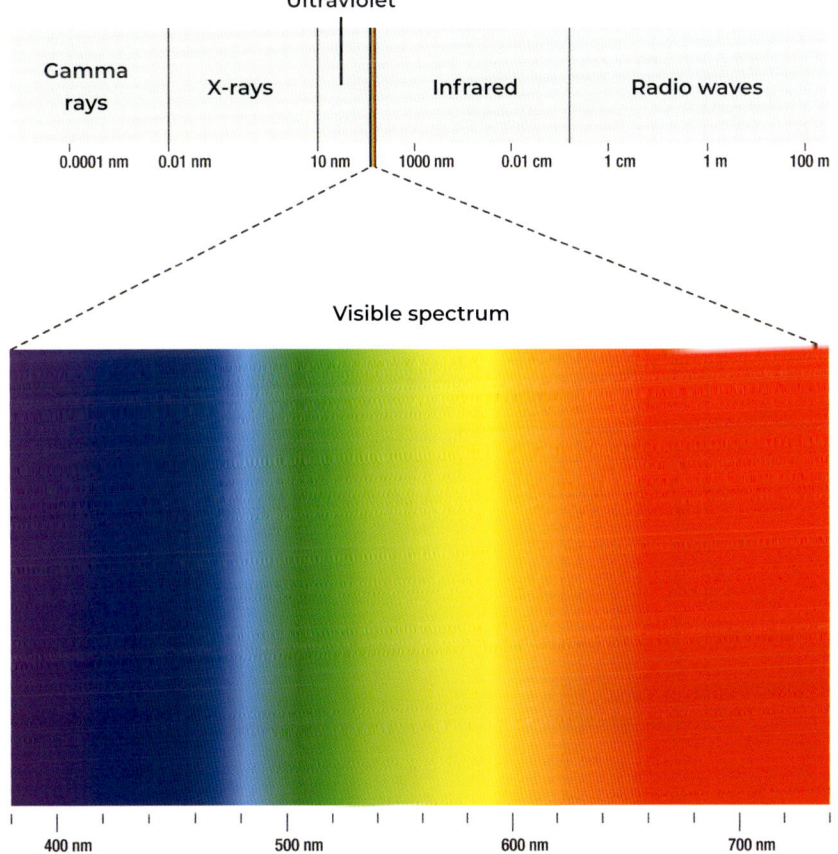

91 Only a small segment of the electromagnetic spectrum is visible to us as color.

BLACKBODY RADIATORS

Let's look a little deeper into "blackbody radiators," the proper term for these commonplace light sources. **Most light sources are actually emitting radiation all across this spectrum, to varying degrees, in fairly predictable ways. We can see how this general distribution occurs below in image 92.**

We don't need to know exactly how this occurs, but having more context is useful to remind us of the full electromagnetic spectrum beyond just the visible light that we see. As you may remember from page 48 of the Color chapter, when we are dealing with light sources, they are rarely emitting just one wavelength but will always be emitting some level of every color. We can also see that as the energy of the light source increases (high kelvin, getting colder in color) the peak of this curve moves to the left, toward blue. In order to see why this causes the color temperature of light sources, let's follow this curve up through the energy levels just in the visible spectrum.

First, let's look at a low-energy light source **(93)**. This might be an old halogen-style bulb or a weak fire. We can see immediately, just from the sloping shape, that there is a huge imbalance of colors toward the warmer end of the spectrum, resulting in a strongly warm, orange light source color.

Now let's observe the light source moving to a medium energy, peaking more in the green **(94)**. We can see that while it's certainly peaking in green, there is a fair balance of all the various colors available in the light. We know that light mixes additively, and when an equal amount of lights mix, we see white – this is why we perceive this "green" peaking light as white instead. This is also the balance of light emitted by the sun, so our eyes are adapted to detect it.

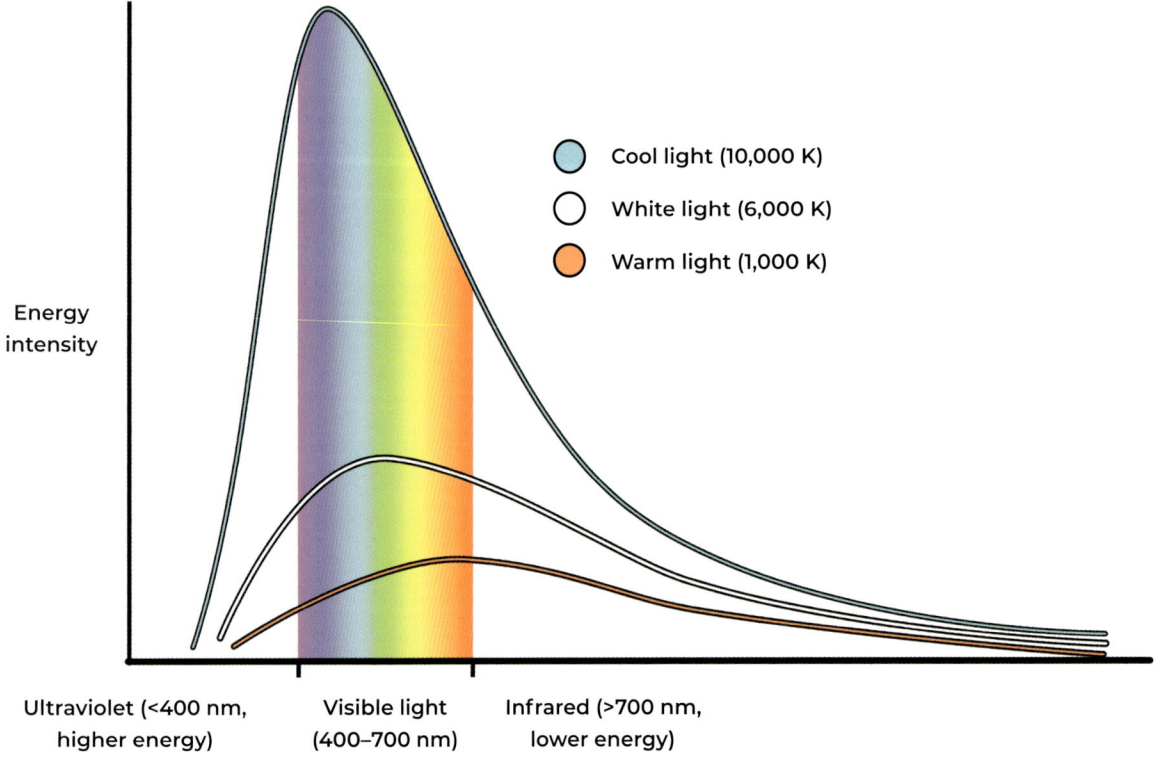

Cool light (10,000 K)

White light (6,000 K)

Warm light (1,000 K)

Energy intensity

Ultraviolet (<400 nm, higher energy)

Visible light (400–700 nm)

Infrared (>700 nm, lower energy)

92 Higher-energy light peaks further to the left, producing cooler light.

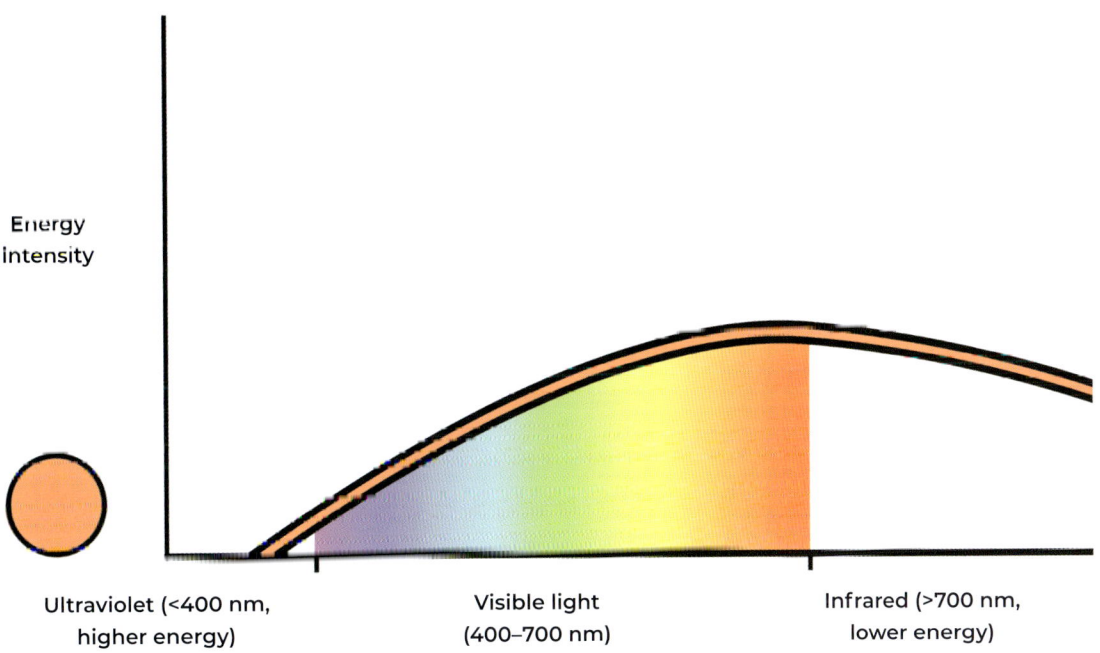

Energy
intensity

Ultraviolet (<400 nm,
higher energy)

Visible light
(400–700 nm)

Infrared (>700 nm,
lower energy)

93 A low-energy light source peaks in the red range, with a high concentration of warm colors.

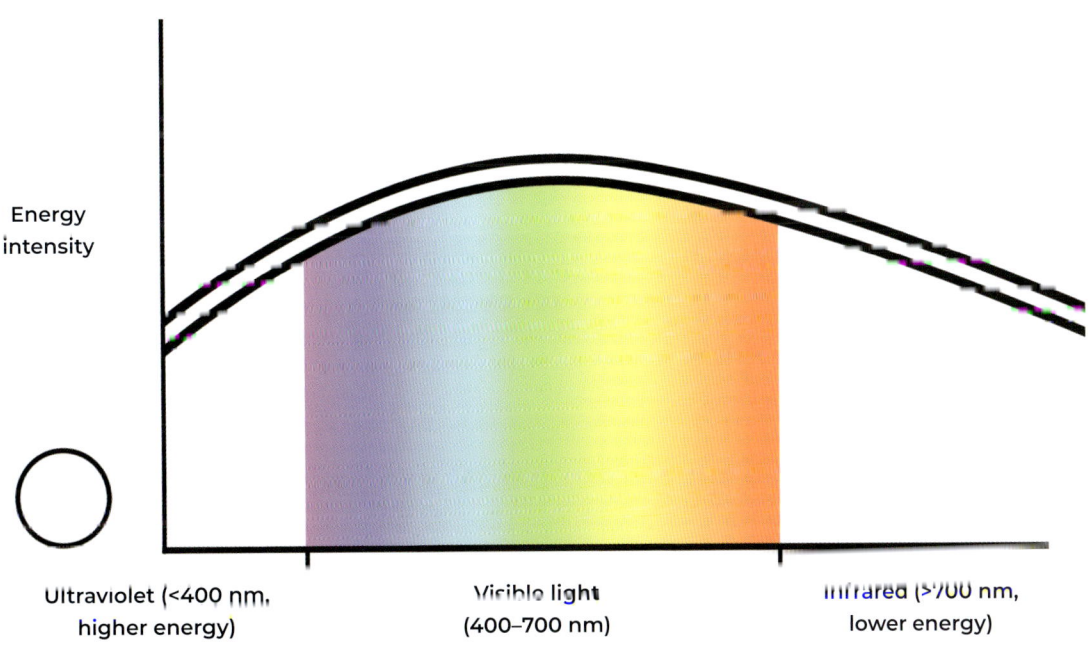

Energy
intensity

Ultraviolet (<400 nm,
higher energy)

Visible light
(400–700 nm)

Infrared (>700 nm,
lower energy)

94 A medium-energy light source peaks in green, which mixes additively to

white. It has more colors available in it and is fairly balanced across them all.

As the light source's energy increases even further, we once again see a strong bias in the balance of colors, this time toward the blues **(95)**. However, while this mimics the orange light source's shape, there is also much more light present at this higher energy. Therefore, this type of light source will not generally be as strongly colored as the warmer lights. This shifting of the curve's peak could continue beyond what's shown here. However, in order to create a high-energy light biased toward violet, the last color in the visible range, you would need an infinite amount of energy, which doesn't exist in nature. This is why we don't see natural violet light sources.

LIMITED-COLOR LIGHT SOURCES

While this is generally how most light sources that we observe will work, it is important to recognize that these are not the only kinds of light source that exist. We know this simply by looking at traffic lights! However, this does tell us that such a different-colored light source would be much less balanced in the colors it emits.

One of these chromatic light sources might look like image **96a**, with a strong peak in one area of the visible spectrum. This is often done by taking a balanced light source and cutting it down with colored filters. This is also how RGB LED light sources work, with peaks in three colors rather than a balance of all colors through the spectrum **(96b)**.

These artificially limited light sources also do not return colors except the ones they emit – so a range of multi-colored objects, revealed under one of these limited lights, would only show colors with content matching the light's color. As we'll see next, attempting to photograph or film a subject under these limited lights can lead to problems in the returned image.

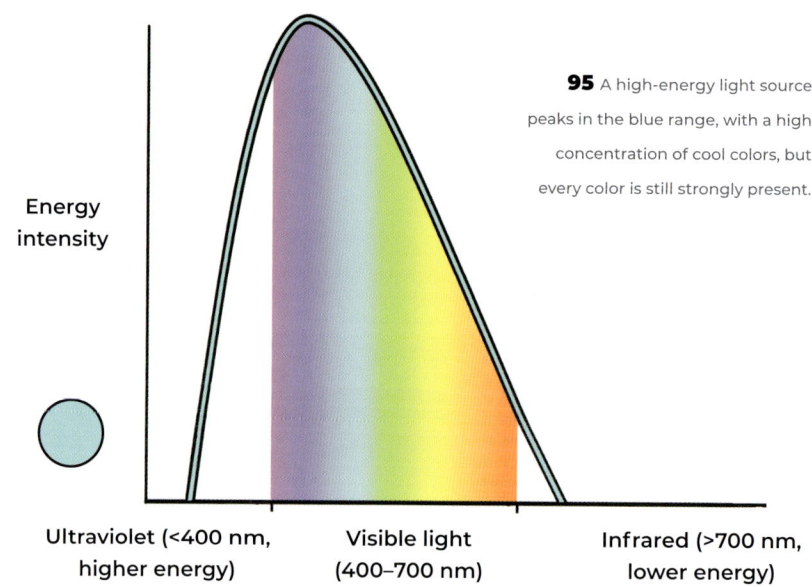

Energy intensity

95 A high-energy light source peaks in the blue range, with a high concentration of cool colors, but every color is still strongly present.

Ultraviolet (<400 nm, higher energy)   Visible light (400–700 nm)   Infrared (>700 nm, lower energy)

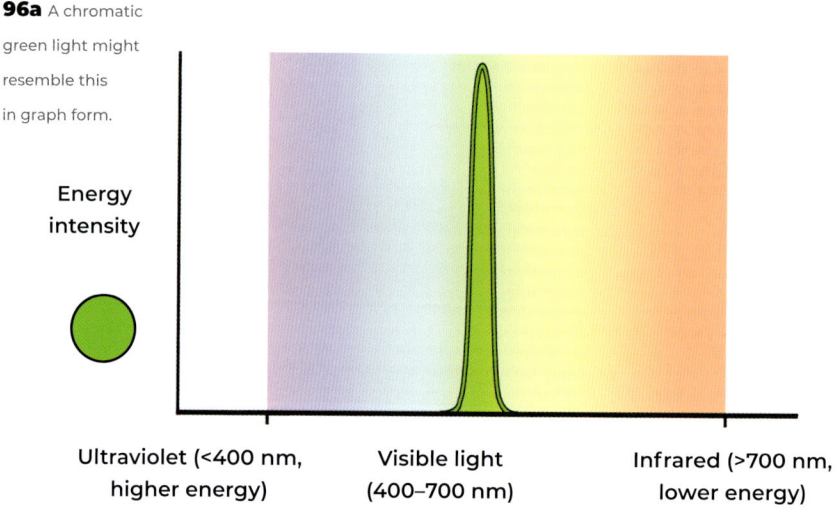

96a A chromatic green light might resemble this in graph form.

Energy intensity

Ultraviolet (<400 nm, higher energy)   Visible light (400–700 nm)   Infrared (>700 nm, lower energy)

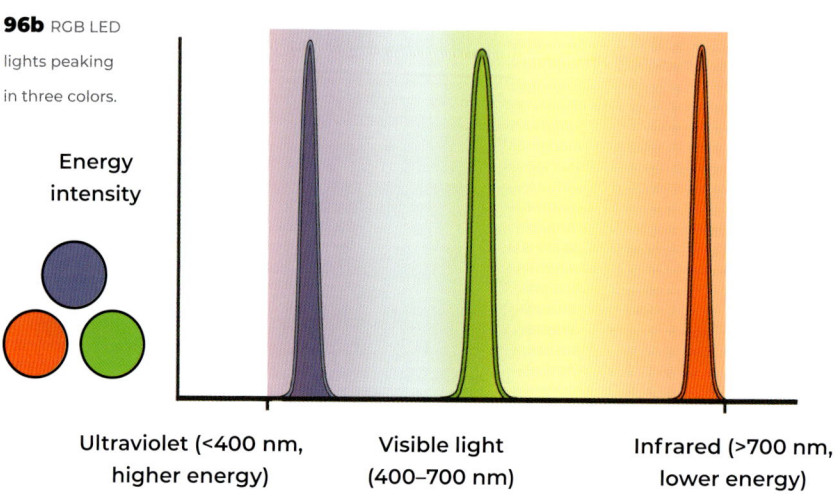

96b RGB LED lights peaking in three colors.

Energy intensity

Ultraviolet (<400 nm, higher energy)   Visible light (400–700 nm)   Infrared (>700 nm, lower energy)

COLOR RENDERING INDEX

In fact, no lights will perfectly conform to this theoretical blackbody curve – not even the sun. Every light source will have some gaps in the colors that it can return. The amount that a light source conforms to this curve is generally called its Color Rendering Index (CRI).

This CRI number is generally what we want to check when buying new light sources for use in an artist's studio. Most good-quality lights lie in the 90+ CRI range, with 100 being the maximum. The CRI and temperature of the light source are the two most important considerations when purchasing lighting equipment for an artist's workspace.

So our most important consideration, when observing a light source, is to ask ourselves whether we are observing a warm, cool, or balanced light. This can sometimes be difficult to work out *in situ*, as our eyes naturally do so much work to adjust to different light sources.

The easiest way to evaluate our environment's lighting with certainty is to use a ColorChecker Color Rendition Chart (sometimes called a Macbeth chart). This is a series of colors in simple squares. By photographing the chart in our lighting situation, we can get a definite sense of what type of light we are working under.

To the right we can see a chart photographed under a few of these different light sources. Observe how the colors returned to our eye change under these different lights **(97)**.

97 A ColorChecker chart is a valuable aid for evaluating the Color Rendering Index of light in a real-life scenario. Here you can clearly see how the range of revealed colors is heavily influenced by the light source's color.

White lights

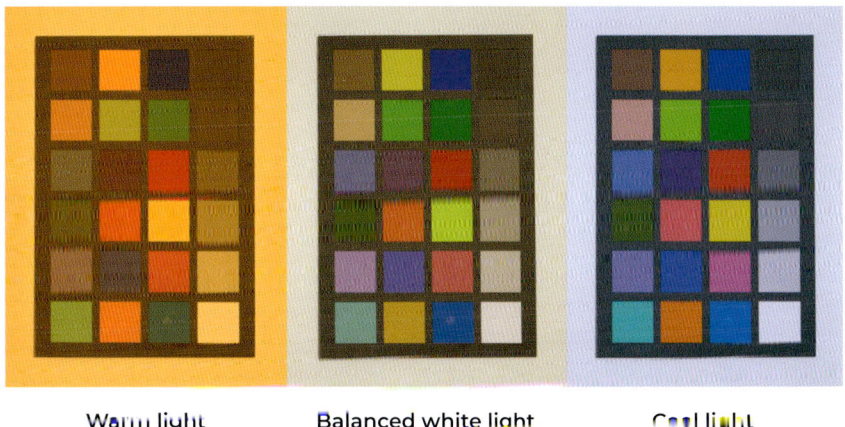

Warm light   Balanced white light   Cool light

Primary-colored lights

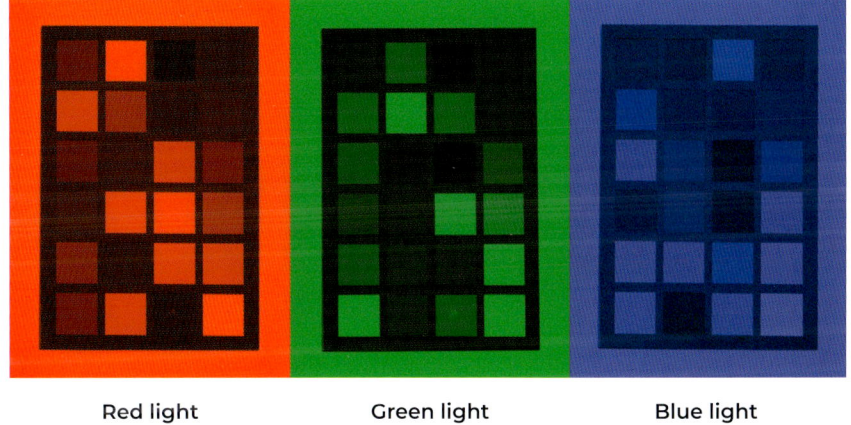

Red light   Green light   Blue light

Secondary-colored lights

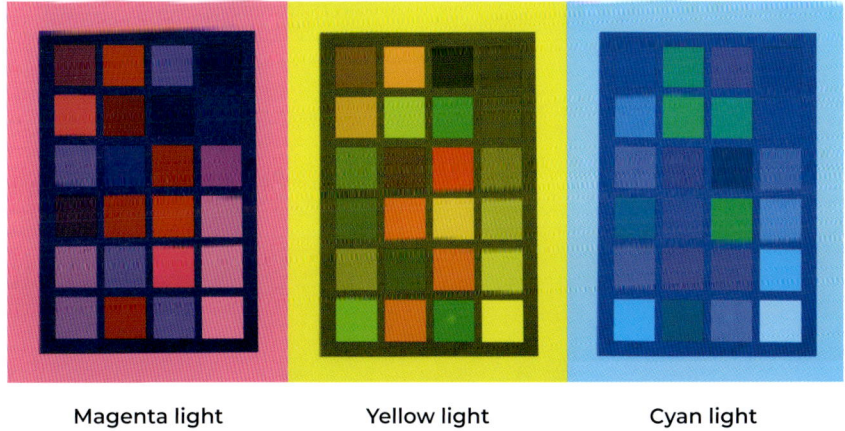

Magenta light   Yellow light   Cyan light

THE PROGRESS OF A DAY

Now you are familiar with the concept of light temperature, but there is one final, most important aspect of the subject that we need to cover: The color of daylight and how it appears to change throughout the day. While the effects of natural light are hugely variable and should always be observed for themselves, it is useful for us to have a working model for the types of daylight we will usually be presented with.

We may think of sunlight as yellow, but it is actually white in space. As it enters our atmosphere, the blue light is scattered and becomes the blue sky, as we'll cover in more detail on page 164. Due to this, on earth we will generally see the sun as a warm light against a cool blue skylight.

We learned on page 100 that the sun is so far from us that it can essentially be treated as infinitely far away. Therefore, we can treat the light rays coming from it as functionally parallel, making the sun the most perfectly direct light source available to us, with none of the falloff of our own local lights (98).

On page 94, we also spoke about the relationship between the width of a light source and how direct or diffuse a light source is. Since the sky is as wide a light source as is possible, the light it gives off can be thought of as the most diffuse light we have access to. The light from the sky is considerably weaker than direct sunlight, so its influence will generally only be felt in the shadows outside, leading to the "warm light = cool shadows" relationship that many painters follow.

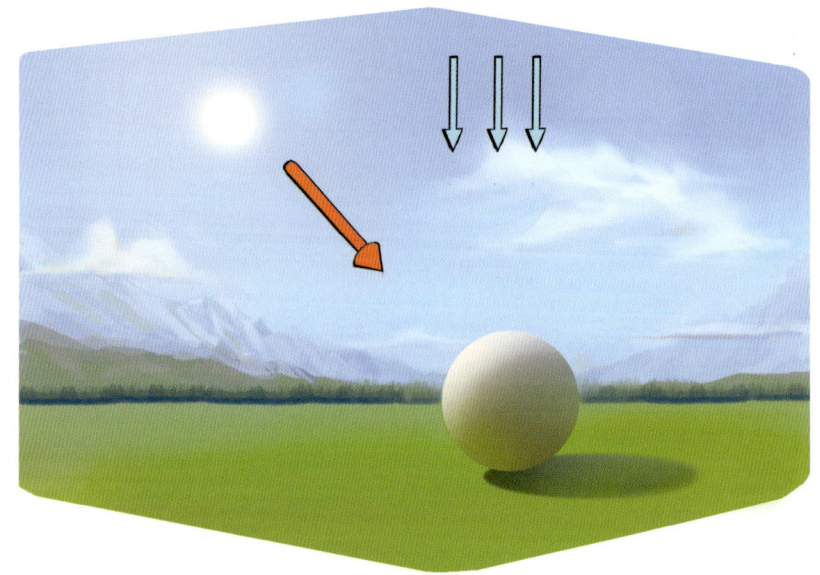

🟠 Warm sunlight (perfect direct light)

🔵 Cool skylight (perfectly diffuse light)

98 We can functionally consider sunlight as the most perfectly parallel, direct light and sky light as the most perfectly diffuse light available to us.

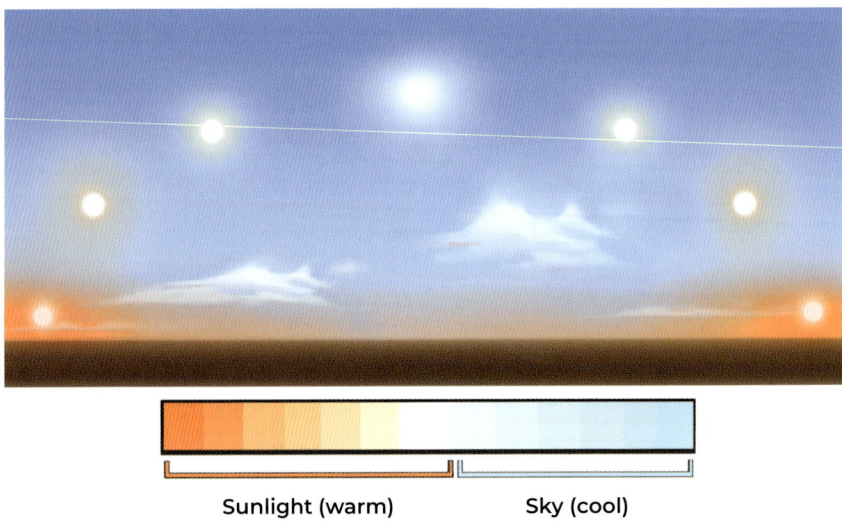

Sunlight (warm)   Sky (cool)

99 As the sun progresses through our atmosphere, the temperature of its light appears to change, as does the temperature of the blue skylight.

SHIFTING SUNLIGHT

One interesting nuance in this general relationship between the sunlight and skylight is that the color of sunlight will also vary throughout the day. This color shift is fairly predictable as the day progresses. The largest part of this shift happens at sunrise and sunset, when the sun gets lower in the sky – the sunlight color we perceive becomes warmer, peaking in the reds.

As the day progresses and the sun gets higher in the sky, it moves closer and closer to a pure white color, peaking in the middle of the day, when the sun is highest in the sky **(99)**. You might notice that this progression of colors follows the blackbody radiation progression mentioned on page 118. In other atmospheres, this effect could be different depending on the color of the atmosphere, but will generally be true on Earth.

The reason this occurs is that as the sun gets lower in the sky, its light enters the atmosphere at a shallower angle. The sunlight has to pass through more atmosphere in order to reach our eyes, leading to more blue light getting scattered out of the sunlight, and therefore a warmer perceived light.

The majority of this shift happens around sunset and sunrise, as captured in these changing light scenarios by Djamila Knopf **(100)**. Most of us have an intuitive sense for how small a fraction of the full day these parts of the day are, not taking more than thirty minutes in most cases. Once the sun is clearly in the sky, its shift toward a balanced white is still occurring, but it's a much slower, subtler shift for much of the day.

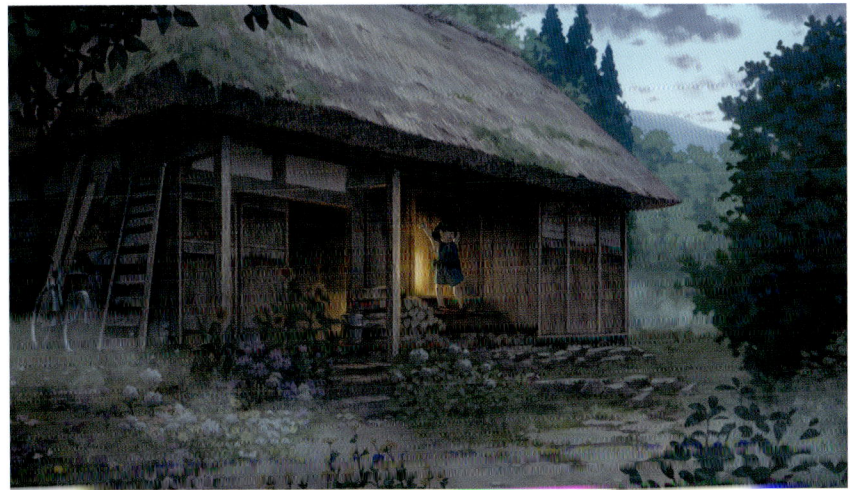
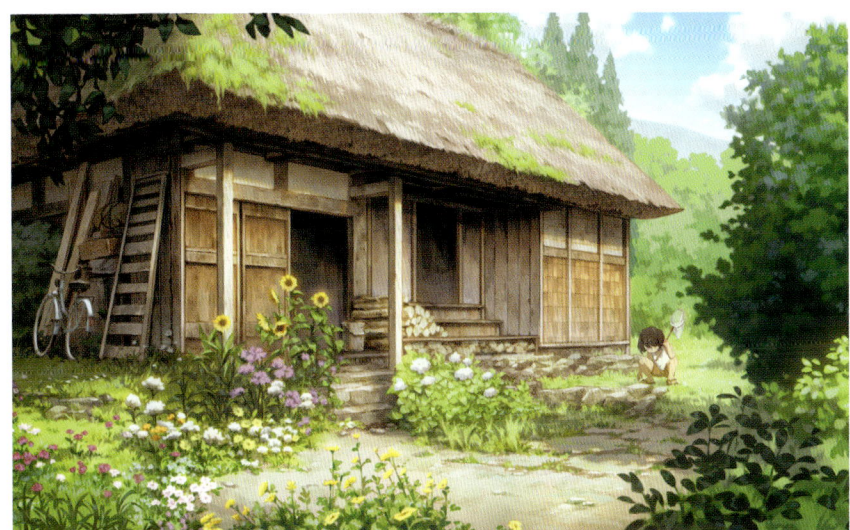
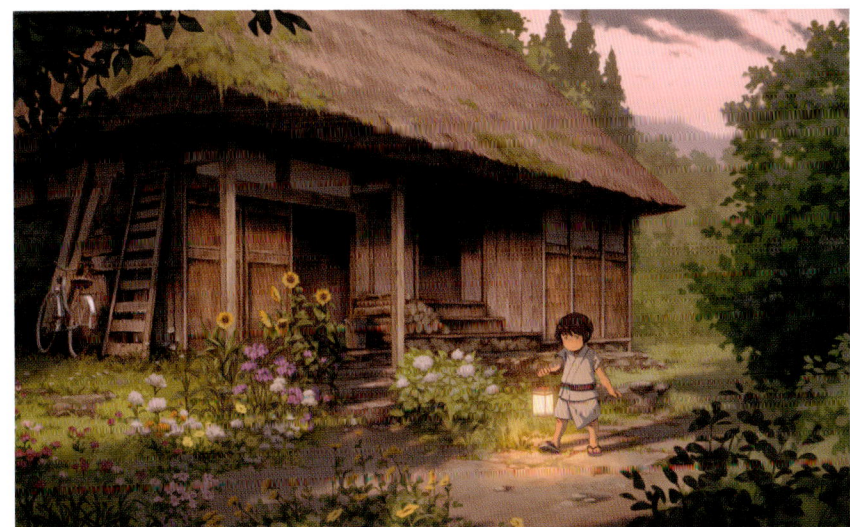

100 These scenes, which you'll learn how to paint in Djamila Knopf's *Day by Day* tutorial (page 208), are perfect examples of how the sunlight and skylight qualities change throughout the day, from early twilight to direct sunlight to sunset.

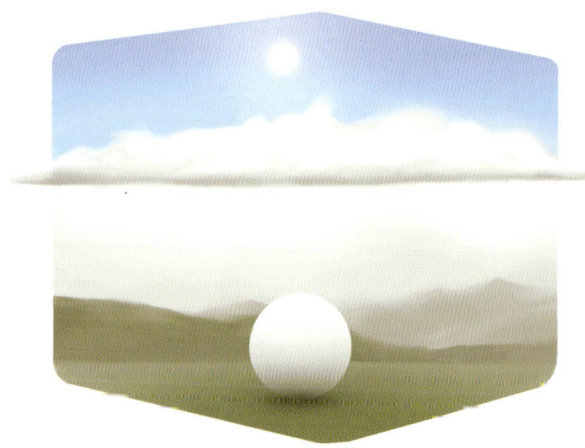

101 On an overcast day, the cloud layer neutralizes the light of the sun and sky into a diffuse light with a balanced temperature.

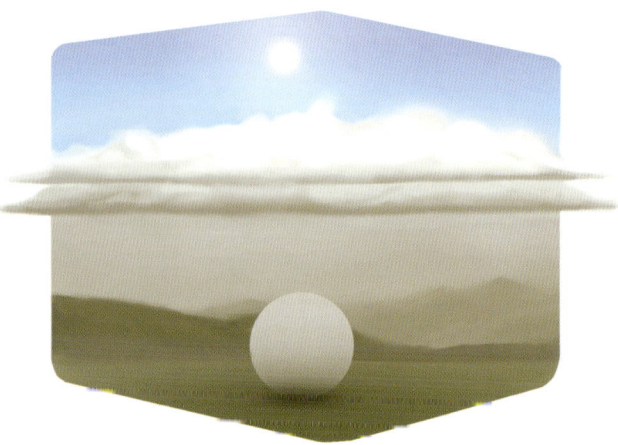

102 The thicker the layers of cloud, the more daylight is lost before it reaches us.

OVERCAST DAYS

Another common type of day that we will observe is the cloudy or overcast day. As anyone who has ever flown in an airplane can attest, the warm light of the sun and blue light of the sky are still present above the clouds. We can think of clouds as being a recombination of these two lights back into the white light of the sun. Due to this, overcast days provide the most balanced white light source we will generally observe in nature **(101)**.

Since the sun is mostly or completely hidden by clouds, overcast light is also the most perfectly diffuse light source we have access to. As these layers of clouds become thicker and denser, more of the light will be lost in the cloud, darkening this light until it finally rains and we return to a sunny day **(102)**.

Due to the balanced nature of this light, objects within it will generally just display their local colors without too many shifts. Many artists employ this as a useful fundamental basis for how they understand lighting. If overcast lighting is well understood, we can simply throw any different kind of light source we want for our piece onto it.

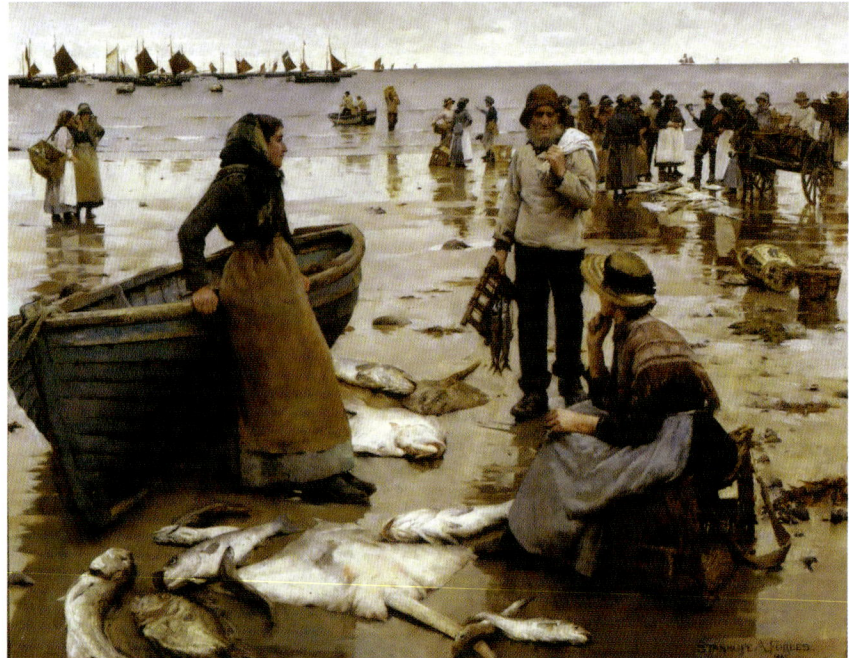

103 In Stanhope Forbes' *A Fish Sale on a Cornish Beach* (1884–85), you can see how the forms and local colors of the subjects are clearly visible and distinct under the cloudy, overcast lighting.

Let's look again at Stanhope Forbes' *A Fish Sale on a Cornish Beach* (1884–85) as an example **(103)**. Note the graphic, simple local colors that it displays, with the colors only getting gradually darker as the forms face downward. Overcast lighting can be one of the most subtle and beautiful types of light, often a favorite of still-life artists.

MOONLIGHT

All days finally move into the night. The most obvious thing that we can say about this situation is that it is considerably darker than the day, only being lit by the moon. However, one thing that people do not generally appreciate about this light is that it is fundamentally the same form of light as the sun **(104)**. Many people intuitively think of moonlight as "cool," but this is not physically true. Moonlight is purely reflected sunlight, moving through the same atmosphere as sunlight does, so there is no interaction that makes it cool.

Moonlight is considerably less intense than sunlight, as it is secondhand. In fact, pure moonlight is so weak that it often lies at the limits of our color vision. Due to this, colors under moonlight appear less chromatic and details are less clear **(105)**.

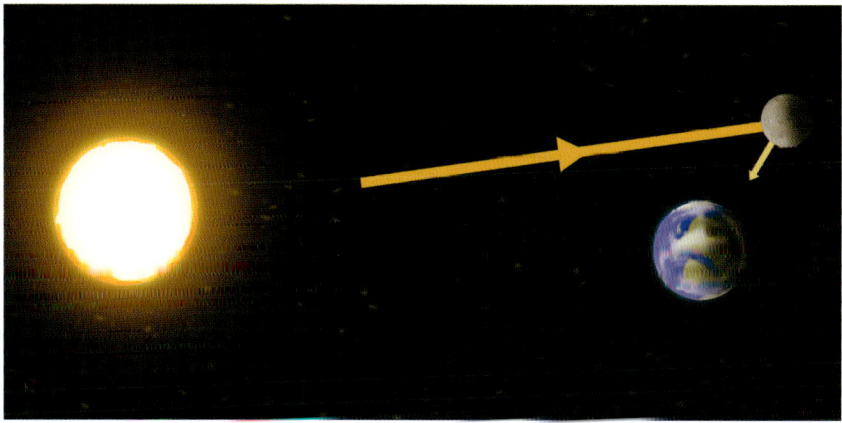

104 We think of moonlight as "cooler" than sunlight, but it's simply reflected light from the sun and is not innately cooler in temperature.

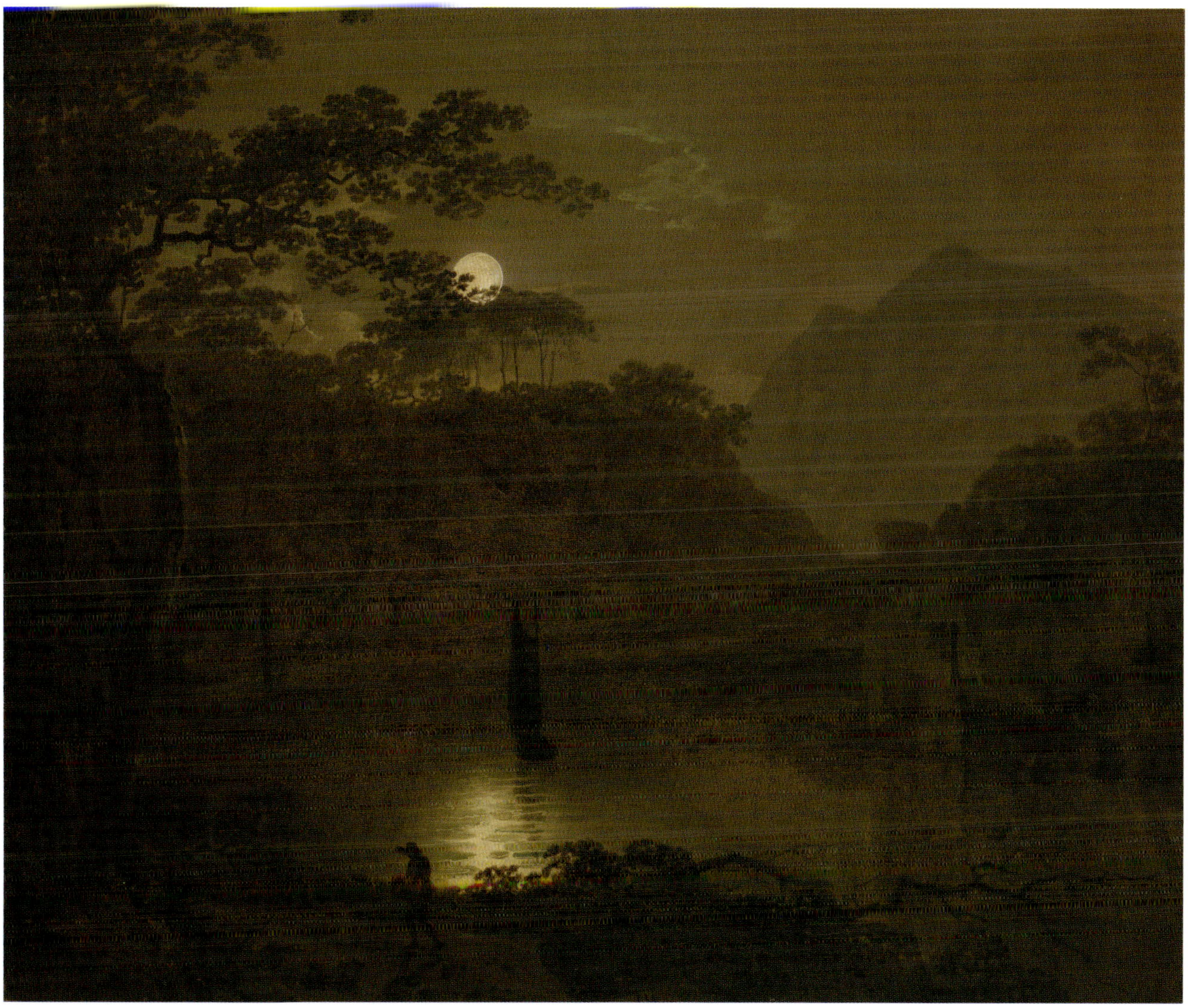

105 *A Lake by Moonlight* (1773–75) by Joseph Wright of Derby is a striking example of a scene lit by the moon, showing its dimness of light and hue compared to sunlight.

LIGHT:
SPECULAR

Specular surfaces, from mirrors to metals, are a challenge for artists new and old. However, like everything else so far, they can be broken down into logical steps that will enable you to tackle increasingly complex subjects and scenarios.

SPECULAR REFLECTION

Now that we have fully discussed the mechanisms and logic behind diffuse reflection and matte surfaces, let's switch gears and talk about the other most common light interaction: specular reflection (01). This form of reflection is often undervalued and thought of as a fringe case by students. However, it is important to realize that all diffusely reflecting objects will exhibit some level of specular reflection, too.

This has a profound effect on the colors we observe in every scene we represent, so it's important that we have a thorough understanding of the logic of specular reflection. This logic will be fundamentally different from the diffuse reflection we have discussed previously – many of the rules we have learned so far will not apply.

The most obvious difference is that specular objects *do not exhibit shadows*. You cannot cast a shadow on a purely specular object. As you can see in **02**, the values of the mirror are the same within the cast shadow as they are in full light. This is because of the first, most important logic of how we will think about specular reflections: Specular objects will display an image of their surroundings.

This image will be reflected at the same angle (relative to the normal of the plane) that it struck the plane with **(03)**. This basic idea will form the entirety of how we think about this type of material.

Since the light never enters the object, there is no influence from the local color of the object, and the colors of the reflection are entirely decided by the environment.

Therefore, when trying to represent specular reflections, it's more important to consider the surroundings than the object itself.

Specular reflections on more complex forms will just be a deformation of this simple image idea. To learn how to work with these more complex forms, as always, we will start by discussing how to tackle the problems on our simple fundamental forms of the cube, cylinder, and sphere.

Before we get into that, we'll take a look at the most simple, planar version of this problem and something we will all be familiar with: the mirror.

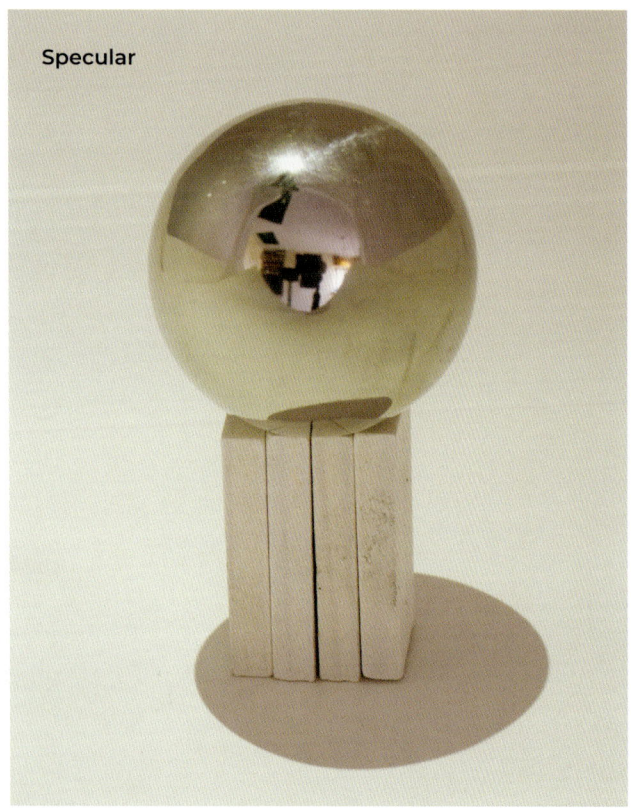
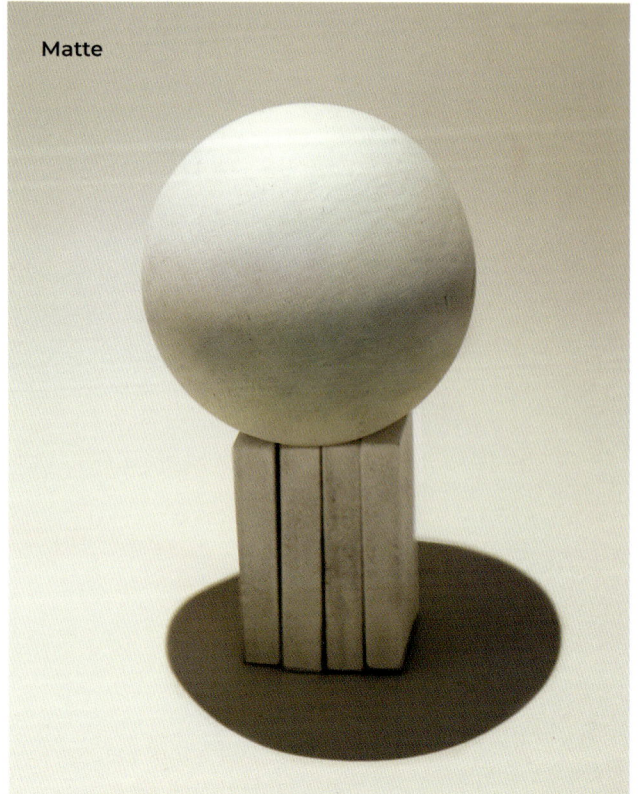

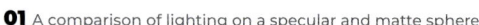
01 A comparison of lighting on a specular and matte sphere.

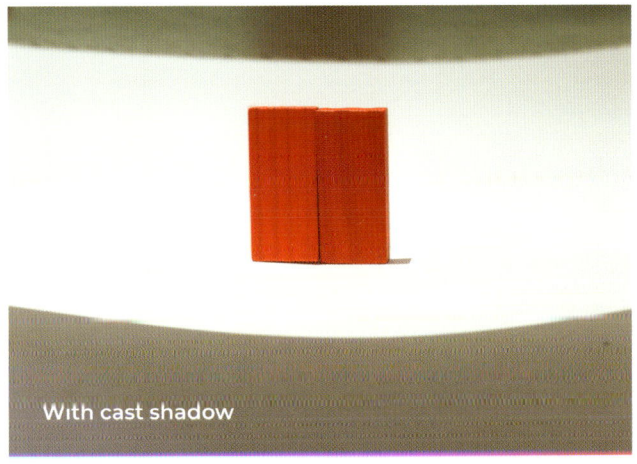

With cast shadow

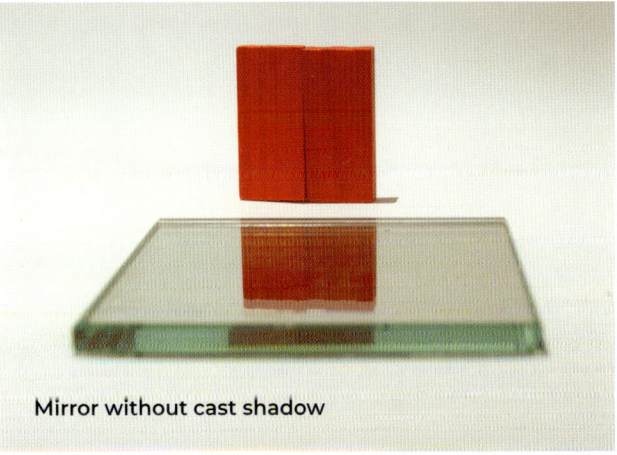

Mirror without cast shadow

02 The overhead object does not cast a shadow onto the specular surface of the mirror.

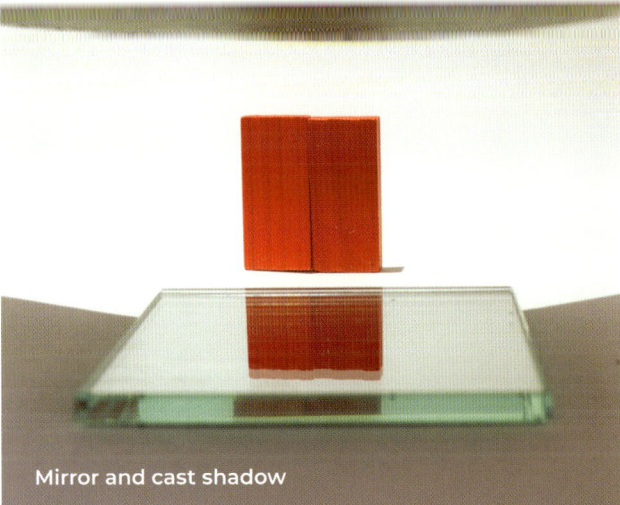

Mirror and cast shadow

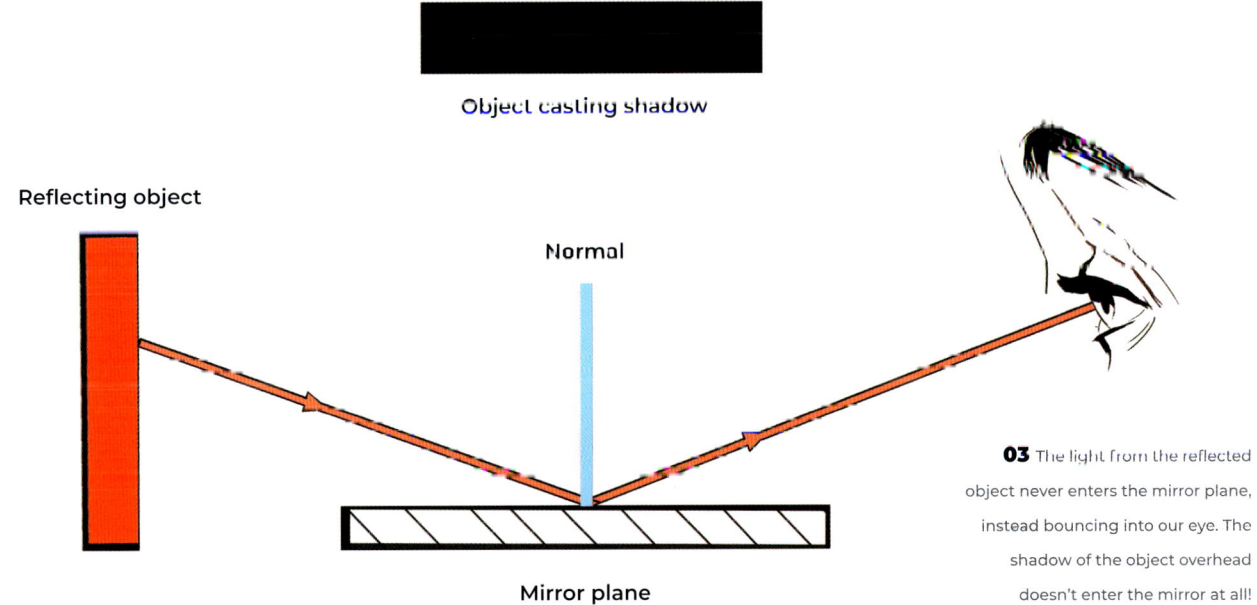

Object casting shadow

Reflecting object

Normal

Mirror plane

03 The light from the reflected object never enters the mirror plane, instead bouncing into our eye. The shadow of the object overhead doesn't enter the mirror at all!

THE MIRROR

In order to fully understand how we can approach mirrors, let's first follow the path of a mirror through a simple 90-degree rotation, so we can see for ourselves how specular reflection affects the image we see in it (04–10).

These colored dominos are arranged in a "clock face" formation, with each "hour" representing 30 degrees. This will enable us to track exactly what we are seeing in the mirror. The mirror is in the center of the circle, with a red line indicating its normal

in the diagram. The reflection's angle is indicated by the blue line from the camera (our point of view).

0 degrees. When the mirror is at 0 degrees' rotation, front on, we get a direct but flipped reflection of our position. Everyone who has looked in a mirror will be intimately familiar with this, so it should easily make sense! **(04)**

15 degrees. Rotating the mirror to the 15-degree position slightly increases the range of dominos visible to us. The red

30-degree domino is now central in the reflection, and we can see part of the neighboring orange domino **(05)**.

30 degrees. If we rotate the mirror 30 degrees away from us, we can see a greater effect on the reflection. The angle of the reflection doubles, which will remain consistent for every angle – though the mirror's normal is facing the red 30-degree domino, we don't see it, instead seeing ahead to the yellow 60-degree domino **(06)**.

Angle degrees

  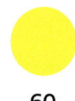   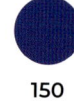

| 30 | 45 | 60 | 90 | 120 | 135 | 150 |

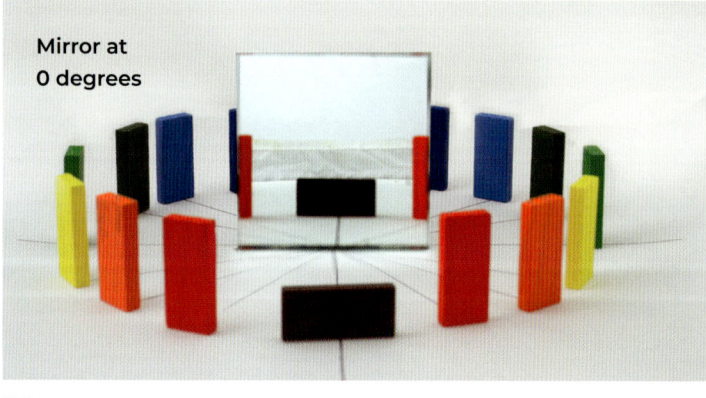 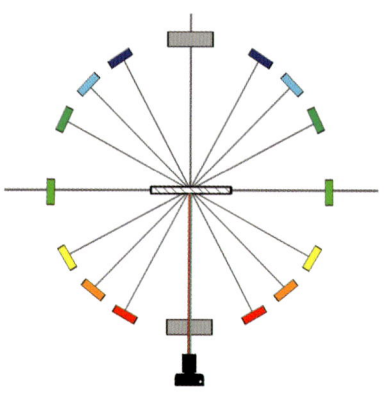

Mirror at
0 degrees

04 With the mirror facing us at 0 degrees, we can see a direct but flipped reflection of what's in front of the mirror and behind us.

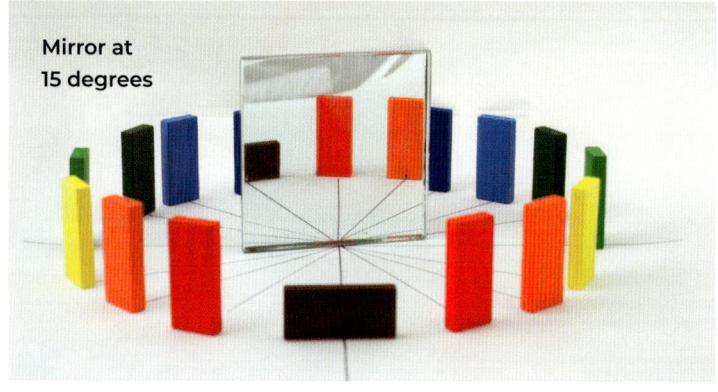 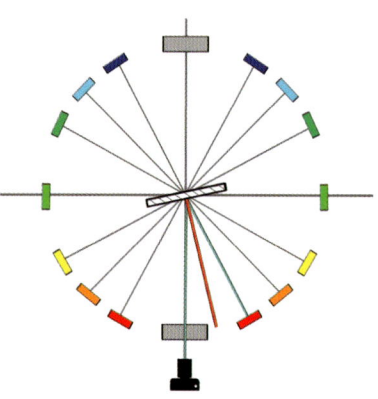

Mirror at
15 degrees

05 With the mirror's normal turned to 15 degrees from us, we begin to see objects that are not directly in front of the mirror.

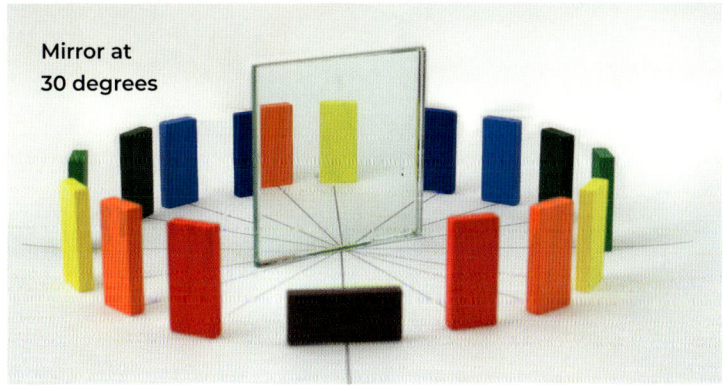
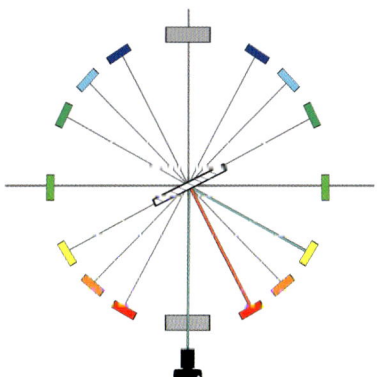

06 At 30 degrees, the effect becomes more apparent as the reflection's angle doubles.

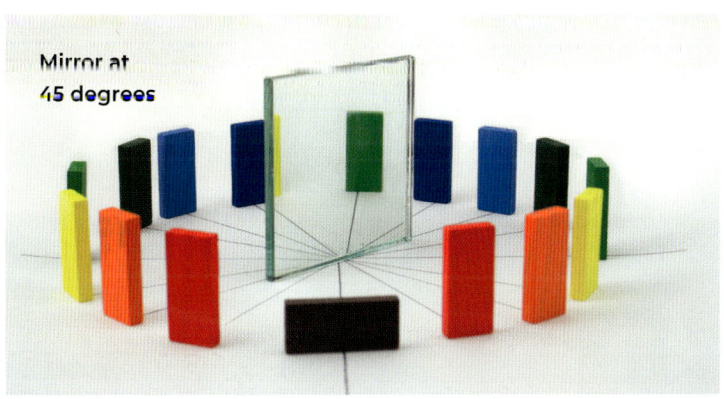
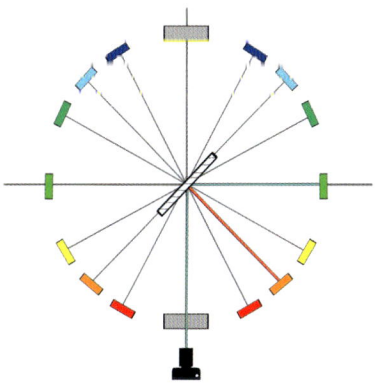

07 At 45 degrees, the angle of the reflection doubles to 90 degrees.

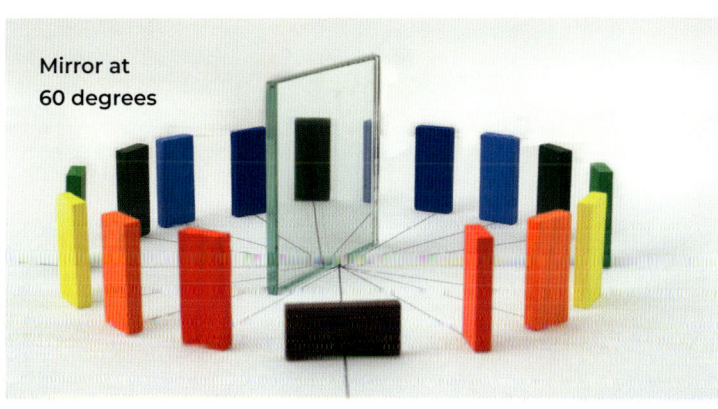
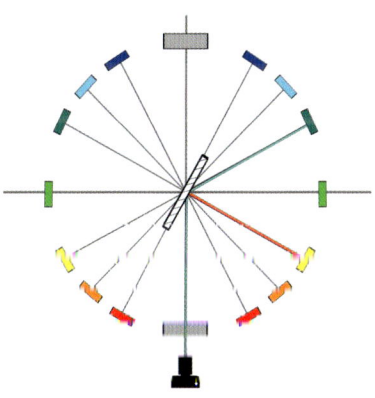

08 At 60 degrees, we begin to see objects that are almost behind the mirror in space.

45 degrees. At 45 degrees' rotation, our angle doubles again. This shows us an image of 90 degrees, or directly to the right of our mirror – the green "three o'clock" domino. This will be a critical angle for us when we work, as it is the first angle where we can't see an image of the environment behind us. Identifying this angle is a key skill in orienting ourselves and working out which parts of the environment we will see reflected **(07)**

60 degrees. If we rotate the mirror to 60 degrees, we begin to see the light blue domino, even though it's in the extreme periphery of the mirror plane. A common student mistake is to assume that if we can see the front of our mirror plane, the mirror must also be reflecting something in front of it. Seeing this angle dispels that idea **(08)**.

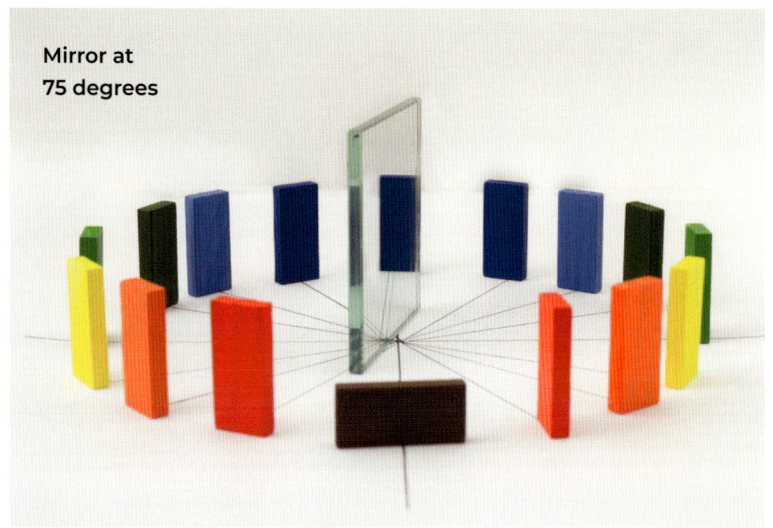 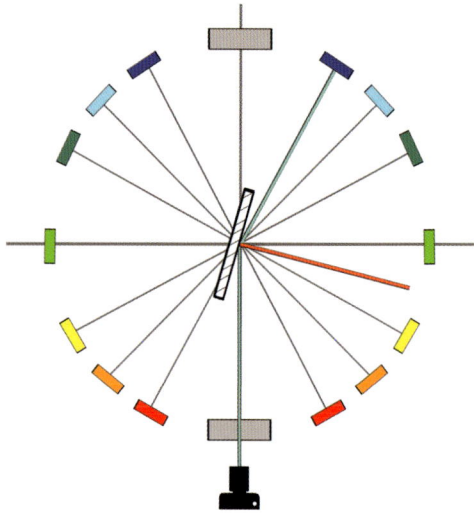

09 With a rotation of 75 degrees, the reflection angle is far beyond showing what is directly in front of the mirror.

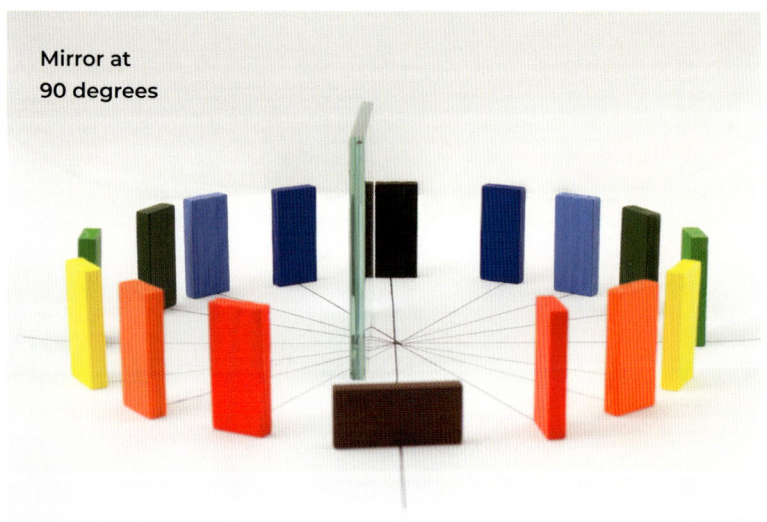 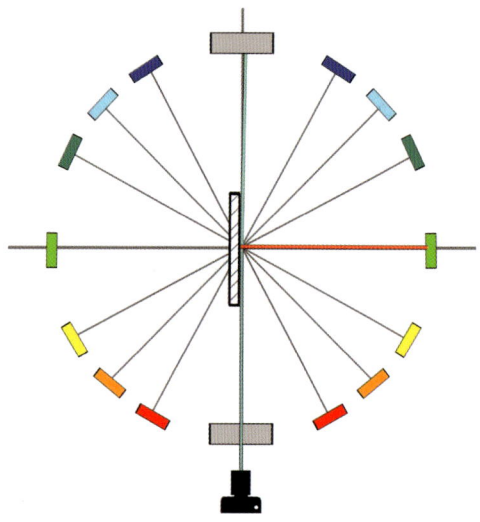

10 At 90 degrees, we see past the flat plane of the mirror and can no longer view a reflection.

75 degrees. If we continue rotating the mirror to 75 degrees, the previous phenomenon becomes even clearer. We don't see a reflection of the orange, yellow, and green dominos that are in front of the of the mirror plane at all. Instead, we can only see the rear dark blue domino **(09)**.

90 degrees. If we rotate to our final position, we can now clearly see past the mirror plane to what is behind our mirror. This leads us to the conclusion that everything that we can see that is not blocked by the mirror will be reflected by it at some angle **(10)**.

The most important knowledge to take forward from this series of images is: If the mirror is angled more directly toward us, the reflected image will show what's in front of the position of the mirror. When the mirror passes through 45 degrees, this changes, and as the mirror continues to turn away from us, the reflected image will begin to show what's beyond or "behind" the position of the mirror.

CONSTRUCTING THE MIRROR, PART 1

How that we understand the relevance of the angle of our mirror plane, and that the 45-degree angle is the most important to orient ourselves, we need an intuitive method for working out what this angle is in our images.

It's important to note that while it is not covered in this book, perspective is incredibly important for all drawing. The more you can understand it, the better you will be able to work in a three-dimensional space. However, there is a useful, simple method we can apply to be sure of the orientation of our mirror plane, through the use of ellipses.

Ellipses are circles put into perspective. If we know what ellipses look like at a few key angles, we have an easy way to work out the orientation of any plane.

The angles we want to understand here are the same angles we looked at on the previous pages, transitioning from fully front-on to perpendicular to our vision (11–17).

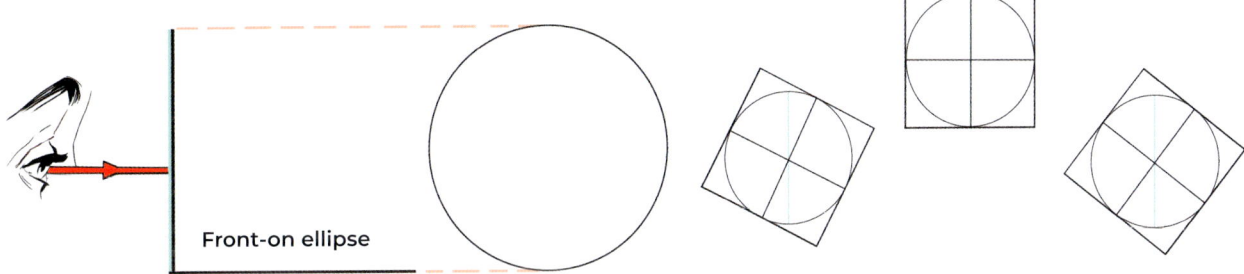

11 The front-on ellipse is simply a 1:1 circle with no foreshortening in any direction. This proportion would only be observed on a square plane facing us directly.

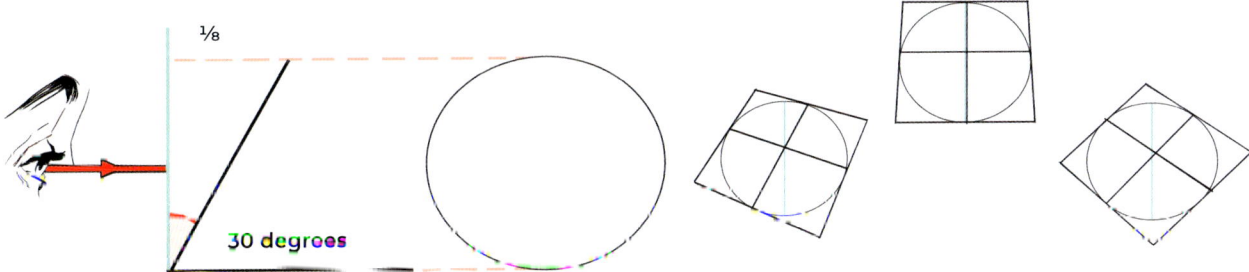

12 At 30 degrees, we see a minimal amount of foreshortening. This degree of ellipse reflects all of the environment behind us.

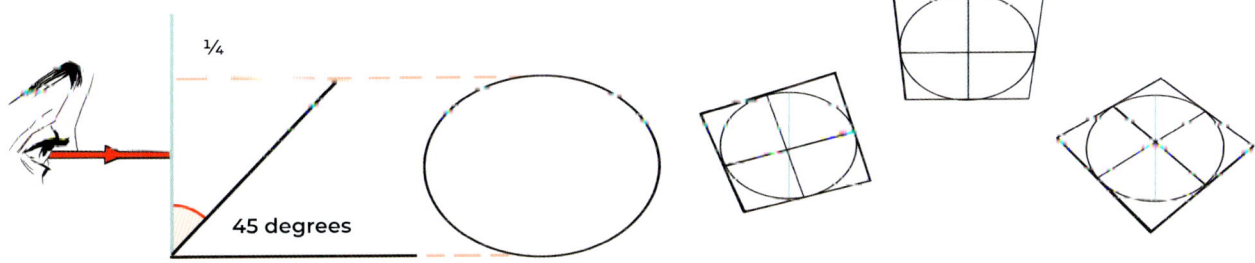

13 At 45 degrees, there is moderate foreshortening, losing about a quarter of the ellipse's height. This will be our key orientation as it marks the point of horizontal reflection. The environment behind us would be reflected with a small amount of foreshortening.

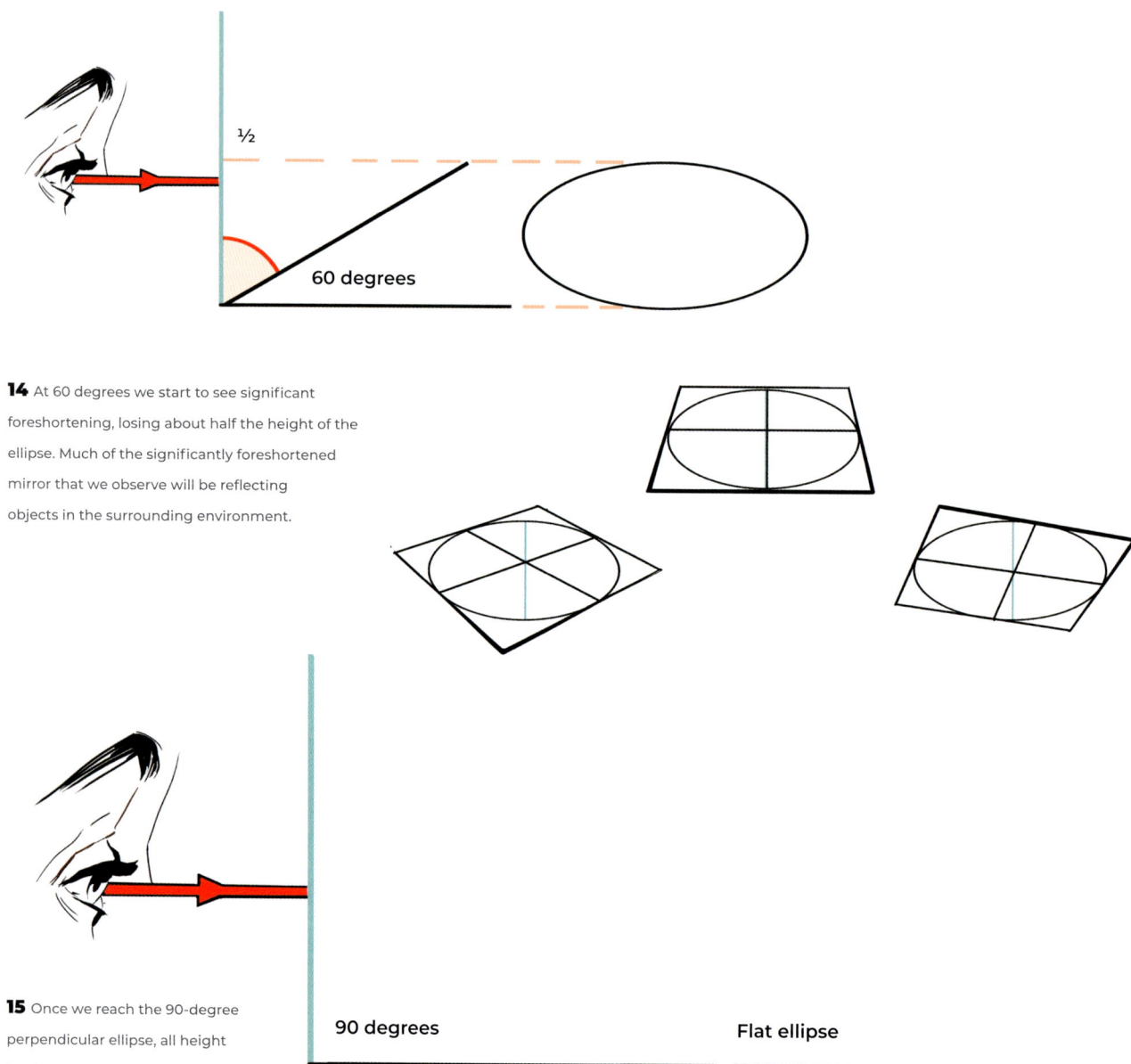

14 At 60 degrees we start to see significant foreshortening, losing about half the height of the ellipse. Much of the significantly foreshortened mirror that we observe will be reflecting objects in the surrounding environment.

15 Once we reach the 90-degree perpendicular ellipse, all height has been foreshortened out and we are just left with a thin line.

PLACING AN ELLIPSE GUIDE

If we can remember these rough ellipse degrees, we can work out the approximate angle of the plane we are looking at by finding the degree of the ellipse that fits on the plane. This is an incredibly flexible and practical way to figure out our reflections

without delving into more complex perspective calculations.

It is important to note that this method will only work on square-proportioned planes, so that our circle is placed within another evenly proportioned shape and we can clearly see how its angle changes.

As we will rarely be dealing with perfectly square mirror planes, an easy workaround is selecting a square portion within the plane and finding the ellipse for that. We can see how this would work in images **16a–c**. Every plane has a square plane somewhere within it, so this method will work well for us.

16a Placing an ellipse requires a square mirror. Luckily, it is easy to find a square segment on this flat mirror shape.

16b Simply portion off a square section of the mirror and locate its center by quartering it.

16c Place the ellipse within the square to find the approximate orientation of the mirror plane.

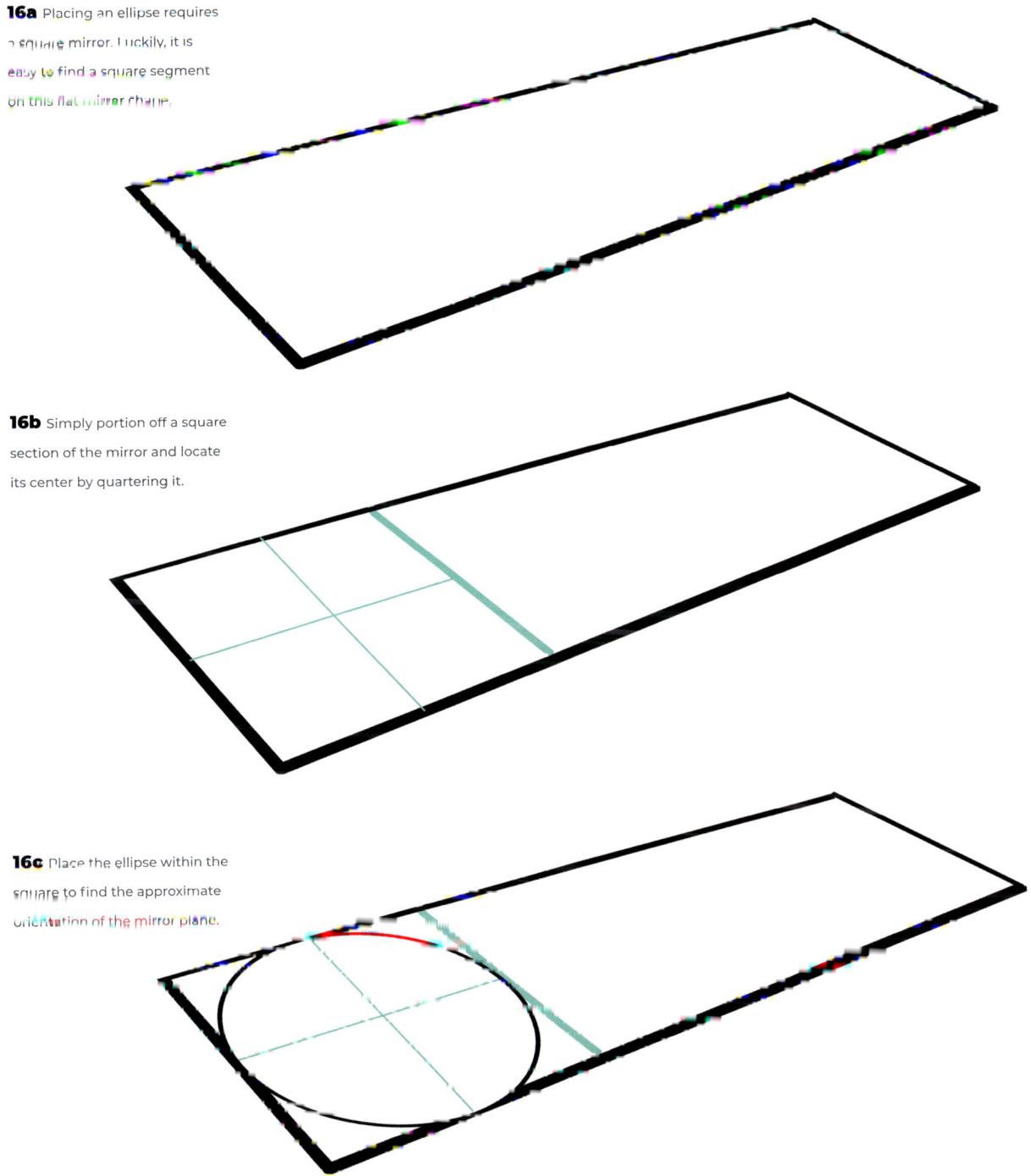

PLACING THE REFLECTION

Now that we have a way of working out the approximate orientation of our mirror, we need a way to map reflections onto it. We know roughly where those reflections should be, but how do we actually place them onto our mirror plane?

THE MIRROR WORLD

Let's begin by looking at a mountain range reflected in a calm lake **(17)**. This example is useful because the large lake can be seen as a functionally infinite mirror that we know is flat to the ground plane of the image.

If we look at the reflection of the mountain ranges, which are also effectively infinitely distant, we can learn two extremely useful lessons. The first lesson is that these reflections all line up as parallel lines (shown in blue below). These lines are perfectly vertical, perpendicular to our mirror plane (the lake). This is the "normal" of the plane, as covered on page 70. So our first lesson is: The reflected image on a plane will always be in line with the normal of the plane.

Each of these reflections lying along the normals are the exact same distance from the horizon (in red below) as the real mountains. The reflection appears as a simple flipped image of the mountains, giving us our second lesson: The reflected image will be a mirrored image of the real object, equidistant from the place it touches the mirror plane. This reflected image can be thought of as its own physical space, with each object reflected at the same distance into the "mirror world" as its real-world distance from the mirror.

THE MIRROR'S POINT OF VIEW

While the reflected mountains seem like an exactly flipped image, this is partly a simplification due to the sheer distance of the mountains from us as the viewer. Let's investigate this by looking at a simple object sitting on a simple mirror **(18)**.

We can see the same two rules we learned are still true. The mirror still reflects an

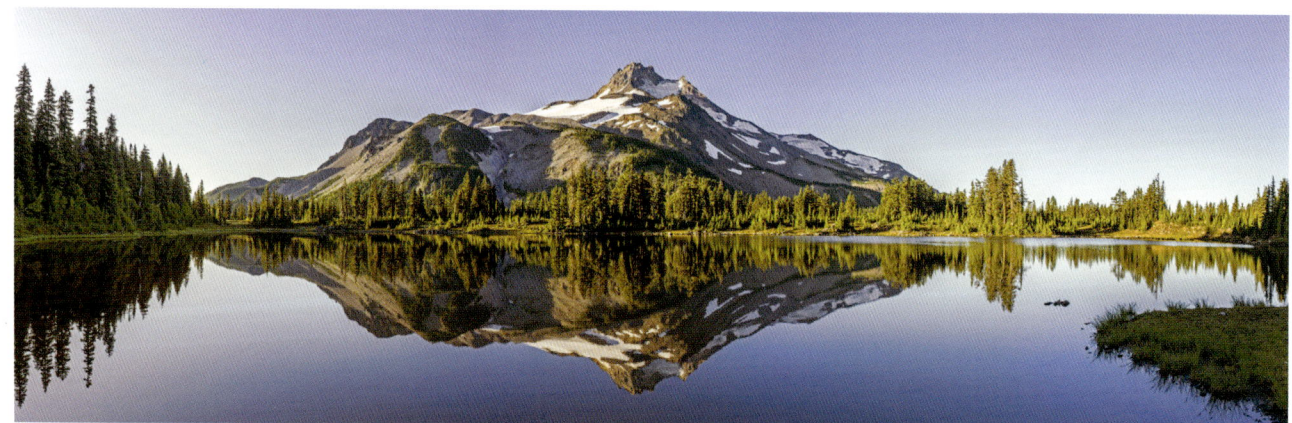

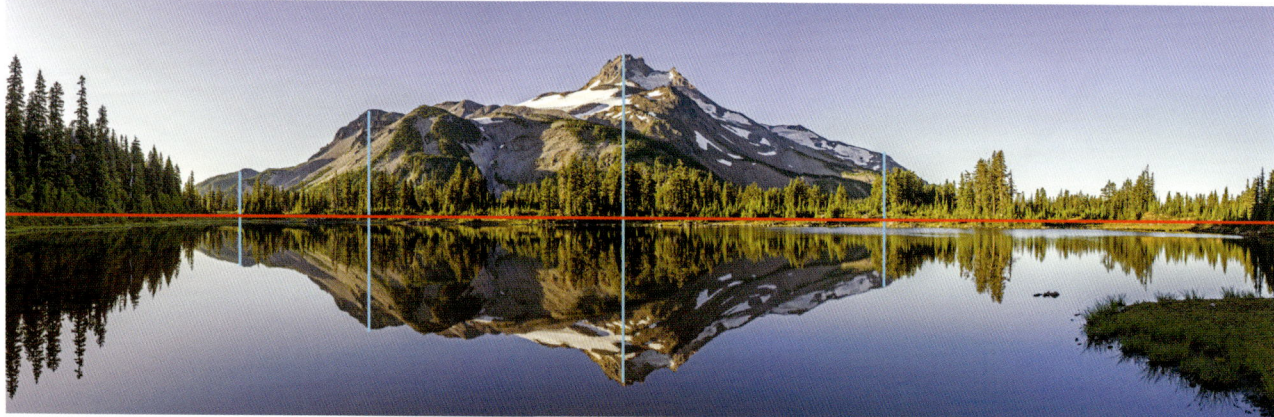

17 The lake in this scene serves as an enormous mirror plane, where we can see the mountains appear to be reflected directly vertically along the mirror's normal.

image along the normal of the plane, and this image is still equidistant from the point of contact with the mirror plane. However, you can see that the reflected image is not an exact "flipped" duplicate of the true cylinder. This is because the reflection we are seeing is the cylinder from the point of view of the mirror plane. Thus we're seeing more of the underside of the cylinder, instead of the top plane that we see in the true cylinder. The reflected image has its own perspective independent of the original object.

Knowing that this reflected image will have a new perspective is incredibly important for us going forward, because it means each new reflected image we paint must be considered carefully. To paint a scene containing mirrors, and to know how to represent reflections from any angle, we need a full enough understanding of how to place ourselves in the scene.

EXTENDING THE MIRROR

So far, we have only dealt with subjects directly in contact with our mirror surface. However, this won't always be the case in our images, so we need another solution for placing reflections. Luckily, this is a simple problem to solve.

As you can see in image **19**, the reflection still basically works in the same way – we just aren't seeing the entire interaction. To find a solution to this, all we need to do is imagine an extension of the mirror plane (shown in blue) that meets the surface of the object, and then project our reflected image in exactly the same way as before. When we paint the image, we simply paint only the required portion of the visible reflection.

However, you may notice another problem: This solution only works if the reflected object is still in contact with the extended mirror plane. What if this isn't the case, like the floating cylinder in image **20**? We can solve this problem in a similar way, except

this time by extending the object down to meet the mirror plane. Once this is done, the same logic still works – the relevant portion of the reflected cylinder is simply the same distance into the "mirror world" as the real cylinder is away from the mirror plane.

Through either of these methods, or a combination of the two, you can work out the reflection for any planar mirror image. This "projecting" into the mirror space will be the most common skill we will use in creating reflections.

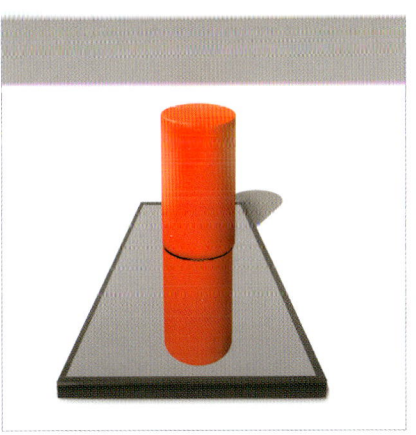

18 The reflected object isn't a total duplicate of the object we see, but an image from the point of the view of the mirror plane.

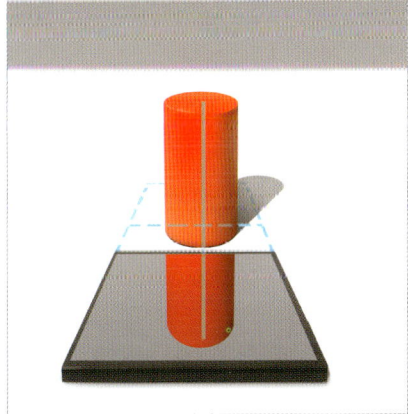

19 If the reflected object doesn't touch the mirror plane, we can place its reflection by imagining an extension of the mirror plane.

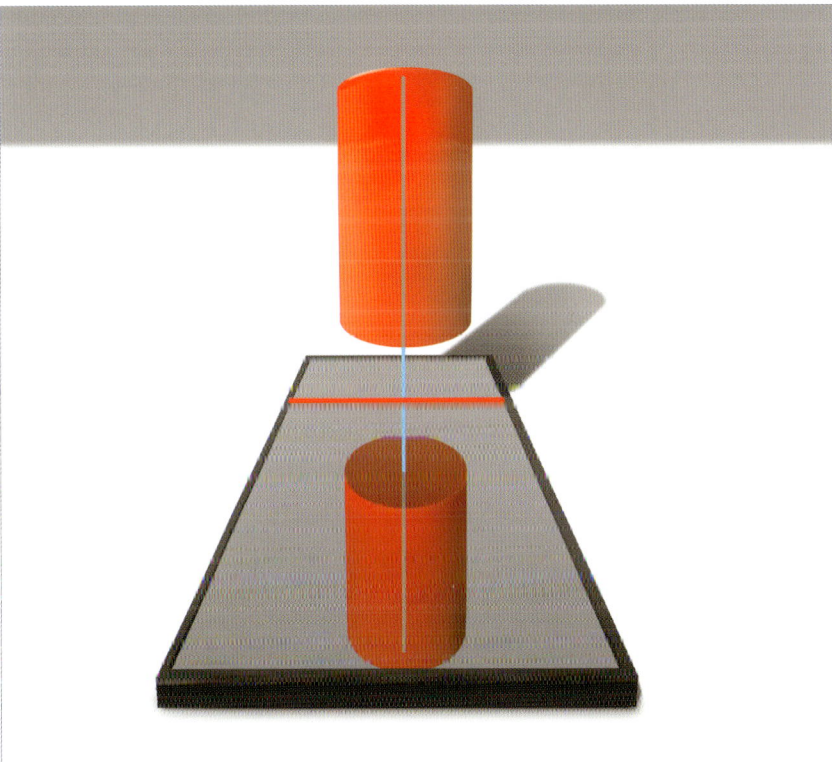

20 We can also imagine an extension of the object to help place its reflection correctly on the mirror plane.

CONSTRUCTING THE MIRROR, PART 2

Now that we understand the basic logic at play when we construct a mirror, let's have a look at how this might play out practically.

We will go through some simple steps to construct a mirror in a basic still life scene, with the mirror simply standing on the ground plane (**21a–f**). We will then look at how to capture a more difficult reflection, with the mirror angled above the scene.

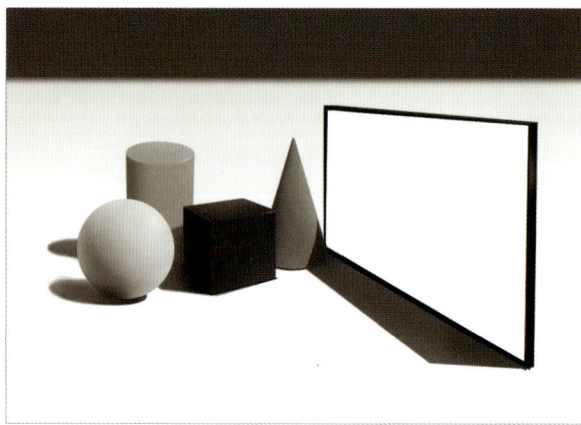

21a Place your mirror plane in the scene. Just place it simply for now – if you have something specific you want to reflect, you can vary this plane later in the process.

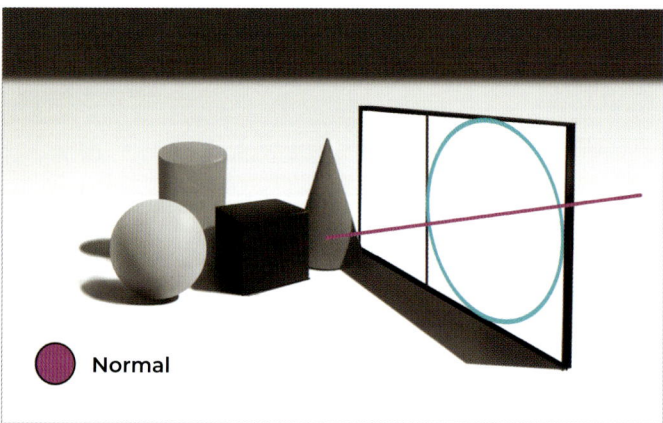

Normal

21b Find a square on the mirror plane and place an ellipse to help find the plane's orientation. In this case, it's a 60-degree ellipse, so we know the reflection will be "behind" the mirror. The short axis of this ellipse will be the normal of the plane, and so this is also the simplest way to find this useful angle.

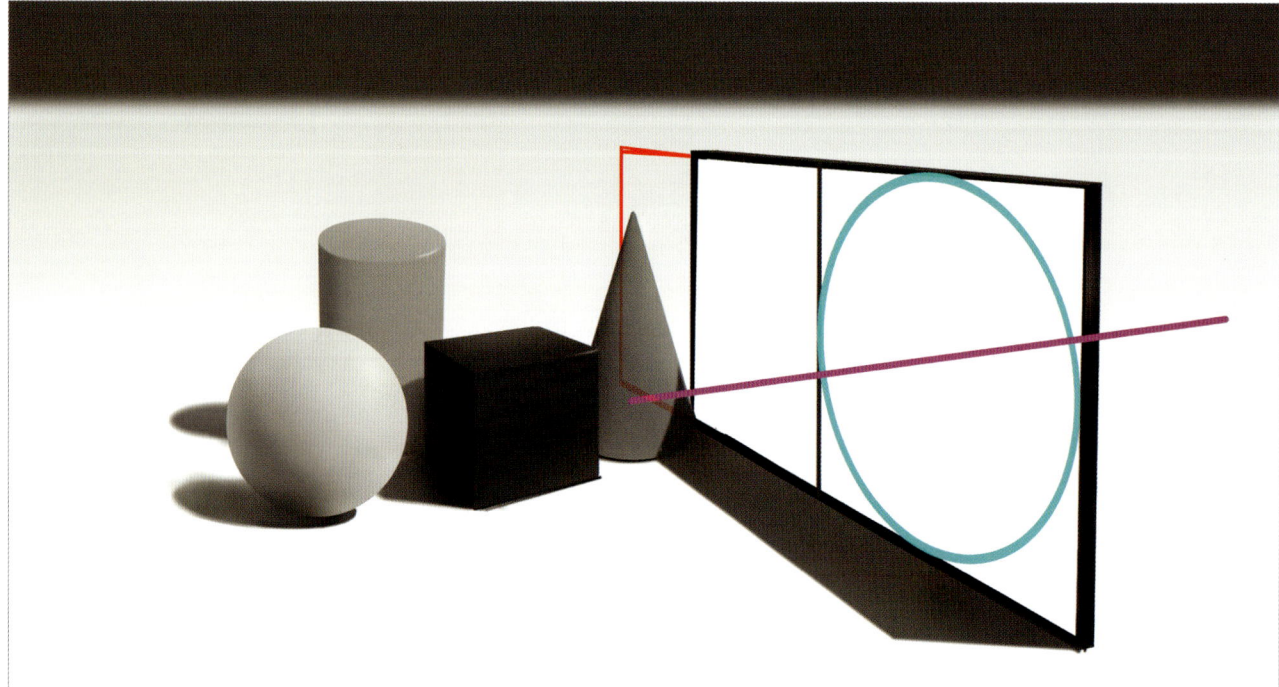

21c As we learned on page 137, add an extension until the mirror reaches past the objects we want to reflect. Extend the mirror (shown in red here) until it either contacts the object or we can extend the object toward the mirror plane along the normal angle.

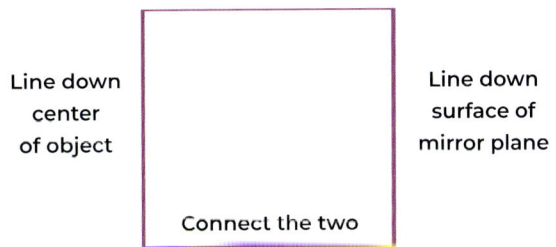

Line down
center
of object

Line down
surface of
mirror plane

Connect the two

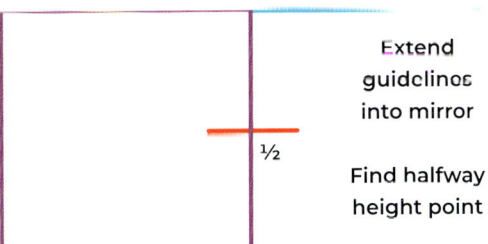

Extend
guidelines
into mirror

Find halfway
height point

½

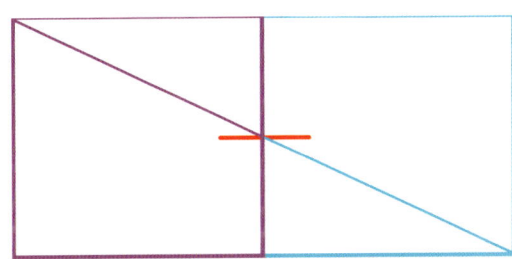

Draw diagonally through middle mark to
find distance of reflected object's center

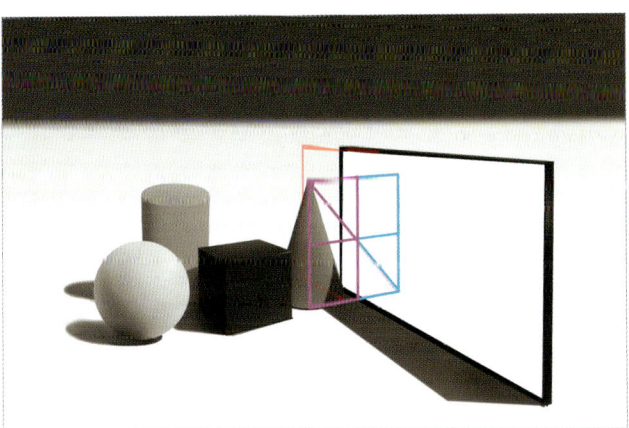

21d We can now use the extended mirror and the normal angle to find the distance of each object into the mirror world. Do this by extending each shape into the mirror plane, as shown in the diagrams on the right.

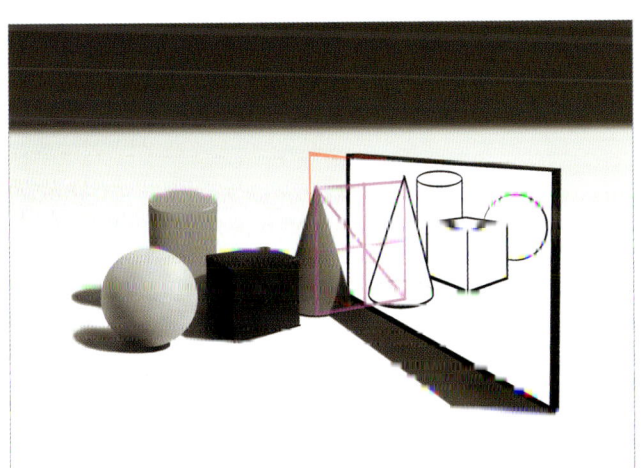

21e Repeat the previous step to place guidelines for each object in the "mirror world," then construct the line drawings for the reflected forms. Remember, this will be an entirely new view of our forms – you can transfer each mark if you are unsure of how to draw it. Eventually you'll be able to visualize this new angle from the point of view of the mirror. Being able to approach this more intuitively will become more important the more complex our subject is.

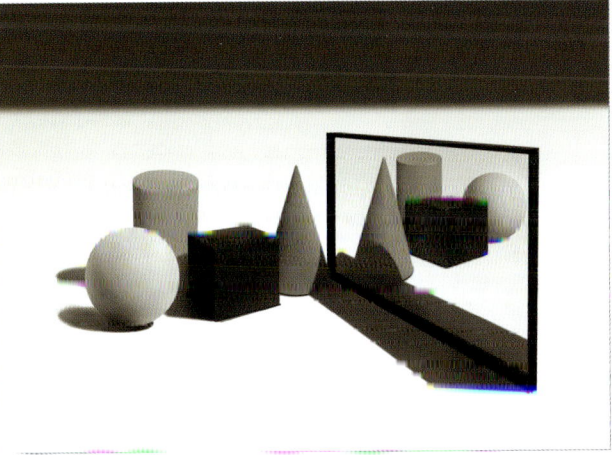

21f Now that the drawings for the reflection are planned out, all that we need to do is render the reflected forms. It's important to remember that no mirror will reflect all light perfectly, so the reflected image will be slightly darker that its real counterpart.

REFLECTING MORE COMPLEX ANGLES

Now let's see how we would apply this simple method to a more complex angle. While the shape that we need to mirror here is slightly more challenging, due to the unusual angle of the mirror, the fundamental logic is the same. We can use the same basic method to insert a mirror plane at any angle into an image and project a reflection onto it from objects in the scene **(22a–g)**.

This will work for any mirror angle that is directly reflecting something in the environment (any angle smaller than 45 degrees). If we are dealing with angles reflecting something outside of the image space, the mirror will still reflect something along the line of the normal – it would just require more planning and visualization of the scenery outside the canvas.

 Normal Form normalized on mirror plane

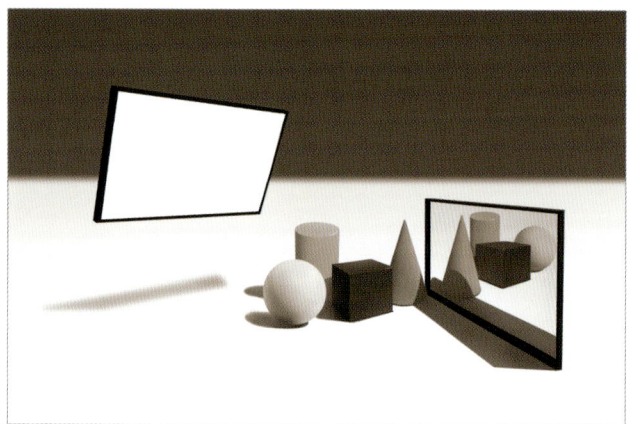

22a Place the new mirror in the scene.

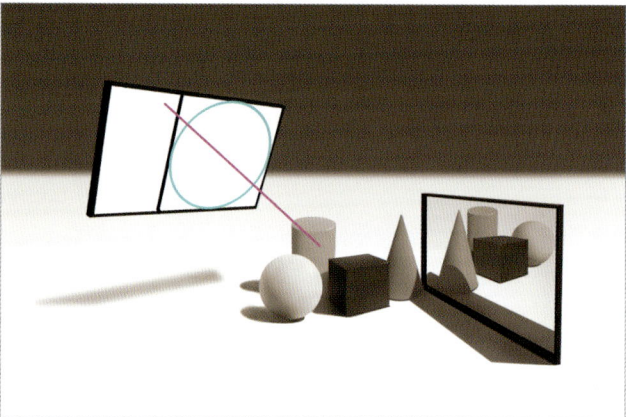

22b As before, find a square on the mirror plane and place an ellipse in it. Draw through the shortest axis of the ellipse to find the mirror's normal.

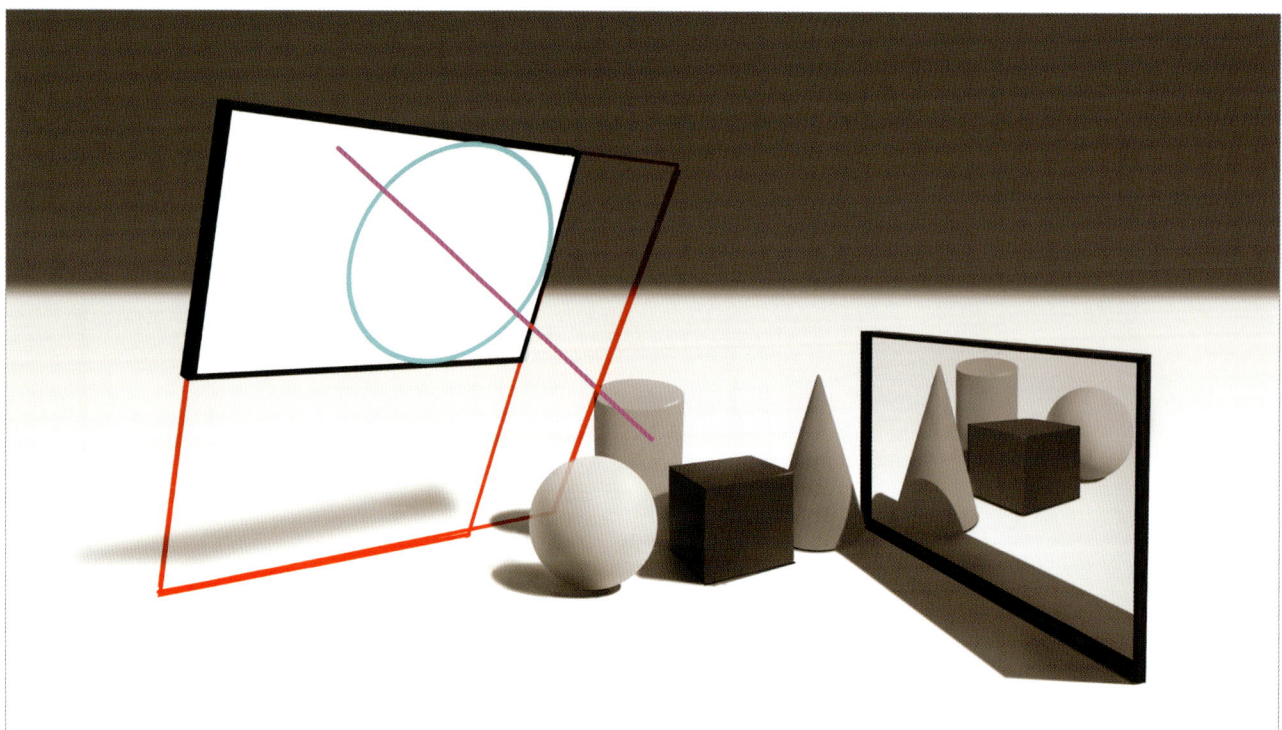

22c Extend the mirror out and down (shown in red) to reach the ground plane and extend behind the objects.

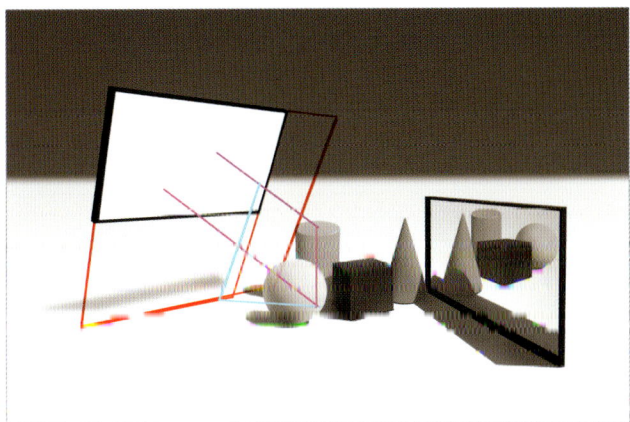

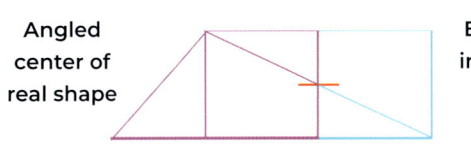

Angled center of real shape

Extension into mirror world

Extended mirror surface line upward

Extend object center line upward

Complete triangle to find center line of mirrored shape

22d The guidelines we use for this complex angle are slightly more complicated, but the logic remains the same. The only new element we need to normalize is the angle of the mirror to the ground plane, and the center lines of the mirrored objects now meet in a triangle.

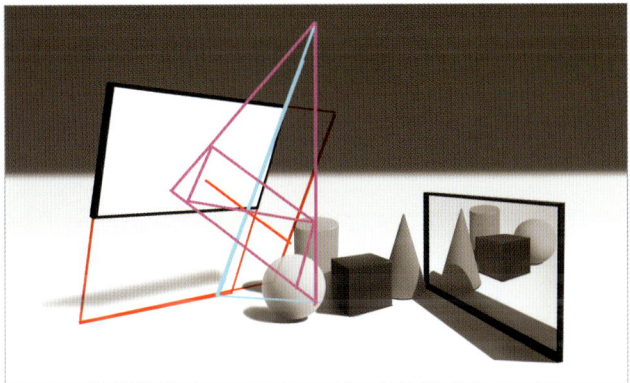

22e Extend the cylinder's center line and normal guidelines up until they meet in a triangle. The other side of the triangle will mark the angle of the reflected cylinder in the mirror world.

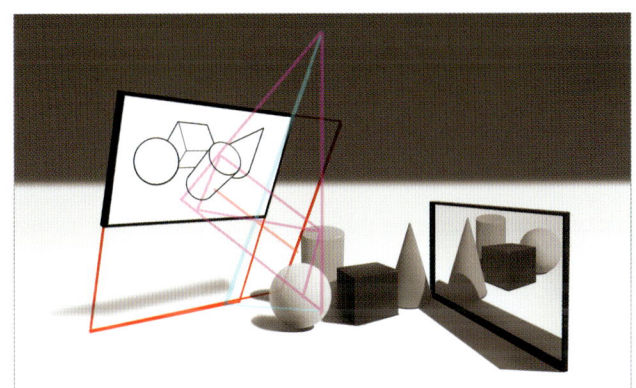

22f Repeat the guideline process for the other shapes until you can sketch the outlines of each object in the mirror.

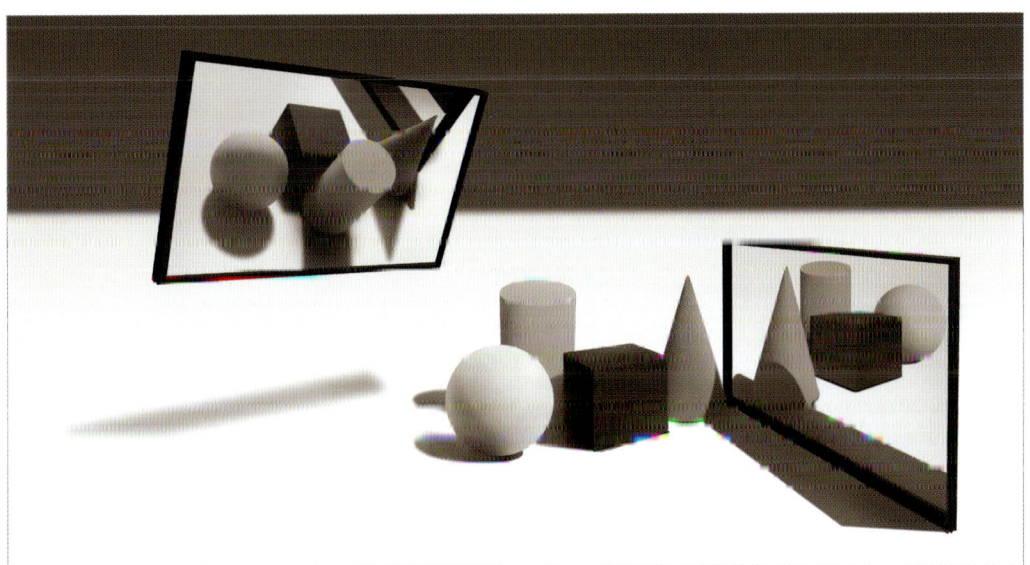

22g Render the shapes in the mirror, again keeping in mind that their values will be slightly dimmer than in the real scene.

MIRROR EXERCISES

A great exercise to practice your mirror skills is to take an existing environment and place various mirrors around the space from your imagination. As you can see below, it takes a little more imagination to visualize the areas of the room you can't see in the original. It can help to draw a top-down floor plan for the space to orient yourself in the exercise, but eventually you will not need this aid and will simply be able to visualize the new view given by the mirrors **(23)**.

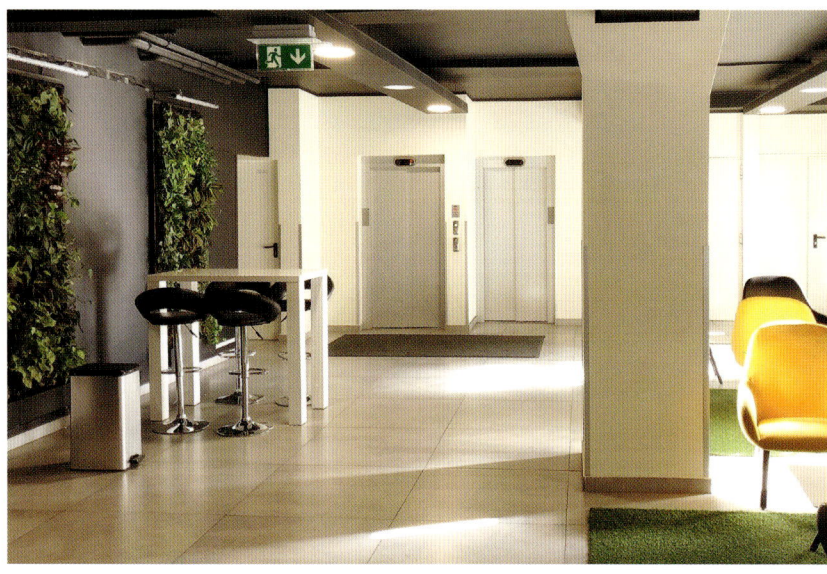

23 An example of a more complex scene with angled mirrors reflecting the surroundings.

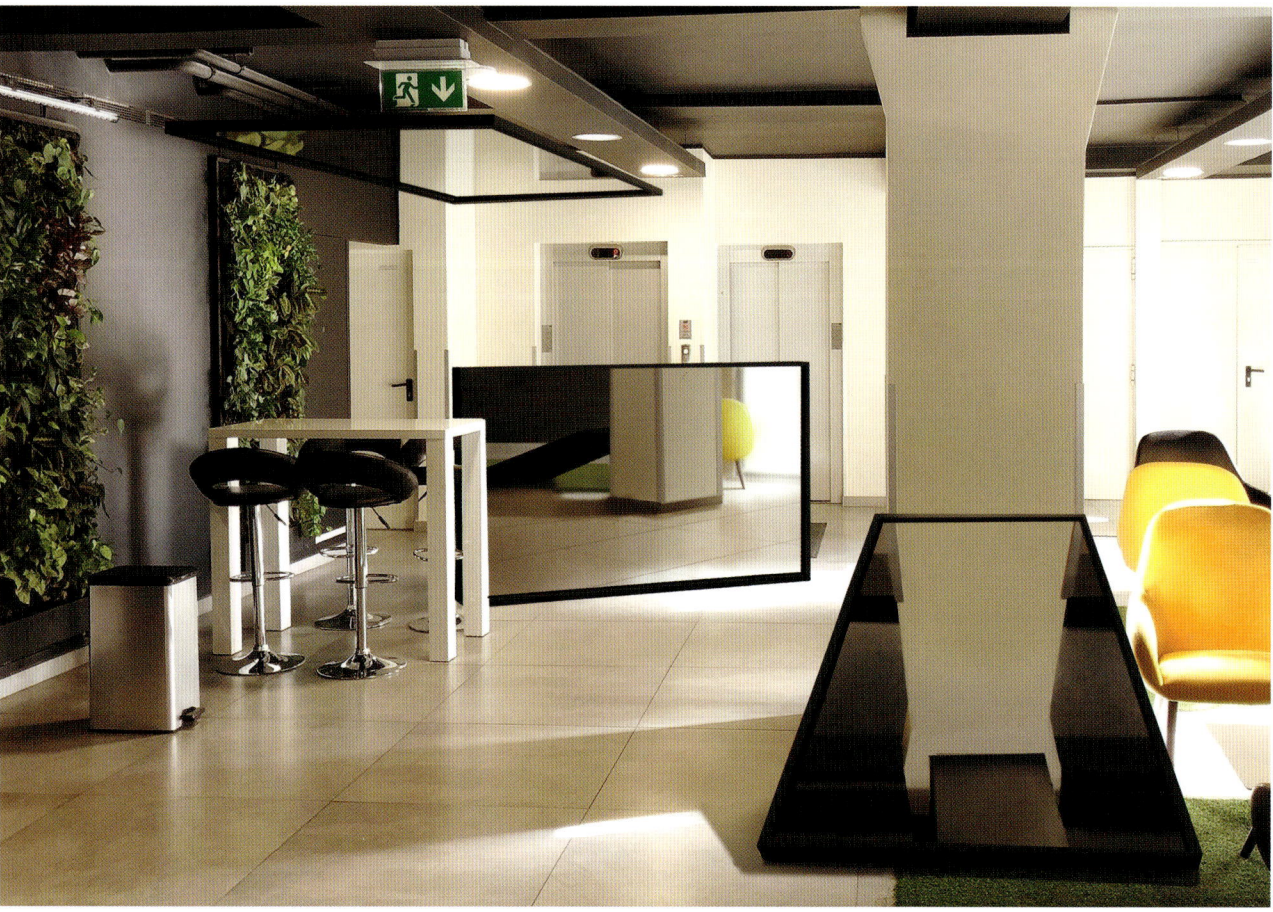

Image 23 photo by David Fintz on Unsplash

CURVED MIRRORS

Before we move into the specular fundamental forms, there is one more aspect of specular logic that we need to understand: The deformation of our reflected image when we are not dealing with a perfectly flat mirror.

THE CONVEX MIRROR

First, let's start with an ordinary mirror plane and see how a simple image changes when we make the mirror gradually more convex (bending outward, like the outside of a sphere). On a flat plane, the light rays bounce back to us directly, and so we observe an undistorted reflection of our subject **(24)**.

As we add convex curvature to the mirror, we begin to see a pronounced distortion of this reflected image **(25)**. We can see clearly that the image reflected in our mirror plane is squashed along the plane we have curved, resulting in the cylinders appearing thinner and closer together. This distortion will be true for all convex surfaces when they reflect an image.

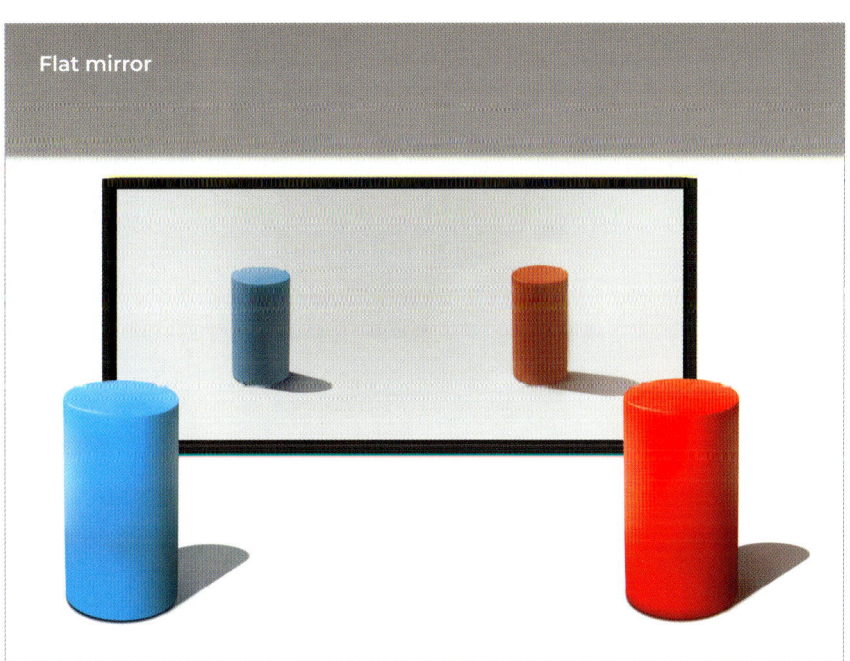

Flat mirror

24 The undistorted reflection of a simple scene on a flat mirror plane.

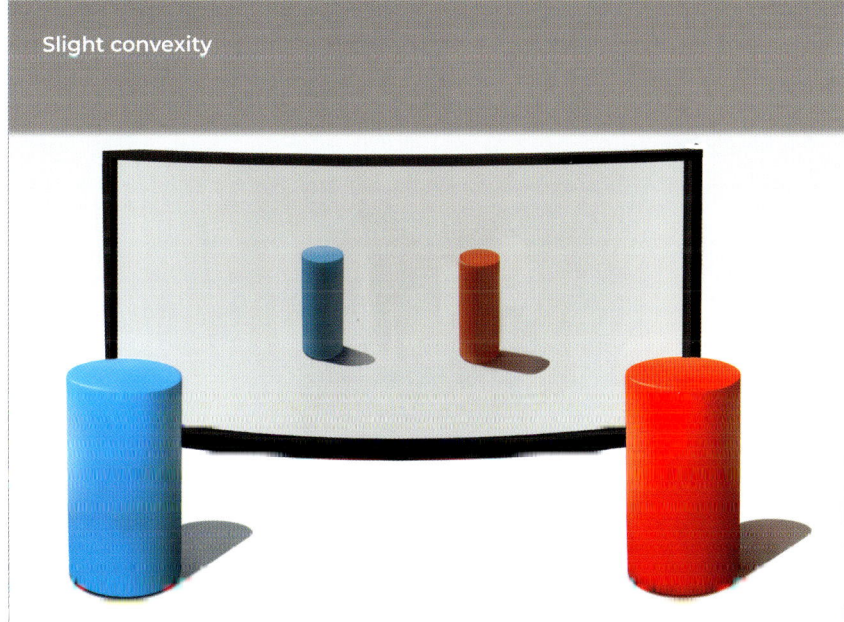

Slight convexity

25 On a slightly convex mirror, the reflected image begins to squash along the curved plane.

The reason for this distortion becomes clear if we look at a simplified version of this interaction **(26)**. If we project parallel light rays onto a flat mirror, they bounce straight back to where they started. If we do the same for a convex mirror however, the light rays spread out once reflected. More of the environment is able to be taken in and reflected by the convex mirror, causing the image to squash to fit everything in.

In images **27** and **28** we can see what happens when our mirror has an even a tighter convexity, increasing the distortion.

It's important to understand how this tightening of convexity works in reality, where no two planes ever move directly into each other. As we'll explore on page 148, there will always be some small convexity on the connecting edge of any two planes on a real object.

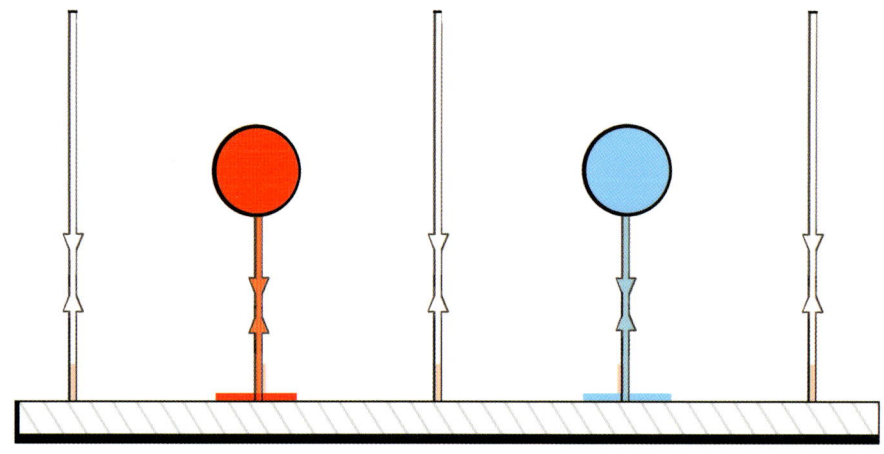

Flat mirror

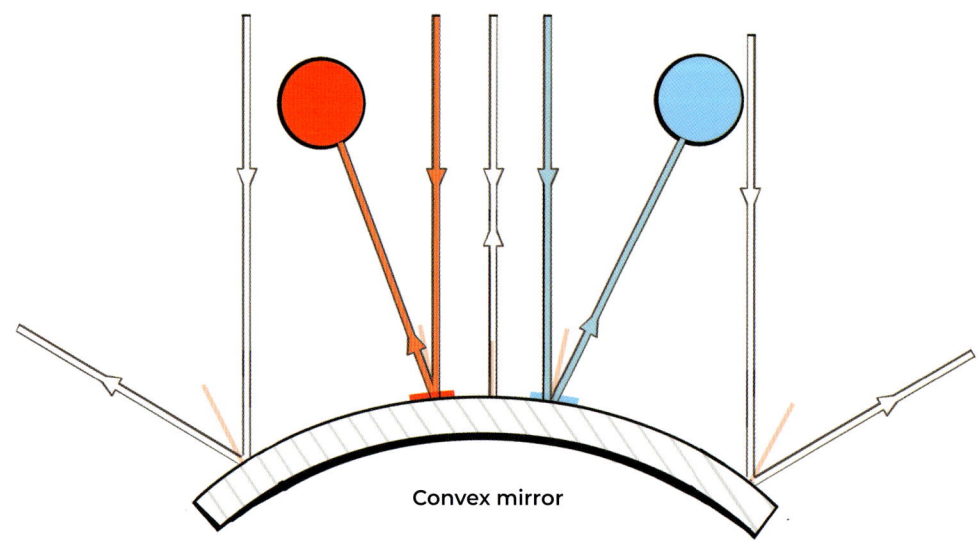

Convex mirror

26 As the mirror becomes convex, the image shrinks along the axis of the curve. This is because the light rays spread out, forcing more of the image to fit onto the surface.

Moderate convexity

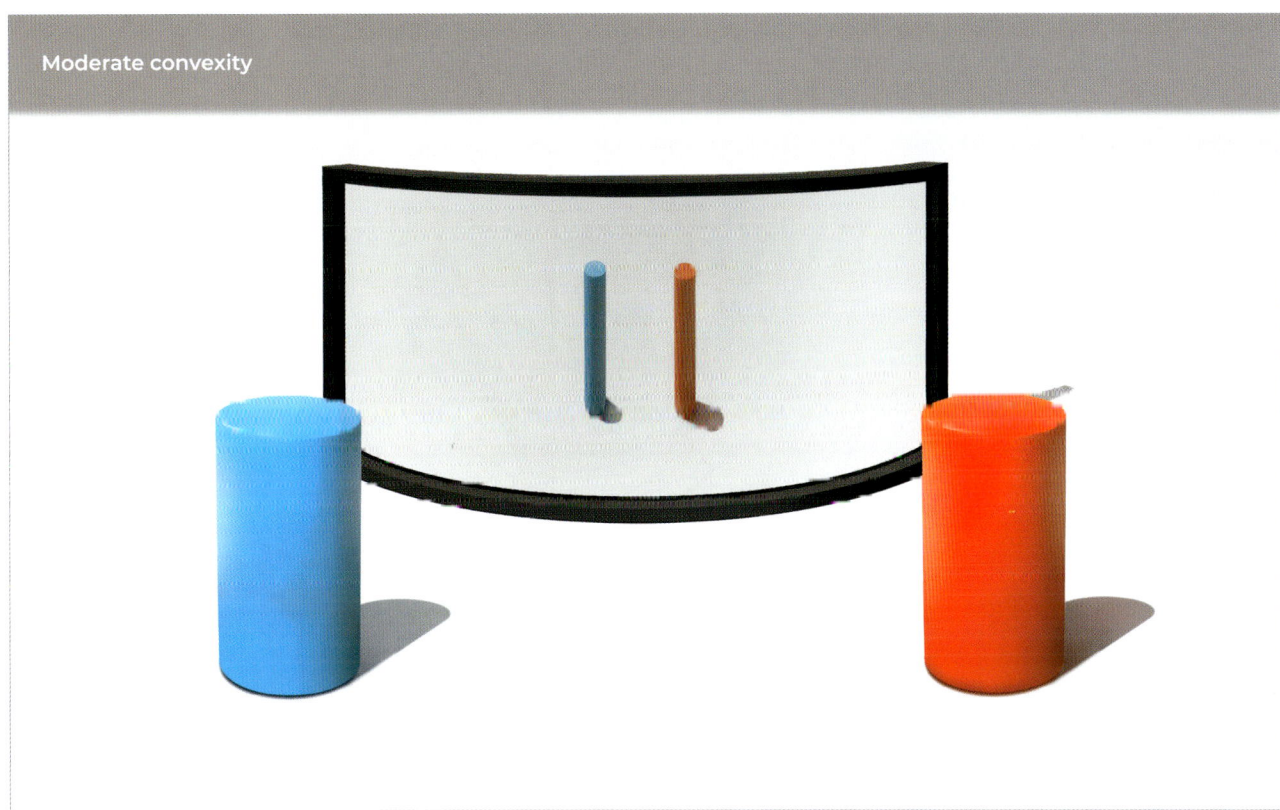

27 As the mirror's surface becomes more convex, the scene becomes even more heavily compressed along the direction of the bend.

Extreme convexity

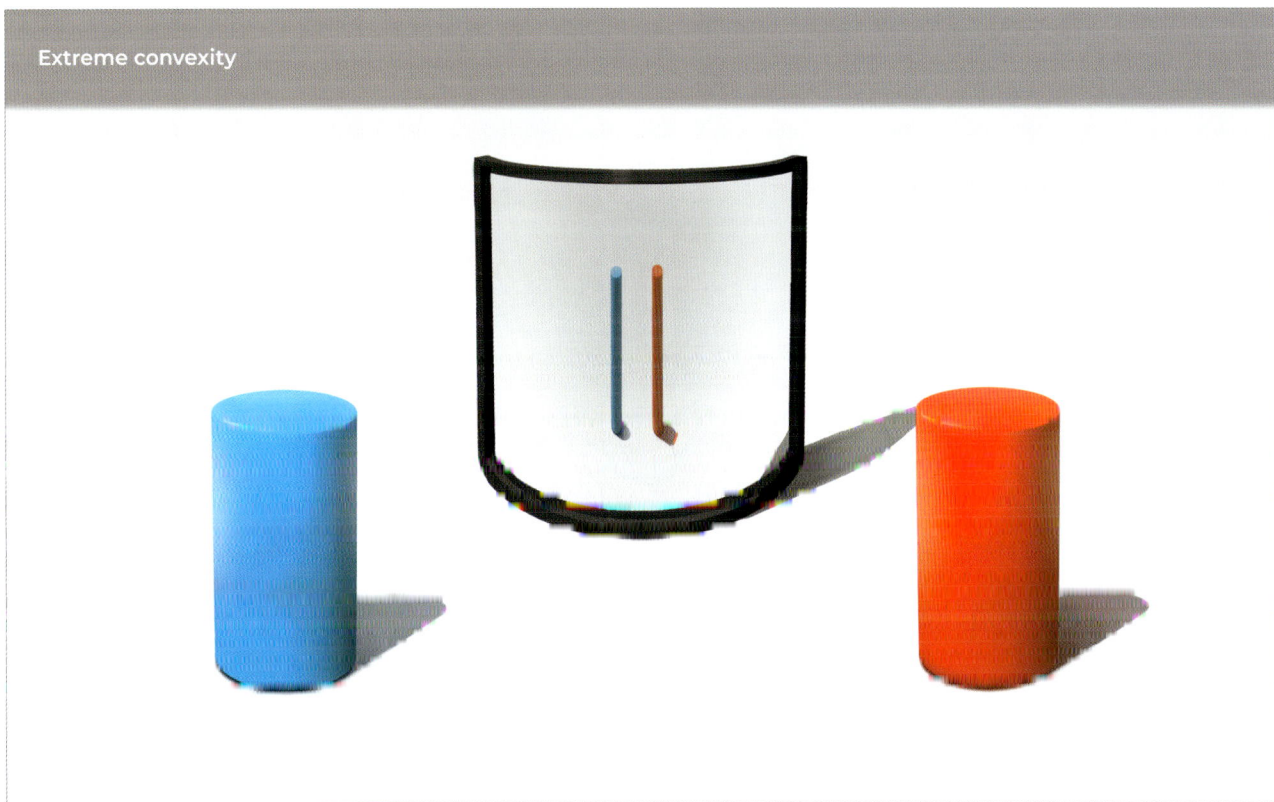

28 On an extremely convex curve, the distortion of the scene is even more profound to squeeze in all the reflected surroundings.

THE CONCAVE MIRROR

Now that we understand the effect of convex mirrors on a reflected image, let's have a look at the effect of the opposite curvature: the concave plane (curving inward, like the inside of a sphere).

If we first take a look at the simplification in image **29**, we can see that this type of curvature has the reverse effect of a convex mirror. Instead of the light rays spreading out, they are collected together. They even meet at a point, which we'll call the "focal point" of the mirror. The more extreme the mirror's curve, the closer this focal point will be to the mirror. There will be a marked difference in the way a subject distorts depending on its position relative to this focal point.

When the subject lies closer to the mirror than the focal point, we can see a distortion that is quite easy to understand in relation to the last type. It's simply a reverse of the previous type of distortion: While convex mirrors squash the image, concave mirrors stretch the image **(30)**.

As our subject approaches the focal point of the mirror, it stretches more and more until it reaches the focal point. When it reaches the focal point, its reflection takes up the entirety of the reflected space **(31)**. Beyond this point the interaction begins to change.

When objects are beyond the focal point, the light rays begin to cross over each other on the way to the subject, causing the reflected image to be flipped. As we can see in image **32**, the blue cylinder on the left now appears on the right of the mirror, and vice versa for the red cylinder. The distortion of the image in this flipped interaction also squashes, in the same way as the convex mirror image, rather than being stretched.

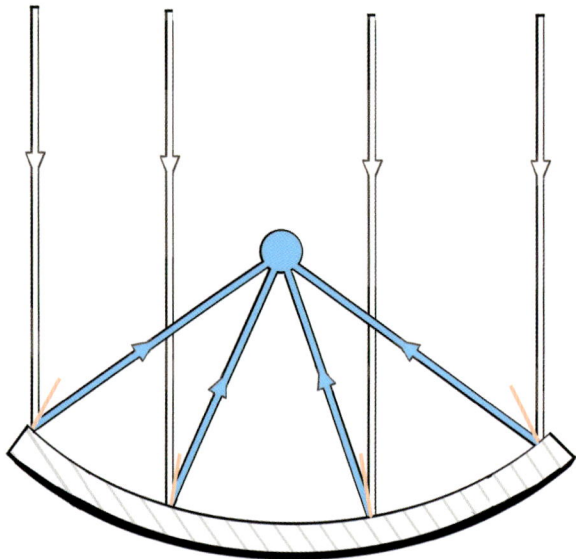

29 A concave mirror causes light rays to converge on a single point called the "focal point."

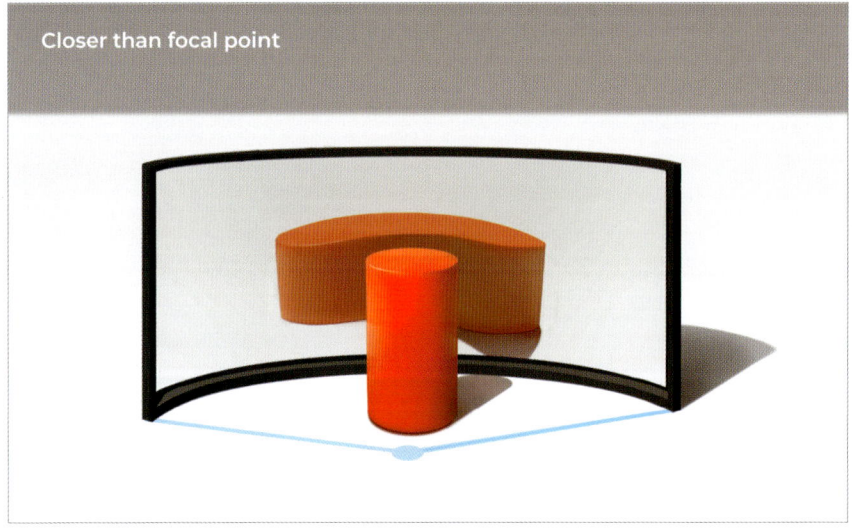

Closer than focal point

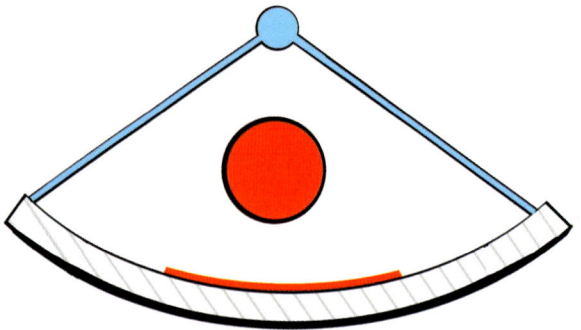

30 When the object is closer to the mirror than the focal point, the image is stretched along the axis of the mirror's concave curve.

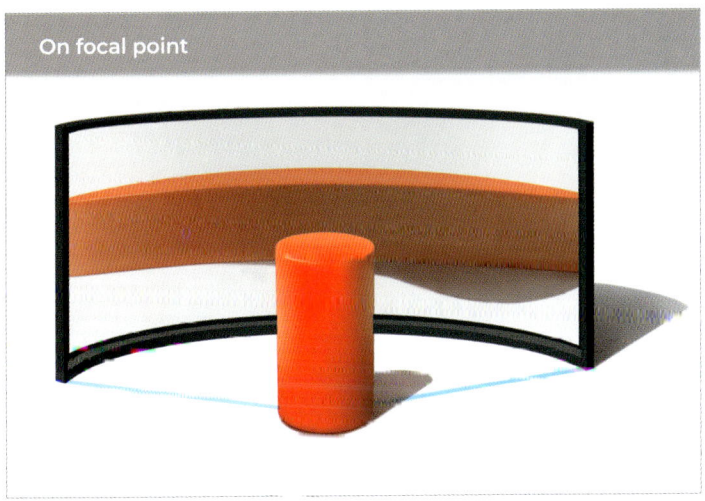

On focal point

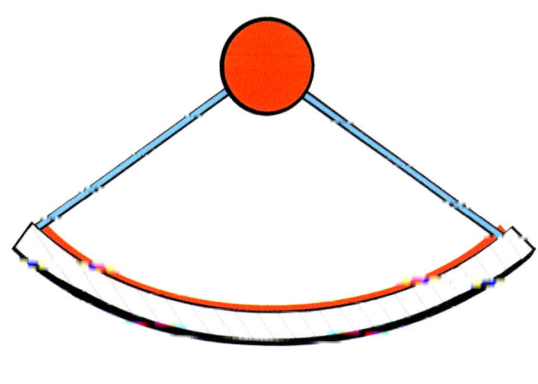

31 When the object is positioned directly on the focal point, the image is stretched along the entire length of the concave mirror.

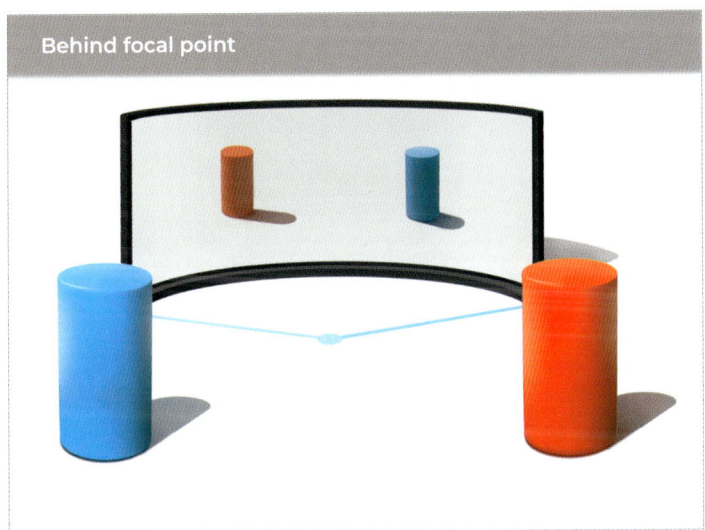

Behind focal point

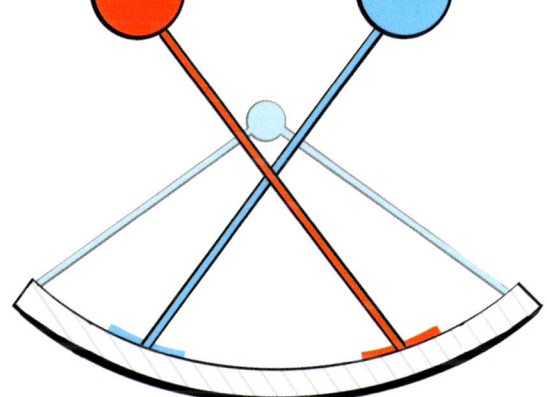

32 When objects are located behind the mirror's focal point, their image is flipped along the axis of the concavity, and squashed rather than stretched.

DISTORTED REFLECTIONS

If you want a way to play with this concept at home, try looking at your reflection in a spoon. See how it changes as you alter the distance. Note how a concave surface stretches your image while a convex surface squashes it. While most mirrors obviously avoid these kinds of distortions, you may also be familiar with these effects in carnival funhouse mirrors!

THE SPECULAR CUBE

Now that we have a full understanding of how to construct mirrors, let's get into how we render our fundamental shapes in a specular form. We'll start, as we did earlier, with the simplest form: the cube.

Now that we fully understand how to construct a flat mirror plane, the basic reflections on a specular cube are just a simple extension of the same method. At its core, a cube is just six planes connected together, so everything that we have learned about planes will apply directly here **(33)**.

However, as you may remember from page 86, the connections between these six planes are never perfectly sharp. If we look closely enough at any cube in real life, there will always be some level of rounding connecting the planes to each other **(34)**. This occurs

between internal planes as well as on external edges **(35)**.

Due to these rounded connections, every reflected object between the two planes will be contained in the bevel between them. Due to the extremity of the bend, this reflected image will be highly compressed, likely appearing as no more than a line of the most contrasting reflected values.

One result of this compression at the edges of the cube is that specular highlights tend to appear on these bevels between planes, since they offer many more opportunities for the light to be reflected. You can see the results of this clearly in image **36**, where there are many different angles where the edges of the cubes reflect the light, but only one angle where the main planar faces reflect it.

As a general rule for all objects, highlights tend to occur at the meeting of two planes. This rule will be incredibly helpful for us when we work from life or with more complex subjects, and will enable us to add more believability and depth to our forms.

This applies not just to basic geometry, but more complex, organic subjects. As we can see in **37**, if we isolate the specular highlights and compare them to the planar construction of the head, all of the highlights occur at the meeting of two planes, both concave and convex. While there are some scenarios where the highlight will cover an entire plane, these highlighted edges are extremely common and are an incredibly useful tool for emphasizing the structure of more complex subjects, whether from life or from imagination.

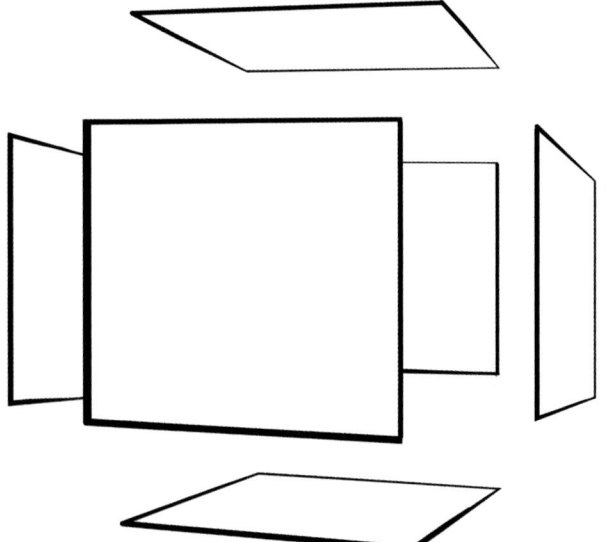

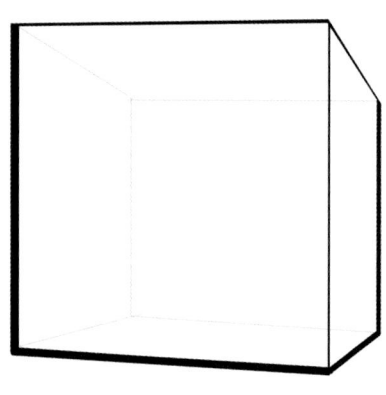

33 A cube consists of six planes to which we can easily apply our knowledge of mirror planes.

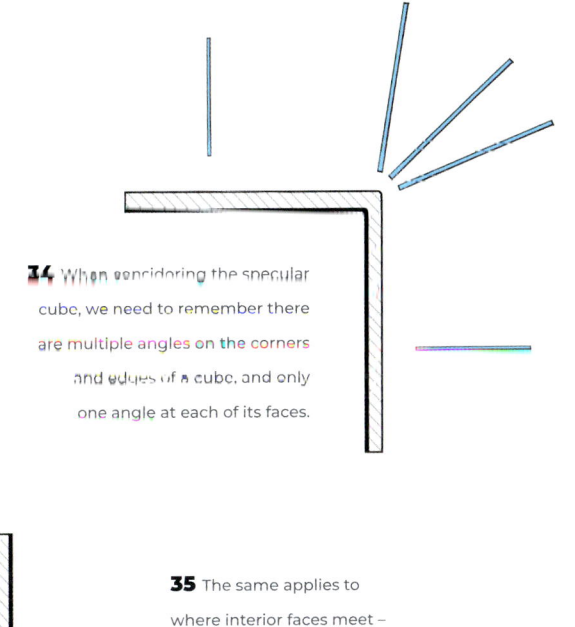

34 When considering the specular cube, we need to remember there are multiple angles on the corners and edges of a cube, and only one angle at each of its faces.

35 The same applies to where interior faces meet – there are actually multiple planes comprising the join.

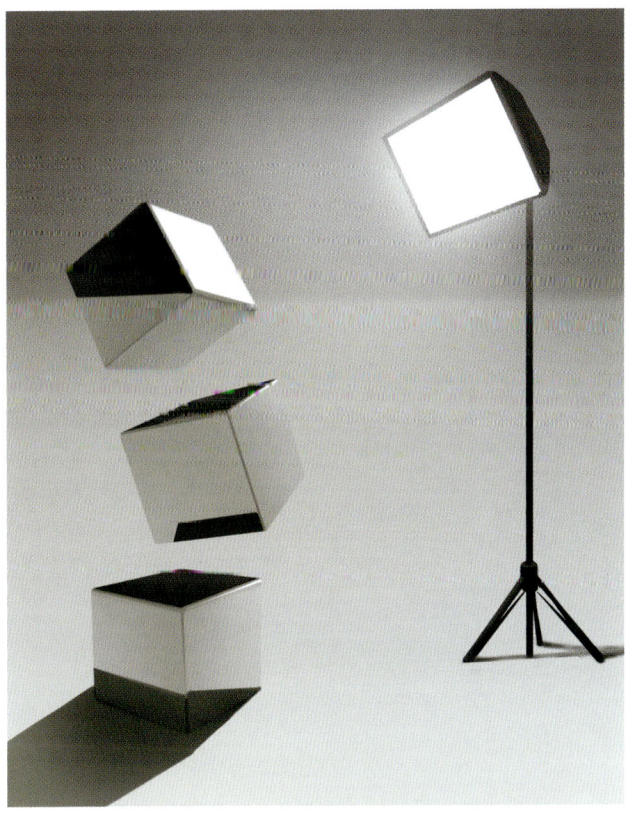

36 The beveled edges of a cube catch the light at multiple angles, while the flat planes are much more limited.

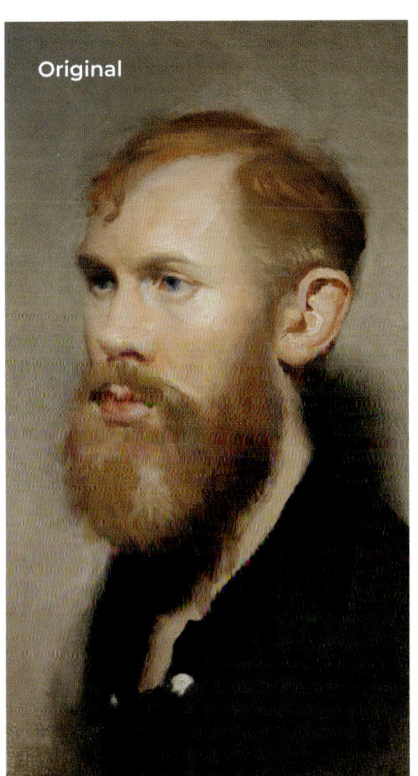

Original

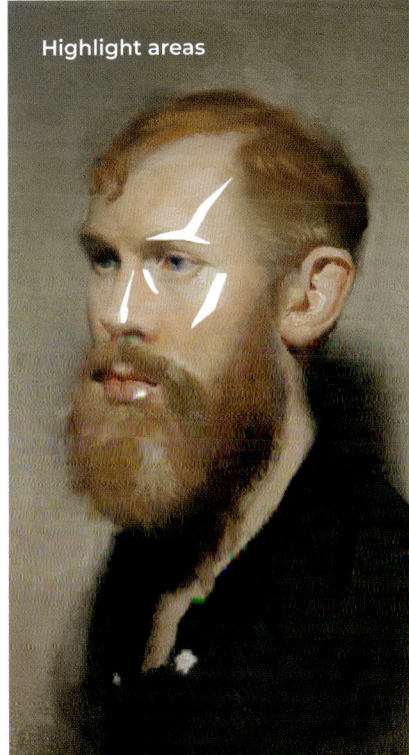

Highlight areas

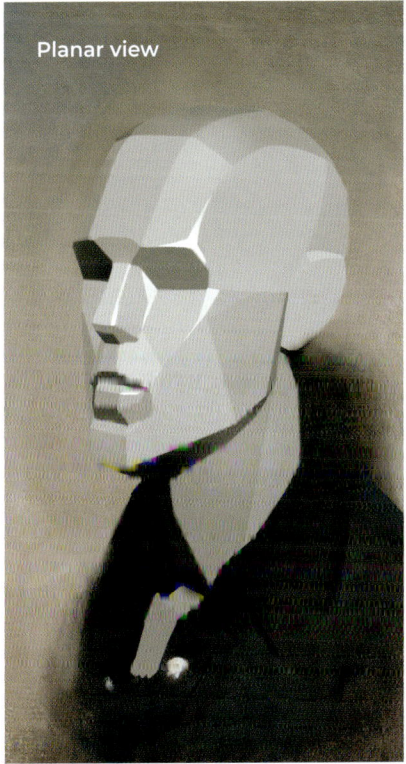

Planar view

37 Even on more complex subjects, highlights tend to occur where two planes meet, as we can see by simplifying this portrait into a planar model.

Based on analysis and principles developed by Devin Korwin for his eBook Creative Fundamentals.

SPECULAR ESSENTIALS TO REMEMBER

Before attempting to render a basic specular cube, let's remind ourselves of a few simple specular rules.

The first is that specular reflections will always be entirely defined by the environment, so it will always be incredibly important that we have a clear sense of the object's surroundings. It can be useful to draw a zoomed-out version of the environment first, so you can plan it in advance and clearly place the major elements in your mind **(38)**. Eventually you won't need to do this, and will be able to

simply imagine the unseen elements of the environment, but it can be helpful when first learning to render specular subjects.

Secondly, when finding the values of the specular reflection, remember that there is always a level of value drop-off on all reflections, so make sure to darken the colors when placing them on your cube **(39)**. When reflecting a colored surface, this darkening will follow the color's saturation path (see page 41).

While the value drop-off will be significant in most areas of the reflection, the light source will generally be so much brighter

than the surrounding environment that it will be far less affected by this value loss – so for chrome surfaces, we won't see the light source darken. Remember that the brightness of the light source will also appear clipped due to exposure (see page 24).

Thirdly, while you can't cast a shadow onto a reflective object, the object itself will still cast shadows onto other surfaces. This means you still need to construct your shadows properly to place your cubes into the environment. These shadows will also often be reflected by the specular object itself, so don't forget to include them **(40)**.

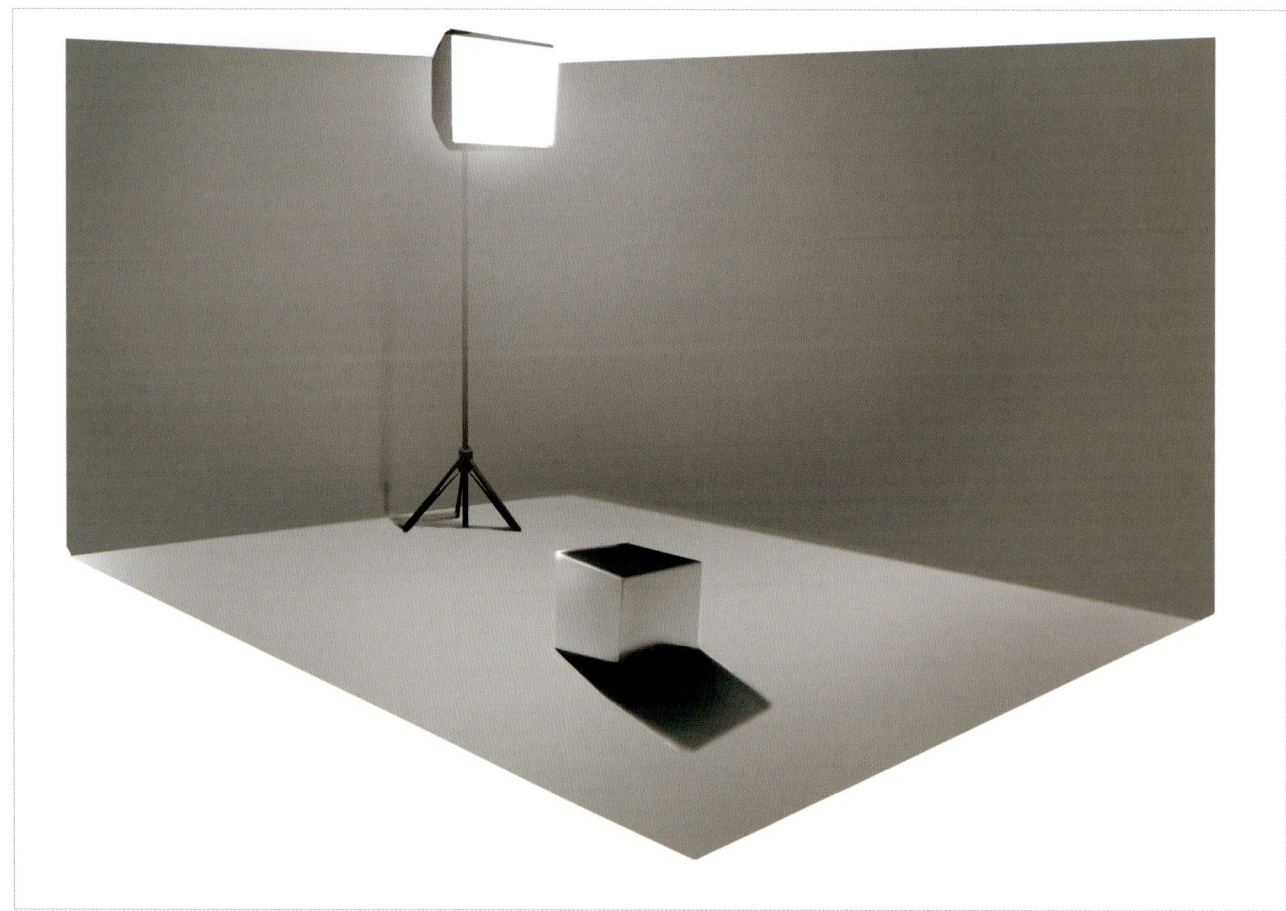

38 Planning out your environment and placing the object in it

can help you visualize how the specular reflections will work.

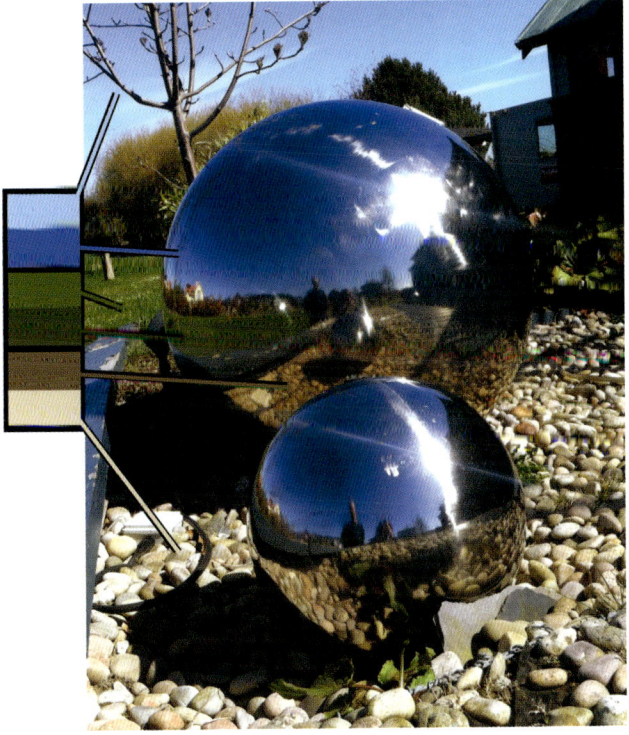

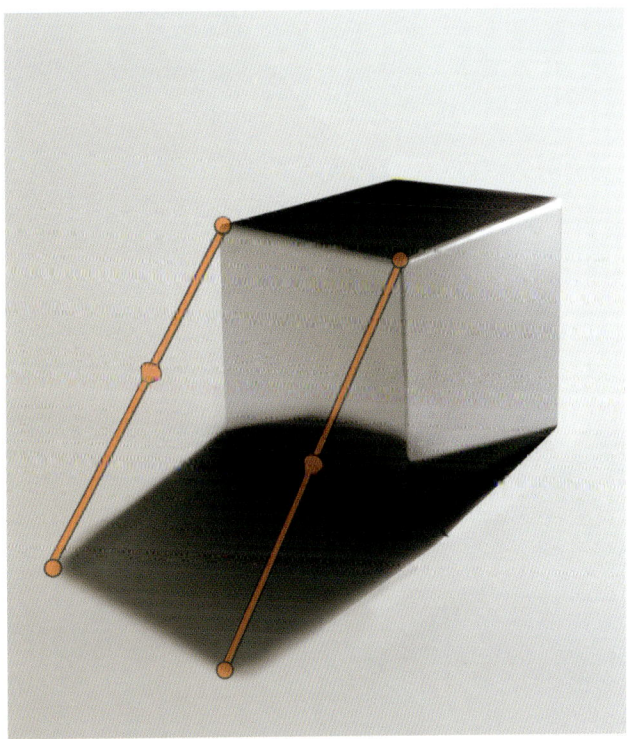

39 When comparing the colors of the real objects to their reflected counterparts, you can see the values on the spheres are much darker.

40 Even though shadows can't be cast onto a specular object, the object itself still casts a shadow that you must account for in the environment and reflected image.

CUBES IN CONTEXT

Now you can practice constructing some of these reflective cubes. Since the way that these are rendered is entirely decided by their surroundings, the environment will always be an important concern, and the best way to practice is to place cubes into existing environments.

You can do this with an environment you have painted from imagination or life if you have them handy. However, the simplest way is to grab a reference photograph or an old master painting and insert your cubes into it. Try to do this in as many environments and with as many different angles as you can, keeping in mind the essential specular rules we just discussed (**41**).

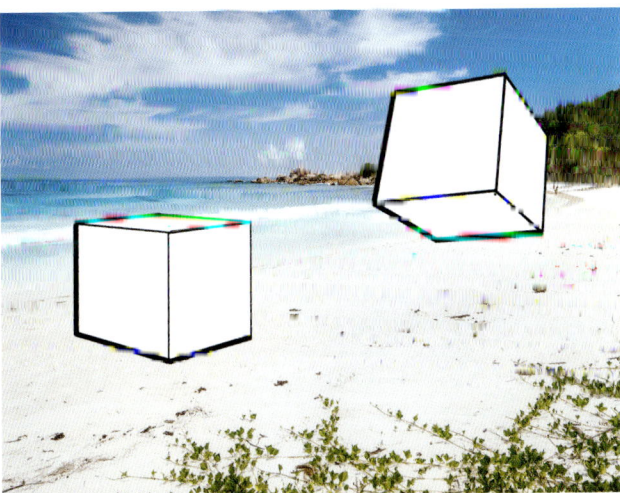

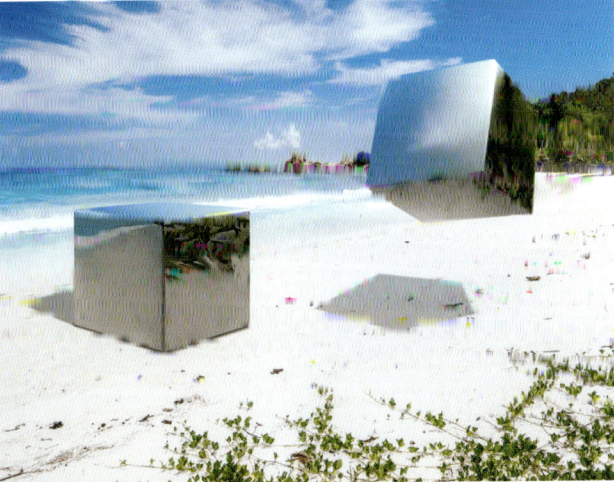

41 Practice rendering specular cubes by dropping them into existing scenery. Photographs and master paintings are perfect for this!

THE SPECULAR SPHERE

Now that we have thoroughly discussed the cube, let's move on to our next fundamental form, the sphere. Everything that we've already learned about specular surfaces is still true – the reflection will still be an image of the surrounding environment, but warped around the surface of the sphere, which curves equally in every direction (42).

If we follow the path of the reflection at the center of the sphere and at the extreme edges, we can see why the reflection spans nearly the entire environment. The farther away the observer, the more of the environment is shown, until we nearly have a 360-degree view of the surrounding environment (43).

It is because of this extremely useful property that VFX (visual effects) artists will often use photographs of chrome spheres as a powerful reference for placing invented objects into a scene. Their reflections are an excellent way to gather all the necessary information about the environment.

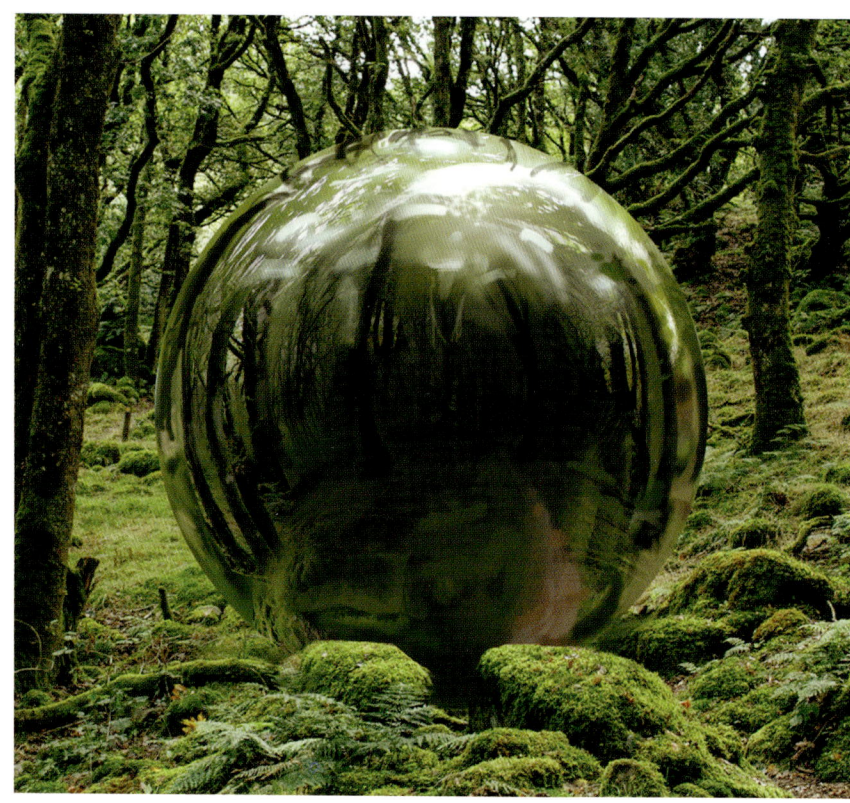

42 A reflection in a specular sphere will show the sphere's surroundings warped around its surface.

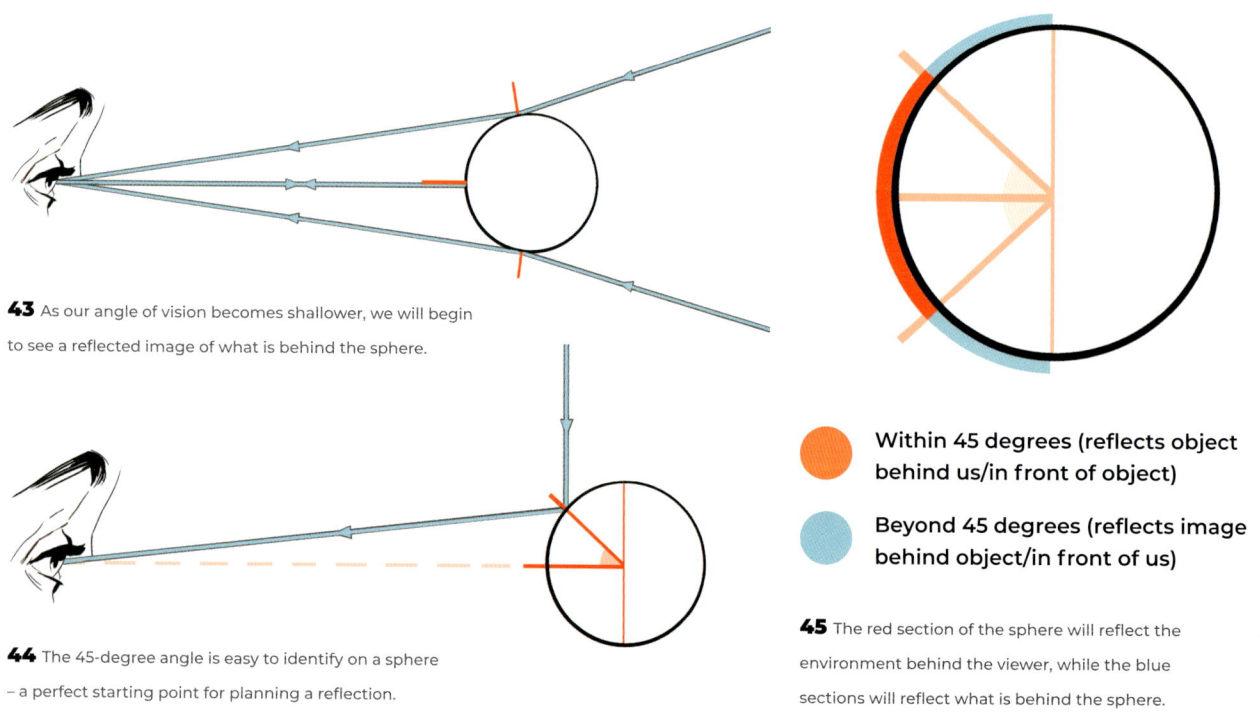

43 As our angle of vision becomes shallower, we will begin to see a reflected image of what is behind the sphere.

44 The 45-degree angle is easy to identify on a sphere – a perfect starting point for planning a reflection.

● Within 45 degrees (reflects object behind us/in front of object)

● Beyond 45 degrees (reflects image behind object/in front of us)

45 The red section of the sphere will reflect the environment behind the viewer, while the blue sections will reflect what is behind the sphere.

Now that we know what we are trying to represent morphed over the sphere, how can we approach it? The distortion that occurs on chrome spheres is an extreme and complex type of perspective ("curvilinear" perspective). How can we begin to orient ourselves and our scene?

The first and most important starting point that we can easily identify is the 45-degree plane. This gives us an extremely useful reference point, as it gives us the perfect horizontal reflection (**44**)

Everything within this 45-degree angle will be reflecting the image behind the viewer, and everything beyond it will reflect an image of what is behind the sphere (**45**). This 45-degree angle will reliably occur three-quarters of the way out from the center, in every direction on the sphere, as represented by the red circle in image **46**.

Students are often surprised at just how far inside the contour this area lands. In image **47** we can see an error often found in student work: The reflection of the red bar is placed directly on the sphere's contour, not considering the rest of the distorted image reflected on the sphere. However, in the correct version, the red bar is reflected about a quarter of the way into the sphere, with

a little of the environment beyond it also shown. Getting this right can go a long way in improving how we render this material.

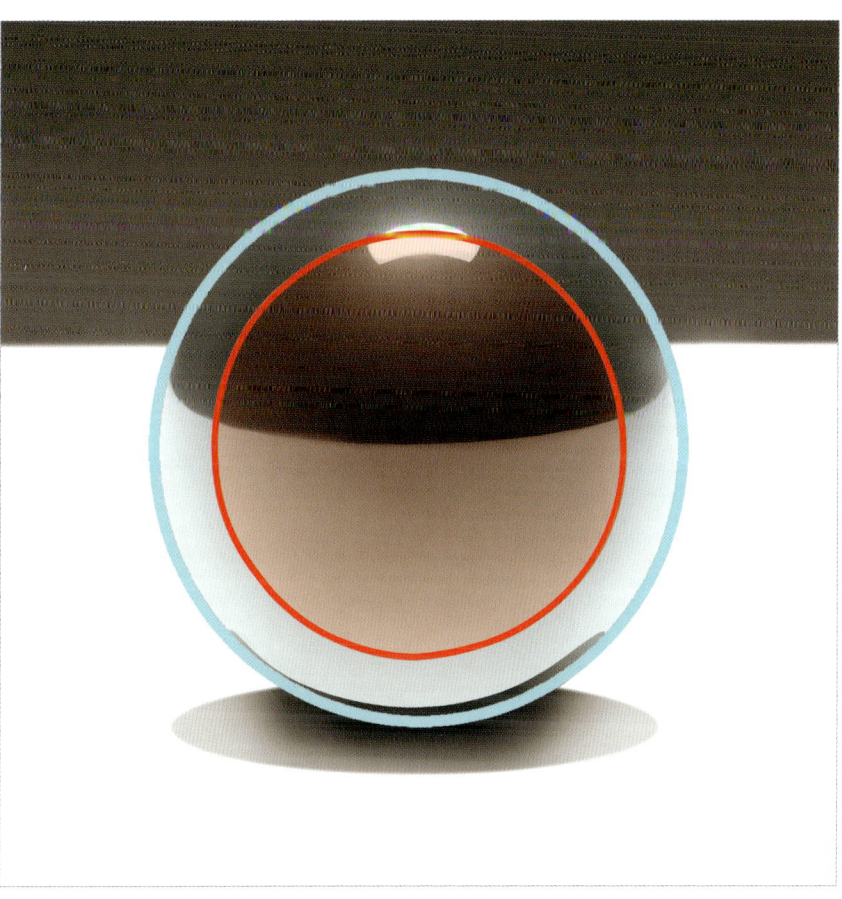

46 The 45-degree area of the sphere occurs about three-quarters of the way out from the center, in every direction.

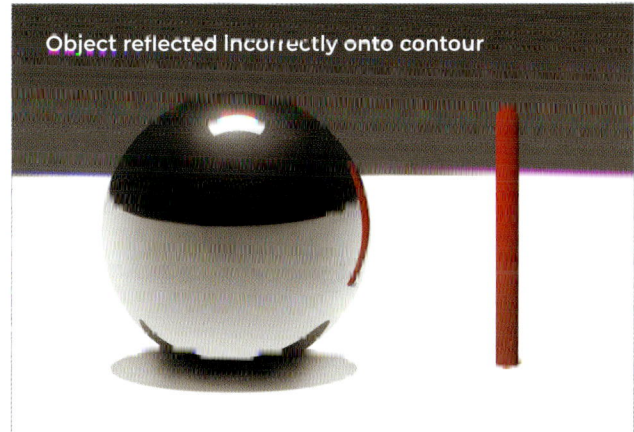
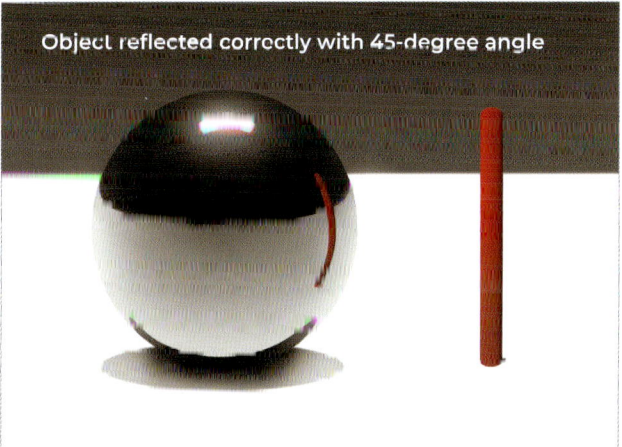

47 A common mistake is reflecting an adjacent object right on the contour of the sphere, not considering the 45-degree angle and the rest of the surrounding environment.

Calculating the correct perspective distortion or the reflection on a specular sphere is a complex problem in curvilinear (often called "fisheye") perspective **(48)**. Achieving a perfect reflection can be a cumbersome process, but thankfully is not often necessary – we don't need the reflections in a painting to be absolutely perfect for them to read clearly as a specular material! With some experience, we can simply eyeball the curvatures for these distortions in our images.

However, it's worth seeing a proper curvilinear perspective grid and trying to use it once or twice for a simple environment, just to get familiar with what these distortions do. Feel free to base yours off the grid in image **49**.

SPHERES IN CONTEXT

Just like with the specular cube, practicing rendering spheres in an environment is the most fundamental exercise to develop our understanding of specular reflection. Try to do this with as many environments as you can – the knowledge gained will be invaluable as we venture into more complex forms. Rendering spheres will be our most important guiding principle for tackling other specular subjects, so it is important to know how to render them well **(50)**.

As mentioned for the cube on page 150, it can be useful to construct some extremely zoomed-out views of the surroundings before getting into the final rendering, to help orient ourselves and develop our ability to visualize the entire scene **(51)**.

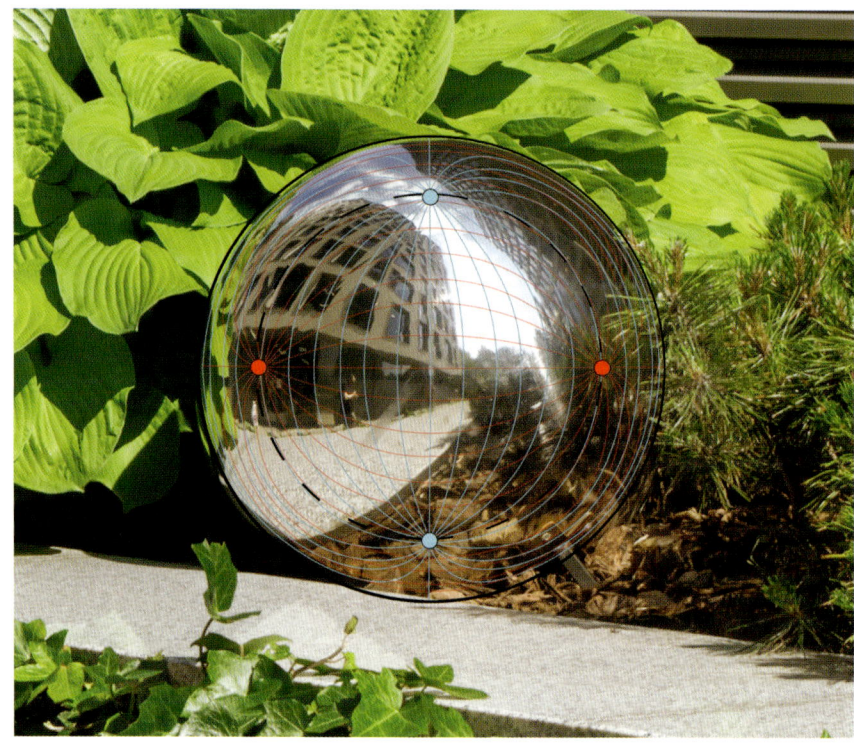

48 Here you can see how the reflected environment bends, showing objects behind the sphere – such as the green leaves – as the image moves beyond the 45-degree area.

Top and bottom vanishing points (45 degrees)

Left and right vanishing points (45 degrees)

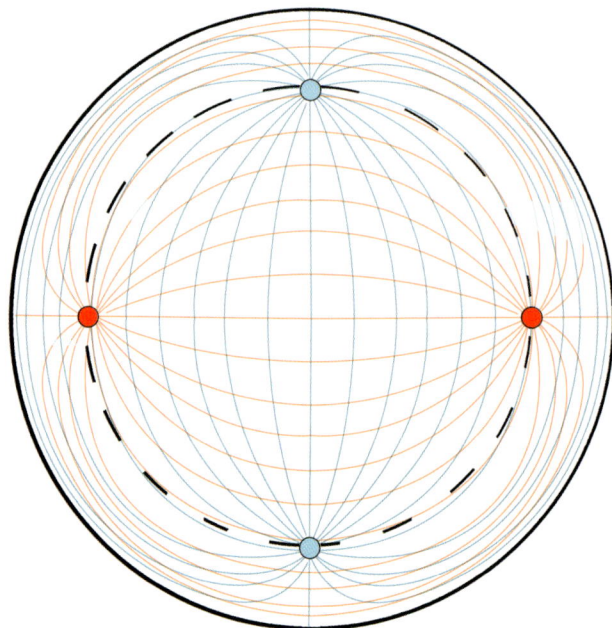

49 Here's the 45-degree curvilinear perspective grid used in the previous image.

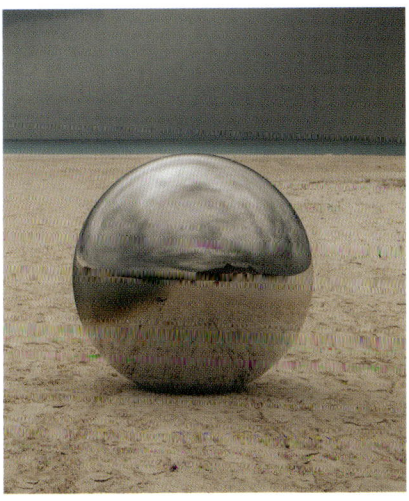
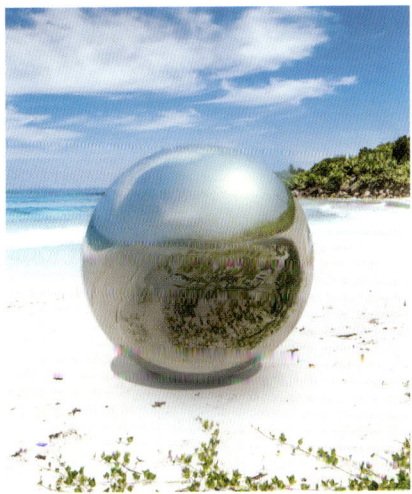
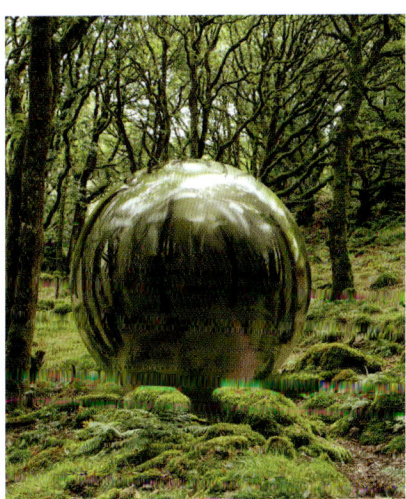

50 Render specular spheres in different environments until you feel comfortable with the process.

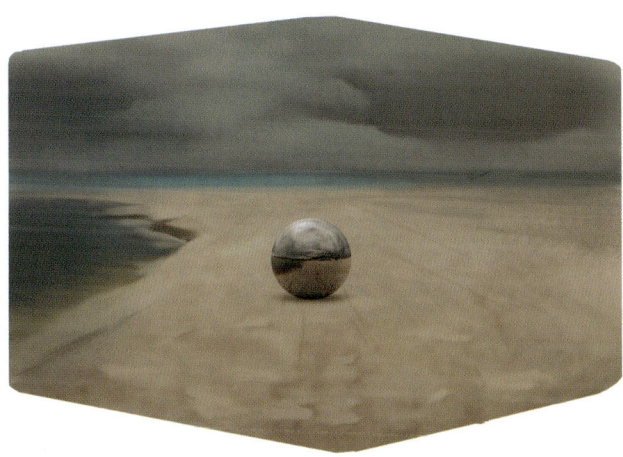

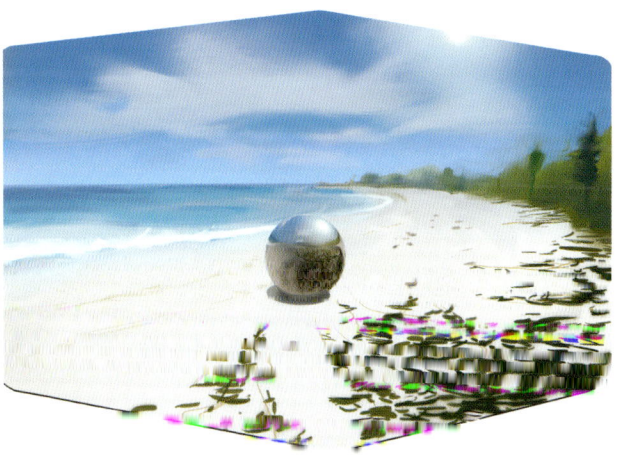

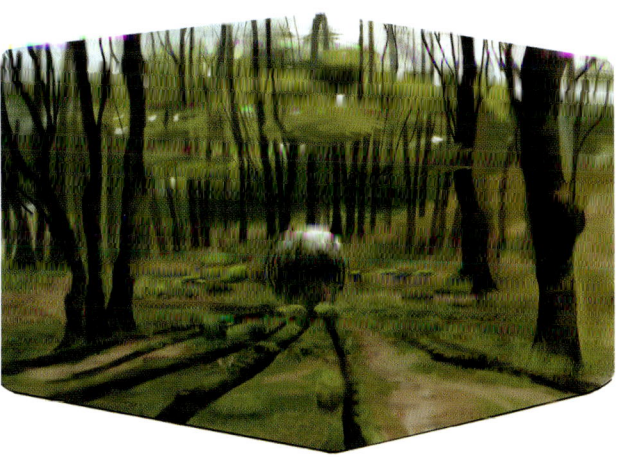

51 Visualizing the layout and lighting of the whole environment can be a valuable aid for planning specular reflection on an object.

COMPLEX SPECULAR FORMS

Now that we have discussed how to render specular spheres and cubes, let's combine those shapes into another fundamental form: the cylinder. Unlike with matte surface shading, where rendering a cylinder is quite predictable, the specular cylinder has fewer consistent features.

THE SPECULAR CYLINDER

From what we have learned so far, we know that the cylinder will show a reflection of the surrounding environment warped around its form. We can also deduce that the image will be distorted and squashed along the curved surface of the cylinder, but will appear flat and clear on the planar ends that are more cube-like (52). The challenge is working out what part of the environment those two axes will reflect.

Luckily there is a simple, intuitive solution to this problem. Since the specular sphere projects an image of almost the entire environment, we can use it as a control for our cylinder's reflections. Based on the angle of the cylinder, we can simply identify the point of the sphere that corresponds with the cylinder's flat plane, and the strip around it that corresponds with the cylinder's curved plane (53). We can then paint an appropriately distorted or undistorted image of the position shown on

the specular sphere. Continuing to use this sphere as a guiding reference, we can paint a cylinder at any angle that we want, keeping them all consistent to the environment (54). In fact, we can use this sphere to orient our

reflections for as many different forms as we like across an image – like with planning matte lighting on page 82, the sphere is our single most useful reference for controlling this type of reflection.

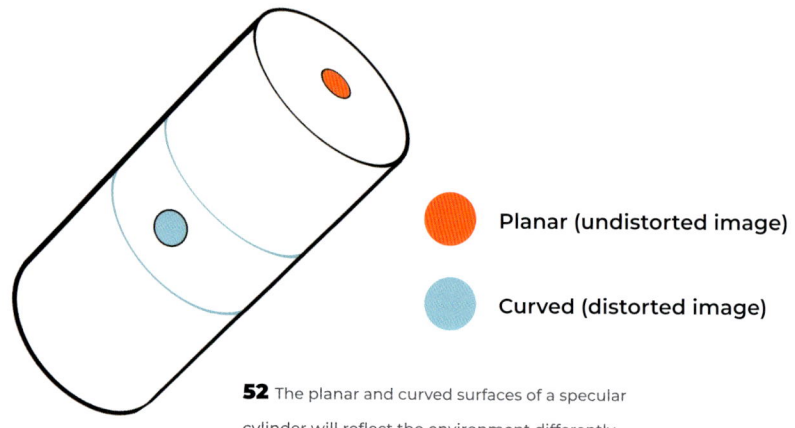

● Planar (undistorted image)

● Curved (distorted image)

52 The planar and curved surfaces of a specular cylinder will reflect the environment differently.

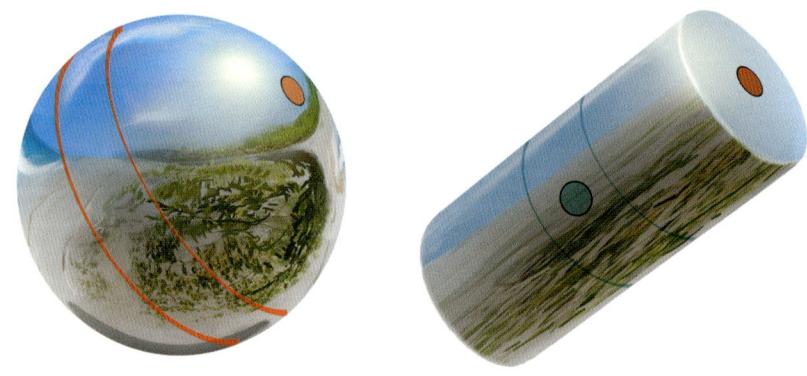

53 The sphere makes its return as a helpful reference shape – this time for locating which areas of the environment the specular cylinder will show.

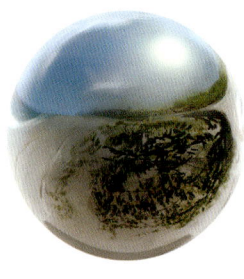
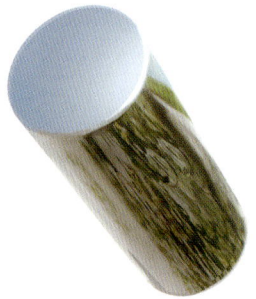
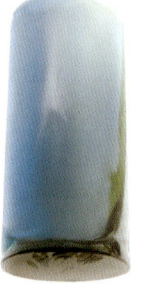
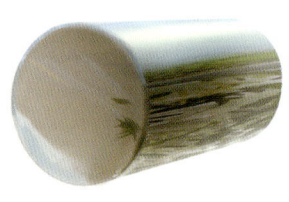

54 Based on the reference provided by our specular sphere, we can render cylinders at any angle while staying true to the surroundings.

SPECULAR DOODLE FORM

As we found on page 88, it is hugely useful to render "doodle" forms to practice our newly learned lighting logic. As with the previous specular shapes, this is best done using an existing environment – whether invented, observed, or photographed – so that you can try to make the specular object sit believably in the scene. Try this out for yourself by painting a random silhouette and making it specular **(55a–d)**.

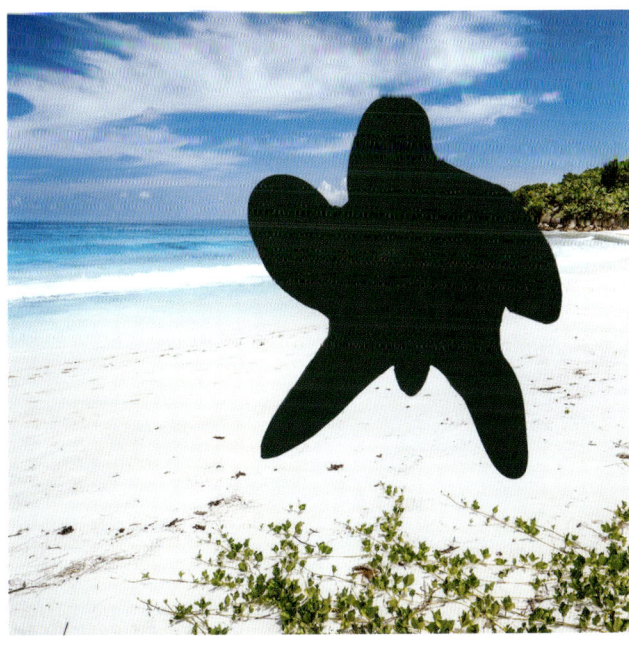

55a Draw a shape. There are no wrong answers here – it can be a specific design or an abstract shape.

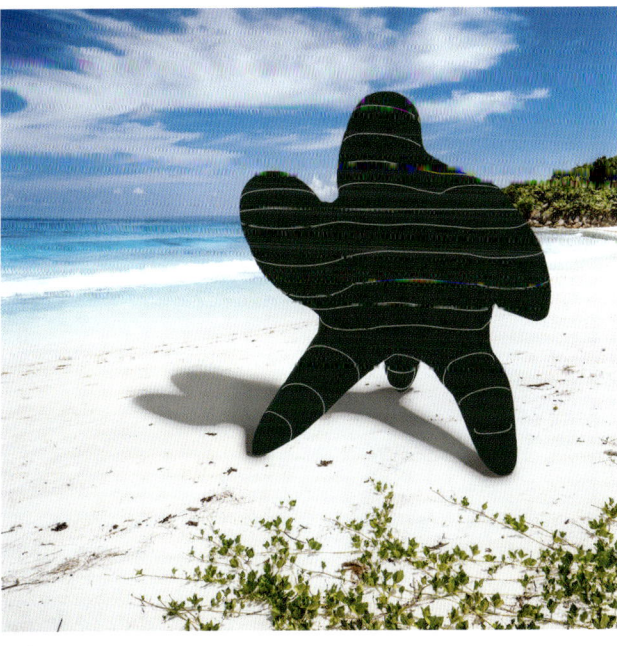

55b Similar to our previous doodle exercises, try to add a 3D "wireframe" structure to the doodle to solidify its form in your mind. This is also a good time to add a cast shadow to help ground the object in the scene.

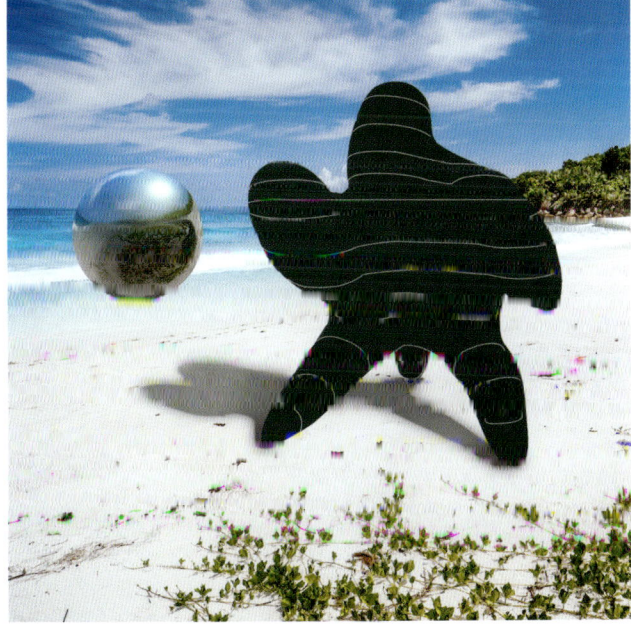

55c Add and render a specular sphere for the scene. This will serve as a reference for the rest of our specular rendering.

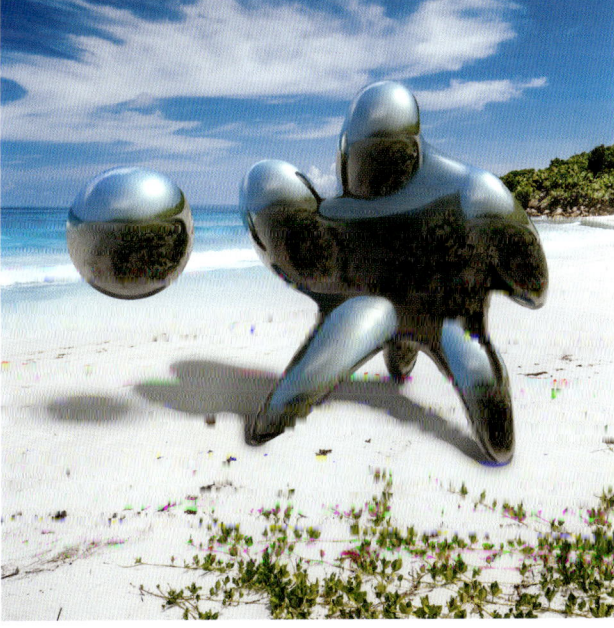

55d Render the doodle form based on the information provided by the sphere. Find each plane's corresponding position on the sphere and then distort that image depending on the doodle form's surface.

SPECULAR COLOR CHANGES

While a specular reflection will always be an image of its surroundings, and this will always be the strongest determiner of the color observed by us, some specular surfaces can also have different-colored reflections and selectively reflect or absorb different wavelengths.

One of the most commonly seen, familiar examples of this kind of colored reflection occurs in gold. The reflections of a gold object are tinted yellow because the material selectively absorbs blue light, reflecting red and green (which additively mix to yellow), as we learned about on page 32. When this happens, what we observe on the specular surface is the reflection of the surroundings mixed subtractively with the local color of the specular object.

The easiest way that we can recreate this digitally is by applying a Multiply layer with the desired color over the specular surface, giving us a convincing effect for any color we want **(56)**. The colors in these reflections will generally be a reflected image filtered down a certain saturation path, but the highlight will usually be so bright that it breaks through this. It's often best to add the highlight back in after applying this general color filter.

However, this local color will rarely totally cancel out all other color shifts. If we apply these color shifts to something specular outdoors, where a greater variety of colors can be observed, you can see that many of the warm-cool relationships survive this color filtering. The opposing color will always be the most affected by this selective absorption. In image **57**, we can see how strongly the blue sky reflection is affected if we change the specular object to gold.

VALUE CHANGES

Alongside this selective color absorption and reflection, specular surfaces can also simply be more or less effective at reflecting light in general. Similar to how white objects are defined by being the most efficient reflectors of the maximum amount of light, a perfect specular reflector reflects light with maximum efficiency.

However, "perfect" is theoretical – no specular surface is a perfect reflector in reality, and surfaces vary greatly in their reflective efficiency **(58)**.

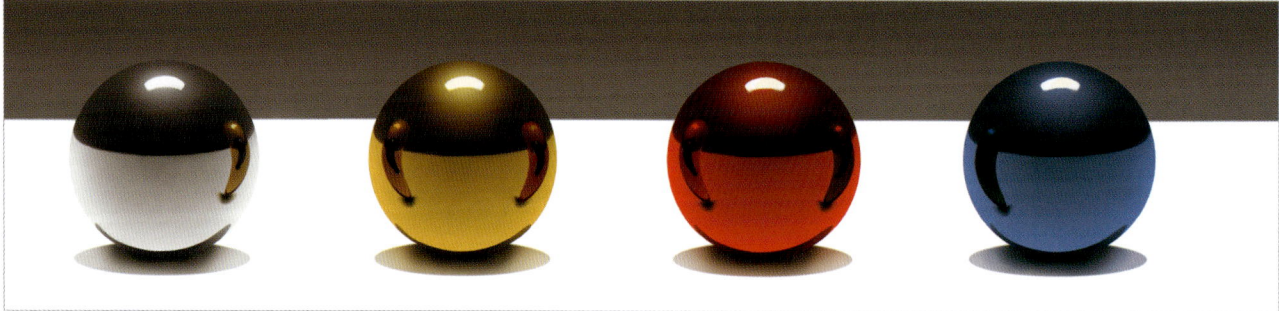

56 When working digitally, we can use Multiply layers to apply any local color to a specular object, to believable effect.

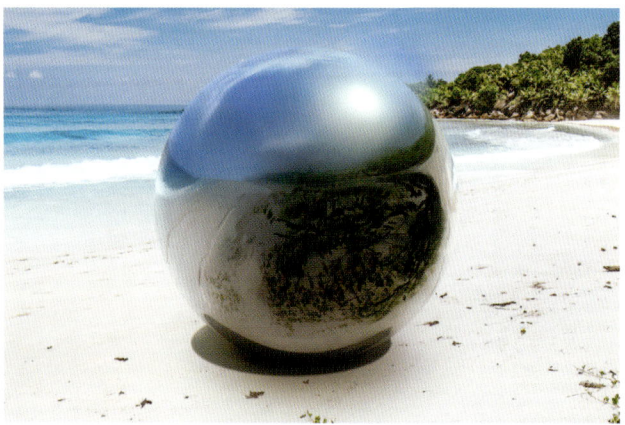
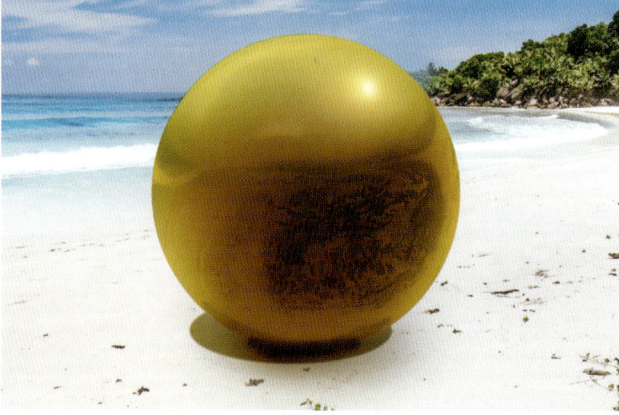

57 The reflected blues change drastically when the object's local color is altered to an opposing gold, but the relative color and value relationships of the reflected scene are still quite clear and legible.

Due to the elements of exposure that we discussed on page 24, light sources are much brighter than we can represent with our materials – they are orders of magnitude brighter than the other elements in the scene. The darker elements of the reflected environment will appear to darken much faster than the light sources. In reality, they darken at the same rate, but the light source is so much brighter than everything else that it takes us a while to notice a change. Eventually the only reflections bright enough to still be seen on the less efficient reflectors are of the light source itself (**58**). This low level of specular reflection is what most matte objects display, since matte objects diffusely reflect most of the light that strikes them. We can see this in image **59**, revisiting the matte spheres from the previous chapter. The spheres' specular and matte reflections have been isolated through the use of polarizing filters, and in the specular isolation, only the highlight is clearly reflected.

As the matte-surface local color of the object darkens, we see the specular information comes into more prominence. This isn't necessarily a result of the specular reflection actually increasing, but more a matter of contrast. On a darker object, there is less light drowning out the specular information, and therefore the specular highlight stands out more.

This leads us to a final, useful rule to follow whenever we combine these two types of shading: As a form lightens, it relies more on matte surface shading information, and as it darkens, it relies more on specular information. You can see these effects exhibited clearly in image **60**.

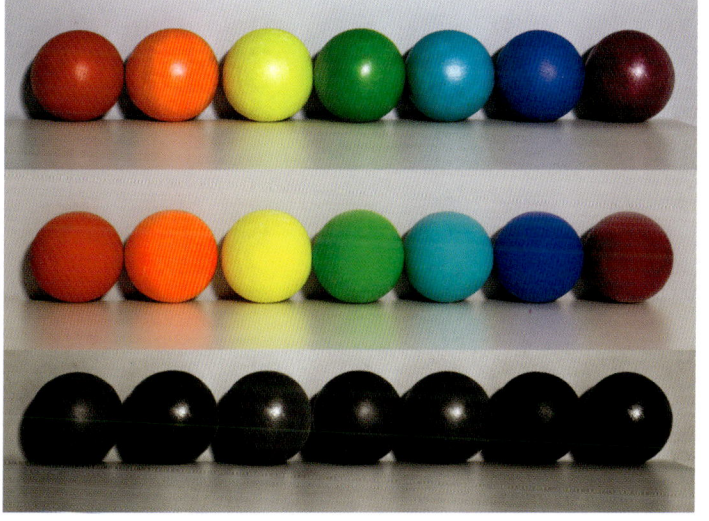

Original

Matte isolated

Specular isolated

Perfect reflection

Imperfect reflection

58 A perfect reflection has clear detail throughout, and bright, chromatic colors. An imperfect reflection has less detail, more contrast, and colors that are less chromatic

59 Even these matte spheres display a level of specular reflection, which becomes more apparent when isolated with a polarizing filter.

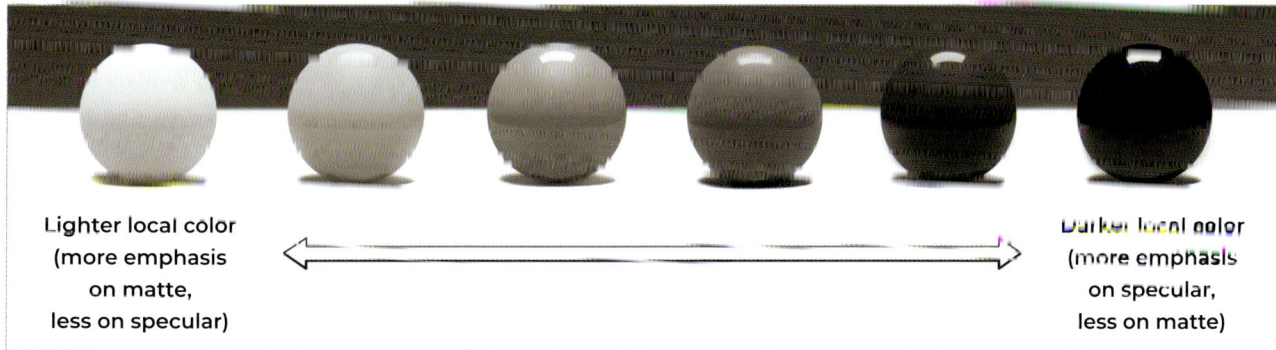

Lighter local color (more emphasis on matte, less on specular)

Darker local color (more emphasis on specular, less on matte)

60 When communicating a form using specular and matte shading, remember that a lighter-colored object will rely more on matte information, and a dark-colored object will rely more on specular information.

LIGHT:
TRANSPARENCY

Now that we have learned how light can be absorbed by a matte surface and reflected by a specular surface, we can turn our attention to the phenomenon of transparency: light being refracted through a clear material. Combining knowledge of matte, specular, and transparent materials will enable you to confidently tackle lighting any subject you encounter.

TRANSPARENT MATERIALS

Transparent materials, at face value, have an extremely simple logic in their basic form. With a perfectly transparent material, all that we see is what's on the other side of the material. However, no material is perfectly transparent – in reality, there will always be some loss of light in every material.

We can examine the effect of this loss of light by layering transparent sheets on top of each other in front of a subject **(01)**. Every transparent material, when made thick enough, will become an opaque material. Because of this, as we layer more and more

material in front of the subject, the colors in the transmitted image become closer and closer to the local color of the transparent material, until we can no longer see the subject on the other side **(02)**.

This leads us to our first strategy for communicating depth in transparent materials: The thicker the material we are observing a subject through, the lower the subject's contrast with the local color of the material. While we are primarily seeing a loss of contrast, it's important to remember that every material will lose some light and therefore be slightly darker, too.

One of the most common transparent materials we will find ourselves painting is glass, so let's take a look at those basic ideas at play in this material. As you can see in images **03** and **04**, the light rays at the edge of the glass have to pass through more material in order to get to our eyes, and therefore they darken somewhat.

This loss of light and contrast due to thickness is often the simplest and most direct way for us to communicate that a material is transparent. As you can see in the painted glass in image **05**, it can be effective even on its own.

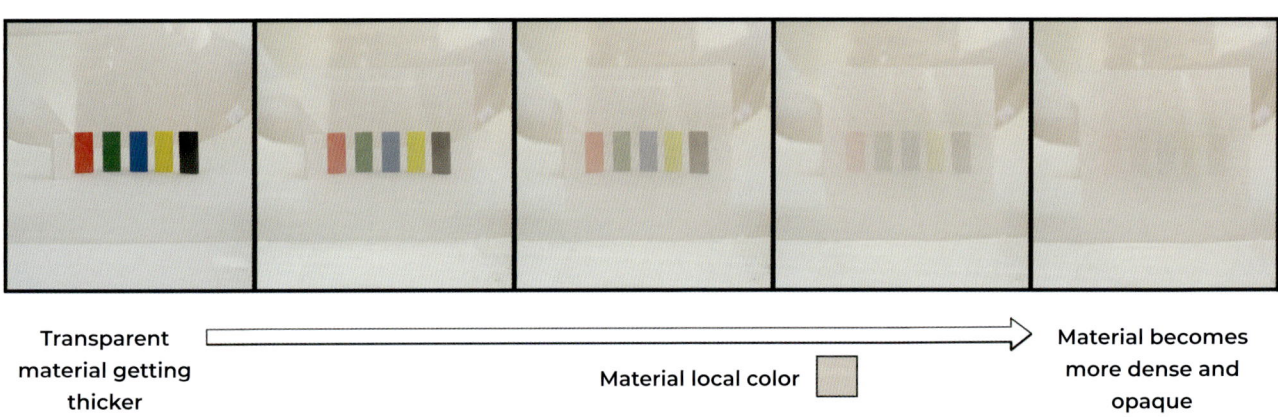

Transparent material getting thicker — Material local color — Material becomes more dense and opaque

01 As the layers of transparent material increase, the scene's contrast becomes lower. The colors mix subtractively until they converge into the local color of the now-opaque material.

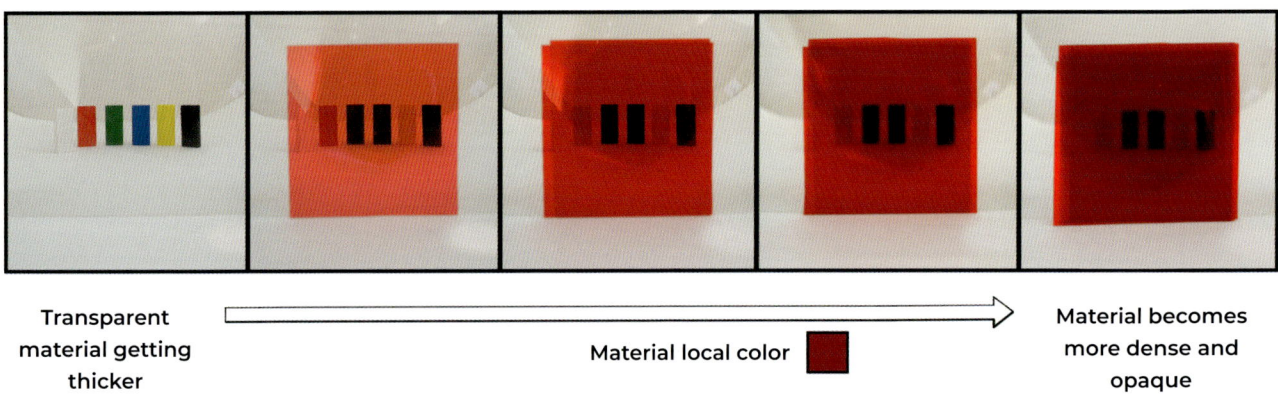

Transparent material getting thicker — Material local color — Material becomes more dense and opaque

02 The same principles apply to transparent materials of any local color.

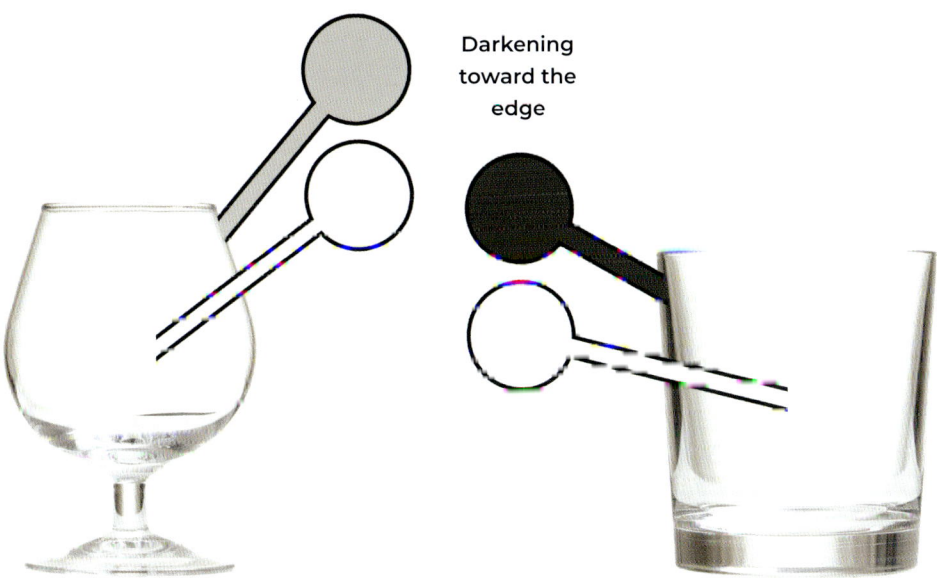

Darkening toward the edge

03 These glasses appear lighter in the middle but dark at the outer edges. Grab a glass in real life and see if you can observe the effect!

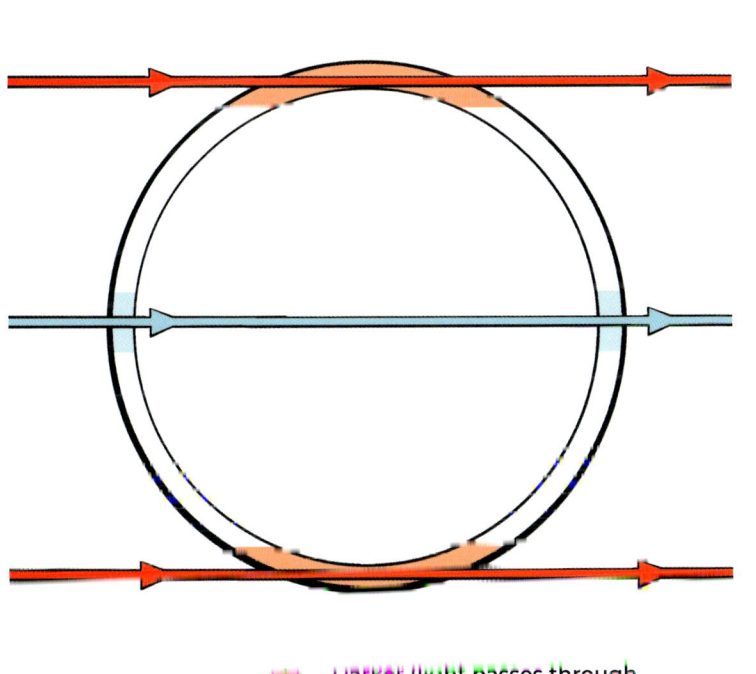

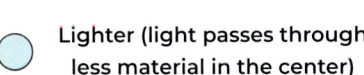
Darker (light passes through more material at the edges)

Lighter (light passes through less material in the center)

04 Light passes through more material on the outsides of the glass than in the center, which causes the edges to appear darker.

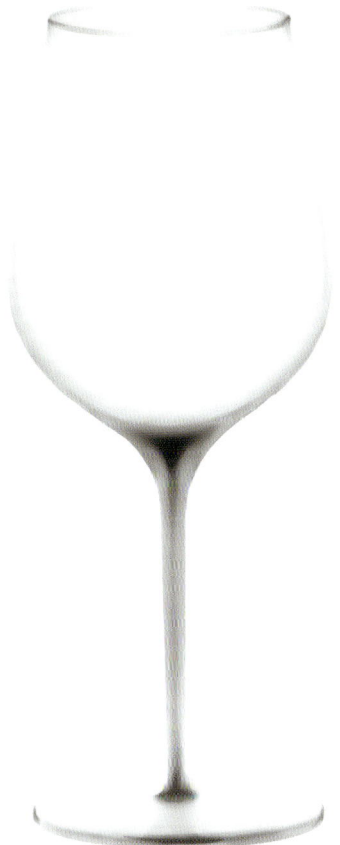

05 Using this edge-darkening effect alone, it's possible to paint a convincingly transparent glass object.

ATMOSPHERIC PERSPECTIVE

One important fact not commonly realized by students is that the air that surrounds us is actually a transparent medium as well. Whenever we observe anything, we perceive it through this transparency. The more air that lies between us and an object, the more we see a loss of contrast.

As painters, this means that loss of contrast is our single most important tool for communicating depth. It is also a very flexible tool for us to use creatively in our work – air could conceivably be thicker anywhere in the environment, or an atmospheric fog could roll into a scene.

In image **06**, the two spheres painted with the same contrast appear similar in distance, even though one is behind the other. In comparison, when we decrease the contrast as one sphere disappears behind the other, and increase the contrast in the foreground, we see a much stronger clarity of depth.

SCATTERING LIGHT

Another interesting aspect of atmospheric perspective is that it's inherently cool. This is because as sunlight enters the atmosphere, the blue (high-energy) light is scattered out and spread over the sky **(07)**. It is common to see sunlight represented as yellow or orange, and this is generally true on Earth. However, sunlight seen from space is entirely white. It only appears yellow to us because of this scattering of blue wavelengths (known as "Rayleigh scattering").

You have probably observed in real life that as the sun sets, it appears progressively warmer and warmer to us. This is because its light enters the atmosphere at a shallower angle, so has to move through more of it, thus scattering out even more of the blue light. You can revisit page 122 to see more examples of this.

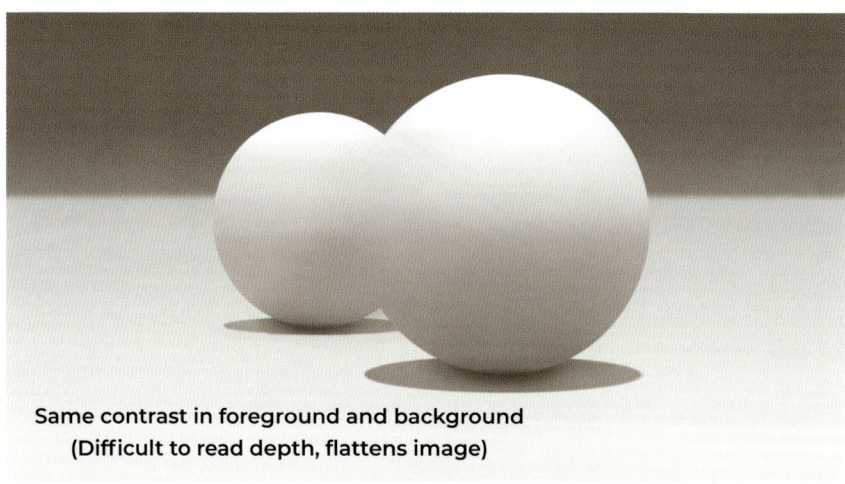

Same contrast in foreground and background
(Difficult to read depth, flattens image)

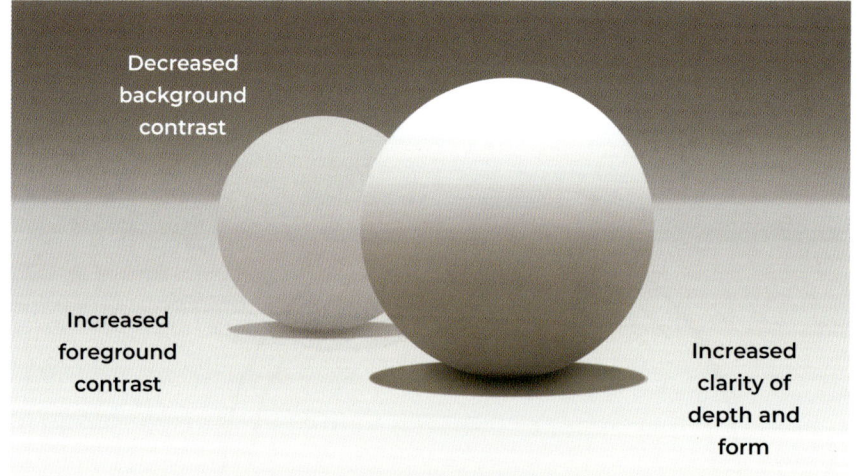

Decreased background contrast

Increased foreground contrast

Increased clarity of depth and form

06 Lowering the contrast of the background sphere makes the image look more three-dimensional and much easier to understand.

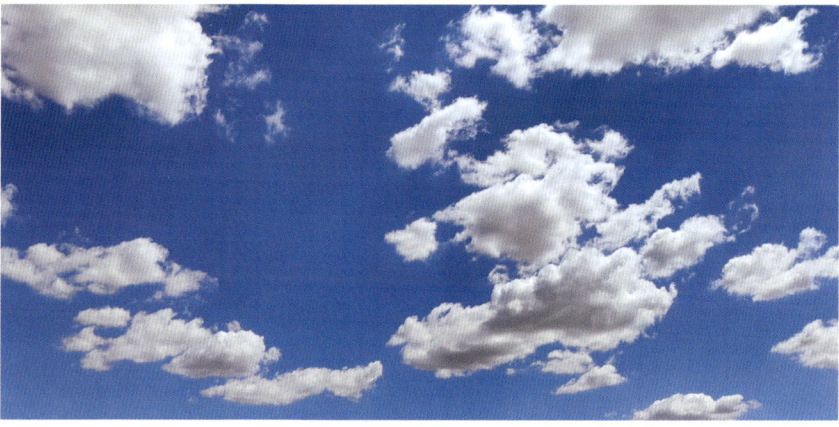

07 The sky appears blue to us due to the scattering of blue wavelengths throughout the planet's atmosphere. This effect also makes white sunlight appear yellow to us.

So, due to our inherently blue atmosphere, cool colors will generally recede and warm colors will advance. The color strips in image **08** are all the same value, but the blue strips appear slightly "behind" the red strips due to this effect. This definitely doesn't mean you can never use warm colors in your backgrounds – as we covered on page 45, all color is primarily about relationships, so this "coolness" is relative and there are many ways in which it can be represented.

We can see atmospheric perspective put to wonderful effect by Djamila Knopf in image **09**. You can clearly see how the distant background is cooler in hue, as well as much lower in contrast with its surroundings (in this case, getting lighter in value), creating an impressive sense of depth and scale. When we view the image in black and white, we can see just how much the value contrast of the scene is controlled alongside this.

As always, value is the most important element of a successful image, and this limiting of contrast in the distance is essential to this visual depth.

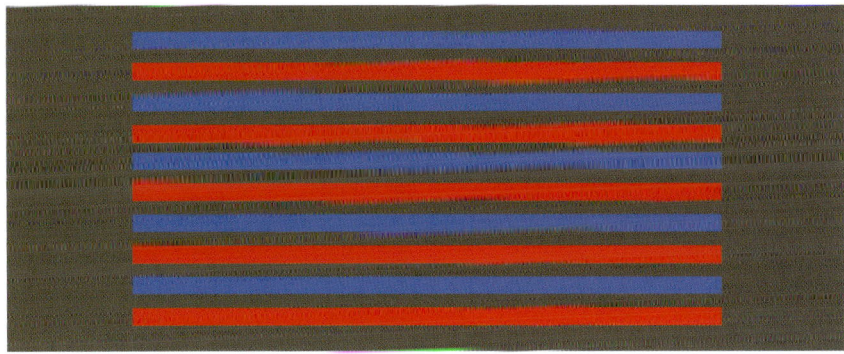

08 When considering our cool atmosphere and warm sunlight, remember that cool colors will "recede" visually when compared to warmer ones. Which of these colors stands out to you?

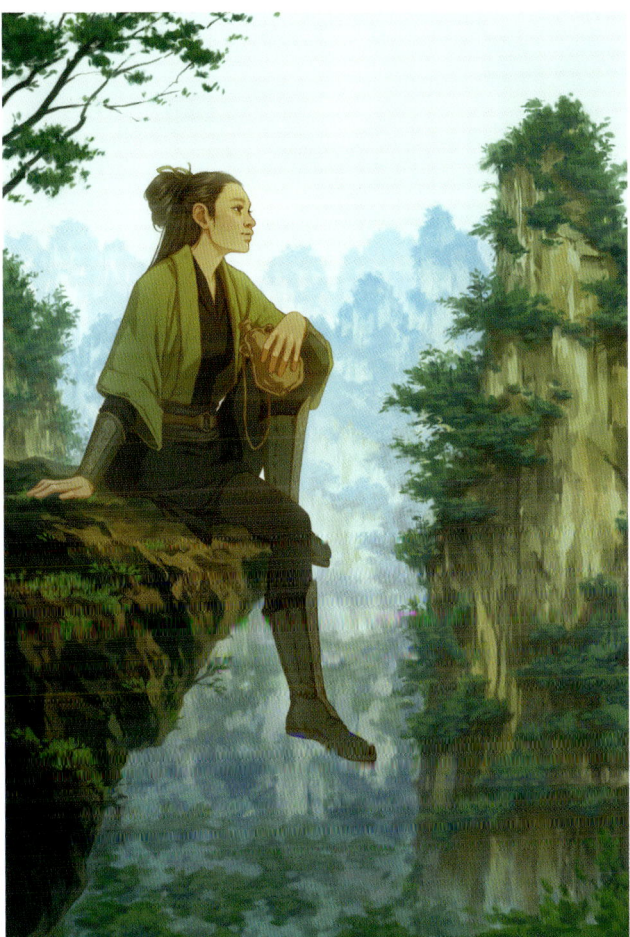

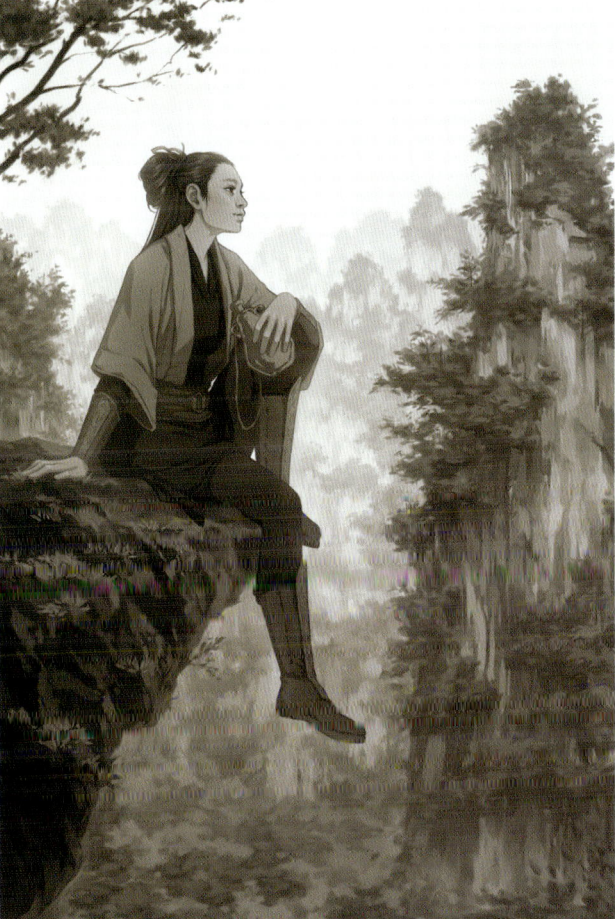

09 In this illustration, you can clearly see how the distant background is cooler in hue, as well as much lighter in value.

UNDERSTANDING REFRACTION

When dealing with transparent materials, it's essential to know about refraction. Refraction is the bending of light that occurs when it moves through materials of varying density, and the distortions that it causes are at play in all transparent materials to some degree. In image **10** we can see how a light beam bends as it moves from the air through the glass block.

The easiest way to understand the mechanism behind refraction is to take the simplified analogy of a car driving from a smooth road directly onto mud. As you can imagine, the car can move at a faster pace on the uniform road than on the rougher mud. If this car drives at an angle from the smooth road to the mud, one of its wheels will hit the mud before the other, causing the two wheels to move at different rates. The faster-moving wheel will swing the car around and change its direction **(11)**.

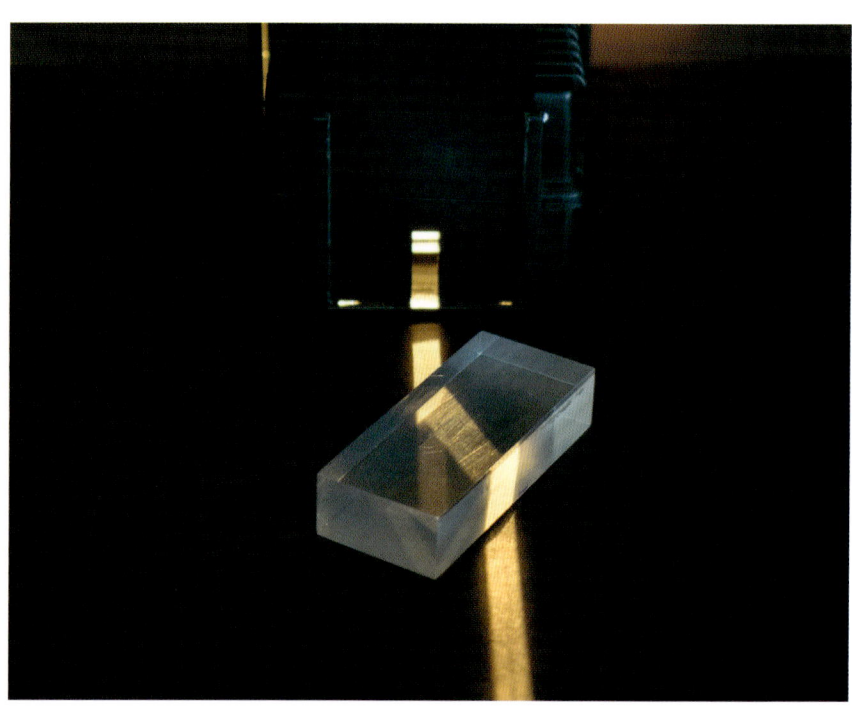

10 This example of refraction shows how much a beam of light is displaced when passing through a thick glass block.

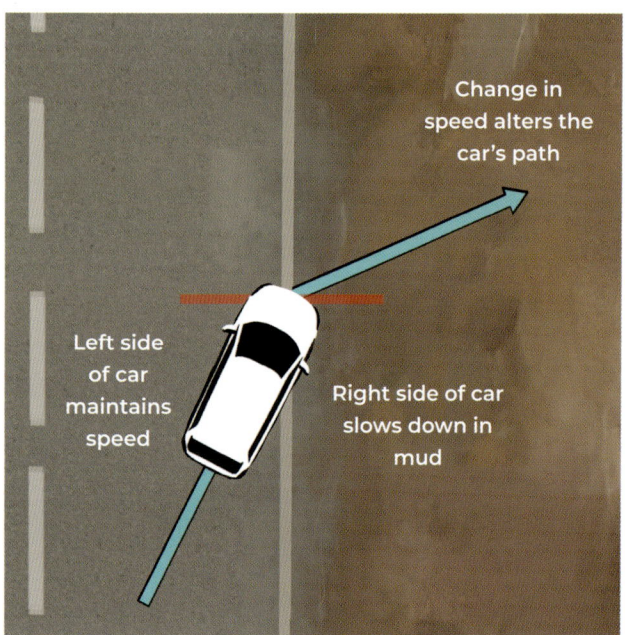

Change in speed alters the car's path

Left side of car maintains speed

Right side of car slows down in mud

11 In can be helpful to imagine a beam of refracted light as a car changing course when one of its sides hits different terrain!

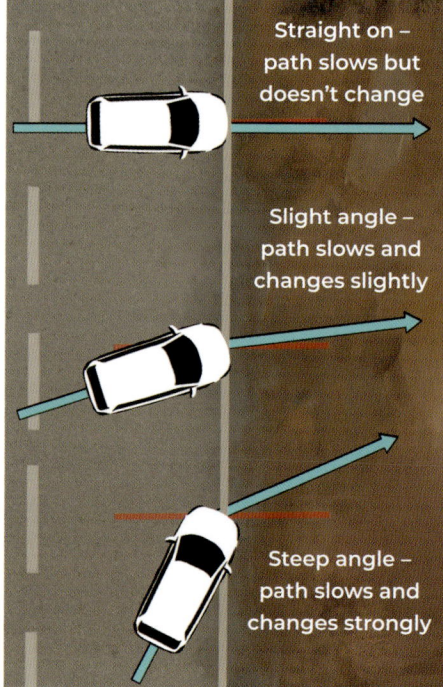

Straight on – path slows but doesn't change

Slight angle – path slows and changes slightly

Steep angle – path slows and changes strongly

12 In this car analogy, the approaching angle of the car (or the light) dictates the angle of the refraction.

One thing to note is that the car's new direction, from this angle of approach, would never become perfectly perpendicular to the transition between the two surfaces (the "normal" indicated by the red line). It would instead be a diagonal.

Image **12** compares three different angles for the car that represents our beam of light. If the car approaches straight on, both wheels hit the mud at the same moment. In this situation, the car would slow down but not change direction. As the angle of approach becomes shallower, with a greater delay between both wheels hitting the mud, the turn in the car's path becomes greater.

All of this is just as true of light. As the light passes into a denser medium, it slows down due to the same effects described above. The same is also true in reverse, when moving from a dense medium to one that's less so.

The level to which refraction occurs varies greatly for different materials, and the level of distortion depends on the degree to which each material refracts light. The level to which a material refracts light is called its "refractive index." While these have been measured precisely by scientists, we don't need to know the particulars of these numbers for our purposes – they can quickly get overcomplicated! It's enough for us to be aware that this effect occurs and varies in intensity. As long as we keep the level of distortion consistent throughout a material, there is a fair amount of creative leeway for us as artists.

For flat planes the refraction can be relatively simple, with the image behind the plane simply shifting slightly to one side. The shallower the angle, the more extreme this shift appears. In image **13**, the amount this image shifts increases as the angle of the glass becomes shallower, with no distortion when viewed straight on.

Let's look at a glass container for an interesting view of refraction and distortion effects varying with angle. In image **14**, the view through the center of the glass is enlarged but barely distorted, while the image toward the edges, where the angle of the plane is shallower, displays a much stronger distortion. We can clearly see how our view of the white tabletop is fairly level in the center but distorts toward the edges.

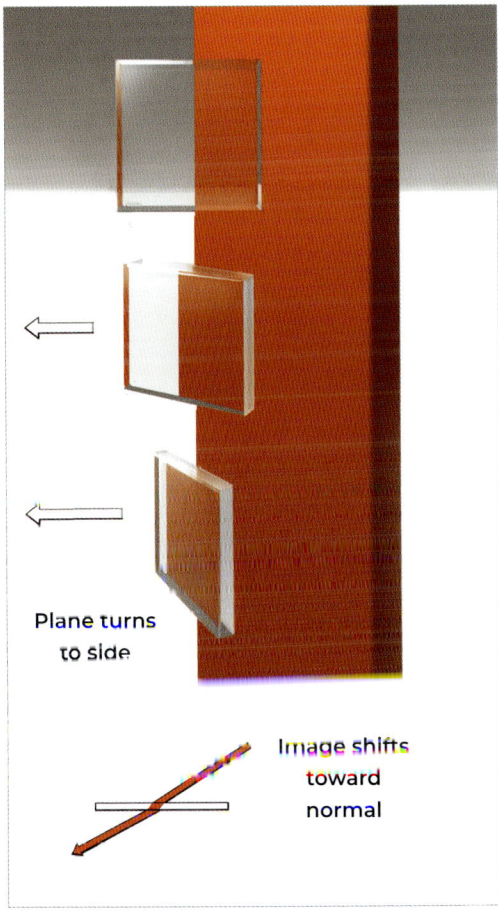

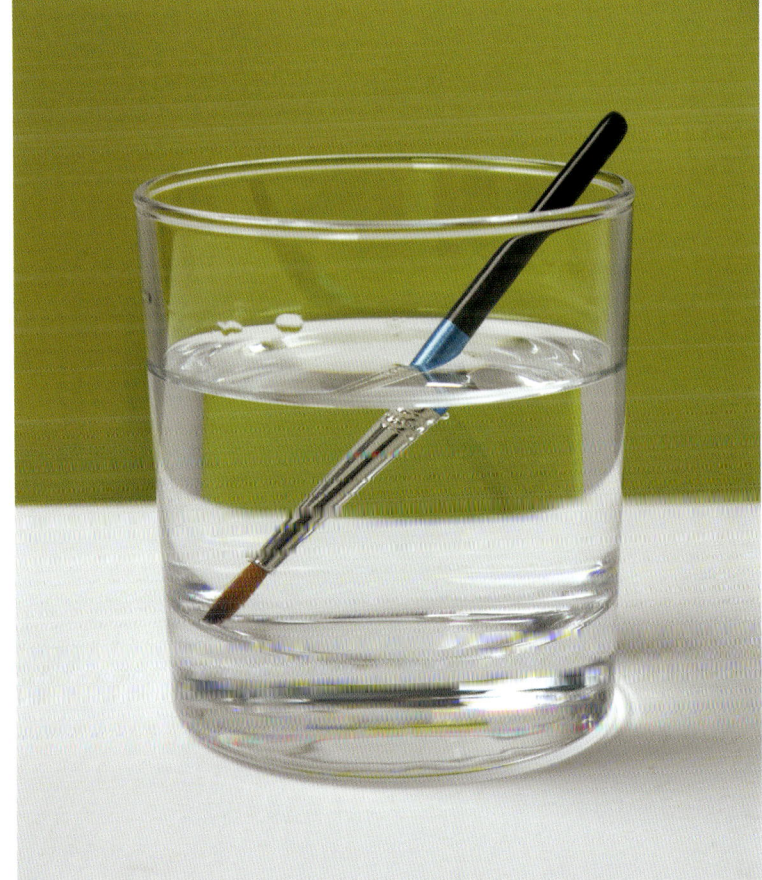

13 In this example, you can see how the refracted image shifts in the direction of the transparent object's normal.

14 The distortion of the image becomes stronger in the areas of the glass at a steeper angle to us (the edges).

TRANSPARENT PLANES AND FORMS

In order to understand how refraction distorts an image through a transparent plane, let's take a look at how an image changes depending on the plane's curvature. In image 15 you can see the simple image we will be distorting.

We can generally think of this distortion as similar to the distortions caused by specular reflections, except reversed. As you can see in image 16, if we project parallel light rays at a concave transparent plane, they spread out, just as they did for a convex specular plane. This means we can expect a squashed image with this type of lens.

Similarly, the convex transparent plane creates a focal point, just as the concave specular plane did. This causes enlarging and flipping depending on the subject's relationship to the focal point:

· If the subject is closer than the focal point, the image stretches **(17)**

· If the subject is on the focal point, it is stretched over the entire length of the lens **(18)**

· If the subject is beyond the focal point, its image appears flipped **(19)**

Using this basic logic, and lessening the distortion toward the center of the plane (where we see it front on), we can construct a believable lens refraction for these basic types of curvature.

By combining these distortion effects with the use of contrast discussed on page 162, we can create convincing distortion and communicate thickness with each of our fundamental shapes, which will always be

our most essential way to understand form and volume.

If the lens becomes perfectly convex, as in a glass sphere, the focal point moves *within* the form, meaning everything beyond it will be flipped in every direction. This results in an image that's flipped both horizontally and vertically **(20)**. However, on a cylinder, where the form only fully curves on one plane, the image just flips on the axis of the curve, as we'll see on page 173.

Don't worry about getting these reflections completely perfect on more complex forms, as those calculations would quickly become very unwieldy. These effects are easily predictable for the sphere but need to be felt out more intuitively for more complex transparent subjects.

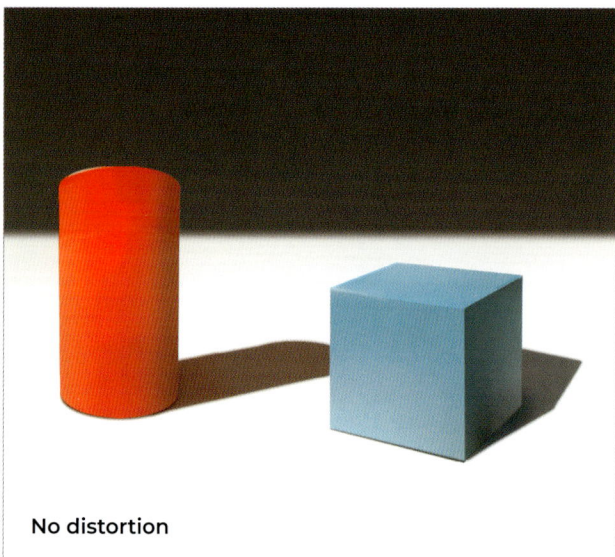

No distortion

15 The undistorted scene we will be viewing through transparent lenses.

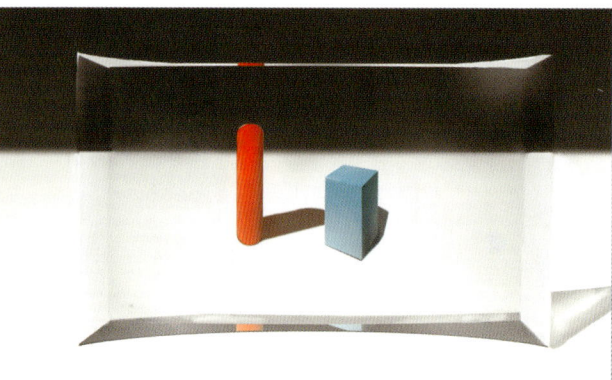

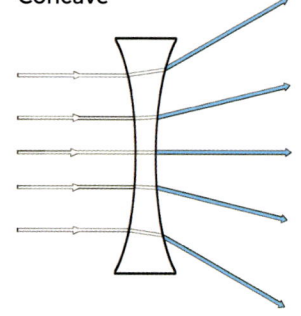

Concave

16 When looking through a transparent concave lens, the light rays are spread out, resulting in a squashed image.

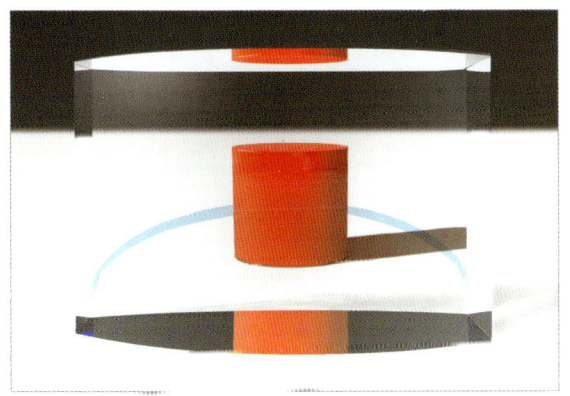

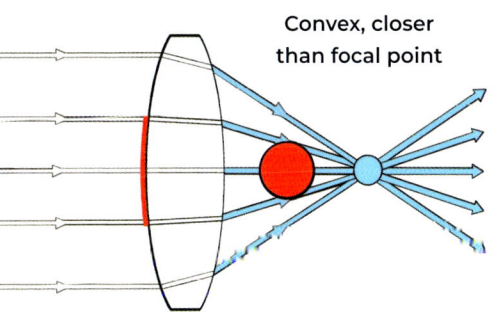

Convex, closer than focal point

17 When the subject is closer than the focal point, its image is stretched evenly across the surface of the convex lens

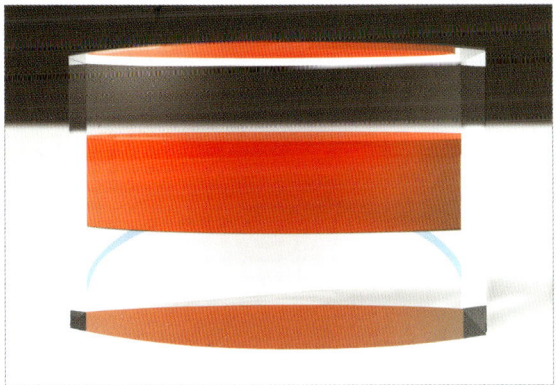

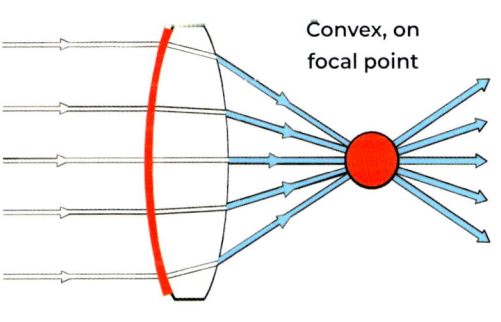

Convex, on focal point

18 When the subject is on the focal point of a convex plane, the resulting image fills up the entire lens.

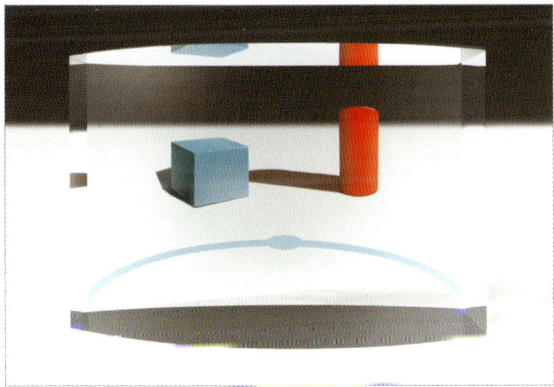

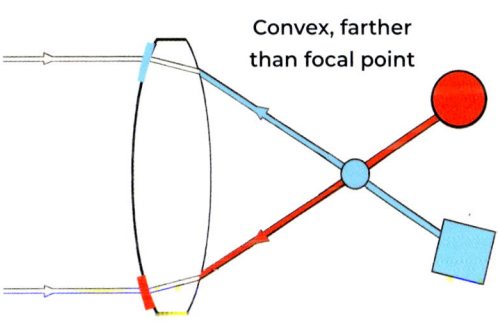

Convex, farther than focal point

19 When the subjects are farther than the focal point of a convex lens, the resulting image appears flipped.

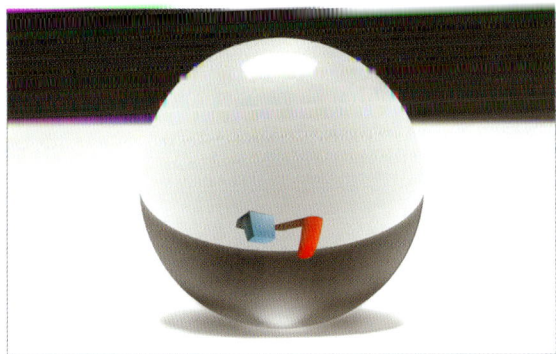

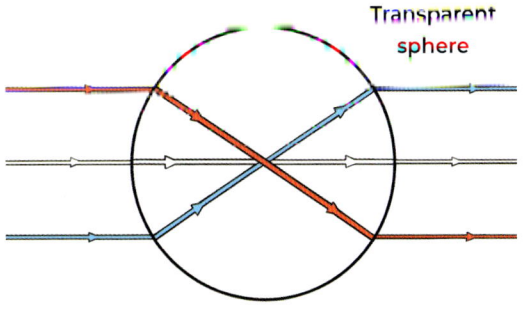

Transparent sphere

20 An image viewed through a transparent sphere will be flipped both horizontally and vertically.

SHADOWS AND CAUSTIC LIGHT

The shadows cast by transparent materials undergo a couple of key changes from what we already know. The first is simple – since a lot of the light passes straight through the material, the object's shadows will be significantly lighter than they would be for opaque materials. As the transparent material thickens, the shadows also increase in darkness.

Another new and quite intriguing effect we can observe in transparent materials is "caustic" light. This refers to the bright spots created by the concentration of light caused by the refraction. We can see this in the center of the shadow in image **21**, and more strikingly in image **22**, where dappled light shines through a glass.

It is important to recognize that these effects will only be simply predictable for extremely basic forms. Due to all of the bending and concentration of light in more complex objects, they will often occur in very unpredictable ways, as you can imagine looking at image **22**! Nonetheless, caustic light can be a beautiful effect to add when we represent transparent materials.

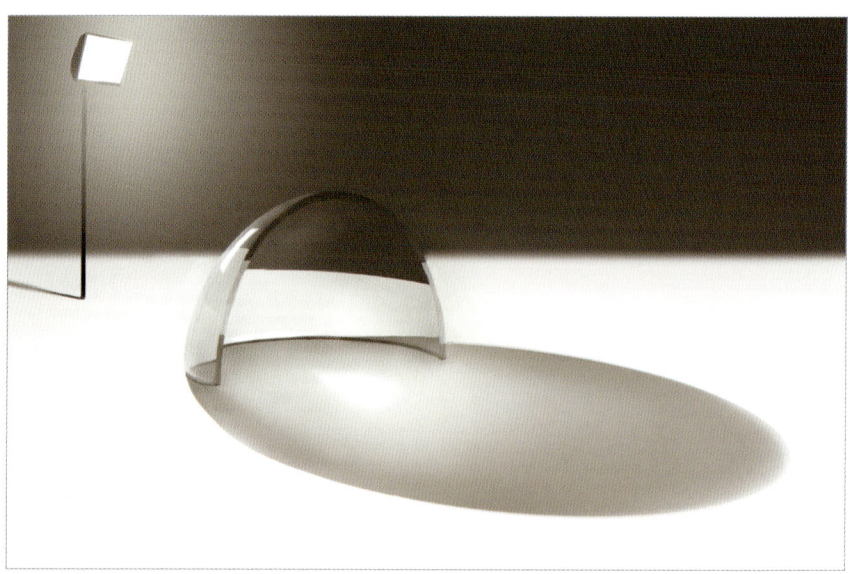

21 Light passes through transparent objects and brightens their shadows. The shadows are darker where the material is thicker.

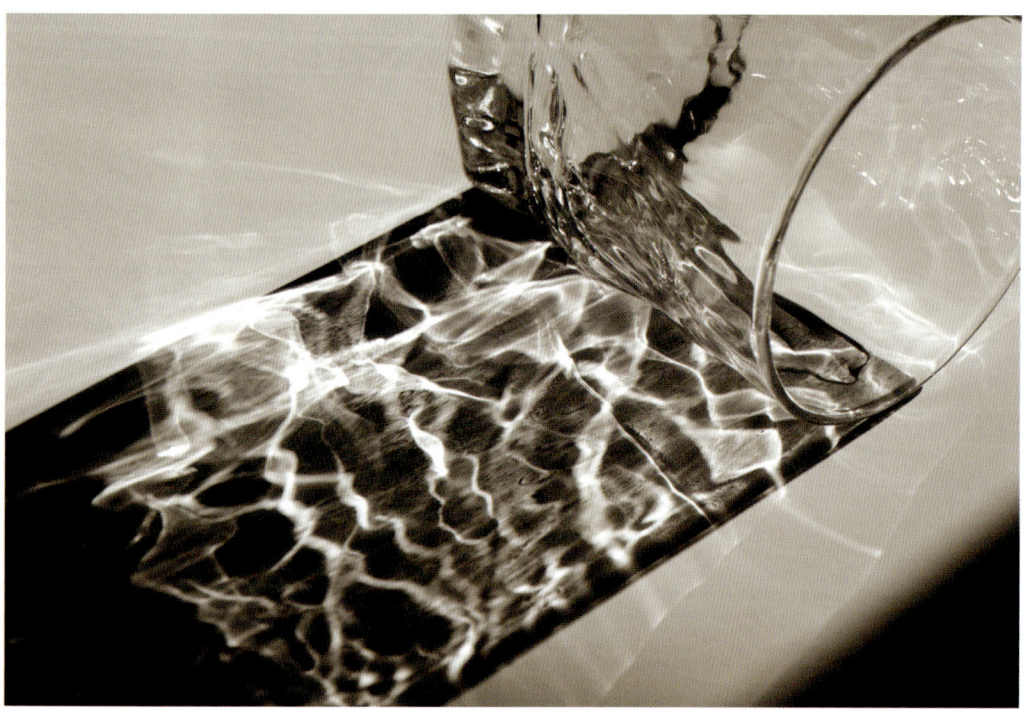

22 Caustic effects are created when refracted light is concentrated into bright spots.

TOTAL INTERNAL REFLECTION

While understanding refraction will go a long way in representing glass, in order for us to properly represent planar objects like the cube, we need to understand one more concept: total internal reflection.

We tend to think of reflection as only happening on the outside of a material, as we spoke about in the specular reflection chapter. However, reflection actually occurs *within* dense mediums as well. As we can see in image **23**, the blue lines on the bottom of the pool are reflected on the surface of the water above.

The reason this happens is related to our previous concept of refraction, except this time in reverse. While before the light was traveling from a less-dense medium (air) into a denser one (glass or water), this time it is moving from water to air, and so it will speed up instead of slowing down.

To understand how this affects what we see and what results in a reflection, let's return to our analogy of the car, this time traveling from mud (slow) to the road (fast). When the car approaches this transition, once again,

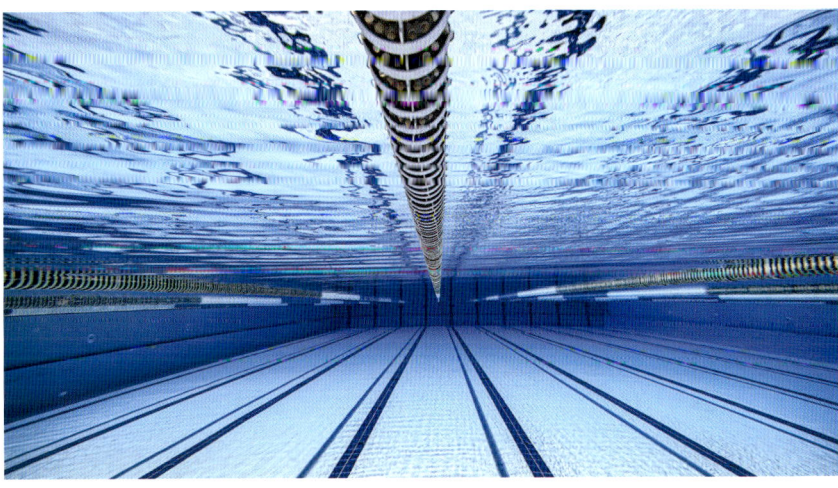

23 The effect of total internal reflection can be clearly observed in this pool, where the image of the pool's floor is bounced up onto the surface above.

one of the wheels will reach the road first. This will cause it to speed up, altering the path of the car in a similar way as before – except this time moving away from the normal of the plane instead of toward it **(24)**.

Eventually, at a shallow enough angle of approach, the car's path will be changed enough that it drives straight along the path of the transition between the road and the

mud. This angle is called the "critical angle" and it varies depending on the material **(25)**. Again, we don't need to memorize the different angles of specific materials – just knowing the concept is enough.

Beyond this critical angle, the path of the car will be changed enough that it ends up diverting back onto the mud. This is what we observe as total internal reflection **(26)**.

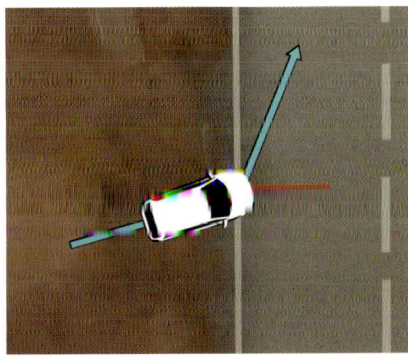

24 In the reverse of the refraction shown on page 166, when the car moves from mud to road, it diverts away from the normal of the plane it touches.

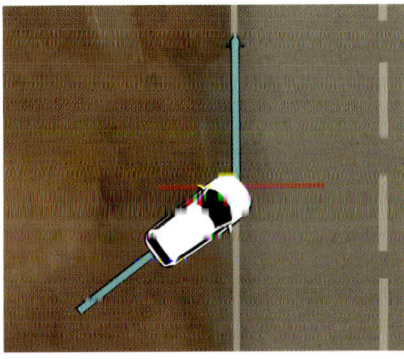

25 With a shallower angle, the car would reach the "critical angle," driving straight along the line between road and mud.

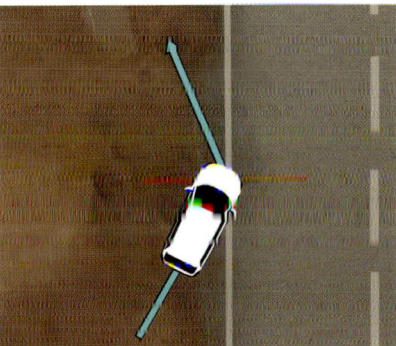

26 Beyond the critical angle, the car's path would divert away from the road and back onto the mud – total internal reflection!

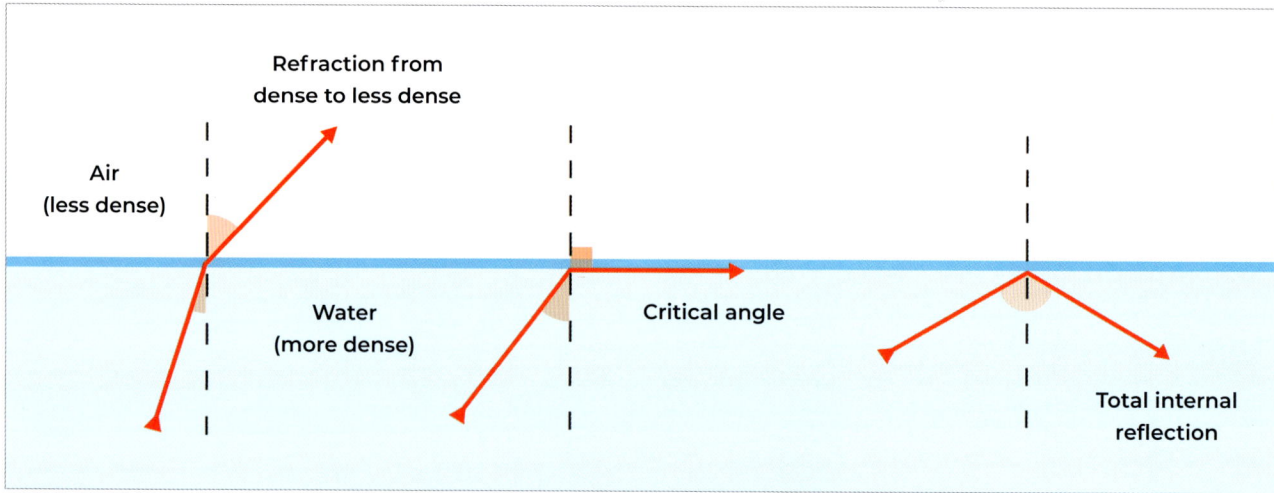

27 When refracting from a dense to less-dense medium, the angle increases, like a reverse of specular refraction. At the critical angle, the shallower light angle stops the light making it out of the water, instead skimming along the surface. In total internal reflection, the light's angle is reflected completely within the dense medium.

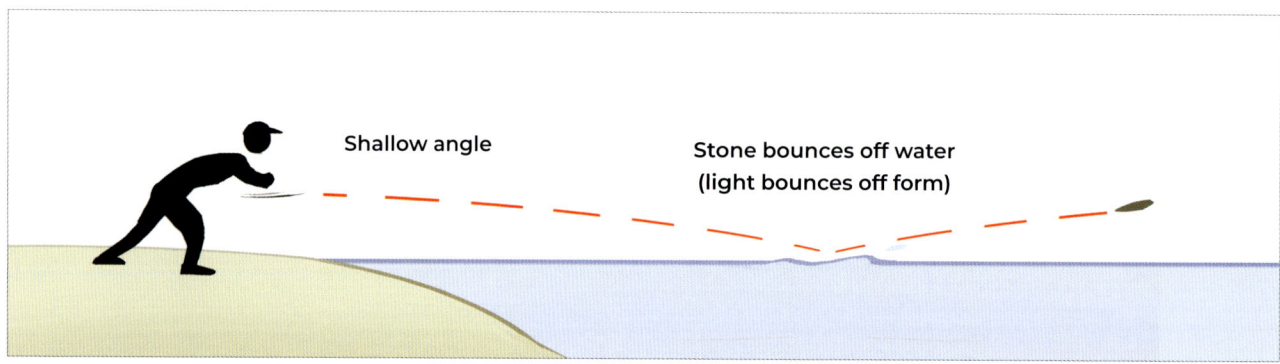

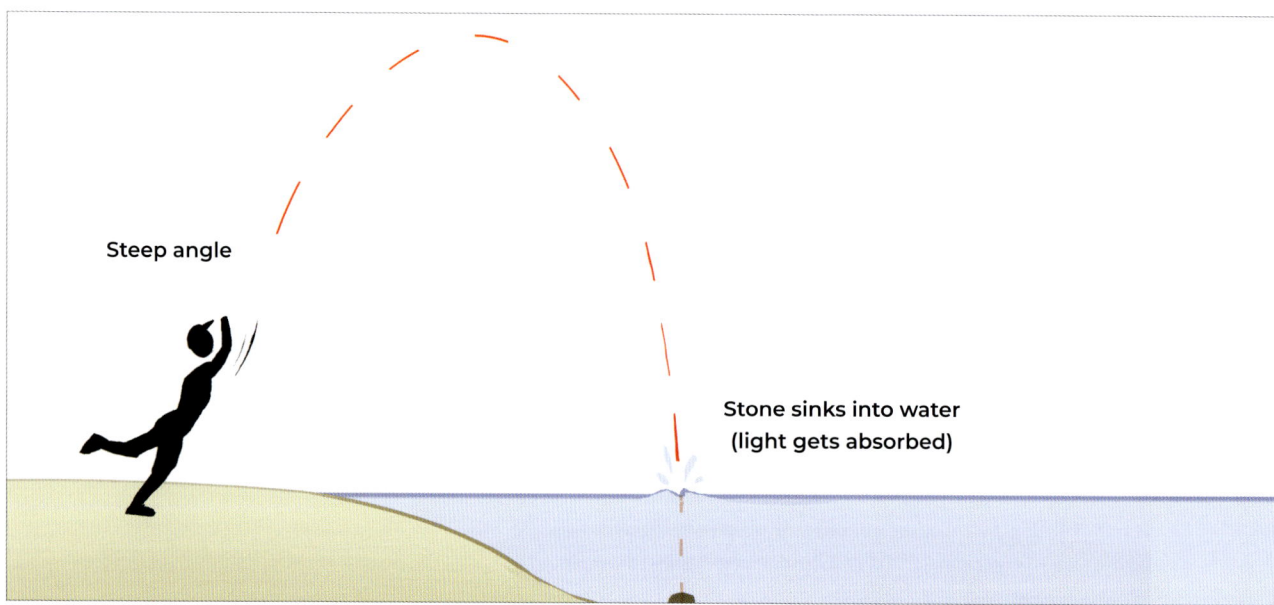

28 Imagine light as a stone skimming across water. Depending on the angle at which it strikes the water, it will either bounce (reflect) or sink (absorb).

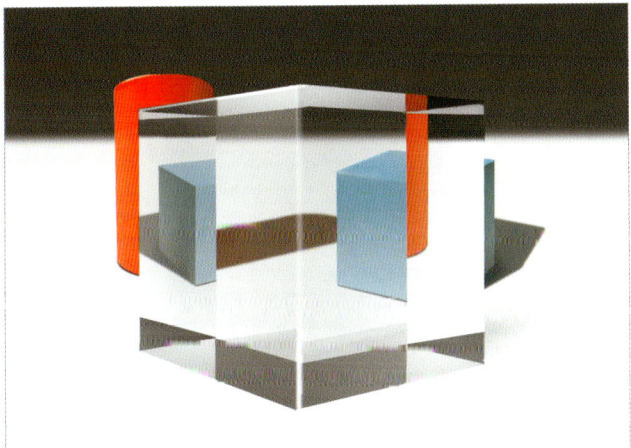

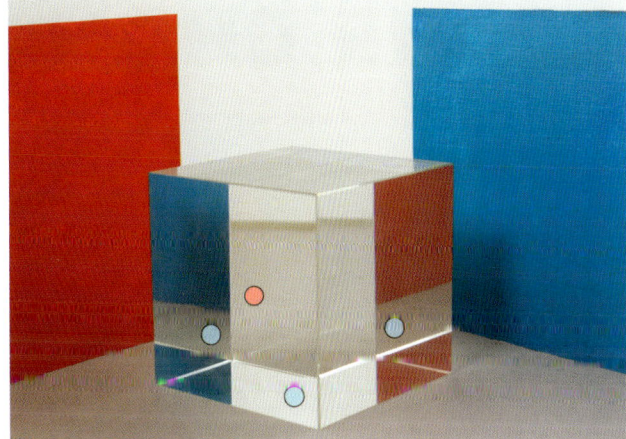

29 What we see in a transparent shape depends on the angle of its planes in relation to our viewpoint.

 Reflected image (where planes are shallow to us)

Transmitted image (where planes are more perpendicular to us)

Image **27** shows a simplified view of each of these interactions occurring in water, though in reality the difference between them is far more gradated. However, for our purposes, we can simply think of each plane as either showing a transmitted image or a reflected one.

Now, the explanation on the previous pages may have felt a bit abstract and difficult to wrap your head around. How can we actually, practically use our knowledge of total internal reflection in our work?

It is helpful to relate this concept to the common experience many of us have of trying to skim stones across water (**28**). In order for the stone to bounce along the surface, we need to throw it at a shallow angle. If the angle is too steep, the stone will simply hit the water and sink. We can think of light in transparent materials in the same way. If the stone would bounce, we see a reflection. If it would sink, we see what's behind the material.

Now we understand the logic behind it, we better understand what we're seeing when we look at a transparent cube or any other planar form. In image **29** we can see that

the internal top plane and bottom plane display this internal reflection, while the more front-on internal planes display a transmitted image of what is behind the transparent object.

Combining total internal reflection with our previously discussed distortion and loss of contrast due to depth, we have enough information to paint each of our fundamental forms in this new material quality, whether planar or curved (**30**).

Now that we have all of the logic to paint any transparent form into an environment, try it out! Similar to the specular forms, this type of rendering will change hugely depending on the environment, so inserting the forms into different environments is the best form of practice. You can do this in your own painted environments or by painting objects into a photograph (**31**).

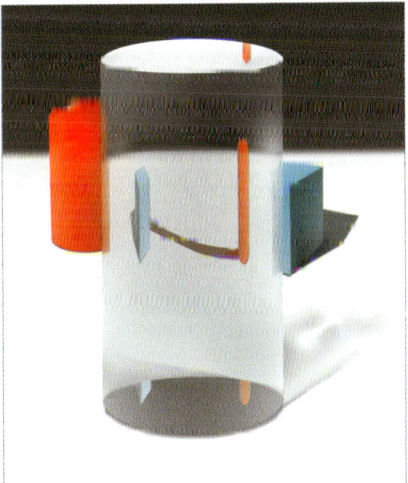

30 This cylinder exhibits total internal reflection, same as the cube, but includes distortion on the curved plane that is now familiar to us.

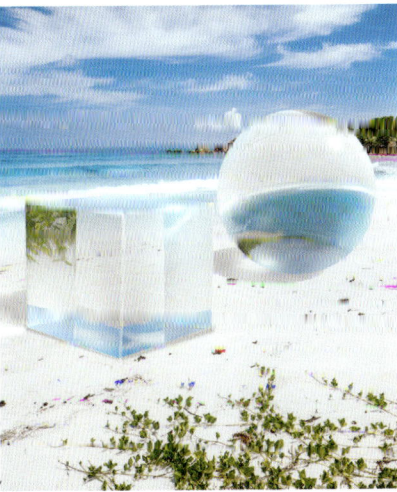

31 Practice painting transparent forms in photographs, as we did with specular lighting on pages 151 and 155.

COLOR CHANGES

Transparent materials can also have specific local colors, which act similarly to what we learned when adding specular color on page 158. The local color acts as a filter that the image passes through, so the result will simply be that image taken down a color's saturation path (32).

Just like with specular color, the easiest way to achieve this in a digital painting is by adding a simple Multiply layer of the desired color. However, there are a few complications that we need to take into consideration when we add this color.

The first is that any specular reflections will generally be unaffected by this color filter and should be treated separately. The second is that, as we discussed on page 162, the more material that the light has to go through, the stronger the filtration of the light. For colored materials, this means that where the material is thicker, the saturation of the color change will be more intense.

If we simply add a Multiply layer on its own, this saturation will be equal throughout – a common error as shown in image **33**. If we instead vary this filter with the thickness

of the material, increasing it toward the center of the sphere, we get a clearer sense of transparency.

These colored transparent materials also mix subtractively – if we layer different-colored transparent materials over each other, the filtered light will mix to black. We can see this in image **34** with different-colored lens filters. If enough of them are layered, light cannot get through, and we simply see black.

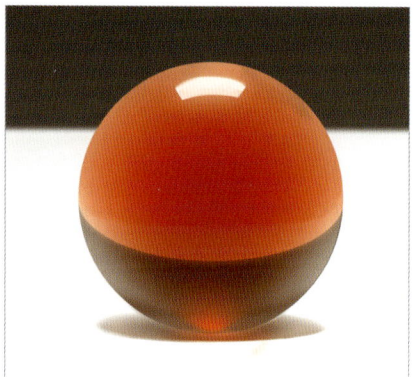
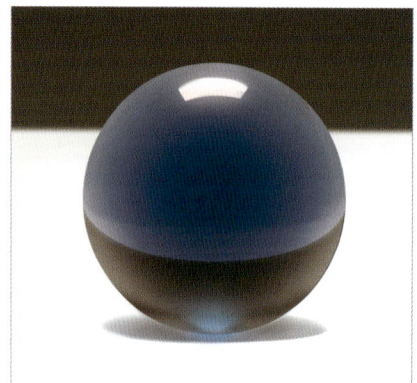
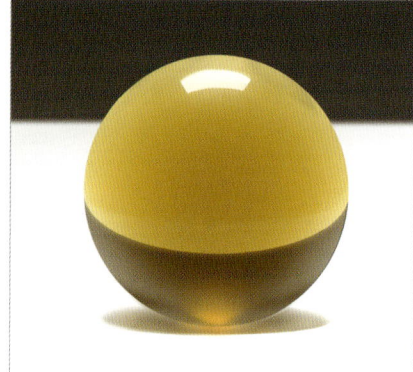

32 Transparent materials can also have a local color – red, blue, and yellow in these examples – that will affect their interaction with light.

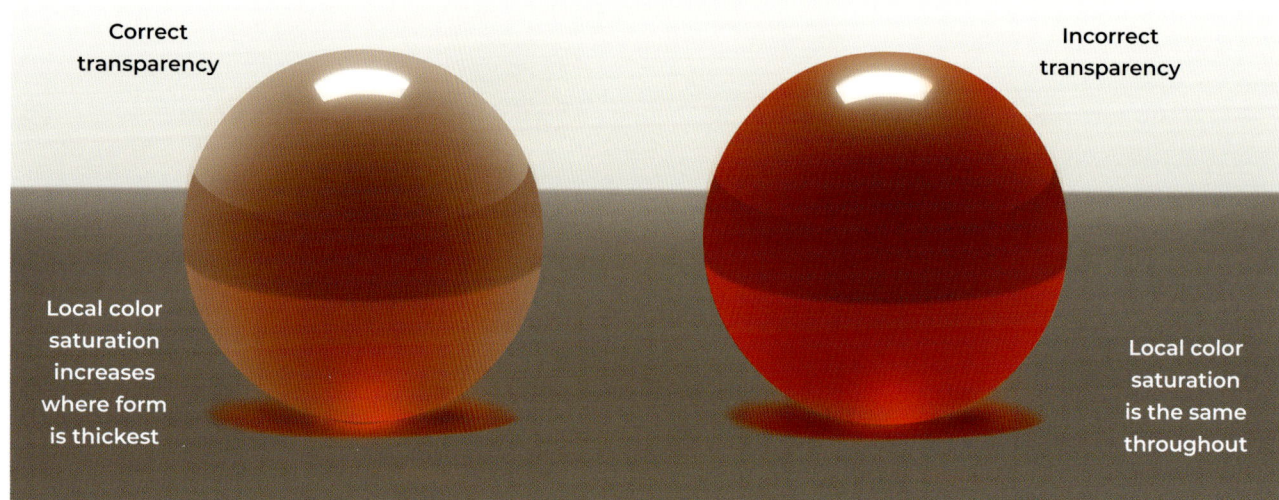

Correct transparency

Local color saturation increases where form is thickest

Incorrect transparency

Local color saturation is the same throughout

33 It's a common mistake to give a transparent object's local color uniform saturation. In reality, the local color should increase where the form is thickest and lose saturation where it is thinnest.

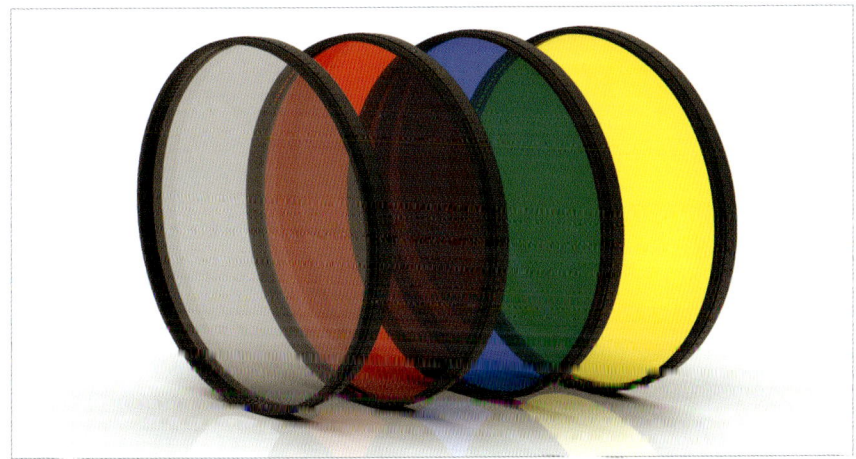

34 Transparent colored materials mix subtractively when layered, as you can see in these colored photo filters.

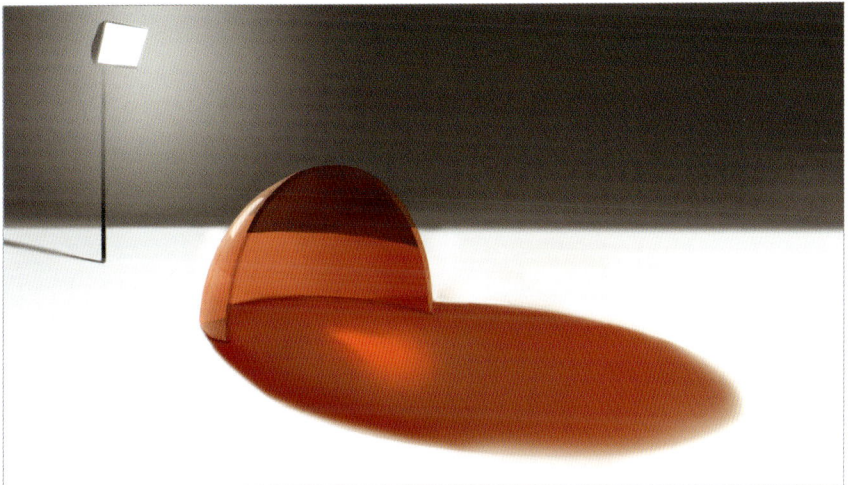

35 The red transparent material creates a red shadow. It's darker and less saturated than the original local color, though still contains a bright caustic hotspot.

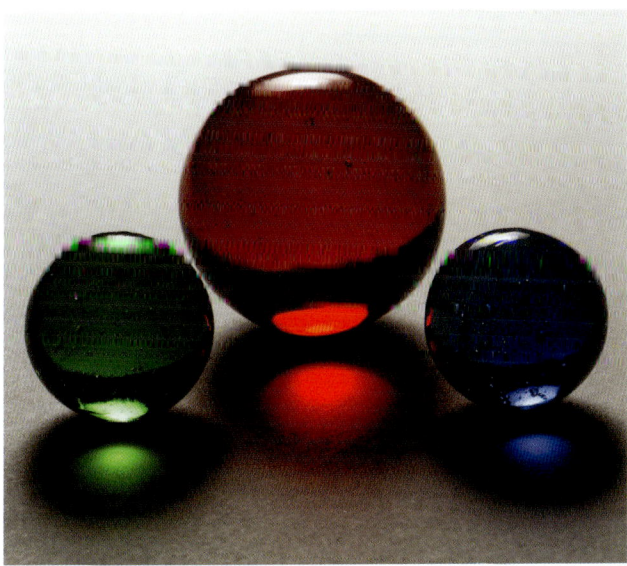

36 Bright spots of caustic light can be observed in these colored glass marbles, both in the shadows and within the marbles themselves.

TRANSPARENCY AND COLORED SHADOWS

As we learned earlier, light travels all the way through transparent materials and always affects the shadow color somewhat. For a colored transparent material, this means that the local color of the object will affect the color of the shadow. In image **35**, the shadow is all red, as the transparent lens only allows red light through. Since this light will mix with any ambient light present, it will also be less saturated than the original object color.

You might notice the exception in the center of the shadow – the caustic effect. As mentioned on page 170, this caustic light is a concentration of the light passing through the object, and so is the most chromatic the local color will allow.

As you can see from the glass marbles in image **36**, these caustic effects can also occur within the object, creating a spot of extreme chroma and brightness within each marble. In spheres, these internal caustic effects will generally be on the other side from the light source, but for more complex objects they are less predictable.

REFRACTION AND IRIDESCENCE

One last aspect of refractive materials to be aware of is that not all colors (wavelengths of light) bend the same amount. In fact, the higher-energy (cool) light refracts faster, while the rest of the wavelengths refract less and less down to the lower-energy (warm) light.

This means that white light will separate out into its component colors if we refract it enough, as we learned on page 31. This is how Isaac Newton first discovered the color spectrum – by diffracting light through prisms. This separation of light will occur whenever light refracts sufficiently through a transparent medium, giving rise to beautiful iridescent effects **(37)**.

Iridescence literally means "rainbowlike," and the rainbow is the most familiar form of this light separation that we will come across. Rainbows occur when enough water droplets in the air refract out the colors in this way. It is also the most easily predictable of these effects – the shape of a rainbow is always the same, always a large circle, caused by our cone of vision. We usually only see a section of this circle, as at least half of it is usually blocked by the horizon. For practical purposes, though, this idea of the rainbow as an arch will serve us fine.

Iridescence can be caused by a great variety of factors, making it extremely difficult to predict exactly how the effect will present itself on different surfaces in our paintings. However, one common factor is that every iridescent rainbow effect will be made up of the same colors of the spectrum in the same order, from red to violet **(38)**.

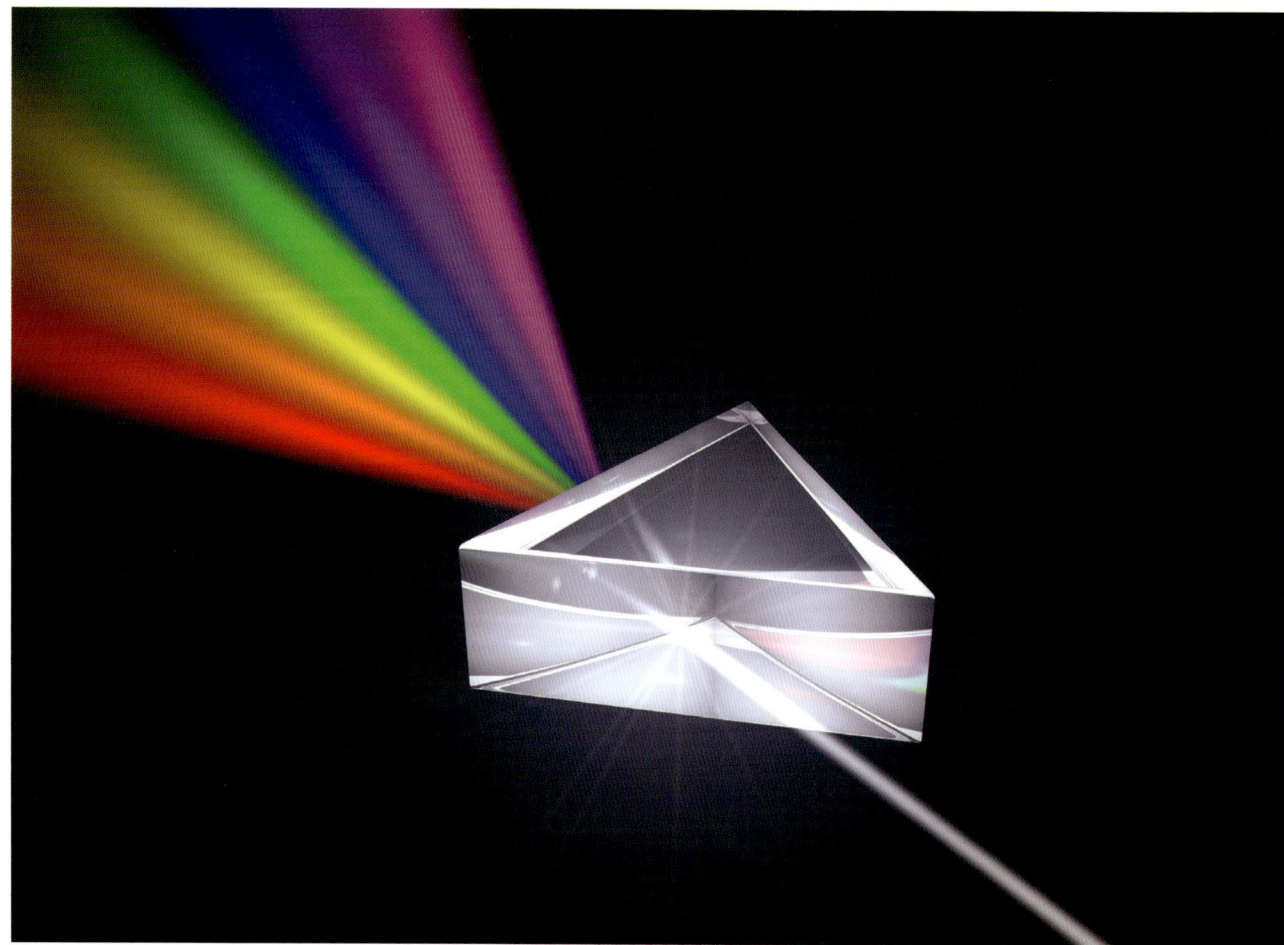

37 As we learned in the Color chapter, white light can be refracted into a spectrum of separate colors.

Iridescence is present in many areas of the animal kingdom, on greasy surfaces like petrol or soap bubbles, and more subtly on glass at certain angles. Despite these varied effects, the visible high-chroma colors will always appear in the same order, like their rainbow namesake **(39)**.

The size and shape of each color will vary wildly depending on the subject, but as long as we keep to this rainbow order, iridescence can be a great way to be expressive in our images. These are some of most chromatic colors present in nature, providing artists a great opportunity to get colorful!

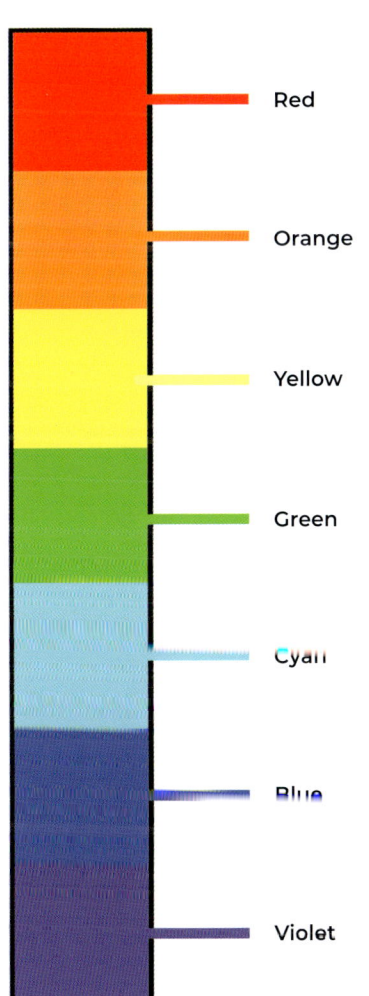

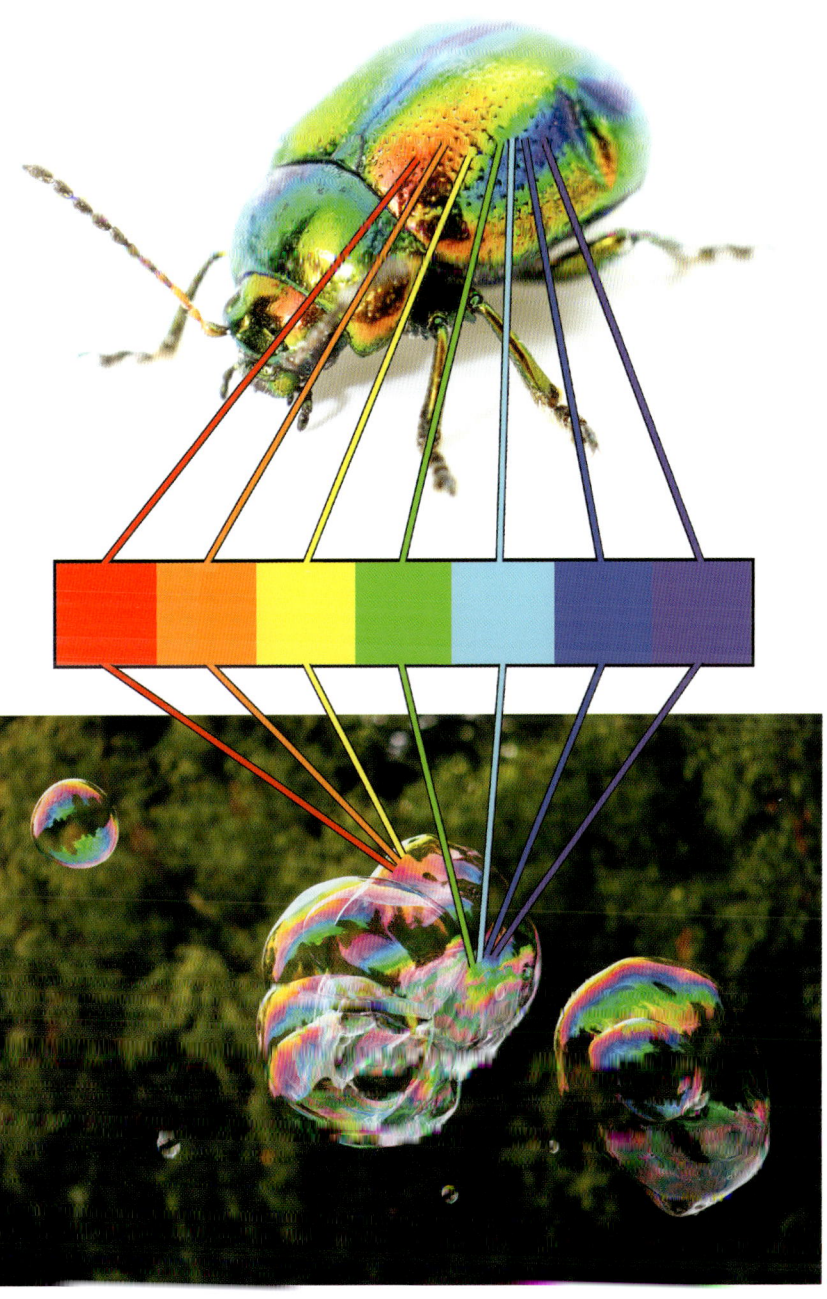

39 Regardless of the iridescent subject, the order of the hues will always be the same.

38 As we learned in the Color chapter, white light can be refracted into a spectrum of separate colors.

TRANSLUCENCY

So far we have been dealing with transparency, where we see a clear image of what is behind an object. It will now be useful to explore what happens when our transparent object moves toward becoming opaque (matte surface shading). Similar to when we add texture to a specular surface, the first thing that happens is that the transmitted image blurs until it's unrecognizable. The object is not yet opaque, but we can no longer see what's behind it. This is when we move into the realm of translucent materials (40).

One interesting thing you may notice about this type of shading is that it immediately looks somewhat familiar. The object has taken on some characteristics of matte

surface shading, with a light shape and shadow shape that depend on the light source. However, there are two major differences that break two of the key rules of matte surface shading. The first is that the "shadow" shape is now brighter in value than the lights. The second is that there's a huge jump in chroma in the shadows. This effect doesn't follow the rules of matte surface shading at all – in fact, it almost appears to be the reverse of a matte surface. Why doesn't translucency follow our previously established rules?

The first difference is easy to explain. The "shadow" side appears bright because the object's material allows light to easily transmit through it. Meanwhile, the

material also reflects very little light, so the "light" side appears dark instead. All of this unreflected light passes all the way through the object to the other side, lightening the "shadow" shape.

To explain the increased chroma of the shadow, it's helpful for us to understand a little of the mechanism behind transparency on a particle level. This simplified diagram shows broadly how particles are arranged for different materials (41). For extremely transparent materials, such as air, the particles are spaced far apart. All this empty space allows light to pass straight through, without, for the most part, interacting with the air particles at all. For the specular materials we looked at earlier, the opposite

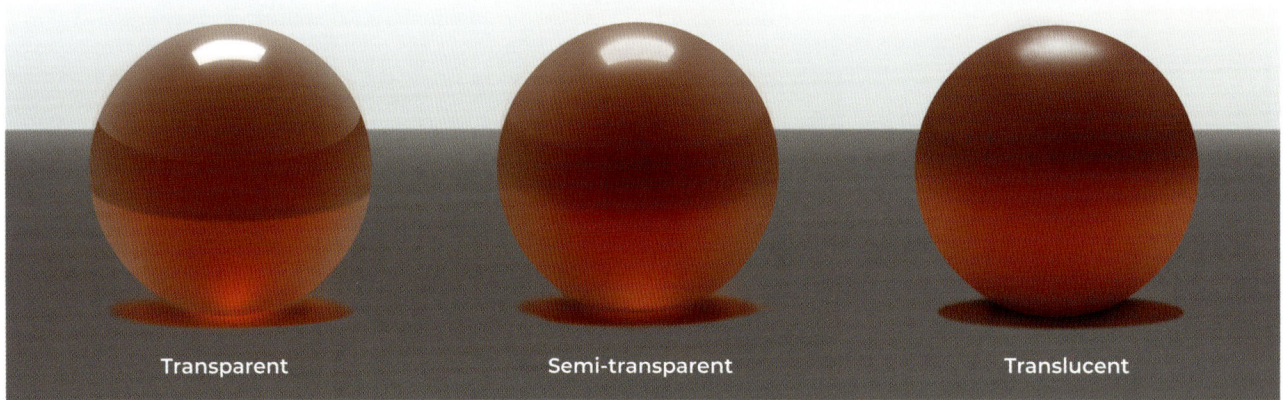

Transparent   Semi-transparent   Translucent

40 As this transparent sphere gains opacity, what would typically be the "shadow" areas on a matte sphere become lighter and more chromatic than the "light" areas.

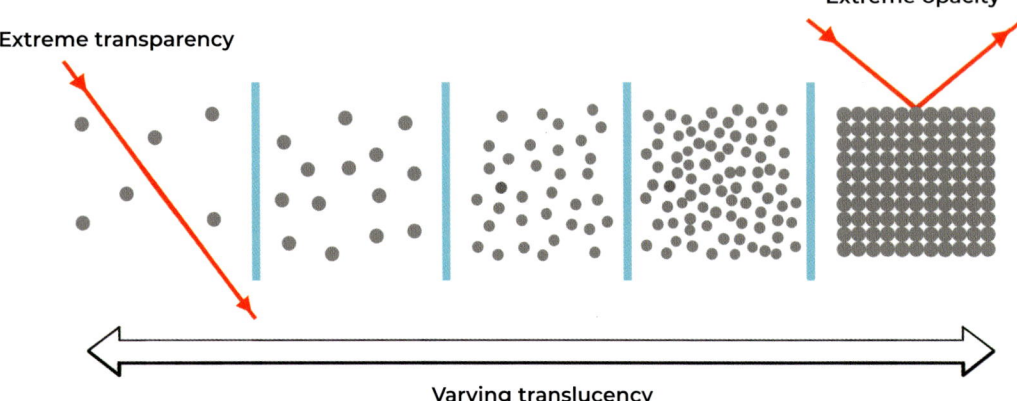

Extreme transparency

Extreme opacity

Varying translucency

41 As the particles become denser, it becomes harder for light to penetrate, until eventually it's reflected. Air and metals exist at the two extremes of this spectrum, with most objects falling in the range in between.

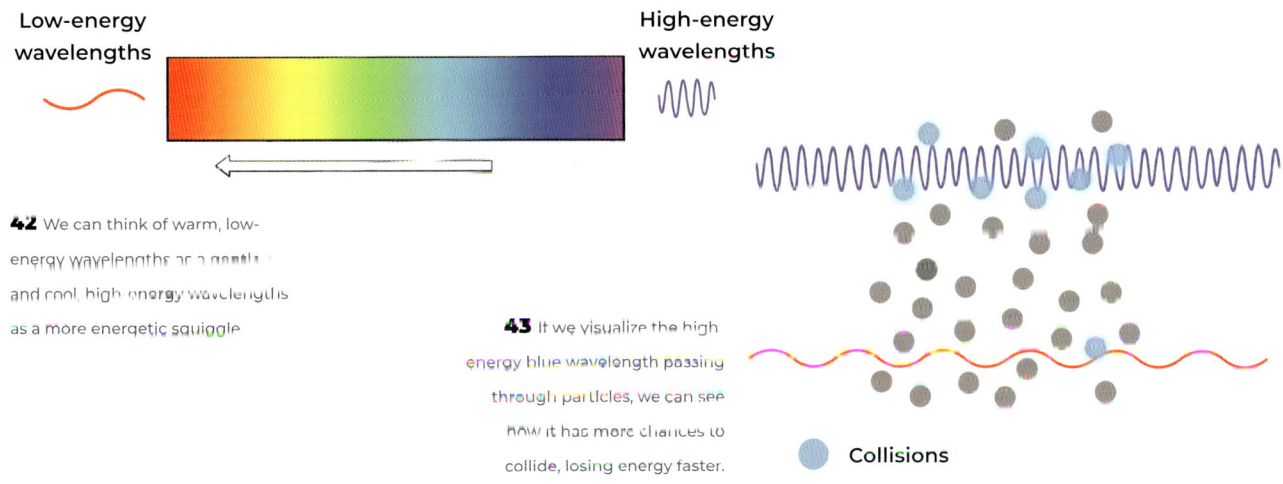

Low-energy wavelengths

High-energy wavelengths

42 We can think of warm, low-energy wavelengths as a gentle and cool, high-energy wavelengths as a more energetic squiggle

43 If we visualize the high energy blue wavelength passing through particles, we can see how it has more chances to collide, losing energy faster.

Collisions

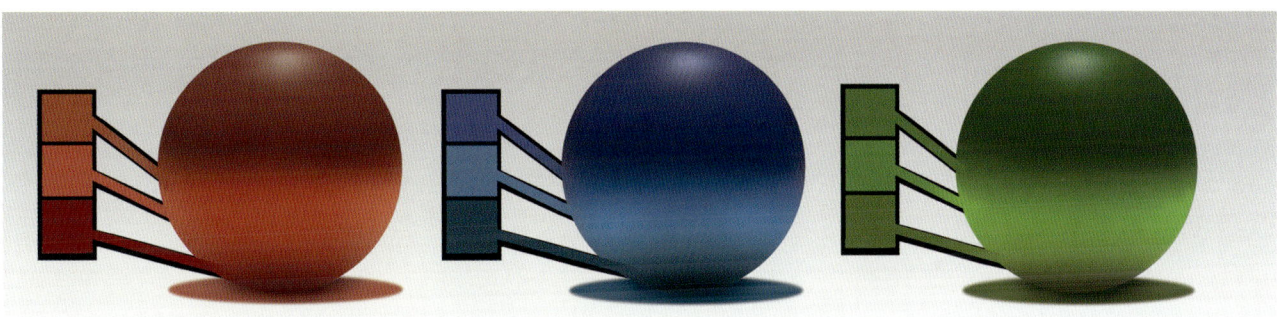

44 Light transmits through these translucent spheres, losing coolness and creating warm, chromatic shadows.

is true – the particles are so tightly packed together that there's no space for the light to penetrate, so it's reflected instead.

In between those two extremes, there are varying degrees to which the light interacts with particles and loses energy. Since there is always going to be some loss of light, for these translucent materials, only the strongest lights make it through the medium unscathed.

WAVELENGTH ENERGY

We have learned already that color, in its physical form, is simply wavelengths on the electromagnetic spectrum. On this spectrum, the warm colors are low-energy wavelengths and the cool colors are high-energy. If we represent these two extreme energy levels with squiggles, as shown in

image **42**, we can imagine that the high-energy colors move around more, while the low-energy colors are more relaxed.

If we insert these two extreme waves over our translucent material particles, we gain an important insight into how light interacts with materials. You can see just how many times the high-energy blue wavelength collides and has opportunities to interact with the material particles (**43**). Upon each collision the light loses some energy until it's fully absorbed by the material. In comparison, the low-energy red wavelength passes through relatively unscathed. This explanation is extremely simplified but works well enough for artistic purposes.

This may all seem quite abstract, and as artists we always need to have a view to the

practical. So what does this mean for our work? We now know that cooler colors lose energy faster than warmer colors – blue light is extracted or "scattered" more than red light. So, as light transmits through a medium, it gradually becomes warmer as the blue light is stripped out. In many materials, this drop-off occurs too fast for us to notice but in translucent materials the effect is on full display (**44**).

When we paint translucent shadows, we must make sure that any shadows with transmitted light shift toward warmer colors. This could mean a hue shift toward red, or an increase in chroma in the shadows if they are already warm in color. In fact, shadows are often where the strongest chroma occurs, due to this translucent material effect.

SUBSURFACE SCATTERING

That warm color shift within translucent materials is called "subsurface scattering," and it's always at play in materials with any level of transparency. In order to understand how to control this beautiful effect, let's have a look at a slightly denser object – a wax candle. Wax is a classic material to showcase this effect. Unlike the fully translucent objects on the previous pages, wax is a much denser material, and so will not allow light to pass through its entire surface (45).

We can see that the longer the light stays in material, the warmer it becomes, as well as becoming darker. As the light penetrates the surface, it progressively falls off into the generic shadow value of the object. The distance that it takes for the light to fully lose its energy in the material is called the "penetration depth" of the material.

The concept of penetration depth gives us a good opportunity to correct a common student mistake. It's common for beginners to view this effect as simply the opposite of matte surface shading. They just flip matte surface shading, making the lightest part the extreme bottom of the form, as shown in image **46**. However, this is slightly wrong. As we can see in the correct sphere, the brightest values in subsurface scattering are the result of the level of depth the light has traveled through the material. Since this penetration depth on a translucent sphere would be shallowest at the edges, as shown in image **47**, the lightest point would actually be the terminator line, with the light decreasing in intensity from that point as the depth of the material increases.

One of the most commonly discussed materials for subsurface scattering is human skin, and the subtle use of this effect is incredibly important when representing this difficult subject. Try holding your hand

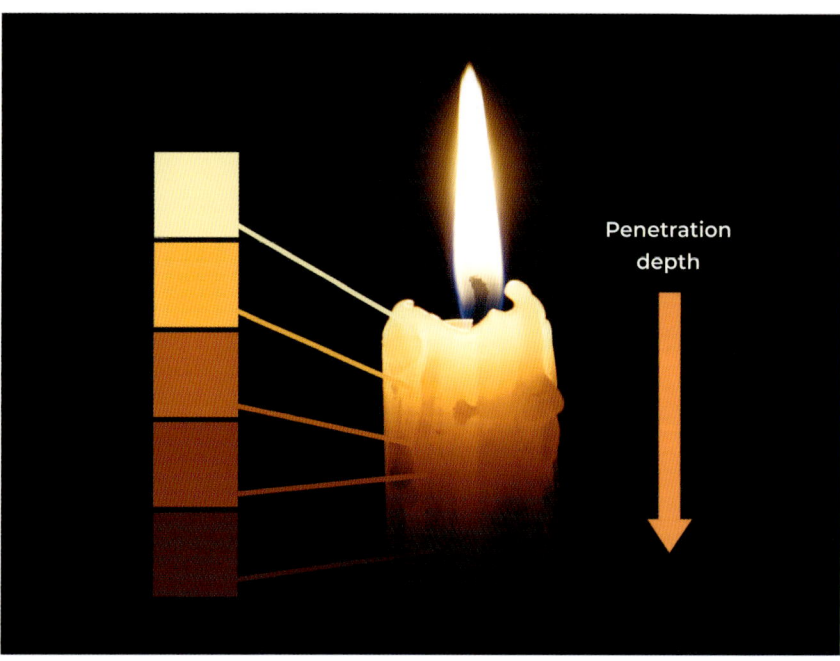

45 In subsurface scattering, colors get more red, more saturated, and darker the farther they penetrate the form.

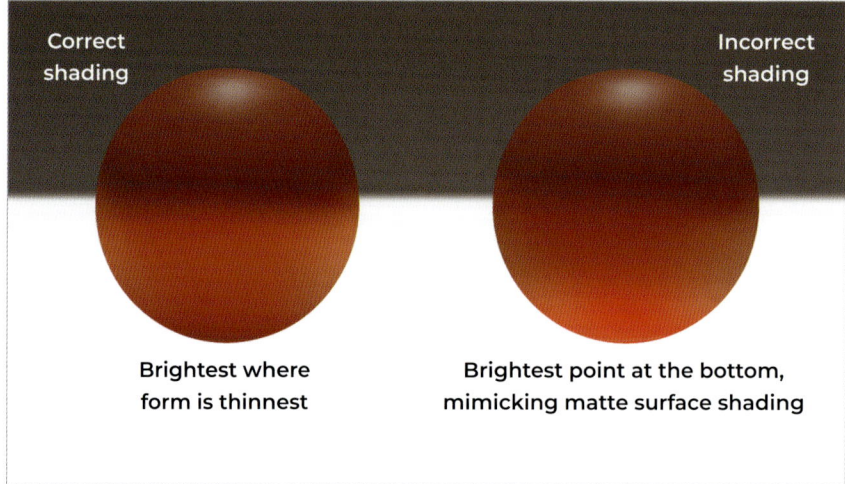

46 It's a common mistake to simply flip matte surface shading on its head when portraying translucent materials, but subsurface scattering works slightly differently.

near a bright light, like in image **48**, and you will see the extremely high-chroma red created by subsurface scattering through the skin. You may also notice that this red glow only exists around the contour of the hand and drops off toward the center. This is because of the denser bones and flesh in the center of the fingers and hand blocking the light. The human form has many varying densities and transparencies all around it, which are not uniform, and will require careful observation to get just right.

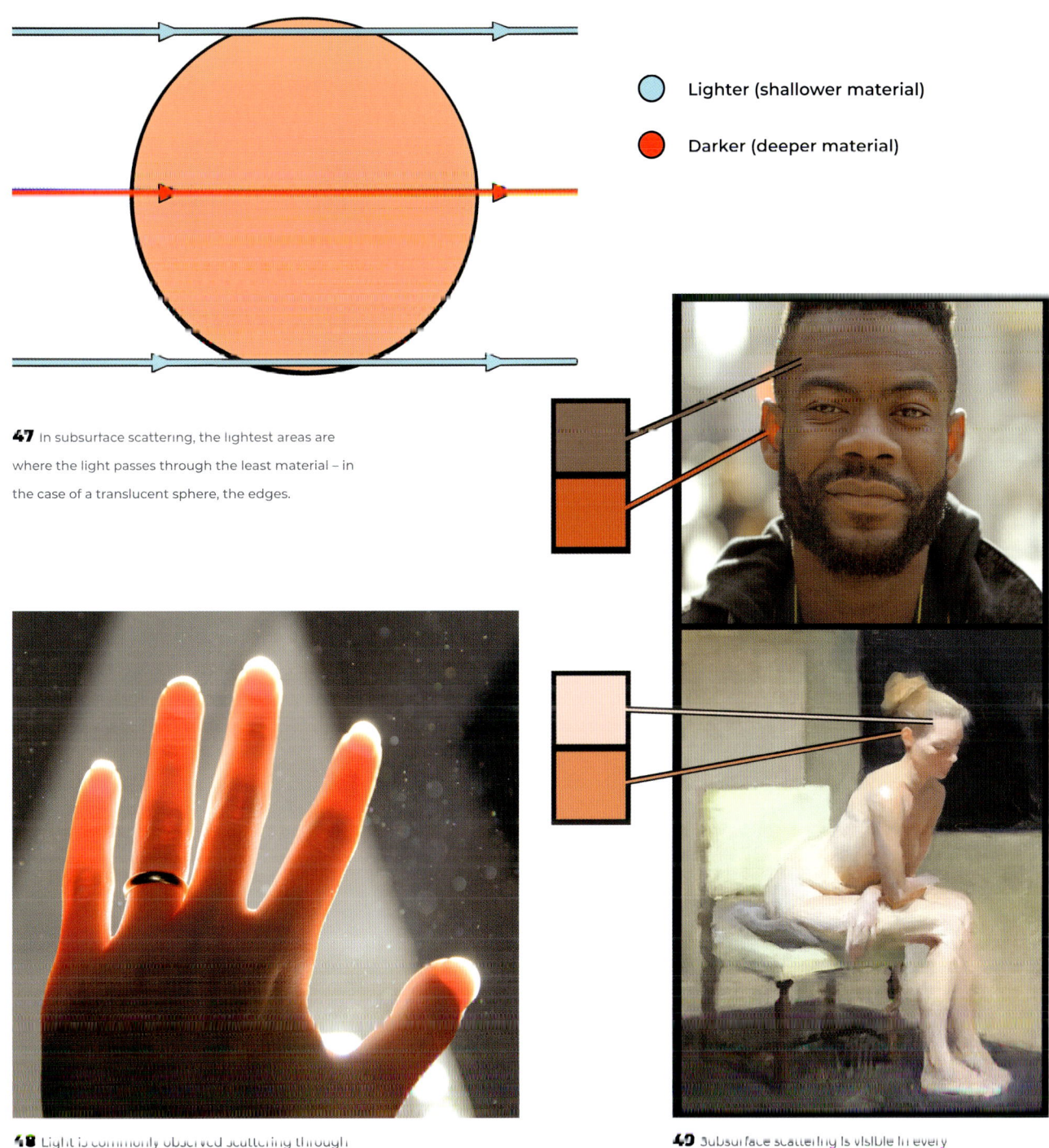

47 In subsurface scattering, the lightest areas are where the light passes through the least material – in the case of a translucent sphere, the edges.

Lighter (shallower material)

Darker (deeper material)

48 Light is commonly observed scattering through thin areas of our skin, such as the fingers and ears.

49 Subsurface scattering is visible in every skin tone and all around the body.

We will delve into skin and skin tones in their own section on page 198, but for now, it's important to note that while subsurface scattering is most obvious in light skin tones, it occurs in all types of skin. The increased melanin that creates darker skin tones can lessen the effect somewhat, but it is always present, as you can see in image **49**. The thin cartilage and skin of the ear is one of the most obvious areas for spotting subsurface scattering, but it occurs in the rest of the skin to a lesser, subtler extent.

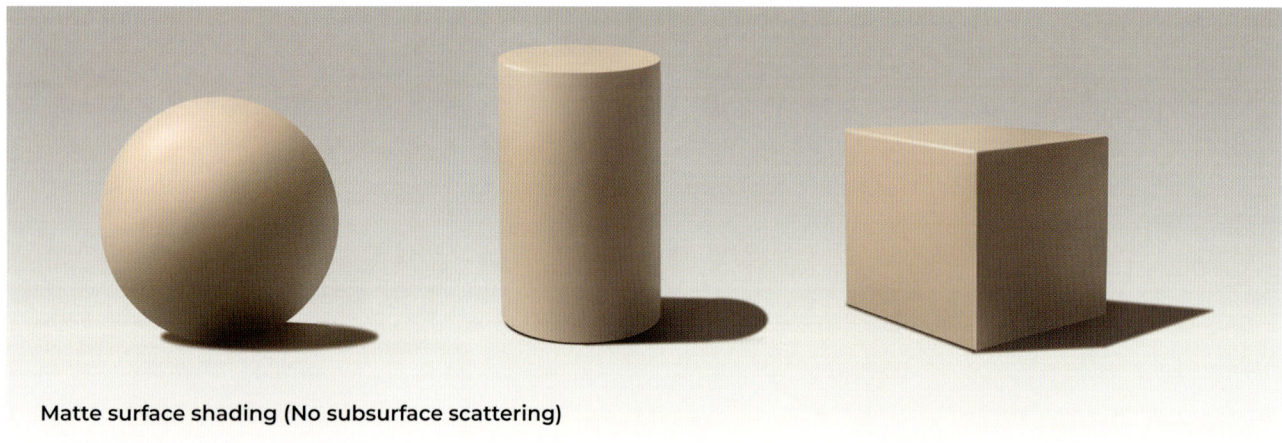

Matte surface shading (No subsurface scattering)

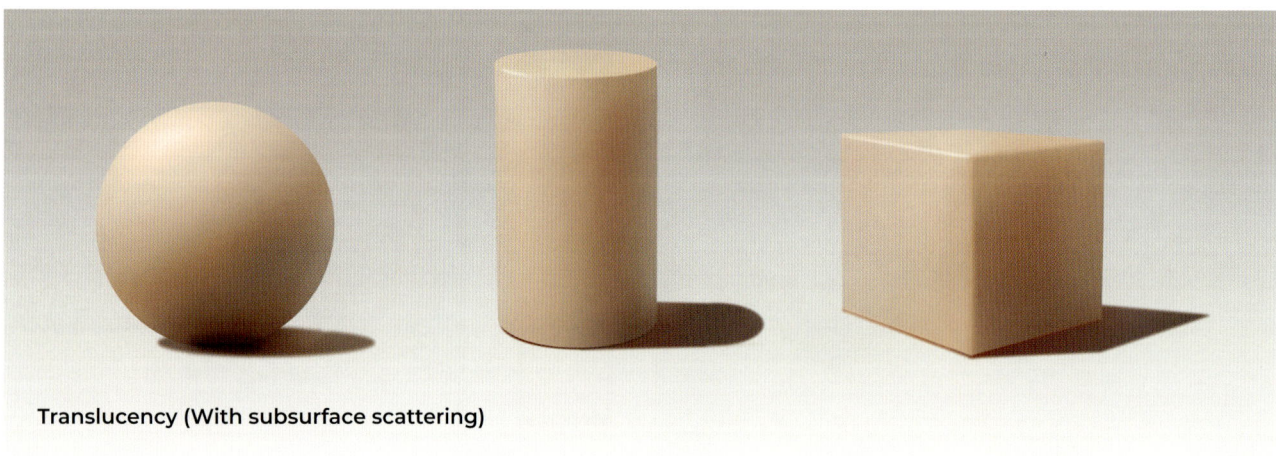

Translucency (With subsurface scattering)

50 Here we can clearly see the difference between a matte-surface form and a translucent skin-like form. Subsurface scattering makes the latter noticeably warmer in color.

SUGGESTING SUBSURFACE SCATTERING

In image **50**, we can see how we might approach applying subsurface scattering to a generic object with a light skin tone, with matte-surface versions for comparison. To achieve the translucent effect, we can simply add a warm shift in temperature and darken the lighter values as the depth of the material increases.

Note that this demonstration is heavily exaggerated to make the effect clear, and in actual figurative paintings, the effect will vary in intensity throughout the form, due to the many varying anatomical structures under our skin.

In image **51** we can see what these varying effects might look like as we scale up the penetration depth of the light. With no subsurface scattering, the skin would appear almost like stone, with no transparency and a dull finish. With too much scattering, there almost appears to be an intense light source within the form itself. Balance is key for capturing this subtle but important effect.

So far we have only assumed a single direct light source acting on our object, but real-life scenarios are rarely this simplified. Ambient light will also be affecting any object in most situations, striking it from all angles and creating subsurface scattering. The light will also randomize strongly under the surface of the object – its exact path is unpredictable.

Therefore, outside of extremely intense, focused lighting situations, we will observe degrees of subsurface scattering all over a translucent form. However, on the light side of the form, this will generally be drowned out by the other light modeling taking place. The scattering will become more apparent as we move into the object's shadows, as shown in the wax candles in image **52**. The shadow color appears generally warmer than the light colors due to this effect, as well as being slightly brighter than they would on a more opaque object.

No
subsurface
scattering

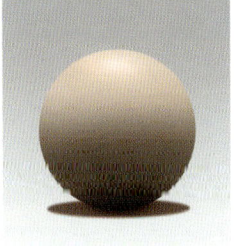
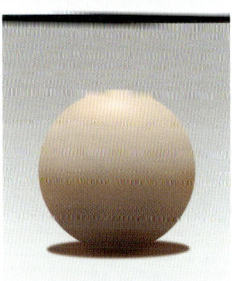
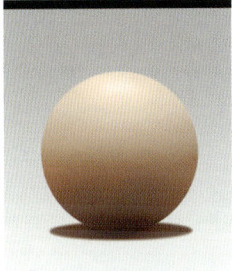
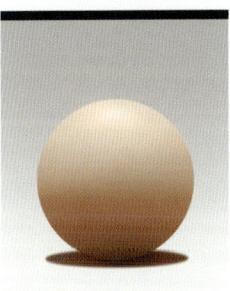

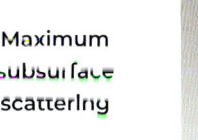
Maximum
subsurface
scattering

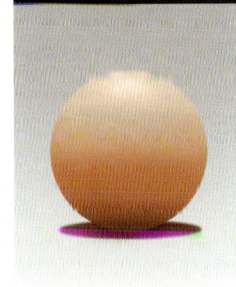

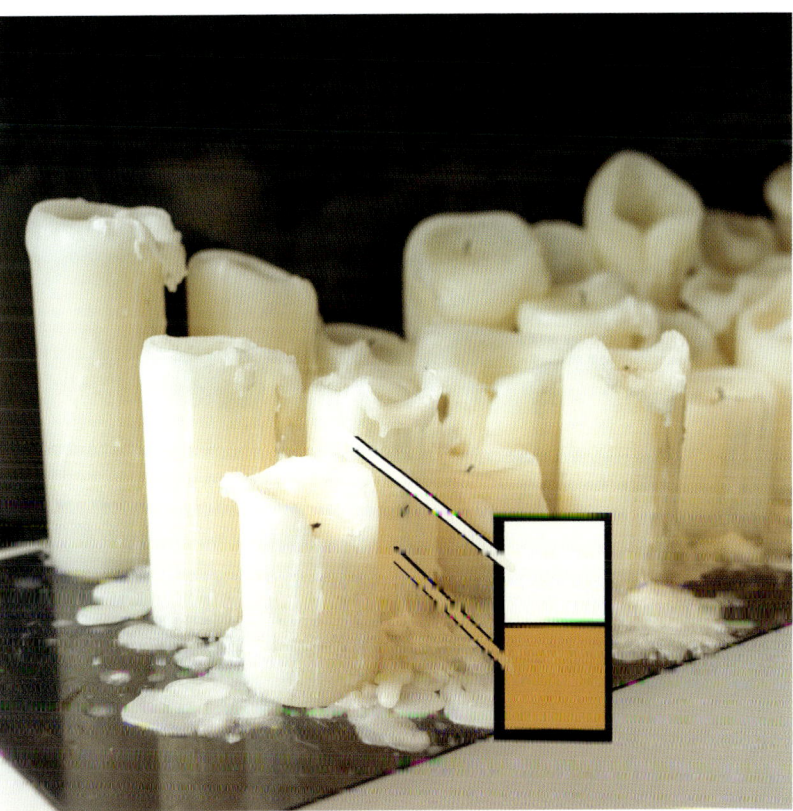

51 In these spheres, with varying levels of translucency, we can see the increasing warmth and influence of light scattering through the material.

52 The shadows on these translucent candles are generally warmer than the ambient light.

LIGHT:
COMBINING MATERIALS

To conclude our journey into the complex and fascinating world of light, this last theory chapter will explore some of the effects that occur when matte, specular, and transparent interactions are combined. No material in reality is ever just one type. While the previous chapters have already given us a solid grasp of how light effects can combine, there are a few more advanced phenomena and specific challenging materials that, if handled right, will give our images greater veracity.

THE FRESNEL EFFECT

Matte surface shading, specular reflections, and transparency never happen in isolation, occurring at the same time on most of the materials you will ever see or represent. Let's look at one idea we need to understand as we begin to use these effects together: the Fresnel effect.

Augustin-Jean Fresnel was a nineteenth-century scientist who contributed greatly to the science of light, most notably in our understanding of refraction and lenses. For our purposes, though, Fresnel refers to a specific effect, most clearly seen across a lake on a clear day (**01**).

If we observe the water's surface close to us, we can see the rocks underneath the transparent water very clearly. However, as we look farther out, we progressively lose the clarity of this underwater image and begin to see the specular reflection of the distant shore instead. By the time our gaze reaches the water on the other shore, the transparency is completely lost and we only see this reflected image.

This effect is a consequence of the "total internal reflection" we learned about on page 171. As our angle of view becomes steeper, more of the transparent image is reflected internally (under the water instead of passing through it) and is unable to reach our eye. As a result, the reflected image comes into stronger prominence until it's the only thing we see. The general rule we can follow here is: A steep angle = a weak specular reflection, and a shallow angle = a strong specular reflection (**02, 03**).

This effect is something we understand quite intuitively for extremely transparent materials. Many people have had the experience of seeing a landscape reflected on a far shore, yet being able to see their own feet if they look straight down into the water.

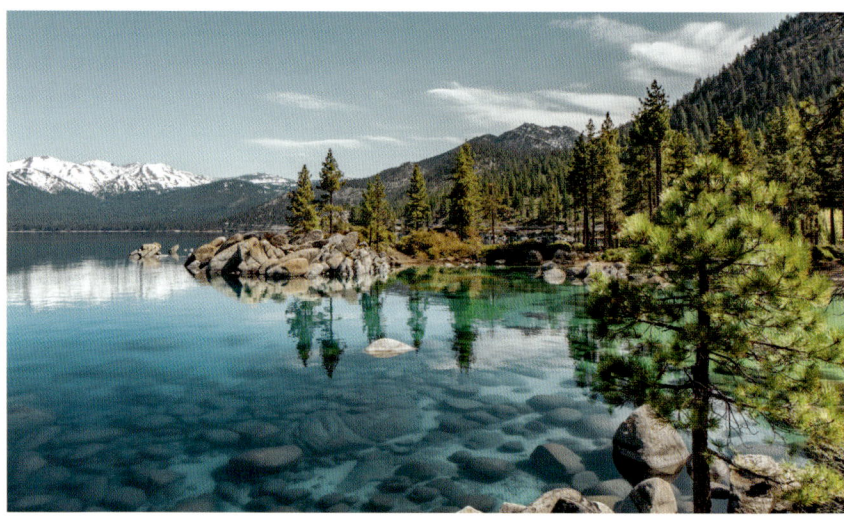

01 The Fresnel effect visible on a lake.

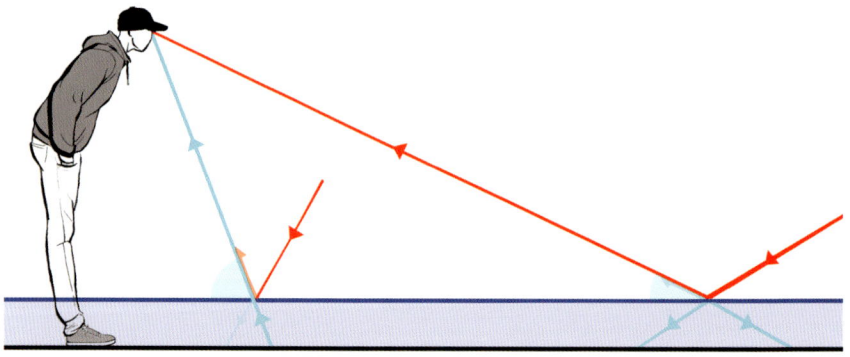

🔵 **Steep angle (weak reflected image, strong transmitted image)**

🔴 **Shallow angle (strong reflected image, weak transmitted image)**

02 A steep angle of view equals a weak reflection and a clearer view into the water, while a shallow angle of view results in the opposite.

What is less understood is that this effect is always present on a huge range of materials, including many with a more matte surface.

We can see this in image **04**. The matte surface shading of the red sheet is extremely prominent when we view it face-on, with no reflected image. However, as the viewing angle becomes shallower, the sheet becomes much more strongly reflective. The reflection becomes much more present, and the color is more dictated by the white backdrop than by the sheet's red local color. Try looking at the smooth surface of a coffee table or similar object in real life, first from directly above and then from a lower angle, and see how much the color and reflection change (**05**).

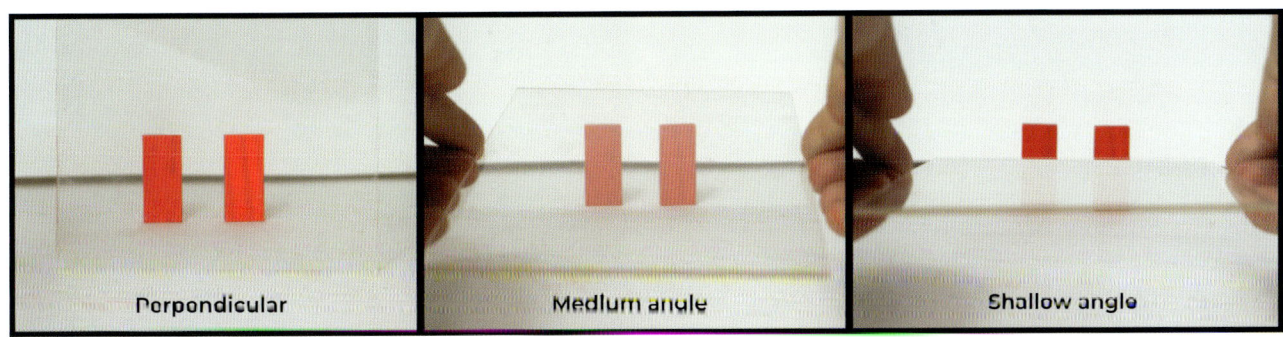

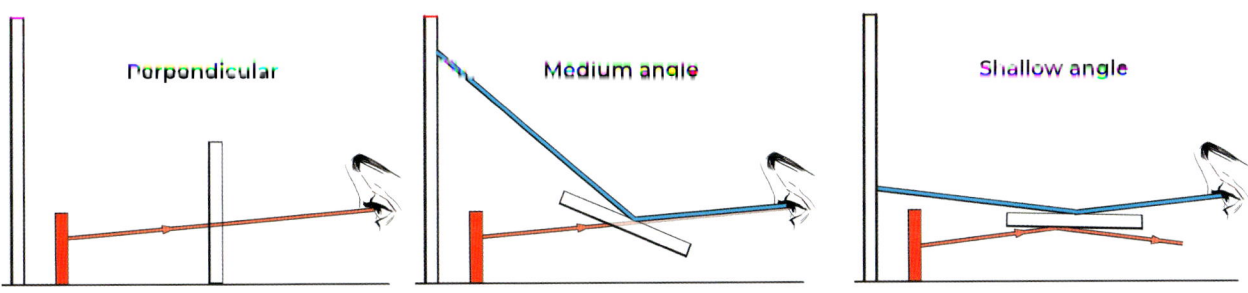

03 When viewing the glass plane at a perpendicular angle, we see the maximum transmitted image with minimal reflection. As the plane turns, the transmitted image becomes weaker and the reflected image stronger.

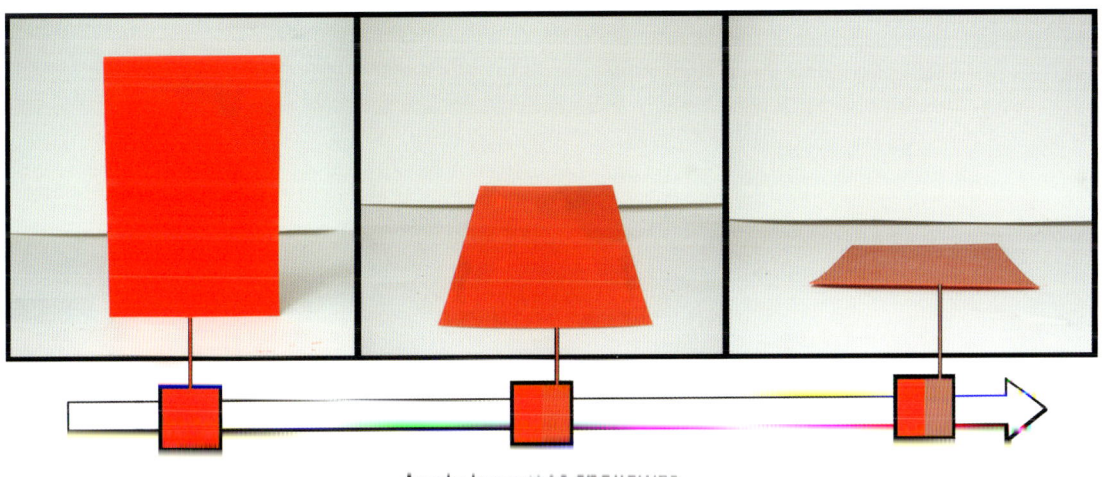

04 As the viewing gets shallower, we see more of the color of the background (in this case, white) mixing additively with the matte surface color of the object.

Angle becomes shallower

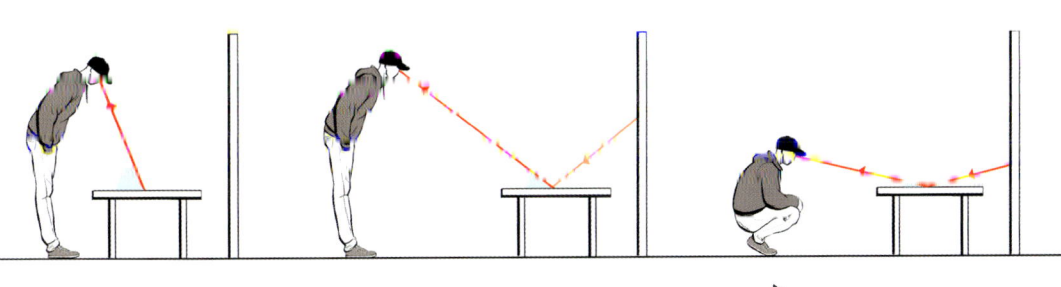

05 Observe various flat surfaces in real life and see how drastically they can change when you alter your viewing angle.

Steeper angle
Stronger matte surface
Weaker reflection

Shallower angle
Weaker matte surface
Stronger reflection

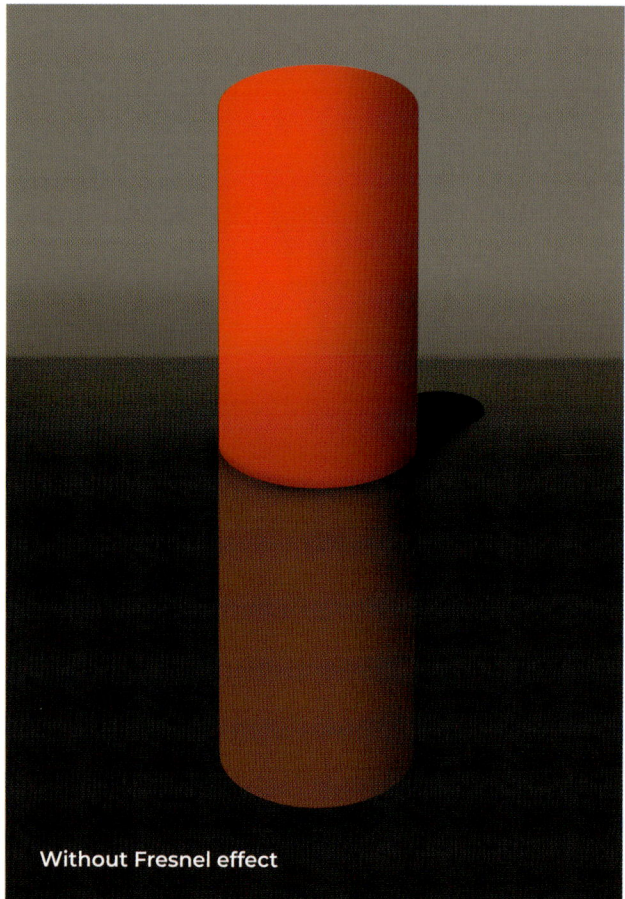
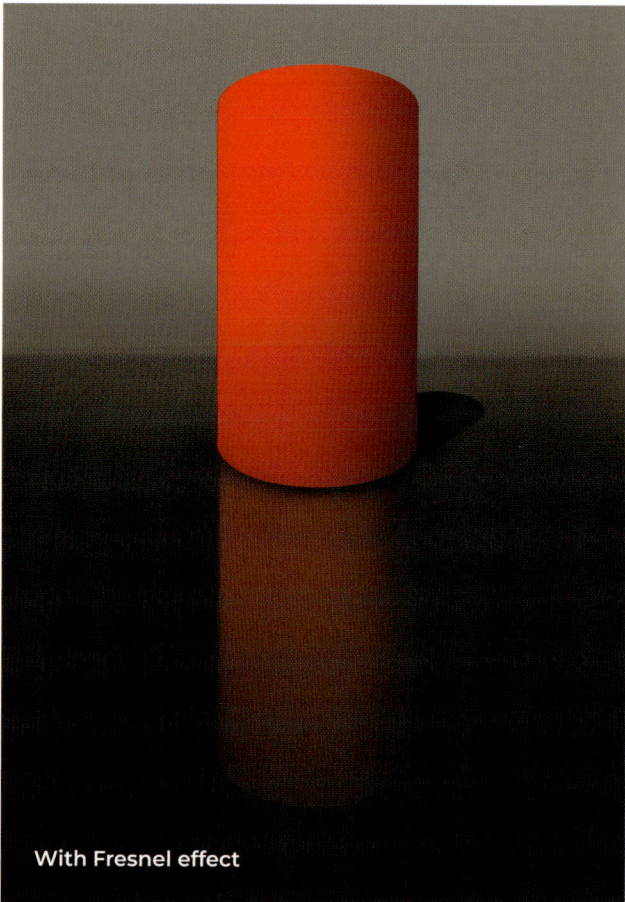

Without Fresnel effect

With Fresnel effect

06 The reflection is somewhat unconvincing to us when it's simply a direct flip of the object. Fading the reflection to suggest the Fresnel effect makes it far more believable.

FRESNEL REFLECTIONS ADD REALISM

We can immediately see the results of this effect when we place objects on a slightly reflective floor. In image **06** you can see a scene depicted without the Fresnel effect, with the reflection simply being a generic flipped image of the object. The results appear somewhat artificial. If we add the Fresnel effect by simply erasing the reflection as it approaches the viewer in space, just a simple gradient, it hugely heightens the realism of the scene.

This type of reflection is more common than you might think – keep an eye out for it on the surfaces around you! The Fresnel effect is happening all the time and has strong effects on the colors that we observe at these shallow angles. On curved forms, especially, we see this idea coming into strong effect. Since curved forms go through every angle before completely turning away from our eye, there will always be some influence of these stronger reflections **(07)**.

If we apply this effect to a simply modeled form, we can see just how much realism it adds to our paintings. In image **08** we can see a basic cylinder modeled purely with matte surface shading, with values and chroma conforming to our simple rules in relation to the light source. The painting has some dimension but it doesn't sit naturally in the scene – it looks like a basic 3D render that lacks realism.

However, when we add specular reflections, we can see how the influence of the environment brings realism to the image. The modeling on a form will always have some color influence from its surrounding environment, and it's important that we consider this whenever we paint.

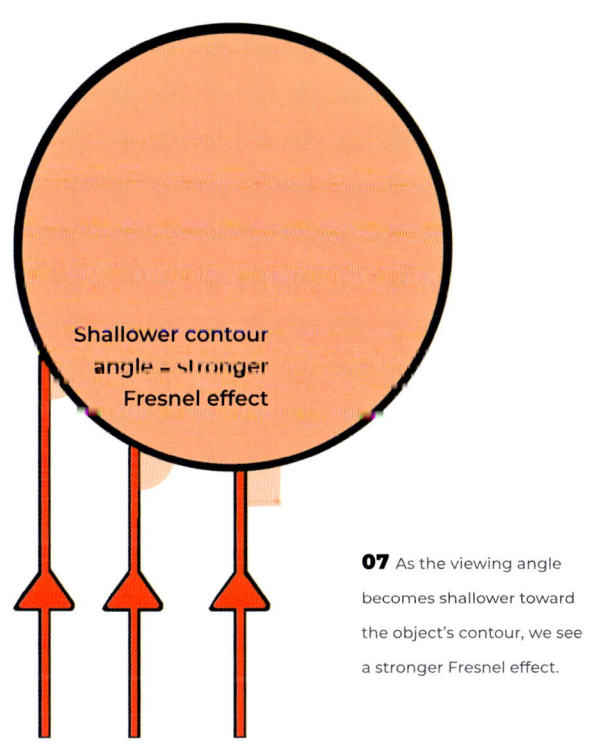

Shallower contour angle = stronger Fresnel effect

07 As the viewing angle becomes shallower toward the object's contour, we see a stronger Fresnel effect.

THE SKIPPING STONE ANALOGY RETURNS

We can think of the Fresnel effect with the same "skipping stone" analogy that helped us understand total internal reflection on page 172. If you could skip a stone off the plane, it would have a strong reflection influence.

As this metaphorical stone would glance off the curved sides of a cylinder, for example, we would see more pronounced reflections on those areas, and less reflection on the areas that are facing our viewing angle directly.

Matte
surface only

Specular
reflections only

Matte surface with
Fresnel reflections

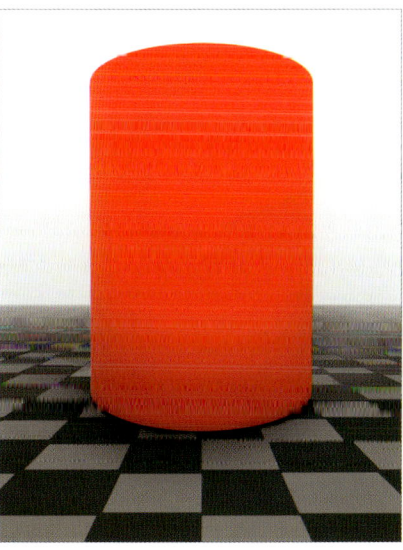

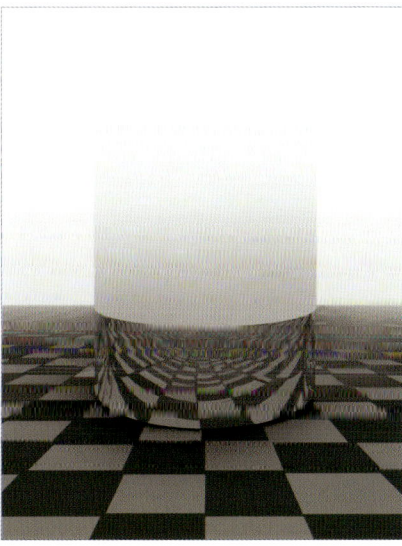

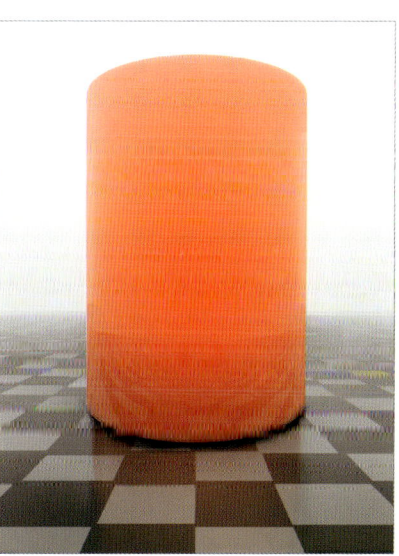

08 The matte surface on its own looks flat and unrealistic. Layering specular information on top in Screen mode, with greater strength toward the edges, gives us much more depth.

SPECULAR EFFECTS ON MATTE SURFACES

Now that we are aware of all varying effects of specular and matte shading, we need to discuss how these different types of shading interact in objects that possess elements of both. No surface will ever be purely matte – some specular shine will always be present – so we need to always keep this in mind when we work.

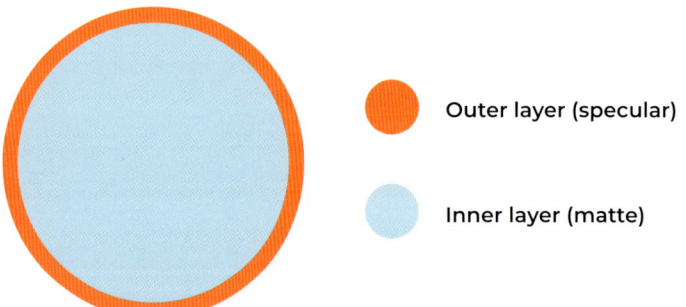

Outer layer (specular)

Inner layer (matte)

In general, as we spoke about on page 102, we can think about these two types of shading as occurring on different layers of a material. We can almost think of the specular shading as an outer shell around the form. One of the wonderful things about creating paintings digitally is that we can even represent this in how we organize our layers, placing a higher specular layer over a lower layer with all the matte shading. In image **09** we can see the two layers I have created for one form, allowing us to examine these interactions.

As mentioned on page 72, if an object displays a lot of matte surface shading, most of the light striking it must be absorbed, making it an inefficient specular reflector. So while we could initially paint its specular layer as a pure chrome object, we would need to remove a lot of the information from the darker elements as we go, which is just not an efficient way to work. Due to this, many painters will only consider the highlight as the important specular information, but it's important to realize that specular nuances are happening all throughout the form.

These two layers mix additively as light on the surface. This means that anywhere that is dark in the specular information will just appear as matte shading. Anywhere where the specular information is lighter, the specular layer will tint the underlying matte surface color. In order to simulate this in

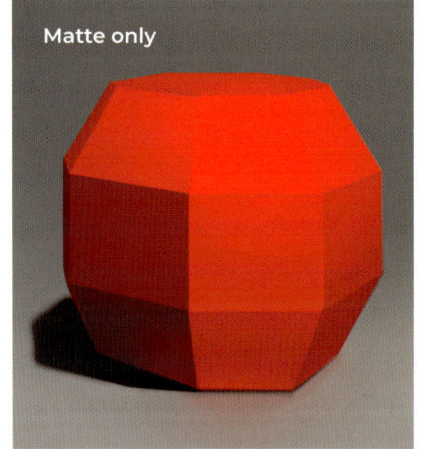

Matte only

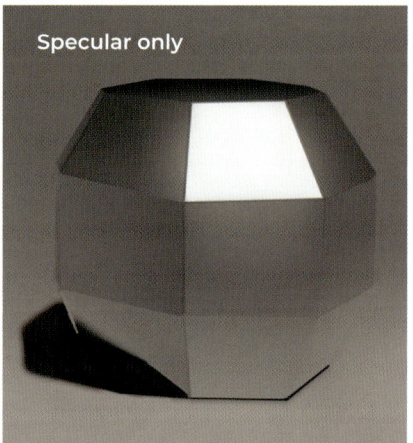

Specular only

09 We can think of matte shading and specular shading as occurring on different layers of an object's material.

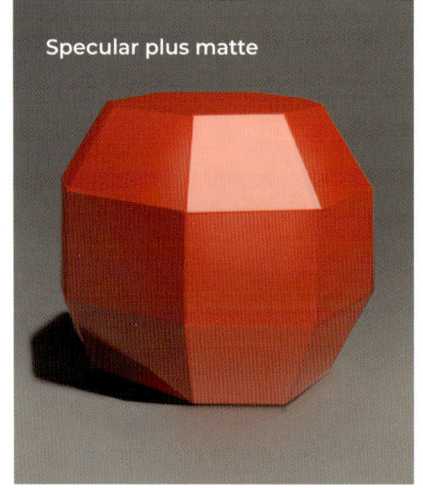

Specular plus matte

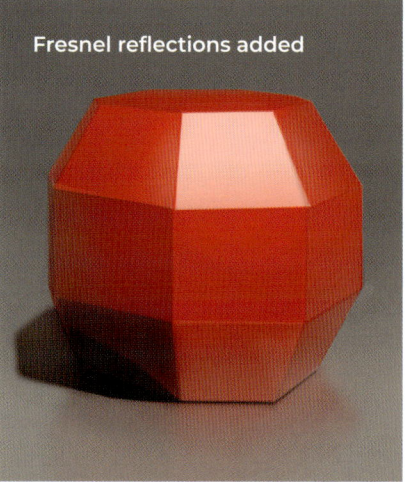

Fresnel reflections added

10 When adding Fresnel, the specular reflection strength is varied, becoming stronger on planes shallower to our vision. These shallower planes also take on some of the background color.

Photoshop, switch the higher specular layer to the "Screen" blending mode.

You can see on the first example in image **10** just how much realism is added by including this specular information, compared to the pure matte version. One side effect of combining these two shadings is that the specular highlight will always be lower in chroma – a brighter tint – than the object's local color. This is incredibly important to consider when we work traditionally, where we can't add this effect with blending modes.

After adding this generic additive layer, it's important to add in the Fresnel effect mentioned on the previous page. In practical terms, this means painting a bit of the background environment's color into the shallow angles of the form. The effect is subtle but vital for placing the object convincingly into the scene – far more important than students often realize.

THE FRESNEL EFFECT AND ENVIRONMENTAL COLORS

To illustrate the degree to which the Fresnel effect influences the perceived colors of objects, let's compare these forms in several different environments **(11)**. You can see just how dramatically the top plane shifts in color toward the color of the surrounding environment, being much cooler in the blue room, warmer in the yellow room, and so on. Remember these environmental colors are still mixing additively with the matte surface color.

In image **12** we can see the "cut-out" appearance of the form if we do this incorrectly. The object appears detached from the scene, like it doesn't belong to its surroundings. Objects will always be strongly affected by their environment's colors, so the importance of this effect for realism shouldn't be underestimated.

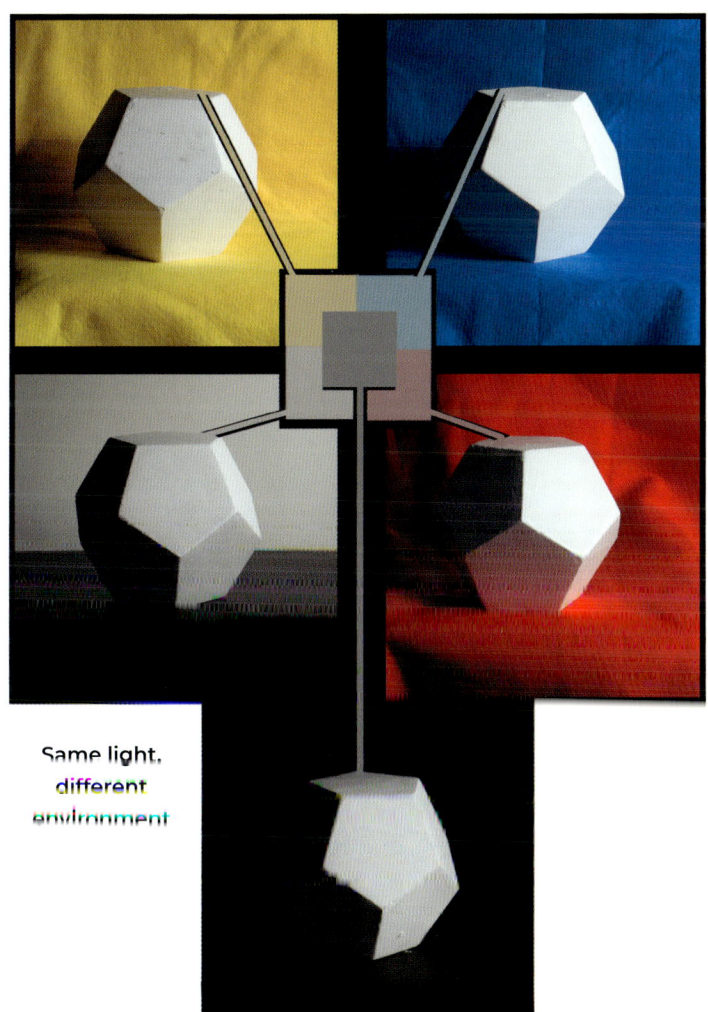

Same light, different environment

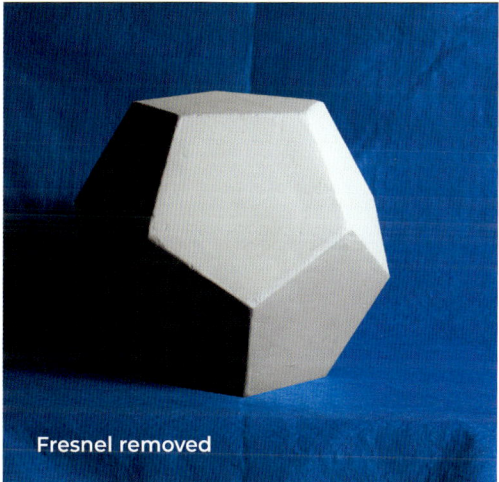

Fresnel removed

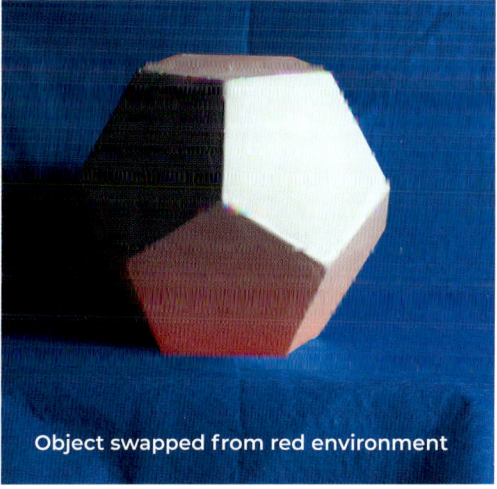

Object swapped from red environment

11 Comparing the top plane color of each of these objects, we can see how the surrounding environment influences the colors we perceive.

12 Here we can see how strongly out-of-place the object looks when the Fresnel effect is not applied or applied incorrectly.

The same effect occurs no matter what the local color of the object is. In image **13** we can see another set of forms in a series of different environments, this time with stronger local colors. The black background influences the spheres' colors the least, so is our "control" version to compare against.

In the other versions, that original color is shown in the outer square, while the inner square is the new color influenced by the colored background. The effect of the surroundings is powerful, though the colors mix as we would expect: In the red environment, the yellow becomes orange, the blue becomes purple, and so on. This is not new information to us.

However, one interesting change is that each of the affected colors is also brighter in value than the neutral original. This is because, unlike many of the color interactions we have dealt with so far, these colors are mixing as light. Therefore, they mix additively and become brighter, rather than losing value as they would if we were mixing paints.

It's also worth noting that the colored sphere that matches the environment color is also the least affected in hue. This is because it's mixing with its own color – so its hue doesn't change, but it does become brighter in value.

HIGHLIGHT TYPES

Since much of the information from the specular reflection will be lost in darkness on most matte forms, the highlight and its proper placement will always be our key concern. In order to understand this placement better, it can be useful to follow the simple path of a light source and track the path of our two important highlights:

- The matte "form" highlight: The point of highest chroma and local value.

- The specular highlight: The point of highest absolute value – a lower-chroma tint of the form highlight.

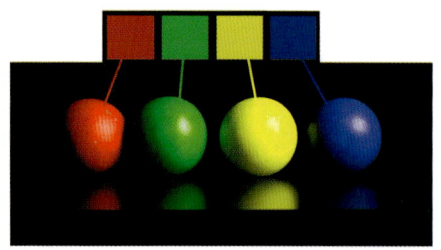

Black background has least influence

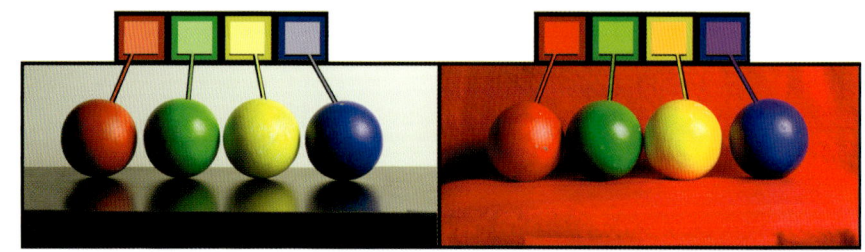

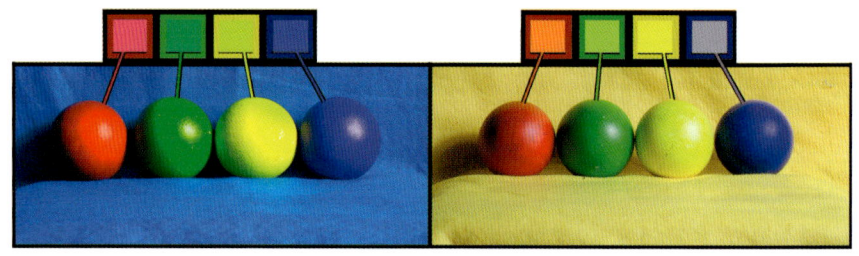

13 The black background has the least influence on the objects' colors, making it an ideal reference for comparison with different backgrounds. In the other examples, the outer color of each square is the original color of the plane, with the new perceived color inside.

Image **14** shows a form viewed from straight on with the light source's position rotating away from us, with the form highlight marked in blue and the specular highlight marked in orange. The form highlight is created by the plane perpendicular to the light, while the specular highlight is decided by our relationship to the light source – the angle of reflection being the same as the angle of incidence (see page 70).

The most common highlighting mistake is assuming that both of these highlights are in the same place. Many people simply paint up to the highlight and leave it at that. However, as we can see in the diagrams, this is simply not the case. This scenario would only occur when our eye is in the same position as the light source. As soon as the light moves from that impossible position, the difference between the two highlights

becomes gradually larger. By the time the light is directly above the object, the form highlight is seen at the 45-degree point, halfway down the form.

As the light source moves behind the form, we no longer see the form highlight, as it's on the unseen side of the sphere – but we still see the specular highlight! Due to the Fresnel effect, this is also where the reflection of the light source is strongest, almost a direct reflection. This type of lighting is called "rim lighting" and is strongly defined by the color of the light source.

This separation of highlights is incredibly important when we work, and identifying the two different types is one of the most important things for us to do early in any painting. This is because all of the form changes need to be painted in relation to the

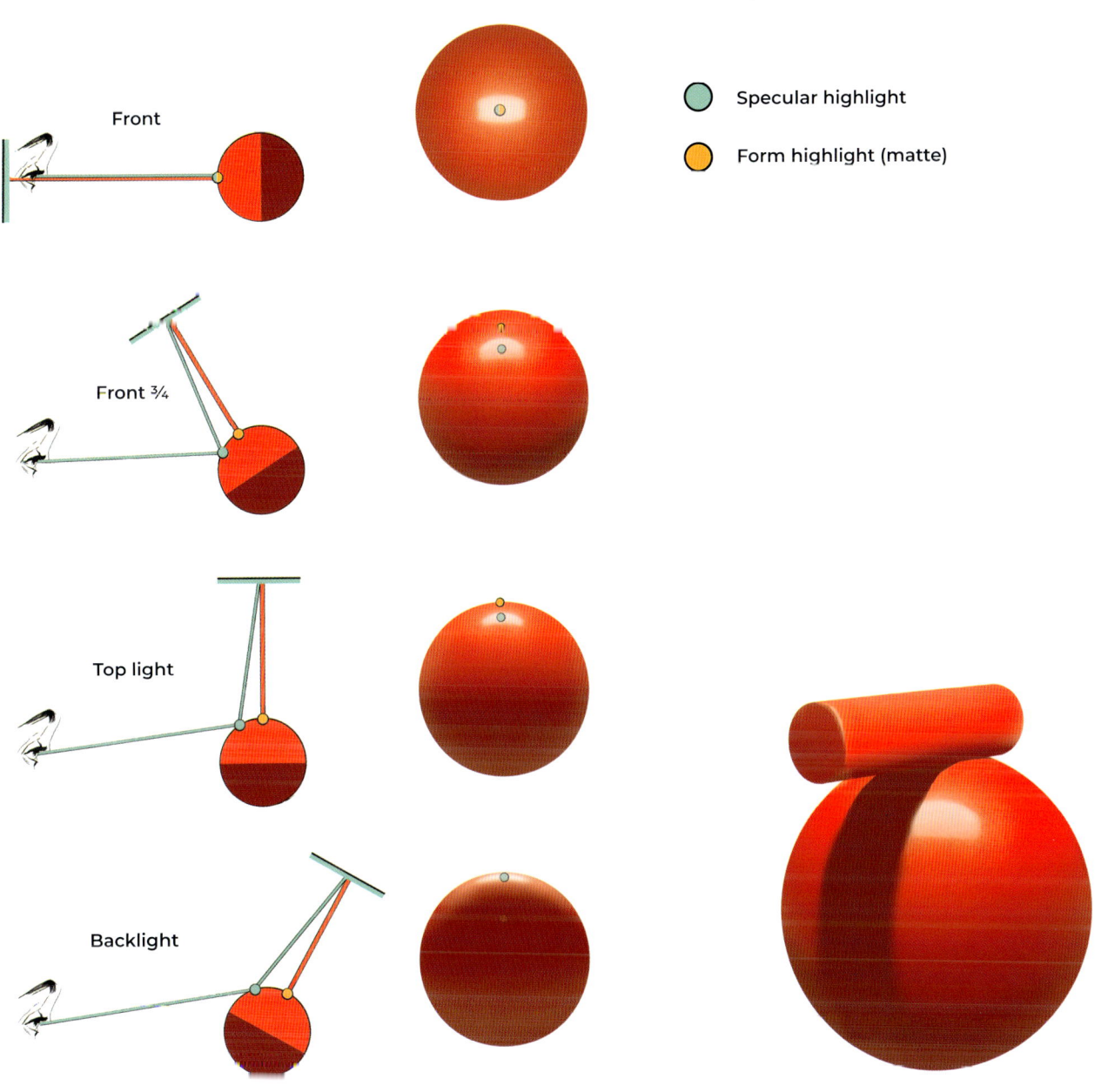

Front

Front ¾

Top light

Backlight

◯ Specular highlight

◯ Form highlight (matte)

14 The two highlight types will always appear in different places, relative to our eye. The only time they would appear in the same position is in a hypothetical, impossible scenario where the light source and our viewpoint are in exactly the same place.

15 The shadow shape and highlight on an object must never meet. The only exception is when the cast shadow from another form blocks the highlight.

form highlight, gaining chroma, while the specular information is just a lighter value added on top of this deeper shading. It's an extremely common area for errors, so it's worth paying close attention to it.

The specular highlight must never enter the form shadow – this is an absolute rule that should never be violated. The two must never touch, and there will always be some light shape between the specular and the terminator. Even in the backlit rim lighting scenario, you can see a fine degree of separation between the highlight and the shadow shape – it's incredibly narrow and subtle, but it's there.

However, a cast shadow from another shape may directly block the highlight. In this case, the specular highlight will continue right up to the shadow shape. These can be some of the most striking, contrasting edges in a painting, but keep in mind that this is the *only* scenario where a shadow shape and a specular highlight make contact **(15)**.

TEXTURE CHANGES

Another important consideration whenever we model objects is the quality of surface texture. When we use the term "texture" here, we mean something more specific than simply what the surface is made from – we mean its surface *quality*. Another way of thinking about this is the surface's level of roughness. Ask yourself what the surface would feel like. Is it smooth or rough? How rough?

While we will generally think of texture as a unique property of a material, it is actually also a result of changes in form and will conform to all the logic that we have discussed so far. While beginners will often attempt to fake texture with a clever use of brushes – and more advanced artists often pull this off – if we are going to represent texture properly, we need to understand that we paint texture in the same way we paint larger forms, just on a smaller scale.

Students can often be misled by the mesmerizing detail of texture and miss the larger forms on top of which texture always sits. To avoid this problem, it's helpful to imagine what the object would look like if covered by thick drapery of its local color, and start by painting that. This is the "large form" of the object.

Start by representing only these large changes in form, then the medium forms, progressively working toward the smaller textural forms. This approach is called working "from general to specific" and is one of the most important core working principles of all modeling.

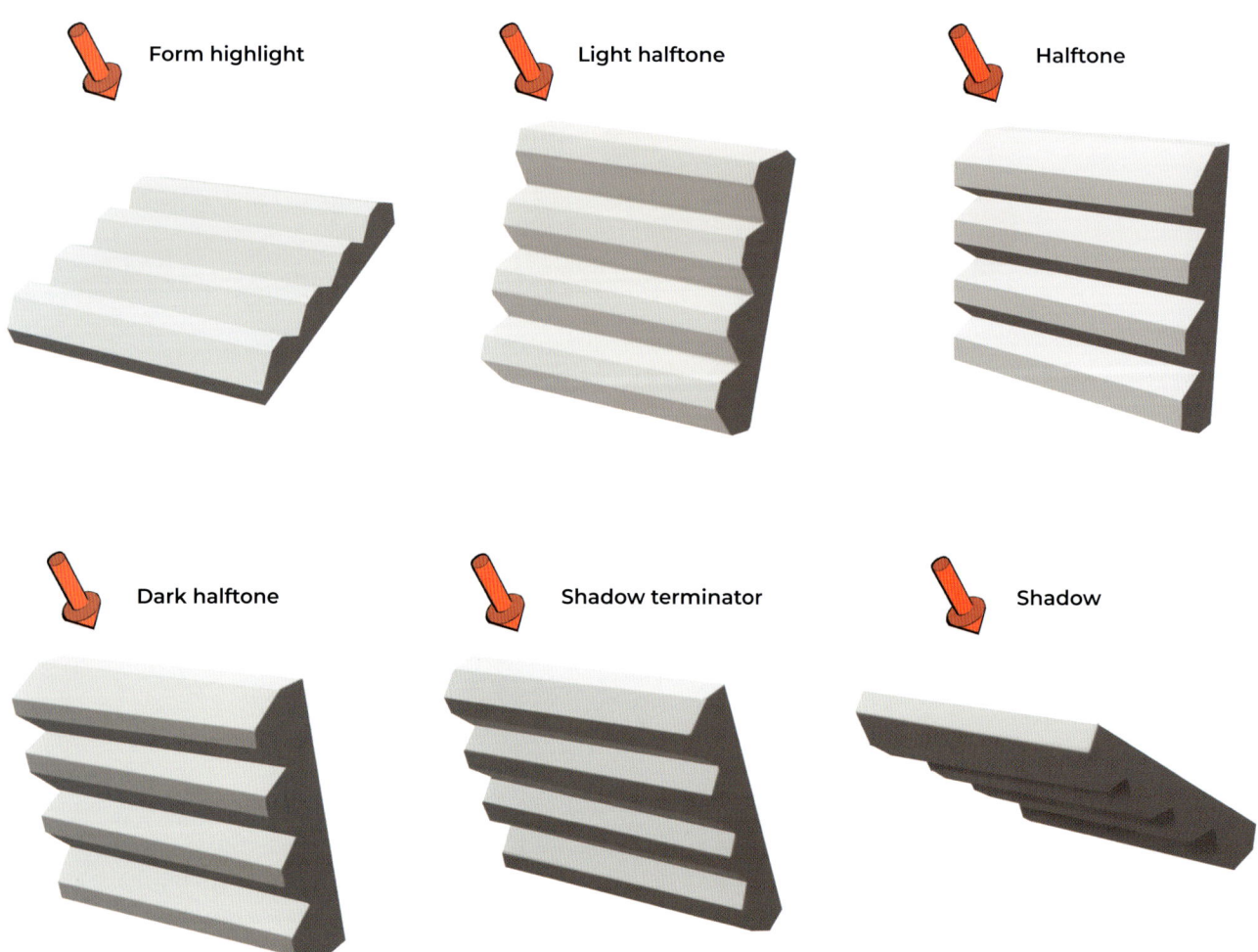

16 A textured plane with the corresponding value group for that angle. Note how the texture starts out less visible, becomes highly visible, then becomes less so again.

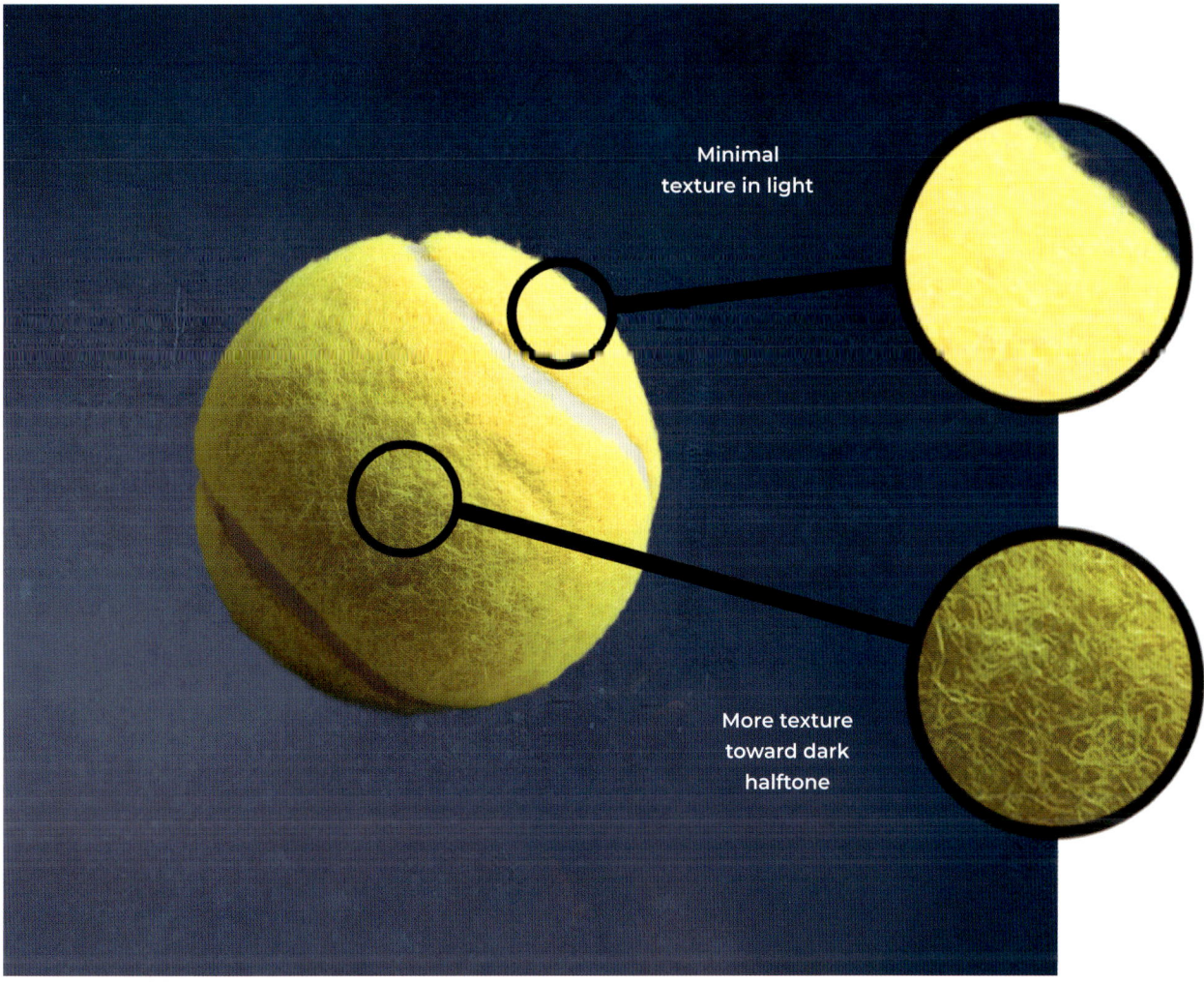

Minimal
texture in light

More texture
toward dark
halftone

17 The tennis ball's fuzzy texture is less visible in the brightest areas.

MATTE SURFACE TEXTURE CHANGES

When we endeavor to represent texture in matte surface shading, it's helpful to examine the case of one simple plane as it turns from light to shadow. For clarity, let's add an angled triangular strip texture, so we can track the changes in modeling **(16)**. If we look at the first form highlight, under full direct light, the texture is extremely hard to make out. The values are grouped very close together, so any changes in form will be within an extremely tight range.

However, as the plane moves down through the angles, the clarity of the texture increases exponentially as we approach the shadow area. At the dark halftone point, we can see the maximum amount of textural information, which leads us to a useful strategy: When representing texture, focus on the dark halftone.

It may be surprising that the plane is not wholly in shadow as it becomes perpendicular to the light source (the dark halftone stage). In order to throw the form entirely into shadow, we actually need to rotate the plane even further away. The exact angle where this effect occurs will vary depending on the level of texture, but it is important to remember that this texture will be felt strongly along the shadow terminator's edge as well.

This general increase in textural contrast as we move down the form will always be true, and is easily observable in photography. In image **17** we can see just how much stronger the tennis ball's fuzzy texture appears as the form turns from the light, reaching maximum clarity at the dark halftone point.

Many artists take advantage of this and focus strongly on adding texture to the dark halftone – in fact, detailing that area is often enough on its own to suggest texture. This is a huge boon that allows us to be much more efficient and effective in our paintings.

TEXTURE ON A SPECULAR SURFACE

So far our discussion of texture has focused purely on matte surface modeling. However, we also learned previously that no material is perfectly matte, so we must learn how texture affects specular surfaces as well. Image **18** shows a perfectly smooth sphere that will be the starting point for our observations here.

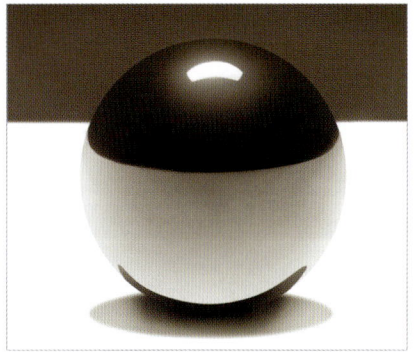

18 This perfectly smooth, chrome, specular sphere will be the basis for our texture exploration here.

In image **19**, we can see some simple texture created on a sphere by adding a couple of scratches in one direction, with a cross-section to clarify exactly what is being done to the form. Each new scratch conforms to the exact same logic that we have learned so far – that a plane at a certain angle will reflect an image of a particular part of the environment.

This means that each angle of the scratch is a color displaced to the right or left, stretching the reflected image in a perpendicular direction to the scratch. If we add more scratches farther around the form, they cannot pick up values from the front of the sphere. On the cross-section diagrams, the angles with matching directions – and therefore, matching colors – are highlighted in red or blue.

If we multiply these scratches over the entire surface of the sphere, we can see the perpendicular stretching effect increase

(20). Since these scratches are small and numerous enough to not register as individual marks, all we perceive are the specular highlight and blurred reflected image stretching in the same perpendicular direction. If we change the direction to vertical scratches, the effect is reversed.

If we combine these two types of texture, the blurring and highlight expands farther as the image stretches in both perpendicular directions **(21)**. This heavily textured surface begins to appear less shiny, and the more texture we add, the more matte it becomes **(22)**. Note that this is not *true* matte surface shading – only the illusion of it. The material is still entirely specular and would require a looser atomic structure to become truly matte. The reflection is somewhat randomized by the surface but is still absolutely an image of the surroundings. We often see this effect on metallic surfaces that have been subject to a lot of wear, such as used armor or an old car. Many metallic

Highlight spreads out perpendicular to scratches

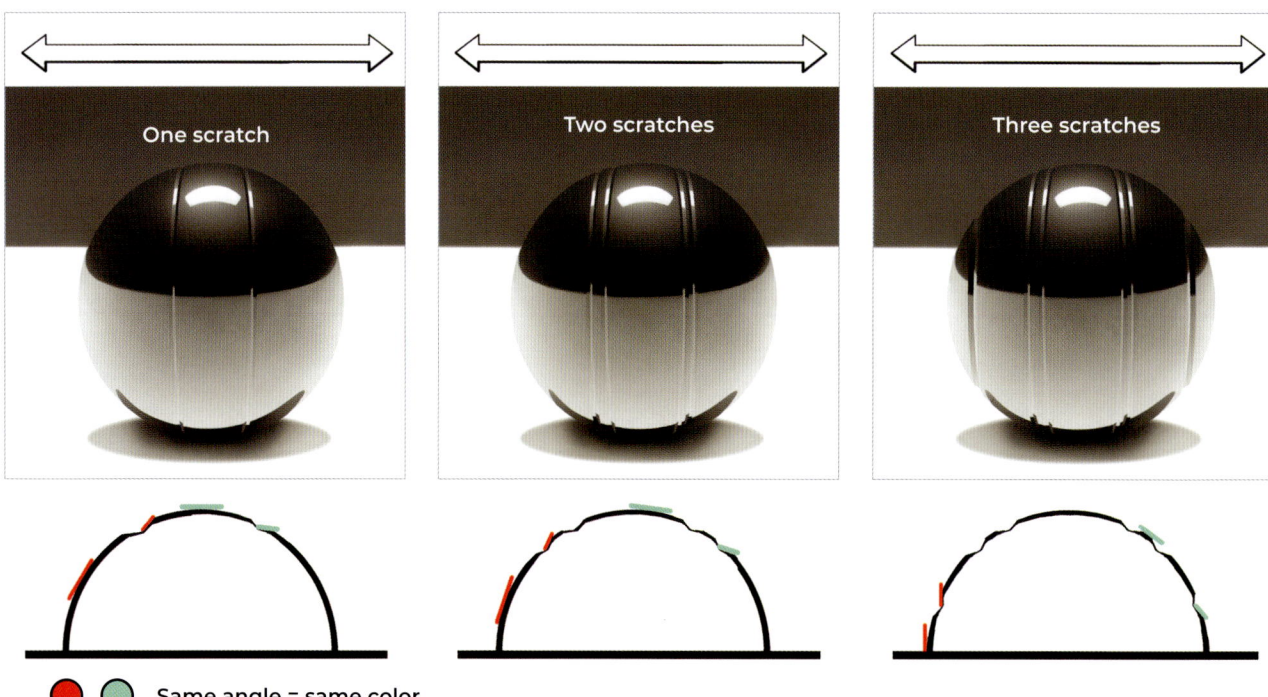

Same angle = same color

19 On a specular subject, the image will be stretched perpendicular to any texture added, and planes facing the same angles will reflect the same colors.

paints also take on this appearance, as they usually consist of tiny shards of metal spread all over the surface of the object, leading to a much rougher surface without obviously changing the object's planes.

As we learned on page 190, these lighting effects will rarely (if ever) be observed in isolation. On most materials, they will be seen together and be subject to multiple logics at the same time. Since objects that are more matte will generally be inefficient specular reflectors, we usually only see the effects of specular reflection in the bright specular highlight. So, as we learned on page 195, representing texture is most efficient if we focus detail on the highlight and dark halftone areas.

Image **23** shows just how much we can vary the appearance of texture by adjusting these two elements on the same subject – our primary strategy for handling texture on most forms.

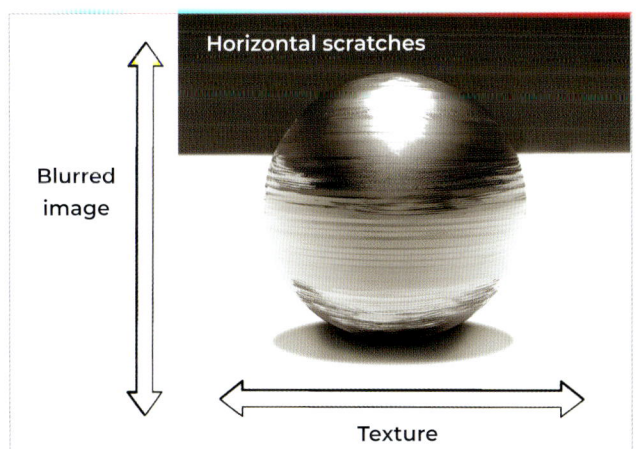

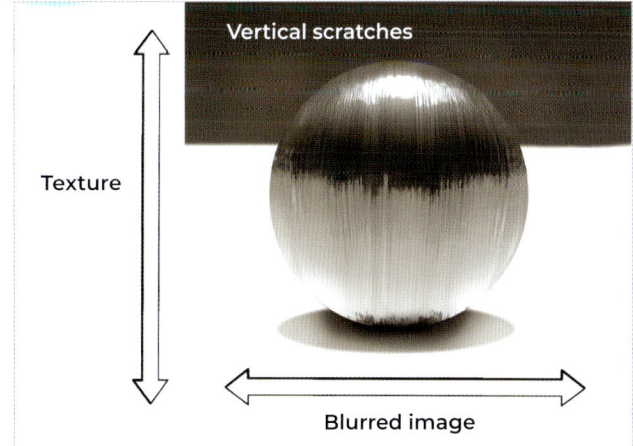

20 If we multiply the scratches to cover the whole sphere, the perpendicular blurring effect becomes more strongly apparent.

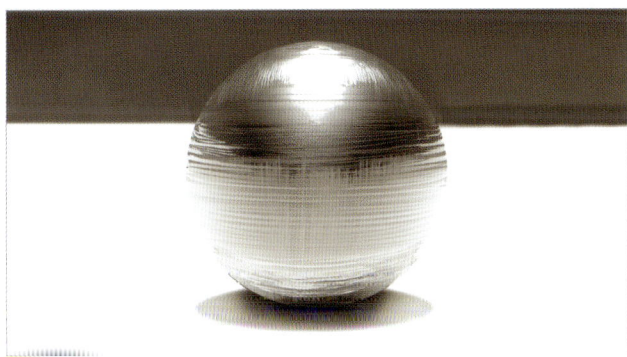

21 If the scratches are layered in both directions, the specular highlight is expanded and stretched both ways.

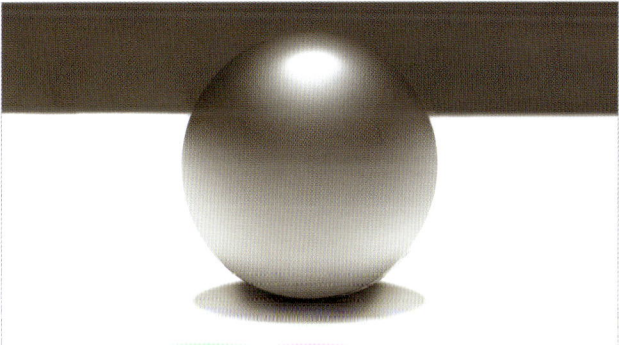

22 A more heavily textured specular surface begins to appear more matte, but remember that it's not truly, completely matte.

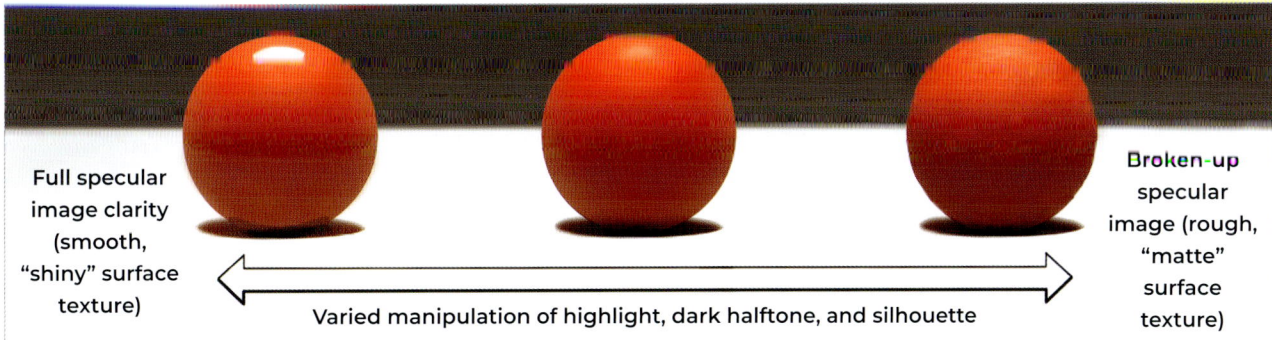

23 Learning how to vary our handling of the specular highlight and dark halftone is key to mastering the communication of surface texture.

COMPLEX MATERIALS: SKIN

Skin is one of the most fascinating and often confusing areas of study for beginner artists. Since most artists will have to interact at least somewhat with depicting people, this is an important material to understand, and a great place to start learning how we can approach analyzing other materials.

Everything we have learned so far will serve as our conceptual framework for understanding this complex subject. There are three basic questions that we must ask when approaching this, or any, new material:

- **What is the local color, or range of local colors?** There could be one general local color or numerous variations. These may be organic or synthetic. We would expect organic color to be more gradated and varied, while synthetic, artificial coloring (such as a tattoo or paint) would change more suddenly.

- **Is this material primarily matte, specular, transparent, or luminescent?** Having this clearly set in our mind is essential, as it will guide us on the general logic to use in rendering the material. There will always be some degree of other types of interaction present in any material, so we must consider the extent of each.

- **What is the material's texture?** Is the texture of the material rough or smooth? What is the cause of this texture, if it's present, and how might that affect our considerations?

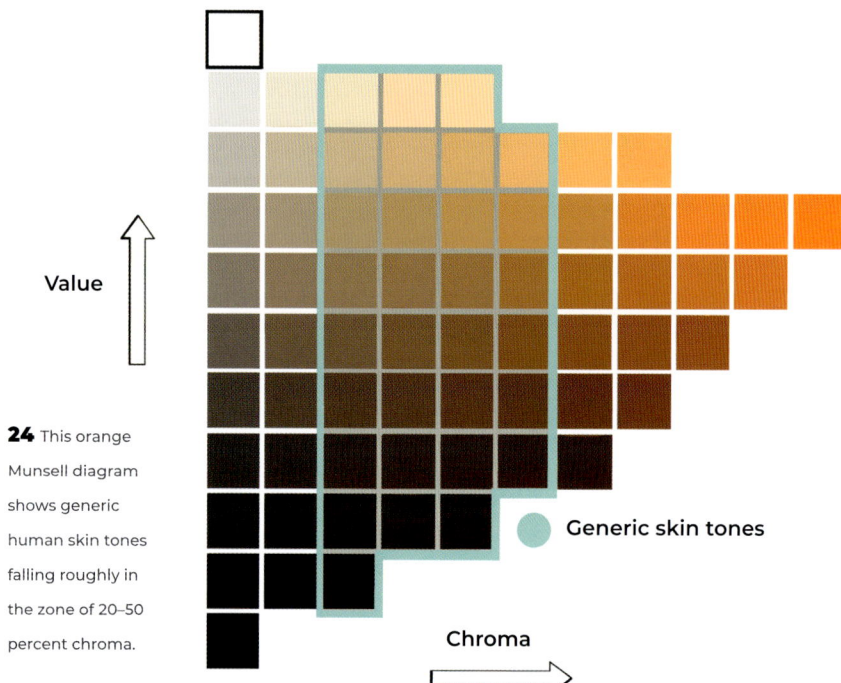

24 This orange Munsell diagram shows generic human skin tones falling roughly in the zone of 20–50 percent chroma.

Generic skin tones

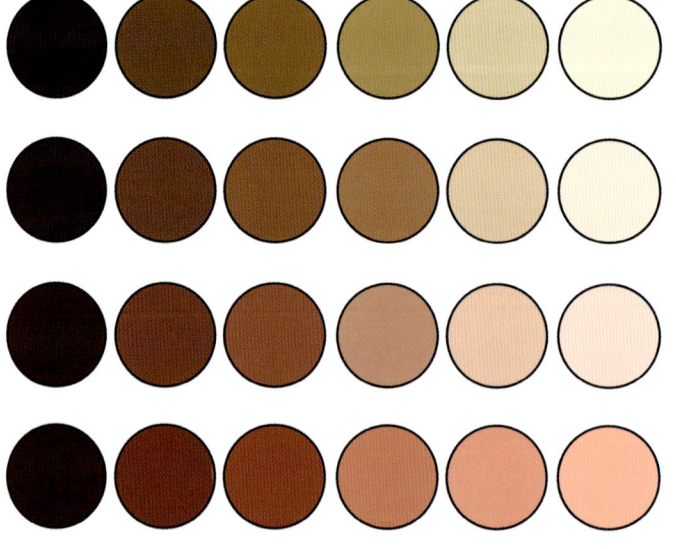

25 Within the generally orange tone of skin, we can observe huge organic variation including reds and pinks.

If we can clearly answer these three fundamental questions about a material, we gain a great head start in understanding how it works. The best way to test our understanding, as always, is by trying to render the material on the fundamental forms of a sphere and cube. So let's look at how we might apply this process to understanding the challenging, varied subject of human skin.

WHAT'S THE LOCAL COLOR?

Our first question of local color is fairly easy to answer when it comes to skin. Skin's local color will generally exist in a predictable and narrow range. In image **24**, the Munsell diagram for a middle orange tone, we can see where this range of skin colors will generally fall. Orange starts to take on the appearance of skin as we lower the chroma, with generic skin tones typically existing in the orange tones below fifty percent chroma.

Keep in mind that when we are working digitally, we are generally working with saturation rather than chroma. This means that darker skin tones will typically be higher in saturation than lighter ones, though they are still roughly the same chroma.

Within these generic skin tones, we can observe wide variations from yellow-oranges to fully chromatic reds **(25)** Many of the oranges and reds come through from the more highly chromatic blood showing through the surface of the skin. These subtle variations sometimes appear to students as greens and reds. For example, people often refer to the veins as being "blue."

However, if we look at some of these variations in isolation, we can see that while they may appear blue, purple, or green in context, they are actually variations of low-chroma oranges, yellows, and reds, and not "blue" at all **(26)**.

Skin is organic, so is always varying in color, often in quite subtle, gradated shifts. Without these variations, it would look like stone or plastic, so it's vital to include them throughout the whole surface. Realizing that these color variations exist in quite a tight range of harmony is one of the most helpful guides for this.

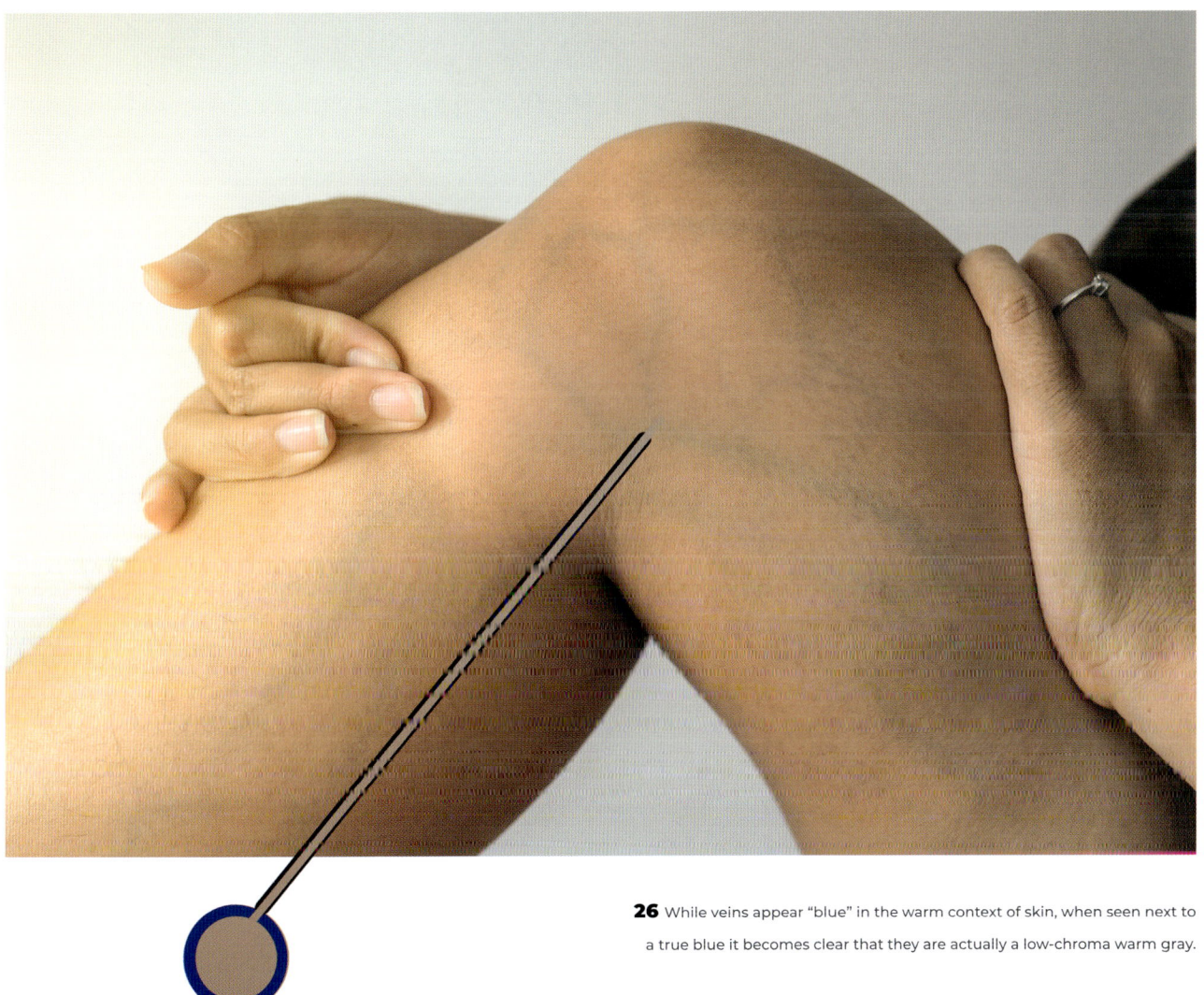

26 While veins appear "blue" in the warm context of skin, when seen next to a true blue it becomes clear that they are actually a low-chroma warm gray.

MATTE, SPECULAR, OR TRANSPARENT?

In general, skin is primarily a matte material, and many artists have made wonderful paintings purely appealing to this quality. However, if we want to be more specific, skin is an opaque but fairly translucent material, and this translucency becomes incredibly important when we get into color.

In image **27** we can see a simplification of the three layers of the human form: skin and fat, muscle and blood, and finally, bone. The changing thickness of these three layers around the human form explains many of the local color variations that we observe. Our skin can appear lower or higher in chroma, and more red or more yellow, depending on the thickness of these different layers.

There are some consistent areas where these shifts can occur. For example, noses and ears generally appear redder due to increased blood flow. However, the exact places where these areas occur are subject to a huge amount of variation, and can even vary depending on emotion. Everyone is familiar with the red flush that comes to an embarrassed face! Due to these countless variations, the best way to get these shifts right is always going to be observing them and learning from life.

Everything that we learned about translucency and subsurface scattering remains true here. Skin shadows are a bit lighter and more chromatic than you might expect. The ambient light will also have a strong effect on the darkest accents in transparent surfaces. Since the only light that can get into these small gaps is entering at extremely shallow angles, many artists decide to paint their darkest colors on transparent materials with extremely chromatic colors. For example, painting a skin shadow down to a chromatic red-orange rather a low-chroma black **(28)**.

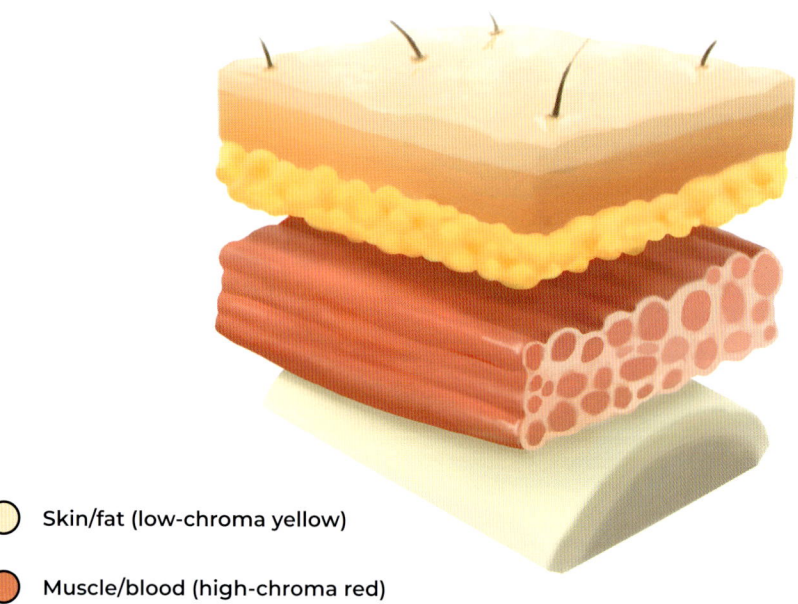

- ⬤ Skin/fat (low-chroma yellow)
- ⬤ Muscle/blood (high-chroma red)
- ⬤ Bone (low-chroma gray)

27 The variation of these three layers creates organic shifts and gradations of local color in our skin.

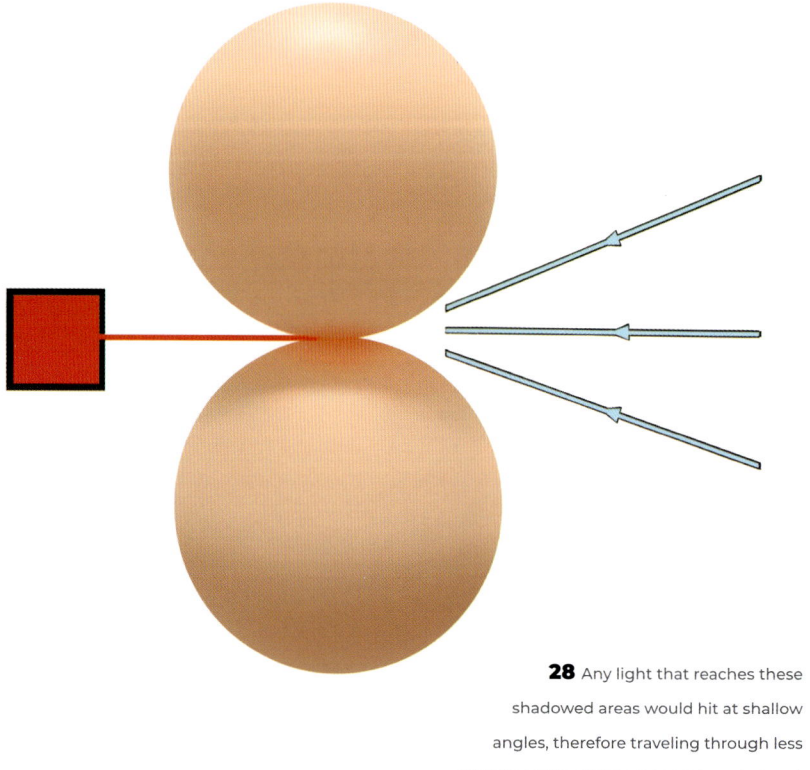

28 Any light that reaches these shadowed areas would hit at shallow angles, therefore traveling through less translucent material and causing a hotspot of high chroma in the deepest darks.

This is by no means the only way to approach figurative paintings. However, it can be an incredibly effective way to encourage ourselves to explore this transparent aspect of skin in our paintings, as shown in image **29**, by Anders Zorn.

All skin will also display some level of specularity, but it is generally an inefficient specular reflector, so we don't need to worry much about specularity beyond the stronger highlights. We will not see much of the environment reflected in skin, aside from some Fresnel color influence.

However, one important point to mention here is the effect of darkening skin tones. Skin gets darker primarily because of an increase in melanin. The more densely packed this melanin, the darker the observed value of the skin, leading to increased specularity and slightly decreased translucency **(30)**.

The difference is subtle but this change will lead to slightly different priorities when approaching painting the different skin types. The feeling of lighter skin tones will depend more on communicating the translucency and darker skin tones will depend more on the specularity **(31)**.

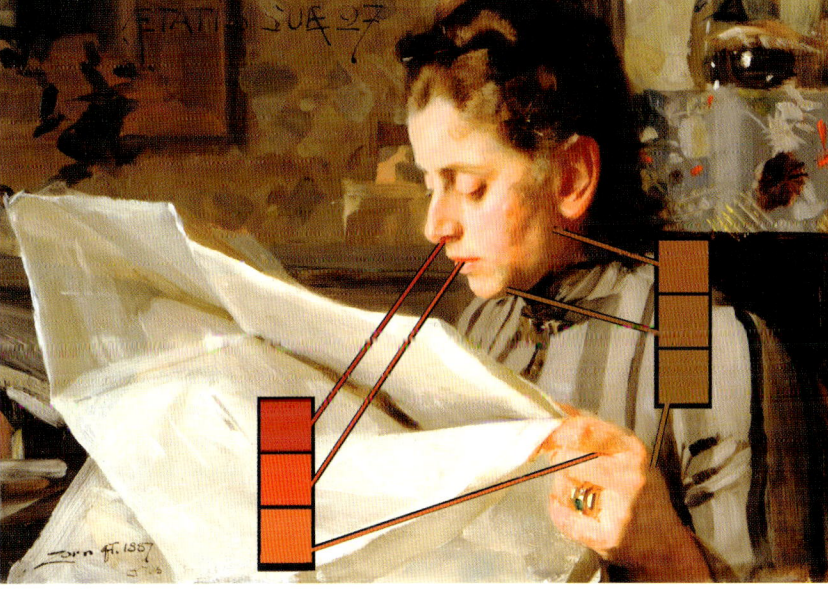

29 In this 1887 portrait, *Emma Zorn, Reading*, by Anders Zorn, the ambient occlusion shadows are warmer and higher-chroma than the general skin shadows elsewhere, due to the higher transparency of areas like the nostrils and lips.

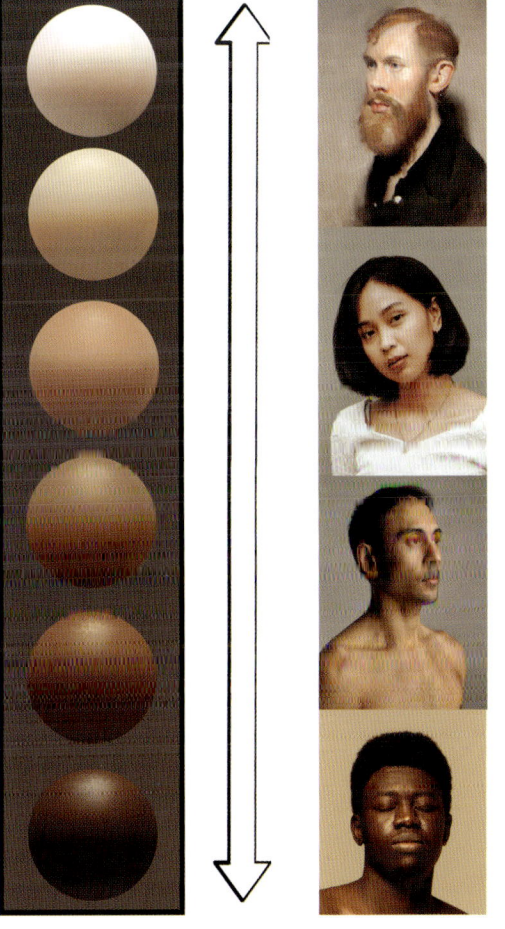

30 The lighter the skin tone, the more transparent it appears. The darker the skin tone, the less transparent (and therefore more specular) it appears.

Less melanin, more transparency

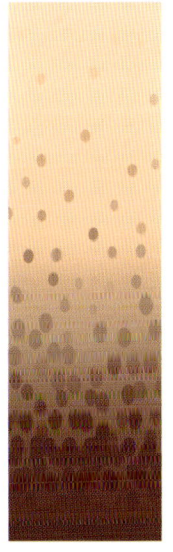

More melanin, less transparency

31 As the melanin becomes denser and the skin tone becomes darker, the skin appears less transparent and more reflective.

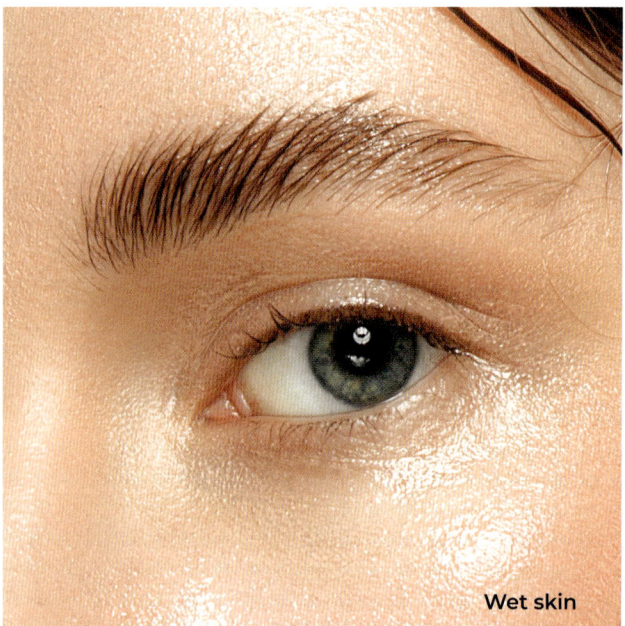
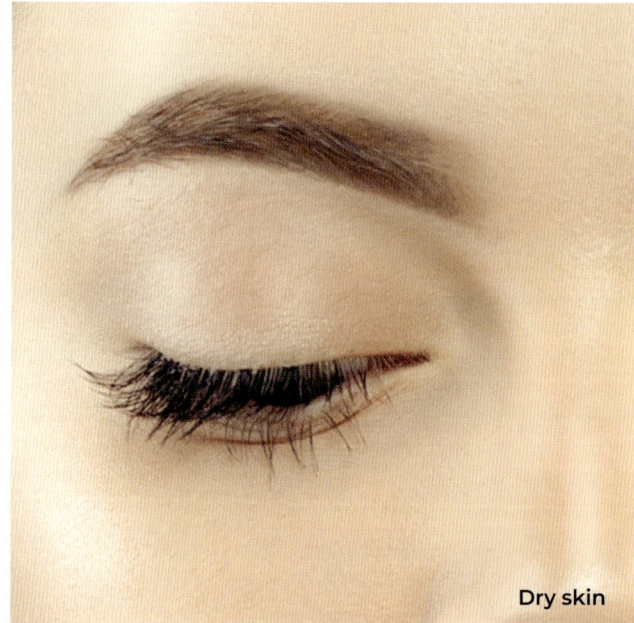

Wet skin

Dry skin

32 Wet and dry skin have very different specular reflections, which must be kept in mind when representing oily or diffuse areas.

WHAT'S THE TEXTURE?

If you look very closely at your own skin, you'll see that it's a fundamentally rough, textured surface, with various pores and tiny wrinkles all over its surface. This texture can be very subtle and is sometimes not even noticed by students. While some artists choose to call attention to this texture, for the most part, we don't need to worry too much about it in our matte surface modeling.

This texture will, however, have a huge effect on the way that specular reflections appear on the surface. As we discussed on page 72, a rough surface will diffusely blur the reflected image, generally leading to diffuse highlights. The smoothness of the surface will also be complicated somewhat by wetness.

In image **32**, we can see that the highlights on wet or dewy skin are sharper and more defined than they are on diffuse or dry skin. This effect occurs at varying levels across our skin, with some areas that are smoother or higher in oil content (such as the nose)

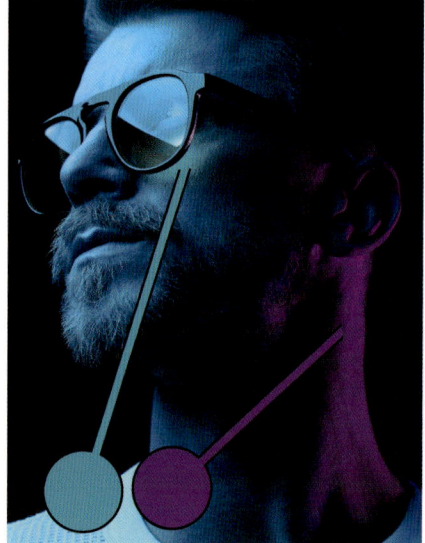
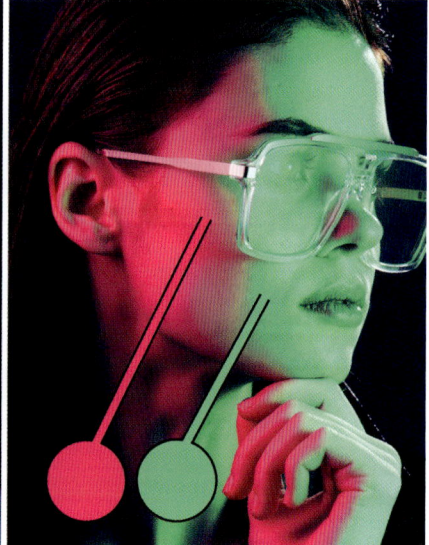

33 Skin is a powerful vehicle for external light colors, offering us great creative scope in our images.

having more prominently defined highlights than others.

On a final note, all our discussion of local color is assuming a perfectly balanced white light, assuming realism is our main aim. However, due to the low-chroma nature of skin, it can display any colored light source (remember, low chroma in light means more colors are "present" in it). Therefore, any

treatment of skin needs to acknowledge that the actual color we see will change to fit the gamut we are painting within (**33**).

The possibilities for "skin color" are actually endless and will conform to whatever color gamut or light we are choosing to paint under. As artists, we cannot allow our understanding of the material to make us inflexible in our color decisions.

COMPLEX MATERIALS: DRAPERY

Now that we've looked at skin, let's explore how we might apply the same approach to other materials. Another common subject you might encounter is drapery, which we can approach with the same three fundamental questions.

WHAT'S THE LOCAL COLOR?

Drapery is far less limited than our previous example of skin tones. Since it's synthetically colored with dyes, it is almost limitless in its range of potential hues and patterns. Any color that we can mix, we can recreate in drapery **(34)**. Another quality to bear in mind is that it will typically be presented in distinct pieces, therefore with distinct shapes of color. There may be exceptions to this, but this will typically be true of most textiles we represent.

MATTE, SPECULAR, OR TRANSPARENT?

Cloth is generally one of the more matte surfaces we will encounter, due to its threaded nature. There are exceptions to this rule, such as silk (see overleaf), but most cloth is matte with a weak degree of specular information. We can see this specular quality isolated in image **35**, but the matte surface shading is the primary driver for this material.

It's often surprising to students that cloth is typically an opaque (non-transparent) material, because everyone has had the experience of seeing "through" drapery. However, this actually has far more to do with the texture of the cloth than its inherent transparency.

If we shine a light through a cloth, we can see this texture more clearly **(36)**. When we see "through" a piece of cloth, it's usually because we are seeing light pass through the empty spaces *between* the woven threads, rather than actually refracting through the fabric in the same manner as a transparent material such as glass.

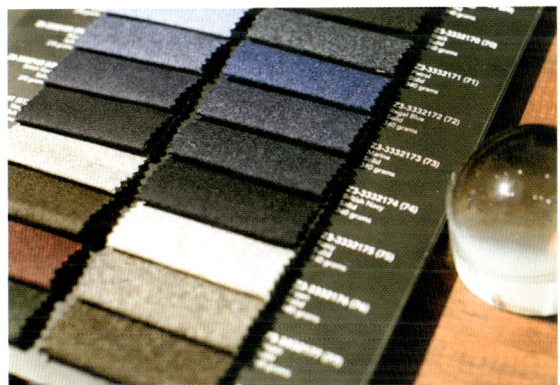

34 Fabric can be found in any color we are capable of mixing, giving us an essentially limitless range of colors (as well as patterns and weaves) for our work.

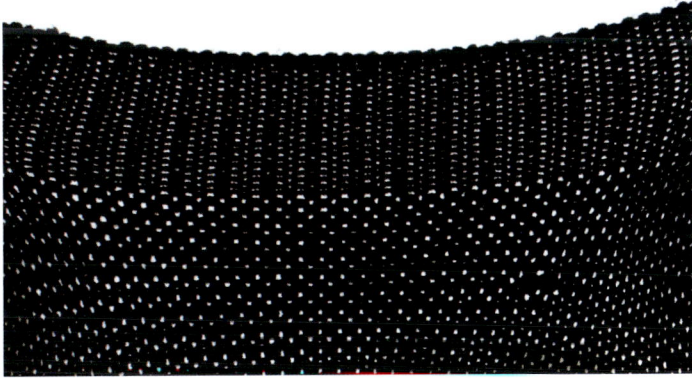

36 Though we've often seen "through" cloth, it's usually due to the weave of the fabric rather than any actual transparent properties.

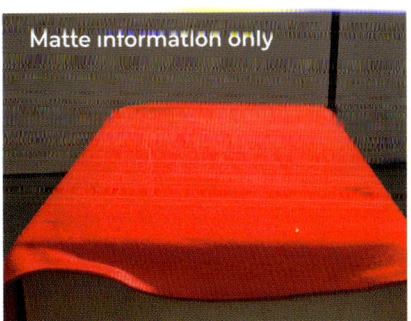

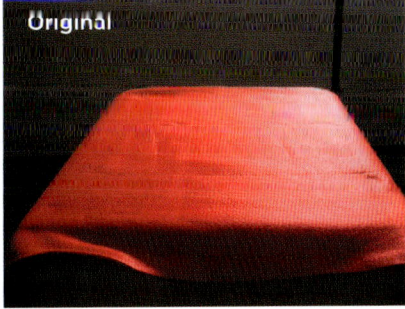

35 Here you can see the matte and specular information isolated with a polarizing filter. While some specular influence is present, the matte surface shading is the primary property.

WHAT'S THE TEXTURE?

The texture of drapery will vary in density, but it will always fundamentally be quite a textured surface, made from tube-shaped threads woven together in various patterns. The exact composition of these patterns will vary depending on the specific properties of each textile, but will generally repeat throughout an individual piece of fabric. The quantity of threads contained in a particular area of fabric is called the "thread count," and the higher this number, the smoother the observed texture will be.

In most cloth that we observe, these thread counts will be high enough that we can't make out the individual details, but it helps to know the structural makeup of these textures, even if we are only suggesting them in practice. Image **37** shows how threads alter the woven texture we see, ranging from an extremely low thread count (such as a handmade knitted cloth) to a higher thread count more typical of what we encounter on a daily basis.

DRAPERY ON FORMS

Other considerations when representing drapery are that it's typically quite thin and often draped over other forms. Due to this, well-painted drapery will always be more defined by the underlying covered form than by the shape of the cloth itself **(38)**. Remember to ask yourself these questions:

- **What forms are being draped over?** Is this fabric covering a rounded, planar, or perhaps pointed shape?

- **What forces are being involved?** Just gravity, as pictured here? Or perhaps the cloth is influenced by something else, such as being pulled or blowing in the wind?

- **Which areas have too little space for drapery?** These areas are where folds will occur.

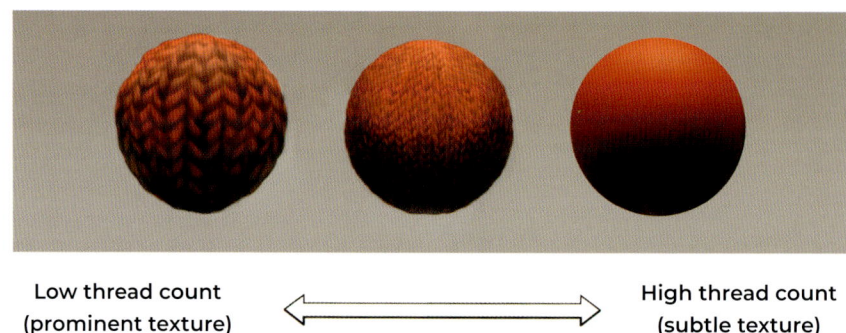

Low thread count (prominent texture) ⟷ **High thread count (subtle texture)**

37 Cloth texture appears smoother as the thread count increases in density. Smoother textures can be more subtly suggested when we paint them.

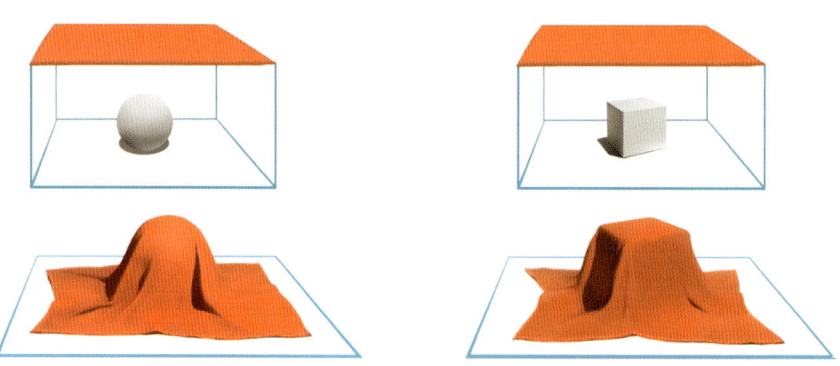

38 We need to consider the shape of the form beneath the drapery, and areas where less cloth will fit, causing wrinkles and folds.

Most of the time, when representing drapery, it will be in the form of clothing. Most of the clothing we encounter is not just made of one continuous piece of cloth, but multiple pieces of varying shapes and sizes, stitched together. The meeting point of two pieces creates a seam **(39)**. Seams will vary greatly depending on the function and style of different clothes, so it's best to observe them from reference. In general, though, they will be placed to avoid excessive folding around the body, and will appear as a slightly raised bump with a deep shadow where the two pieces meet.

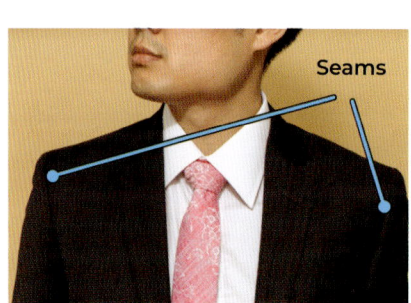

Seams

39 Clothing will also feature seams and stitching that influence the shape and direction of the fabric.

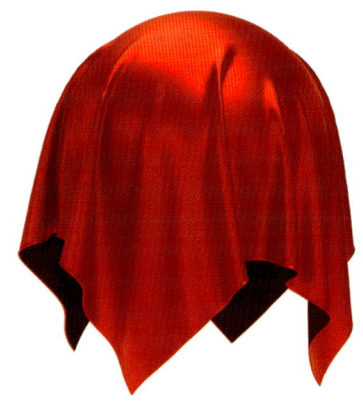

40 Silk has a very finely woven, highly specular finish that is very different from most fabrics you will observe in everyday clothing.

OTHER TEXTILES

One of the notable exceptions to the usually matte nature of cloth is finely woven silk. This fabric displays a large amount of specular reflection due to the extremely fine weave that creates its nearly perfectly smooth surface (40).

So it's important to keep in mind that most of the examples given here are only fully true of typical cloth materials such as cotton, while many other interesting and more unusual textiles exist. A plain, matte fabric is a helpful base for approaching the fascinating subject of drapery, but it can only ever be

an introduction. Within fashion, people strive for variability – the differing qualities with textiles and garments are vast, and the different types need to be approached in their own way. It is always helpful to look at references and try to discern these differences for yourself.

OTHER COMPLEX MATERIALS

Beyond skin and cloth, the broad world of materials that surrounds us at all times is functionally infinite and sometimes overwhelming. What you have learned in this book is an introduction to this wonderful world, and using the logic laid out so far, you will be able to analyze surfaces, light materials, and render colors easily in your own work.

Remember to ask yourself those three questions ("What's the local color? Is it matte, specular, or transparent? What's the texture?"), gather references, and try to apply each new texture to the fundamental forms we have discussed throughout this chapter. Add your texture objects into environments and lighting scenarios. These practices will give you full and confident control over each new material.

Image **41** below shows examples of what these studies might look like for three other materials. How many others can you discover around you?

WEATHERED IRON

This worn metal is technically specular, but its roughness, due to weathering, makes it practically matte. Its local color is a low-chroma, low-value cool gray, but rust from moisture has also formed, introducing some warm, chromatic tones. This play of warm and cool is crucial to capturing the overall effect of the material.

WOOD

This wood is primarily matte, with a local color of low-chroma brown in the yellow-red hue range. Wood textures are highly variable depending on treatment, but this

example is fairly smooth. Due to the way trees grow, wood generally has a dark grain following a particular direction, and keeping this consistent is important for conveying the material.

WAX

Wax is a primarily translucent substance, as we saw on pages 180 and 183, displaying a high level of subsurface scattering. This example is a high-value, low-chroma warm yellow, and the material texture is generally smooth. As wax melts, runs, and cools, it creates drips – these long, thin forms are an excellent opportunity to show translucency.

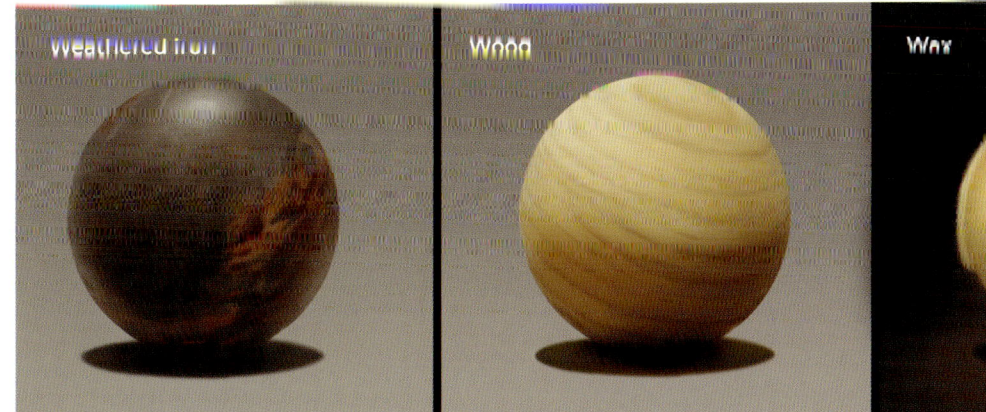
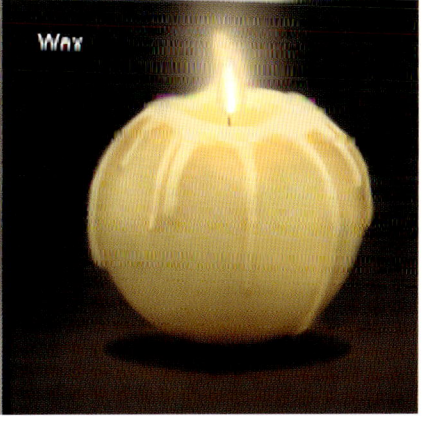

41 Using everything we've learned about matte, specular, and transparent surfaces, we can analyze and learn to paint new materials.

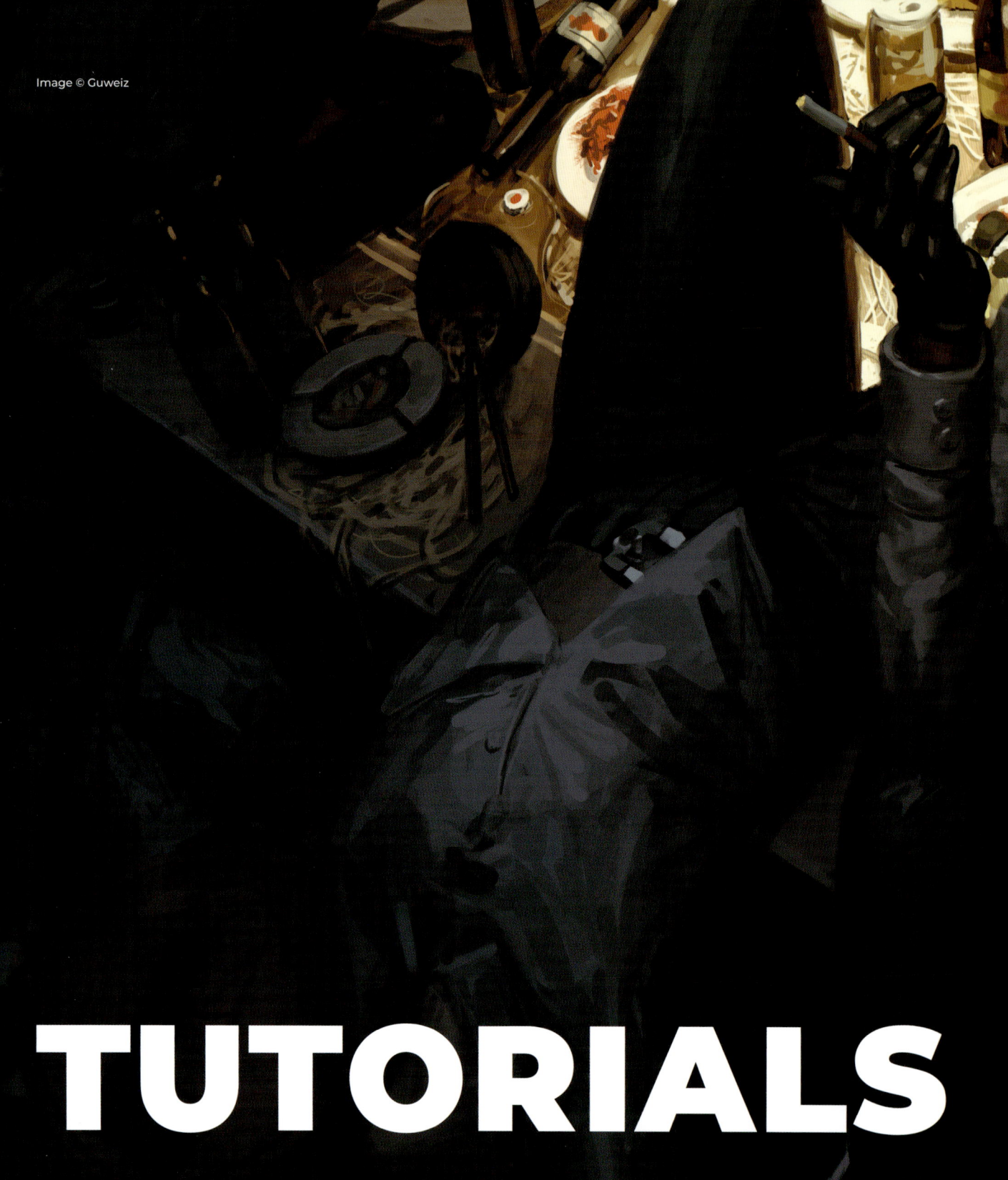

TUTORIALS

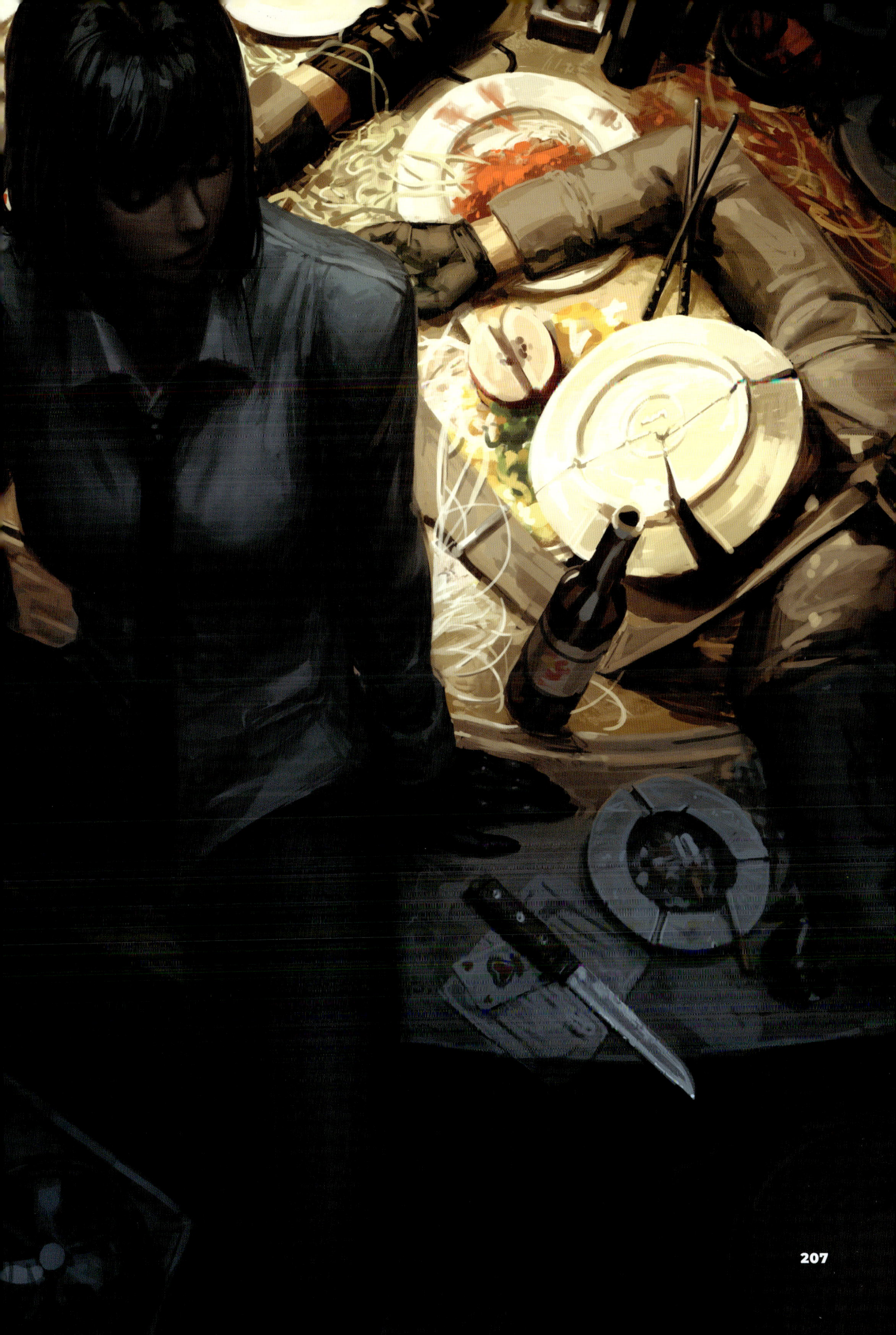

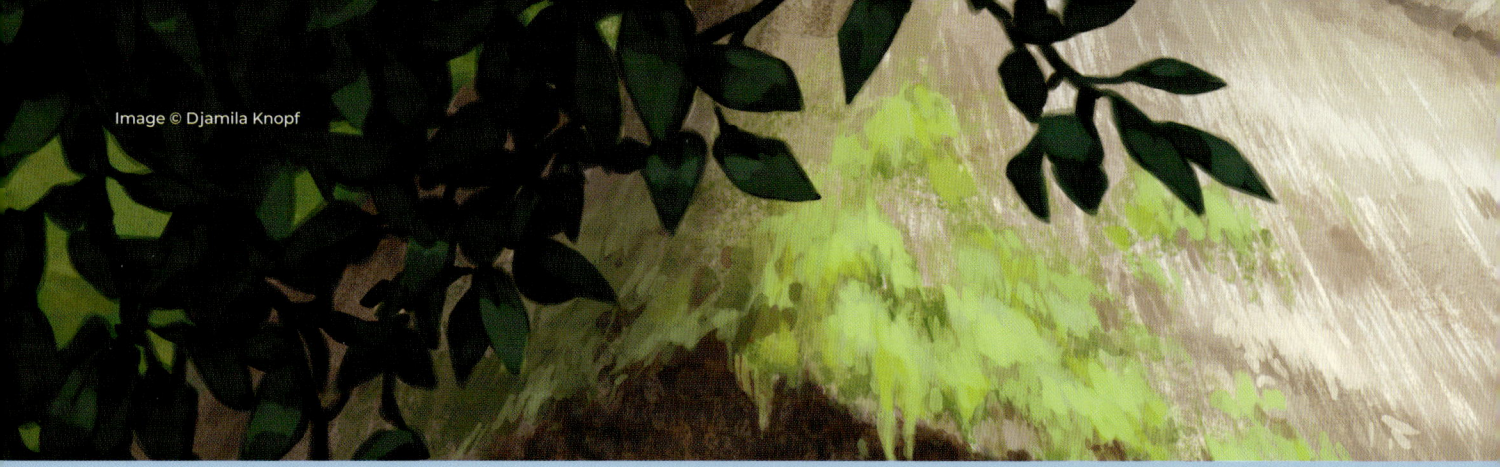

DAY BY DAY

DJAMILA KNOPF

In this tutorial, I will be painting the same summer's day in five different lighting scenarios: overcast, bright sunlight, early morning, sunset, and rain. For each version, I will opt for a different mood and story. Since I am starting out with a simple, muted setup with overcast lighting, you may think, "Hey, this is supposed to be a color and light tutorial! Where's the color?" but I promise, after laying the foundation, I will quickly introduce more vibrant palettes.

Color and light are powerful tools for evoking emotion and telling a story. They are also closely interconnected with environments, and with that, different seasons, weather situations, and times of day. When I am painting a landscape, sooner or later I'll ask myself, "OK, what are the circumstances here? How warm or cold is it? How much sunlight is there?" Playing with these aspects is incredibly fun, and I love seeing how drastically a scene can change when you see it in a different light – literally.

I am using Photoshop for this project, but the techniques can be adapted to any other painting software, as long as it supports layers and blending modes. And, of course, there are lots and lots of different approaches when it comes to color and light. This is just one of them.

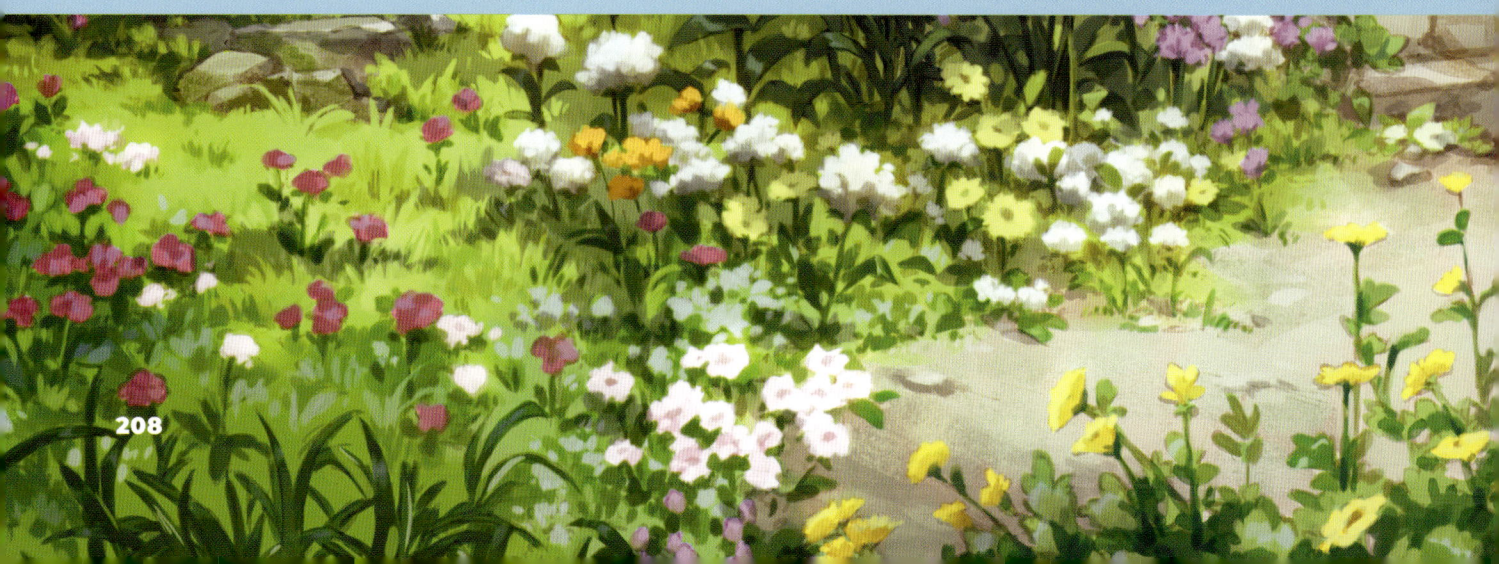

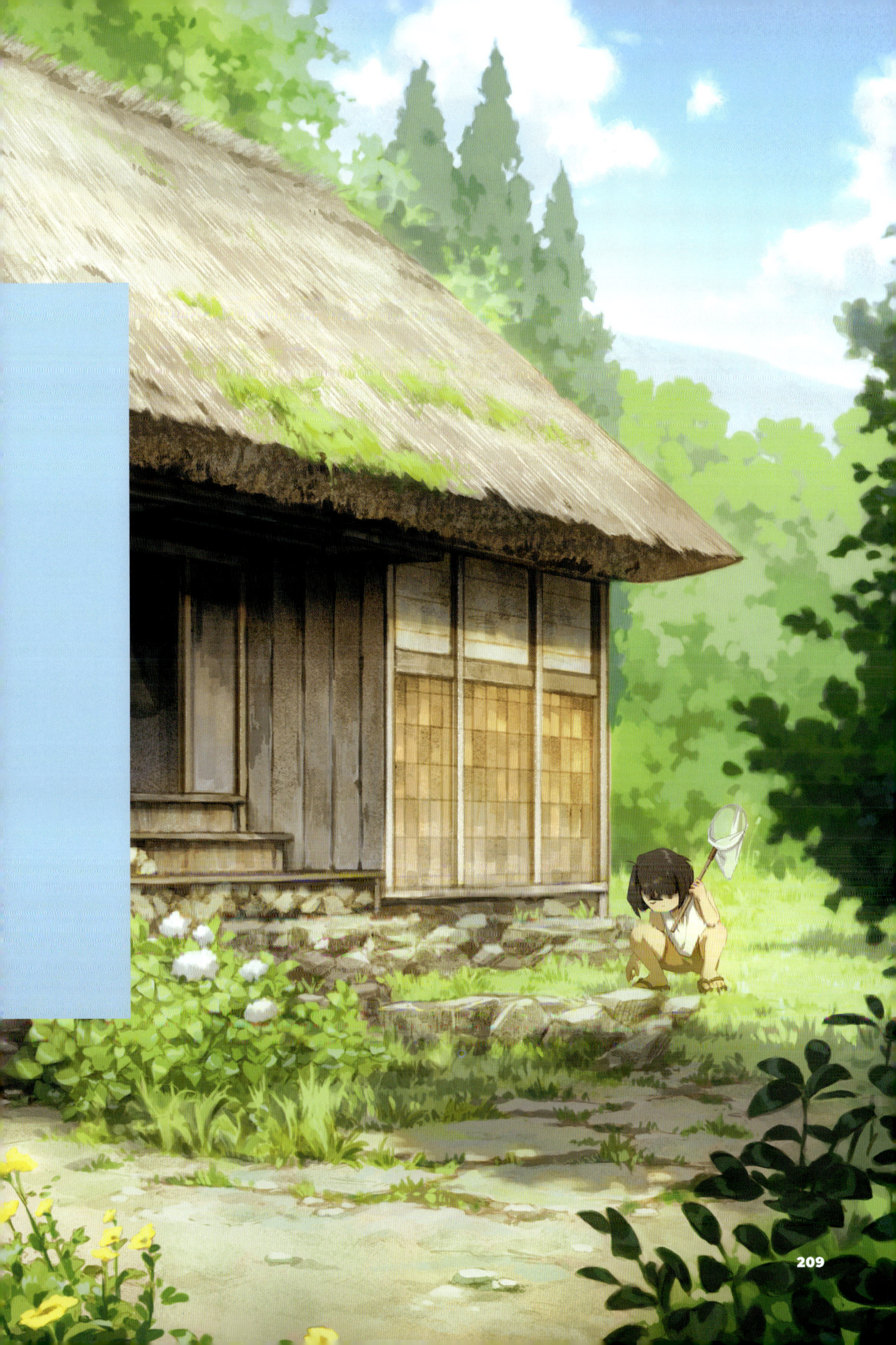

01 A DETAILED LINE DRAWING

Whenever I start an illustration, I always begin with a detailed line drawing to solve any structural issues upfront, such as environment design, perspective, and possibly character anatomy and body language. This gives me a solid base that I can use to test out different color schemes and lighting scenarios later on. The drawing is a safety net that allows me to be more free and experimental in my color choices.

From here, the drawing can go in many different directions, depending on what palette and mood I choose. I always go by this rule of thumb: "The line drawing tells you what you are seeing; the color tells you how to feel about it." Throughout this chapter, we are going to explore a few different ways to "feel about" the same scene.

LIGHTING SCENARIO: OVERCAST

We are going to start out with the simplest of lighting scenarios: overcast lighting. Imagine a day without any direct sunlight. All you are seeing is a thick layer of clouds that are white or light gray. These clouds act like a giant photographer's softbox that diffuses the light coming from above, creating an even illumination around the entire scene. It is bright enough that you can see every object in detail, and in the absence of direct sunlight, there are no harsh shadows.

02 SETTING UP AN OVERCAST DAY

I like to think of overcast lighting as the "purest" way of viewing our environment, without any shadows or other elements stealing away our attention. It's a drama-free lighting scenario, almost like a matter-of-fact statement that just says: "Look, this is a house."

My first step when it comes to any kind of color palette is to get rid of the white canvas. It's hard to judge colors against white, so I immediately replace it with something neutral and slightly darker. In this case, the light-gray sky provides a good base. I make sure every new color I introduce fits in terms of saturation, lightness, and temperature.

I try not to go too vibrant, but also not too dull. I place every new color on its own layer, and if one of them stands out too much, I use Photoshop's Hue/Saturation adjustments to tone it down.

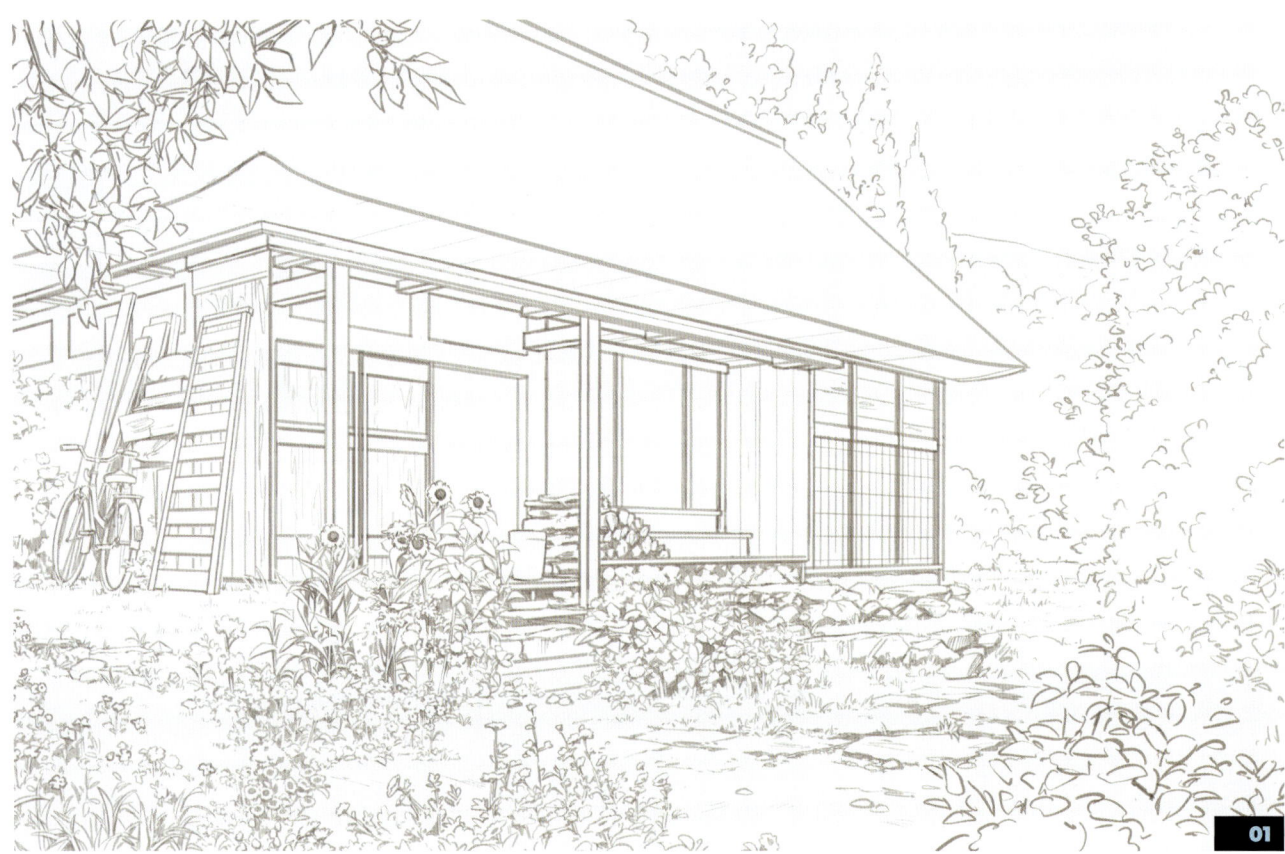

01

01 In any software, I always set my line layer to "Multiply" mode and paint on a new layer underneath it. This way, the sketch will remain intact, no matter how messy I am with my colors.

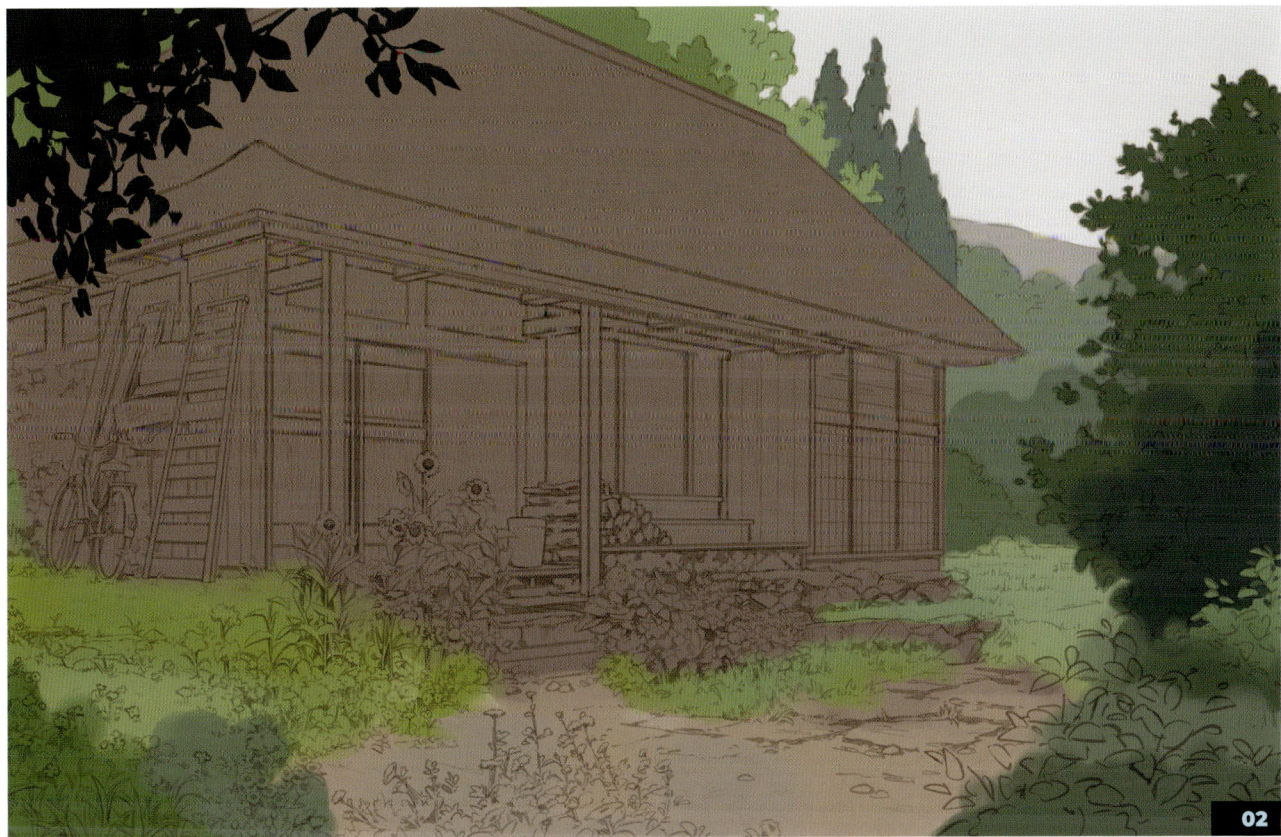

02 While building the color palette, I also start establishing a value scheme that separates the foreground, middle ground, and background – going from dark leaves in the front, all the way to the light-gray sky in the back.

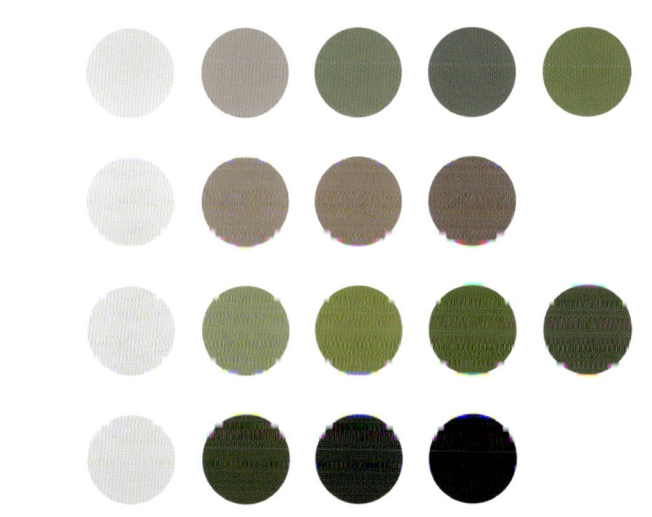

Choosing my palette. These are some of the colors I am introducing in relation to the original light-gray base. My goal is to create a broad value range and a variety of hues for visual interest, with a mix of light and dark colors for the ground, cabin, and foliage.

ADDING NEW COLORS

Selecting new colors can be tricky. If you want to add a green object and go straight to the "paint bucket" version of green, it will likely look out of place in the color scheme. Instead, I pick a pre-existing color from my canvas that is closest to what I have in mind, and use it to form my decision. I ask myself three questions about the new color I'm looking for:

· Is it cooler or warmer than the original color?

· Is it lighter or darker than the original color?

· Is it more or less saturated than the original color?

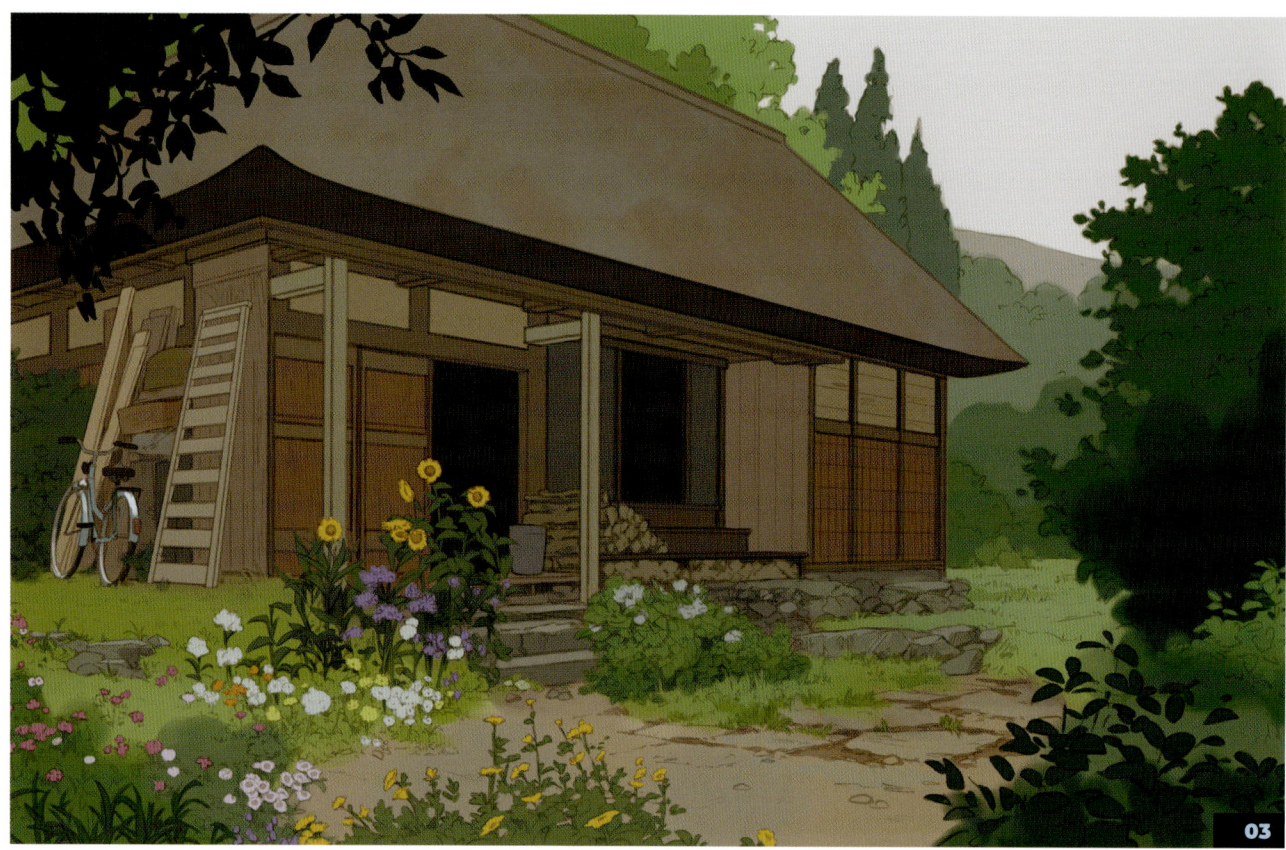

03 You can see an example of the subtle hue variation I was talking about on the roof and ground.

03 A FULL PALETTE

I now color every element in the painting using lots of neutral tones, especially for the house. I love painting wooden houses because the natural material fits perfectly with a lush green environment, and it provides a good resting place for the eyes. Neutral tones are also a great backdrop for more vibrant colors.

People often avoid neutrals and grays because they don't want their paintings to look dull or boring, but I love them! If you avoid grays altogether and make every element in the scene extremely saturated, everything screams for the viewer's attention, and as a result, nothing stands out. But if you maintain a balance between neutral tones and some strategically placed, vibrant focal points, that's when they complement each other. You can use this approach to draw the viewer's attention and create a rhythm in the scene.

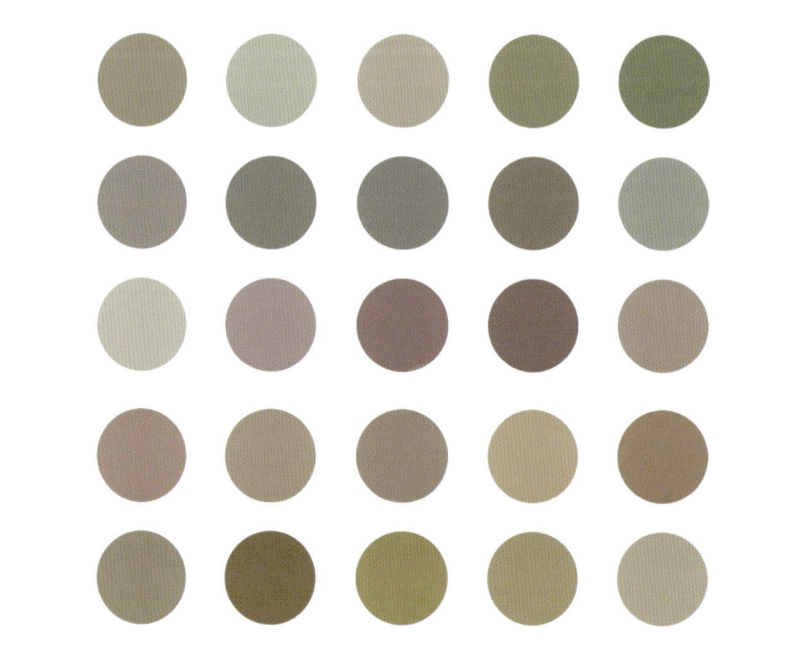

Playing with hue. Gray tones deserve more love! If you work with subtle hue variations, they can actually look quite colorful. This is an example of the variety you can achieve.

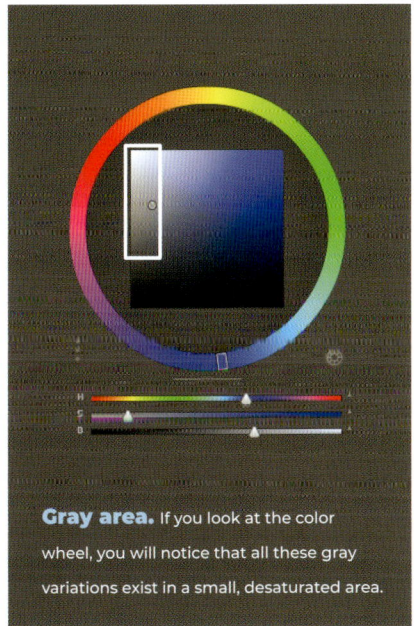

Gray area. If you look at the color wheel, you will notice that all these gray variations exist in a small, desaturated area.

04 THATCHING THE ROOF

At this point, I am happy with the basic color palette, and am moving on to paint details and textures. Right now, everything looks flat, but my goal is to give the illusion that the roof is thatched and the beams are made of wood. Textures become even more important when there is no dramatic lighting in the scene to provide extra visual interest, so I am giving each surface close attention. Leaves will become smooth and shiny, and stones will become ragged.

I don't usually have a fixed order in which I paint things. I often start with either a big area that I can cover quickly to pick up momentum, or whichever unfinished area bothers me the most. This time, in both cases, it's the roof!

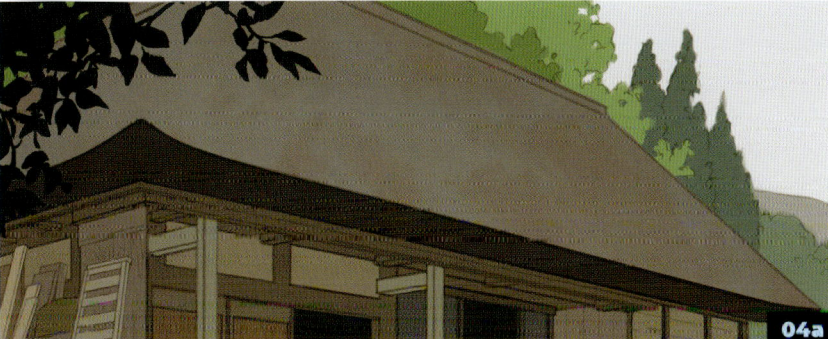

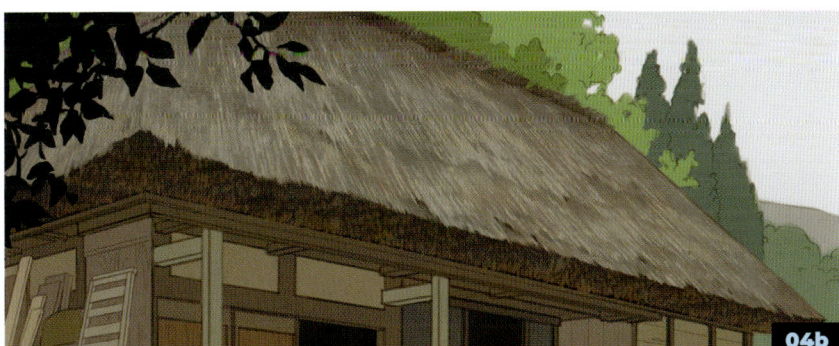

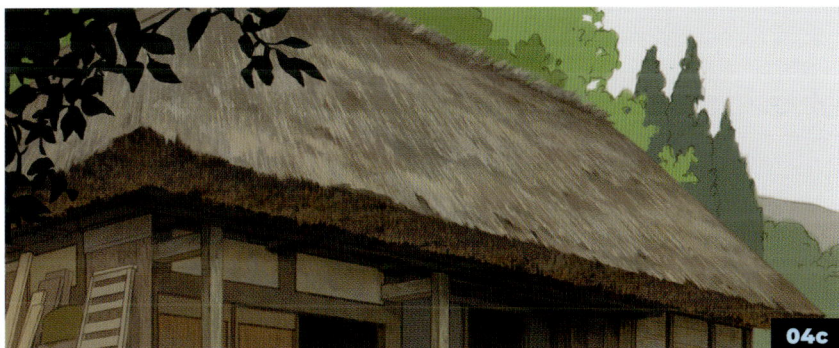

04a – 04c I am adding lighter strokes and darker shadows to indicate the thatched material, making sure that their direction follows the perspective of the roof.

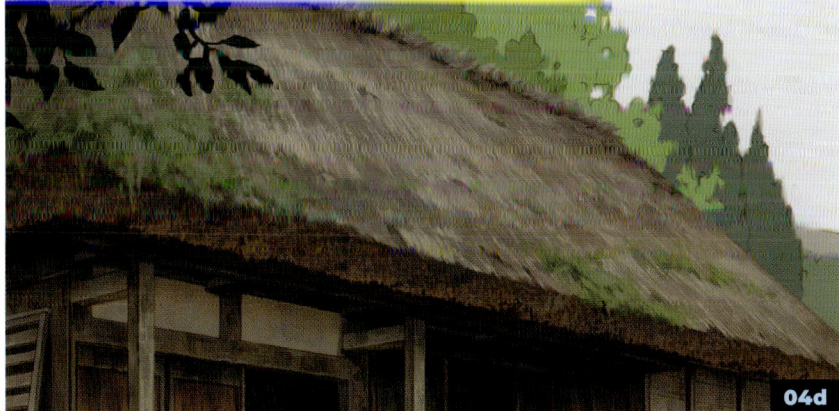

04d The roof still looks boring to me, so I break it up with some vegetation. Adding a bit of green creates that vital visual interest.

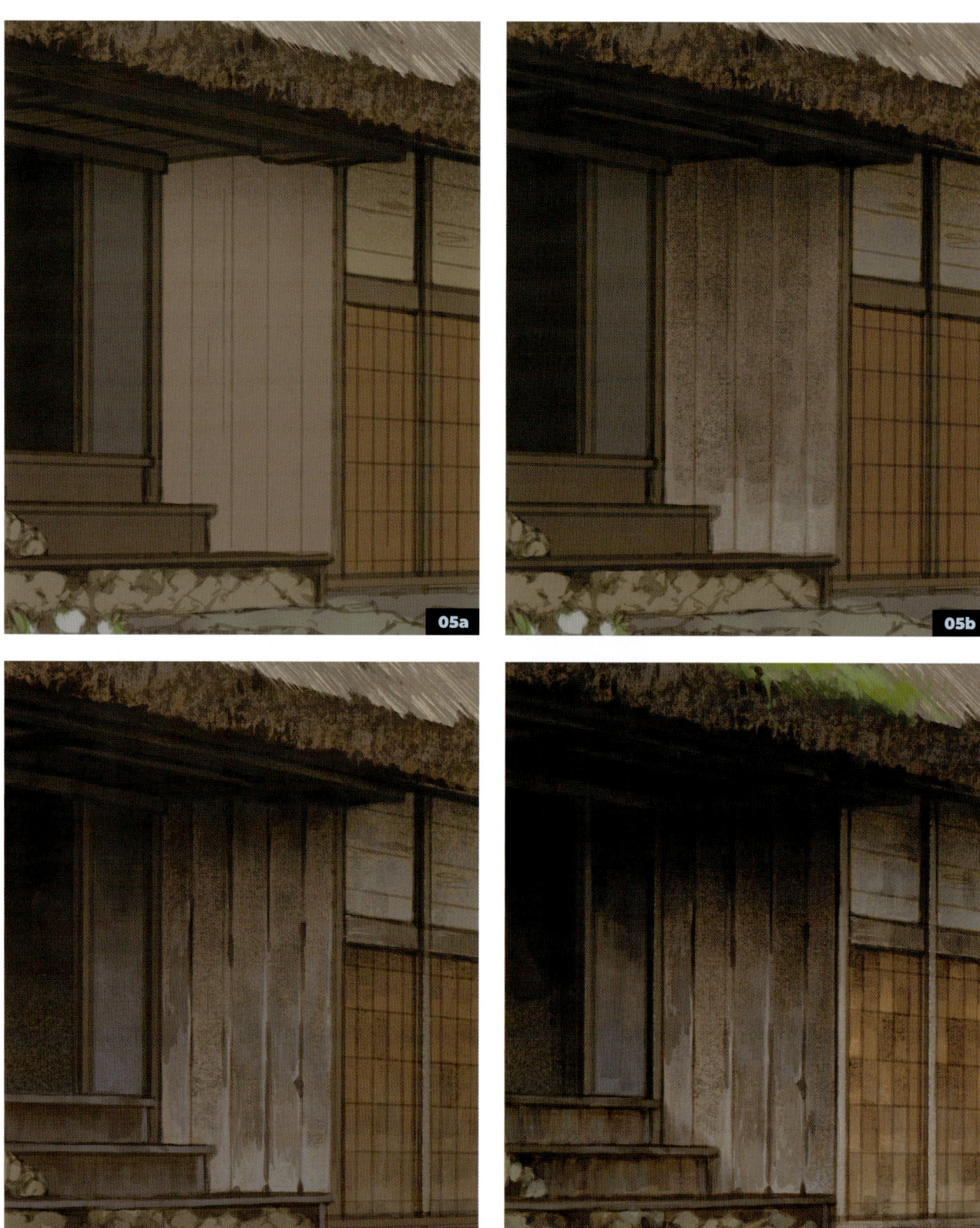

05a – 05d I make sure the planks actually look flat, not curved or warped, which can easily

happen if lighter values are used in the wrong places. This process is all about precision and subtlety.

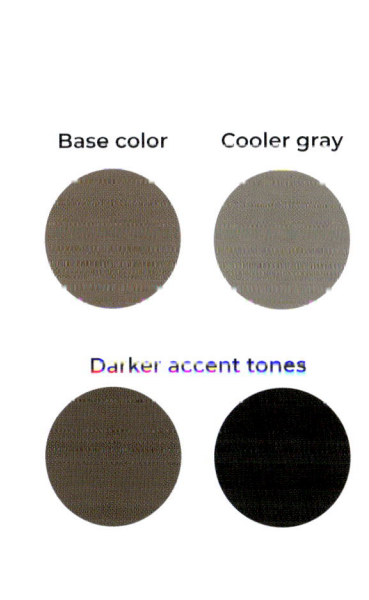

Building up tones.

Starting out from the base color, I add a cooler gray tone followed by some darker accents. Overall, though, I keep the value and color range fairly narrow.

05 WOODEN PLANKS

Generally, with every element that I paint, I want to highlight its volume and structure. I used to make the mistake of being too heavy-handed in my use of values, but I have come to learn that a little goes a long way. I like to keep the contrast within a single surface fairly low at first, and just focus on introducing different hues. Then, step by step, I bring in subtle gradients, shadows, and indentations to suggest texture and three dimensionality.

Wooden planks aren't the most exciting subjects to paint and are certainly not the focal point of this illustration! I want them to be just detailed enough to create some "noise" in the overall illustration, but not so much that they are the first thing you notice.

06 IN PRAISE OF SHADOWS

Shadows are fundamental in creating the illusion of three-dimensionality. Since we are dealing with an overcast lighting scenario, we don't have any harsh separations of light and shadow. Instead, at our disposal are soft gradations that get darker as they turn away from the light source (in this case, the giant softbox that is the cloudy sky). The main goal is to make use of these "form shadows" to highlight the structure of each element in the scene.

This is also a good time to mention a phenomenon called "ambient occlusion," which refers to those dark corners and crevices where little or no light gets in. It is commonly seen in deep folds of fabric or where furniture touches the floor. You can even notice it when you bend your arm and look at where the skin pushes together. You can learn more about ambient occlusion and how it's formed on page 96.

In this particular scene, the area below the roof is most affected by these two shadow types. It won't catch much light, and neither will the corner over to the left, where the bicycle and boxes are stored, with all its little nooks and crannies.

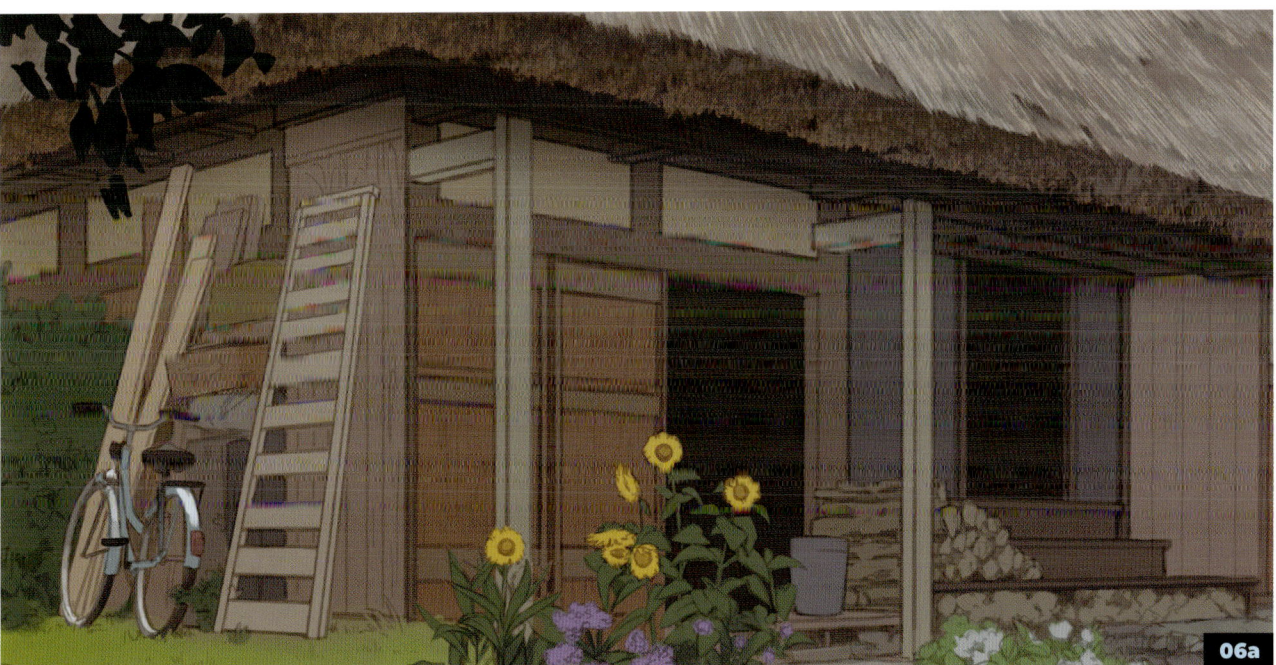

06a A simple, soft gradient can be a great starting point to indicate shadows and suggest depth. I make sure to integrate shadows and textures as I go, so that they both work together.

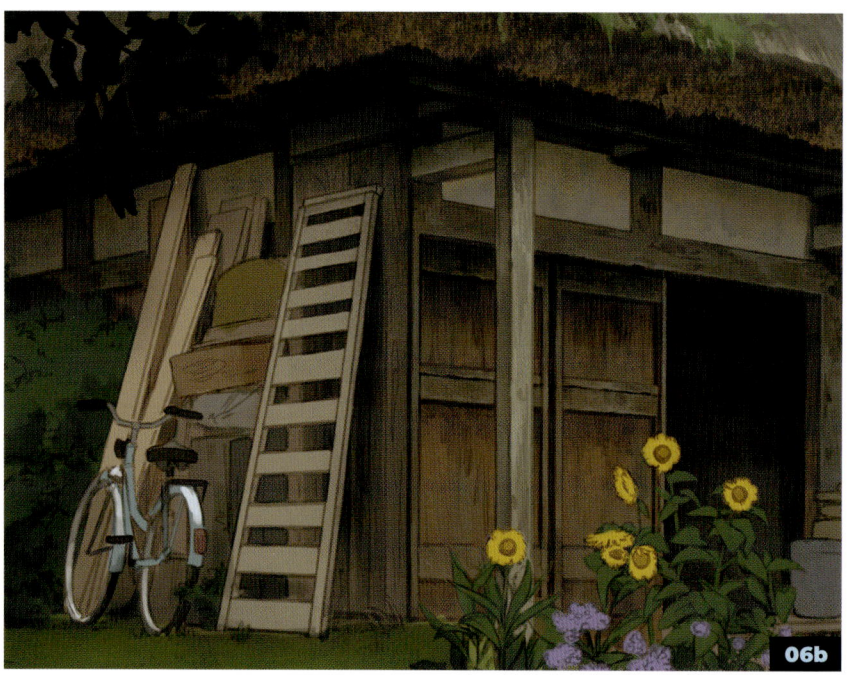

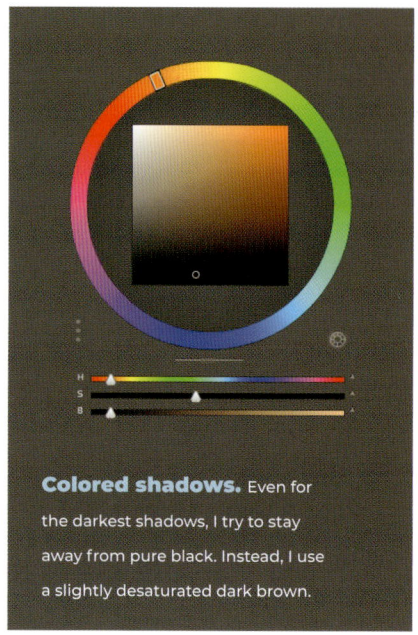

Colored shadows. Even for the darkest shadows, I try to stay away from pure black. Instead, I use a slightly desaturated dark brown.

06b While I am painting and detailing all the different surfaces, I constantly remind myself that the light is coming from above.

07 COOL FOLIAGE HIGHLIGHTS

On an overcast day, planes that are facing up toward the sky appear cooler in color temperature. This effect is especially noticeable in foliage – at least in the kind with a shiny surface. Leaves facing up will reflect and bounce back that cool skylight, which makes them appear slightly more blue. Even though this scene's sky is gray, it is still on the cooler side, and I personally like to exaggerate this effect because I like the way it looks.

In the tip on page 211, I demonstrate how I often introduce a new color by using a pre-existing one as my starting point. In this case, I pick the foliage color from the canvas, cool it by shifting it toward blue, make it lighter, and decrease its saturation. The difference is extremely subtle, often just a five- to ten-percent change in brightness, but combined with the tweaks in hue and saturation, it is very effective.

As I move forward, I apply that same process not only to foliage, but also to the stones on the ground and other surfaces that are facing up.

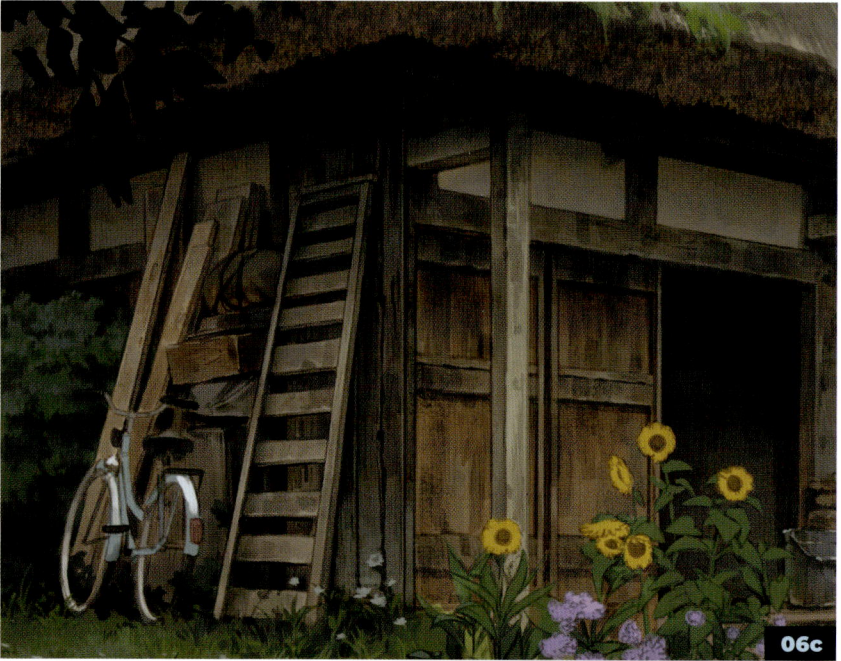

06c As the light on these sheltered objects comes from above, everything gets lighter toward the bottom. You can see this most clearly in the ladder and screen doors.

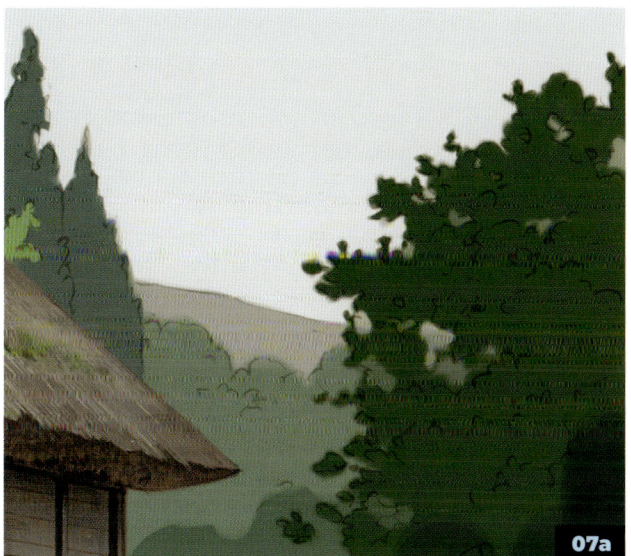

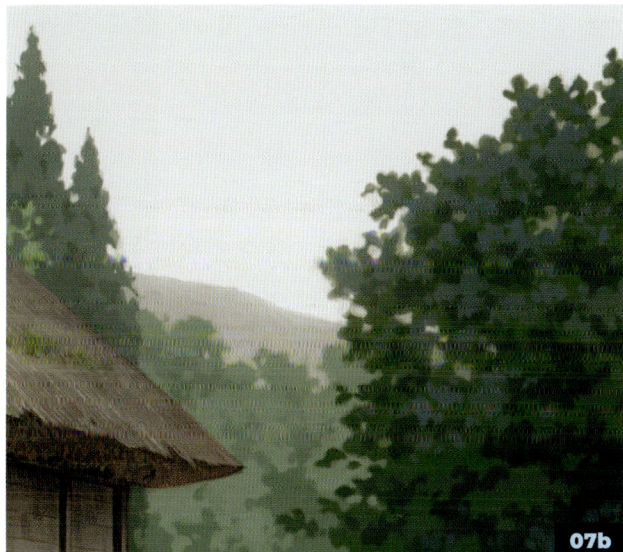

07a – 07b Shifting the foliage highlights toward blue creates color variation and reinforces the idea of a cool atmosphere in the absence of sunlight.

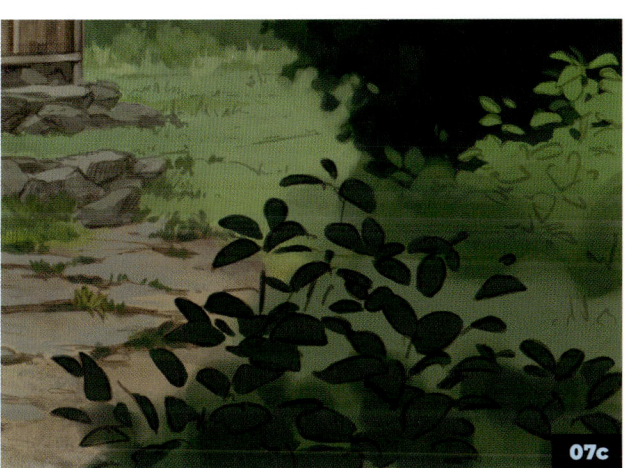

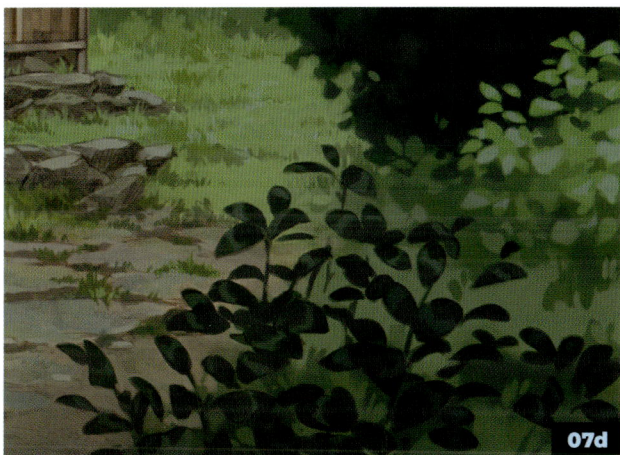

07c – 07d The cool highlight effect will stand out especially clearly on objects with a shiny surface, such as these smooth leaves.

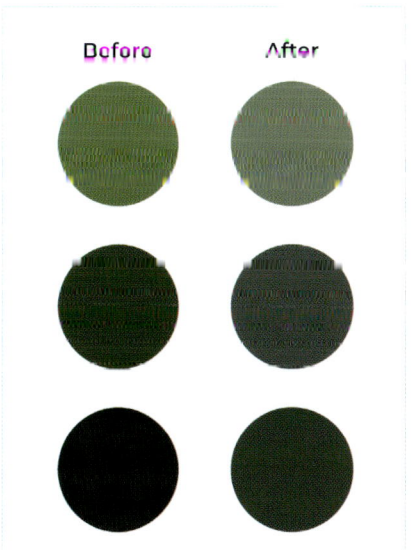

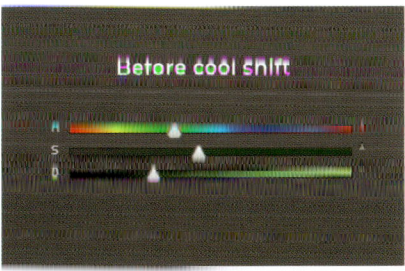

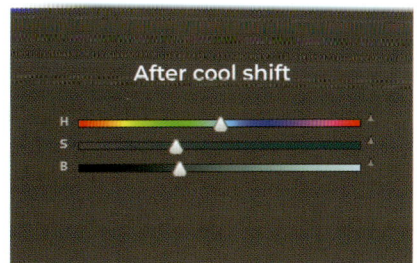

Cool highlights.

Here are some examples of different foliage base colors (left column) and the corresponding highlights (right column). The HSB sliders represent the swatches in the middle row, and how subtle the difference is between them.

08 ATMOSPHERIC PERSPECTIVE

When you look at the trees, bushes, and the mountain in the painting, you will notice that they gradually become lighter the farther back they go. Each element's local color still comes into play, but there is a general tendency for them to get lighter as they recede.

This is known as "atmospheric perspective" and it's an important phenomenon to understand when it comes to painting landscapes. Air is not actually crystal clear and one hundred percent see-through. Instead, it's filled with dust and moisture that affects the light. This causes distant objects to appear increasingly bluer, lighter, less saturated, and lower in contrast. The farther back things go, the stronger the effect, until they eventually blend into the sky. You can learn more about this effect on page 164.

You can see this at work most clearly in the bushes and mountain behind the house. I have made them much lighter than, for example, the edge of the house, to create the illusion of distance between them. I apply the same principle to the bush on the right – by making it darker, it appears to be closer to the viewer.

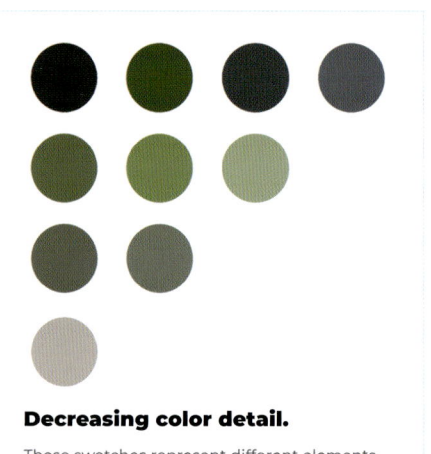

Decreasing color detail.

These swatches represent different elements in the scene. I sampled the top row from the large bush on the right, the second and third row from plants in between, and the bottom row from the mountain. Notice how I use fewer and fewer colors for each element.

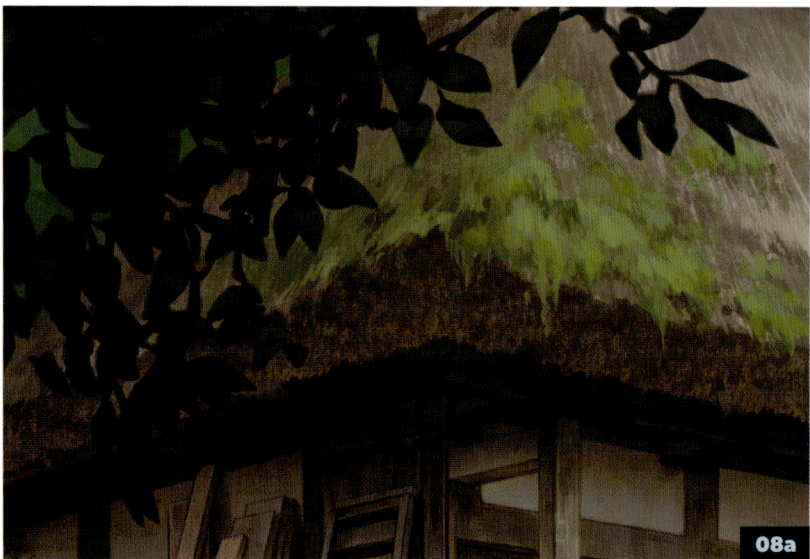

08a The leaves in the foreground are the darkest in the entire composition, because they are the closest and therefore the least affected by atmospheric perspective.

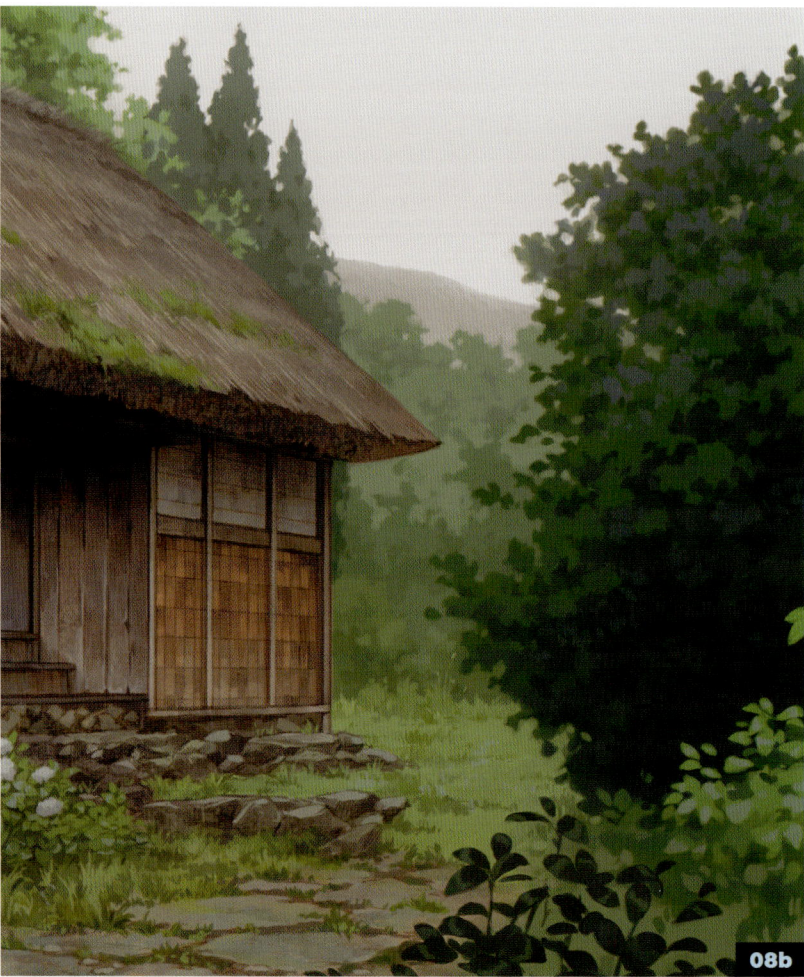

08b Local colors are also at play, so some things can still appear light even though they are close by – for example, the little pale-green plant at the bottom right.

09 A SPLASH OF COLOR

You may have noticed that I'm a big fan of hue variation, but to drive that point home, take a look at the image on the right. It shows the foliage in a flat, monochrome green compared to the previous step. To me, this looks dull and lifeless – two things I try to avoid!

In a scene like this, which has a simple lighting setup, it is even more important to play with local colors, and all the different plants provide a perfect opportunity for this. I make sure to include various shades of green in the trees and grass, as well as different types of flowers. While greens and earth tones dominate the palette, the flowers provide a pop of color, and their intricacy acts as a further counterpoint to the dense foliage. The aim of all this is to play with harmony and contrast, juxtaposing smaller areas against bigger ones, saturation against gray tones, and light against dark.

As I work on this painting, and especially toward the end, I constantly ask myself:

· Does the color scheme look balanced?
· Could certain areas be emphasized or toned down?
· Is the lighting believable?
· Is the light source consistent?
· Have I succeeded in telling the story – does this actually look like a house in the woods on an overcast day?

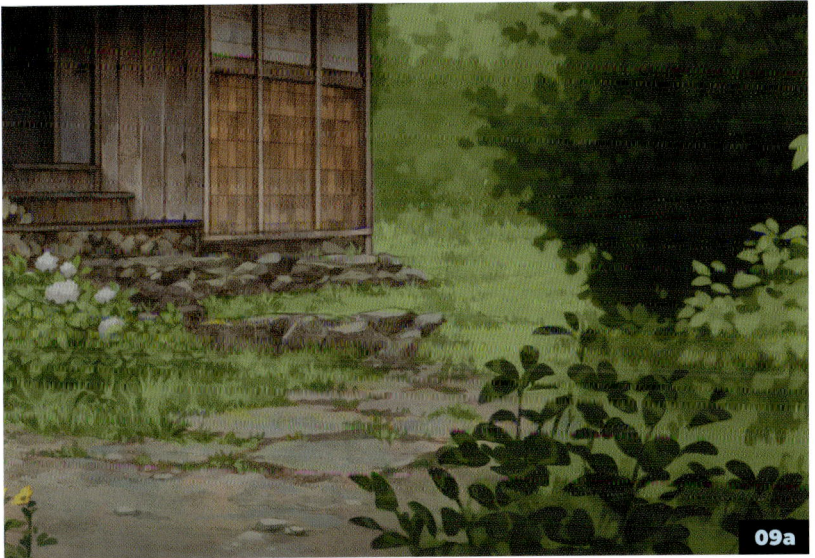

09a Look at the foliage without any hue variation – characterless and dull!

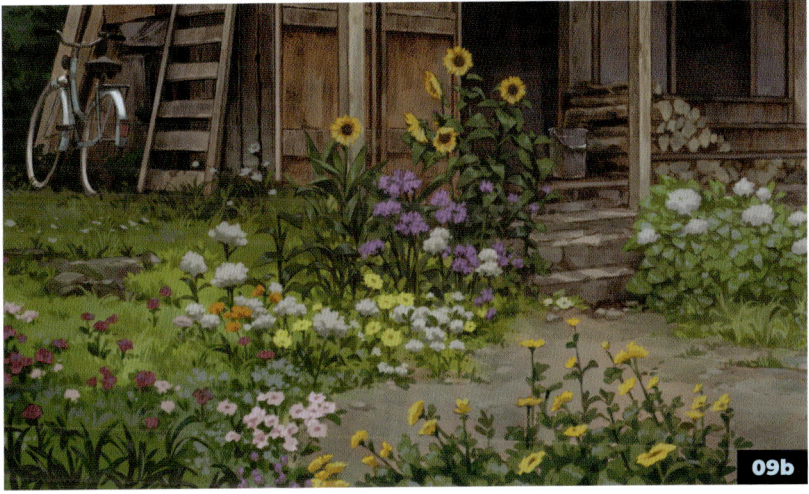

09b This is the most detailed area of the entire painting. It also includes the widest variety of colors.

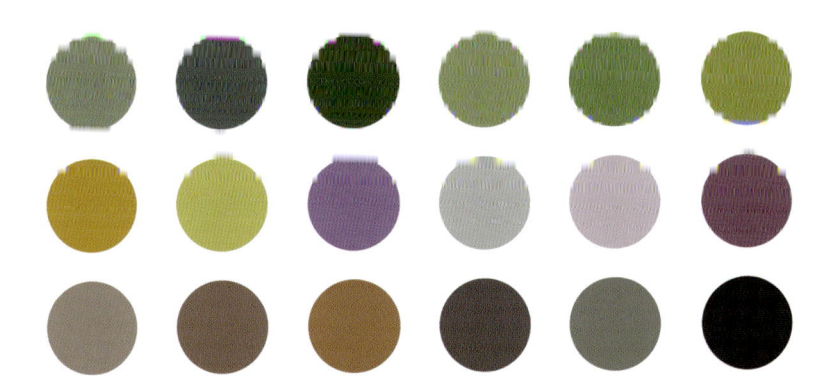

Final palette overview.
Here is a simplified version of the final palette. Among the predominant greens and earth tones, the hues of the flowers provide a colorful visual break.

LIGHTING RECAP: OVERCAST

Let's review what we know about overcast lighting. We know there is no direct sunlight in the scene. Instead, the light is scattered through a giant layer of clouds that stretches across the sky and covers it in gray. This provides a soft, even illumination from above that creates subtle gradations between light and shadow. Highlights (especially those on surfaces facing upward) appear cooler in temperature, and in comparison, shadows appear warmer. There is enough light for us to see objects clearly and in detail.

Now that we know all this, it is worth asking how we can use this technical knowledge to inform our storytelling and evoke an emotional response. What kind of mood does this lighting setup create? In what situation is it appropriate to use? Of course, this is up to you, but here are some of my suggestions and observations.

On one hand, like I mentioned earlier, overcast lighting can be very matter-of-fact. It highlights an object's structure and texture, which makes it ideal for showing off designs. If you are not too concerned with evoking a mood, and just want to present an environment in its neutral form, it is a good choice.

On the other hand, with the right emphasis, an overcast sky can create a very bleak, dense, and oppressive atmosphere. The thick blanket of clouds can potentially reflect the heaviness of a character's emotional state, if you pair it with the appropriate body language. There is something about an overcast lighting setup that makes it seem like it could start raining any minute, as if things are about to get worse.

While we usually associate a cloudy day with negative feelings, it can also suggest the hope for better times and for the sun to come out again. All of this depends on the setting you choose and how you have your characters interact with it. In some instances, it might even be the perfect setup to create a sense of mystery, suspense, and otherworldliness. There is no "one size fits all" and that's what makes it fun – that is where your creative freedom as an artist comes into play!

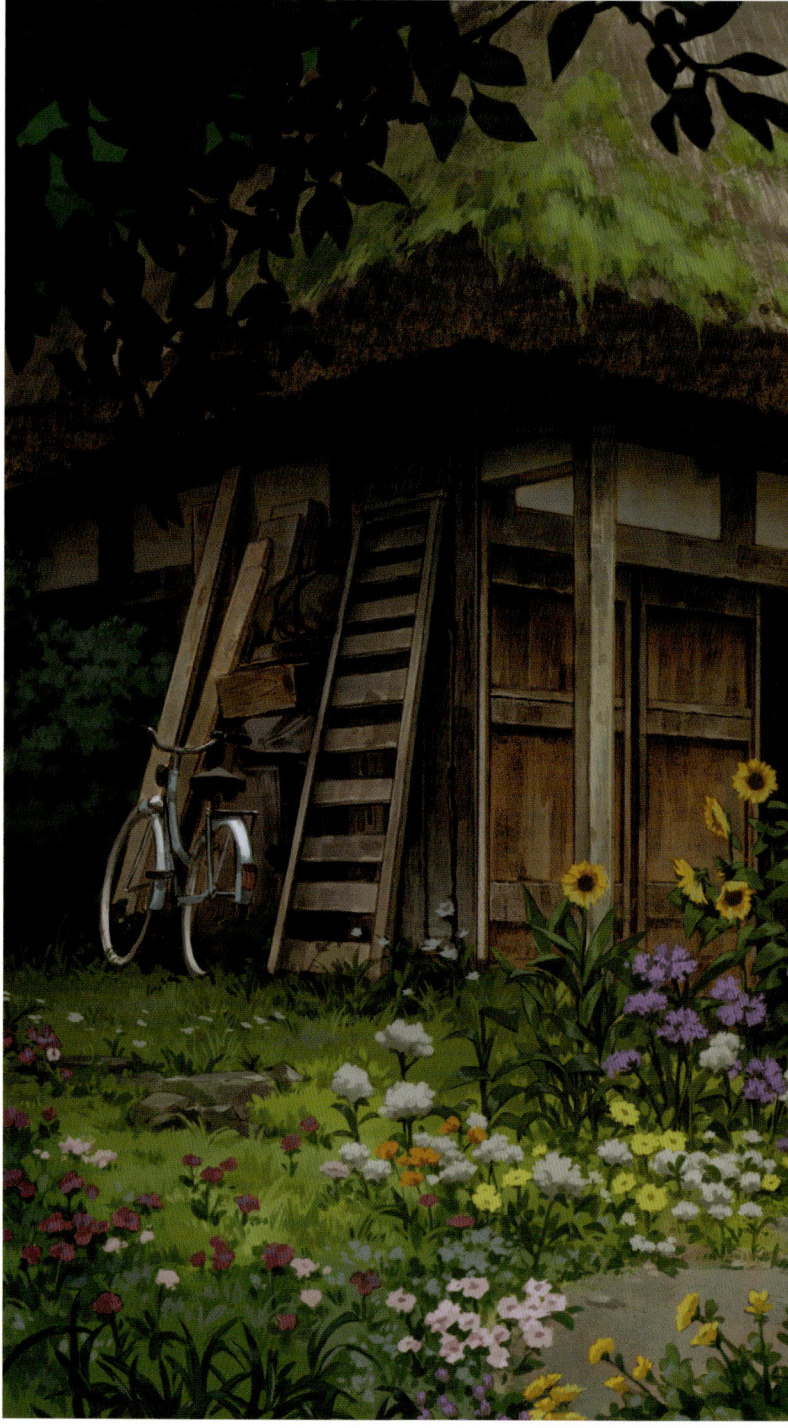

A typical overcast day. I did not include any characters in this scene, because my goal was just to design the environment and to keep it simple.

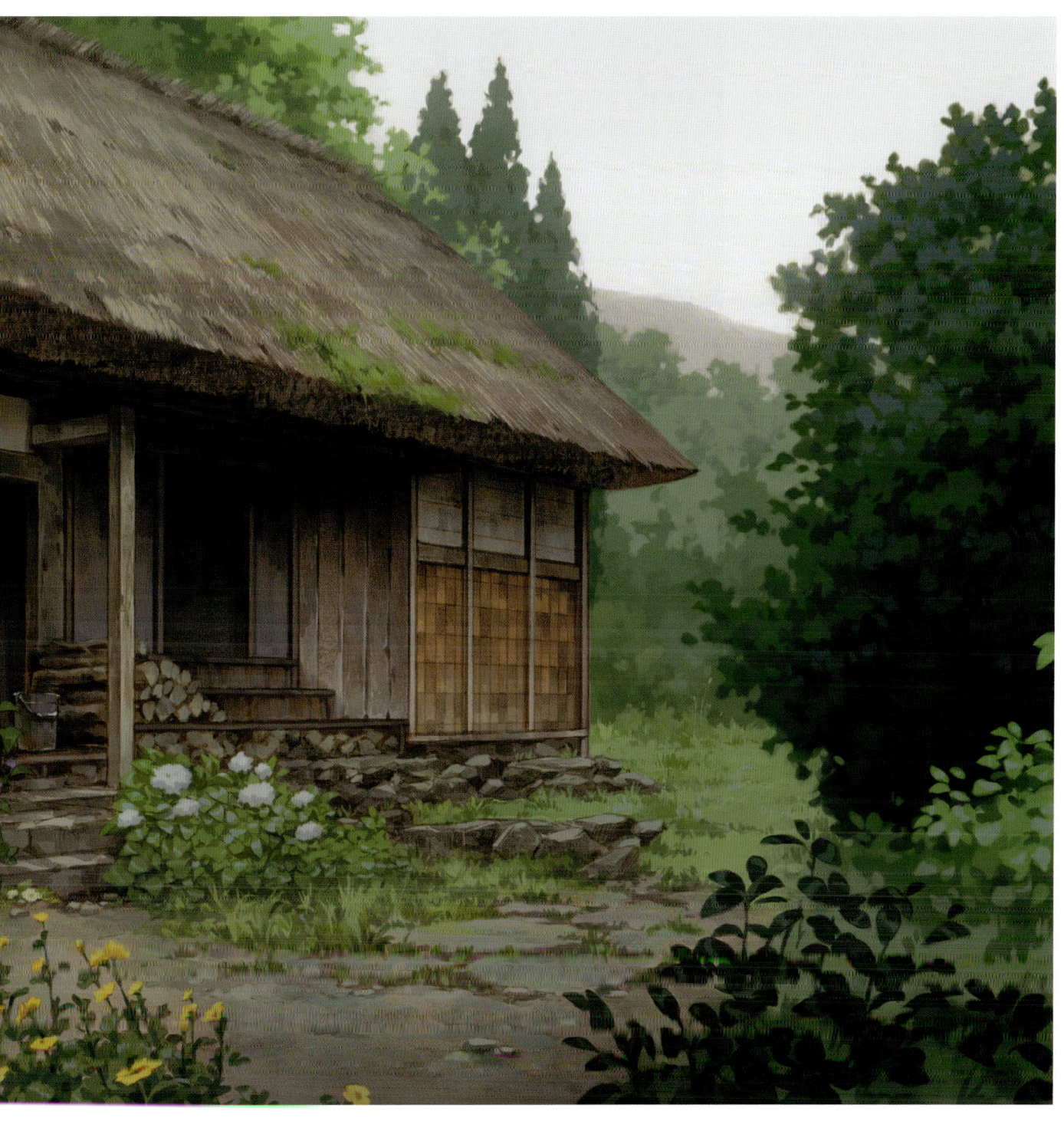

LIGHTING SCENARIO: BRIGHT SUNLIGHT

Now it's time to introduce some color! Step by step, I am going to flood our overcast scene with bright sunlight and make a happy and cheerful alternate version of the image. This is by far the lighting scenario that I feel the most comfortable with and that I use most often in my work. I love its warm, positive atmosphere and vibrant colors. Since we get to play with contrast and shadow patterns, there is more opportunity for drama and interesting compositions, but at the same time, it is also more complex to paint.

10 HERE COMES THE SUN

To paint a bright, sunny day, we can build on the foundation we laid in the overcast setting and continue using a lot of the same principles. The major difference is that there are now three light sources at play: the warm, direct light from the sun (our new, extra-powerful light source), the bounce light, and the blue light reflected from the sky. We will deal with all these in detail as we progress.

For now, my first concern is deciding what needs to happen to this overcast scenario to convince you that you are looking at a warm summer's day. The obvious answer is that it needs to be lighter and warmer, which I am fortunately able to do with just two simple actions. I use two of Photoshop's adjustment layers to make this change: one to increase the warmth and one to bump up the lightness.

You will also notice that I've introduced a small character to bring more life to the scene. This can be done at almost any stage of the painting process, thanks to the flexibility of digital layers, but I'll go into more specific detail about it on page 228.

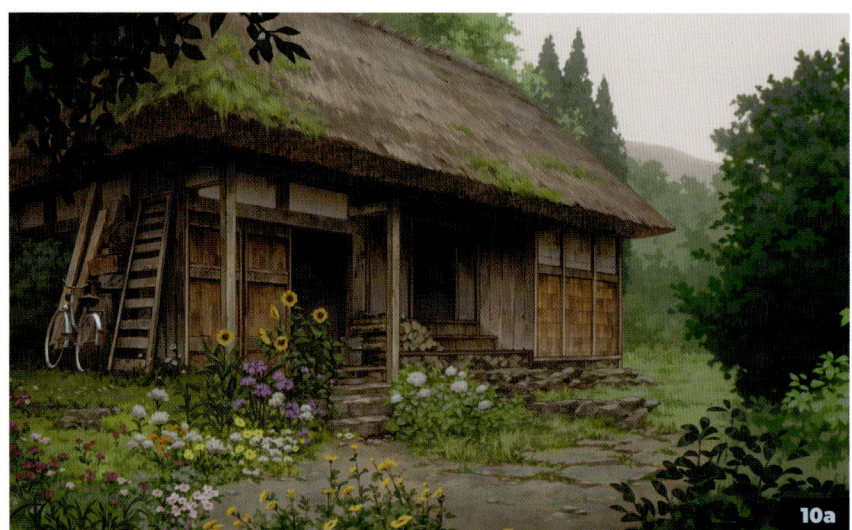

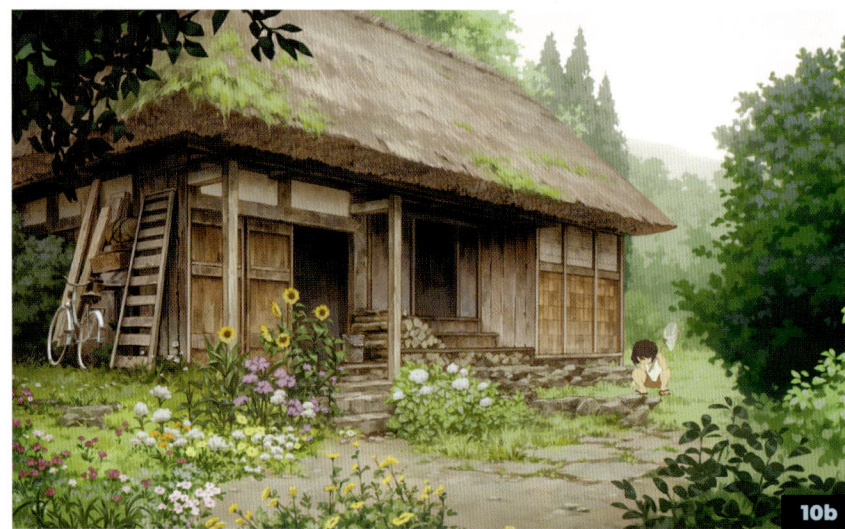

10a – 10b The scene before and after applying the adjustment layers. Even this first step changes the scene drastically, though there is still a lot of work to be done.

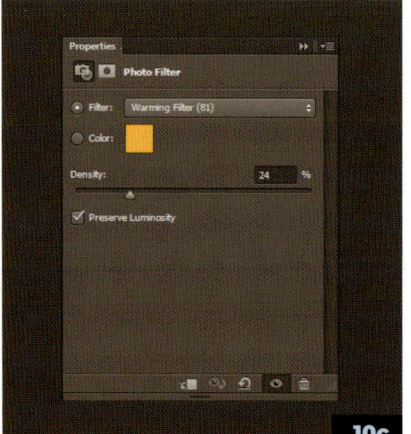

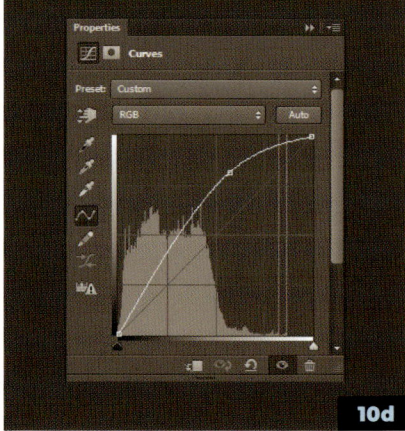

10c – 10d I apply a Photo Filter adjustment to bring in more warmth, and then a Curves adjustment to lighten the painting. I deliberately leave the darkest areas alone because I like the strong contrast.

ADJUSTMENT LAYERS

We will be using Photoshop's adjustment layers often as we explore color variations for our scene. Adjustment layers are effects that you can place anywhere between your painting's layers, enabling you to make quick changes to colors and values. They come with a mask that enables you to erase areas of the effect or to lower its opacity if needed. They are also non-destructive, so you can toggle the adjustments on and off, edit them at any point, and delete them without damaging your painting. They provide great flexibility and give you an easy way to make quick color explorations.

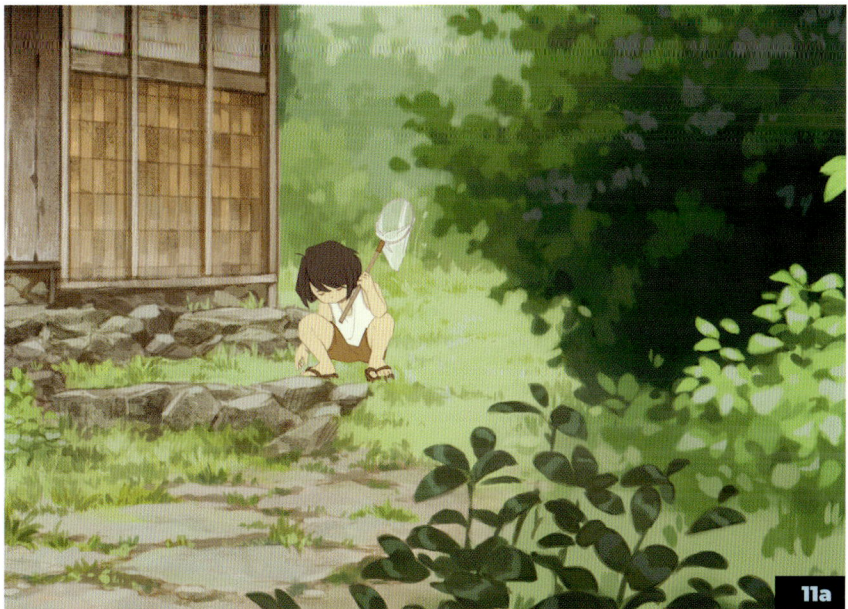

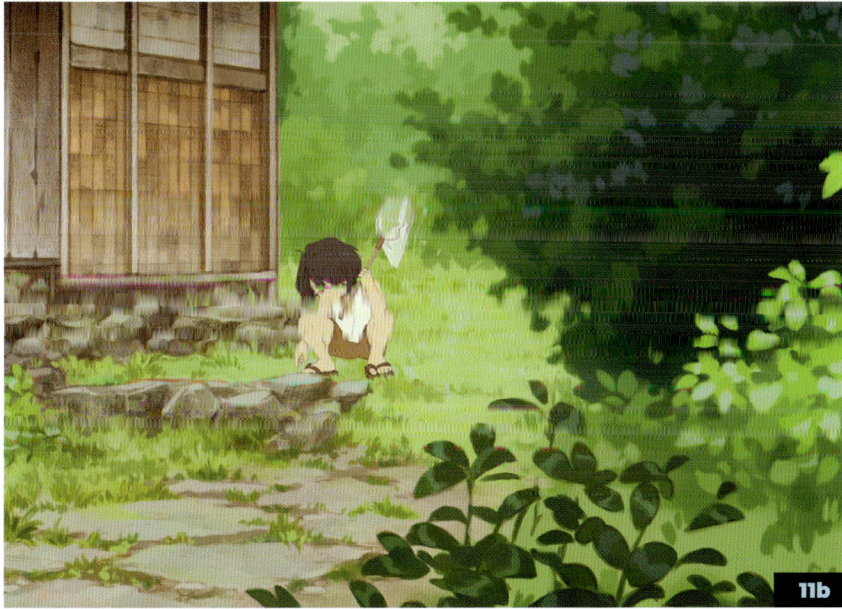

11a – 11b In a Vibrancy adjustment layer, I add +60. In a Selective Color > Green adjustment layer, I shift the greens +65 toward yellow. This is the result.

11 VIBRANT SUNSHINE AND FLUFFY CLOUDS

Everything is still looking quite dull, so we need to introduce some more color. I want this version to look very different from the previous one. I use more adjustment layers to increase the vibrancy and add warmth to the green tones in the painting.

What makes the biggest difference is bringing in a bright blue to replace the overcast sky (see next page). It immediately adds a new dominant color to the scene and completely changes the mood. Since the original sky is so light, I can just create a new layer, set the blending mode to Multiply, and paint the blue color on top.

By this point, I am starting to believe that what's in front of me is actually a beautiful summer's day. To reinforce this impression, I also want to add some fluffy clouds.

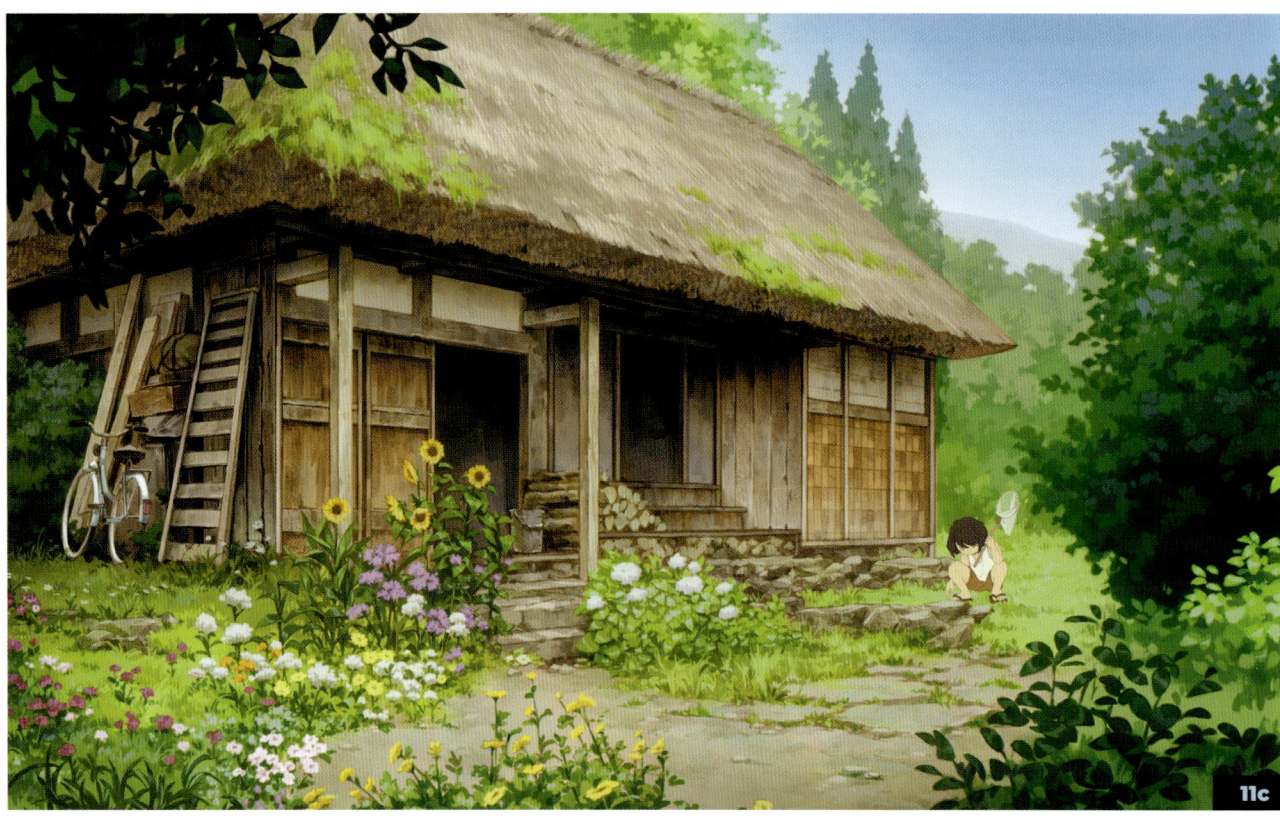

11c If you compare this to the overcast version of the painting, we are already seeing a big difference in atmosphere.

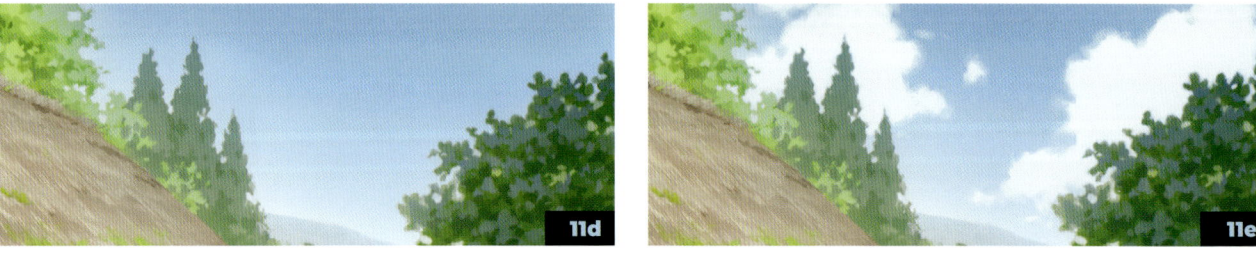

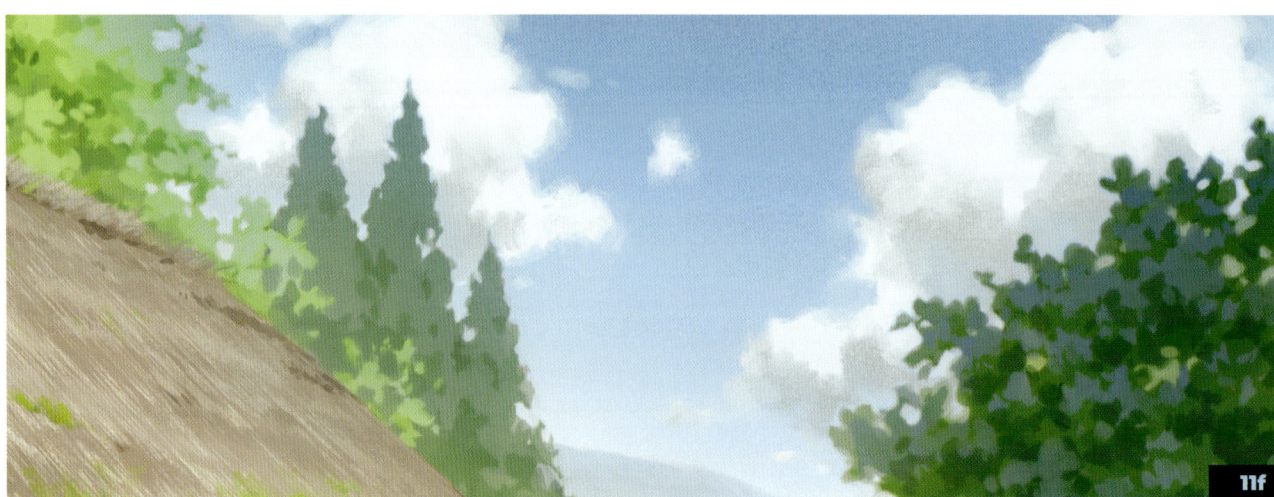

11d – 11f When it comes to the clouds, I keep the contrast between light and shadow quite low, as I don't want them to look too dramatic. I finish them off by adding a hint of the blue sky color to their undersides.

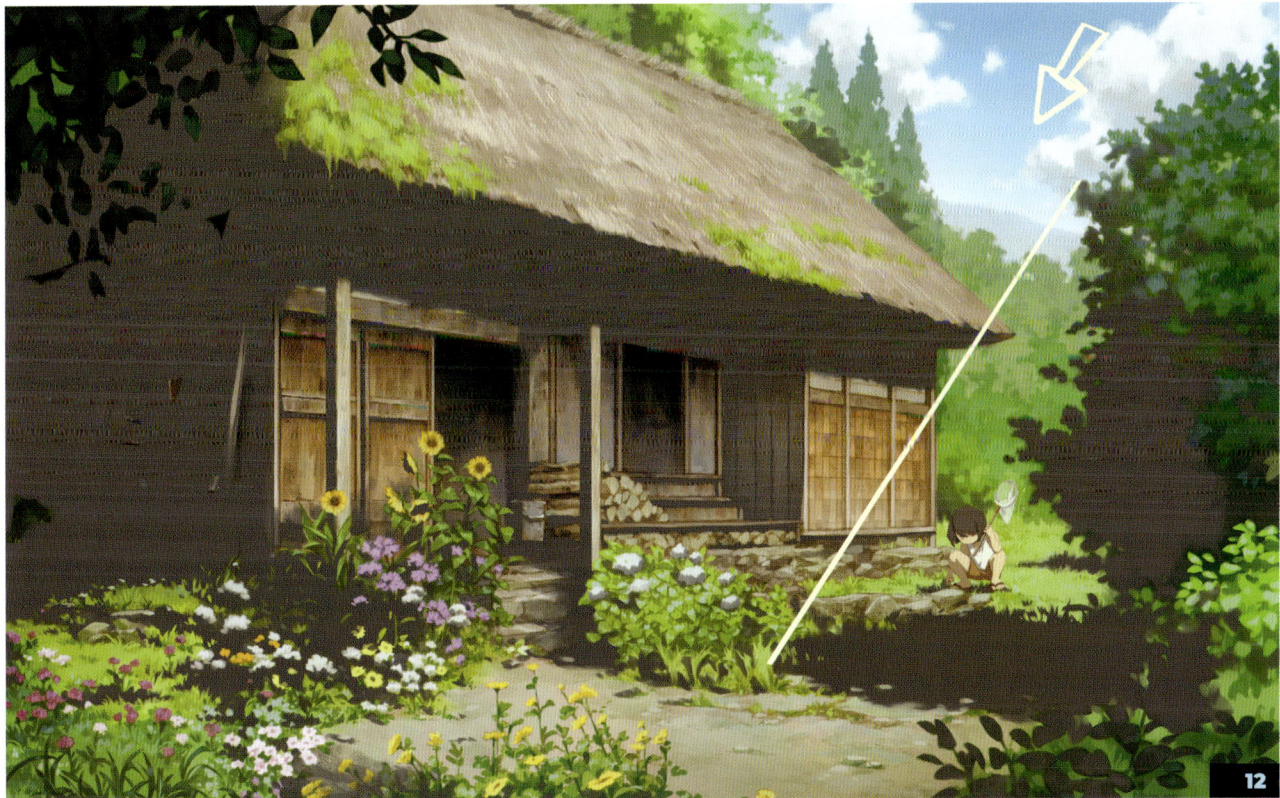

12 The dark areas indicate the cast shadows that I have added to the scene, before a blending mode is applied, and the arrow represents the sunlight's direction. The higher up it is, the shorter the cast shadow becomes, and vice versa.

My favorite method for painting clouds is to focus on the contours and edges first. Initially, I only paint with a single color (in this case, light gray), until I am happy with the basic shape. Next, I create a clipping mask and attach it to the layer that holds that shape. This keeps my strokes within the confines of the cloud contour, so that I can focus on adding shadows and creating three-dimensionality inside that area.

12 CASTING A LONG SHADOW

So far, the scene is looking brighter and friendlier, but what's missing are some more shadows. We still have the form shadows caused by the skylight, but now that the sun plays a major role as well, there should be some cast shadows caused by objects blocking the direct sunlight.

When I am working with cast shadows, I always try to map out where the light is coming from, and I think about which elements would be "getting in the way" of it. It can be useful to draw an arrow on your painting to keep the light's direction consistent. However, I am not too worried about getting this exactly right – sometimes I even sacrifice accuracy for visual appeal, if I think it serves the painting.

I approach shadows almost like graphic design elements where I am trying to create interesting shapes and patterns. They can be great compositional tools that guide the viewer's attention, and can even involve objects casting shadows from outside the frame. Shadows can also give a painting more depth, allowing the artist to simplify and group certain areas together.

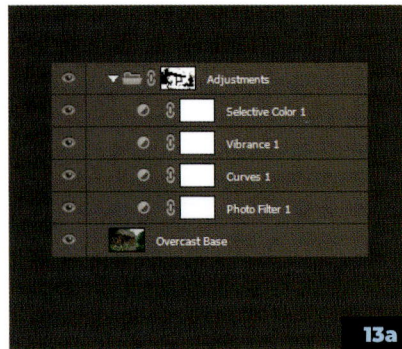

13a

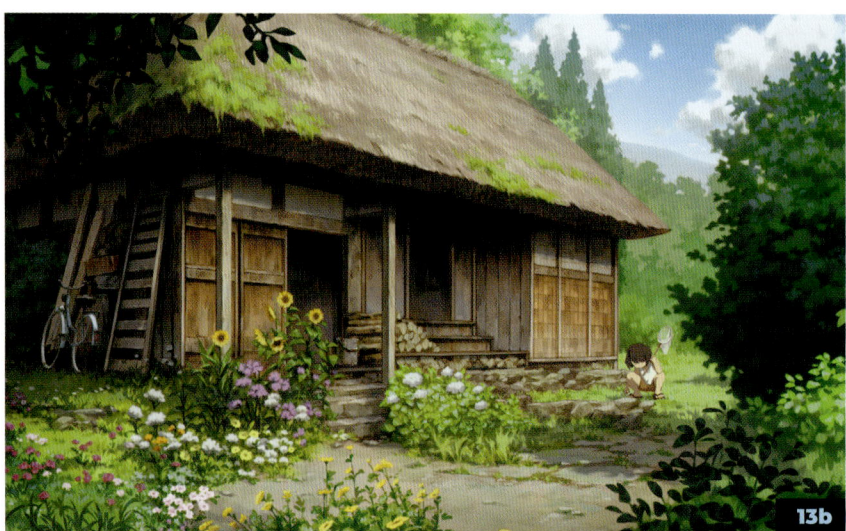

13b

13 SWITCHING OFF THE SUNLIGHT

It can be difficult to determine how light or dark a shadow should be and what color it should have. I am not one for exact science, so when it comes to sunlight, I generally use a shadow color that is slightly cooler (with tints of blue or purple) and roughly twenty to forty percent darker than the light area.

However, in this case, we will peel back the couple of layers that we have just added to reveal the overcast setting underneath. This will serve as our shadow, almost as if we are switching off the sunlight in those areas.

When painting shadows, it's good to keep in mind that a hard light will cast shadows with a hard edge, and that soft light will cause shadows with a soft edge. Distance also plays a role – the shadow of a tall tree on the ground will have a much softer edge than the shadow of an average-sized person. I sometimes break this rule on purpose, especially when I draw characters, but more on that later!

14 BOUNCE LIGHT

Another thing to take into consideration is bounce light. Since sunlight is so bright and strong, most surfaces will reflect it and cause it to bounce around the scene. You can clearly see this effect on the underside of the roof, where light finds its way back up from the ground and warms up the surface. On a sunny day, planes that are facing down are warmer in temperature, and even though

13a – 13b I erase parts of the sunny adjustment layers to reveal the original darker scene. Since I put all the layers in one folder, a single mask allows me to paint in the shadows (black) and to leave the light areas (white) unaffected.

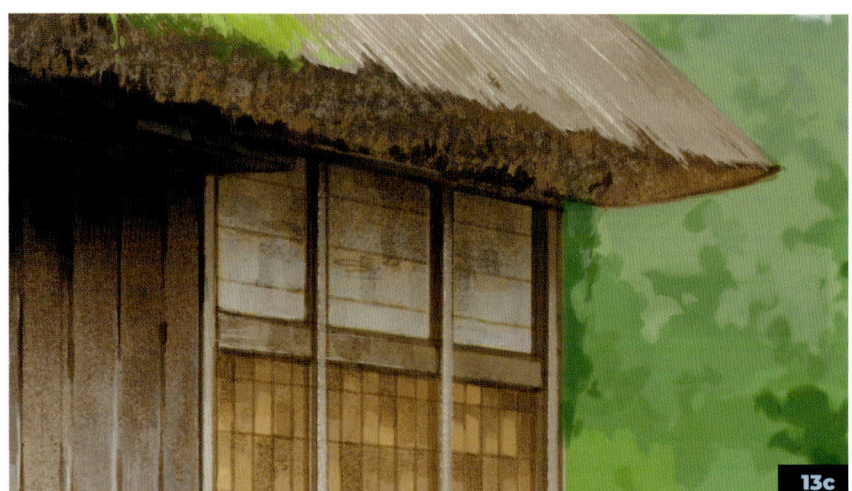

13c

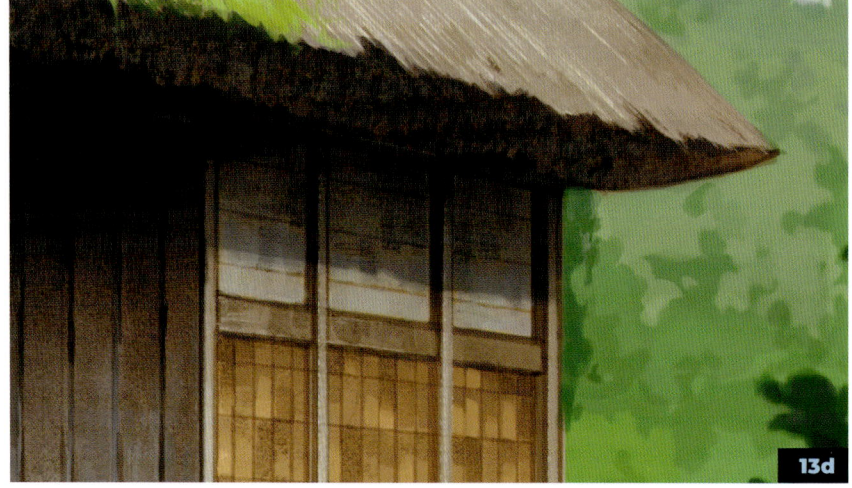

13d

13c – 13d Adding cast shadows makes the scene look more three-dimensional.

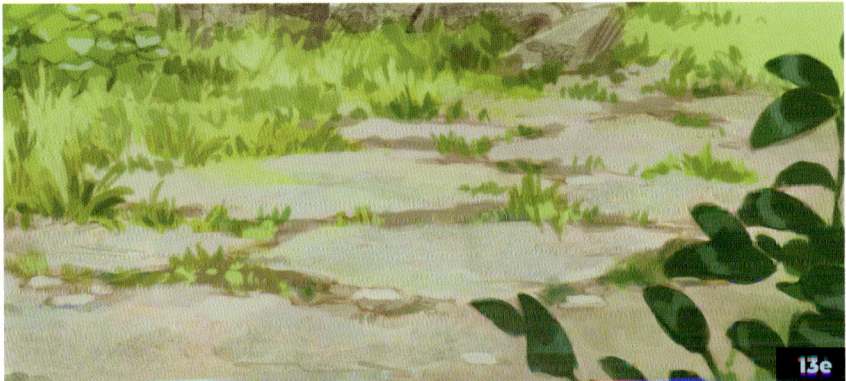

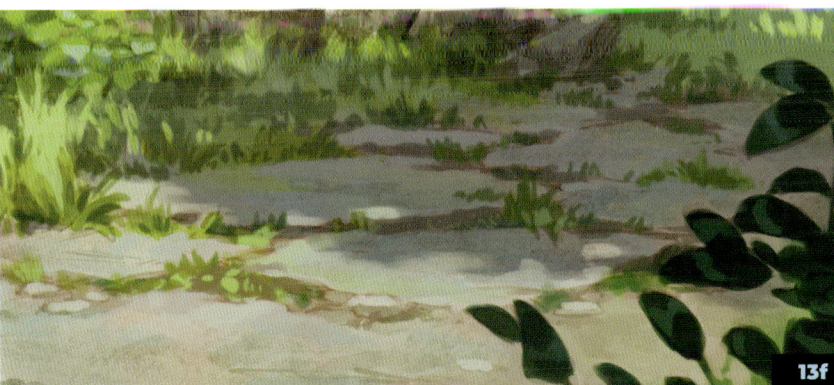

13e – 13f Cast shadows created by strong sunlight will have a harder edge.

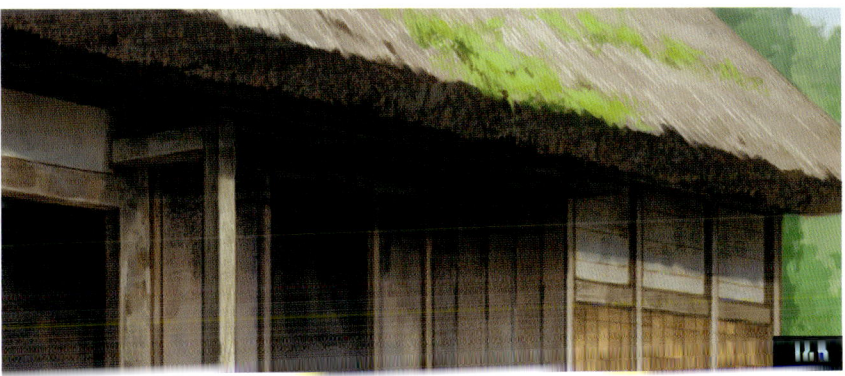

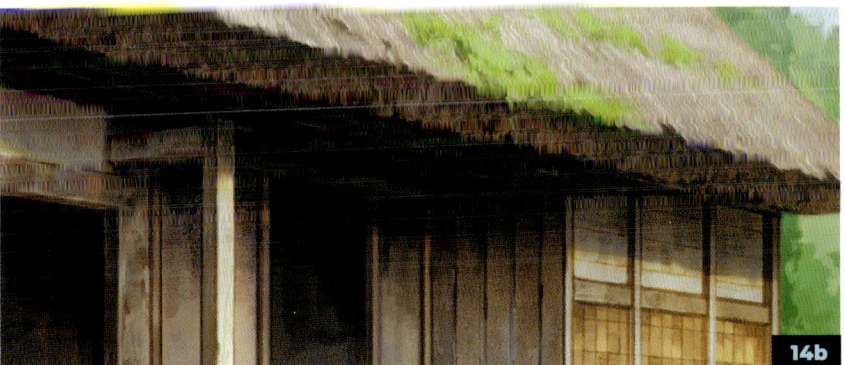

14a – 14b The effect is subtle, but introducing more bounce light creates a warmer atmosphere and makes the sunlight more believable.

we mentioned earlier that shadows tend to be cooler, some warm light can still sneak into them. Keep in mind that bounce light is always weaker than the light coming directly from the primary light source – it's easy to overdo!

When in doubt, follow this useful guideline: The lightest parts in the shadow areas are always darker than the darkest parts in the light areas. You can see this at play when you look at the roof. The light and shadow sides are both clearly separated, and the warm bounce light doesn't get any lighter than the darker areas on the light side (I am not counting the deeper crevices here, because I consider these shadows).

While we are on the subject of warm light: I am also adding an orange tint to the areas where light meets shadow, because these edges tend to be warmer and more saturated.

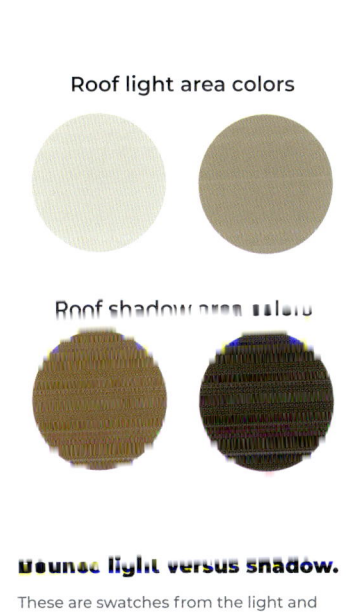

Roof light area colors

Roof shadow area colors

Bounce light versus shadow.

These are swatches from the light and shadow areas of the roof, with the lightest and darkest color from each. Notice how the lightest part of the shadow (bottom left) is still darker than the darkest part of the light (top right).

15 BLUE SKYLIGHT

We have now covered two of the three mechanics we mentioned in the beginning: direct sunlight and bounce light. This leaves us with blue skylight. Fortunately, we already know how it works from the overcast section: Planes that are facing up toward the sky appear cooler in temperature, which is to say, slightly bluer.

However, since the sun is the strongest player in the scene and easily takes over with its warm light, the blue skylight is only visible in the shadows. When the sky is clear, the effect becomes more pronounced because there is more blue to go around.

If we combine this knowledge with the principles of bounce light, we are left with a simple rule for painting shadows on a sunny day: Planes that are facing up appear cooler and bluer, while planes that are facing down appear warmer and more orange.

16 INTRODUCING A CHARACTER

Now that we have addressed the basic principles at play in the environment, it is a good time to talk about the character. For each variation of this painting, I want to

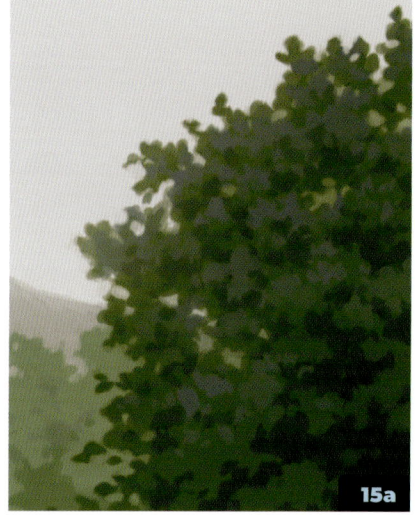
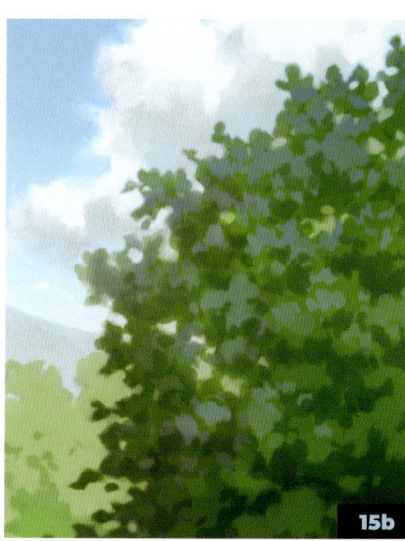

15a – 15b You can see how, in each setting, the leaves facing up pick up some of the sky color.

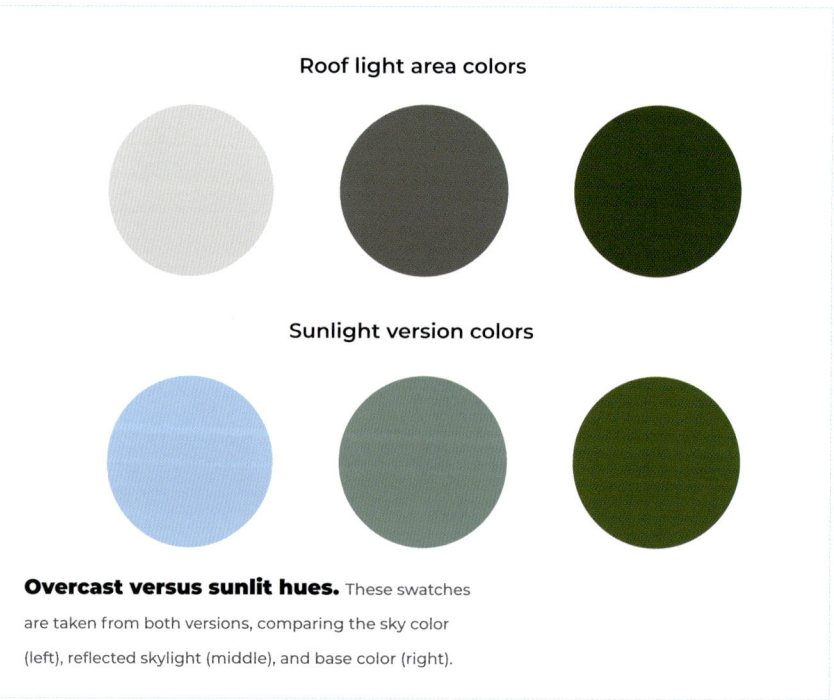

Roof light area colors

Sunlight version colors

Overcast versus sunlit hues. These swatches are taken from both versions, comparing the sky color (left), reflected skylight (middle), and base color (right).

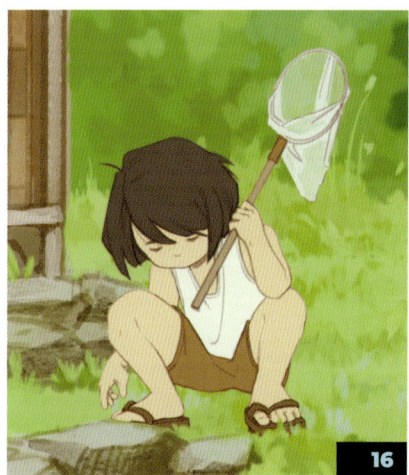

16 I choose a very simple, limited color scheme for the character, and I keep everything flat to begin with. The only extra thing I do is mask out part of the net to create a transparent effect.

add the same character, but in a different situation, therefore telling different stories.

Since we are looking at a traditional Japanese house, I want to showcase a simpler, old-fashioned lifestyle. I gather some photographs taken in the Shōwa era (1926–1989) for inspiration. During my search, I am reminded that Japanese children love to go bug-catching in the summer, which seems like the perfect fit for this scene.

This story also informs my color choices: I think it is appropriate to apply some camouflage, because if you are catching bugs, you'd probably want to blend in with the environment and wear neutral colors. A simple color palette for the clothing also underlines the old-timey feel of the scene. I look around the painting and select colors that would work for the character, sometimes creating subtle variations, and keep the colors flat for now.

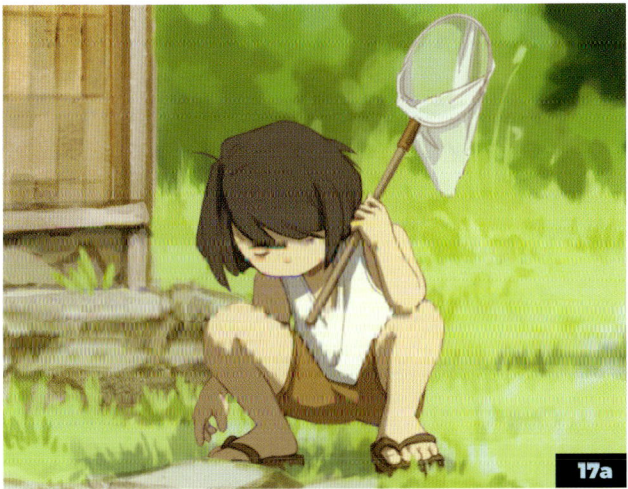

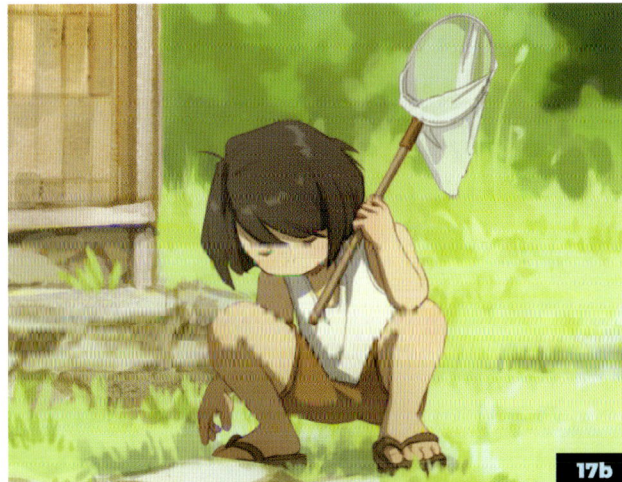

17a – 17b This is what the character looks like before and after adding shadows, details, and subtle gradients. These harsh shadows aren't very realistic, but I love how they introduce a sharpness that helps draw focus to the character.

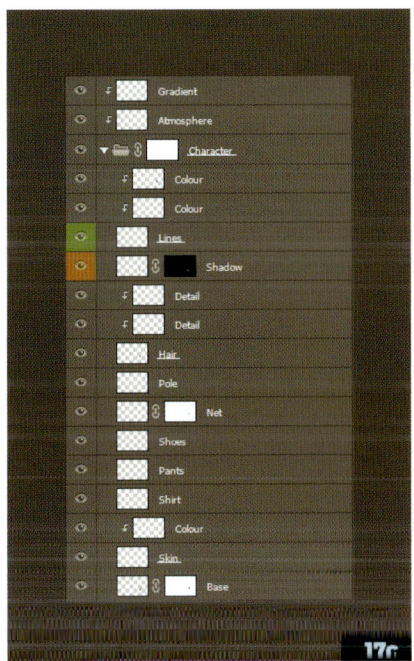

17c This is my layer breakdown for the character. If I want more details (like a subtle gradient across all layers), I can attach more clipping masks and adjustment layers to the whole folder.

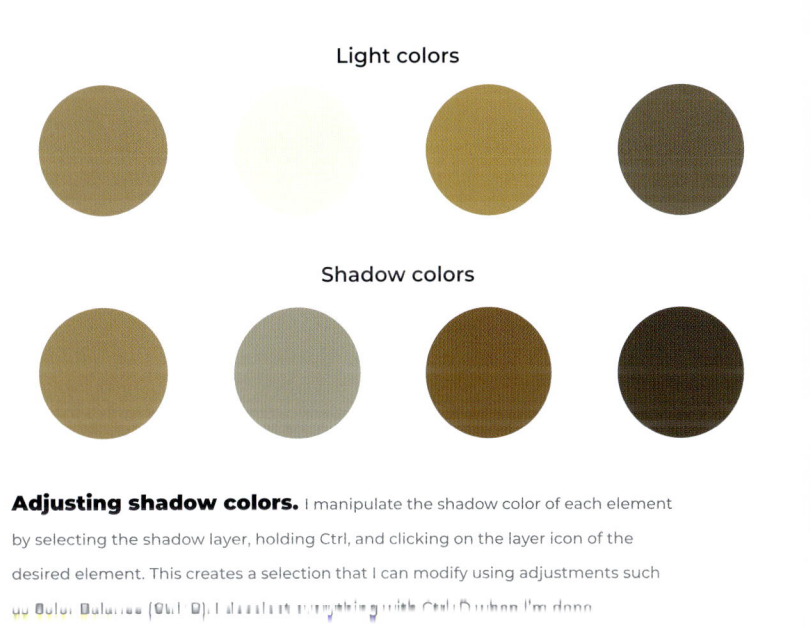

Light colors

Shadow colors

Adjusting shadow colors. I manipulate the shadow color of each element by selecting the shadow layer, holding Ctrl, and clicking on the layer icon of the desired element. This creates a selection that I can modify using adjustments such as Color Balance (Ctrl B). I deselect everything with Ctrl D when I'm done.

17 CEL SHADING

When it comes to painting characters, I use a technique called cel shading – a term that comes from way back when animation frames were hand-painted on celluloid. My process is quite simple: I set up a base color for each element of the character, then choose one shadow color to go on top of everything. To be able to change these around easily, I keep each element on its own layer and name it accordingly. I add another layer above all these, fill in the whole silhouette of the character, and set it to Multiply so it becomes the shadow. Using a mask and a hard-edged brush, I erase parts, or bring them back if needed, until I feel happy with the shadow shape. While I am doing this, I pay attention to the light direction in the environment.

Next, I create clipping masks and attach them to any part of the character that I think needs further detailing. For example, I use clipping masks to add a bit of redness around the cheeks, knees, elbow, hands, and feet, and I paint in some highlights on the hair. I also use clipping masks to vary the color of the line art in certain places. To finish the character off, I tweak the shadow color for a couple of elements – for example, making the shadow on the shirt slightly bluer.

229

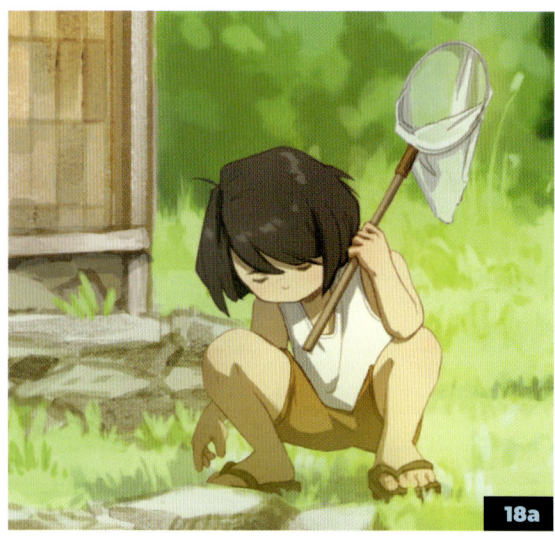

18a Adding a glow around the character enhances the impression of bounce light in the sweltering heat.

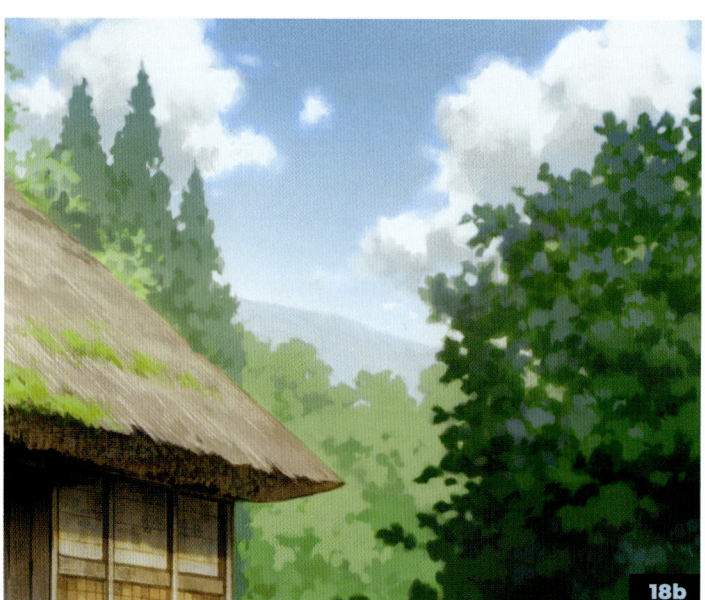

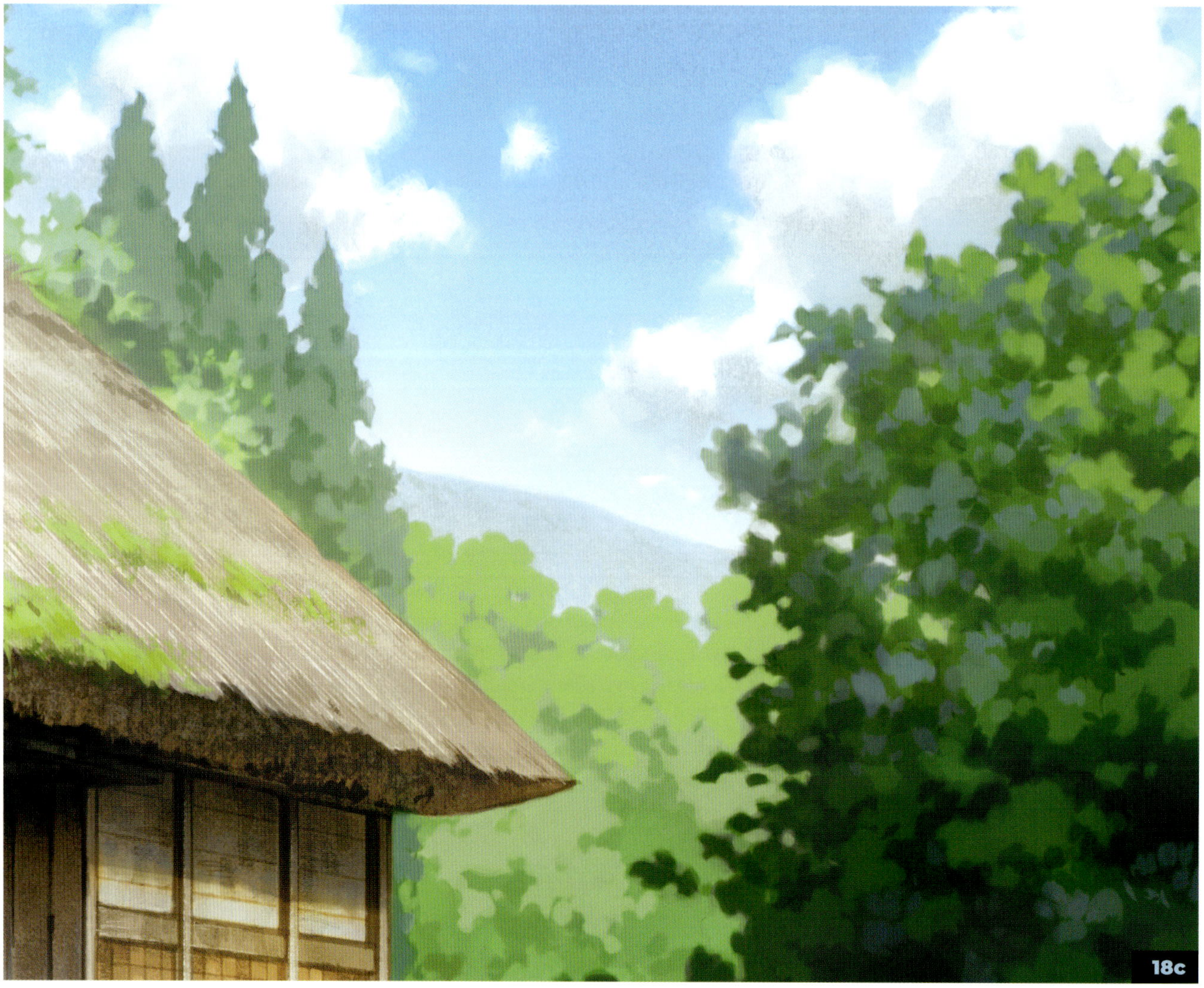

18b – 18c It's another small change, but painting in those warmer greens in the light areas makes the foliage look more interesting and believable.

18 FINAL TWEAKS

The summer's day painting is nearly complete – I just need to make a few final tweaks. Most importantly, I want to apply a warm glow that enhances the feeling of sunlight and adds a slightly overexposed effect. I use more adjustment layers to bring out the highlights even further, and use a yellow color and a big, soft brush to paint warm light around the character.

In addition to these lighting tweaks, I finish off the illustration by hand-painting the foliage on the right. I introduce some more light spots in vibrant green tones to really sell the idea of sunlight hitting the leaves.

During the whole process, some areas have lost their texture. This is a natural trade-off that just happens: To create the illusion of bright sunlight, you end up sacrificing textures in the light areas. In a similar way, to paint a night scene, you sacrifice clarity and contrast for moodiness.

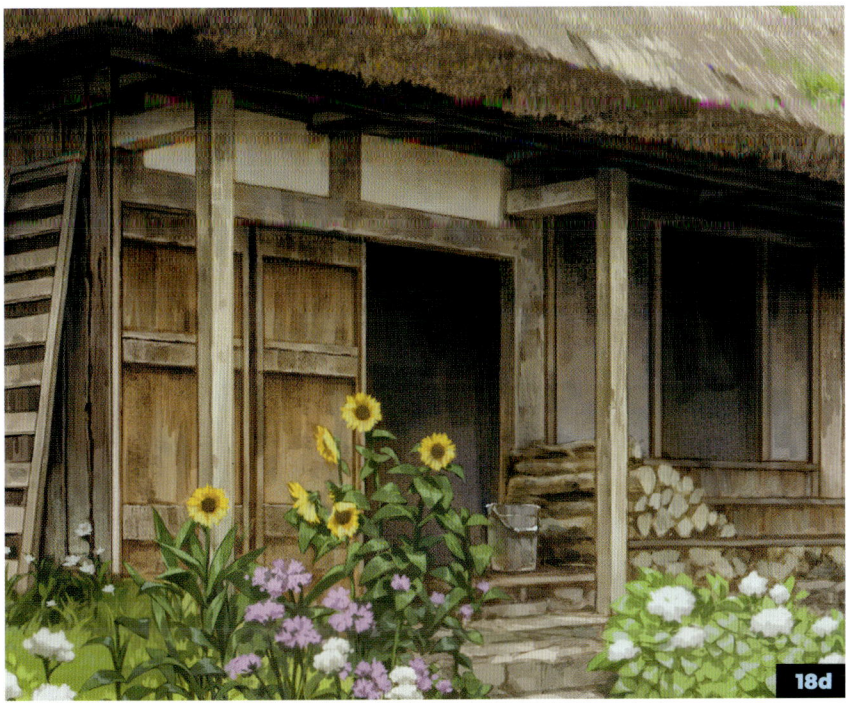

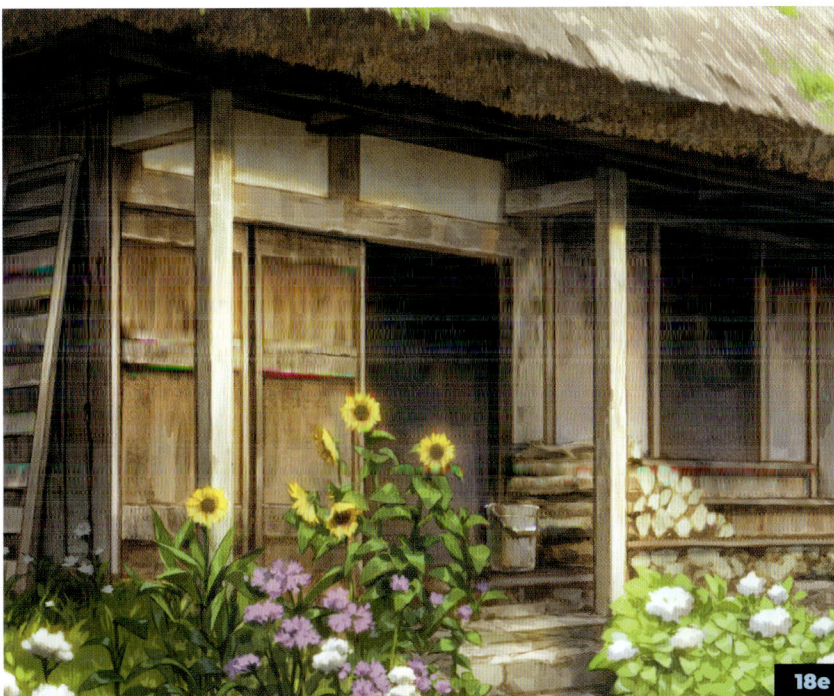

18d – 18e If you look back at an earlier version of the painting you can see that the wooden beams used to have a lot more texture.

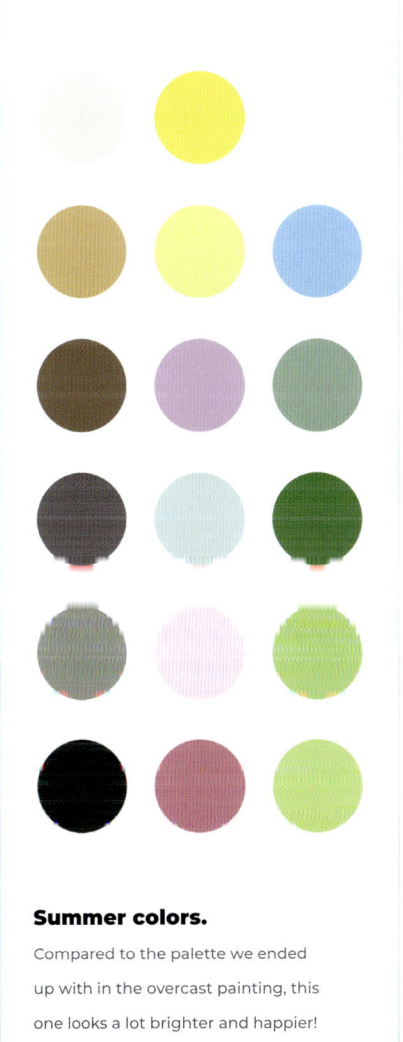

Summer colors.

Compared to the palette we ended up with in the overcast painting, this one looks a lot brighter and happier!

LIGHTING RECAP: BRIGHT SUNLIGHT

Let's summarize what we've learned again. In direct sunlight, we are dealing with three light sources: direct sunlight, bounce light, and blue skylight. Out of these three, direct sunlight is predominant, causing cast shadows throughout the scene. The main thing to pay attention to is keeping the direction of the light consistent.

The overall color scheme of this version is warmer and more vibrant than the overcast setting, and it has a "purer" quality to it. It also has more contrast, with the light areas being a lot brighter than before, while the deeper shadows stay about the same. I tried to recall the atmosphere of a hot summer's day and channel it through the artwork. Looking at the illustration, I want you to be able to hear cicadas chirping, to feel the heat in the air, and to imagine the grass under your feet.

Just like I did with the overcast scenario, I am going to delve into storytelling and give you a few suggestions about when to use bright sunlight in your artwork and what it might communicate.

To me, bright sunlight is the epitome of warmth, positivity, and openness. It can make a scene come alive and have it buzzing with energy. It is perfect if you are telling a story that has a friendly and inviting tone. I also believe that nature – especially greenery – looks best in bright sunlight.

However, on the flip side, sunlight can also suggest unbearable heat and blinding light that can be very unpleasant, if your story demands it.

Lastly, sunlight provides an excellent opportunity for creating drama, as well as interesting shadow patterns and compositions. You can use these to highlight or tone down parts of the painting. If your initial sketch is lacking some visual interest, you can bring in strips or spots of light as extra focal points and to guide the viewer's attention.

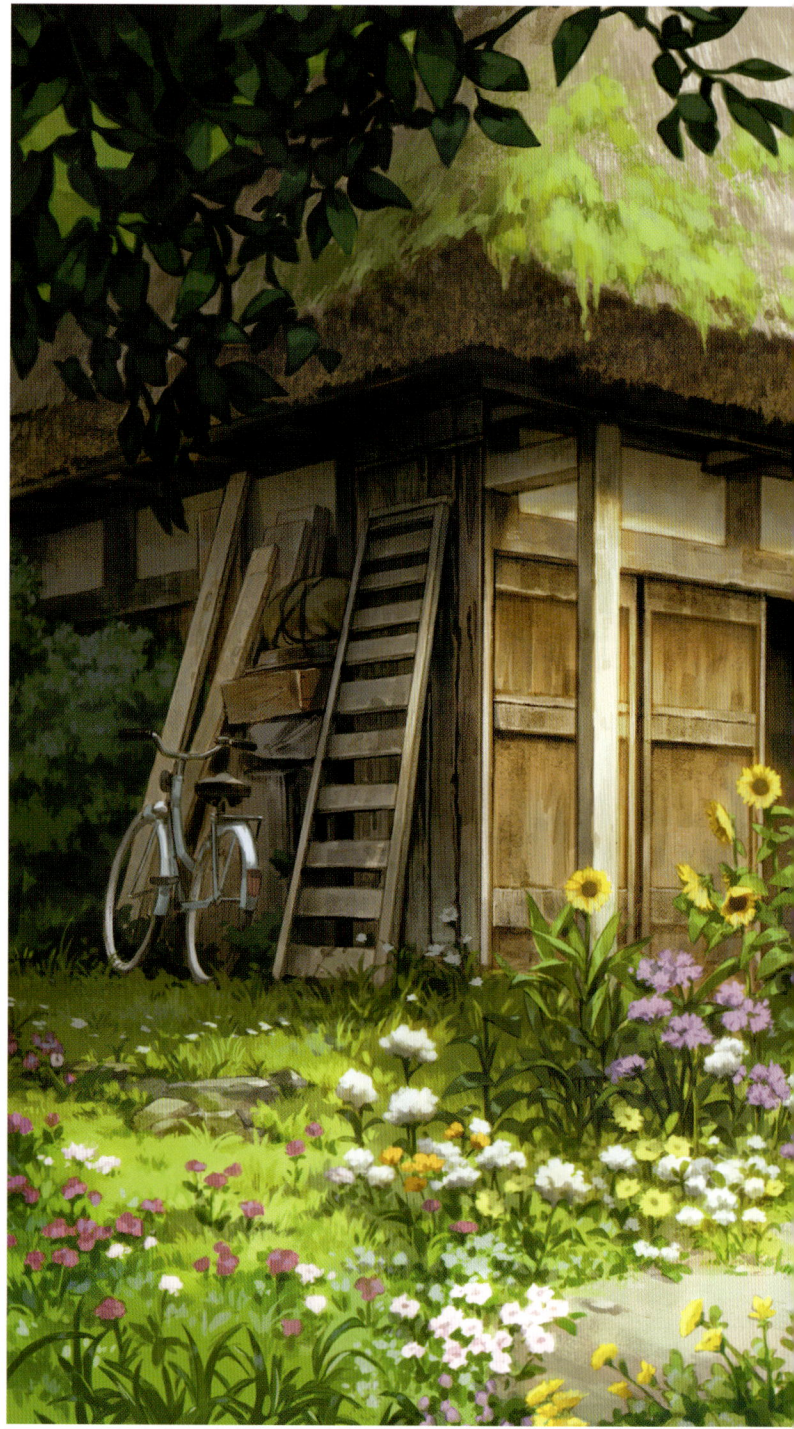

A clear, warm, sunny day. The final painting of a child catching bugs on a summer's day. Everything feels bright, lush, and vibrant.

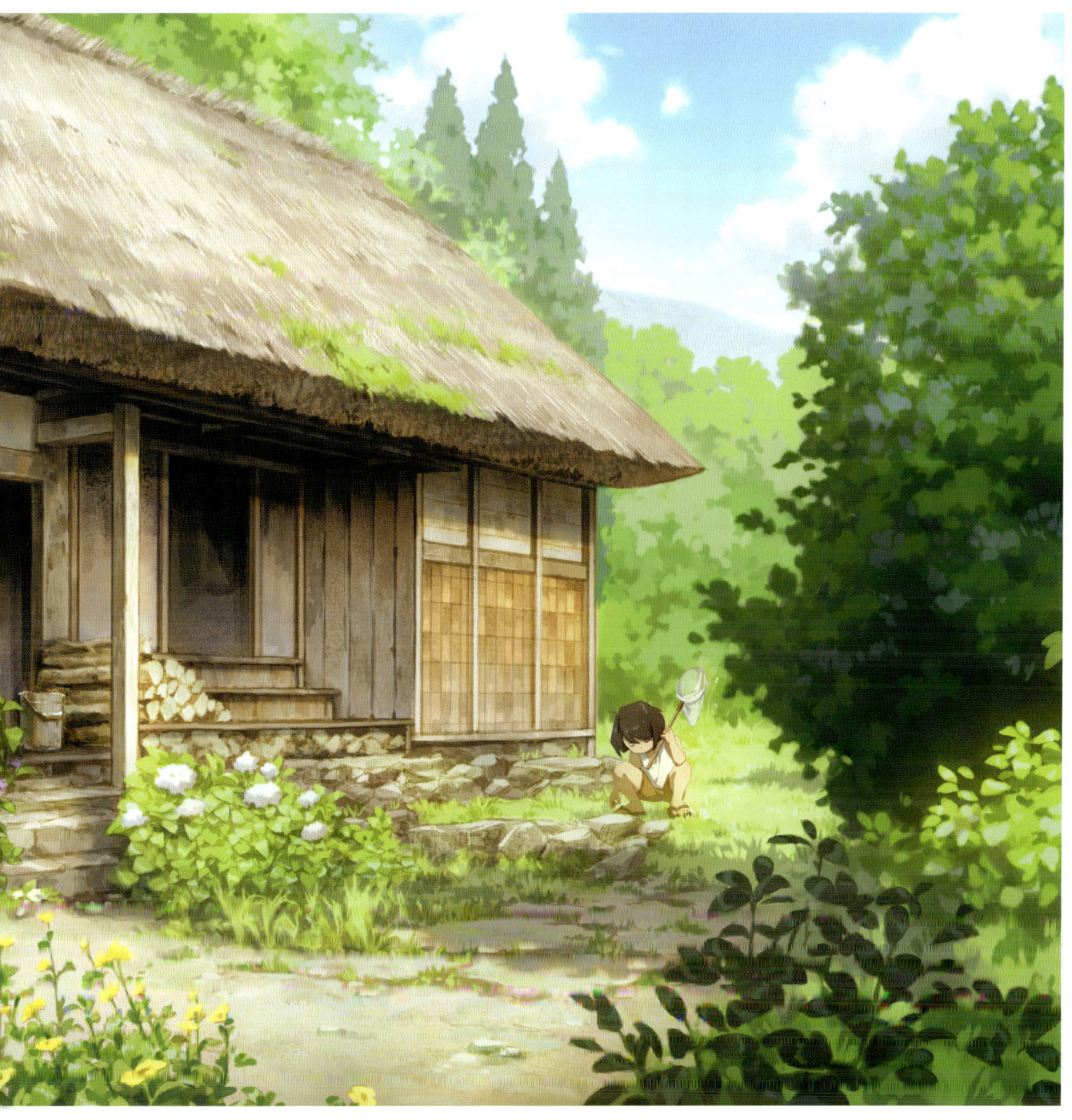

LIGHTING SCENARIO: EARLY MORNING

The next time of day I want to tackle is the early morning. There are many ways to approach this, perhaps the most obvious being a warm sunrise. However, I associate the start of the day with being calm, quiet, and cool. To embody this, I will paint the so-called "blue hour," which occurs during twilight, when the sun is still far enough below the horizon that the light's blue wavelengths dominate.

19 THE BLUE HOUR

To me, the early morning is when you can take a moment for yourself, before the world around you comes alive. That is why I choose to tell the story of a character who is yawning, stretching, and just waking up. During the blue hour, the color scheme will be predominantly blue, and in the absence of direct sunlight or any streetlights, the scene will also be quite dark.

To accomplish this, I go back to the overcast version of the scene and start tweaking the colors and values. I use a Color Balance adjustment layer to add more blue to the scene, then use Selective Color to shift the green tones toward a darker magenta.

20 PALE SHADOW

Now I can start to think about shadows and light sources. Just like before, we have diffused light coming from the sky, which reveals the forms of all the objects in the scene. However, it's weaker this time, and more areas will drop into shadow. In the early morning, we are basically just one step away from nighttime, so the ambient lighting is bound to be darker – but that doesn't mean that we can just ignore the sun.

Since I am painting the same place at different times of day, I have to take into consideration where the sun rises and sets, for consistency. This isn't usually something I think about, but in this case, where I am depicting variations of the same setting, it's

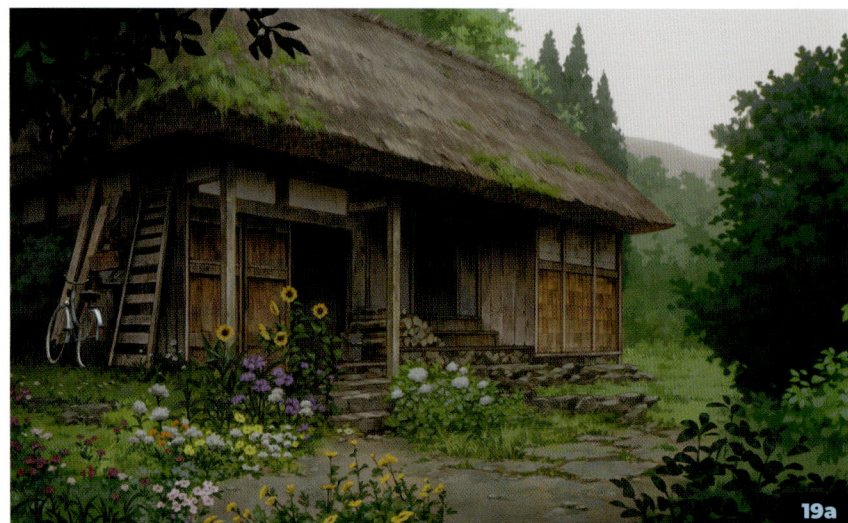

19a

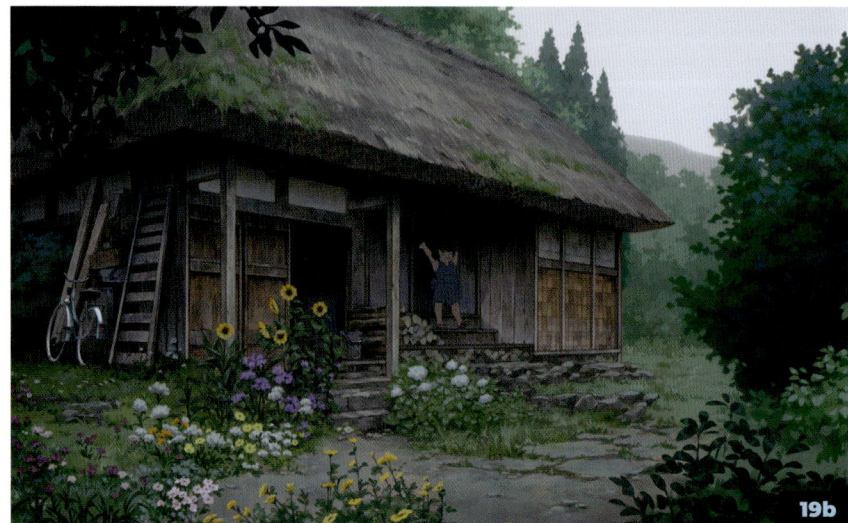

19b

19a – 19b The first step is shifting the whole color palette toward blue and neutralizing the green hues with a complementary color.

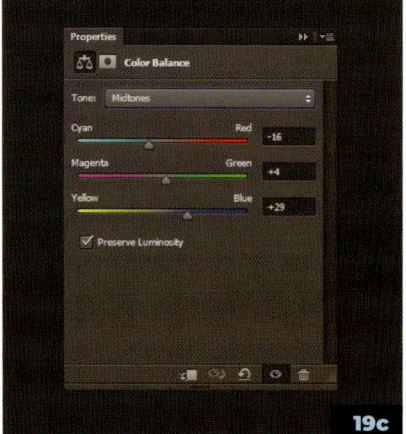

19c

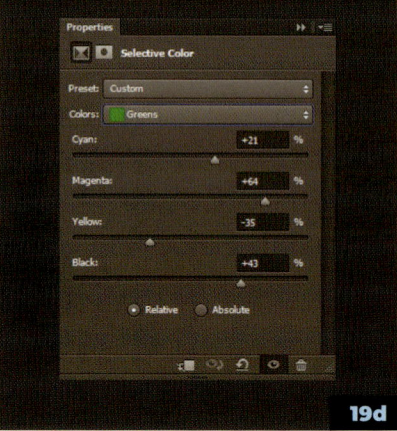

19d

19c – 19d Color Balance and Selective Color adjustment layers enable me to make nondestructive mood changes very easily.

worth paying attention to. The sun follows a set path: It rises in the east, makes its way across the south, and it finally sets in the west. Judging from our daylight scene, I conclude that the right side of the painting is south. That makes the distant mountains east and the "front" of the illustration west. I use this information to plan the lighting setup. I am going to include a faint light behind the mountain range, where the sun will eventually rise.

21 FEELING BLUE

The palette needs to be much cooler, so I go back to the same technique I used in step 11 for the sky in the bright sunlight setup: I add a new layer, set it to Multiply mode, and use a big, soft brush to paint in more blue. I apply it over the sky and all the plants in the scene, because they look richer and moodier when they are darker. The trees and bushes on the right in particular create a good contrast against the sky.

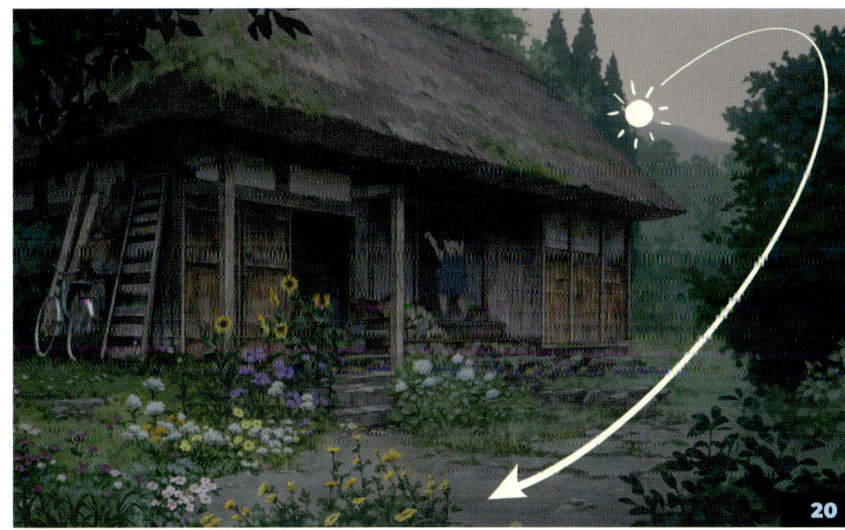

20 This diagram maps out how the sun travels through the painting over the course of the day.

I also drop the entire middle ground (the area around the house) into deeper shadow. This might take away some of the clarity and detail, but it reinforces the mood and story, and that is what's important to me. This change also allows me to visually group the house area together, prepping the composition for the focal point I am about to introduce in the doorway. Last, I use Color Balance to add a subtle purple tint to the shadow areas, to cancel out some more of the green hues.

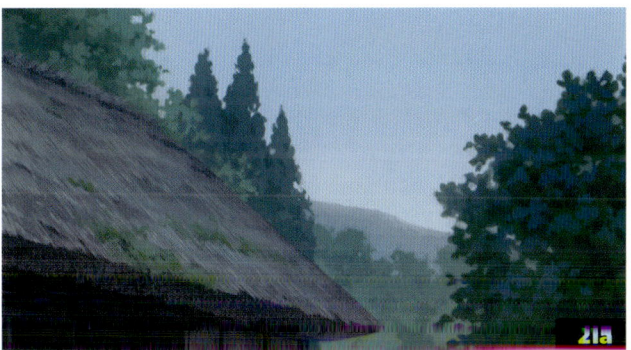

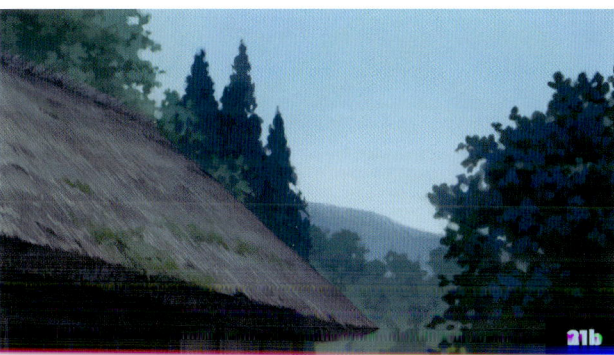

21a – 21b Darkening the trees reinforces the impression that the sun is somewhere behind them, and that they are not catching much light from above.

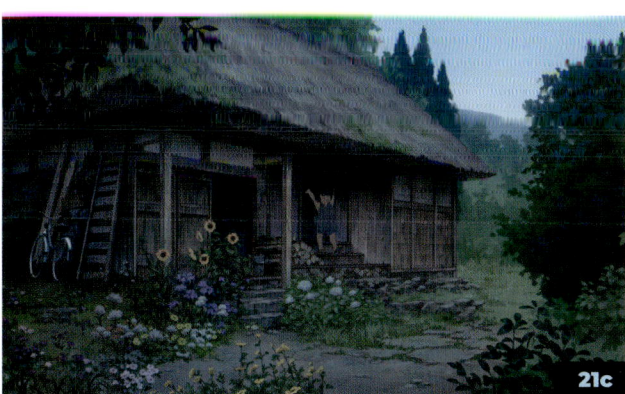

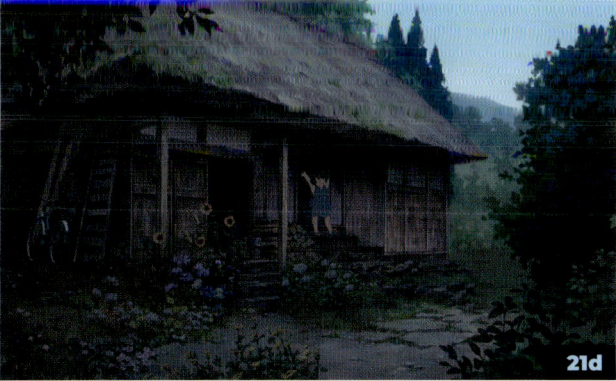

21c – 21d I introduce deeper shadows and more purple into the painting, canceling out more of the green.

22 A NEW LIGHT SOURCE

The scene is looking quite dark now, which means that it is the perfect time to introduce a new light source. When I paint any illustration, I always look for opportunities to include interesting moments and focal points. I assess each environment and lighting setup and ask myself what stories it has to offer. I particularly like strategically placed lights, shadow patterns, and weather phenomena. I can use all these to my advantage and to enhance the composition.

In this case, I see a great opportunity to add a warm light inside the house. Before sunrise, it is still dark outside, so it makes sense that someone would turn on the light or make a fire. Since this is not a modern scene, I lean toward the latter.

This light introduces a new focal point and fulfills a few purposes: It adds a warm accent in the overall cool color scheme, which serves as a point of contrast against the big, dark shape of the house, as well as framing the character and helping to bring out their silhouette. I had this potential scene in mind from the beginning, when I positioned the character in the doorway.

23 ADDING HIGHLIGHTS

Now that there is an extra light source in the environment, it will affect the character. I usually approach lighting characters in one of two ways: I either start with a light base and add darker shadows, or I start with a dark base and add bright highlights. In the bright sunlight setting, you may remember that I added the shadow to the character to indicate the light source, but in this case, I am choosing the opposite approach: I paint in the light. This is because the light makes up a very small area of the character compared to the shadow.

I create a new layer above all the character's base colors and set it to Color Dodge mode.

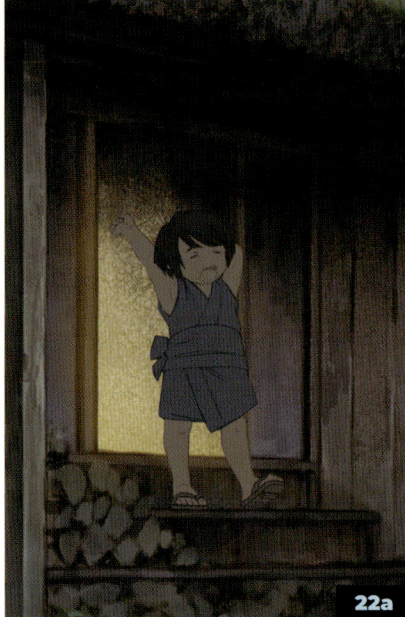
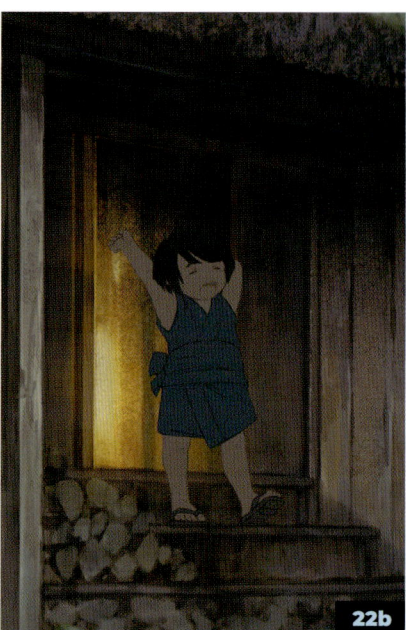

22a – 22b I block in a simple yellow gradient behind the character, then add warmer colors and light accents to give the illusion of firelight. I also darken the character.

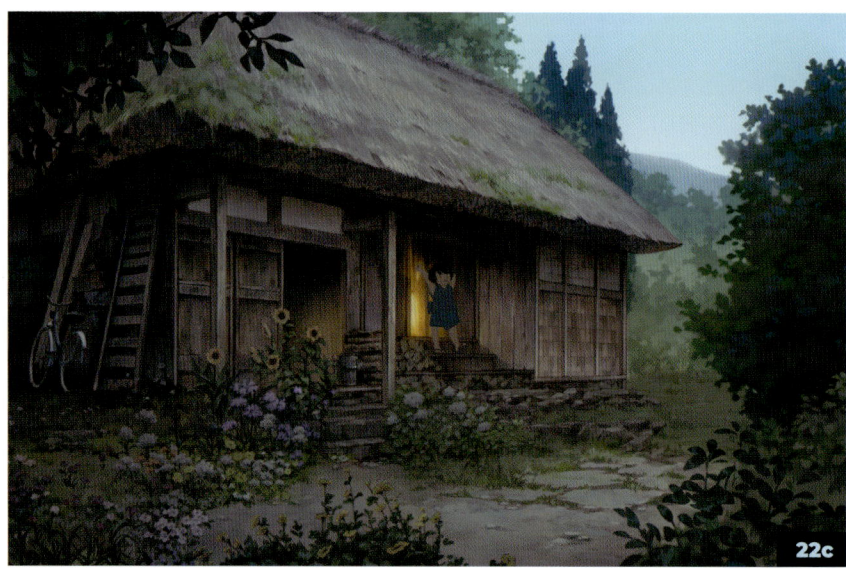

22c Just this small change has a big impact on the overall composition.

Then I use a desaturated ochre to paint in the light – anything brighter will look blown out because Color Dodge can be very intense. I am happy with the overall look, except for the hair. Since the hair should be quite reflective, I want the highlights to be brighter and more pronounced, so I shift that area of the Color Dodge layer to be lighter, warmer, and more saturated. To

emphasize the light even more, I copy the whole layer and change the blending mode to Overlay to enhance the effect.

I also paint a few deeper shadows on the clothing using a Multiply layer. To finish the character, I use a few clipping masks to add details and color variation to the different elements, such as redness around the cheeks.

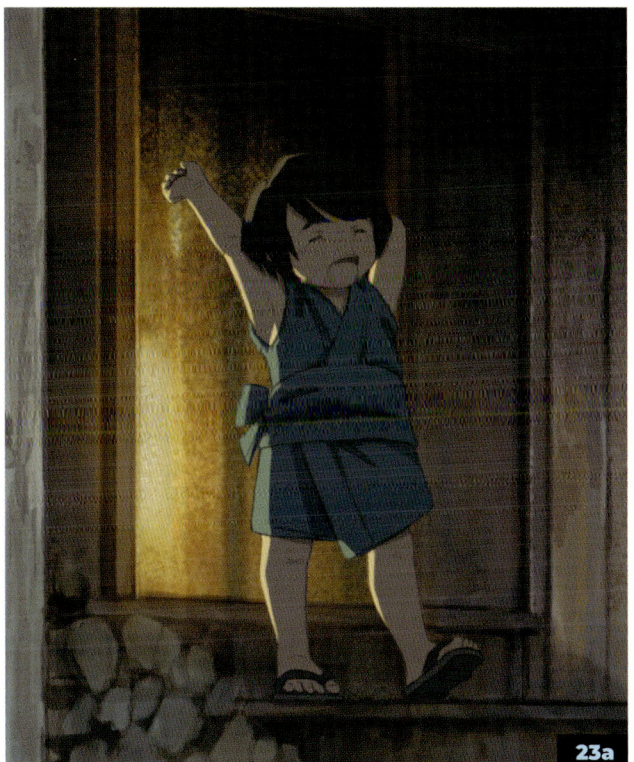

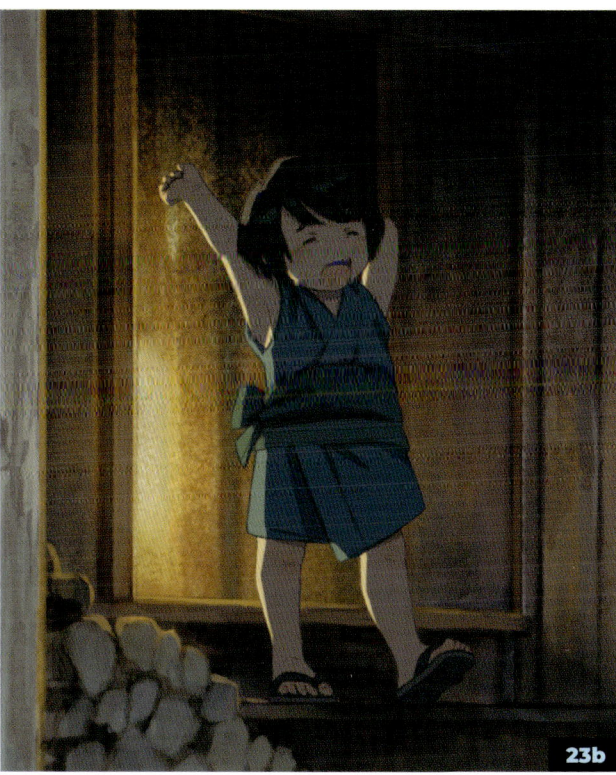

23a – 23b Using Color Dodge can be tricky, but if done right, it can be extremely useful for adding highlights. I love how the same ochre color interacts differently with the clothing and the skin.

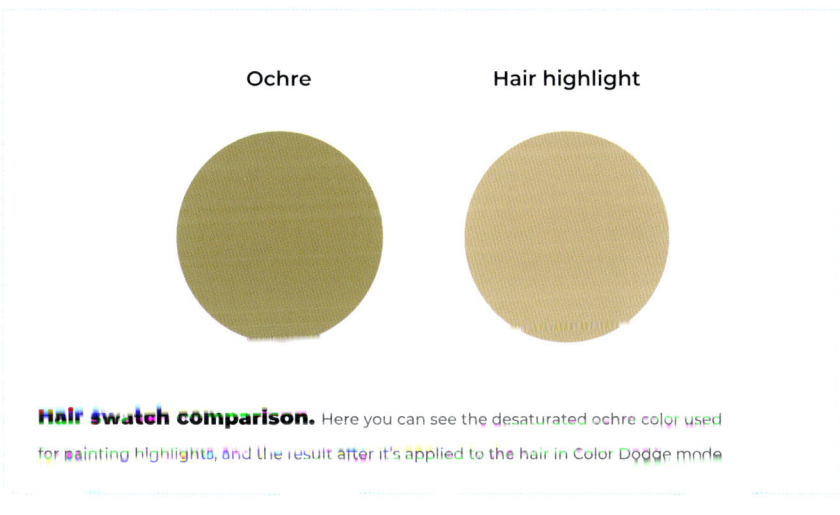

Ochre

Hair highlight

Hair swatch comparison. Here you can see the desaturated ochre color used for painting highlights, and the result after it's applied to the hair in Color Dodge mode

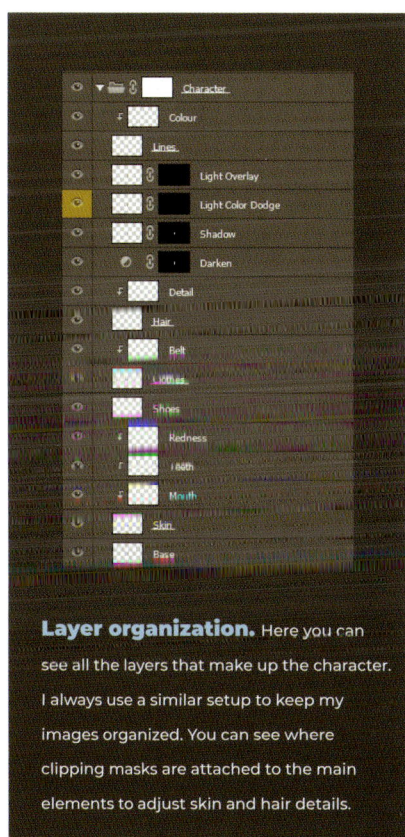

Layer organization. Here you can see all the layers that make up the character. I always use a similar setup to keep my images organized. You can see where clipping masks are attached to the main elements to adjust skin and hair details.

CONTROL THE ILLUSTRATION

As a painter, you have complete control over your creation. You get to decide where to place the light sources, what color the lighting is, and how strong it is. This applies to both outdoor and indoor scenes. I like to think of it as staging a scene in a movie. You position your actors and use the lighting to enhance the story and mood as best as you can. Most of it is carefully choreographed rather than just a happy accident.

24 SMALL LIGHTING TWEAKS

At this point, I am happy with the mood and color palette that I have developed, and I feel like the painting is heading in the right direction. I have made all the drastic changes, and now it is time to look around and see what smaller tweaks can help sell the concept of "early morning light."

I notice that the vegetation on the roof still looks too light and colorful, so I adjust it with a Multiply layer. I also realize that the stones and some of the flowers in front of the house need more contrast, so I sample the sky color and lightly brush it on the upward-facing planes to reinforce the lighting.

At this time of day, it is too dark for natural bounce light to occur, so it doesn't feel right that the lower part of the house gets lighter. I darken those areas because they wouldn't be catching any extra light reflected from the ground.

Last, I reinforce the light inside the house. I make sure that nearby elements catch some of its warm glow, painting a dark orange color along the edges of the logs by the door, as well as the bucket and the wooden beam.

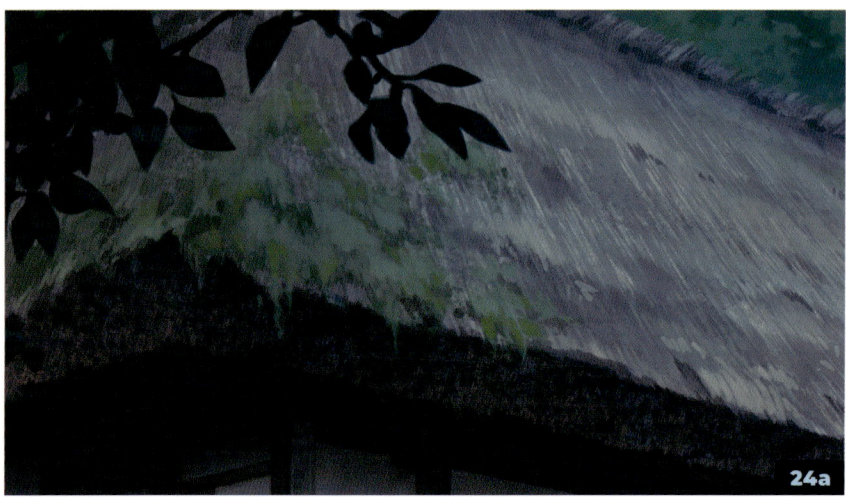

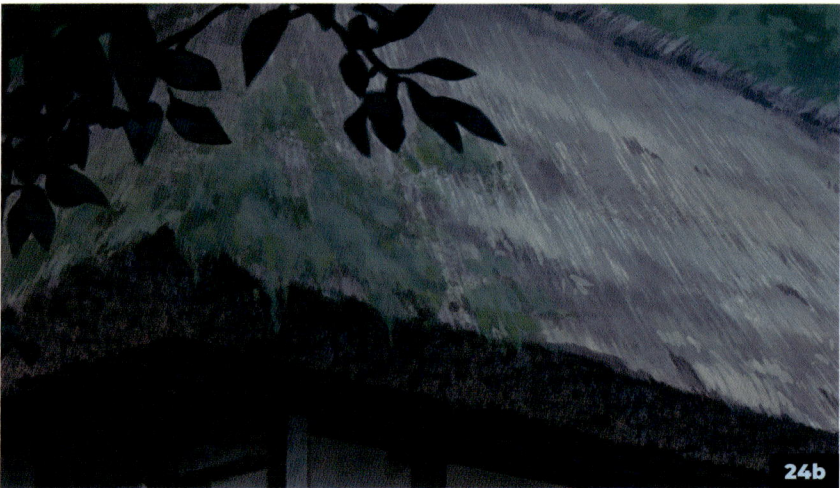

24a – 24b A Multiply layer darkens the vegetation on the roof to make it look less conspicuous.

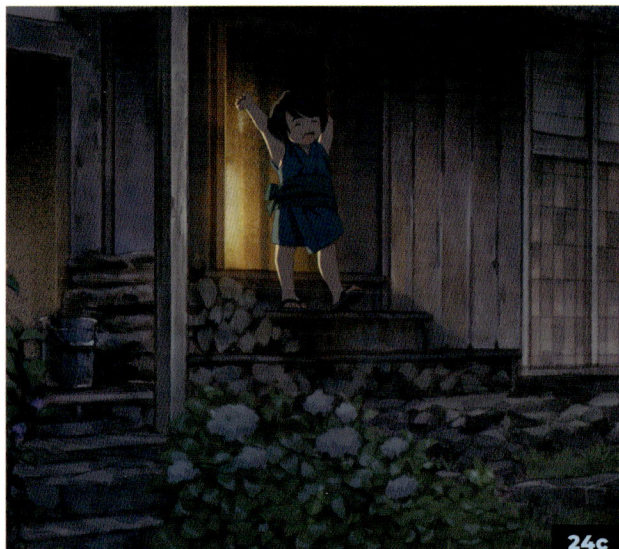

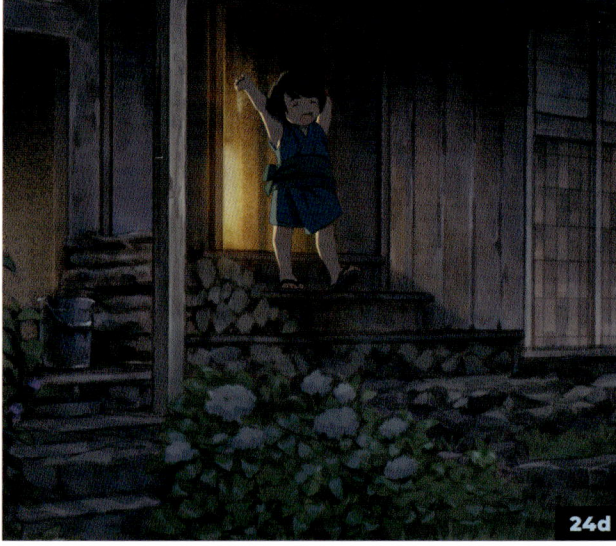

24c – 24d Small tweaks like these make the lighting situation come together and look more convincing.

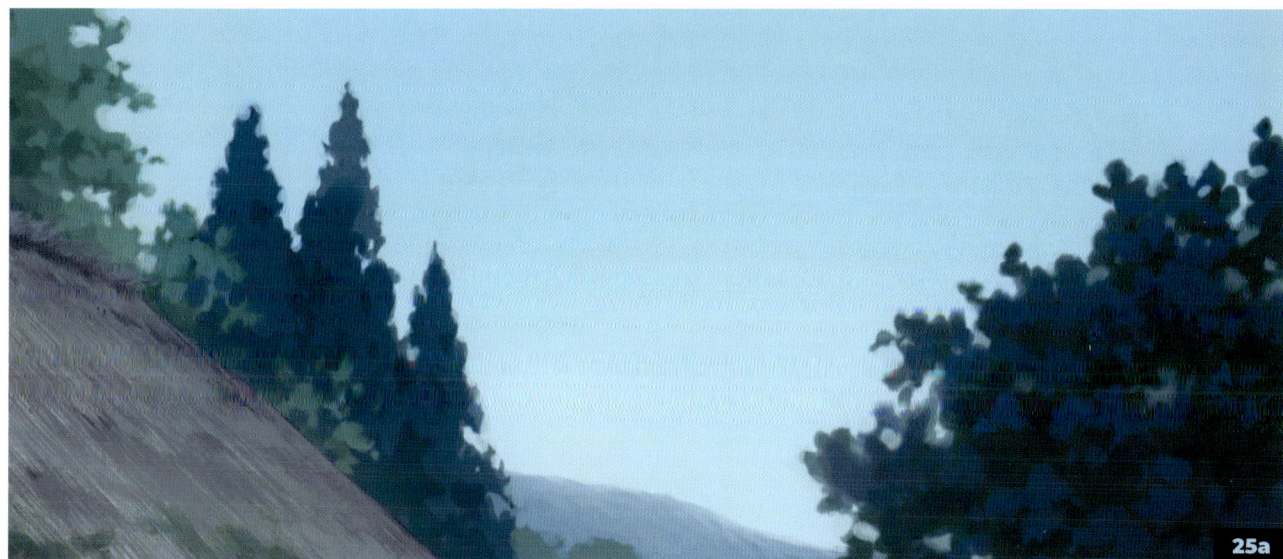

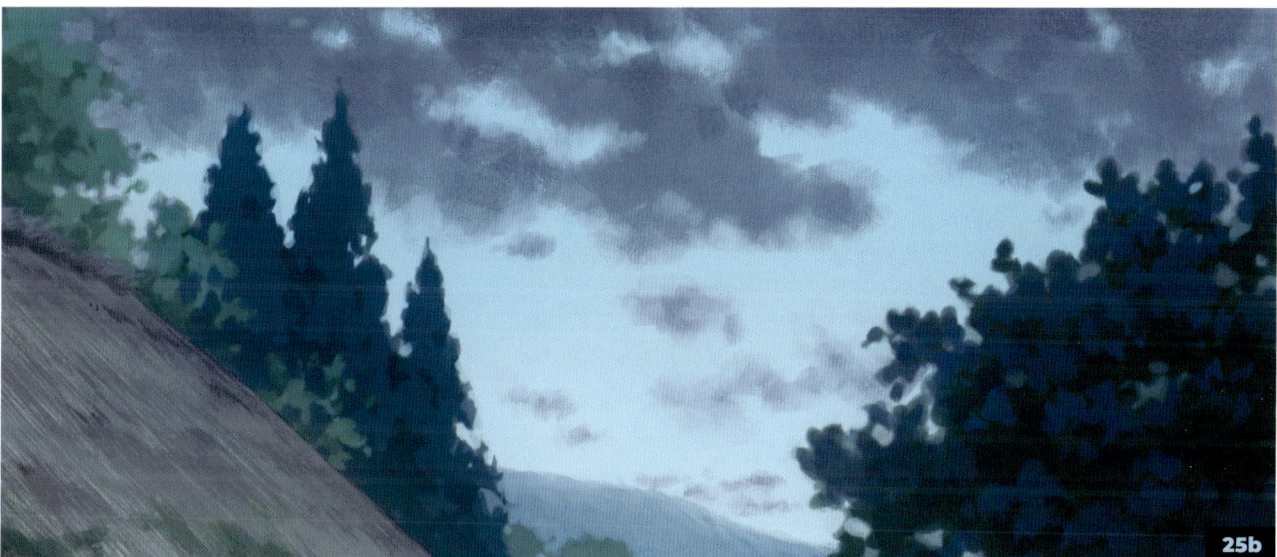

25a – 25b For the clouds, I use the same process as before: I paint in the rough shape, then attach a clipping mask to it to add more of the sky color underneath. I also add a slightly darker blue across the top.

25 A SILVER LINING

Again, I have saved the most fun part for almost the last: painting the clouds. Clouds are extremely versatile and can be very useful for reinforcing a certain mood. Thanks to their various shapes and types, and contours that are easy to manipulate, they can make a scene look dramatic and threatening, peaceful and dreamy, or even epic and awe-inspiring. When you paint a person or a building, for example, you're beholden to the basic laws of physics. If you push the subject too far, it stops looking like the thing you're trying to portray. However, with clouds, most bets are off: They are perfectly malleable, which makes them ideal compositional elements, offering a variety of colors as well as shapes.

I decide to use the clouds to add some drama, breaking up the sameness of a big area that contains little contrast. I don't want the sky to look like a thunderstorm is approaching, because my goal is still to tell the story of a quiet morning, but the added contrast and light-dark pattern create a nice rhythm.

These clouds are smaller and thinner than the ones I painted in the bright sunlight scenario. I want them to look like they are receding in space, back behind the mountain range, toward where the sun will eventually rise.

I also make these clouds a darker color because they are not lit from above (because of the sun's position below the horizon).

239

26 MORNING MIST

The last thing to add to the scene is some morning mist on the ground. This addition will create an air of mystery and beauty. I most commonly see this phenomenon on fields, desolate roads, or around forests, so I think it reinforces a feeling of seclusion that is very fitting for this little house in the woods. The hazy quality of the mist can even be seen as a reflection of the character's hazy state of mind at this time of day. From a compositional standpoint, the light mist color provides another visual break among the dark areas of the painting.

I use a very simple technique to create the mist. On a normal layer on top of the scene,

I use a big, soft brush and a pale blue color to paint in the mist. I then add a mask to reveal some areas again, like the leaves in the foreground. On the same mask, I also use a textured brush to make the mist more transparent and to add a subtle noise effect.

27 ORANGES AND BLUES

If you compare the color palette to the bright sunlight scenario, you will notice that there is a lot less variation. Most of the colors in the early morning version are desaturated blues that are close together on the color wheel. The two major accents are the light blue of the sky and the warm color of the light inside the house. Due to the drastic shift

in temperature and the dim environmental light, the flowers that used to provide pops of color are far more muted now.

It sounds like we are losing a lot of what originally made the image appealing, but we are trading that colorfulness and vibrancy for something else: moodiness. This simplified, limited palette is much more suited to tell this particular story of the blue hour. The use of contrast and complementary colors (blue versus orange) also provides enough visual interest for the image to work on an abstract level.

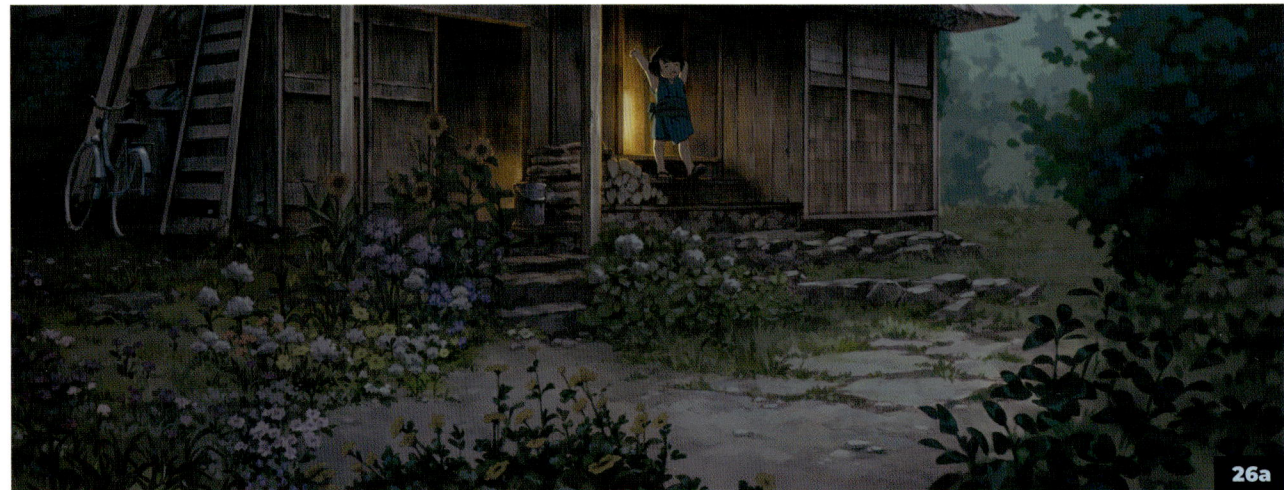

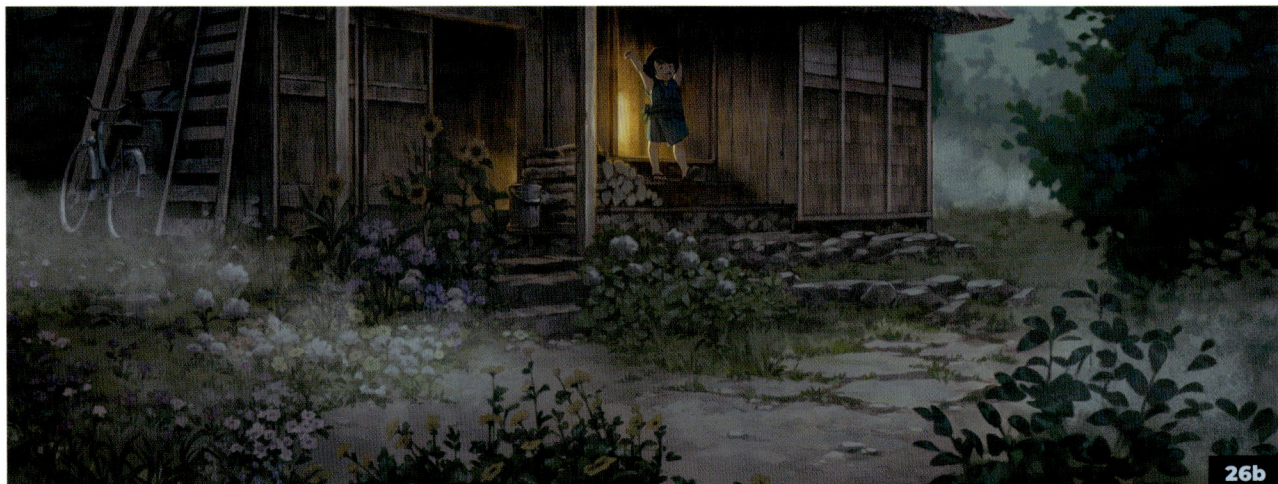

26a – 26b Adding mist to the ground makes the scene look a lot more atmospheric.

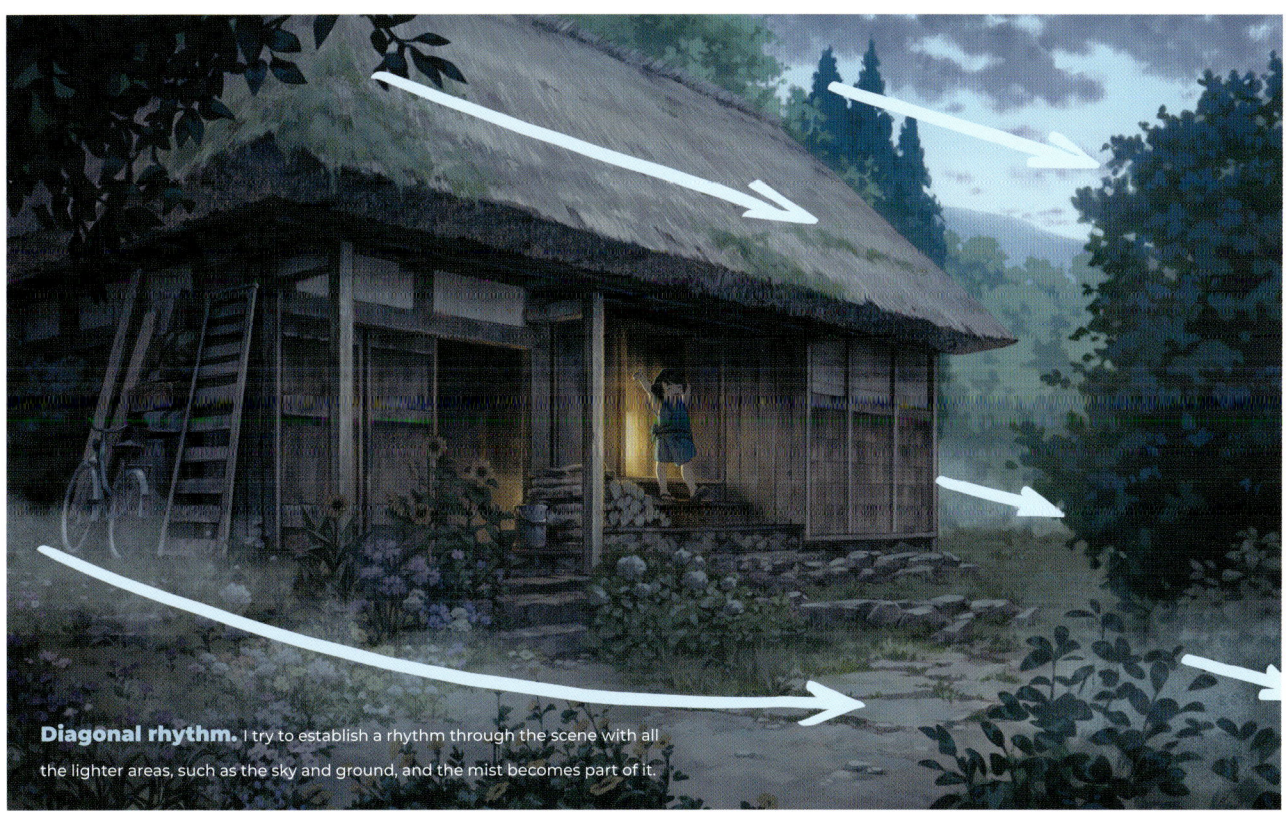

Diagonal rhythm. I try to establish a rhythm through the scene with all the lighter areas, such as the sky and ground, and the mist becomes part of it.

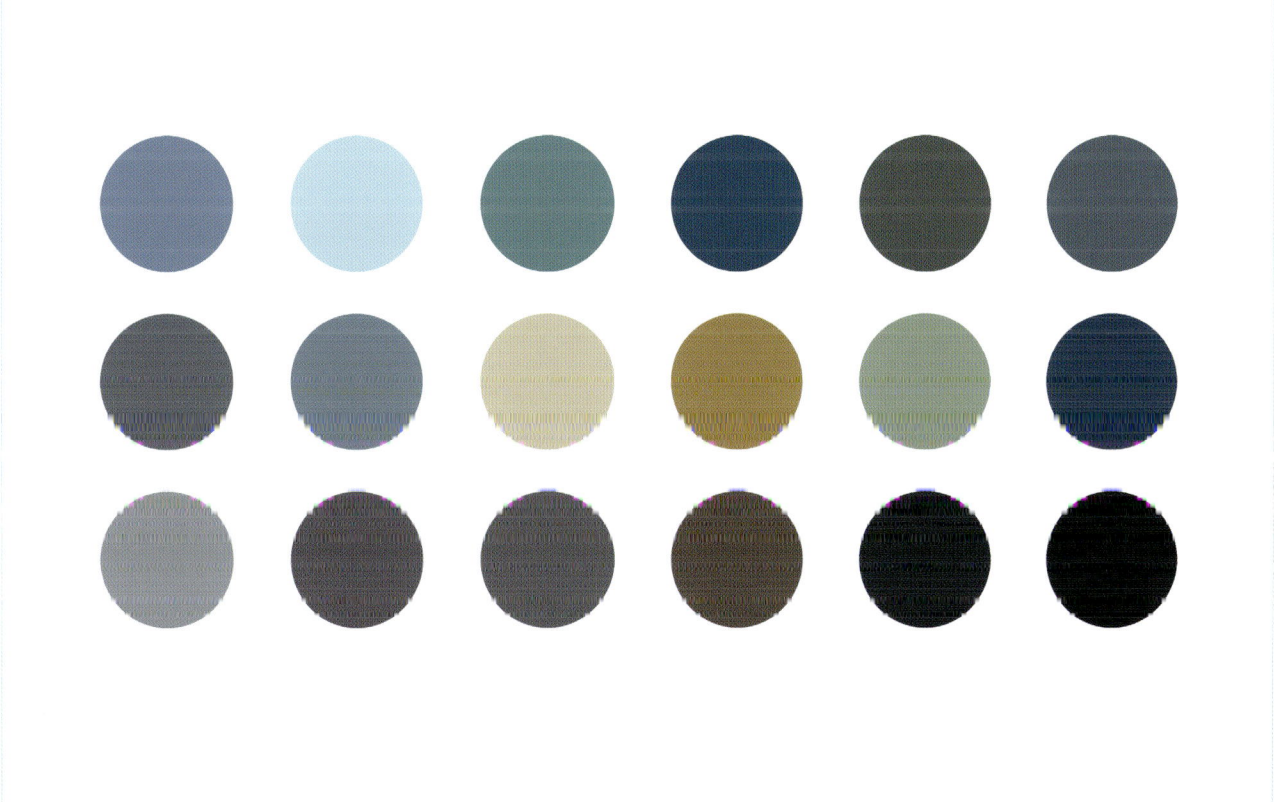

27 In the final palette, the warm accent of the firelight clearly stands out from the sea of blue.

LIGHTING RECAP: EARLY MORNING

This is the moodiest scenario that we have tackled so far. In the blue hour, color variety becomes less important and makes room for darker, more desaturated hues. We are just one step away from nighttime, so the sun is still below the horizon. Assuming there is no artificial light source, this means a large portion of the scene will drop into shadow. There also won't be any bounce light because the diffused light from the sky is too weak. Scenes appear hazier and less clear compared to the daytime, and the overall contrast is a lot lower than it would be in direct sunlight.

Just like the previous scenes, this lighting setup is very evocative, and provides a variety of opportunities for storytelling. To me, the early morning is a time for solitude, before the hustle and bustle of daily life begins. When I think about waking up in my city, the following scenario comes to mind: The streets are empty, except for a couple of people heading out to work, and a few lost souls wandering around after a night out. The air is fresh and clear, and you hear birds singing. It is a time for new beginnings, opportunities, and a fresh start.

However, I also associate the blue hour with insomnia and lying awake while the night fades away, still unable to fall asleep. It can be a time for soul-searching, important decisions, and turning points. Being so close to nighttime, the blue hour can also set the scene for strange encounters and weird occurrences. It is a mysterious time, and the dim light has a glowing and ghostly quality to it.

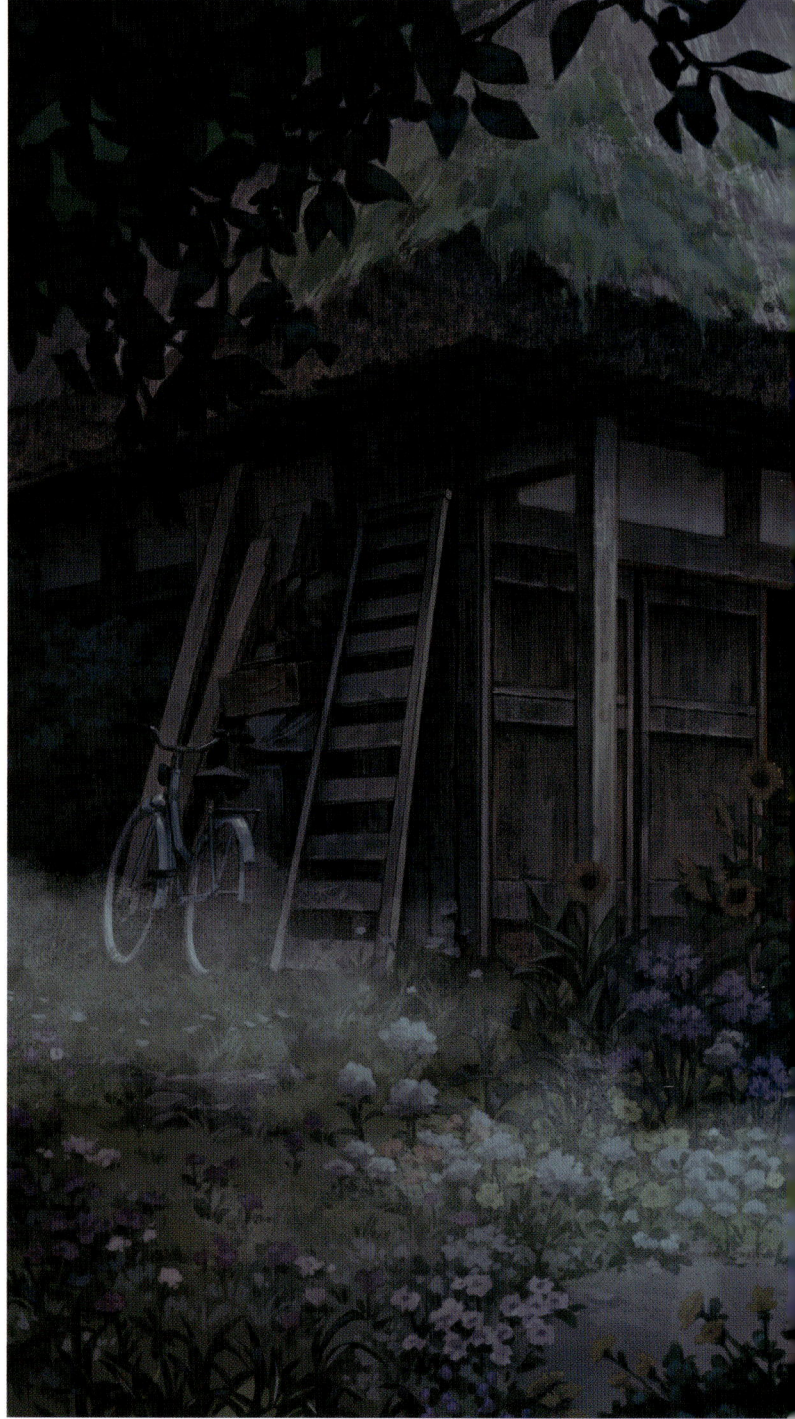

Cool blue twilight. The final result: Our little character having a stretch in the light of the early morning. The sun hasn't yet come over the horizon to clear the mist.

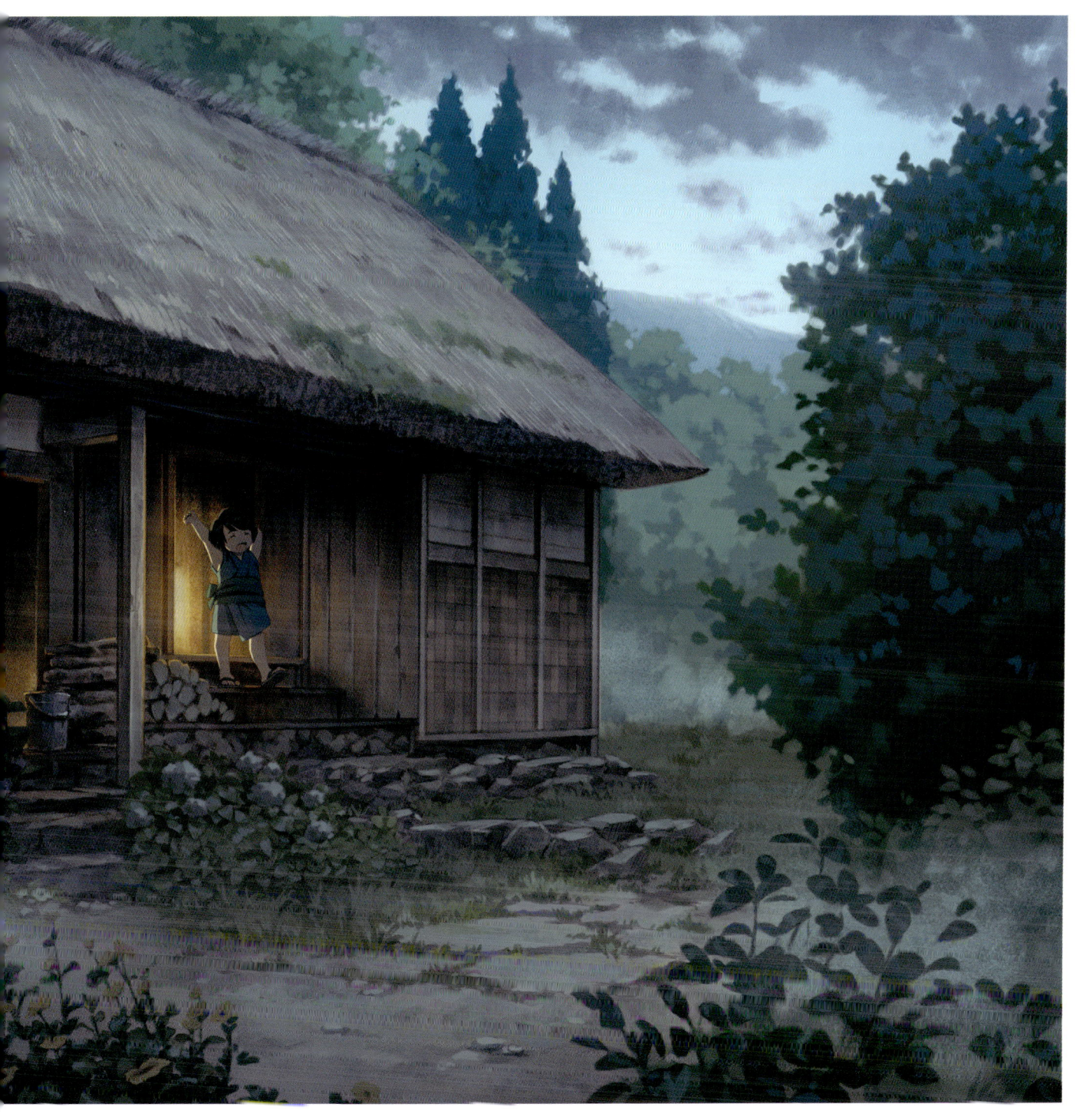

LIGHTING SCENARIO: SUNSET

Our last major lighting scenario is a sunset. Around this time of day, you can observe a variety of warm and vibrant colors. I immediately associate sunsets with dramatic skies, offering endless possibilities to play with different cloud shapes and color variations. Sunsets give you creative license to push the color spectrum of a scene quite far. As long as you are including some warm colors – anywhere between orange and purple – I think you can get away with a lot.

28 SUNSET

I naturally gravitate toward cooler tones, so my interpretation of this scenario is going to be more on the pink side, rather than orange. Just like before, I am using the original overcast setting as the base. My first step is to apply a red Photo Filter to start shifting the color palette in a pink direction.

Like I did with the other paintings, I am looking for a story that fits the setting and that allows me to bring in some interesting visuals. I decide it would be a good idea to give the little character a lantern to carry around. This makes for an appealing story, as well as a good focal point in the composition. Where are they going this late?

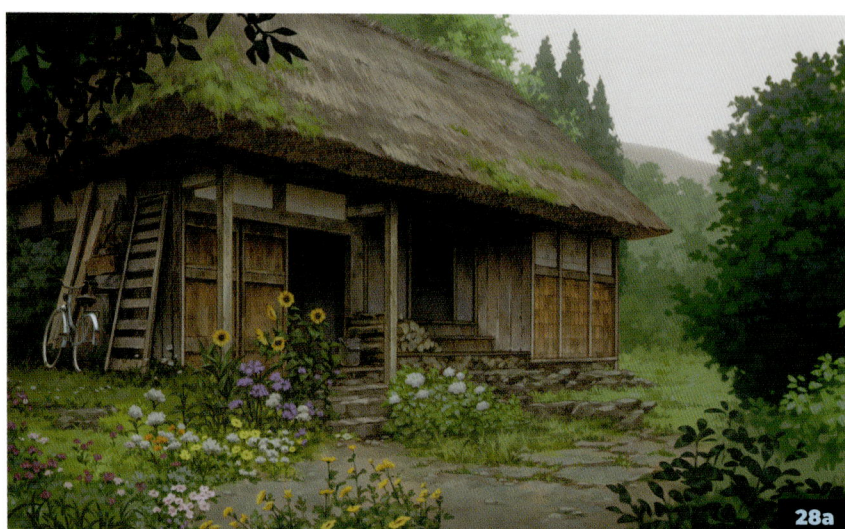

28a

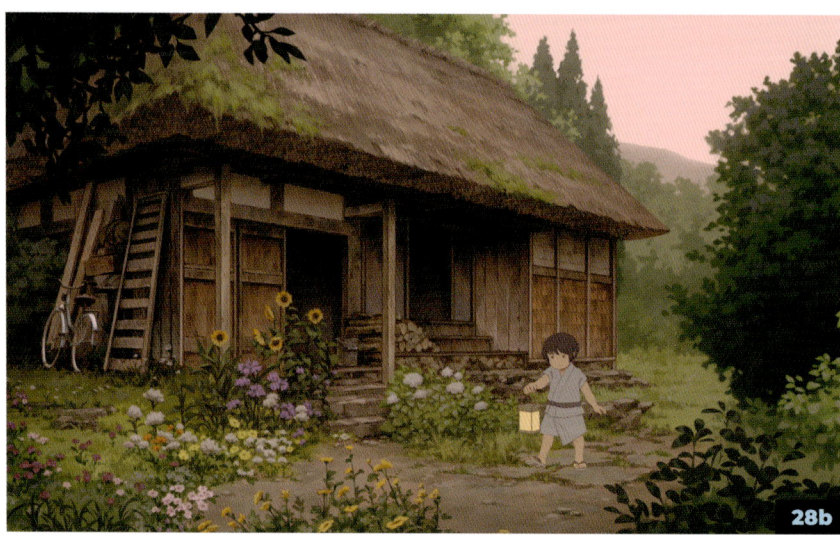

28b

28a – 28b Just this first step completely changes the mood and creates an interesting effect in the sky.

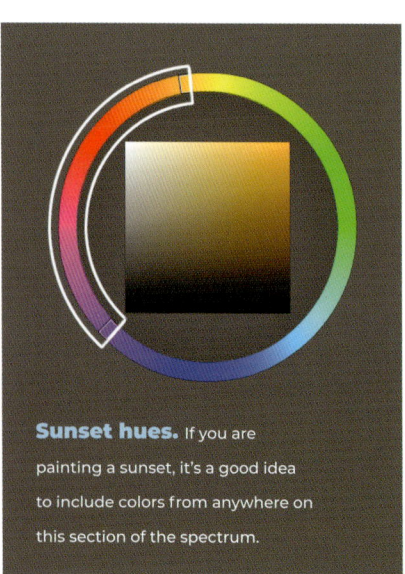

Sunset hues. If you are painting a sunset, it's a good idea to include colors from anywhere on this section of the spectrum.

29 COMPLEMENTARY SHADES

In the previous section, I briefly touched on complementary color palettes. To create a complementary palette, you can simply combine two colors that are opposite each other on the color wheel. Classic combinations are orange and blue, yellow and purple, or green and red. This does not mean that you should always use fully saturated versions of those colors – the hues that you choose can simply "live" in those areas of the color wheel.

I wasn't planning on using a red-green complementary palette, but I stumbled upon it when I introduced red to the scene and saw how well it interacted with the greenery. Of course, the red tint also affects the character, so I make sure to choose a pinker skin tone and a warm gray for the clothing. I also choose a more purple version of the hair color, rather than blue.

Even at this early stage, I think the colors and values look good, but I know that I need to introduce cast shadows next. I prepare for that by making the scene a bit lighter using a Levels adjustment.

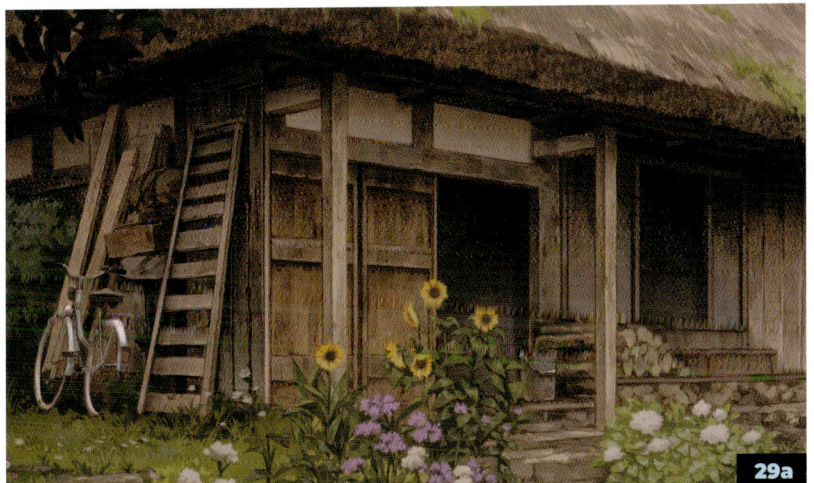

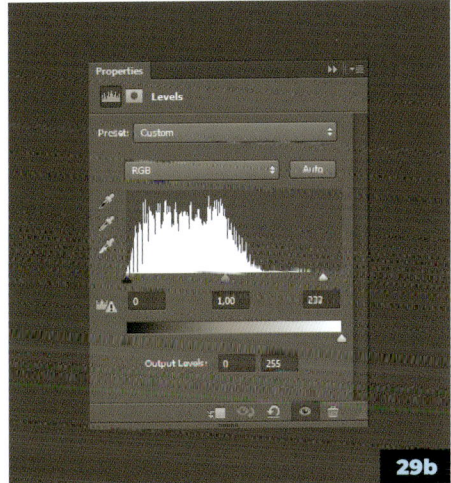

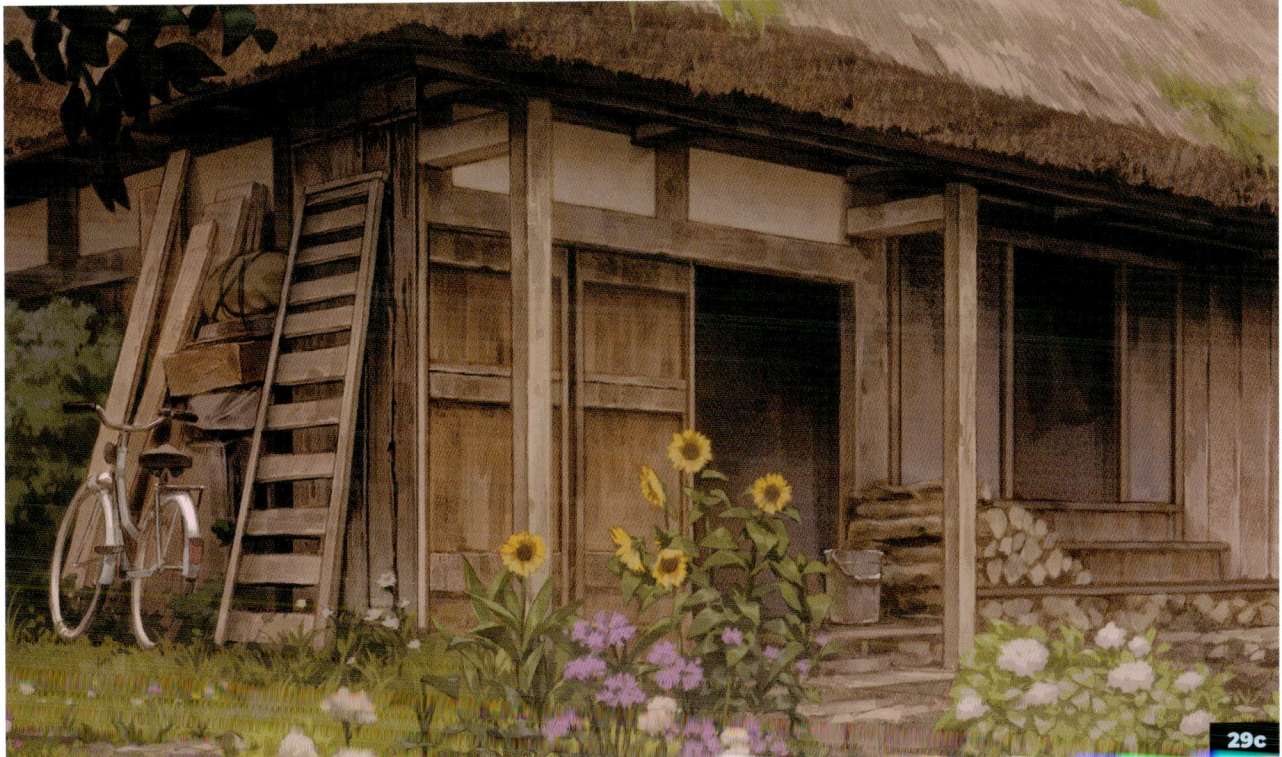

29a – 29c In the Levels Adjustment, dragging the slider toward the left lightens the painting – especially the highlights.

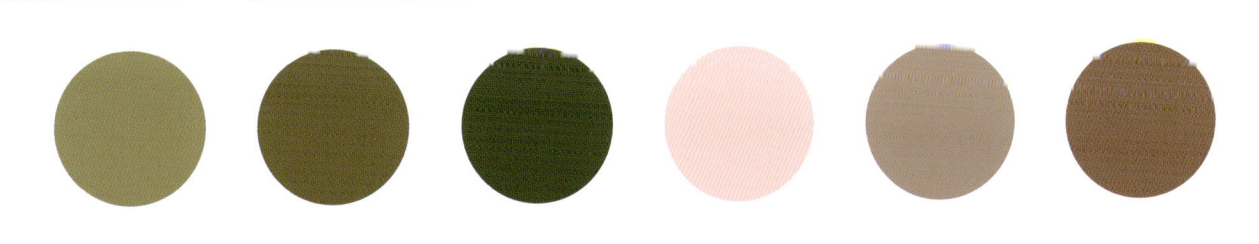

Complementary hues. Red and green hues dominate this new palette, but in subtle variations.

Notice how the greenery has become a lot warmer compared to the previous versions of the scene.

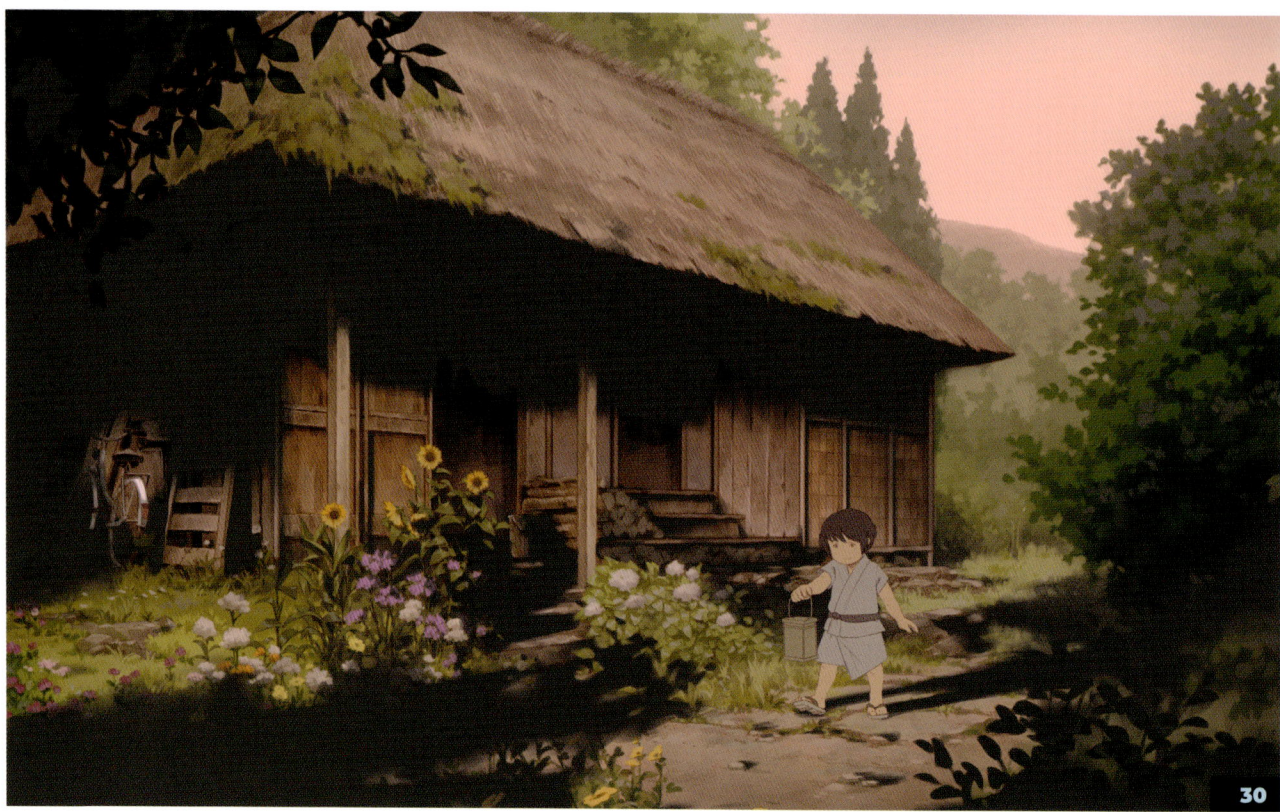

30 Here you can see a version of the painting that highlights where I've applied shadow areas.

30 LONG EVENING SHADOWS

Besides warm lighting and dramatic skies, sunsets have another characteristic feature: long shadows. The lower the sun's position in relation to the horizon line, the longer the shadows will be. Painting those shadows will make the lighting setup look more convincing and add depth.

According to the sun's position that I established earlier, it would set in the "front" of the scene, on the side closest to or behind the audience's viewpoint. Just like before, I want to keep the shadows' direction consistent, and look out for elements that are blocking the light, both within the composition and outside of it. This is another opportunity to create interesting patterns and rhythms.

Compared to the warm light in the scene, the shadows are going to appear cool and quite dark, without much bounce light. The simplest way to achieve this is with a Multiply layer and a mask: I fill the layer with a dark, desaturated blue and mask out the shadows. Even though the shadow areas are dark, I don't want them to appear black, which would be too stark and unrealistic. A shade of blue is more subtle and convincing.

PHOTOS VERSUS REALITY

One might think that photos provide perfect depictions of reality, but that isn't the case. If you have ever tried to photograph the vibrant colors and nuances of a beautiful sunset and were disappointed by the result, you will know what I'm talking about! Subtle variations often get lost or are flattened by the camera.

Photographs are a great resource to study from and to use for reference, but it is important to know their limitations. If you are trying to achieve a lot of hue variation and subtle value shifts in your work, it can be a good idea to do some *plein air* painting. If that's not available to you, take a closer look at plein air paintings by other artists. Observe the variety of colors they are using compared to what you would see in a photo.

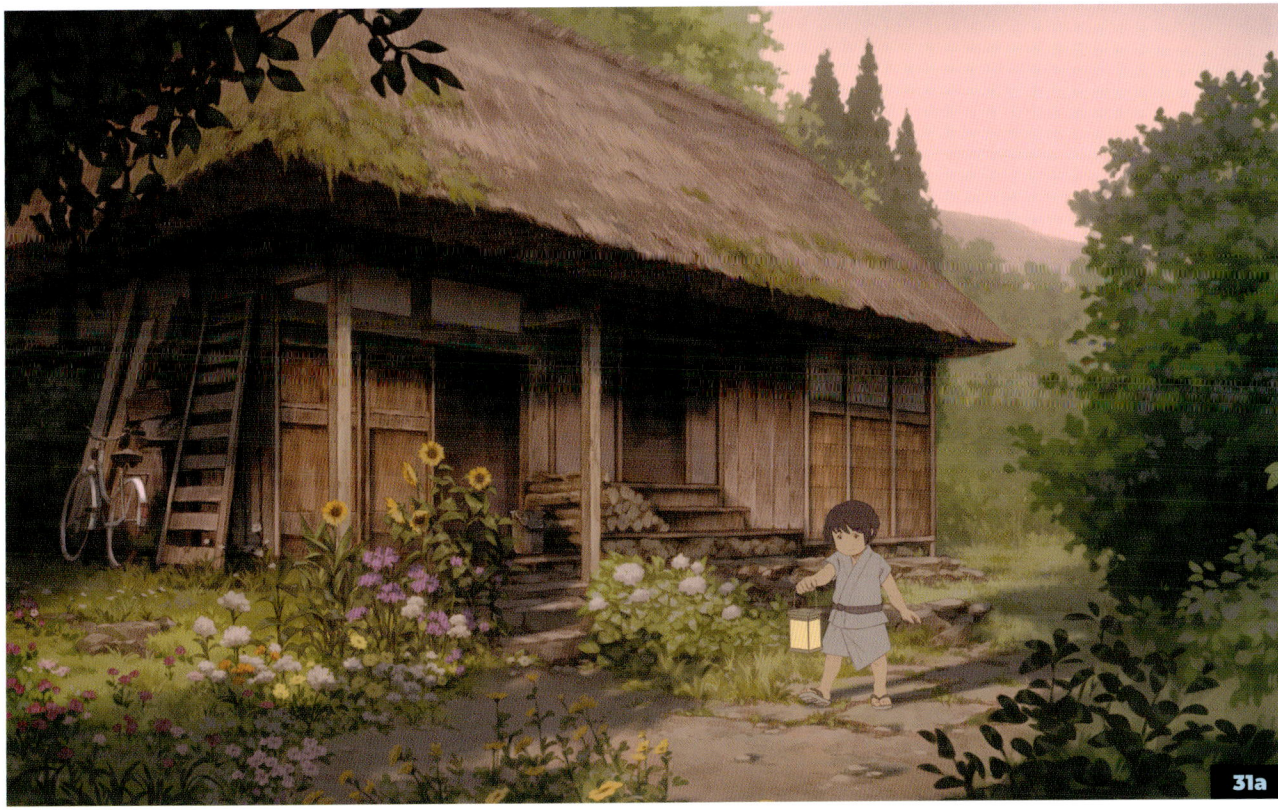

31a This is what the painting looks like after applying the cool shadows.

31 NEW VISUAL INTERESTS

While going through different lighting setups for the same environment, I notice that each setup highlights different parts of the scene. I love these unexpected happy accidents – they make the painting process even more fun and surprising.

In this case, one of my favorite moments occurs in the left corner, where the bicycle, boxes, and wooden planks are stored. I put the upper half of it in shadow, and this creates a dramatic gradient: It turns a mundane area of the scene into something far more interesting, drawing attention to this corner that had been neglected in the previous versions.

I also enjoy some of the shadow patterns on the ground that create a rhythm of light and dark, especially around the flowers in the foreground.

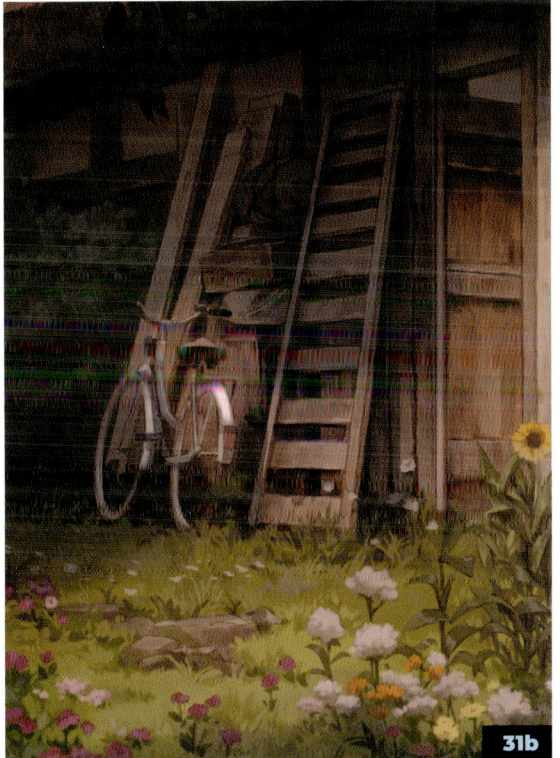

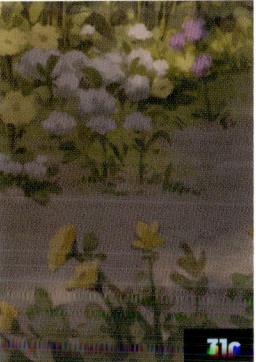

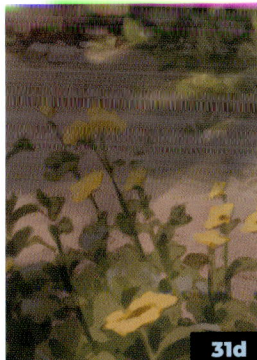

31b – 31d I love how shadows can enhance even the most mundane-looking areas of the painting.

32 ON CLOUD NINE

Next, I will introduce the clouds. Since the shadows are so long, it would be interesting to have long, narrow shapes reflected in the clouds. My plan is to create sweeping lines across the sky that look almost like ribbons, especially compared to the rounder-shaped clouds that I used in the previous versions. I try to establish an interesting pattern in which lots of the major lines head in the same direction.

I keep the colors simple. The patch of sky we are looking at is basically in the opposite direction of where the sun is setting, so there is not as much going on in it. I choose a slightly darker, more purple, and more desaturated version of the sky color for the clouds. At the top edge, I add a subtle pink glow. I like how the darker color also mirrors the shadows on the ground.

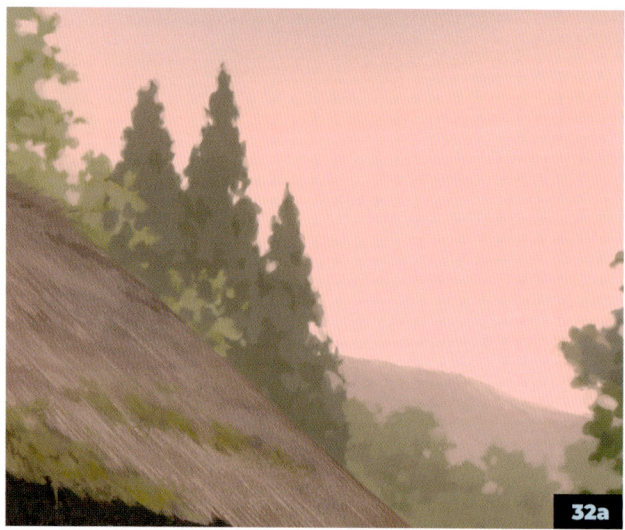 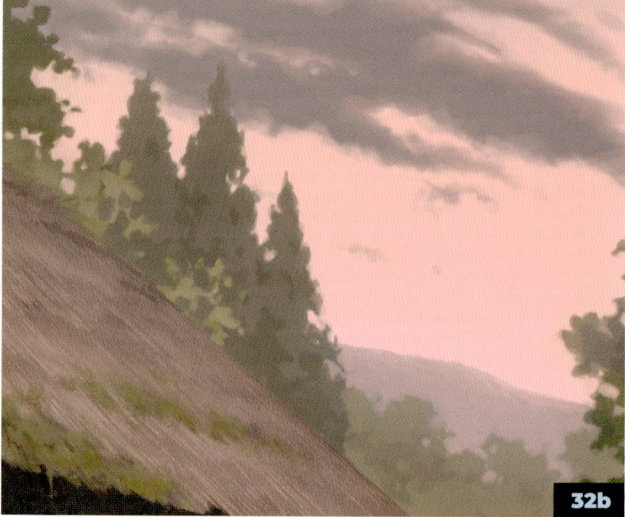

32a – 32b Adding the clouds to the sky gives it more depth and contrast.

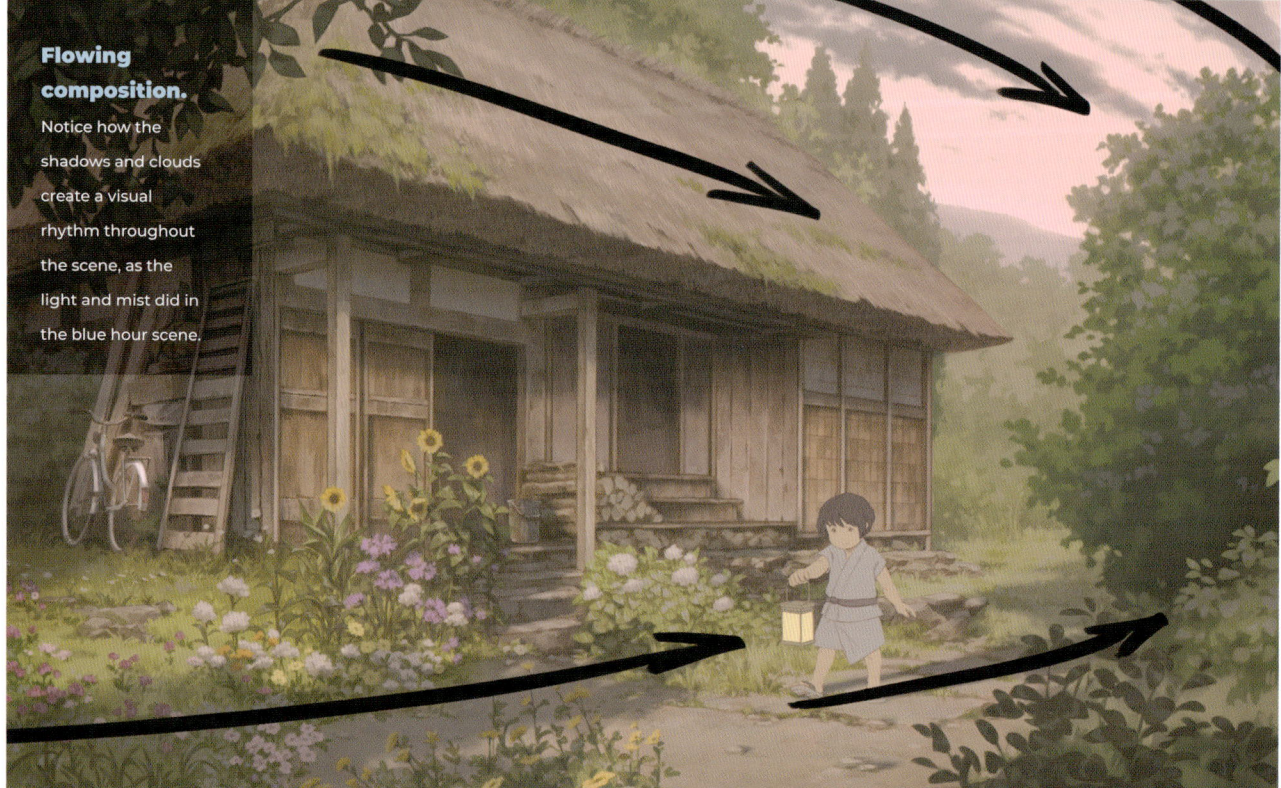

Flowing composition. Notice how the shadows and clouds create a visual rhythm throughout the scene, as the light and mist did in the blue hour scene.

33 TURNING ON THE LIGHT

Once I am happy with the environment, it is much easier to integrate the character into it. My priority is to "switch on" the light from the lantern and make sure it illuminates the character.

To achieve that, I go with the same technique that I used in the early morning setting: I create a layer in Color Dodge mode and simply paint in the light. It works well to establish the light source, but it brightens the character more than I'd like. To darken them again, and to make them feel like they're part of the environment, I attach a Levels adjustment as a clipping mask to the entire "Character" folder, and I paint more shadows on a Multiply layer. The shift in values makes a big difference, and also adds richer colors.

And lastly, I add the usual detailing to the character: Highlights in the hair, red cheeks and knees, and some deeper shadows here and there.

Sky swatch comparison. Here are the skies of the three scenarios for comparison: Bright sunlight, the early-morning blue hour, and warm sunset.

Bright sunlight

Blue hour

Sunset

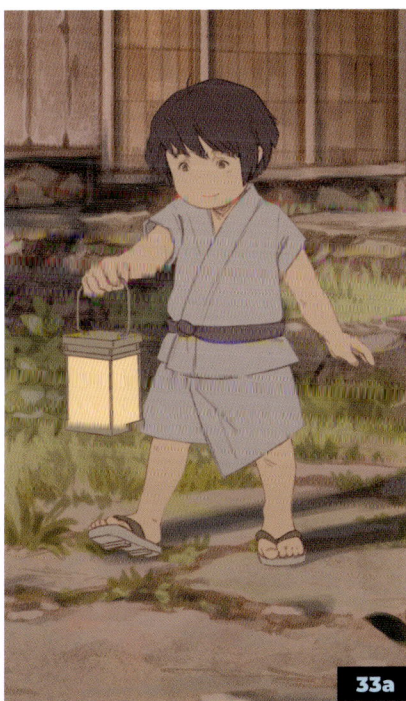
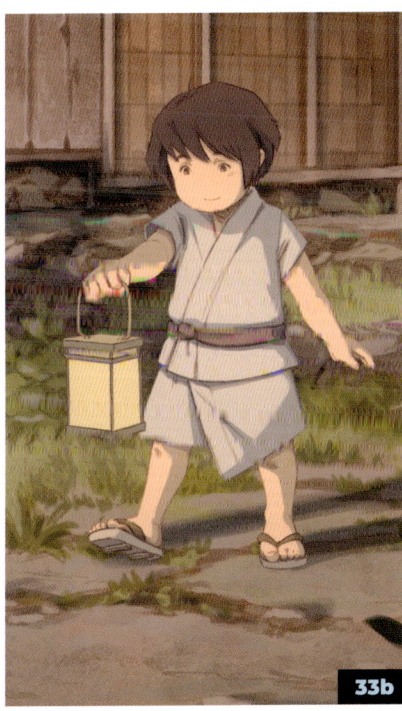
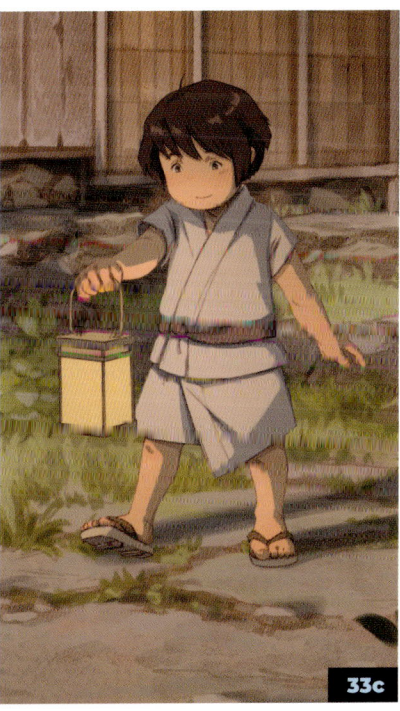

33a – 33c Adding light to the character makes them fit into the scene more seamlessly, but I still need to tweak the lantern light.

34 BLENDING THE CHARACTER IN

One of the biggest challenges when it comes to illustrations like this can be integrating the character into the environment. The artist must explore perspective, scale, values, colors, and lighting to address this problem. I usually ask myself these questions:

· Does the character share a common horizon line with the environment?

· Is their size believable compared to the other elements in the scene?

· Does the character fit into the environment's lighting scenario?

In this case, in order to make the character and the surroundings feel like they are part of the same world, I am exaggerating the lantern light. I want it to affect the character, the air around them, and the ground. That way, it connects those elements, emphasizes their relationship with each other, and makes the scene more believable.

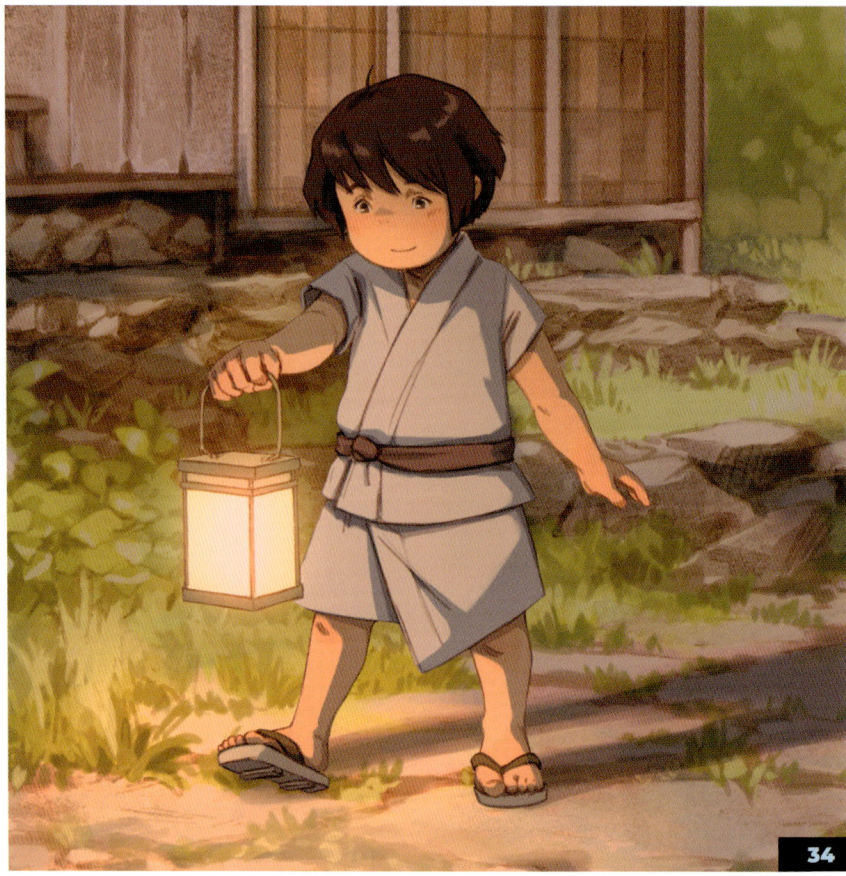

34 The stronger lantern light increases the contrast and makes the character more of a focal point in the scene.

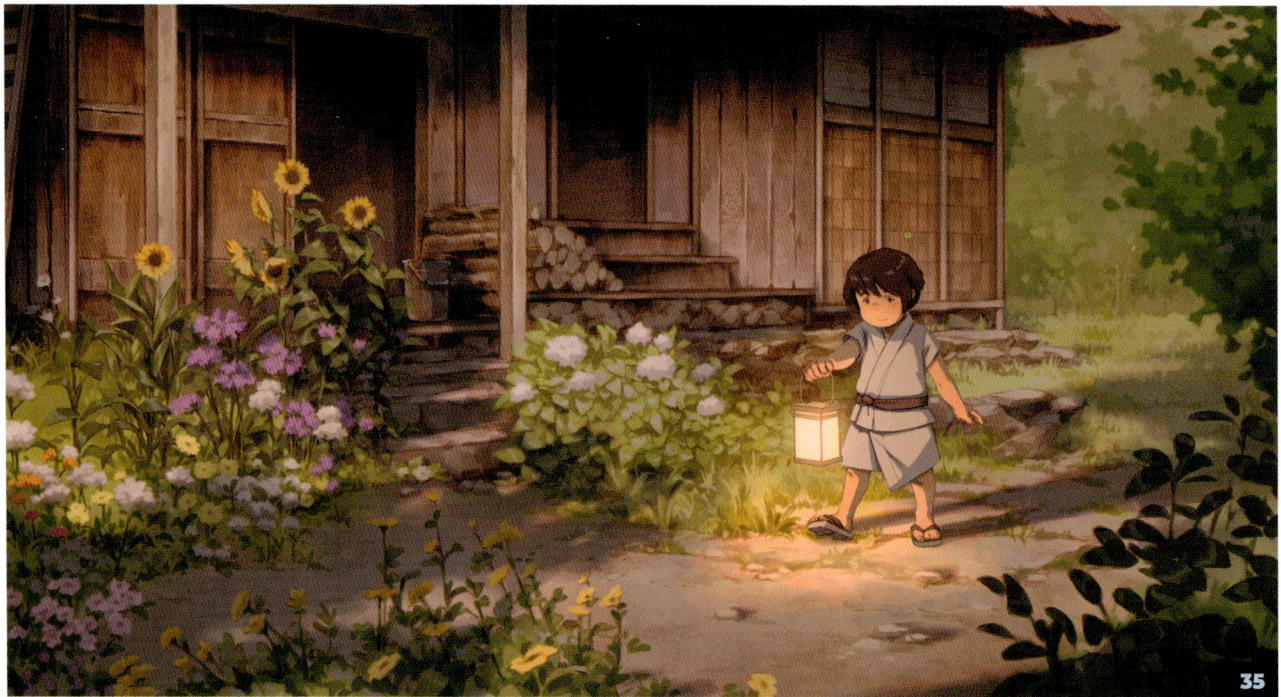

35 The character primarily catches the attention, but I want the area around them to look vibrant and interesting as well.

I also add a brighter specular highlight to the character's eyes and a little shadow above their nose, as if cast by the lantern light. Tiny details like these really matter, even if we are dealing with a stylized representation of reality.

35 A NEW ACCENT COLOR

While emphasizing the lantern light, another interesting thing has happened: I have introduced a new accent color. The warm light's interaction with the plants has created a warm green that is different from the other greens in the scene. Again, this is one of those happy accidents that I didn't plan, but that benefits the visual impact of the painting. The warm green broadens my color palette and enhances the focal point of the character.

To punch up the colors even more, I use a Hue/Saturation adjustment layer to boost the Saturation until I feel happy with the richness in my color palette.

36 A WARM PALETTE

Before I reveal the final version of the painting, I want to take a moment to sum up the color palette: We are looking at a limited palette that "lives" in the color range between purple and warm green. You will not find a single blue tone in the entire illustration. Anything that appears blue is actually a very desaturated purple. Excluding such a big part of the color wheel might seem like a sacrifice, but it actually makes it easier to maintain harmony and to create a cohesive, moody atmosphere.

Back in the blue-hour setting I applied the same principles, but with different colors. That palette stretched from yellow-orange to blue. Red, purple, or pink were nowhere to be seen. I rarely use the full range of the rainbow, unless as a way to achieve a very specific effect. I find limited palettes extremely appealing. They offer a lot of variety, depending on the hues you choose within each color and how you balance the ratio between them.

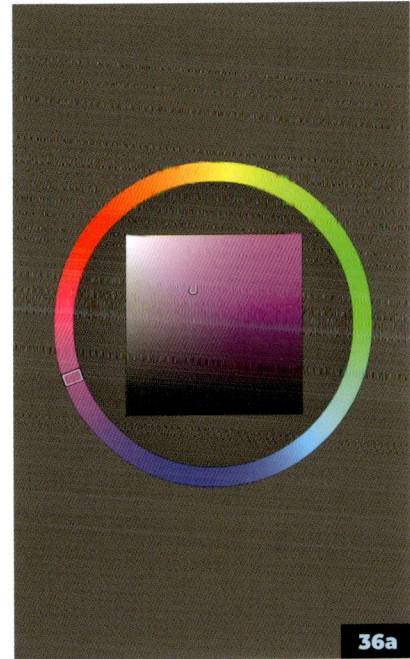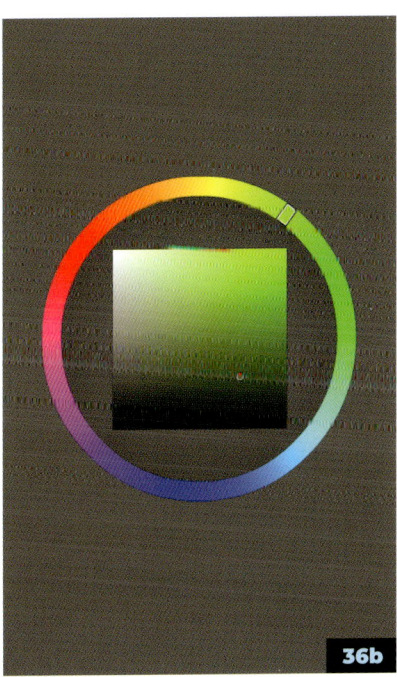

36a – 36b In my limited complementary sunset palette, the warmest tone is a pink-purple and the coolest is a dark green, avoiding the cooler blue half of the wheel completely.

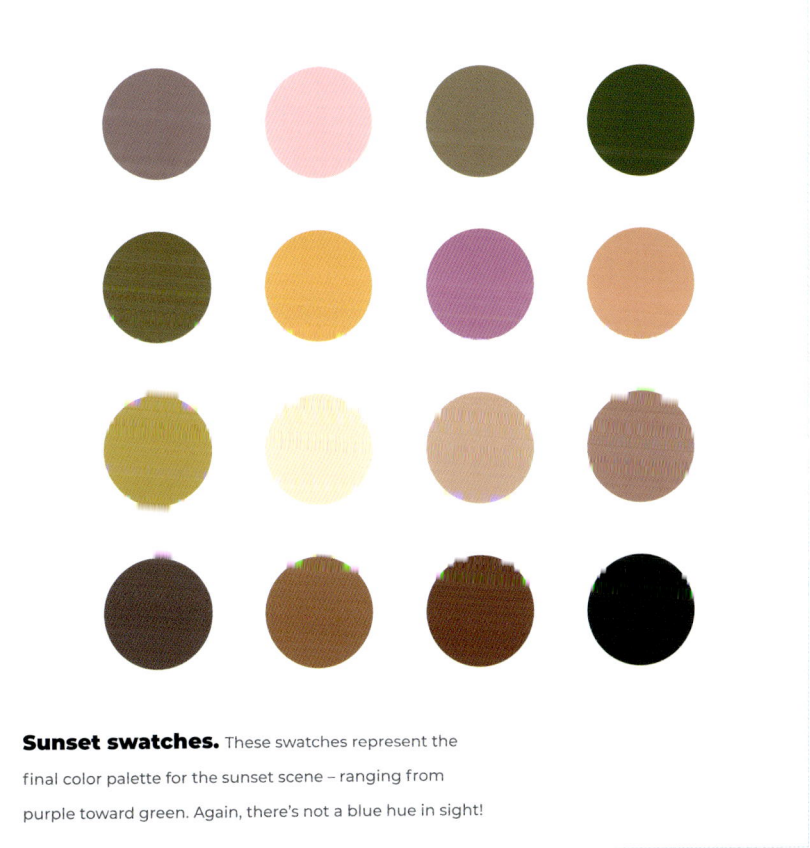

Sunset swatches. These swatches represent the final color palette for the sunset scene – ranging from purple toward green. Again, there's not a blue hue in sight!

LIGHTING RECAP: SUNSET

Let's make one last recap to summarize the sunset setting. Warm and vibrant colors are characteristic for this type of lighting scenario. The sunset provides the opportunity to put a special focus on the sky, and to highlight different cloud shapes and patterns. It features colors from anywhere between orange and purple. Shadows in the scene appear elongated and cool, and there is not much bounce light.

Sunsets are visual spectacles, providing some of the most beautiful sights nature has to offer. They provide a sense of drama, connecting even the most distracted person to their surroundings. In terms of storytelling, they can be a great tool to depict events of major importance, or to symbolize a break. One example that comes to mind is at the end of a battle in a fantasy epic: When the evil has been defeated, you might imagine the hero "sailing into the sunset," things finally right with the world.

Visually speaking, wide, open skies can be great compositional elements. If used intentionally, they can make characters seem heroic or even godlike. They provide a perfect backdrop for strong, dark silhouettes. Imagine a figure walking toward the viewer, the sun setting behind them – all you would see is their shape, but no details, creating great tension and anticipation.

I associate sunsets with a period of transition. They fit perfectly as a backdrop for train journeys or for walking home at the end of the day, before the setting changes to the dark of night.

Lastly, sunsets are very fitting for a romantic setting. Warm colors, especially reds, are associated with love and affection. A sunset can make you see your surroundings in a whole new light, just like how you might see a person differently at the beginning of a new relationship.

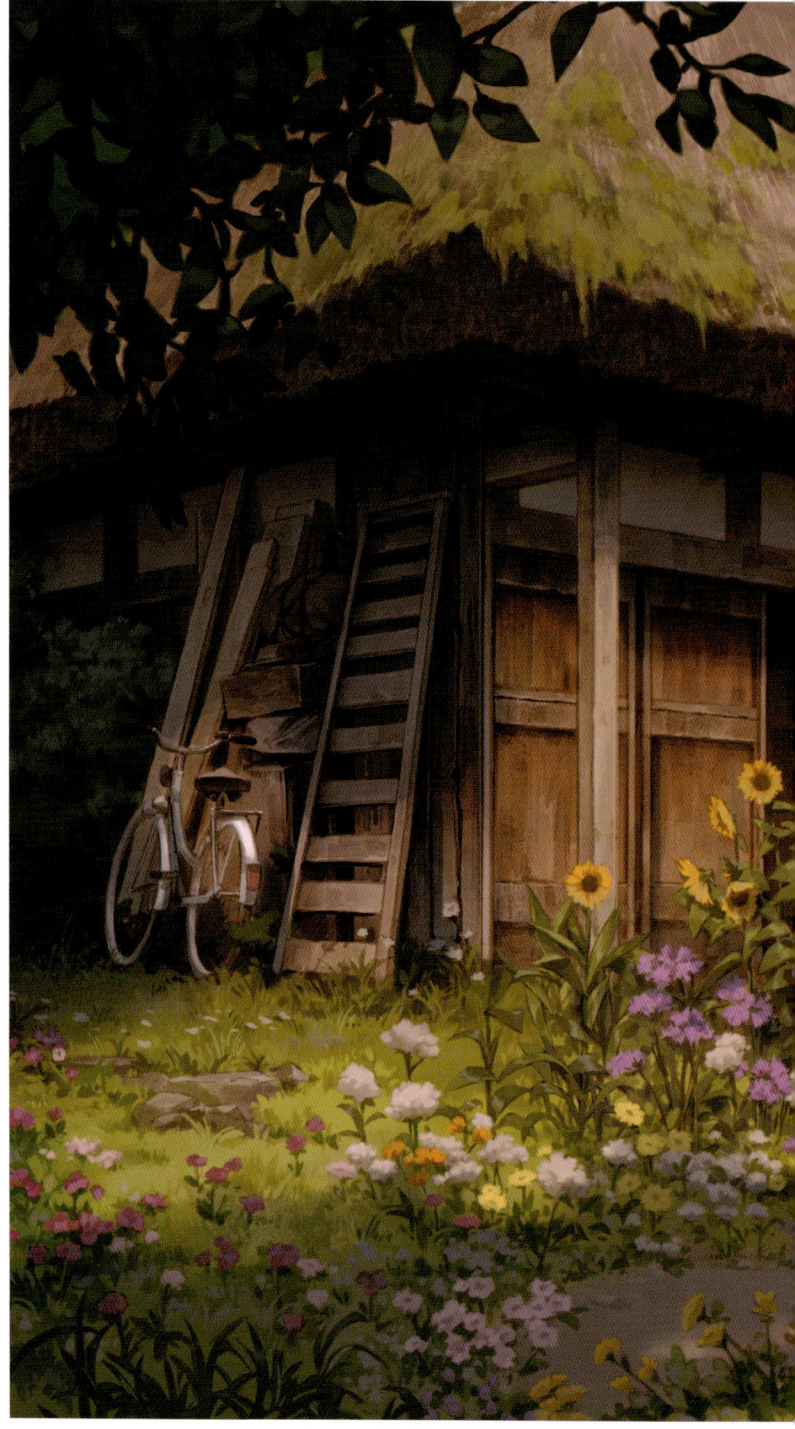

A sunset scene. The final painting of a child carrying a lantern at sunset. The environment glows with warm, cozy, pinkish light.

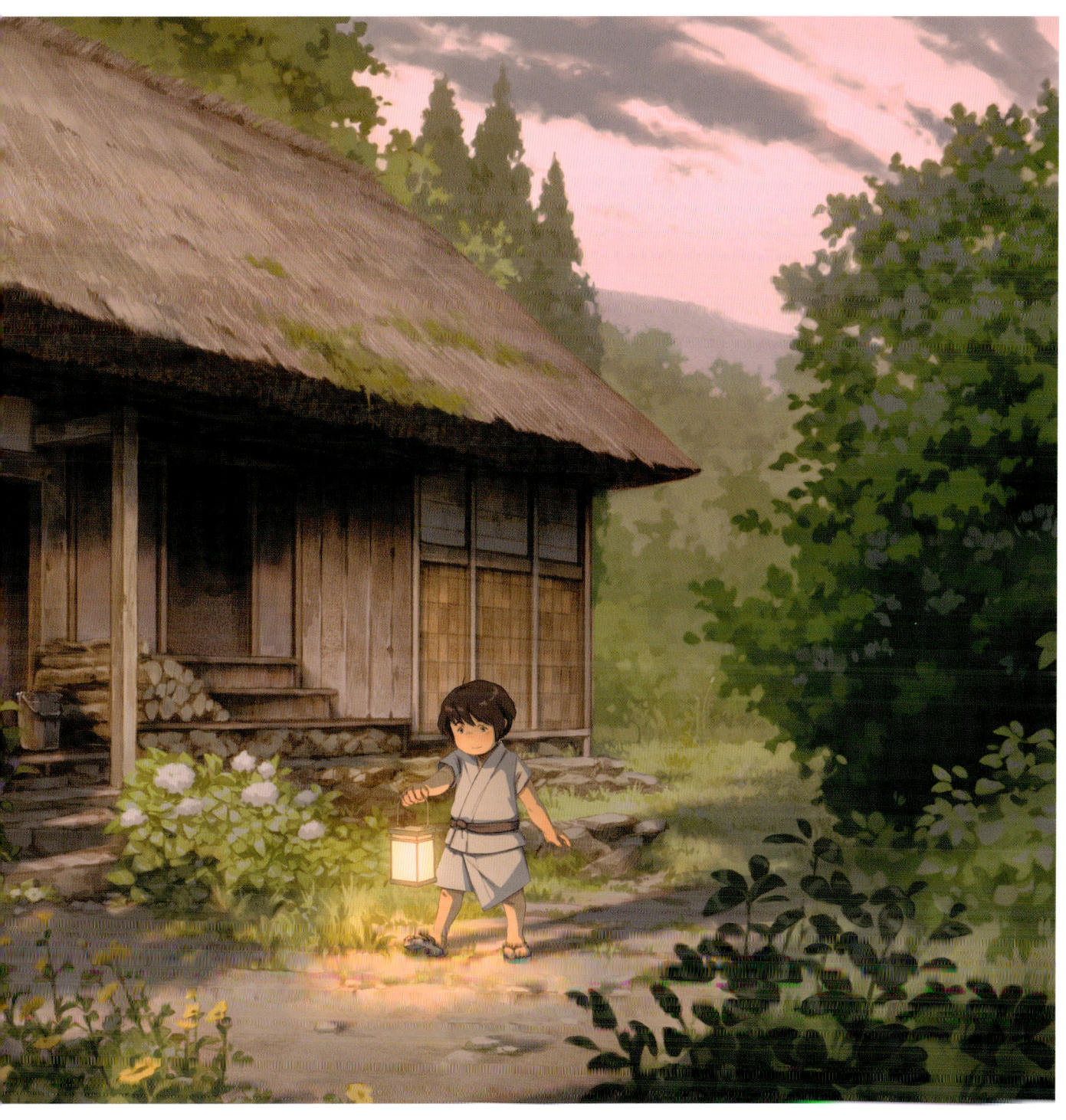

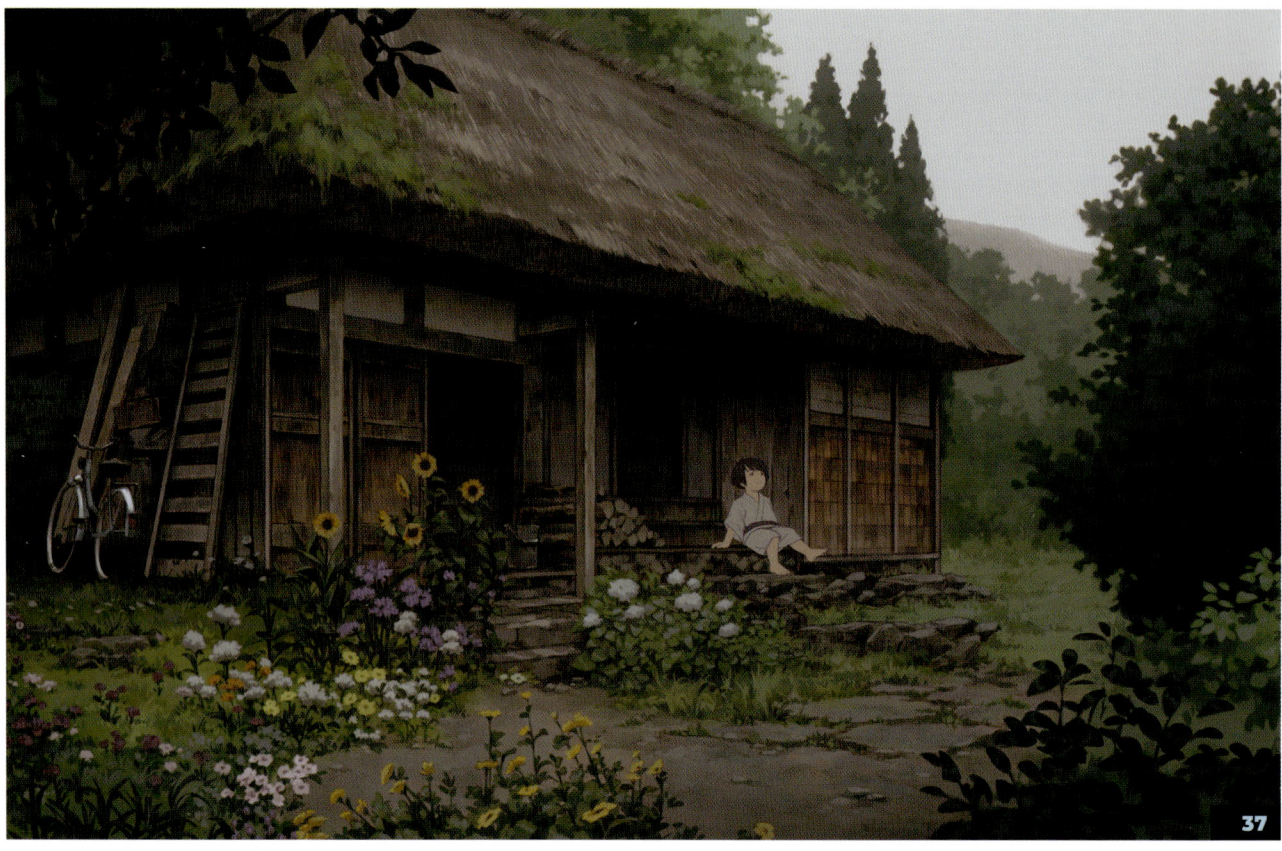

37 I am already reminded of rain when I look at the desaturated painting!

LIGHTING SCENARIO: RAIN

As a bonus scenario, I am going to transform the overcast setting into a rainy scene, to explore how weather effects can also influence light and color. It will be quicker and easier to create than the other three variations, but will also lack a bit of their visual excitement. Of course, that's just the case with this particular scene and setting – if you imagine a rainy night in a neon-lit city, the reflections and vibrant colors would be a very different result!

37 A RAINY DAY

Here, I am aiming for a version of the scene that is quite desaturated, low in contrast, and very moody. I also think it might be fun to juxtapose the dreary, gray colors with the character's attitude toward the weather. I want their body language to suggest that they feel happy.

The first thing I do to establish the palette is darken the scene and desaturate the colors, using layer adjustments as I have done in previous steps.

38 CREATING A GRAINY TEXTURE

Next, I shift the whole color palette toward blue/green and add some details to the sky. I want the sky to look quite uniform, but with a hint of detail. I use a couple of textured brushes and noise effects to add a grainy texture to it. I also establish a gradient from a gray-blue tone at the top toward a color that looks more yellow-green at the bottom.

The darker the painting gets, the more the character feels out of place. To rectify this, I add a few darker shadows to the character to make them feel like they are a part of the environment again. Even this simple change has a drastic effect: It gives the character more three-dimensionality and weight, and it grounds them in the scene.

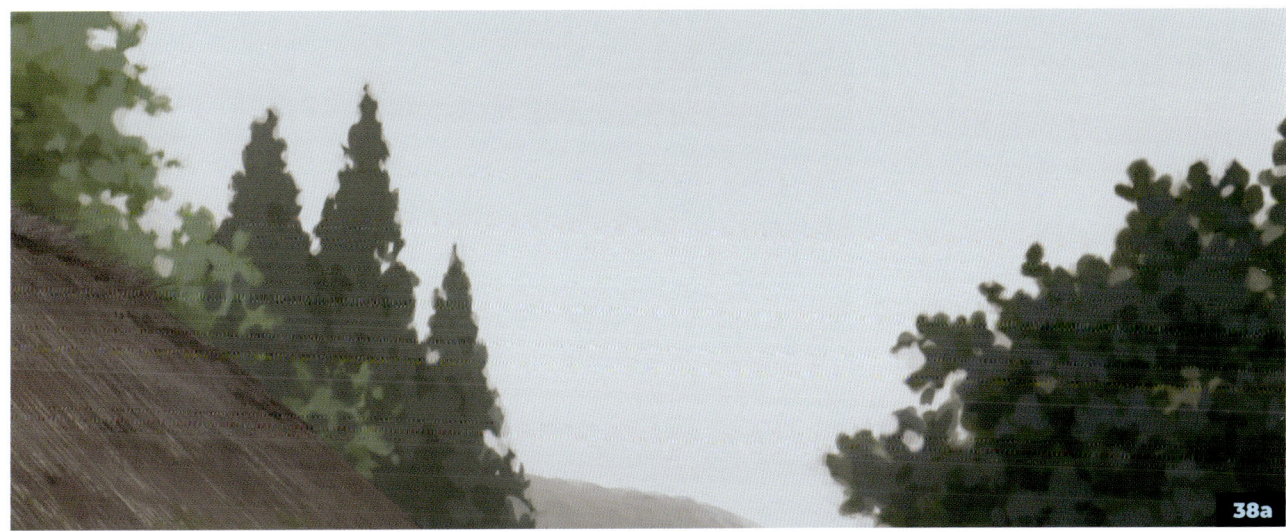

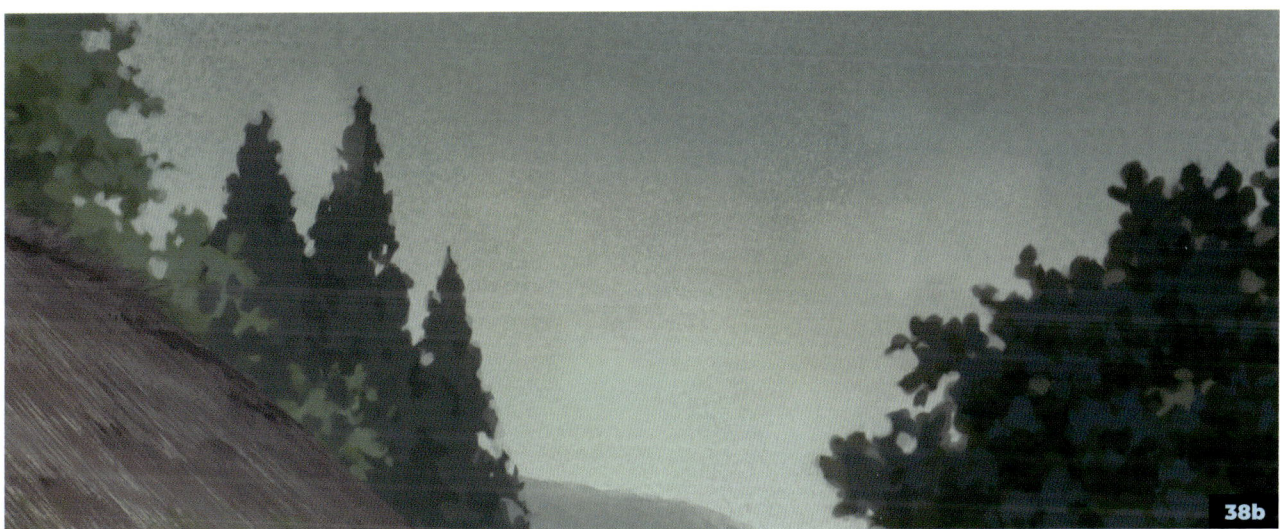

38a – 38b I purposefully make the sky darker than in the overcast setting, using a textured gradient. I want it to look like a dense layer of dark rain clouds.

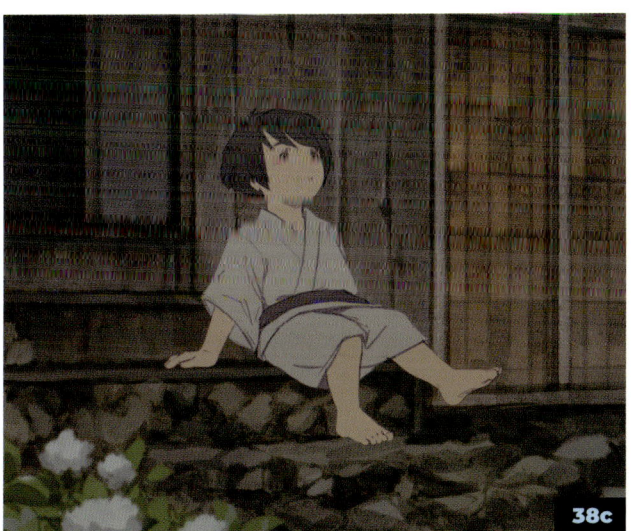

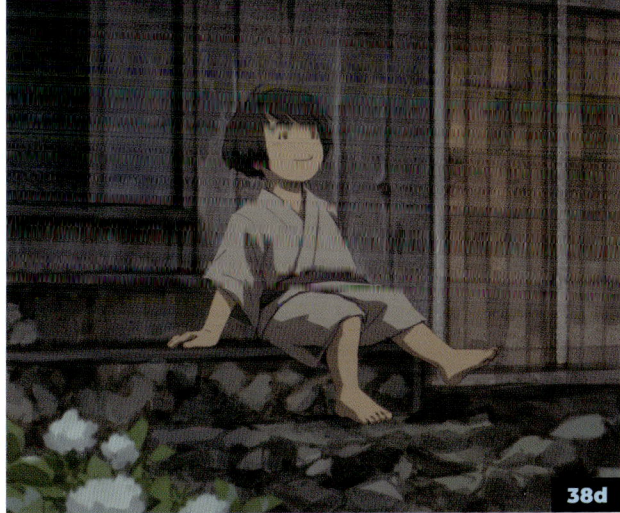

38c – 38d By adding the shadows, I create a stronger connection between the character and the environment.

39 PREPPING THE SCENERY

Before I actually add the rain, I prepare the scene for it, and consider the effect the water will have on the environment. I add a soft haze around different surfaces, where drops would hit and scatter. I also paint water dripping off the roof. I add a few reflections to the ground, lightening the top planes of the stones in front of the house to make them look wet.

The overall palette I have established is a lot more muted than the others. There is no obvious accent color, and the point of highest contrast is the sky. Shapes blend into one another and everything becomes less distinct, but that's exactly the appeal of a rainy scene. There is something peaceful in the way the rain washes over everything.

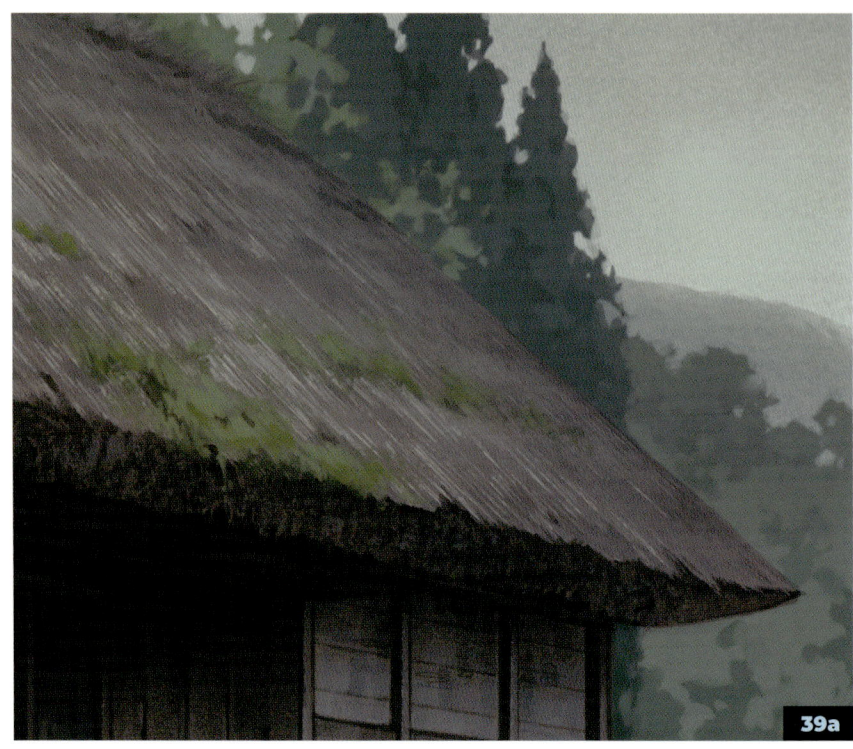

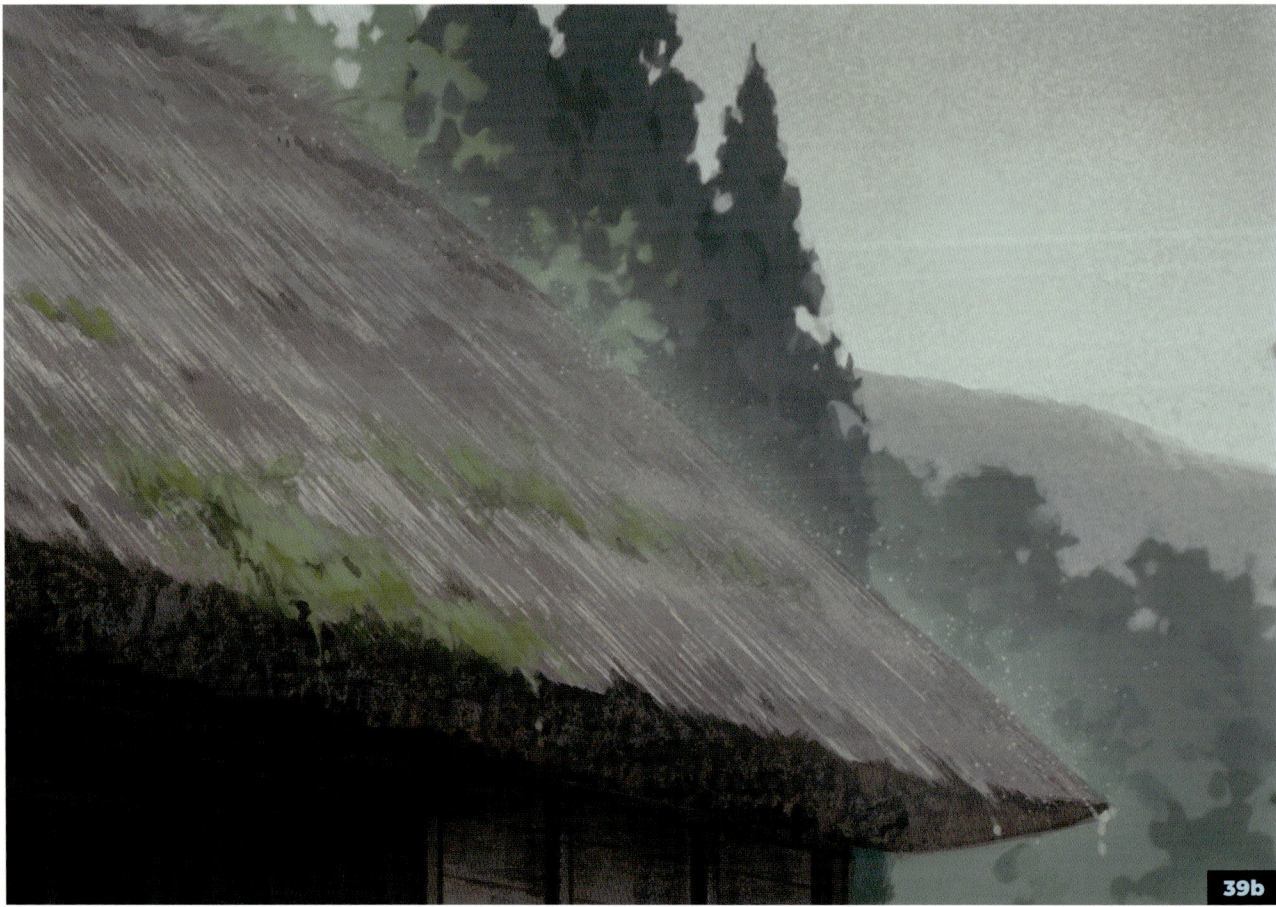

39a – 39b I add a misty haze of rain bouncing off the thatched roof. These small details enhance the mood and atmosphere.

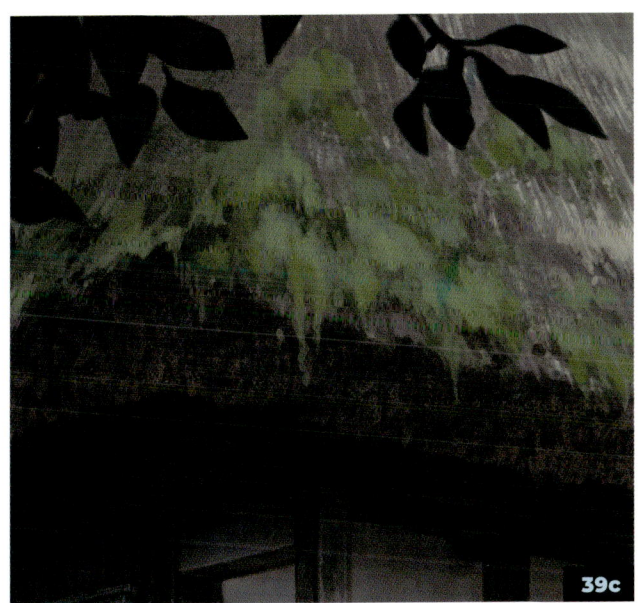

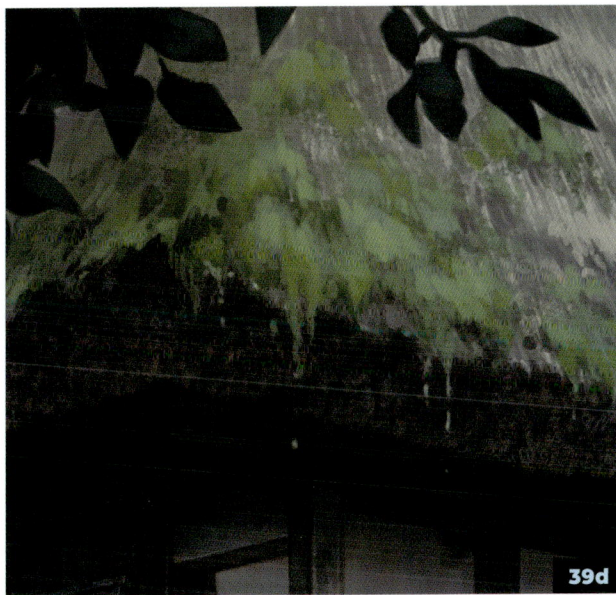

39c – 39d I add water dripping from the edge of the roof, catching the light as it falls.

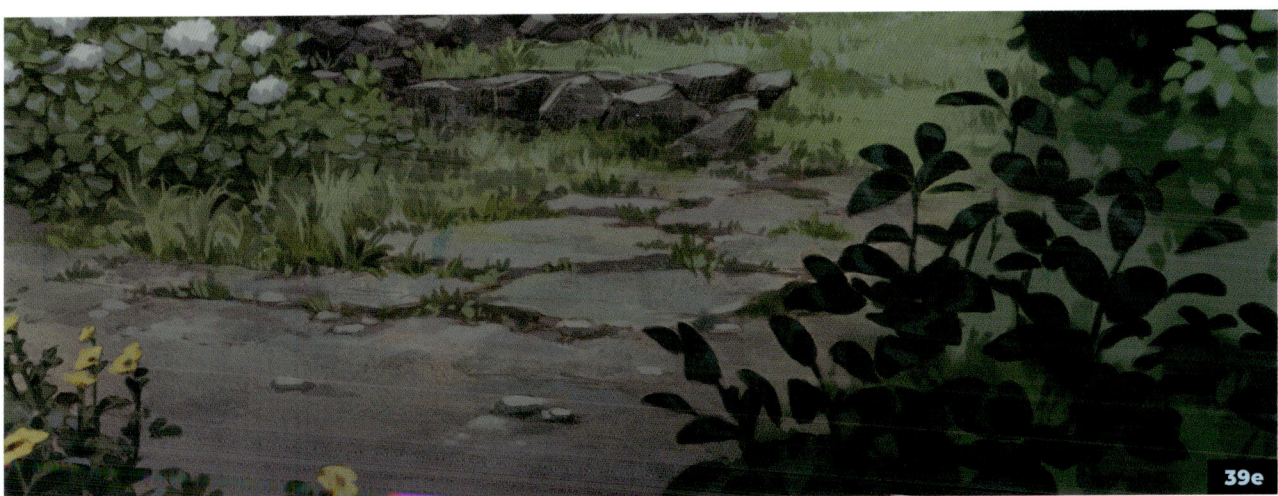

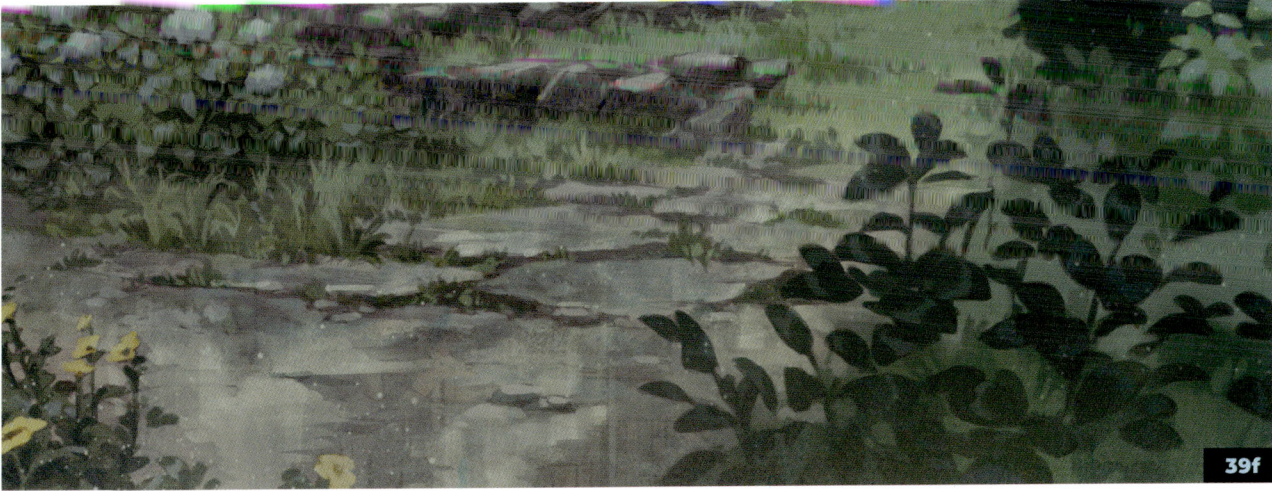

39e – 39f The flat, upward-facing planes of the stones take on a wet shine in the rain.

40 ADDING THE RAIN

Now there's only one thing left to do: add the rain. I place it on a layer above everything else, to make sure that it covers the environment as well as the character. I use very thin, vertical strokes, and try to keep them as irregular as possible. Instead of using pure white, I select a desaturated blue. That finishes off the painting!

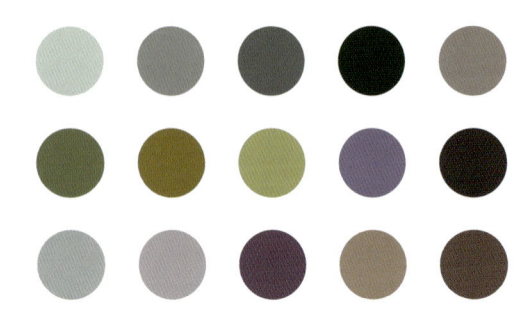

Rainy swatches. Here's my rainy-day color palette. It's similar to the overcast palette, but less saturated, with a greater emphasis on blue and gray hues.

LIGHTING RECAP: RAIN

When it comes to storytelling, rain can suggest many things. In movies, it is often used in the climax, when events finally culminate. It features heavily during fight scenes, or when two people finally profess their love for each other. It can be a sign of determination, like facing the pouring rain, doing what you have to do, and overcoming an obstacle. Rain can also symbolize resignation, depression, or desperation – all these things coming down on a person, just like heavy raindrops.

In a completely different context, you can think of rain as a release and a symbol of freedom. For example, you would welcome it after a long drought. In that case, it feels cleansing and becomes a sign of life, rebirth, and renewal.

Visually speaking, rain brings movement to any scene, and can look beautiful in combination with reflections on the ground.

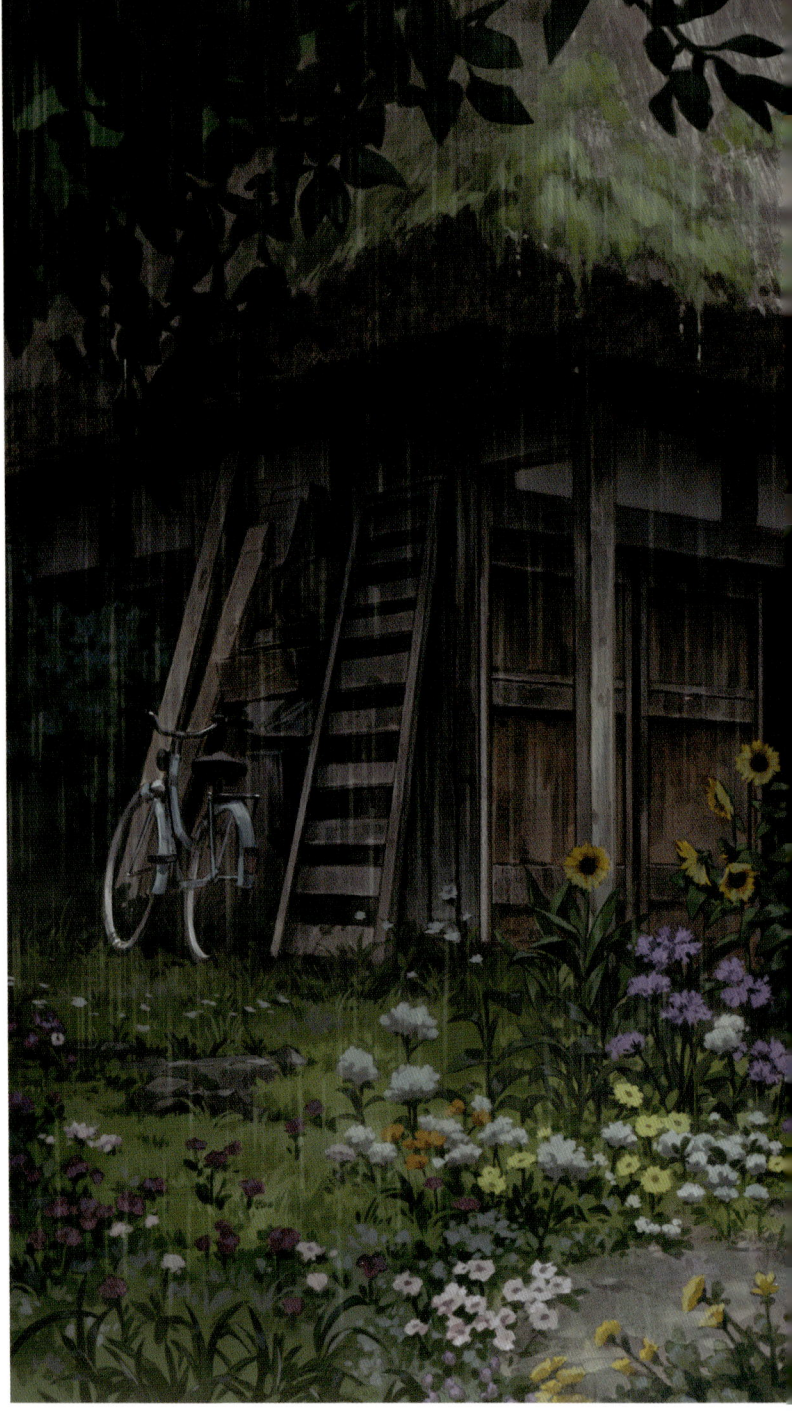

40 Here's the final variation: The little character is enjoying the rain. Water bounces off the house and environment, creating a soft haze.

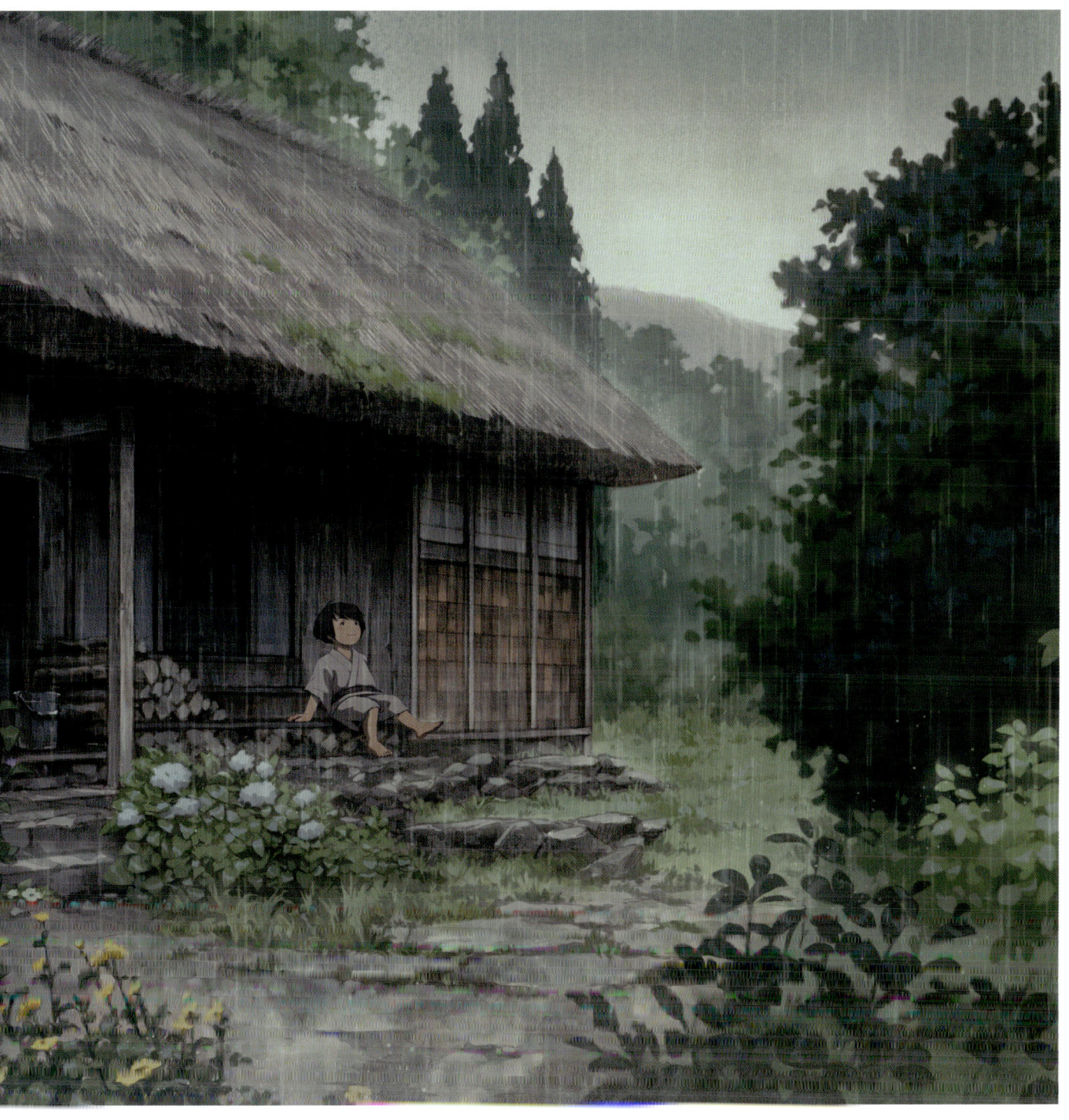

Final image © Djamila Knopf

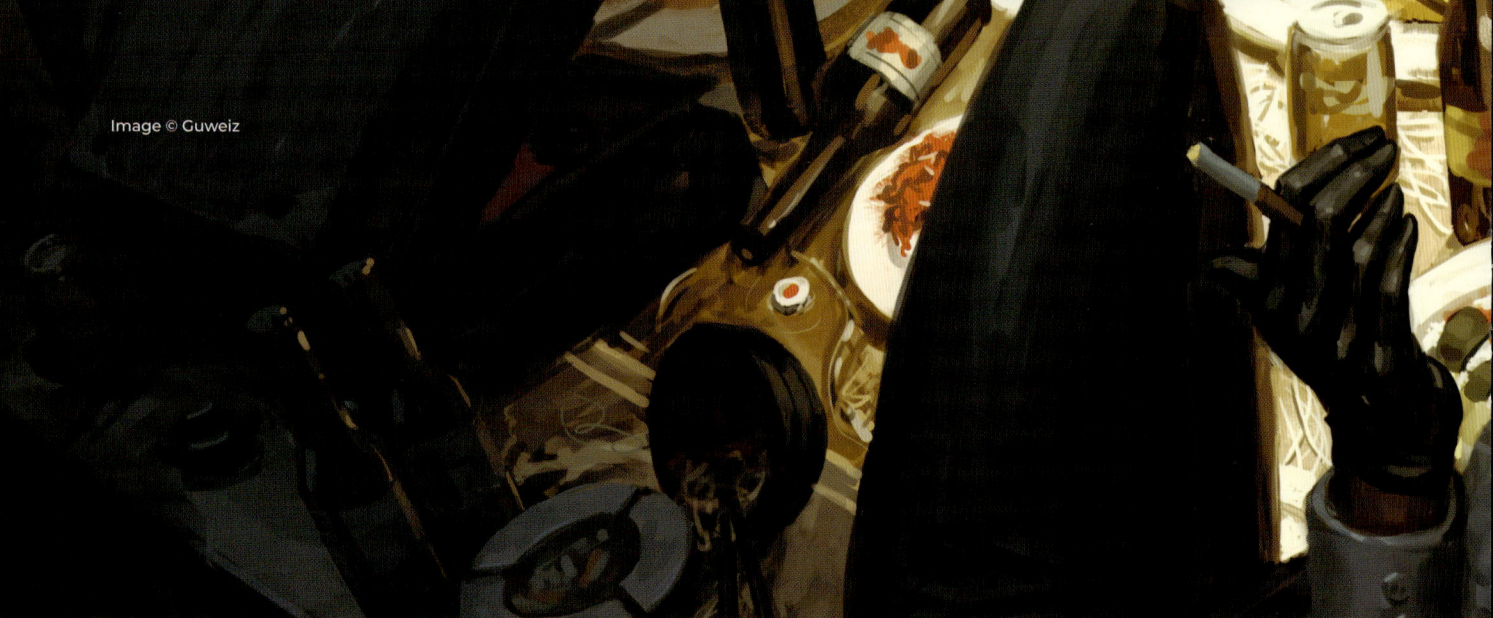
Image © Guweiz

DINNER

GUWEIZ

In this tutorial, I'll be painting a character scene with a dark atmosphere driven by value and moody lighting. We will cover stages such as planning the scene and selecting a viewpoint; placing a perspective grid; mapping out values, ambience, and colors; rendering volumes, textures, and occlusion; all the way through to finishing-touch light effects such as bloom and highlights that will bring the nocturnal scene fully to life. Photoshop is used for this project, though you can follow along with your painting program of choice.

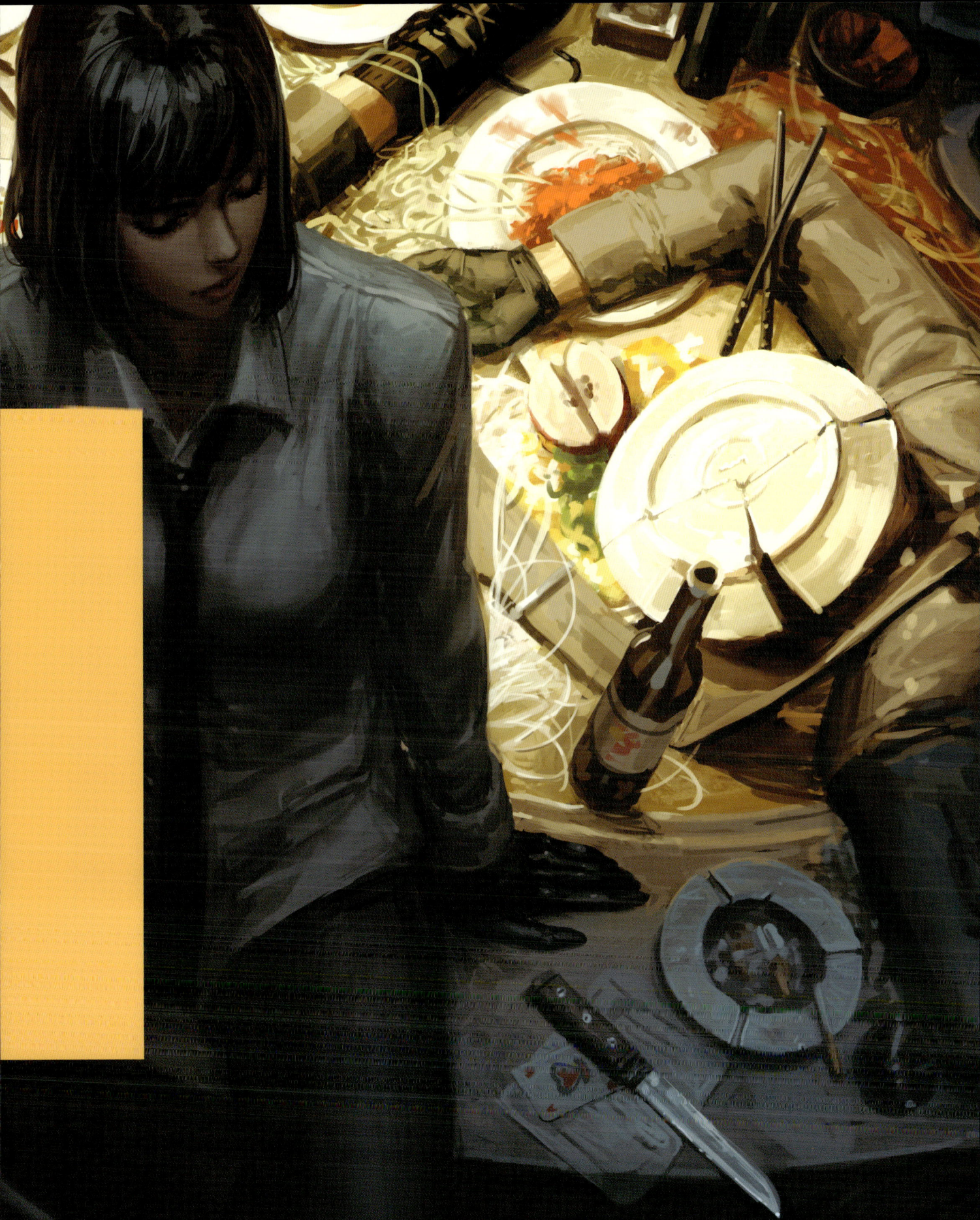

01 WHAT DO YOU WANT TO CREATE?

The beginning of every piece is often a really exciting part of the journey – the options are unlimited and there is infinite potential for creating whatever you want. I very much enjoy letting my mind run wild with possibilities at the start, daydreaming up all kinds of interesting shots that could be realized in the process to come.

At this stage, there's no need to constrain yourself or plan too far ahead; I find it best to simply enjoy the freedom of imagination and visualize in your own mind what you would want to see come into reality. Have you recently watched and been inspired by a film with amazing scenery shots and would like to capture the same awe-inspiring impact in your work? Perhaps you've heard an excellent soundtrack that has prompted you to paint something with a similar mood.

There is no right or wrong idea to jump-start a project. If you genuinely enjoy a concept, that becomes a great motivator to keep you excited and eager as you work.

02 QUESTIONS TO ASK YOURSELF

Once we have formed a rough mental picture of what we would like to paint, things get a little more technical. After all, to transform any idea into a realized image, we have to crystallize the ephemeral concept into something actionable. This means we have to start thinking harder about what our image is going to be, where the interesting parts are, and how we are going to create it. I find that answering the following set of questions is a great place to start:

- What are the focus and purpose of this piece?

- Am I showcasing a character, pose, location, or a combination of these to inspire a feeling in the viewer?

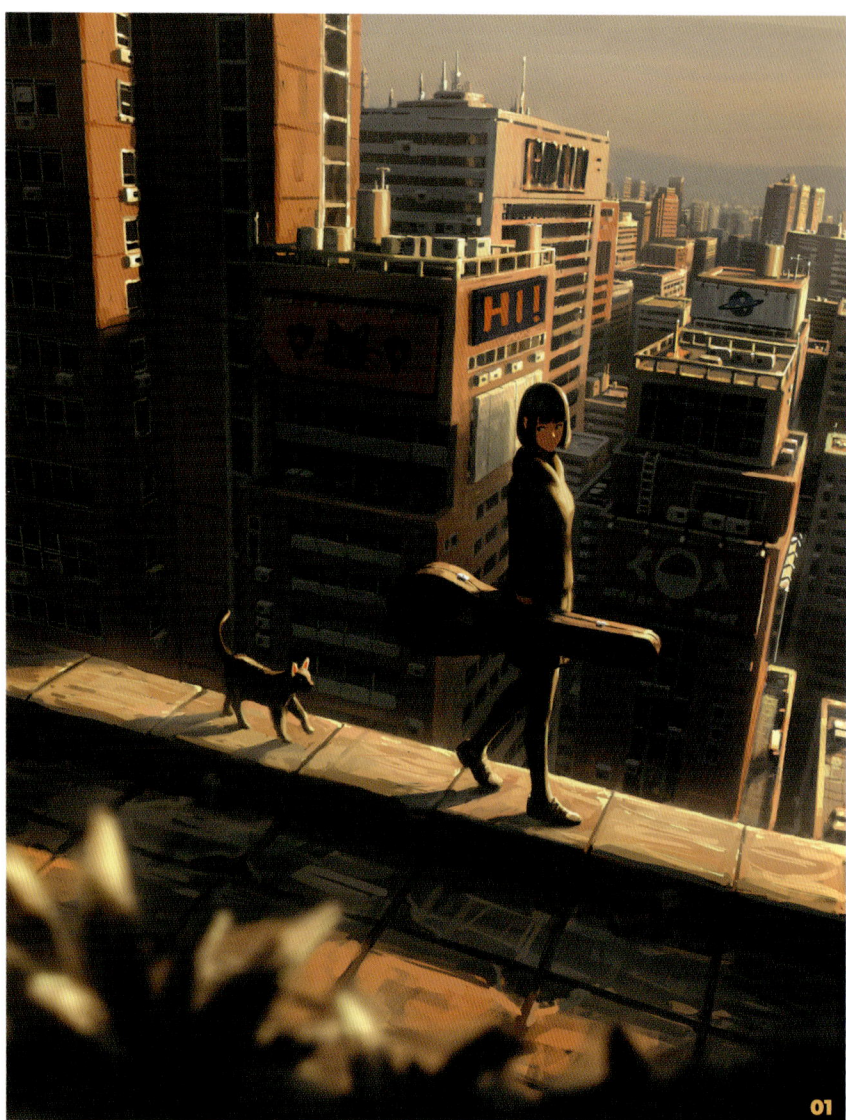

01 An example of a scene that I daydreamed up and locked in on right from the start. Keep your options open and explore different possibilities at this stage.

- Where do the interesting elements lie, and why? Do they coincide with the scene's focus and purpose, or do I need to realign them?

- What makes the picture interesting? The lighting? Location? A unique and beautiful character design, costume, or pose?

- Are there enough of these interesting elements? If not, can I add more?

- How familiar am I with what I want to draw? Will I need references?

- If I want to draw a difficult pose, how much time should I expect to spend on it?

These aren't easy questions if we take them seriously, but they can help us resolve many potential problems early on and contribute greatly to our confidence as we start our painting process.

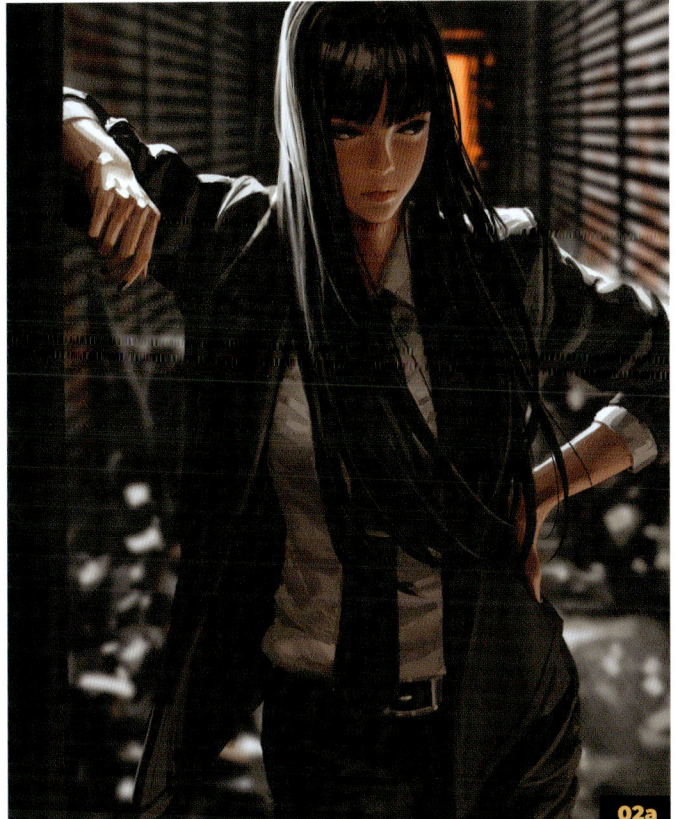

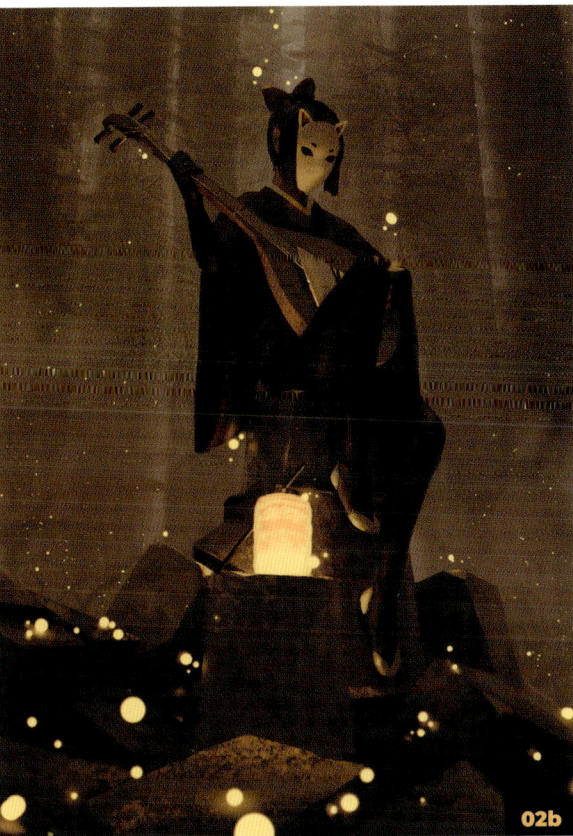

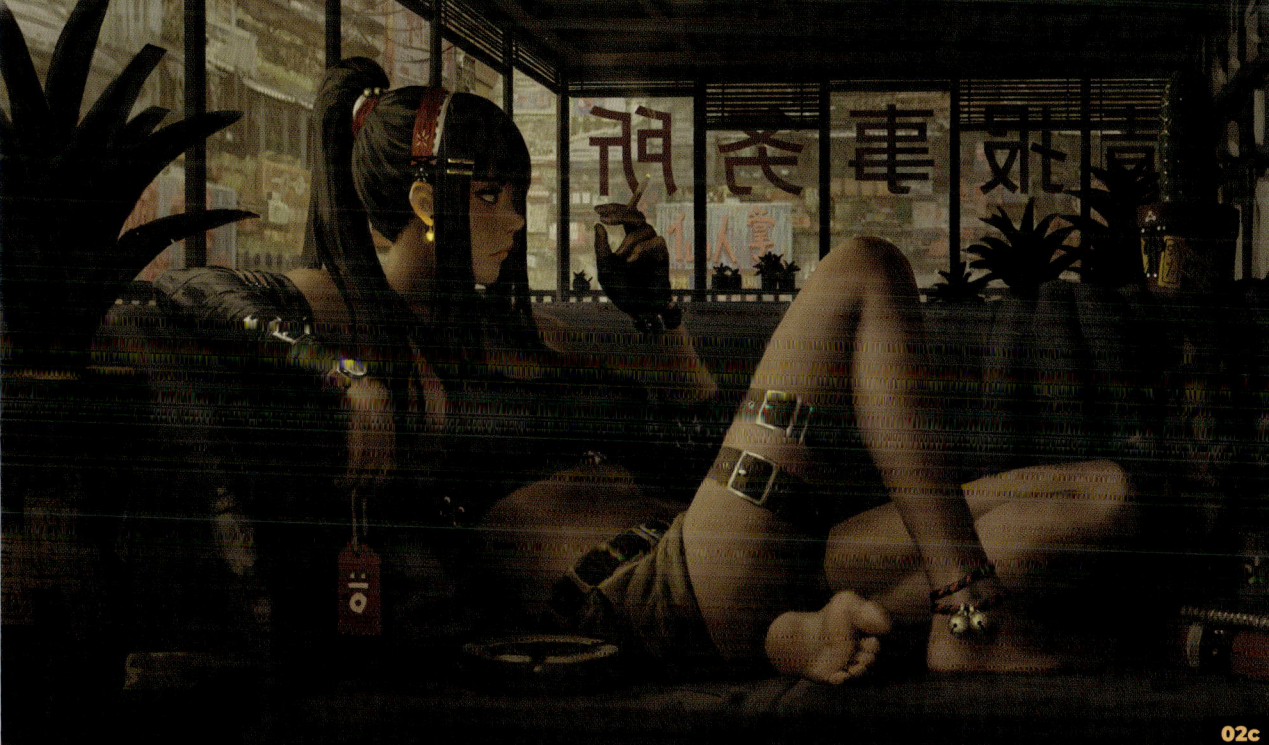

02a – 02c Think about how your idea will be executed before you even begin. Will it be a character- or environment-driven scene? What will be the focus, and why? What elements will make it interesting?

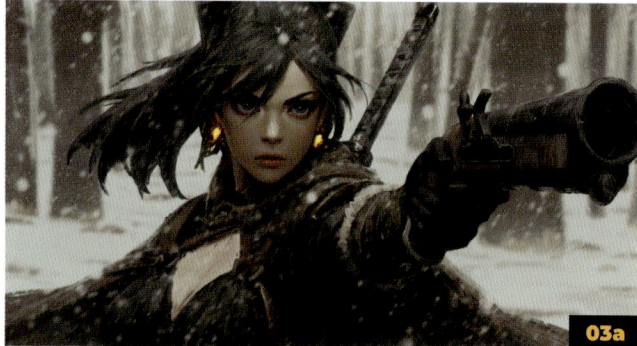

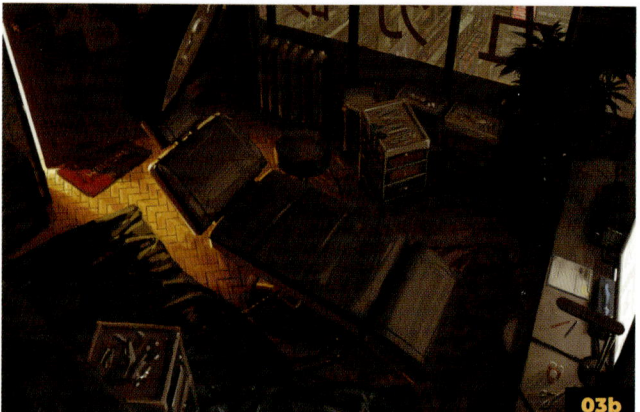

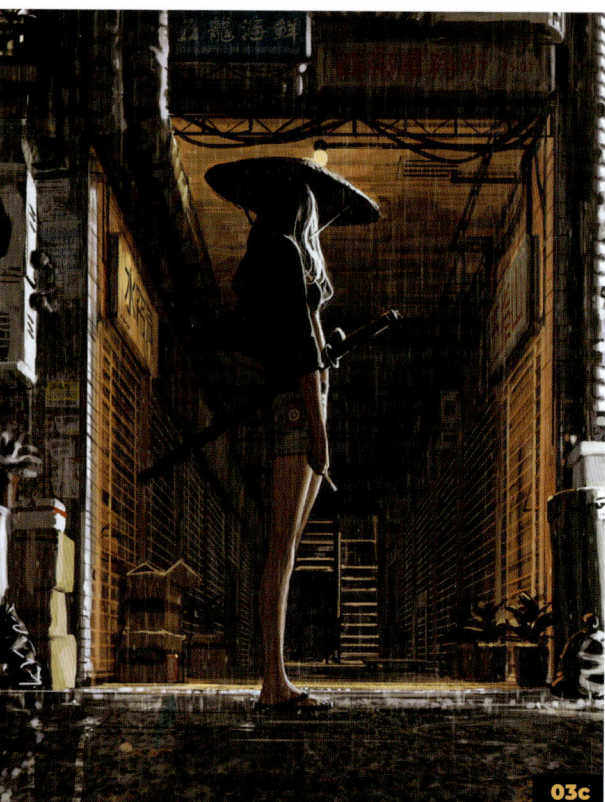

03 Examples of a straightforward, low, and high angle. Each image has a very different dramatic effect for the viewer.

03 PLACING A POINT OF VIEW

Now that we've planned out what elements will be in our piece, we need to decide how we want viewers to perceive them. Despite seeming straightforward, this actually requires some thought and care – selecting a camera/eye position for our point of view (POV) and a corresponding field of view (FOV) is a brief but hugely impactful step.

To help us do this, we first have to figure out what kind of placement is best for our case. While there are infinite places in the scene where we can insert our point of view, we can narrow them down into a few meaningful categories: straightforward, low, and high angles. Each has different uses.

Straightforward angles tend to bring you into an eye-level view, or bring you close to the characters' faces, as if you were standing in the scene itself. Low angles tend to make

the scene feel oversized, like how toddlers see the world as far bigger than adults do, and are great for showcasing size and expansiveness. High angles give the viewer a commanding look into the scene, and generally feel more distanced from the action. I find them great for quieter scenes, but a lot of the fun lies in discovering what each angle does for you personally!

Once we've chosen our desired angle, we must also check off two more items: distance from the scene and field of view. These are more self-explanatory. A short distance between the viewer's eye and the subject makes the scene feel more intimate. A wide field of view simply allows you to see more in the periphery of the scene. What all these aspects have in common is their overall purpose. They are meant to portray your chosen focus in the piece in the most effective way possible, and that should always be the top priority.

04 ANCHORING DOWN PERSPECTIVE

We are finally ready to start the physical process of creating the illustration! For the piece I am creating in this tutorial, I have chosen to use a high-angle, moderately close shot of the scene with a wide field of view. My next step is to make sure I lay the perspective groundwork to help me properly execute this.

A key part of mastering fundamental skills is being able to draw a scene in perspective consistently, making sure the appearance of every volume and surface corresponds to the same eye position. Using a perspective grid gives us a very reliable mathematical guide that can be used to great effect in making a correct drawing and lighting it well.

Let's take a look at the three POV parameters we picked out earlier, as they will help us decide how to create our grid. As of now, we are able to configure our grid to match two of the requirements. The blue lines run along the vertical axis, while the red and green lines form a horizontal plane, setting up the scene's high-angle shot. To indicate that a wide FOV is being used, the axes converge substantially on-camera.

To indicate our POV's actual distance from the scene, however, we would need to draw something for scale.

05 PLACING THE FIRST LINES

With the grid in place, we can finally begin putting our idea onto the canvas. At this very early stage of sketching, the main priority is to put down a version of your idea that is clear enough for you to use for visualization, but rough enough that it doesn't take too much time and effort.

In this case, I have established several key elements of my idea: the character's pose, visually substantial elements like the large bar table and stool, and the two beaten-up extras. With intuitively recognizable elements of the sketch (human figures especially) giving us information on scale, we've also locked in the third and final part of our perspective setup – distance between the POV and the scene.

This step only took about fifteen minutes, but it gives me enough information to confirm that the idea is a workable one that I can further commit to. It also prompts me to start thinking about solutions to different parts of the composition that I only discovered thanks to the sketch.

During this process, we can also easily make changes to any part of the composition as well, which is the big advantage of a "low-cost" sketch. It's important to note that sometimes it's practical to begin straight off with a sketch to help you brainstorm ideas, but for the purposes of this tutorial we have taken a more linear approach.

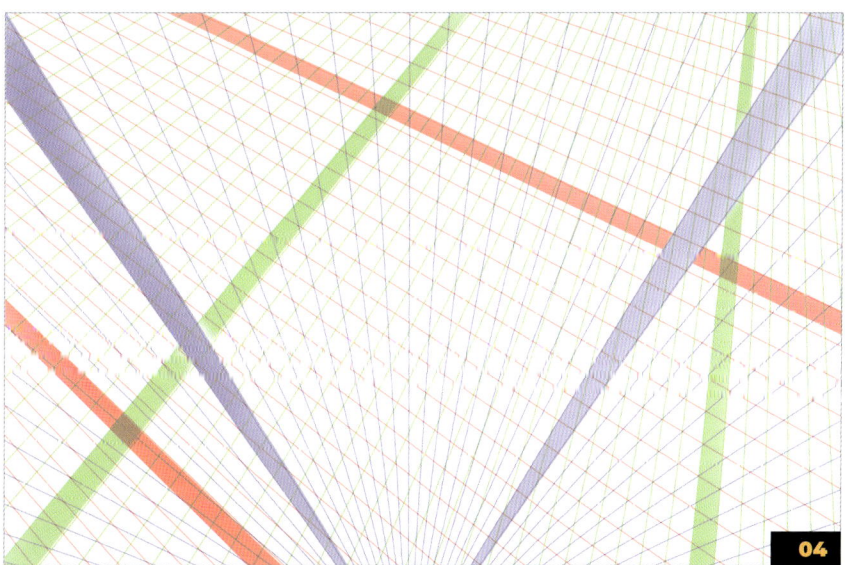

04 The axes at this stage aren't fixed – they are based very much on your own needs. Pick ones that will align to major elements in your composition.

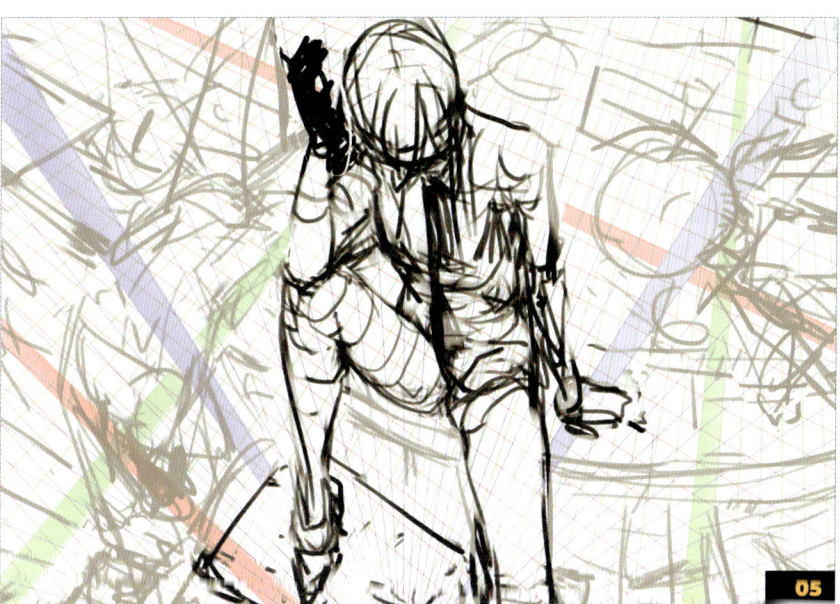

05 This sketch is extremely rough, but captures the gist of the idea.

REFERENCES AND WHEN TO USE THEM

References can come in all shapes and sizes, from searching for relevant images online to looking around your own room or in a mirror. References can be used to kick-start your imagination or to supplement and improve a design or composition. A good habit is to be goal-oriented when using them – understand why you are using a certain resource and extract the most useful parts from it. For example, instead of drawing a supermarket shelf exactly from reference, observe how certain patterns, shapes, and variations in density help make the scene look visually interesting.

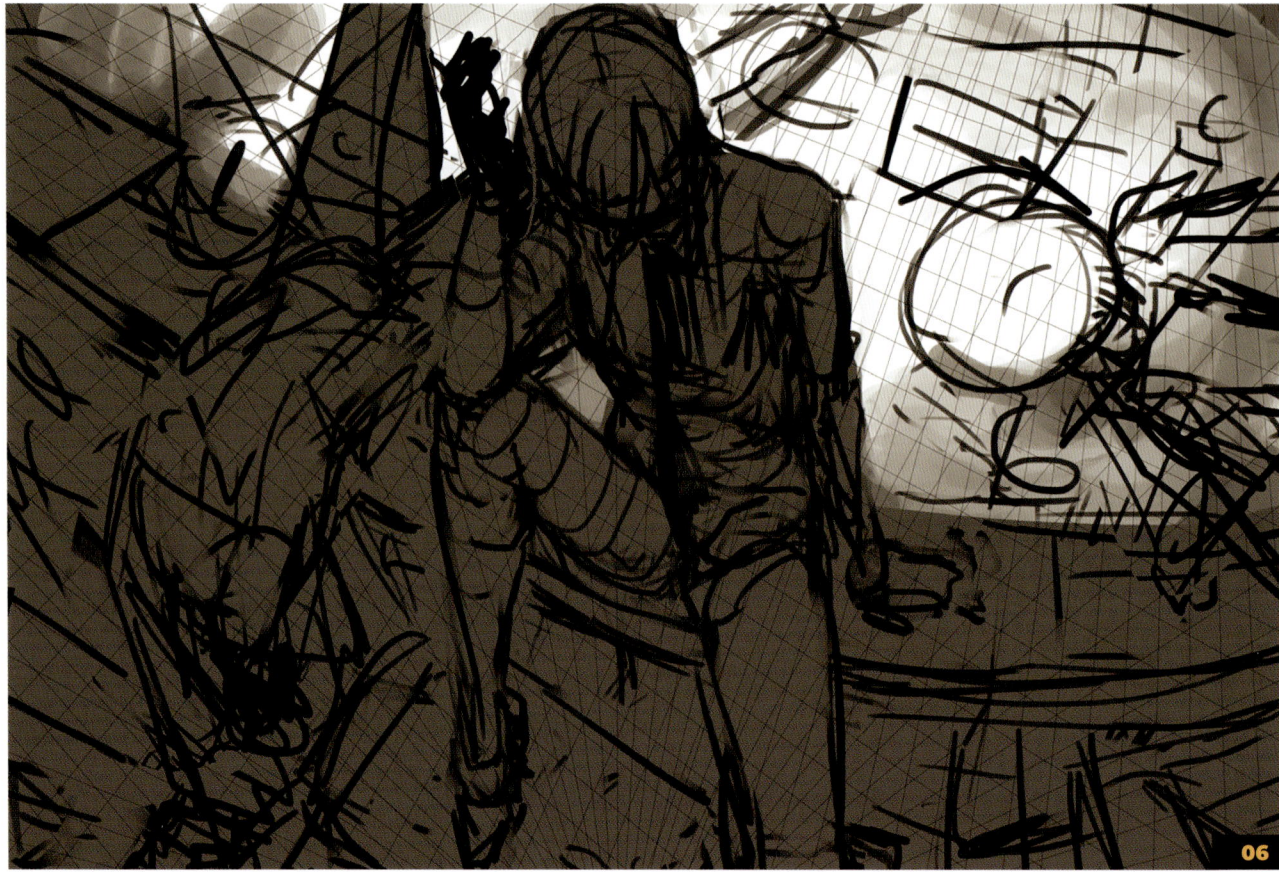

06 Using roughly two different values to discover our desired composition.

06 FORMING BASIC VALUE BLOCKS

With our idea now visualized in a very simple form, the next step is to essentially extend that process to introduce and employ more of the fundamentals that will be the foundation of our painting.

Using a separate layer to paint under the sketch lines, I block in a very simple setup to indicate the basic lighting. The key is to very gradually build up our lighting and volumes step-by-step, starting with the most visually substantial and dominant parts of the composition, assessing their viability and quality as we go.

Since I planned for there to be one strong, major light source illuminating the table behind our main character, I split the image into two value blocks: one to account for the aforementioned main light source, and the other to account for all the areas the light doesn't reach.

It is very important that the relationship between these two blocks is kept clear and at the top of the image's visual hierarchy. As you learned on page 16, a strong value read is the most important part of any image, so, regardless of anything else, the most obvious thing in the composition should be this particular set of contrasting brightnesses.

07 ADDING ADDITIONAL BLOCKS

Keeping to that principle of "biggest first," we can now proceed to the next most important set of value blocks. This next pair captures the relationship between the areas lit by the moonlight coming in from above, and the areas that the moonlight can't reach.

The main change here is that I add a darker value to the side-facing surface of the bar table, separating that region of shadow from the tabletop, character, and stool seats that are in moonlight. Notice that I don't brighten the value of the moonlit areas at all. This is very important to maintain the relationship between the strong table light and the rest of the scene, which, as we have established, is of primary importance.

Of course, as we develop the image later on, the values are likely to change as we paint. The rationale for the careful discipline now is to ensure that we can tackle the later painting stages with all our key compositional elements and relationships solidly in place.

08 INTRODUCING LOCAL VALUE

With the main lighting relationships blocked in, the next step is to start on local values. Local values are essentially based on the reflective capabilities of the various materials. Black fabric, dark hair, wood, and skin all reflect differing amounts of light, thus appearing to have different innate brightnesses to our eyes. For example, if we were to assign them numbers, the local value of white porcelain might be 60, while a pair of black trousers might be 15.

These local values will have a significant impact on our composition, so we want to tackle them early in the process as well. This can be done by using a Soft Light or Overlay layer to paint over areas that have the most extreme local values, such as dark fabrics and bright ceramics.

At this point, there is no need to be too thorough and paint every single different material with its own local value. Once again, the key for now is to highlight and visualize the most prominent elements of the illustration.

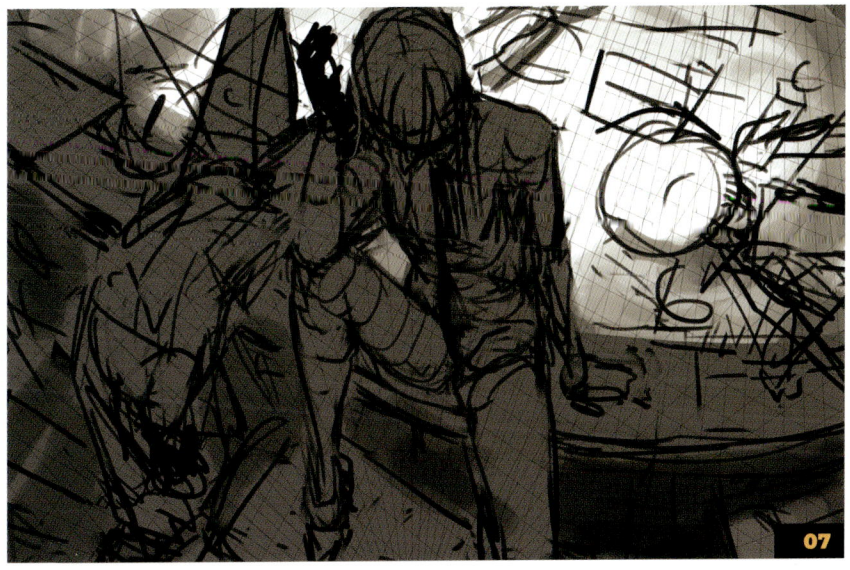

07 A third value block representing the darkest areas adds more nuance to the basic composition.

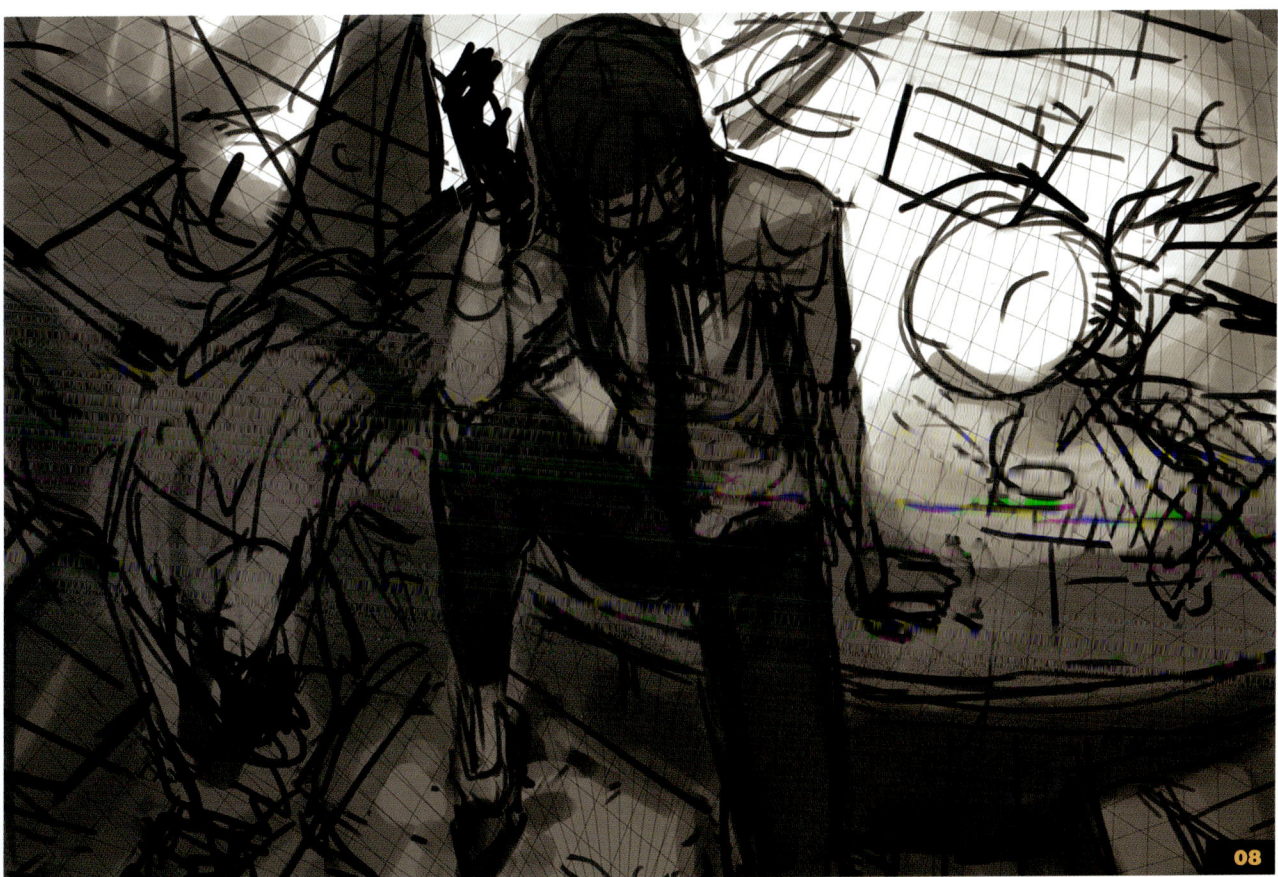

08 The image with important local values added, separating major materials such as the main character's dark trousers.

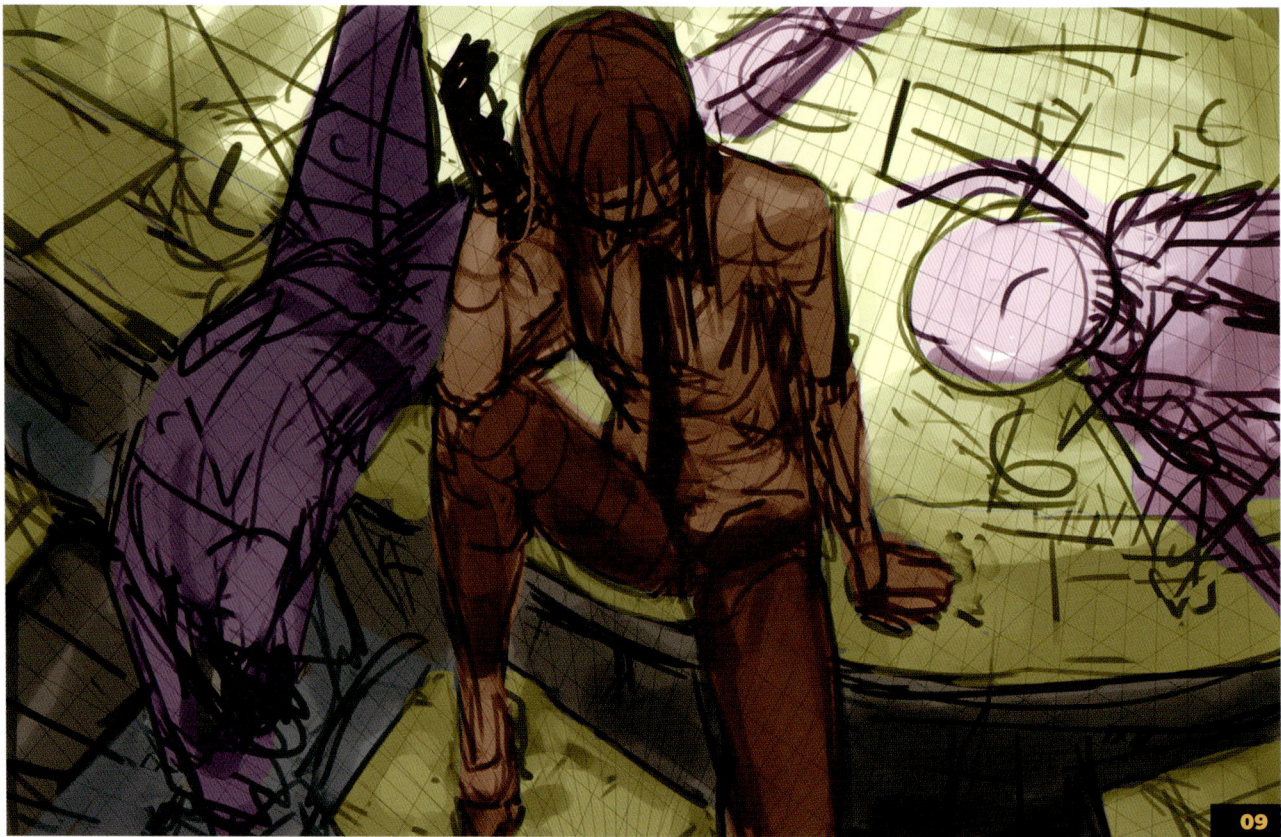

09 Breaking down our composition, we can more easily visualize and manage our elements.

09 MANAGING SHAPES AND KEY ELEMENTS

Now that our sketch is basically a colorless, simplified version of the final product, with all the essential value information in place, we can make another full assessment of the composition, in the same way as when we first created the line sketch.

Identifying and clarifying major "physical" elements in the image is a good place to start. At a quick glance, just to demonstrate for the purposes of this tutorial, I've divided the image into:

Brown: The main character. We want to check that she has a strong position in the composition, and that interesting areas like her head and hands are in regions of high contrast and focus.

Purple: The defeated extras. It's important that their body language and placement makes clear exactly why they are there and what has happened to them.

Yellow: The table and stool surfaces. These areas, while seemingly simple, will hold a massive bulk of visual information that makes our image more convincing and immersive to the viewer.

Blue: The floor, debris, and miscellaneous items. These areas are unlikely to be very prominent, but we still need to pay some attention to them and make good use of them to enhance our story.

Shape management is a topic commonly talked about, but context is key – every composition has its own unique shape needs.

Now that we have outlined our objectives, we can tailor the shapes we use to achieve them. A few examples we can see here are:

· Using the curved edge of the table to converge attention on the main character of the story.

· Covering one of the extra's faces with a visually prominent round plate to imply they lost the fight.

· Using the characters to break up the yellow region into smaller, organically shaped bits, avoiding strange tangents or misleading shapes in the thumbnail.

USING THE HARD ROUND BRUSH

The massive amount of options we have at our disposal in Photoshop – or really any other modern painting and editing software – is staggering. It can sometimes be very intimidating as well. Brushes alone can be a headache for newer artists to get a handle on, and it can often feel like you're missing out on secrets unless you somehow discover and use certain brushes.

While there are reasons why many advanced and fancy brushes exist, they contribute an extremely tiny amount to a piece compared to the knowledge and application of fundamentals in the creation process. Brushes are just a tool for us to transfer our ideas onto a canvas, and as long as we have a good grasp of fundamental knowledge – such as hue, value, and lighting – any brush can be used to create amazing pieces. Of course, as we develop and practice, we can also continue to explore new brush options to suit our preferences.

But to begin with, the basics are no doubt the best place to start! Photoshop's default Hard Round brush can sufficiently fill any role in an artist's arsenal, whether it is for linework, solid coloring and shading, painting a fine gradient, or micro-details. This brush can do it all competently. Not only is it versatile, it's also fast – it can achieve any stroke size and opacity on the fly by making full use of pressure sensitivity on your pen tablet. Using the Opacity slider, you can instantly customize it for more specific uses, such as for painting tiny, opaque details or lightly shading large areas.

The simplicity and versatility of this brush also allows you to quickly and smoothly switch your focus between various parts of the painting without having to change brushes or settings. It's an underrated brush that quietly makes painting a more pleasant experience.

Last but not least, the Hard Round brush is also "texture-neutral" in that it doesn't have a texture overlay by default. This can be a boon in helping to avoid overtexturing early on in the painting, enabling you to focus on more fundamental forms and lighting. This means it can be a little inefficient when used for the final polish – for example, creating a rusty metal surface can be done much more easily with a custom textured brush.

Overall, no matter if you are sketching lines, painting a black-and-white draft, or adding details, the default Hard Round brush is flexible enough to produce a good result, so don't worry about it holding you back.

Pressure sensitive. Without changing any settings, we can achieve the effect of any one point on this brushstroke simply using pen pressure.

Easily customizable. The opacity and size settings unleash even more potential and have easy hotkeys to manage them on the fly.

Versatile. The soft shading on the left and hard lines on the right are both created with the same brush, simply by adjusting stroke size and opacity.

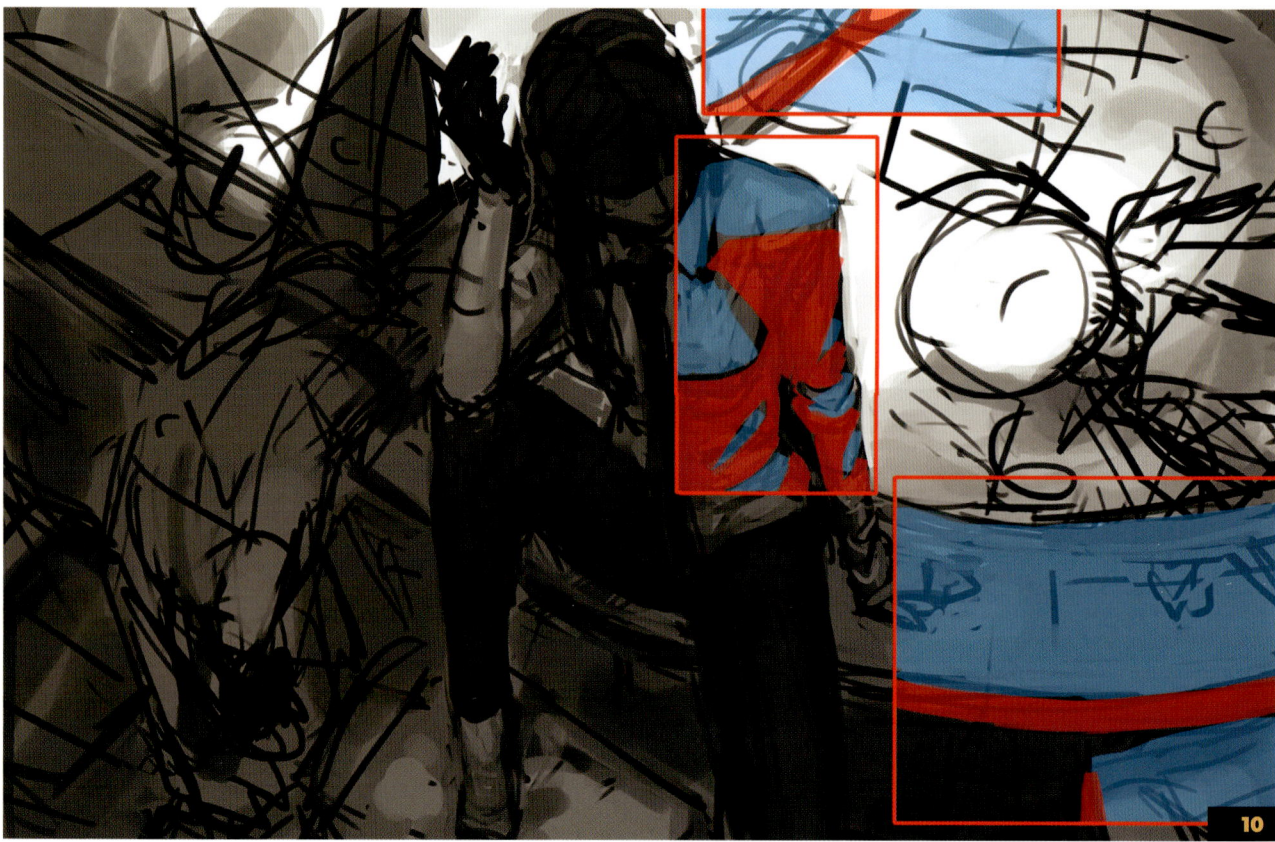

10 In our lighting setup, the top-down split of surfaces is very helpful in depicting form.

10 DIFFERENTIATING SURFACES TO CREATE FORMS

A key method we have been using so far in the drawing process is going from "big to small," tackling the broad, sweeping aspects of the composition first. Now that we have made the big choices, it's time to look at and work on the piece at a higher resolution.

I start breaking down large areas into smaller, more precise ones. Above, I have highlighted the upward-facing surfaces in blue and side- or downward-facing areas in red. I am differentiating them this way because the direct light source comes from the top of the scene, and this will help me decisively paint each surface according to the amount of light they receive and reflect.

Our two direct light sources (the table spotlight and moonlight) are the most prominent light sources in the composition, so they are first up for consideration as we categorize our surfaces.

As we move along in this "big to small" pipeline, we will break the blue and red regions down into even more precise ones. For example, upward-facing surfaces that are completely perpendicular to the direction of lighting, and upward-facing surfaces that face slightly away but not enough to be considered side-facing.

11 MAINTAINING COMPOSITIONAL BACKBONE

As we start subdividing our surfaces and assigning them different values to represent more accurate volumes, there is always the chance that we accidentally "exceed" our value range limits while adding new values. This commonly shows up in the form of the image starting to become "muddy" – things seem to look correct in specific parts of the composition, but the image as a whole becomes confusing and hard to figure out. Let's take a look at how we can detect and prevent this.

Recall that we have carefully determined and are committed to maintaining the relationship between our three big value blocks. The spotlit region must always be brighter than the rest, while the moonlit region, although darker, must still be visibly brighter than the third, darkest region that's shaded from both light sources.

In the process of adding values to subdivide smaller areas, such as the character's shoulder, we have to be very careful not to use values that are too bright or dark for that value block. It's easy to get tunnel vision and try to boost the contrast in the area we are

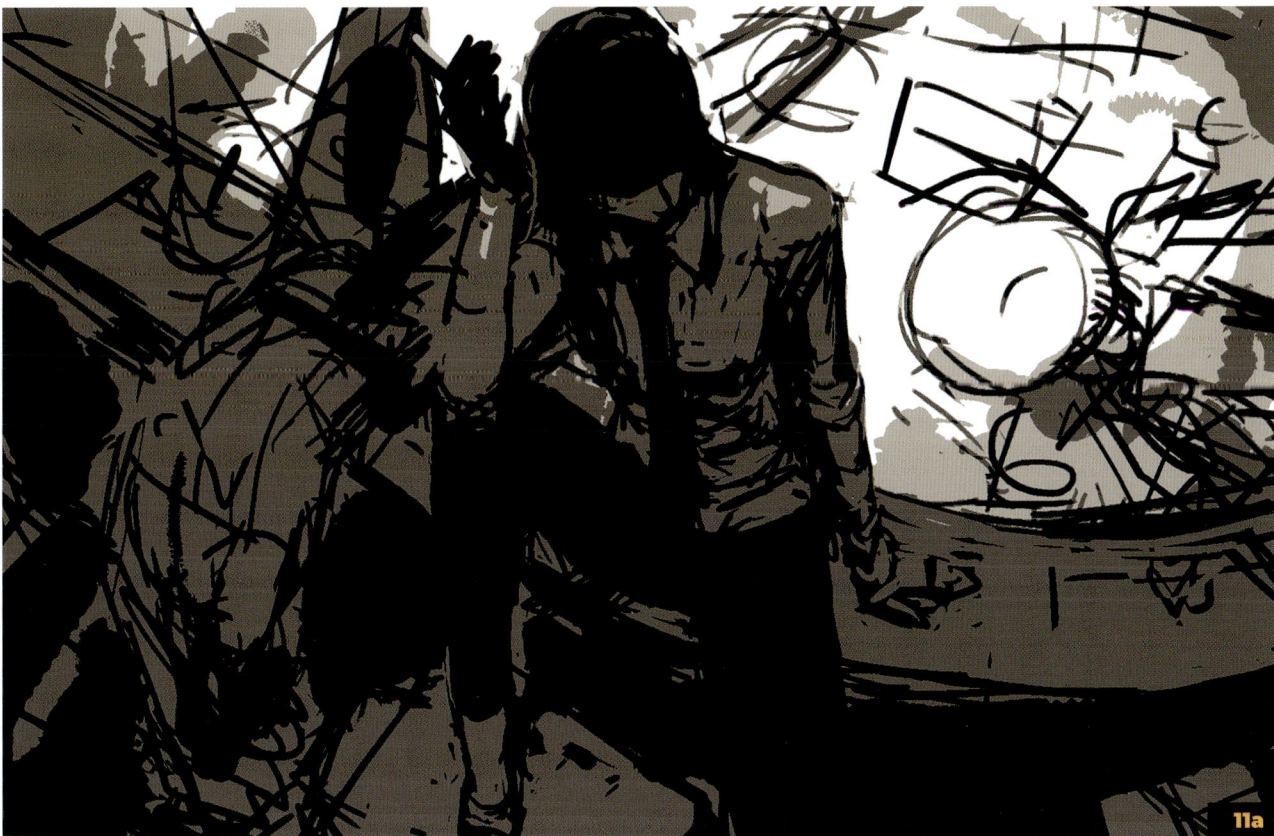

11a – 11c Using Posterize, the image is split into your chosen number of distinct values. In this case, it shows four values.

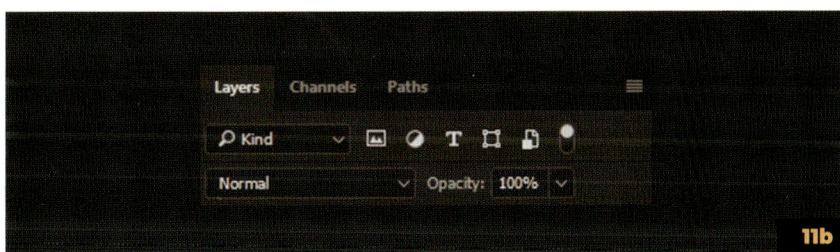

Solid Color...
Gradient...
Pattern...

Brightness/Contrast...
Levels...
Curves...
Exposure...

Vibrance
Hue/Saturation...
Color Balance...
Black White...
Photo Filter...
Channel Mixer...
Color Lookup...

Invert
Posterize...
Threshold...
Gradient Map...
Selective Color...

currently painting – this may not seem to be a problem in isolation, but in the larger context of the painting, it can disrupt our top level value block relationships.

To help check the integrity of these relationships, I recommend using the Posterize tool in Photoshop. This is especially helpful when you feel the image is getting muddy and "gray" but are not sure why. Posterize is a filter layer that mathematically simplifies the entire draft into a set number of values. For example, I have it set to four values above, and that is how it now

represents the sketch. Notice that it still keeps very strictly to our original plan, and the areas receiving the brightest moonlight (the shoulder and wrist area of the white shirt) are only barely equivalent to areas partially receiving the brighter spotlight (slightly darkened areas on the main table).

Using Posterize, we can quickly detect if certain areas have exceeded their allotted range of values. Then simply undo Posterize and correct the image to make sure the overall value hierarchy and layout is maintained as we planned it.

271

12 PAINTING IN VALUES

Taking all that we have learned in the past few steps, we now enter a more organic, free-flowing painting phase for our value base. Our goal here is essentially to get the image into a state where every element in the composition has undergone our "big to small" process pipeline – with the overall focus still on the more prominent elements, of course. The process of organically painting and refining the value sketch will get it ready for the color draft.

At this stage, I decide to expand the canvas out a little, while maintaining the same perspective grid. This increases the field of view without moving the point of view, making us feel more "zoomed out" and showing off a bit more of the scene.

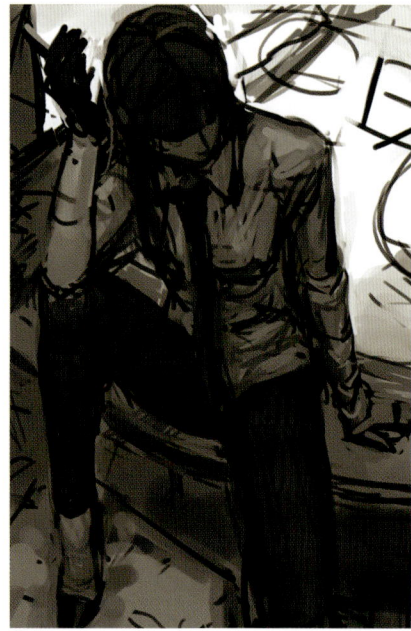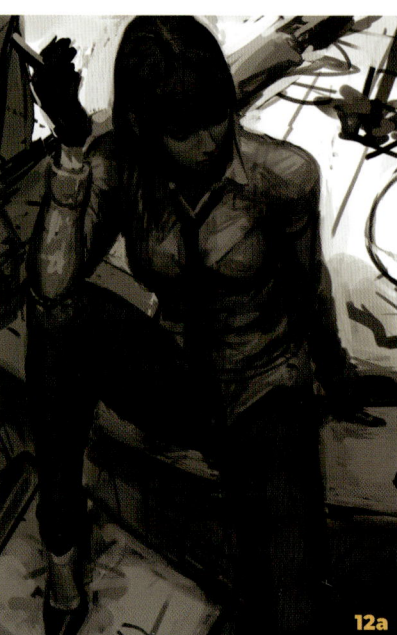

12a When painting over a line sketch, especially a rough one, pay attention to the forms you are indicating. Accidentally removing wanted forms causes the painting to look "worse" than the sketch. Revisit page 80 for guidance on rendering essential geometric forms.

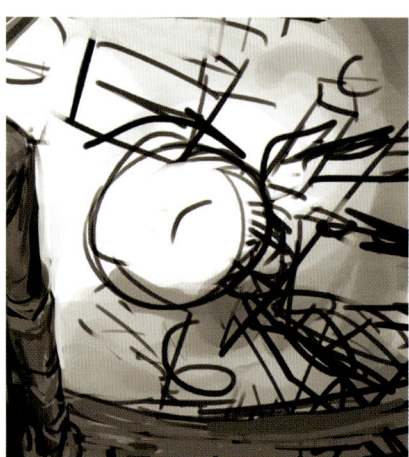

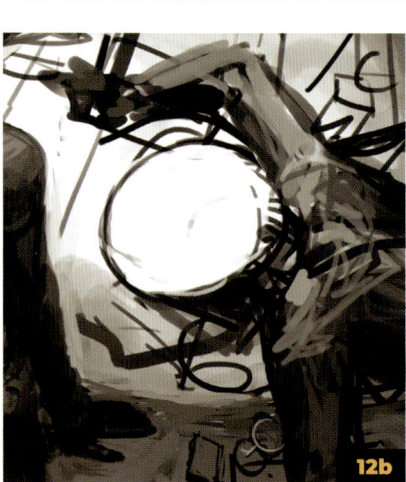

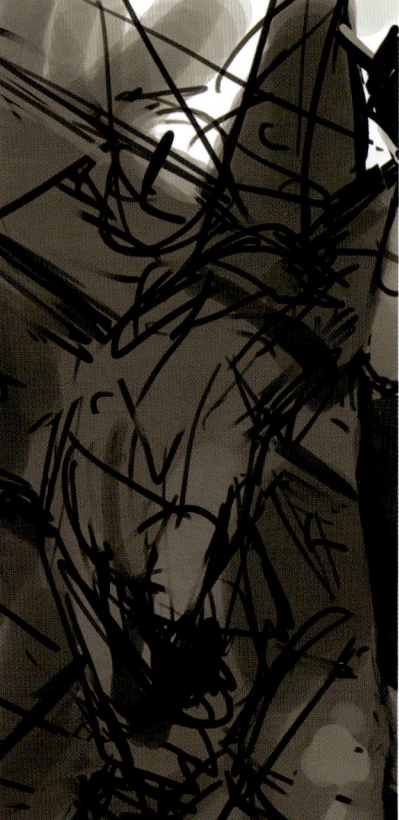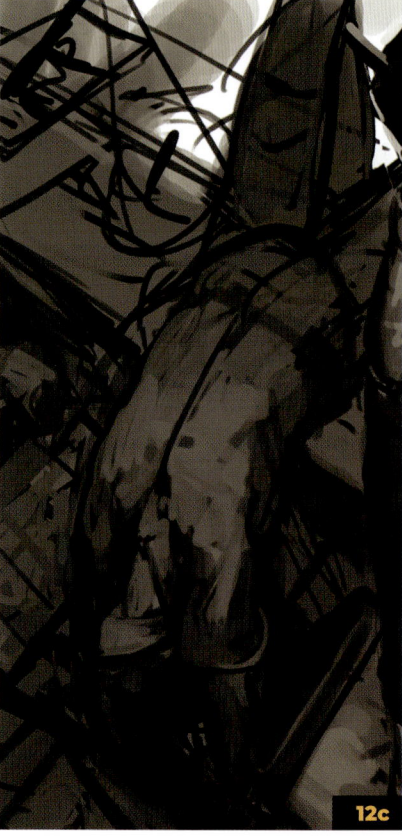

12b – 12c For secondary focal points like these, our main objective is to indicate the overall form and volume, using the perspective grid to help us. For example, we can first draw the torso as a cuboid aligned with the grid, and then subdivide and complexify it into a torso.

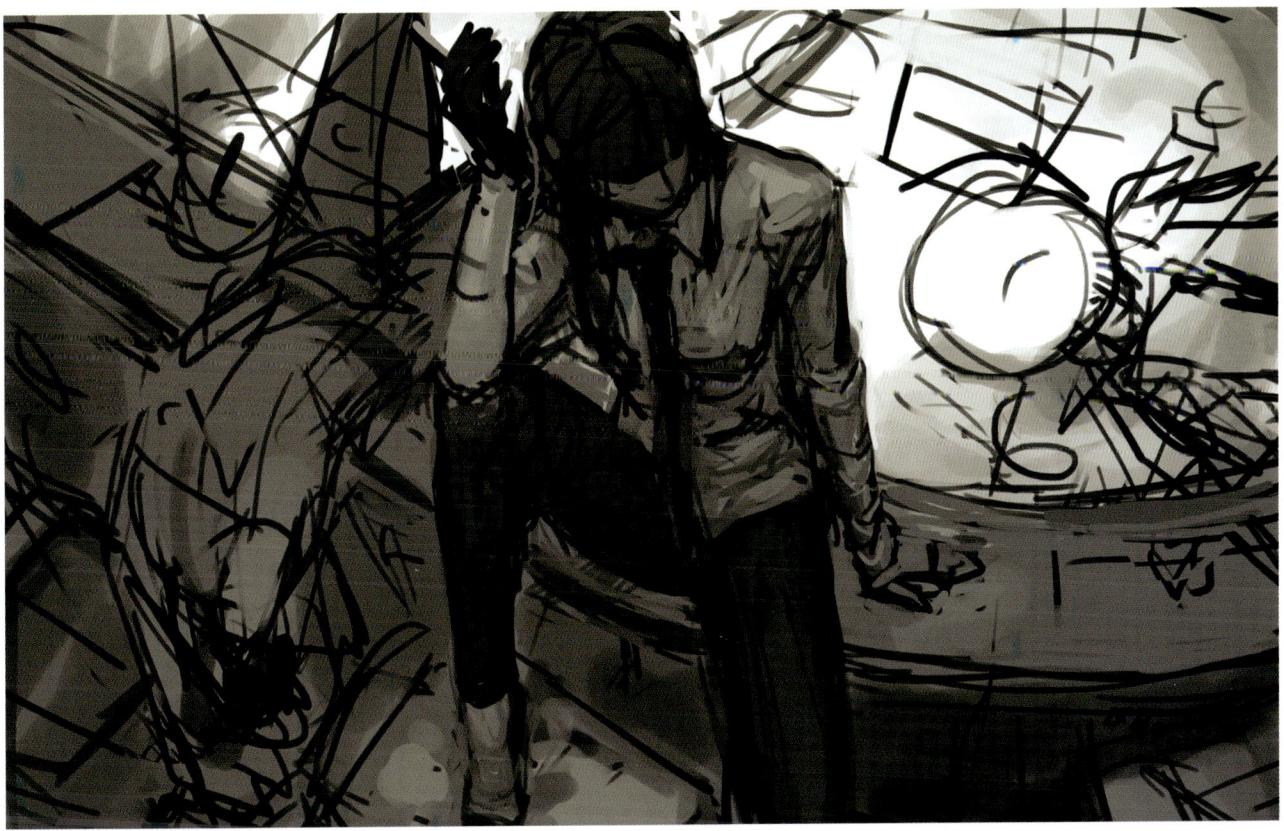

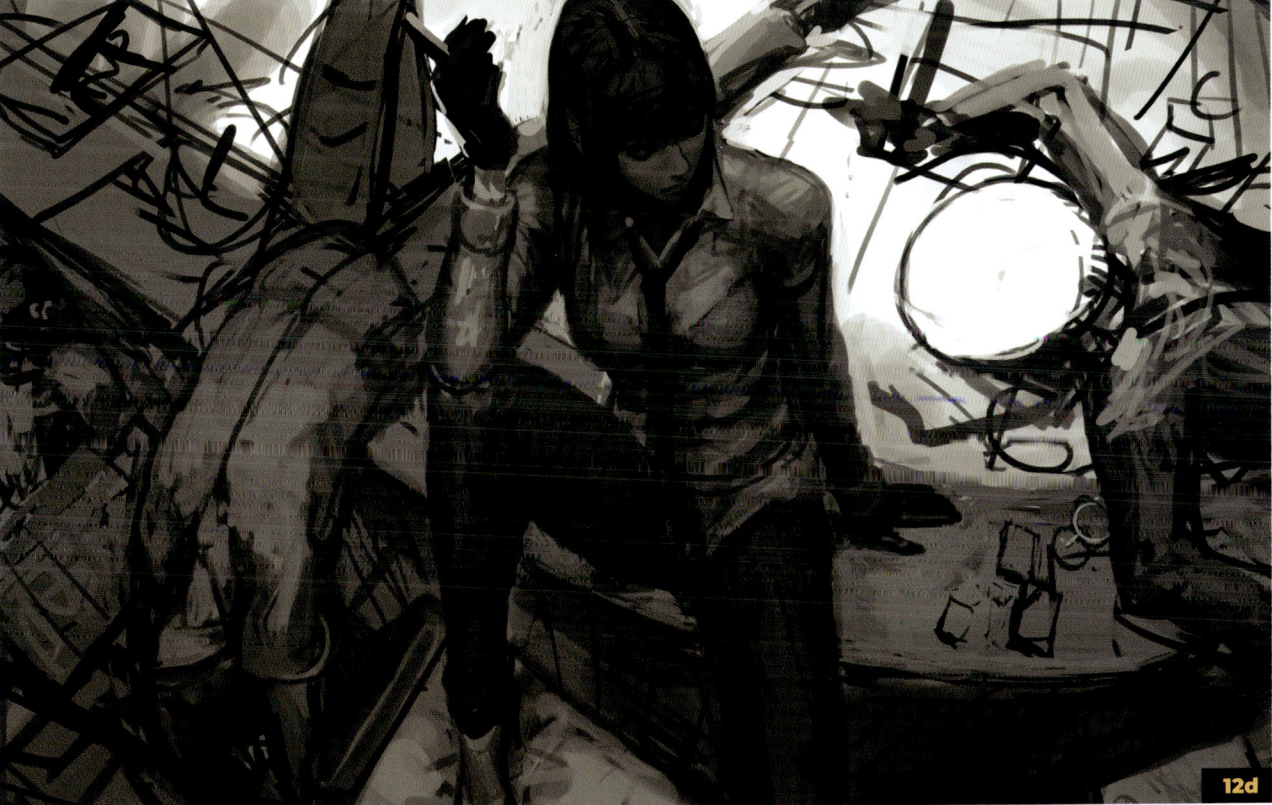

12d Slightly expanding the FOV lets viewers take in more of the scene, although we do lose a little of the "up-close" feeling.

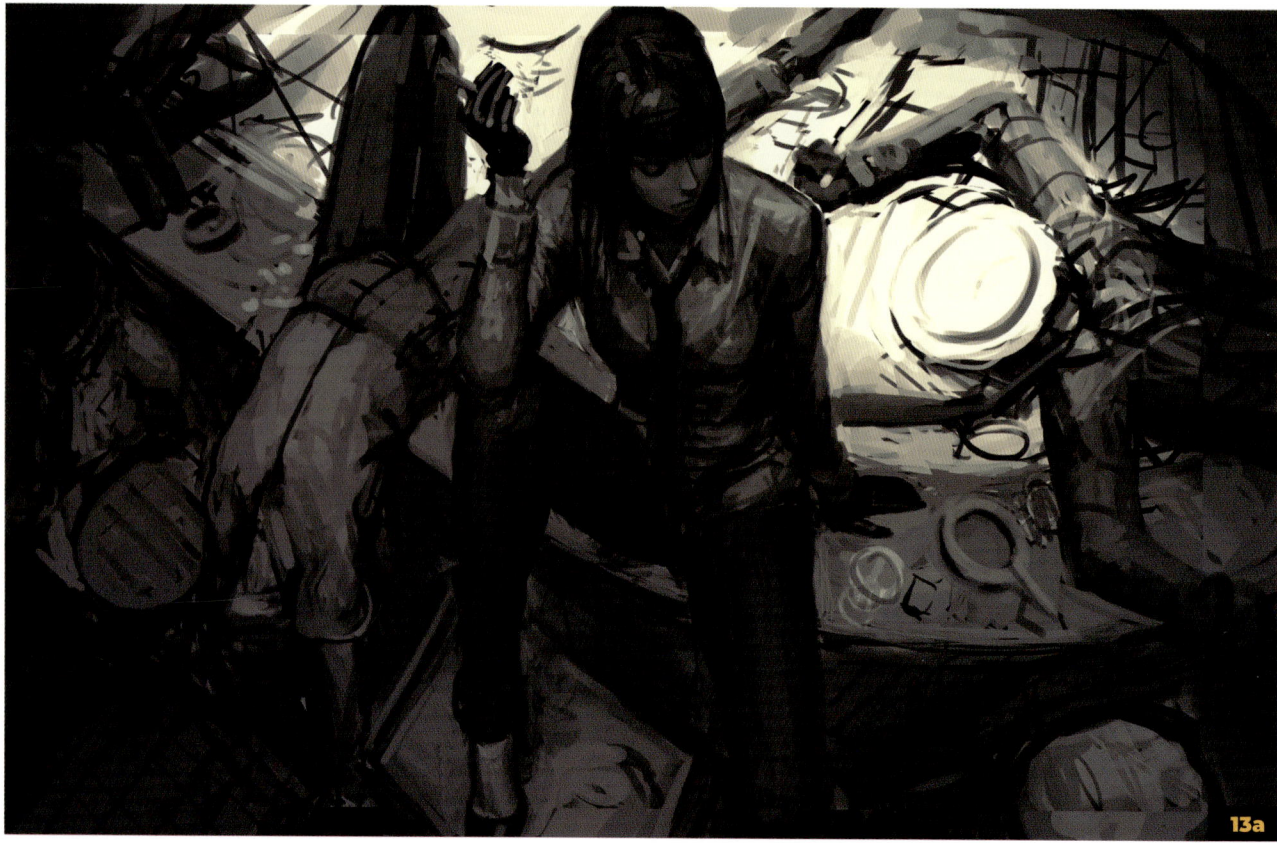

13a – 13b The Selective Color tool is quite intuitive – feel free to just play around with the sliders to get a good feel for it.

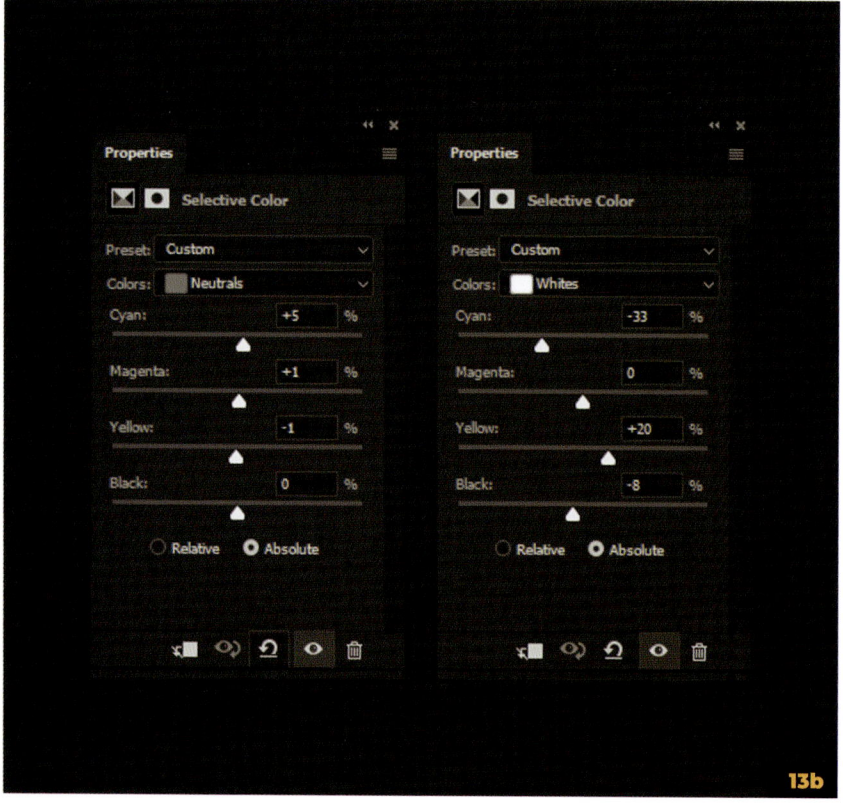

13 INTRODUCING BASIC COLORS

After a substantial amount of value painting, our piece is now ready for the process of adding color! This process varies from artist to artist based on personal preference, so I will be focusing more on explaining my reasons behind each step.

I like to begin by adding a Selective Color adjustment layer to introduce some base colors to the image. Choosing the colors to add, however, takes some figuring out. We have two main sources of lighting in the image: one an artificial lamp, the other natural moonlight. Depending on your composition, there could be any number of light sources with any color. Aside from using lighting strength to differentiate the effect of each source, color temperature is also an excellent option available to us.

In this case, I want the lamp to emit a warm-colored light, while the moonlight takes on a relatively cool color. This means the areas where the lamplight doesn't reach are generally going to appear more bluish than the areas where it does. To establish this relationship, we can tune our Selective Color layer as pictured.

With "Neutrals" selected from the Colors dropdown, we can raise the cyan and magenta sliders, while tuning down the yellow. This gives the entire image a cool tint, with the exception of the darkest and brightest areas. Next, with "Whites" selected, we can turn up yellow and turn down cyan and black, creating a warm look while giving the brightness a little boost at the same time.

14 EXPERIMENTING WITH ALTERNATIVES

We've been steadily making linear progress so far, which is great for making a clear and comprehensive tutorial, but it doesn't quite represent an important part of the digital painting process. So I think this is an excellent time to demonstrate and address a useful aspect of digital painting – the ability to branch off at any point in the process and test new ideas quickly and safely.

Using the same Selective Color adjustment layer, we can play around with the sliders to test out various color setups. Here I try out a more extreme version of our existing lighting color, but the colors feel like they come on too strongly. The limitations of the Selective Color layer mean that blues are added in areas where there shouldn't be any. But this is no problem – we can simply restore the sliders to their previous state or try something else.

The digital medium enables us to explore alternative compositions, colors, designs, and anything else at any time. You never know what great compositional and color choices you can discover – it's quick and risk-free, too!

WARM AND COLD COLORS

Warm and cold colors are not just limited to yellows versus blues – temperature is all relative. Within each color itself, there exists comparative warmth and coolness. For example, maroon could be considered a cooler red, and cyan a warmer blue. Aside from using these relationships to pick out interesting blends of local color, we can also use them to harmonize colors when colored light sources come into play. For example, objects of different colors, under the common influence of warm light, tend to present a warmer variation of their local color. This behavior can help clarify and differentiate the influence of differing light sources.

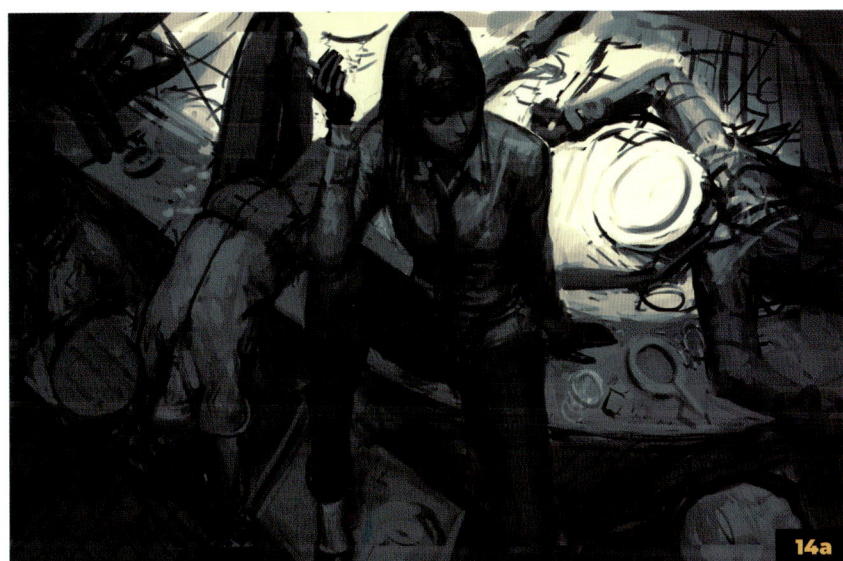

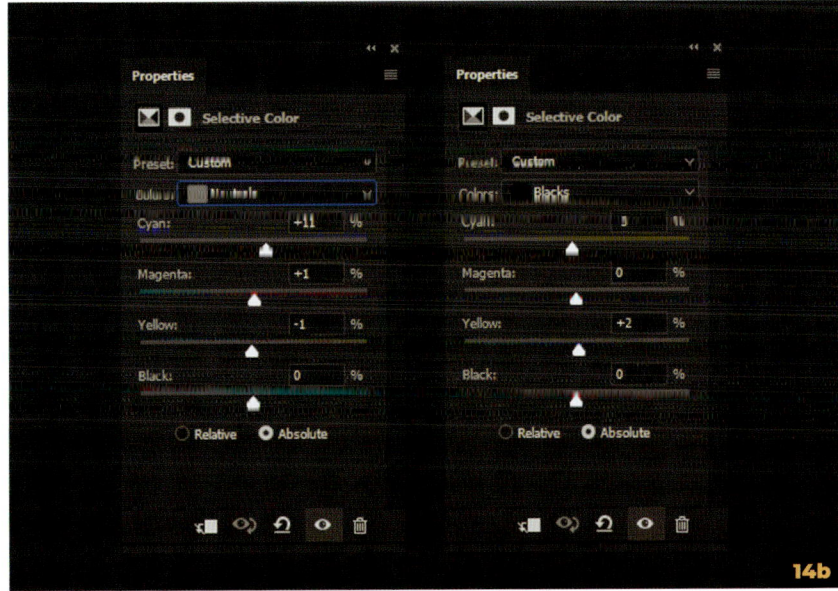

14a – 14b Each option in the "Colors" parameter adjusts a different part of the image. Apply changes in the "Red" category if you want to specifically adjust that color range, and so on.

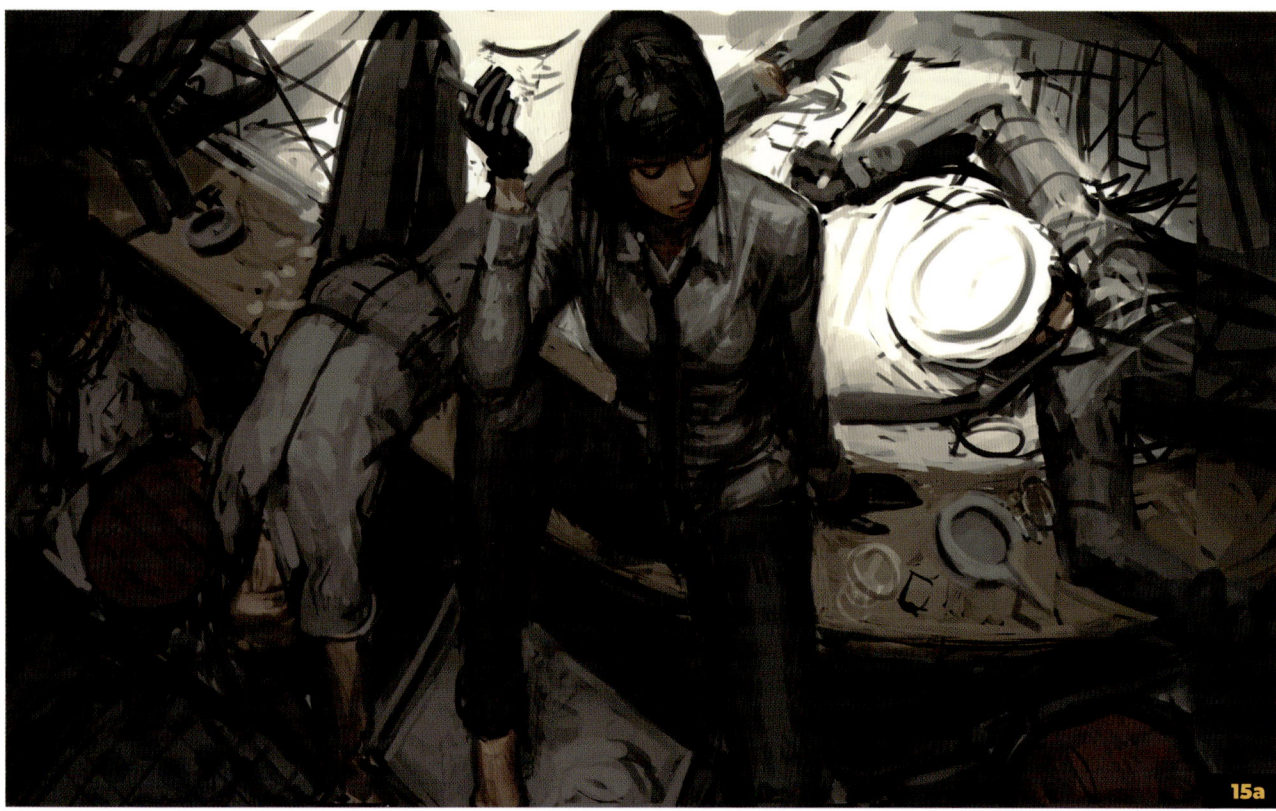

15a

15a – 15b The same image with the initial color setup, with local colors added into the mix using a Soft Light layer.

15 INTRODUCING LOCAL COLOR

After playing around with Selective Color options, I decide to stick with a minimal color scheme for the lighting, leaving some breathing room for our next step – adding local colors.

Local colors are essentially colors innate to materials – for example, gold bars and ruby gemstones have different local colors, regardless of what lighting they are seen in. You can learn more about how we see local colors on page 32. In this initial step, the relevant local colors are the colors of the table, skin tone, and stool seats.

In this first stage, we will start by applying these "anchor" colors – the ones that we know definitely need to be locked in. In this case, these important colors include skin, clothing, and the base colors of the furniture.

To do this, I add a new layer and set it to the Soft Light blending mode. Then I paint over the relevant areas using a solid brush set to each area's respective local color. I find Soft Light mode the most suitable and versatile for this purpose as it allows us to fine-tune the resulting hue, saturation, and brightness of the painted areas.

Immediately we can see the benefit of adding the anchor colors to the image – while the painting still looks a little bland, we've completely lost the monochrome and "unreal" feel of the earlier stages.

Pass Through
Normal
Dissolve
Darken
Multiply
Color Burn
Linear Burn
Darker Color
Lighten
Screen
Color Dodge
Linear Dodge (Add)
Lighter Color
Overlay
Soft Light
Hard Light
Vivid Light
Linear Light
Pin Light
Hard Mix
Difference
Exclusion
Subtract
Divide
Hue
Saturation
Color
Luminosity
Pass Through

15b

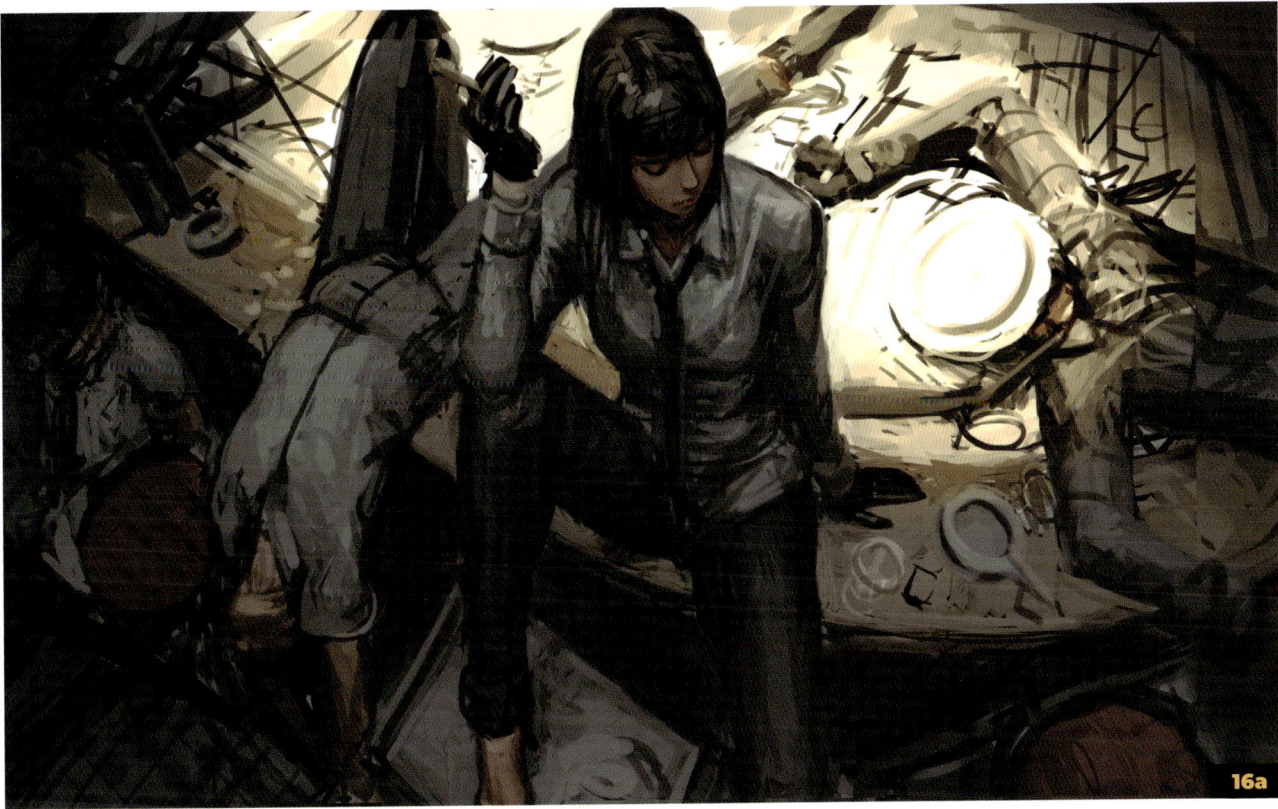

16a – 16c Use a Color Dodge layer and Color sliders to adjust colors and values at the same time.

16 MANAGING THE LIGHTING COLORS

With the local colors now in the mix, the color difference between the lamplight and moonlight feels too suppressed, and no longer as clear as it should be. While there is still a noticeable yellow tint to the bright light in the previous step, it's a little weak for our needs. To ensure this key pair of lighting blocks maintains its distinctiveness, I want to boost the color strength of the lamplight.

To do so, I add another layer set to the Color Dodge blending mode. Using Color Dodge is a great way to brighten an area and simultaneously add vibrancy to its midtones, but we must be careful not to use a color or value that is too bright.

To bring the image to the stage shown above, I use the settings pictured left. Notice the Brightness value (the "B" slider) is only set to 33, as Color Dodge can easily make colors too bright and intense, I lightly brush this color on with a soft airbrush to make sure it doesn't overwhelm the area with pure white.

The image now looks far more developed – the two key light sources are easily distinguished and many of the scene's elements have been assigned their appropriate local colors.

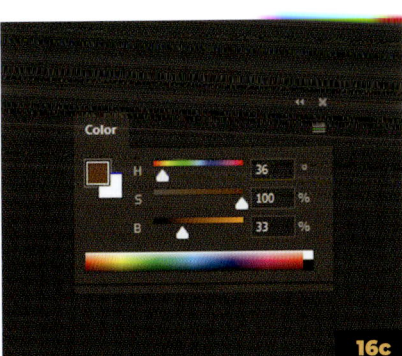

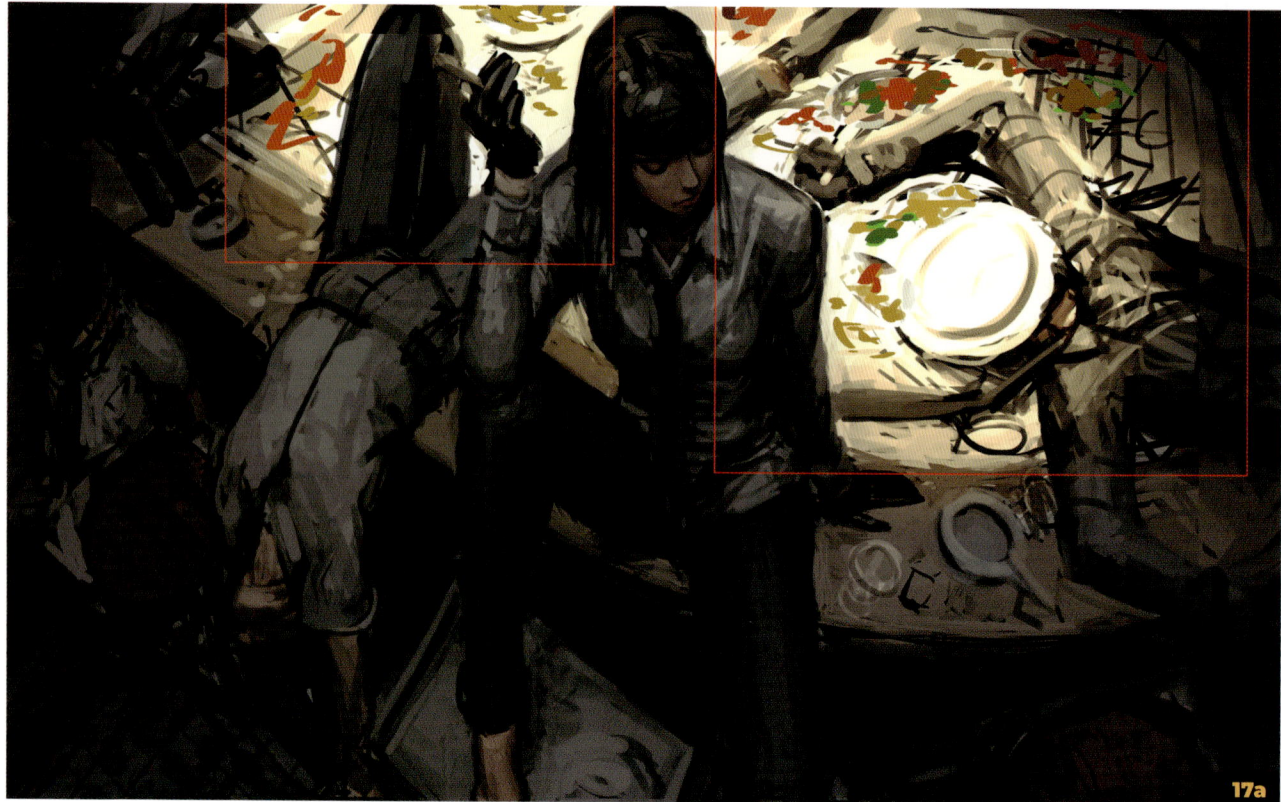

17a – 17b Working proof of the composition with the additional food colors added. They aren't painted in detail – these are simply placeholder strokes!

17 FILLING IN ADDITIONAL COLORS

We aren't quite done with adding colors yet! Our objective is to create an illustration essentially showing the aftermath of an action scene, so we need a lot of food-related debris to be strewn over the table for the image to work as intended.

I use some very rough brushstrokes to quickly find out where and how I should place my colors, and to make sure they are balanced with the composition. I change and move around the brushstrokes until I feel they are in satisfactory positions.

For the moment, this extra layer of food color acts as a "working proof" or placeholder that we can easily return to later when we are painting the actual food debris in detail.

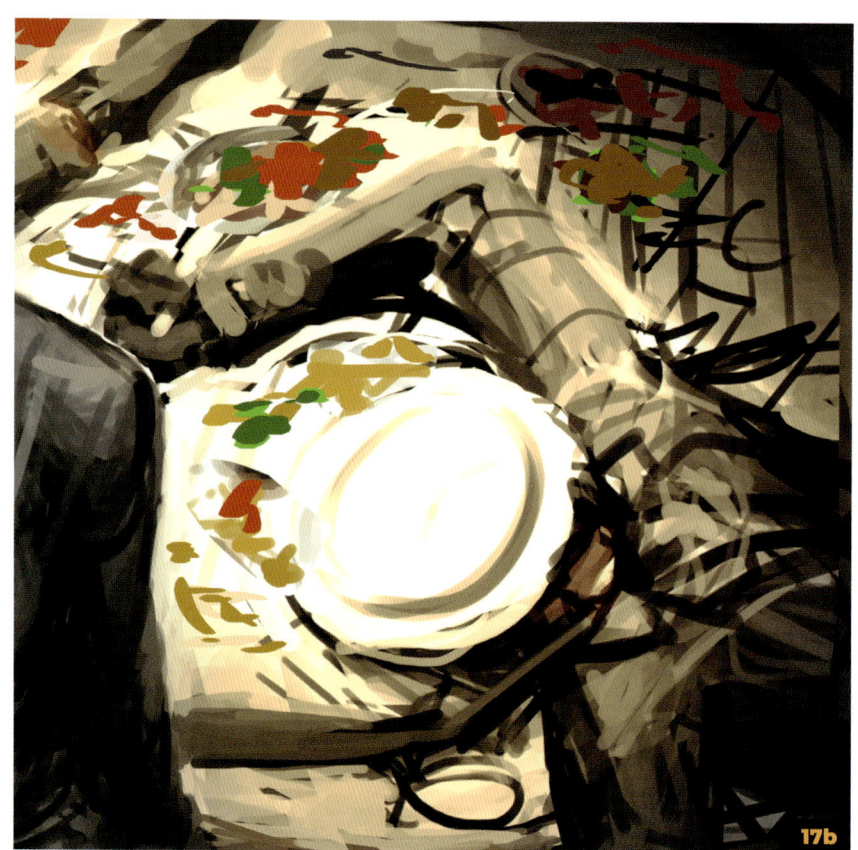

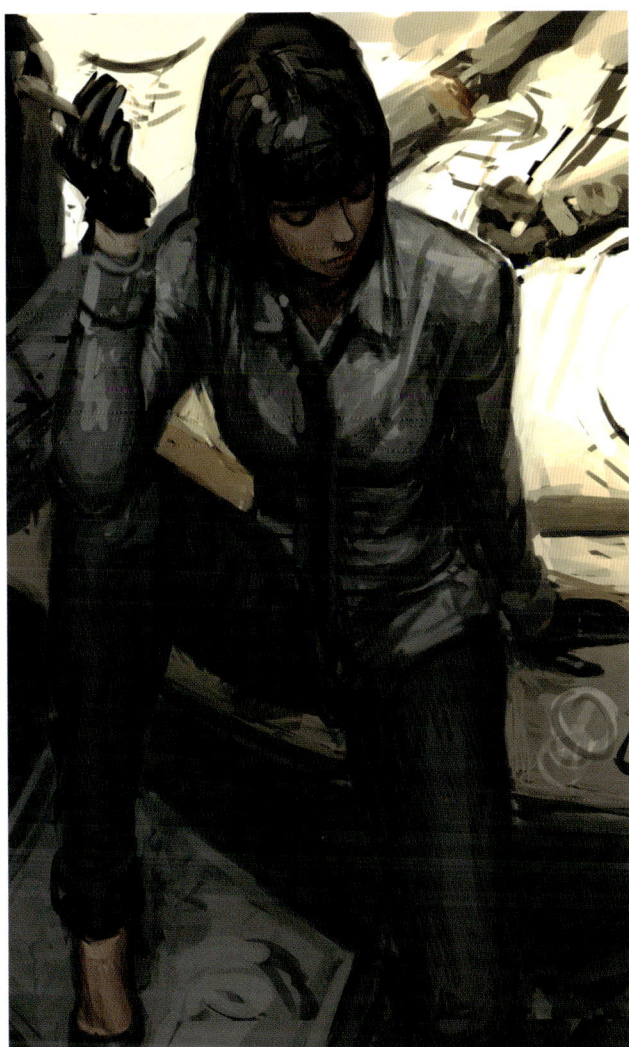
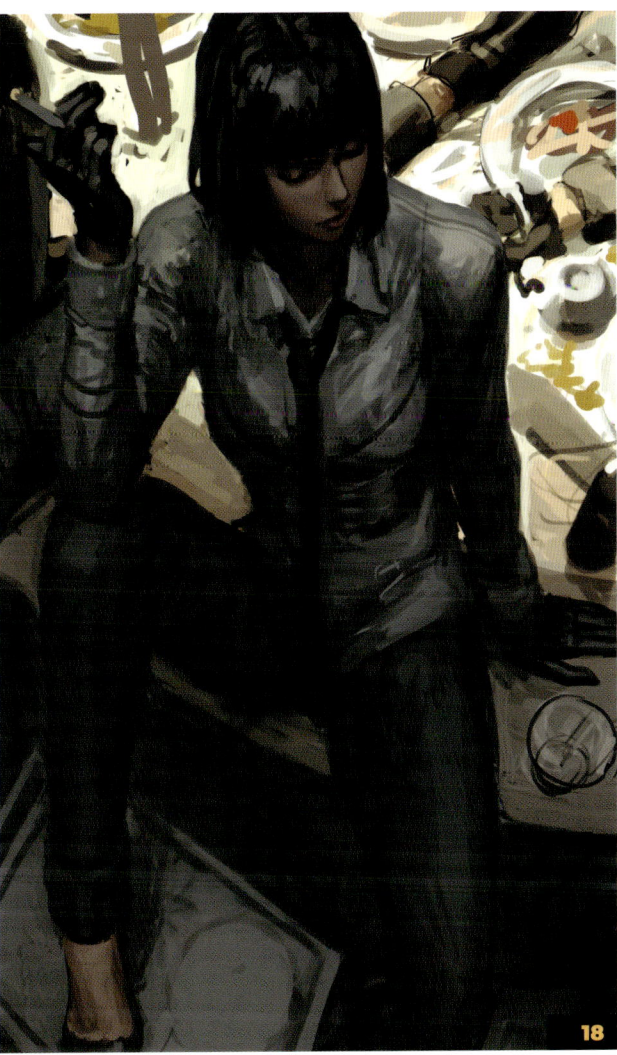

18 Before and after shots of the initial painting process phase.

18 PAINTING CHARACTER COLORS

By this point, we've developed the sketch to a state where there are no longer a lot of large, sweeping changes left to make or major elements left to add. This is when I feel ready to start painting in full color.

We are still applying the same concepts we have used so far, but because the value and color schemes of the composition are already well established, we can easily and organically paint in new objects using existing colors and tones as reference. In this part of the tutorial, I will start breaking down and going through some of the important changes that are made during this painting stage.

In this phase, I start actively trying to correct minor issues that have cropped up since the final black-and-white stage in step 12. I noticed earlier that the character's shoulders were a little too rounded and hunched, so I adjust her to be sitting more upright. During this phase we can also clean up the presentation of the forms already present, such as removing any thick, leftover sketch lines. This will make any future revisions and tweaks a lot easier.

THE SOFT ROUND BRUSH AND LASSO COMBO

While the default Hard Round brush discussed on page 269 is amazingly versatile, it's not always the optimal choice for certain situations. When painting elements that are more sensitive to overtexturing, we might not want our brushstrokes to be very visible. Some materials could look quite strange with a lot of textured brushstrokes: for example, a very smooth matte material, skin, or a highly polished specular surface, as we looked at in the Light chapters earlier.

If the subject is a complex form with a difficult silhouette, it can be inefficient or unintuitive to paint it stroke by stroke with a hard-edged brush. A simple sphere would be unnecessarily tedious to paint using single brushstrokes. Softer shadows and lighting, such as ambient occlusion effects, also face the same difficulties.

This is when the default Soft Round brush and Lasso tool come in. The Soft Round brush allows us to create very smooth, airbrush-like transitions, and to manage gradients intuitively and easily, but it tends to spill over due to its diffused nature. However, using the Lasso tool, we can very quickly and precisely restrict the area in which the airbrush can act, allowing us to efficiently manage both gradients and edges wherever needed.

The example here shows this combo in action: I use the Lasso tool first to draw out the silhouette of a stone, and then I switch to the brush. With a few simple strokes, I am able to easily indicate quite a complex form consisting of widely varying surfaces. A large brush size allows us to smoothly paint the large top surface and its overall shape, while a smaller brush size takes care of the beveled edges. To finish off, I add a smooth shadow on the left side with one large stroke.

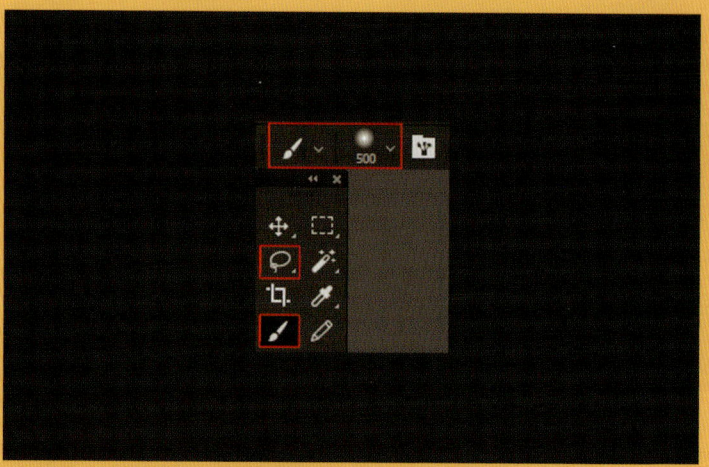

Soft Round brush and Lasso. The Lasso tool, Soft Round brush, and varied brush sizes make a great combo for painting smoother surfaces.

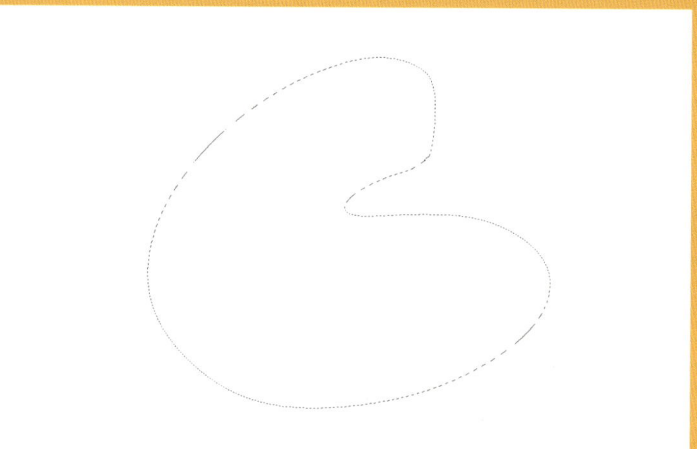

Lasso a shape. Selecting the target area can also be done with the Magic Wand or Quick Selection tools if needed.

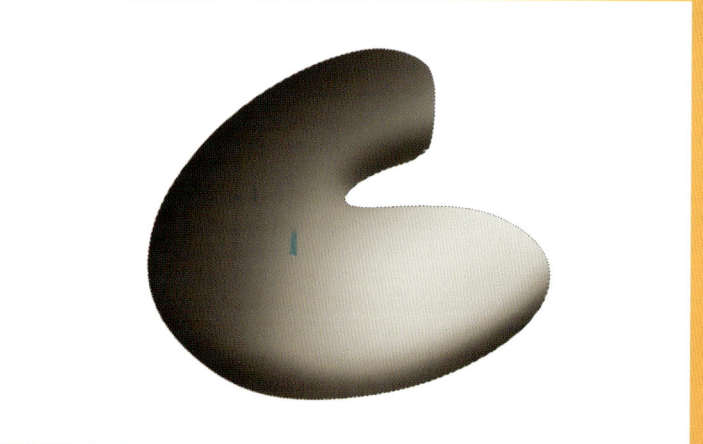

Soft shading. The results of airbrushing the selected area, using the Soft Round brush at a larger size for the big gradients and at a smaller size for the firmer edges.

19 SECONDARY FOCAL AREAS

We now repeat the same process for our secondary characters – cleaning up unwanted thick lines, defining forms more precisely, and making small changes to improve their general presentation. Small details do a lot to make the scene more convincing, such as the necktie flopping across the table, the ash in the ashtray, and the folds in the characters' shirts.

20 CONVEYING A STORY

Taking a closer look at this extra on the right, I introduce a couple of details to make it clear that they are not just lying there of their own volition. The plate under the left arm and the food spilling from the plate onto their face add a messy, scrappy look to the situation. I also add a couple of extra dishes and bottles in the upper right corner, to fill in the awkward empty space and give the impression that the character landed on a packed dinner table.

HOTKEYS AND LAYERS

Hotkeys are great tools that can help make your digital painting process a much more pleasant one. Don't be afraid to assign hotkeys to suit your preferences – if you find yourself frustrated at having to click several times to access a function you use often, give it a hotkey.

Layers are more of a double-edged sword – make full use of them to separate parts of the drawing or save versions as you go, but beware you don't clutter your file up to your own detriment!

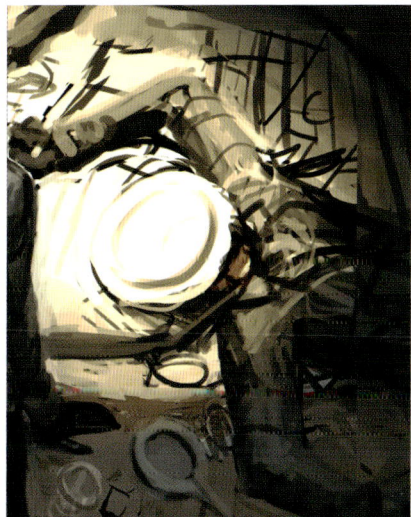
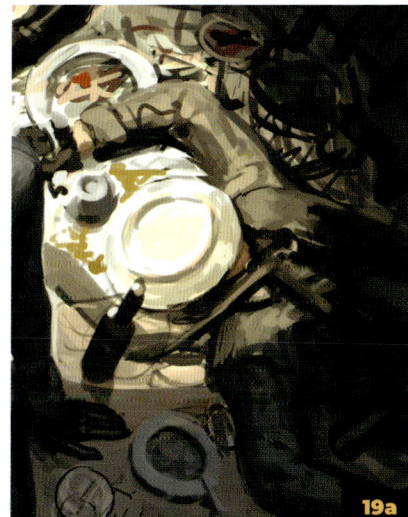

19a

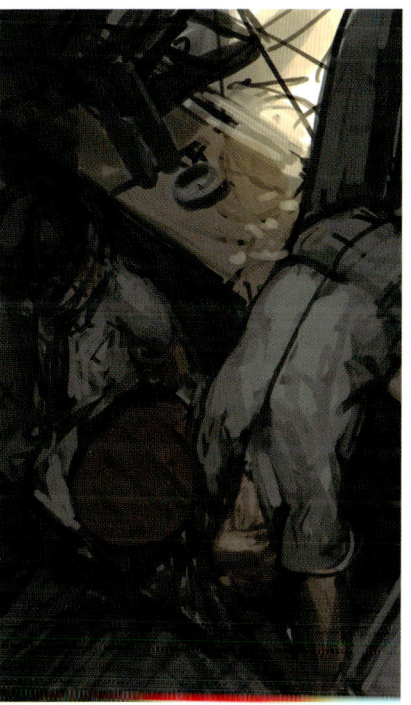
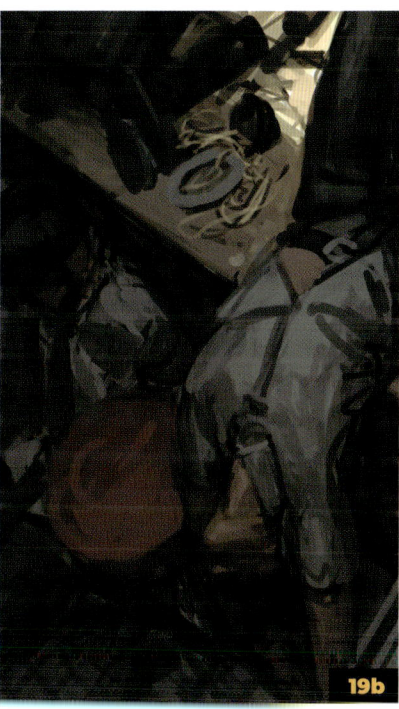

19b

19a – 19b A quick glance at the overarching changes at this stage. Untucking one half of the character's white shirt makes it look like they got knocked out after a tough fight!

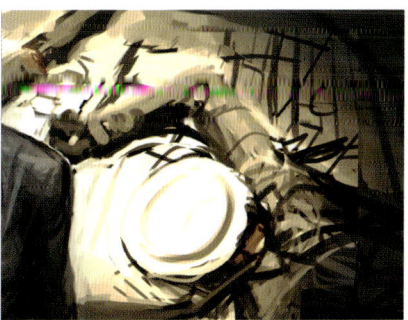
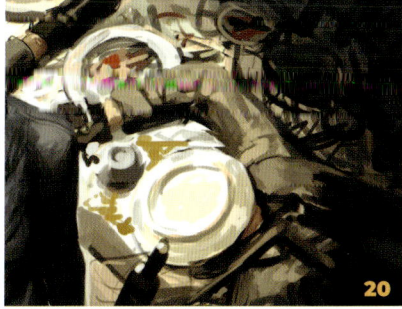

20

20 Although rough, these additional objects develop this area of the composition substantially.

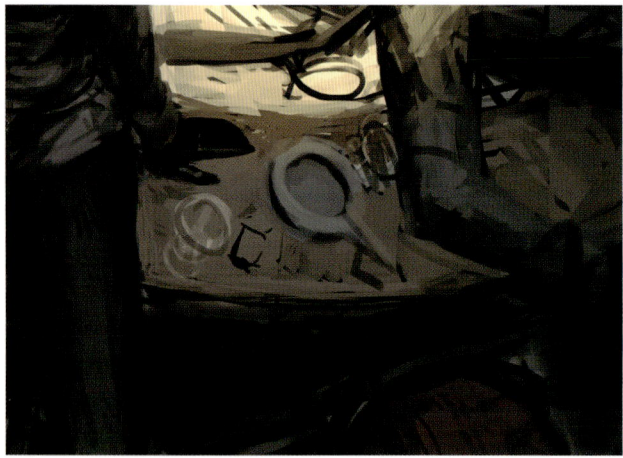
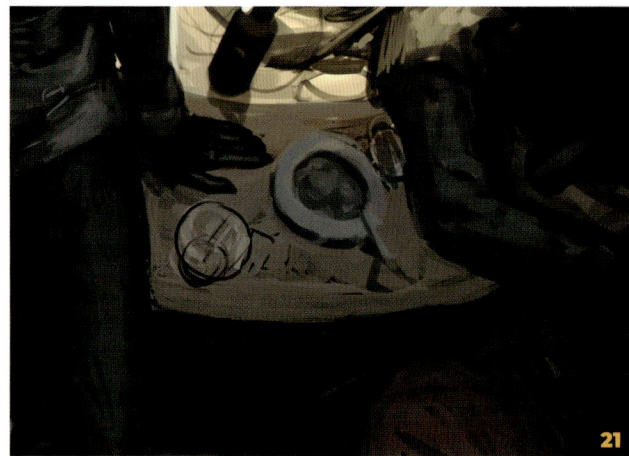

21 Notice how the stool's top looks much more correct and in perspective when we remove the rough sketch line.

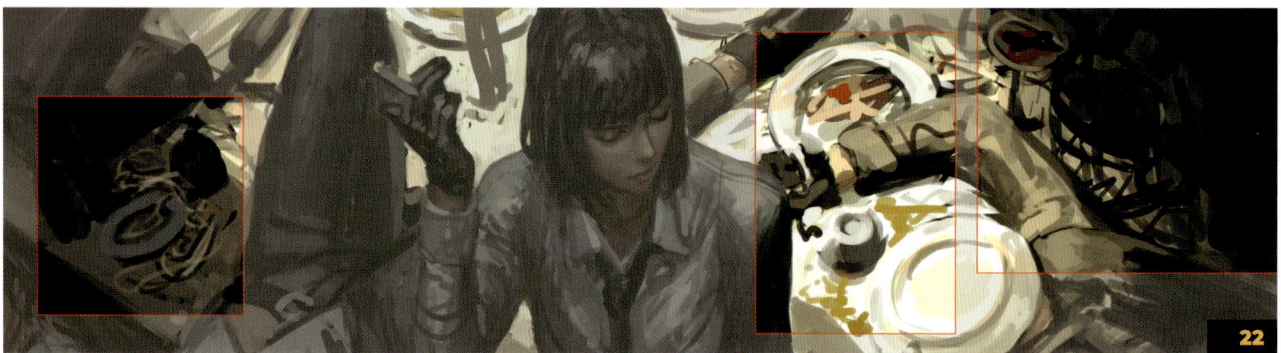

22 Some areas of interest to which we've added visual complexity.

21 CLEANING UP ROUGH AREAS

We have been working quite roughly up until very recently, focusing on the big picture, which of course is key to the image's success. However, at this stage we can start taking the time to add more precision to the piece. If we look at the tabletop surface above, the rough strokes do not represent its actual form very well. At a glance, they add a few unintentional jagged and randomly beveled edges, which we don't want. To resolve them, we can paint over any unwanted brushstrokes, especially near sensitive areas such as the edges.

22 ADDING COMPLEXITY

Another aspect of the painting process I want to draw attention to is the addition of visual "noise." Real places and things often exist in much higher detail than paintings can reasonably replicate one-to-one. Logically, it's much more feasible to capture the *impression* of realism rather than literal realism, which is where visual noise and density come into play.

By introducing little bits and pieces of very densely packed and well-drawn detail at strategic areas in the composition, we create the illusion that the entire piece is drawn at an equivalently high resolution. This gives us leeway to be a bit looser with the bulk of the details, especially those not in the center of attention.

Well-controlled visual noise gives a strong impression of a high level of detail without overwhelming the image or the viewer, which helps the resulting scene look more believable and realistic.

At this point in the painting process, our goal is to plan our high-detail sites and decide on which areas we will commit to drawing more accurately.

23 PROGRESS CHECK-UP

It's been some time since we started painting freely, so let's review our progress by zooming out to a thumbnail-sized view and taking a wider look at the piece. The first thing you may notice is that the before and after shots look quite similar – if you squint, they look nearly identical! This is actually a good sign that we are progressing as expected. It shows that the deliberate choices we made during the planning and drafting processes are still in play, and that we have retained all the important aspects of the composition, even after the rigorous process of painting, cleaning up, and detailing.

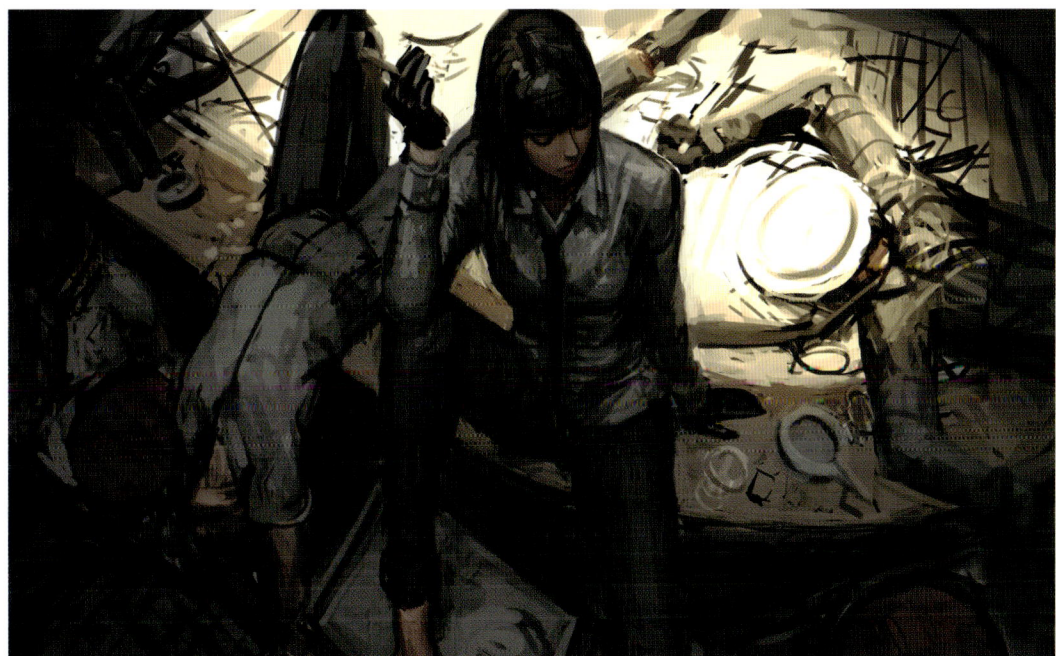

23 Comparing the before (above) and after (below), we can see that the overall composition is preserved, but the scene and story have been greatly developed.

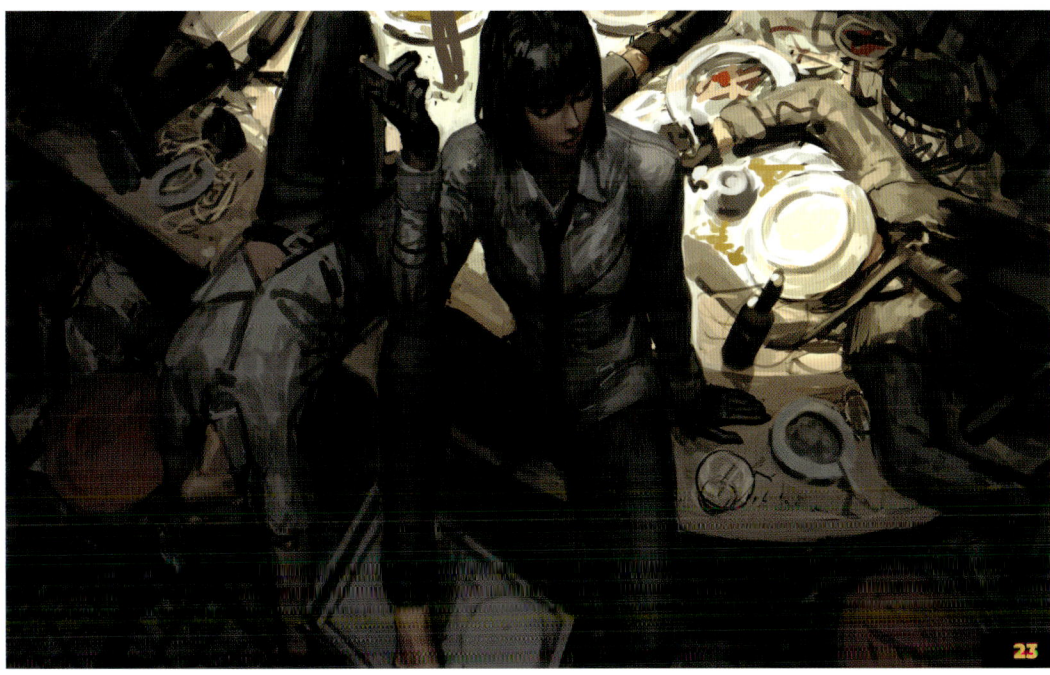

Importantly, this means the protection of key elements – such as the value relationship between our light sources and shadows – has contributed greatly to maintaining the composition's integrity. In the event that the thumbnails don't quite align – especially if the new thumbnail has ended up looking "worse" – we may need to review our recent progress. This is where Photoshop's layers are very useful – we can quickly bring up an earlier state of the painting to superimpose over the current image and check where undesired deviations have occurred.

However, not all changes are bad. Sometimes a well done painting pass can add surprise improvements to a piece. If you think the new thumbnail works just as well or even better than the original plan, feel free to stick with it!

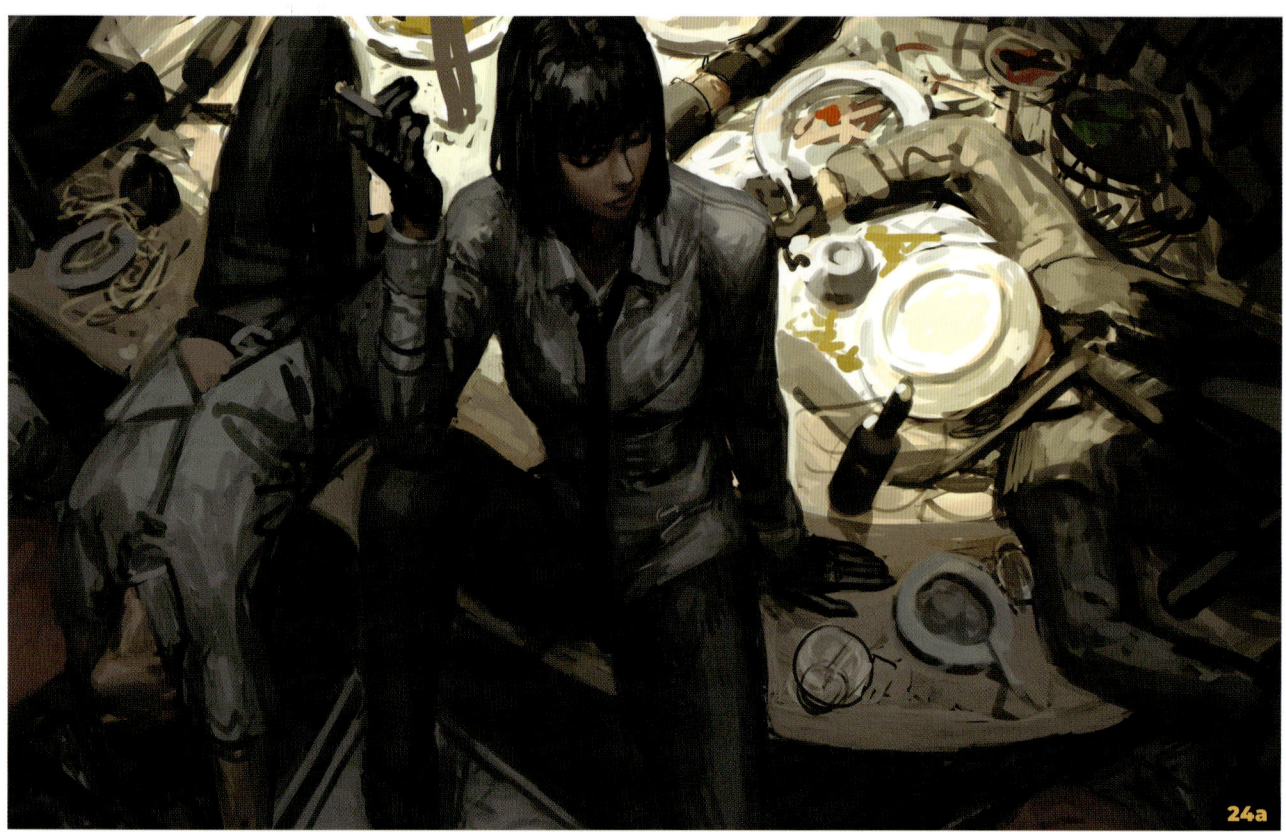

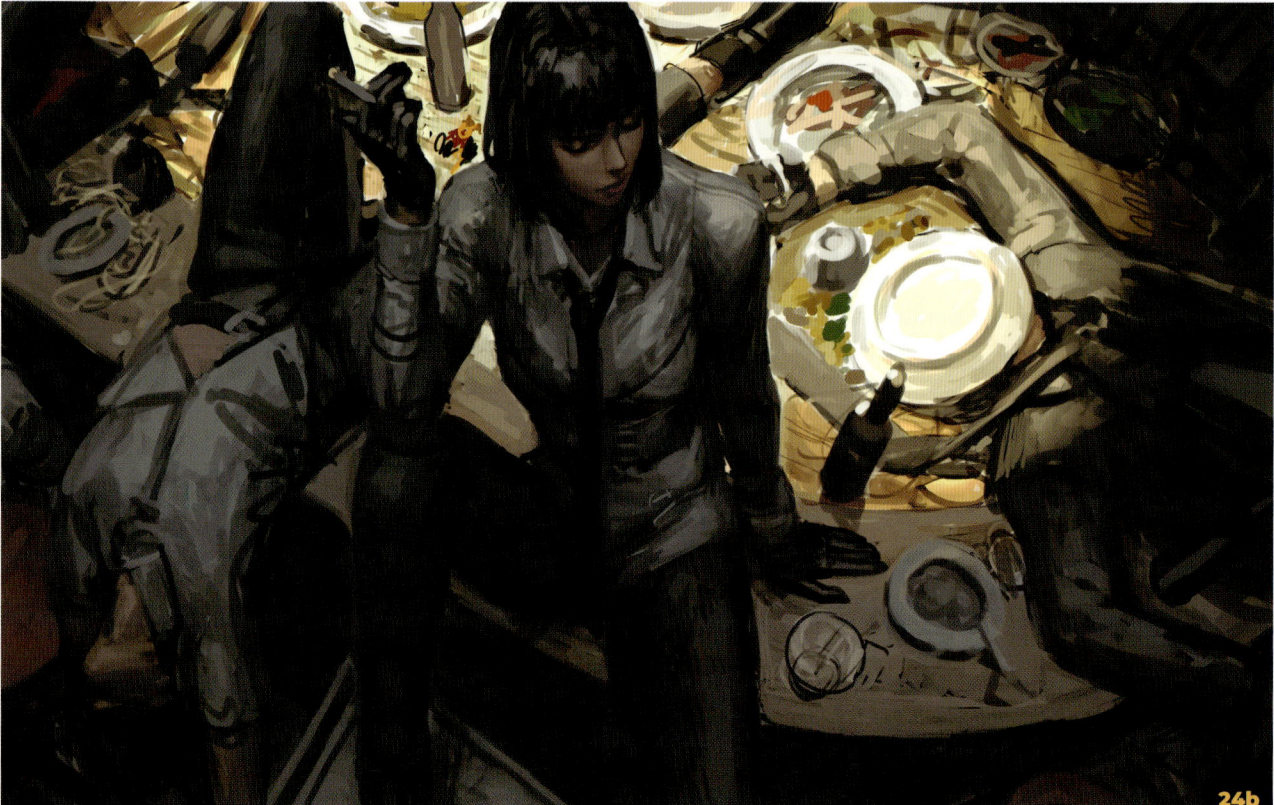

24a – 24b Strengthening the local color of the table surface to give it a distinct wooden look.

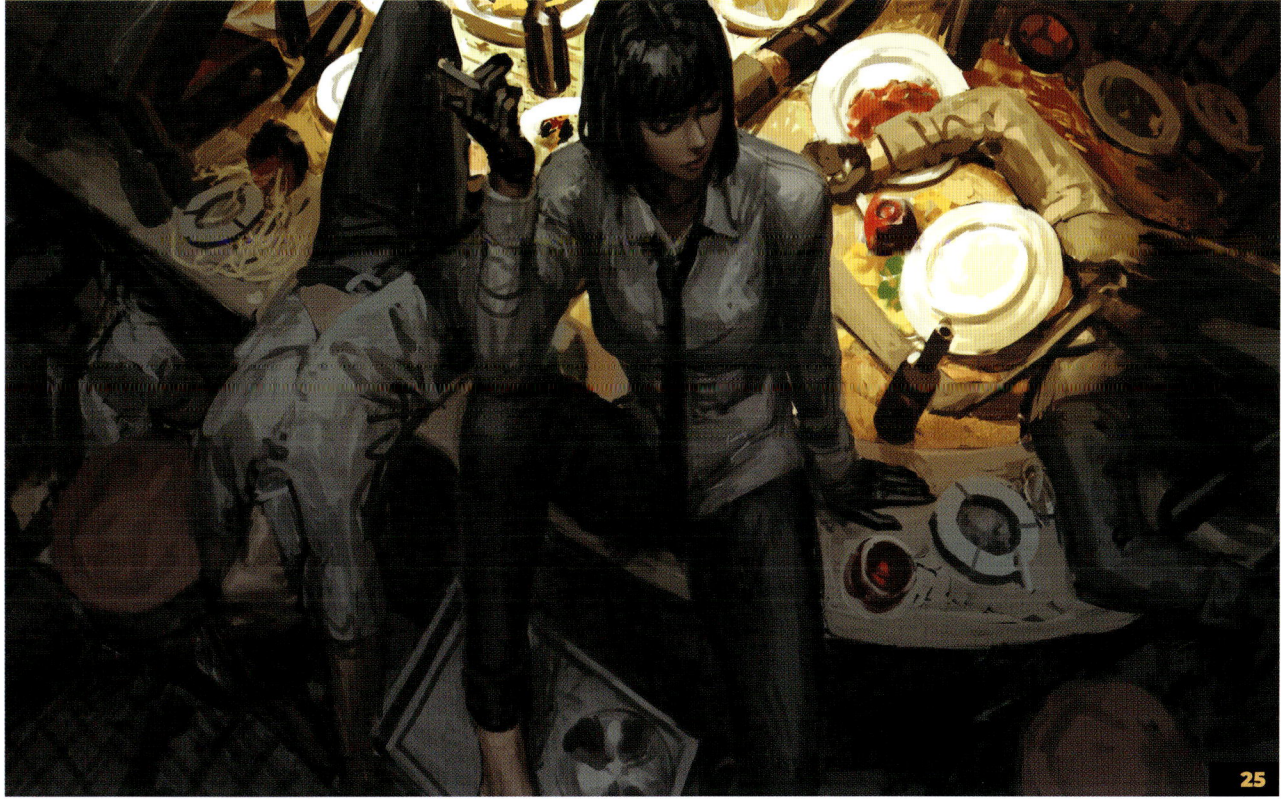

25 Upping the warmth of the light to create a stronger contrast.

24 TROUBLESHOOTING

So far we've done well in maintaining the composition and color scheme as the painting has developed. Moving forward, however, we also have to actively notice and solve problems to further improve the piece.

First, let's take a look at the most vibrant part of our piece: the brightly lit part of the table surface. A quick glance tells me that something feels a little off. Comparing the table surface color to the porcelain plates and food debris, I realize that it shouldn't be this odd, almost ceramic shade of beige, especially when there's no tablecloth.

To resolve this issue, I add a Soft Light layer and apply a solid brown to the relevant areas to give the table a clearly wooden look. This slightly darkens the brightness of our original value plan, but makes the area look much more believable and gives the table a more definitive material.

25 READJUSTING THE LIGHTING

Having resolved the bleached color of the tabletop, another issue appears. At this point, the presence of many local colors in the spotlit area has slightly overshadowed the lighting color. While this occurrence is not necessarily "wrong," I want the lamplight to have a more dominant and vibrant presence in the composition.

To make this adjustment, I add another layer with the blend mode set to Overlay. This allows me to add a tint of bright yellow to the table using a soft brush, as well as adding an appealing bit of color bleed to the edges of the lit area.

I also take the chance to paint up and develop the elements in that area to fit the new lighting and color scheme. For example, I add a few splashes of red and give the beer bottles a deep-brown, translucent color.

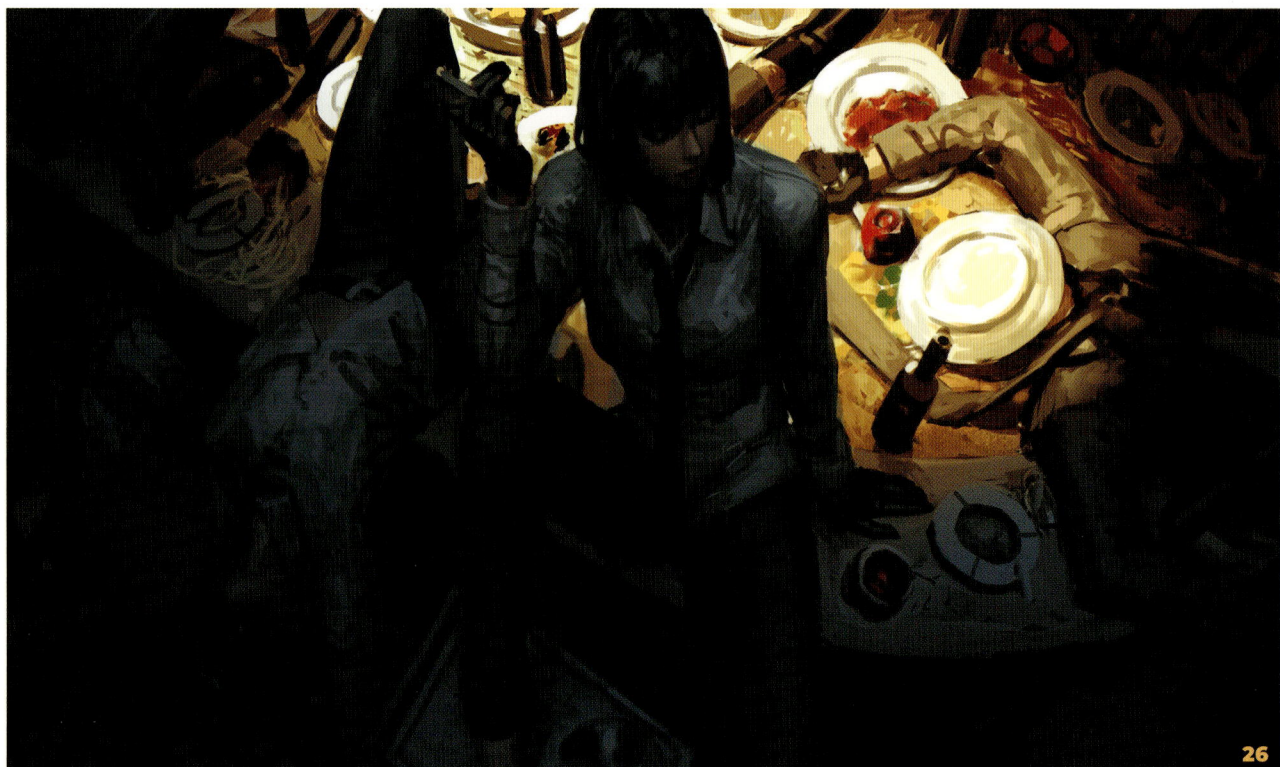

26 Matching the increased warmth by adding blues.

26 BALANCING COLOR TEMPERATURE

Having just adjusted our warm light source and spotlight area significantly, we should also take a look at their impact on the overall image to make sure we have not affected the composition in unintentional ways.

One thing I notice is that with the slightly dimmer yellow lamp light (compared to the paler, brighter tone it had previously), the moonlit and spotlit areas are now blending a little too close together in value.

To recapture our original intention of giving the viewer the impression of an isolated oasis of warm light in the gloomy night, I decide to overlay a dim, strongly bluish tone over the areas that the spotlight can't reach. This makes it much clearer that the scene is set at night. Comparatively, the previous image looks as if it could just be a rainy day outside – which isn't a bad idea in itself, just not our intention for this piece.

TIME MANAGEMENT AND BREAKS

Sometimes it's really easy to get into the zone and work for hours, but other times it's tough to even pick up your stylus and start drawing. It can be frustrating for artists to experience art blocks or fatigue, exacerbated by the very personal nature of creating art. I deal with it by reminding myself that my work is a marathon, not a sprint, and I am allowed to slow down and rest.

When I feel like a painting is not working out, I like to take some time off, browse Pinterest for ideas, or take a nap. My personal rule of thumb is that I should be enjoying myself while creating art – if I found my work constantly miserable, it definitely wouldn't last!

27 CHECKING PERSPECTIVE

Before we continue to develop the piece, I think this is a good time to talk about using the perspective grid correctly. The perspective grid has been a loyal companion to us for our journey thus far, keeping our parallel edges properly aligned and serving as a helpful guide as we sketch in new objects. The more accurately our objects are placed in perspective, the more easily we can light and paint an immersive scene.

However, despite its ease of use, as we start to finalize a lot of the objects in the scene, a bit more attention needs to be paid when using the grid. Consider the three bottles shown here, which all seem to correctly follow the grid. However, the first looks a little too stubby, while the third looks a little too stretched. This is because these two examples were created solely to follow the grid, without taking into account the actual angle and POV from which they are seen.

In the middle example, we understand that we are looking down on the bottle from a high but not extreme angle, and therefore we can foreshorten the sides of the bottle to make sure they're to scale. Too short and it looks like a really stubby bottle; too long and it looks too tall and thin to be believable!

In conclusion, it's important that we keep in mind the full surrounding context, even when drawing small items, and not leave our decisions completely to the grid.

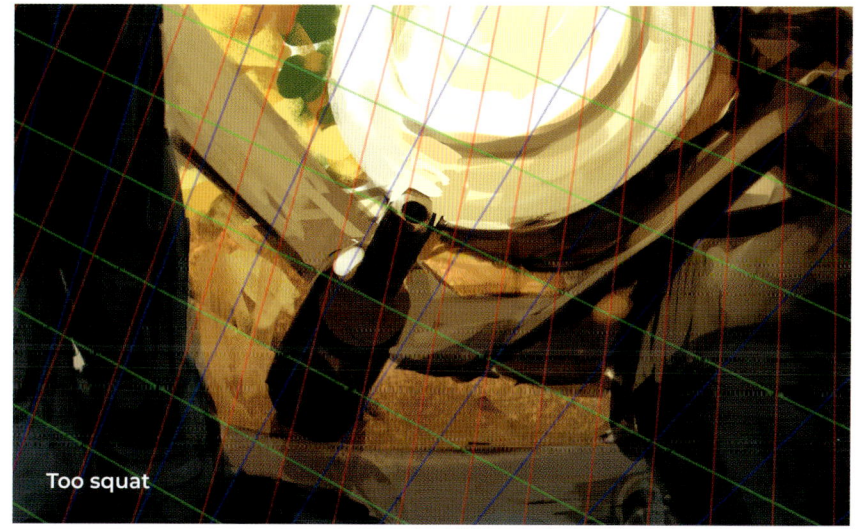

Too squat

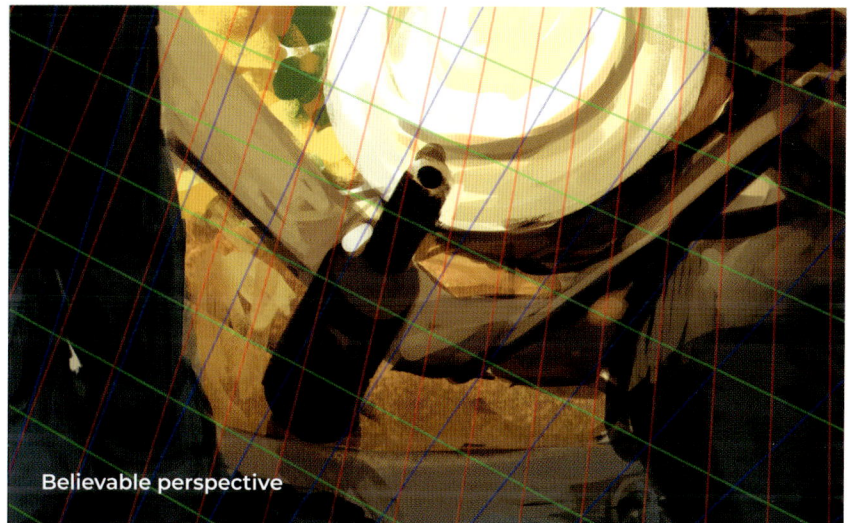

Believable perspective

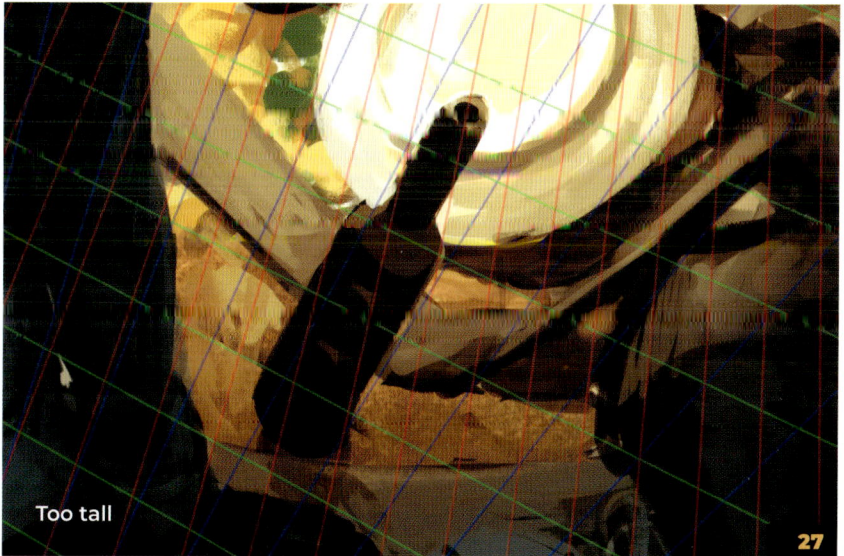

Too tall

27 Comparing the same bottle, drawn according to the grid, but taking different contexts into account.

CREATING REALISM WITH ROUGH PAINTING

Painting roughly isn't just a way to save time and energy, which are obviously important resources to manage, but it can actually help create a carefully crafted illusion of reality.

Right after you turn off your lights before going to bed, take a careful look around your room and try to actively distinguish one object from another. It's likely that in darkness you will find a lot of colors and shapes become fuzzy and blend together. We don't really notice this phenomenon in daily life – it's something we just subconsciously understand and accept. We simply don't see well and can't distinguish details in the dark. This is where rough painting shines: To give an illusion of reality, our image should aim to replicate how we, as humans, see. Thus painting a dark area to be rough and fuzzy in detail is perfect for our purposes.

In the first two images on the right, notice how in dim light and dark shadows, we can get away with leaving things a little rougher. The opposite applies for brightly lit areas, where the image has to be rendered up to a certain level of precision and sharpness to align with our expectations of "reality." When we are looking at a brightly lit desk in real life we expect what we see to be clear and well defined, with plenty of details easily visible to us.

In the second image, we can see how these principles hold true. The brighter area has been given more attention and sharper highlights, and it still looks like it needs more fine-tuning to look realistic! The shadowed area looks fine, even though it is painted very roughly.

This particular relationship between brightness and an "acceptable" level of roughness holds true consistently throughout the composition. In the third image, most of the scene is well lit by moonlight or the table lamp, so I have painted most of it quite sharply to meet viewer expectations. However, the areas on the character that are in shadow, such as the neck region, look satisfactory despite the rougher brushstrokes used.

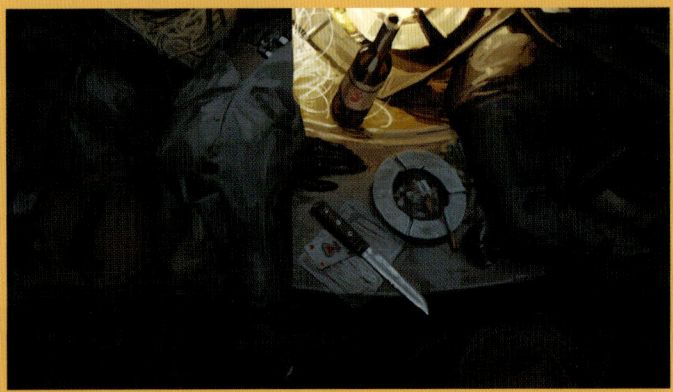

Detail levels. Compare the level of detail between dark areas and brightly lit ones. The allowable discrepancy is quite visible!

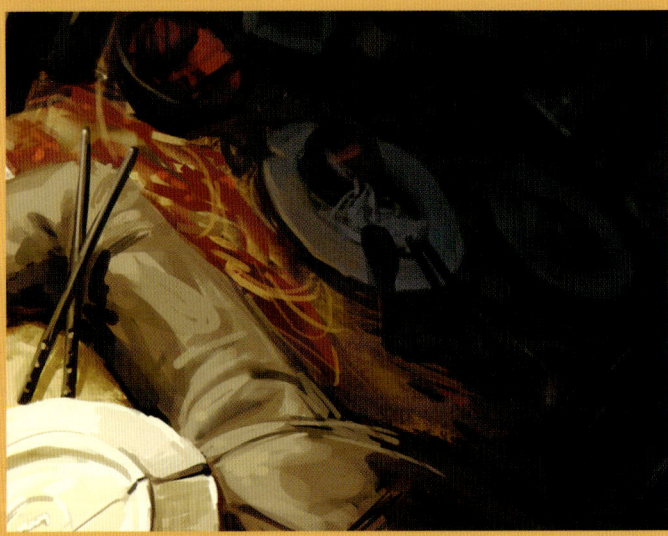

In the shadows. Getting away with rough strokes in the dark areas.

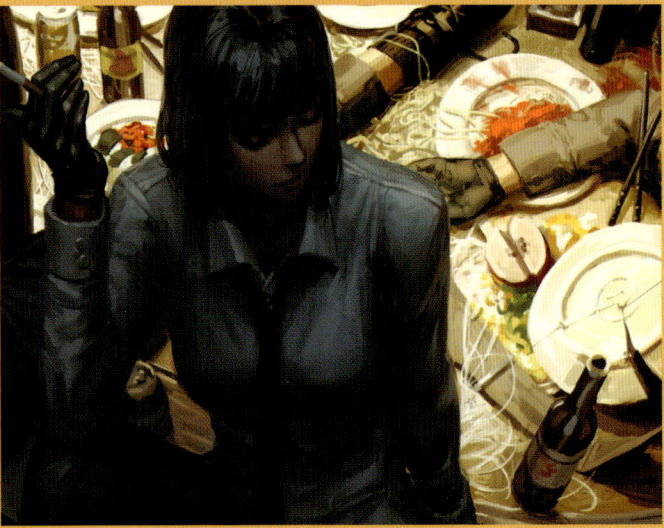

In the spotlight. Brightly lit focal areas require maximum clarity and polish.

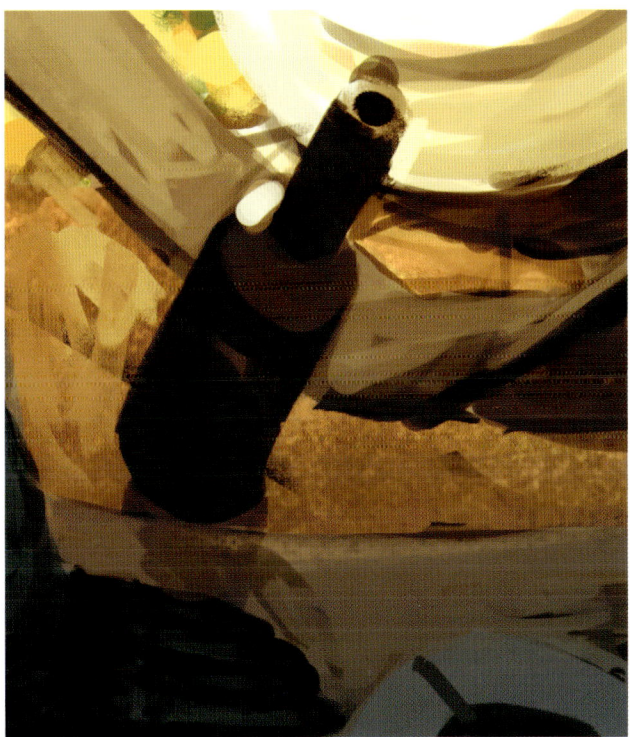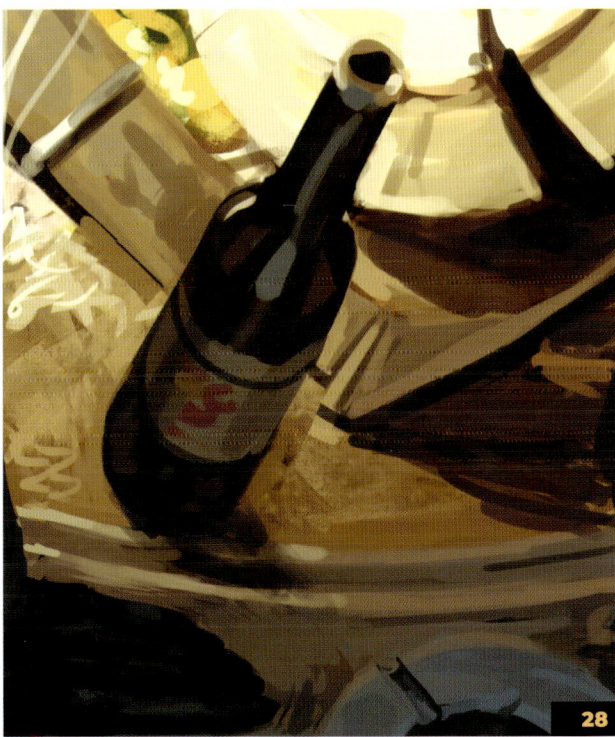

28 The rough sketch compared to a developed version, after taking into account material properties such as specular lighting.

28 VARIOUS MATERIAL PROPERTIES

To make the objects and the scene as a whole look authentic and believable, the trifecta of form, color, and material must be complete. When constructing the piece, we started by painting forms in grayscale, and then added color, but we haven't yet dedicated time to ensuring all the materials' properties are established. At this late stage in the process, we need to start paying extra attention to this – especially for smaller objects that we are likely to have sketched in roughly.

A very important aspect of differentiating materials – essentially how surfaces appear to us – is understanding the concept of reflective properties, as we explored in the Light chapter. These properties consist of two major components: specularity and roughness. Specularity refers to the amount of light a particular type of material, such as plastic, rubber, or metal, reflects. Roughness dictates how sharp or diffuse these reflections are.

Here are some commonplace examples of specularity and roughness that may already be familiar to you:

· Your reflection when using a smooth plastic board as a mirror (medium specularity, low roughness) will seem rather faded, but sharp.

· The same reflection using an actual mirror (high specularity, low roughness) will be intense and sharp.

· Your reflection in a brushed metal sheet (high specularity, high roughness) will capture the intensity of the light being reflected, but with very little clarity.

Now let's take a look at applying these concepts to our piece. A good example to start with is the beer bottle, which we can assume is made out of regular dark glass. We can reasonably determine it to be moderately high in specularity and low in

roughness – therefore the reflection should be fairly intense and sharp. To indicate this, I add a clear blue highlight to account for the skylight that the glass bottle would reflect. The highlight is not quite as bright as the light source itself would be, however, as we have to remember that the specularity of this glass bottle is not as high as that of a perfect mirror.

As we add additional objects with different materials, such as the paper label on the bottle, we have to deliberately paint them according to their respective reflective properties as well.

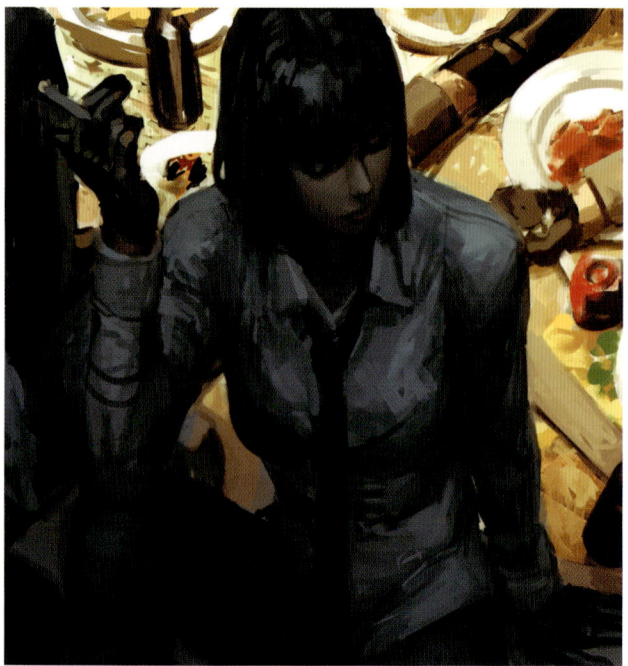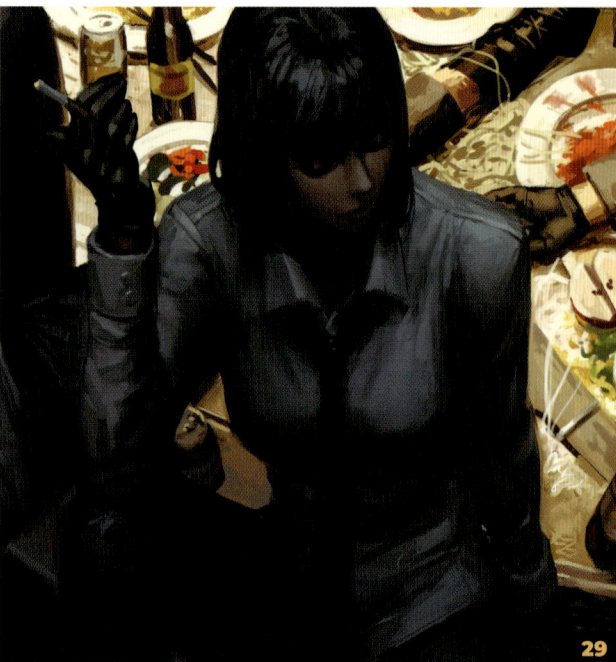

29 Before and after the polishing process; a lot of roughness in the brushstrokes has been cleaned up, in addition to the extra details.

29 POLISHING THE FOCAL AREA

Having covered these extra aspects that we need to take note of during this stage of the process, let's see how we can apply them alongside our fundamentals to continue improving the piece.

Resuming the general painting process, I once again return to focus on the main character. While the brushwork up until now has sufficed in representing the relevant forms, it's not quite good enough when placed under scrutiny. As this region of the composition is a major focus and will be looked at closely, it's important to take it one step further and properly paint elements such as clothing folds and hair textures. You may also notice that a lot of the character's immediate background has also received more attention to detail.

While it can sometimes be helpful to blur or roughly paint areas in service of directing focus to the foreground, it isn't always appropriate. In this scene, the things going on on the table are just as narratively important to showcase as our main character. Furthermore, with the table being well lit by the lamp, viewers will subconsciously be expecting to see a lot of fine details at high resolution. Painting the area according to those expectations will help convey a first impression of realism.

30 POLISHING THE SECONDARY FOCAL AREAS

The same treatment, albeit to a lesser degree, is also required for the secondary areas of focus. While we can get away with slightly rougher brushwork thanks to the dimmer moonlight, we still have to make sure that the forms are accurately drawn and that there is a sufficient level of detailing.

Pictured top right, notice how this extra's clothing receives a bit more attention – the proper reflection is added to the metallic belt buckle and the shirt's form is better defined. The visible slice of the table also has a good amount of extra detail added. Recall that brighter lit areas tend to require such treatment, especially if they are strongly juxtaposed against largely dim surroundings.

Continue refining objects to indicate their respective material properties – for example, the two upright bottles next to the ashtray now reflect a bit of light from the table lamp.

31 MANAGING FINE DETAILS

Next, I adjust the vibrancy of the table's surface to prevent oversaturation of yellow. I want to add a large amount of detailing to increase the "noise" factor of this well-lit area. However, adding and managing detail does take planning.

For a huge portion of this process, ever since embarking on the line sketch, we have looked at many technical aspects and fundamental requirements of producing a competent piece. As we start to wrap things up, however, it's time to return to something we did in the very first step of the tutorial: visualizing the scene as a viewer and thinking about what makes the scene really interesting and enjoyable to look at. To help myself do this, I distance myself from the image and try to pretend I am looking at a photograph instead.

This allows me to think beyond what's on the canvas. For example, we can see that the initial splotches of red don't intuitively read as food or as belonging on a table. The addition of spaghetti immediately helps the red stuff become recognizable as spilled food debris, implying some kind of action has taken place. Similarly, the yellows and greens near the flipped plate look very ambiguous – but if we add some Chinese noodles, they now appear as a scrambled egg and vegetable dish!

Another example is the extra's tie, where adding a visibly metallic tie clip gives the tie a more distinct presence. This prevents viewers from being unable to tell its material apart from the densely packed food and table surface.

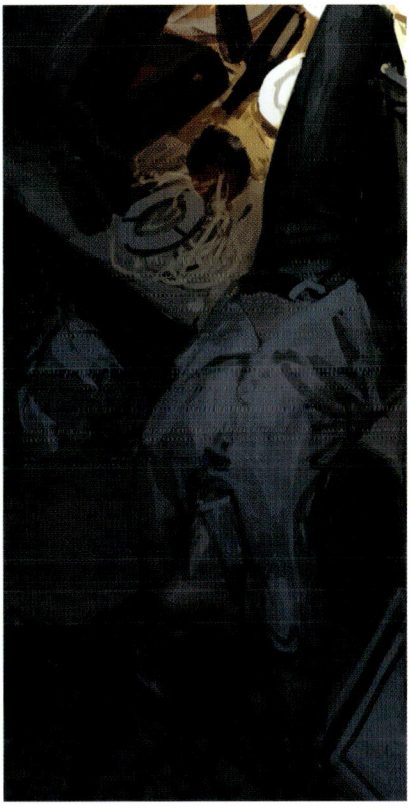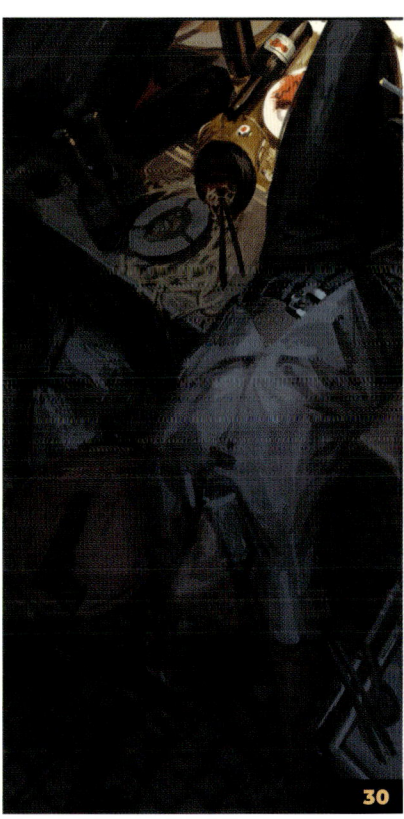

30 Before and after the polishing process. Note the added objects and increased rendering of forms.

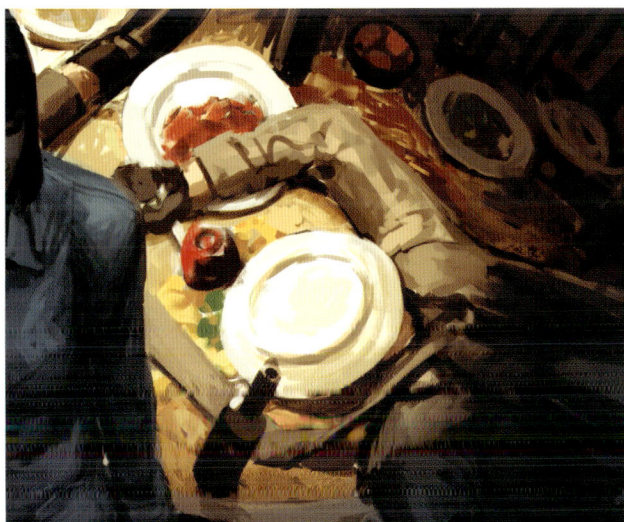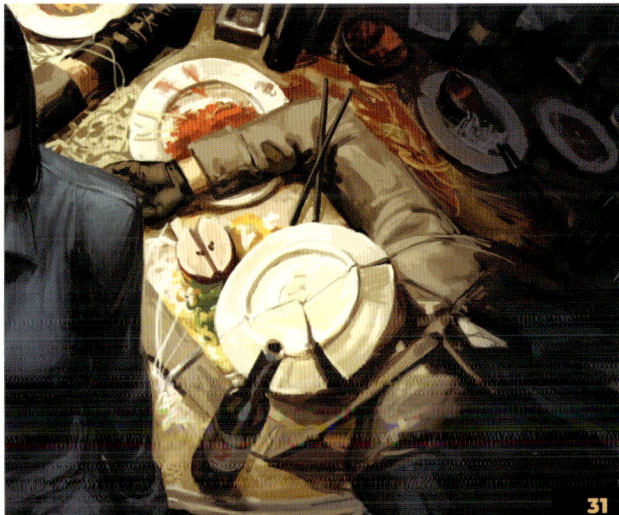

31 Managing details and considering what exactly to depict is important in properly expressing your message. Put yourself in the viewer's shoes to help pinpoint details that could be working better.

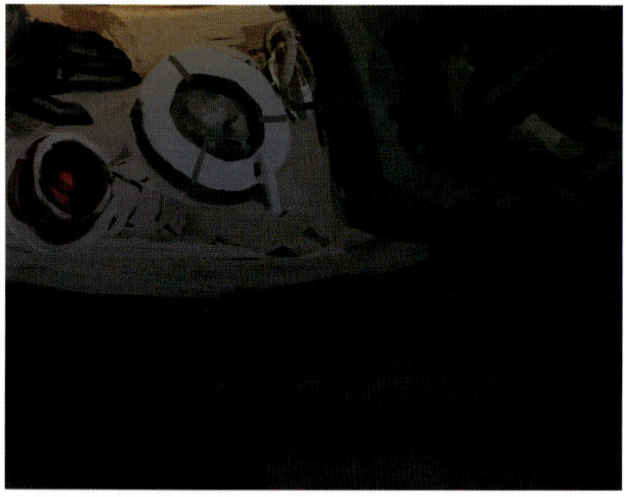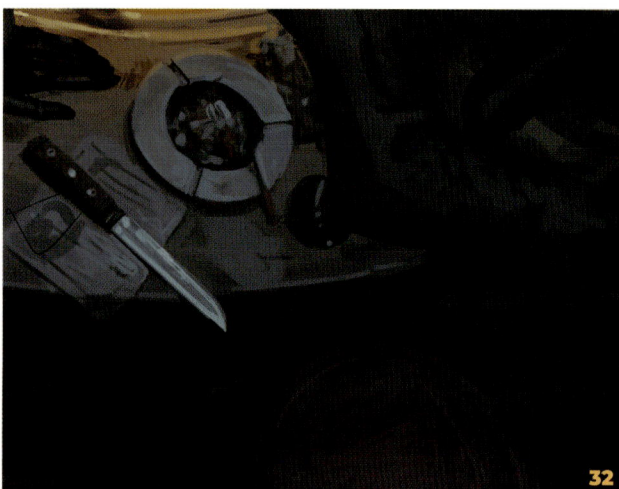

32 Detailing not only conveys a narrative, but is also essential in preparing the image for close-up viewing.

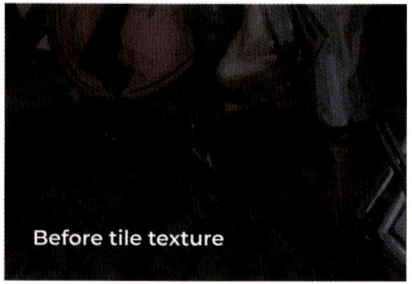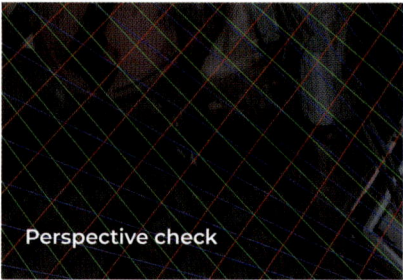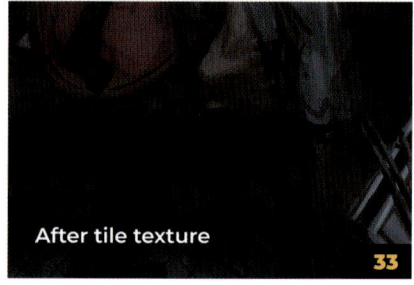

Before tile texture

Perspective check

After tile texture

33 It's quick and easy to line up a pattern thanks to the perspective grid.

32 EXTRA NON-NARRATIVE DETAILS

Aside from some of the central narratives we've created in the previous step, there are also areas where we can add details more freely. A good question to ask yourself is: *"How can I make this area of the composition more interesting?"*

The countertop area around the edge of the table can't be packed as densely as the center of the table, but we can choose to add a few more elements to spice it up. I swap out the wine glass, which was hard to recognize at this viewing angle, and replace it with a knife, which conveys a clearer, immediate concept to the viewer.

I also give the materials in this area the standard refining treatment, distinguishing the marble ashtray, wooden tabletop, lacquered bowl, and metal knife from each other. Even having done that, the bare areas of the countertop need a bit more attention. However, as I want the overall shape and curve of the counter to remain prominent in the composition, adding more objects on top of it is out of the question.

A good solution is to use brushstrokes to create texture in the form of scratches, creases, and surface irregularities. This helps break up large, empty spaces and prevents them from looking unintentionally blank. We can see this in play on the ashtray, countertop, and stool cushion. You can revisit page 194 for some pointers to keep in mind when rendering texture under light.

Last but not least, by adding an extra wooden step lining the transition from counter to table, we are able to up the realism of the furniture while emphasizing this particular curve's place in the composition.

33 PATTERNED SURFACES

Now that the focal areas are dealt with, let's turn our attention to some less noticeable parts of the composition and give them a light touch-up. While the quality of painting in this area isn't high on our list of priorities, we should still give it a once-over before calling the image done.

A very quick and easy upgrade comes in the form of "tileable" patterns – patterns that can repeat seamlessly at the edges. They are excellent when you have a large blank surface that would otherwise remain empty.

For example, adding tiling to walls and floors, where applicable, not only adds pleasant visual detail to the environment, it also overrides any minor brushstroke or lighting errors that may be distorting your image's perspective.

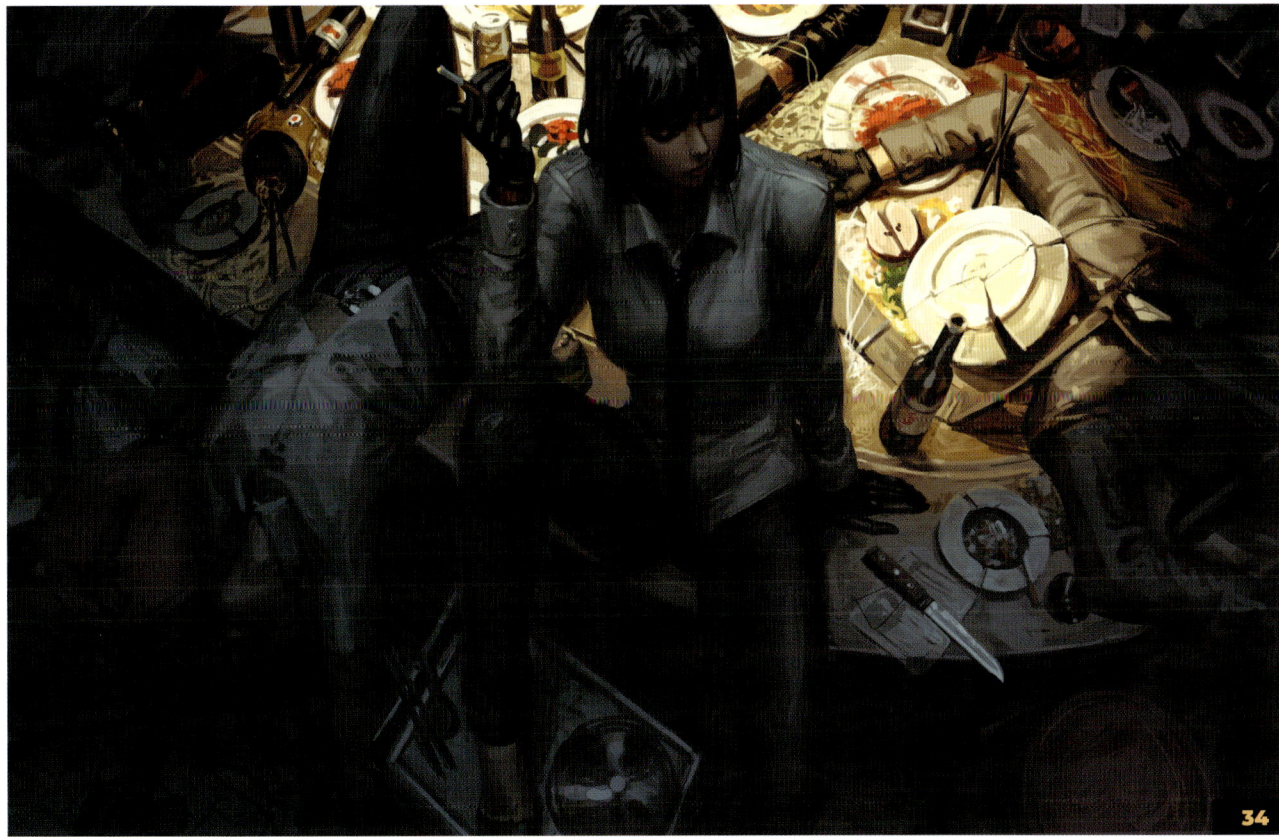

34 Our piece as it stands at this stage. It's nearing completion but there are still some final checks and refinements we can make.

Speaking of perspective, the grid comes in very handy for this part. On a new layer, we can use the Duplicate function to quickly generate a grid of tiles from a single line, meaning we only have to paint one small row of tiles first.

We can then use Transform > Distort to align the pattern to the ground plane. The tile pattern is essentially a grid, which helps us easily add in the rest of the small details in perspective, like the cables lying on the floor.

34 ASSESSING THE THUMBNAIL

As we head into the final stages of wrapping up the illustration, let's regroup and take a look at the big picture. The best place to start with this is a zoomed-out thumbnail view, because it's a great representation of the viewer's first impression of the piece. It also forces us to consider the image as a whole,

which can help uncover problems that would otherwise stay hidden but negatively affect the overall impression.

So, to check if the image works as it should, zoom out really far, so the image is around two inches on the long side. Then we can ask ourselves these questions:

· At first glance, can we describe exactly what is happening? If not, can we at least see enough interesting things to prompt a closer look?

· Is there anything in the composition that can be easily misidentified, or seems like something else when zoomed out?

· If the piece is character-centric, does the character look natural – in terms of gesture, anatomy, and proportion – from a thumbnail view?

· Do the colors look balanced? Do any of the light sources look too muted or too dominant?

This list can of course be expanded depending on what kind of illustration we are creating, but the core ideas would remain the same.

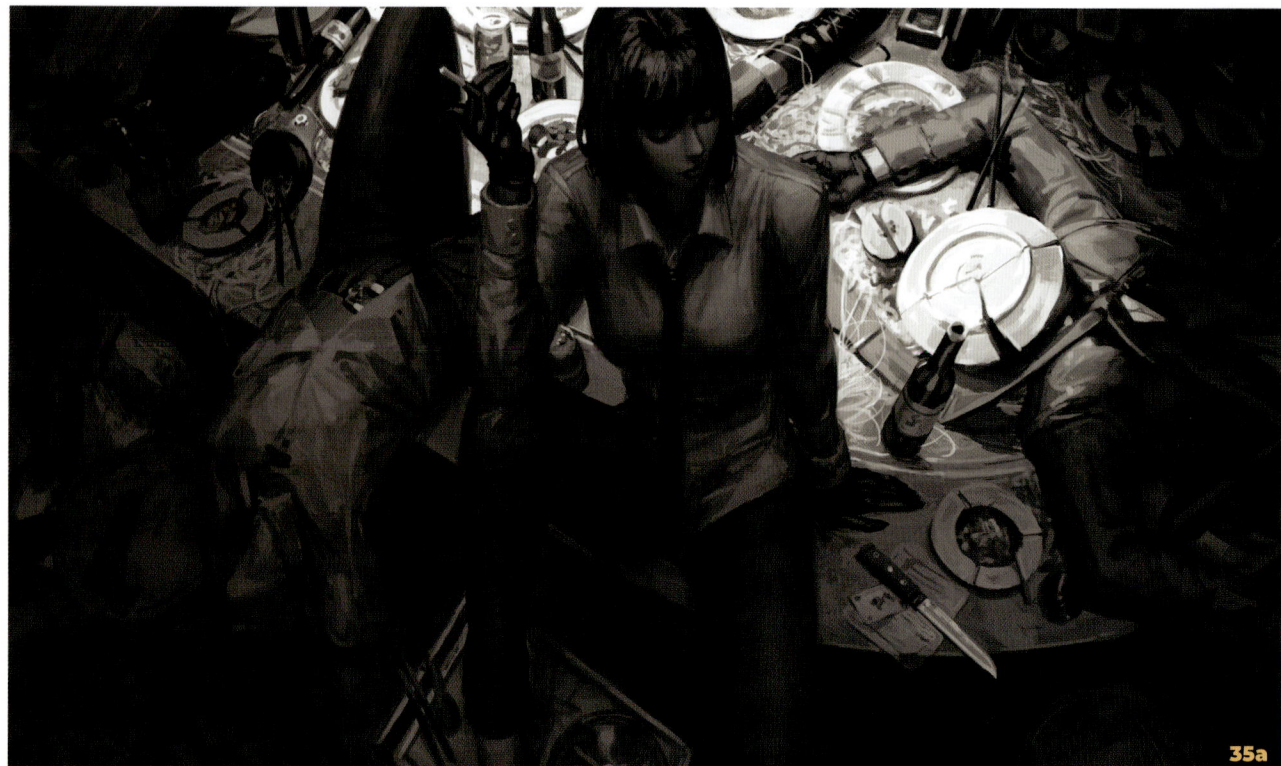

35a Checking the image with a Black & White adjustment layer over it. We can see it's still clear and sticks close to our original value plan.

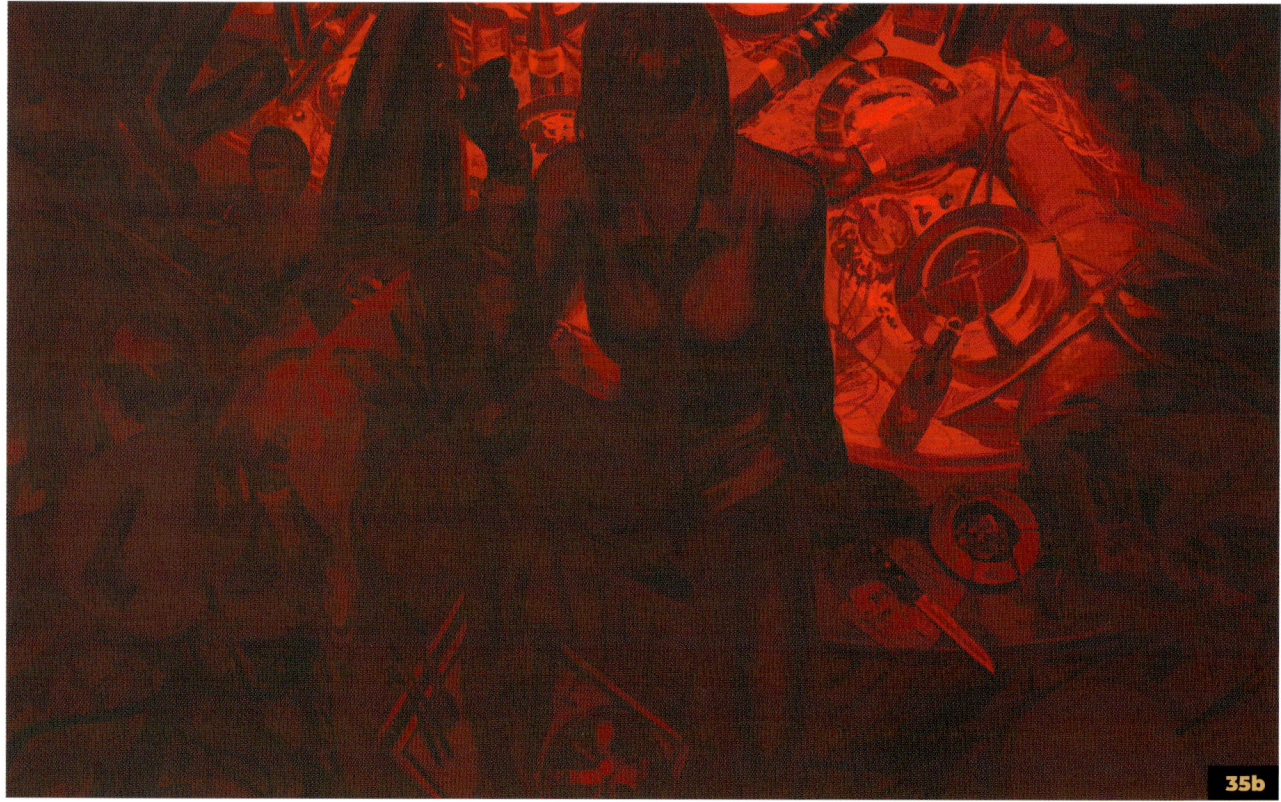

35b Setting the image layer to Saturation on top of a solid-colored layer creates a useful vibrancy map. The brightest reds here represent the most saturated areas.

35 VERIFYING TONES AND VALUES

Another very useful thing to do is to check the overall value layout using Photoshop's "Black & White" adjustment layer option. This is helpful not only to make sure we stick to our initial value-planning and blocking, but also to resolve discrepancies in lighting at any point during the painting process.

Recall that at the beginning of the tutorial, we started out by creating a couple of key value-block relationships that defined the entire lighting setup for our piece. Now that we are at the tail end of the project, let's see how those plans have held up.

As we can see on the left, the strong lighting on the table is working as planned, as is the silhouetting of the main character against it. The level of contrast here tells us that the relationship between strong light and shadow is also intact. In areas where the table lamp's light doesn't reach, we have also successfully maintained the presence of moonlight coming in from above, saving the darkest values for the areas that neither light source can reach.

I also have a method for checking color vibrancy, that's less commonly used or even necessary, but is still interesting to mention. By creating a solid red (or any colored) layer under our image layer, and then setting the image layer's blend mode to Saturation, we essentially get a map of where our color saturation is higher.

This can be very helpful when you feel that some of your coloring is "off," but are not sure exactly where or why. A good rule of thumb is that color is the most vibrant under strong (but not overexposed) lighting, and is decreasingly vibrant the darker the light source gets. In the example here, the most vibrant and saturated colors are located in the brightly lit region, while the dim, moonlit areas are less saturated in color. The areas mostly in shadow are almost invisible on the saturation map. If we had accidentally oversaturated a color in a dark area of the scene, this map would quickly reveal the problem spot for us to resolve.

36 CHECKING THE IMAGE PART BY PART

The last method I want to share with you is something simple but interesting: inspecting one part of the composition at the time by hiding other areas of the image. When working on large compositions with a lot of active parts, it can be very easy to get lost working on certain busy areas of the image, inadvertently missing potential issues in less noticeable areas.

By inspecting small segments of the image in isolation, we can very quickly detect things that are not right or not quite complete. The main things to look out for here are unintentionally empty spaces, insufficiently painted forms, and places that need more detail to be believable. They can be surprisingly hard to find when everything is visible at once, but when fixed, can improve the image substantially.

If we look at the individual blocks below, one thing we can see is that every image block is more or less self-sufficient as a mini-illustration. They each hold at least some interest on their own without looking incomplete in any way.

Of course, this process is only done in service to the bigger picture, so be careful not to overdo it and affect the big picture negatively – for example, low-interest areas of the composition don't need to become colorful or vibrant just for the sake of it.

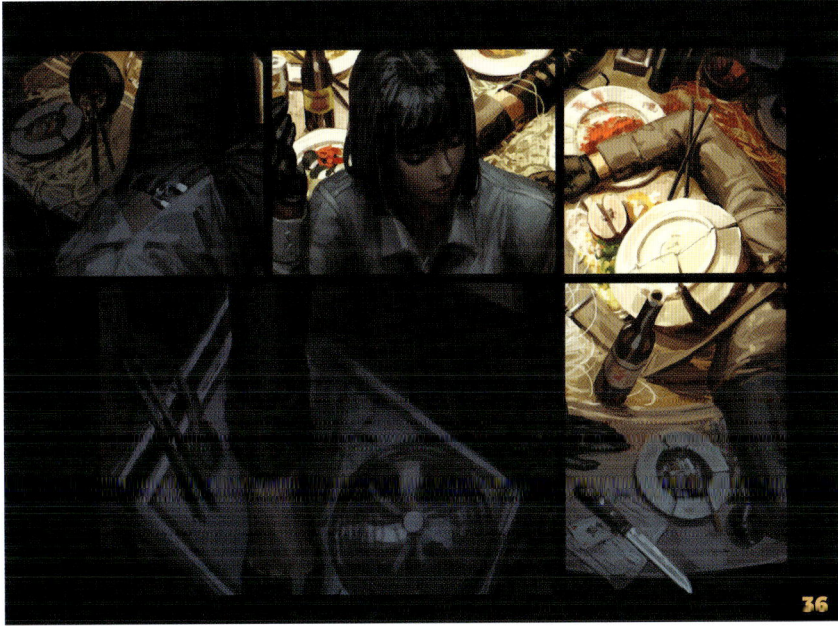

36 We can get a much closer and focused look at each area of the composition one at a time by forcing "tunnel vision."

USING THE TRANSFORM TOOL

The Transform tool, and specifically the Warp option, is an amazing tool that often seems to go under the radar. While you may be puzzled as to why we would need this particular tool when we can just perform regular rotations and transforms, Warp actually brings a whole new set of options to the table.

Let's first take a look at one of its more intuitive uses: wrapping texture around curved volumes. It can be difficult to manually draw textures that wrap around curved surfaces accurately, especially when perspective is in play as well. It can take a lot of mental energy to figure out how all the lines should converge and how the curved lines should look nearing the edges. With the Warp tool in play, we can easily create a flat texture and then superimpose it onto the target surface.

Warp conveniently affords fine, independent control of different parts of the texture that is being warped, allowing us to carefully but intuitively work the pattern into place. In the example below-left, it took less than thirty seconds to create a grid, and then another thirty to line it up with the cylinder. Consistency and uniformity are great strengths of the tool – things that are not easy to achieve manually, especially with repeating patterns.

Lastly you can see a practical application of the Warp tool below – I drew the flowers manually, and then used Warp to fit them to the contours of the character's clothing. No guesswork or difficult perspective drawing needed!

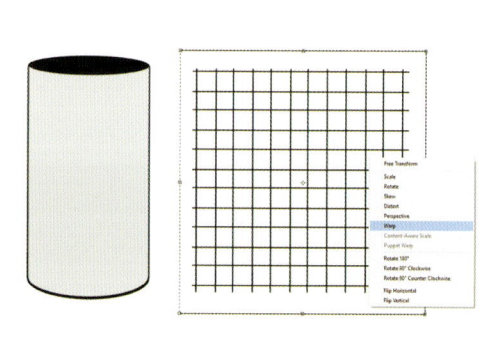

Flat grid. Preparing a simple hand-drawn grid for wrapping is quick and easy. Simply select, Transform, and Warp.

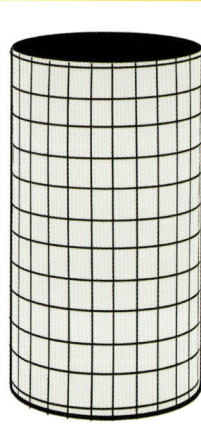

Wrapping. It only takes thirty seconds and a little effort to transfer this texture onto the curved plane of a cylinder. We can get an even better result if we spend a little more time tweaking.

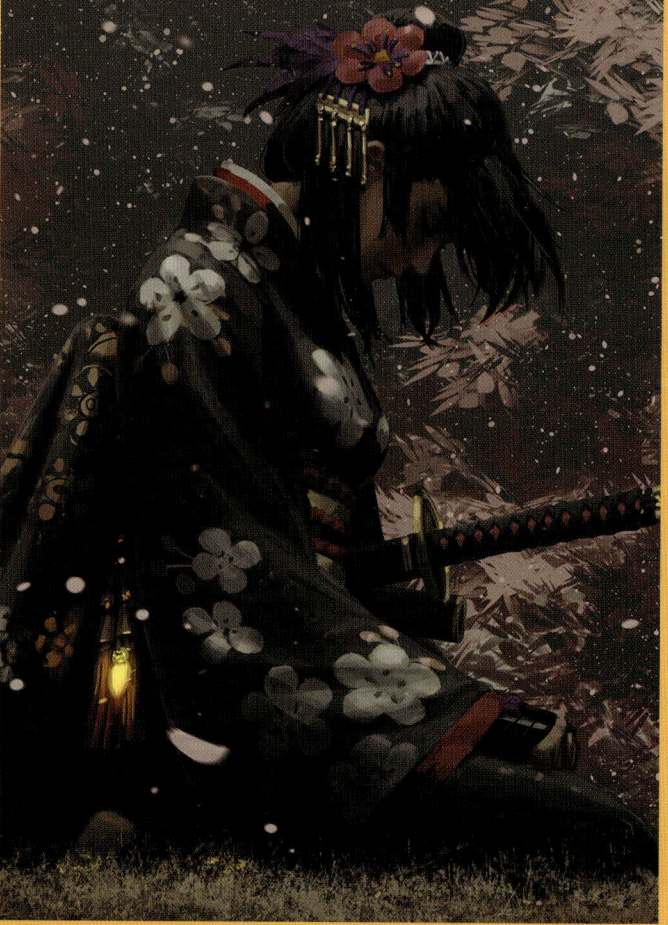

Warp and wrap. In this example illustration, the Transform and Warp options were used to wrap the floral patterns around the complex draped forms of the fabric.

37 RESTING AND REVISITING

At this point, we can call the image done, but what I like to do – if time allows – is return to the piece after a day or two working on something else. Fresh eyes and fresh energy can help you discover a few more minor areas of improvement.

Micro-details are the sort of thing that a fatigued artist would miss out on. Coming back to the piece with newfound energy, I go through a lot of the smallest objects to give them more detail and clarity. For example, I add highlights to a few select strands of noodles, as well as drawing in notches and highlights for the chopsticks. With a big piece like this, this step is not always a must, but it does add a nice touch – for smaller pieces with fewer elements on display however, it can be more important to ensure each of them get the full treatment, lest the piece feels incomplete.

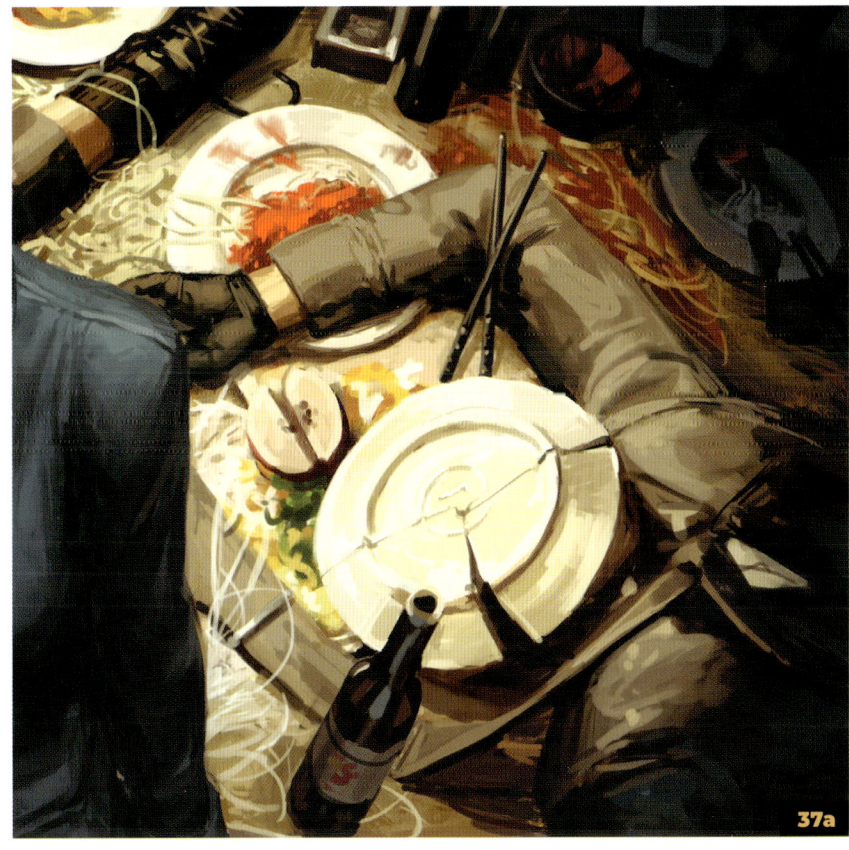

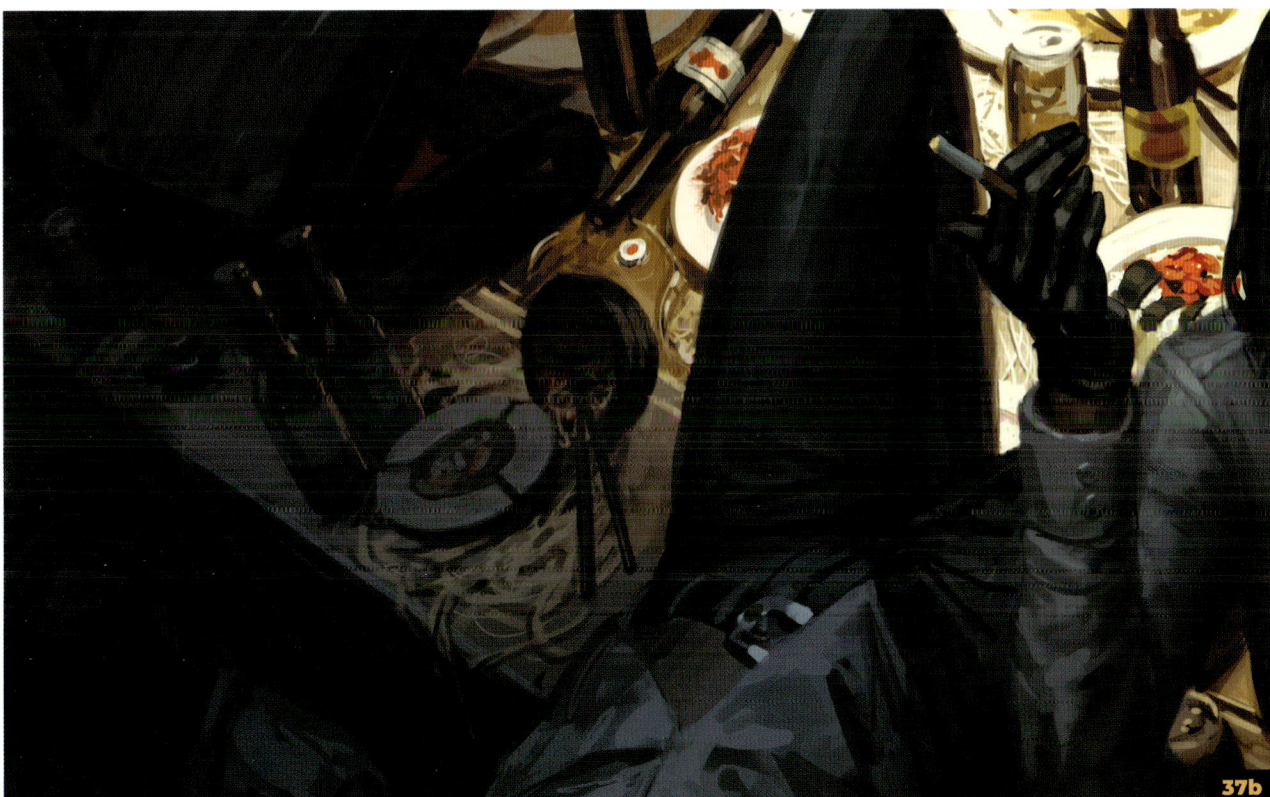

37a – 37b Upping the detail level on select areas to enhance the piece. This is much easier to do after a short break to refresh your view of the image.

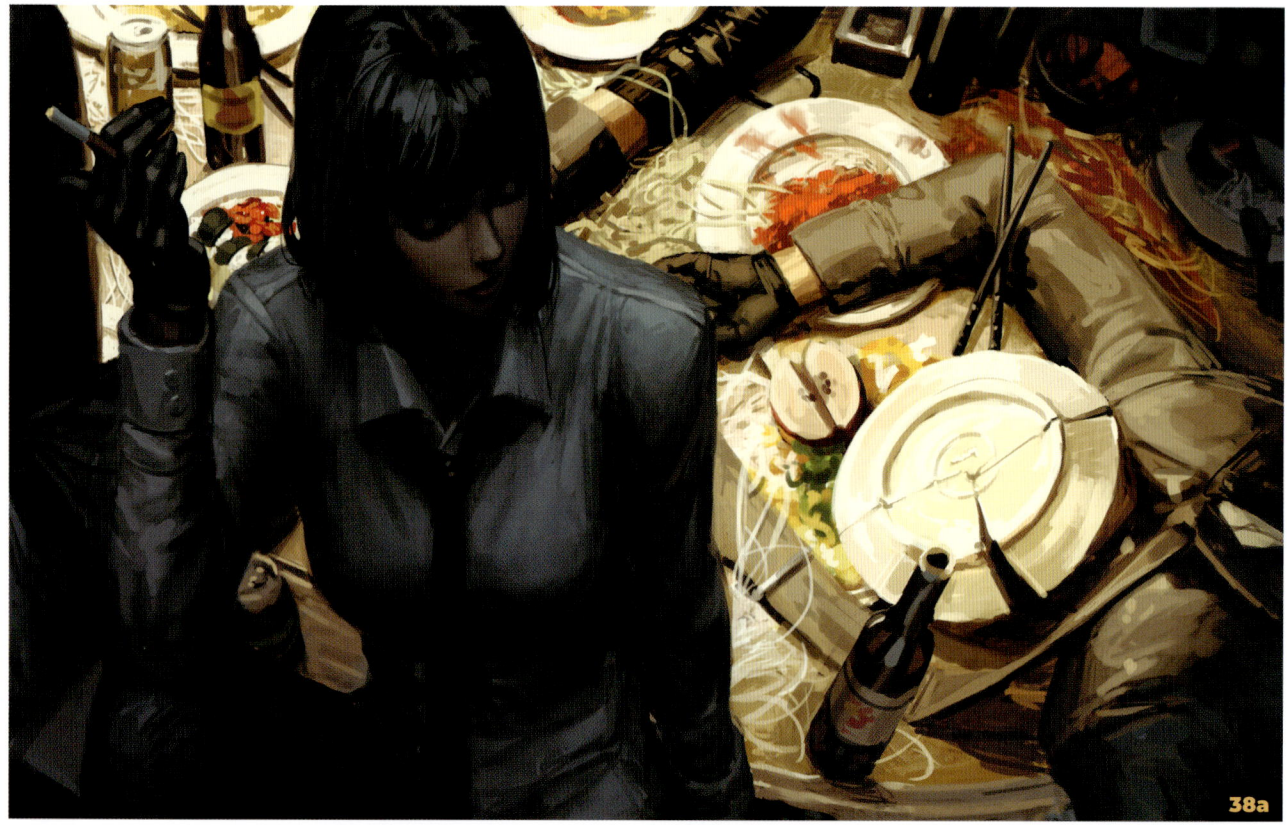

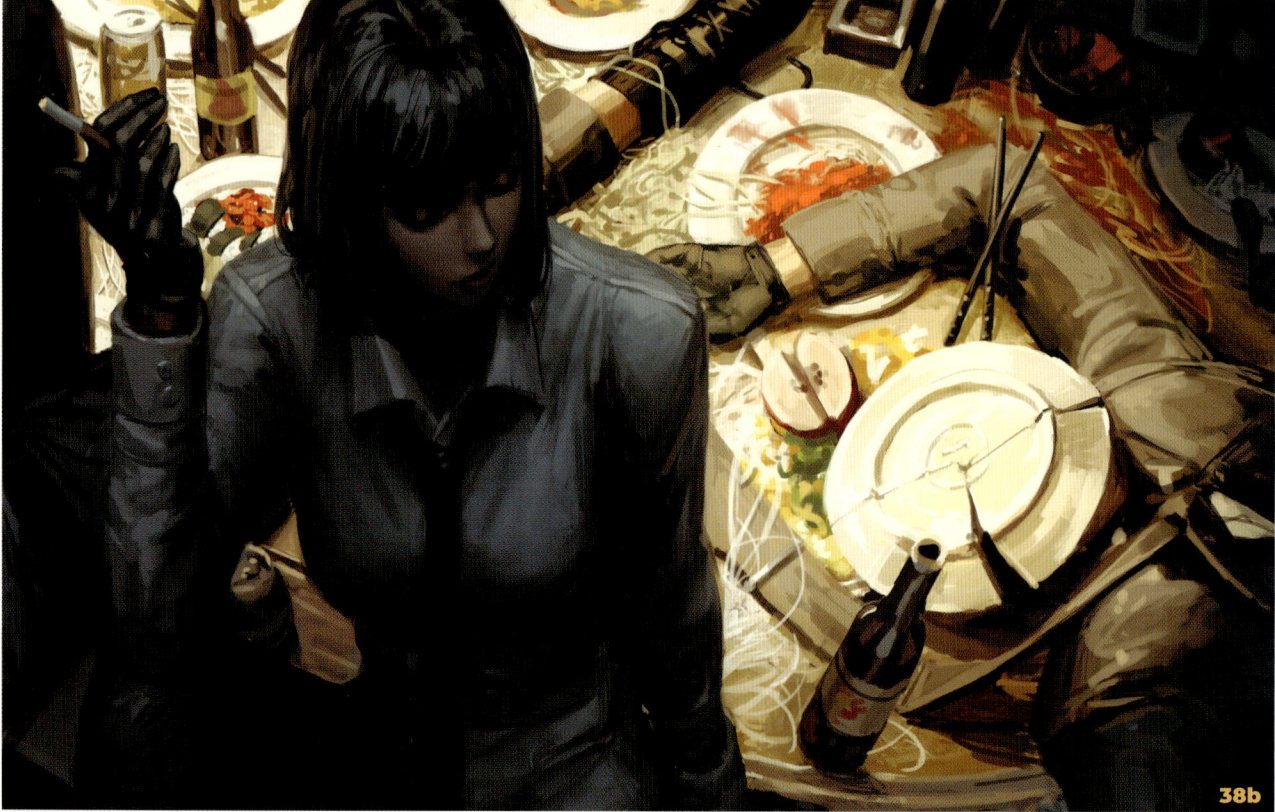

38a – 38b Adding a "film of light" effect to the brightly lit area. This bloom is subtle but adds an extra touch of believability.

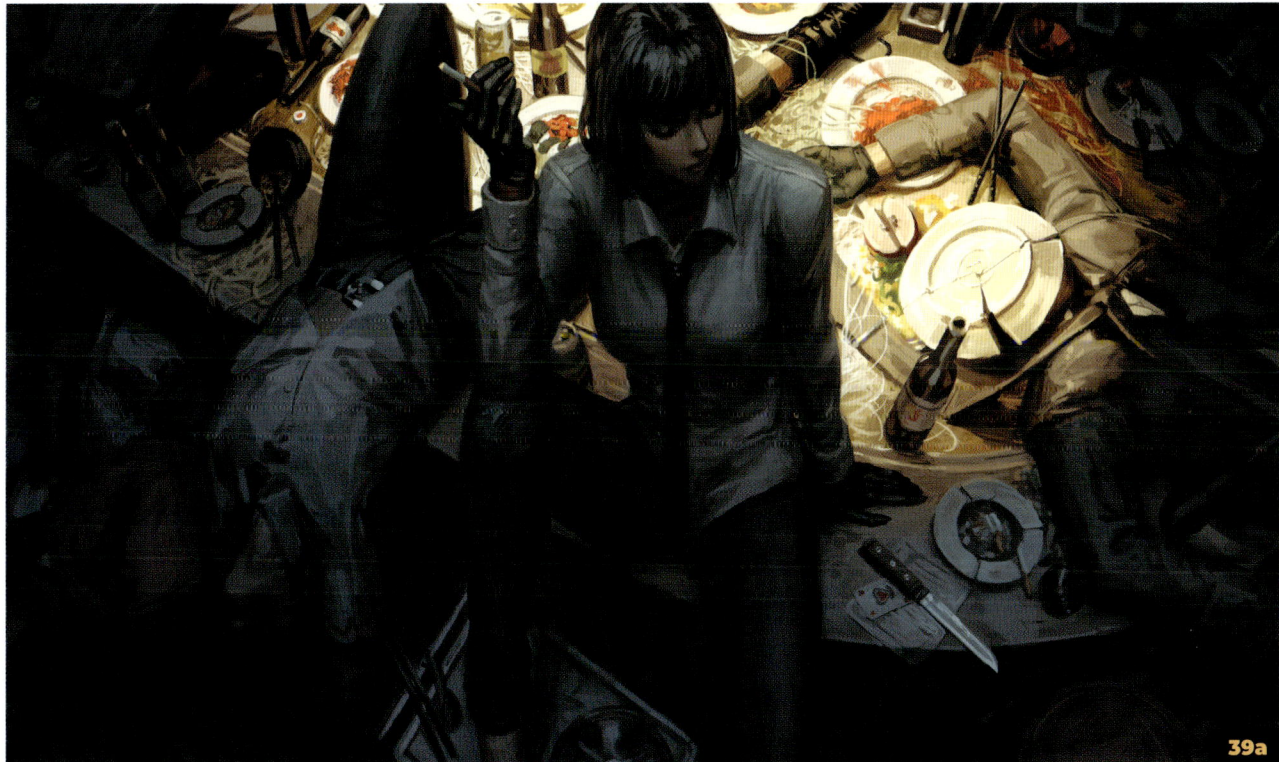

39a

38 ADDING A LIGHT BLOOM

I want to take the opportunity to boost the lighting and give it some bloom to create a more realistic effect. In real life, if we look at a brightly lit area in an otherwise dim room, it is likely we see some level of glare or bloom that a camera would not actually pick up. The effect is almost as if there's a film of light between our eyes and whatever we are looking at.

To create that effect, I very lightly paint over the table on a layer set to Soft Light mode. The change is most visible on the darker objects, such as the shoe and glove of the background characters, mimicking that "film of light" feeling we get when seeing bloom in real life.

39 PLACING EXTRA SHADOWS

I also add in some extra ambient occlusion to some areas that need it. As we learned on page 96, this kind of occlusion refers to

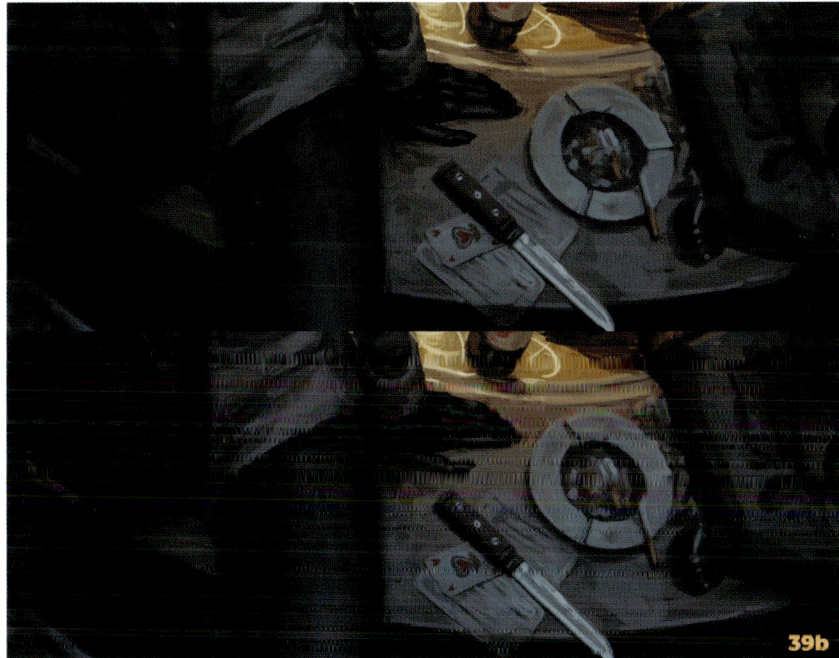

39b

39a – 39b Before and after ambient occlusion, which helps to create a visual suggestion of close proximity between affected forms.

the phenomenon where an area receives less ambient light because objects in close proximity are blocking it out. In the images above, you can see the places where our

main character comes into contact with the counter, such as between her hand and leg, have been subtly darkened to represent this light occlusion.

THE COMPLETED IMAGE

After a few more fine touches are added with pixel-thin brushes, it's time to finally call the image done! Throughout this journey, we have used many different methods, drawn a wide variety of different subjects, and completed several challenging phases, but my key takeaway for you is to not take all of this at face value. I am simply providing a tiny slice of the possibilities you can explore in the wide world of art.

At the core of this, however, we still have our fundamentals to thank, for they lay the foundation and act as the logic behind all these processes. It's only with close consultation and making full use of the fundamentals such as light and color theory that we can construct robust and appealing works.

Lastly, fundamentals are not just something you learn once and are done with. They are something you have to use in every single piece you paint. It is incredibly rewarding as you increase your own grasp and mastery of them. I am still learning and practicing myself!

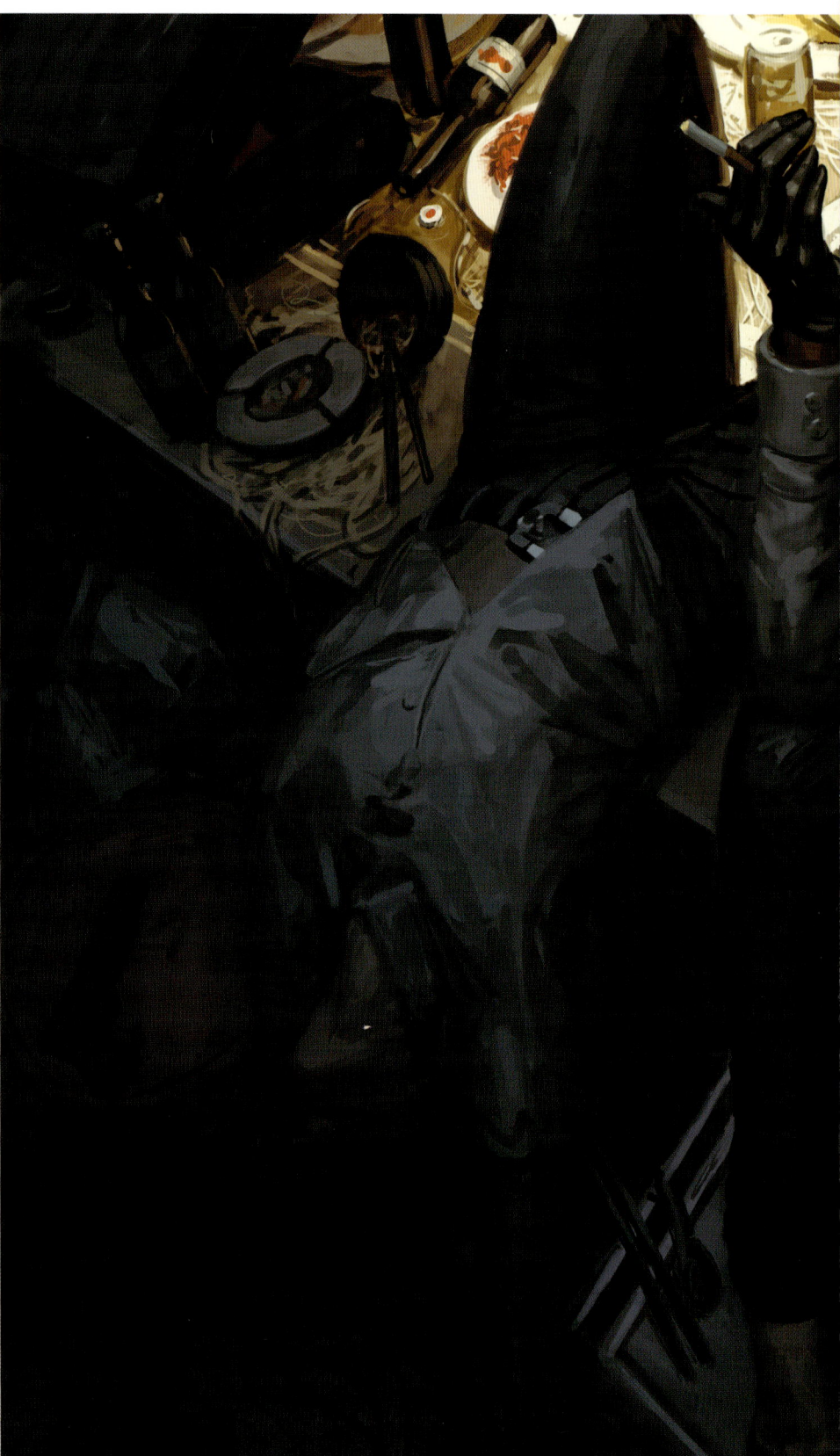

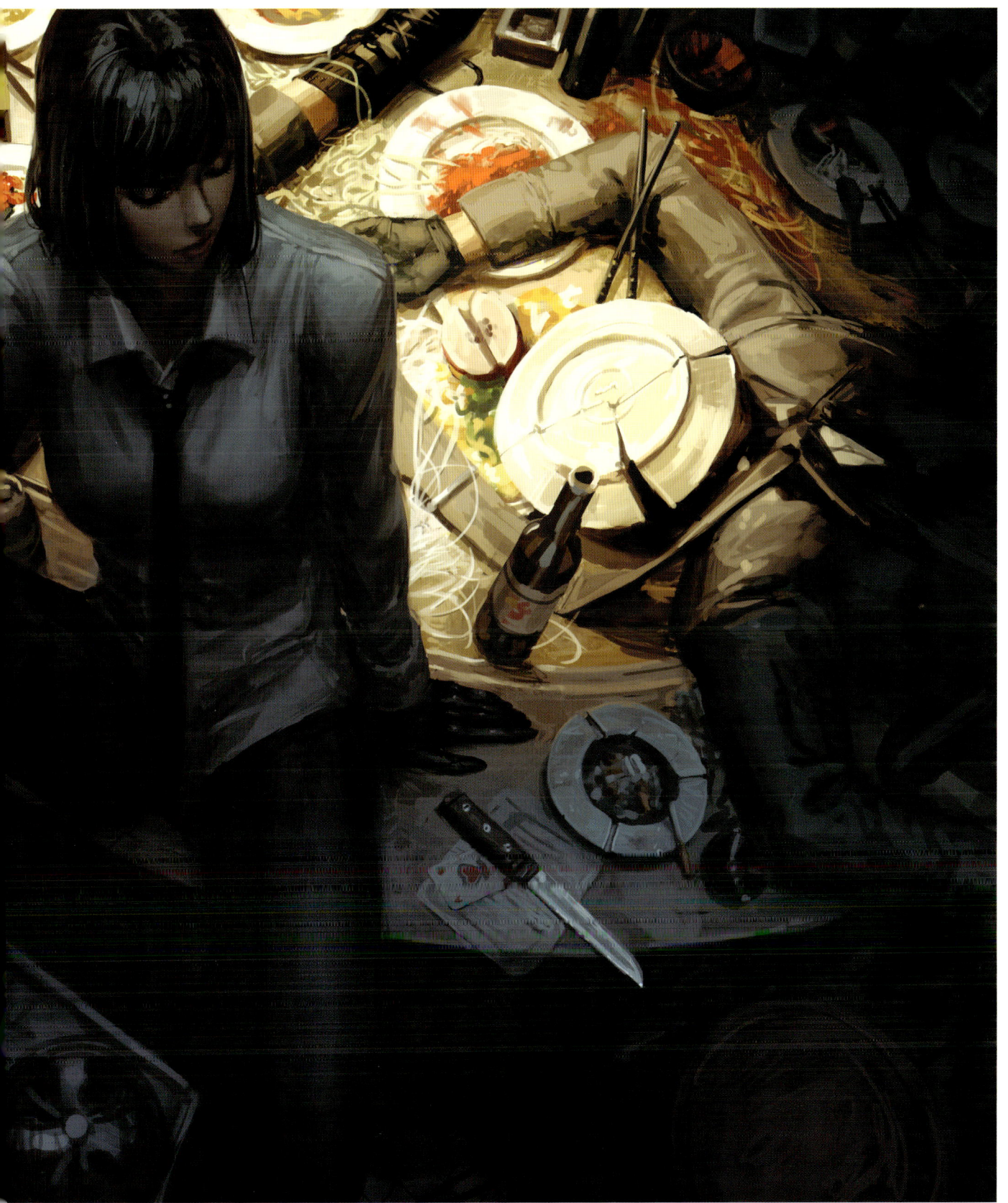

A dark story. The completed image, using value control, color temperature, and levels of detail and texture.

BALBOA SPIRE

NATHAN FOWKES

As a kid growing up in California, I was always taken by the rich warms and cools of the landscape. When I became an artist in my teens, I strived to discover what it was that made those vistas so luminous. This has been a goal of mine ever since, and I am excited to demonstrate some of my solutions for you!

I will be painting a distinctive landmark that is situated near the Californian coastline in San Diego. I will show you how sunlight interacts with vibrant and neutral colors to create a remarkable level of visual interest. This demonstration will be of benefit to both digital and traditional painters. I will use the versatility of digital painting to rough out my initial idea based on a photo reference, and will also refer to traditional sketches done on location. Then, I will paint my finished piece with a combination of watercolor and opaque white gouache.

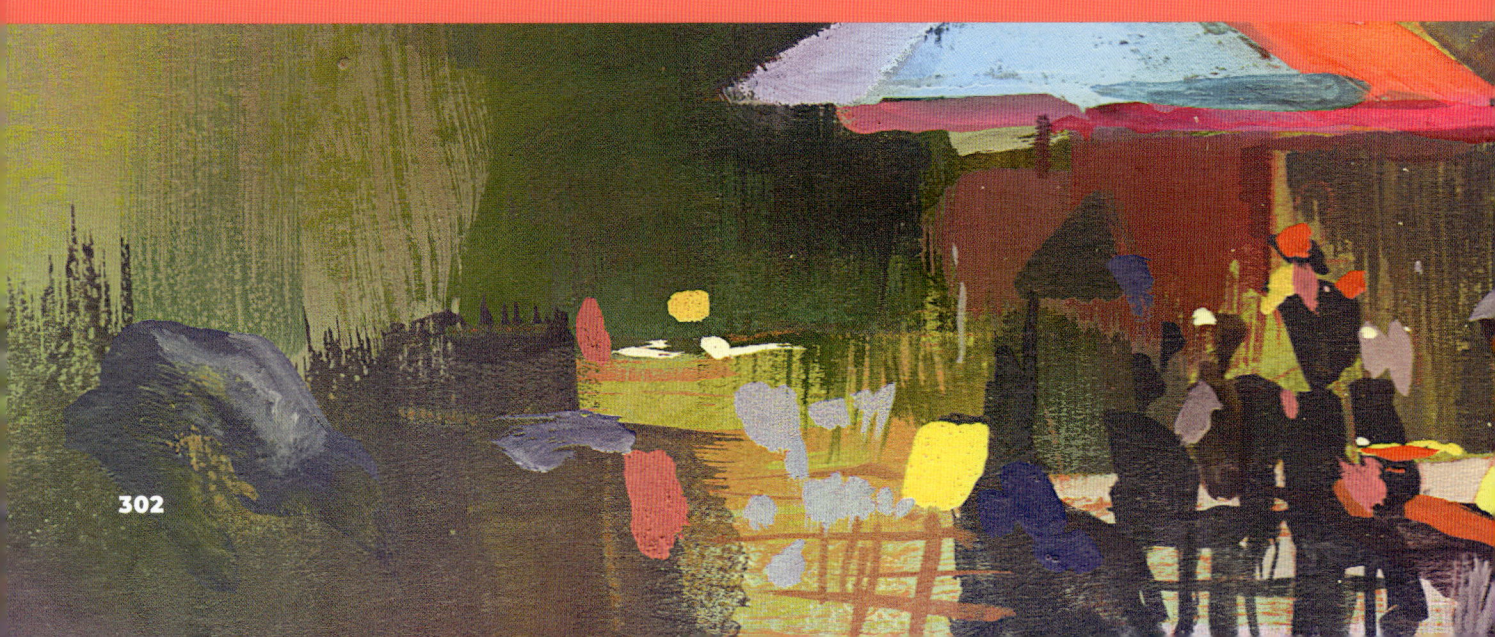

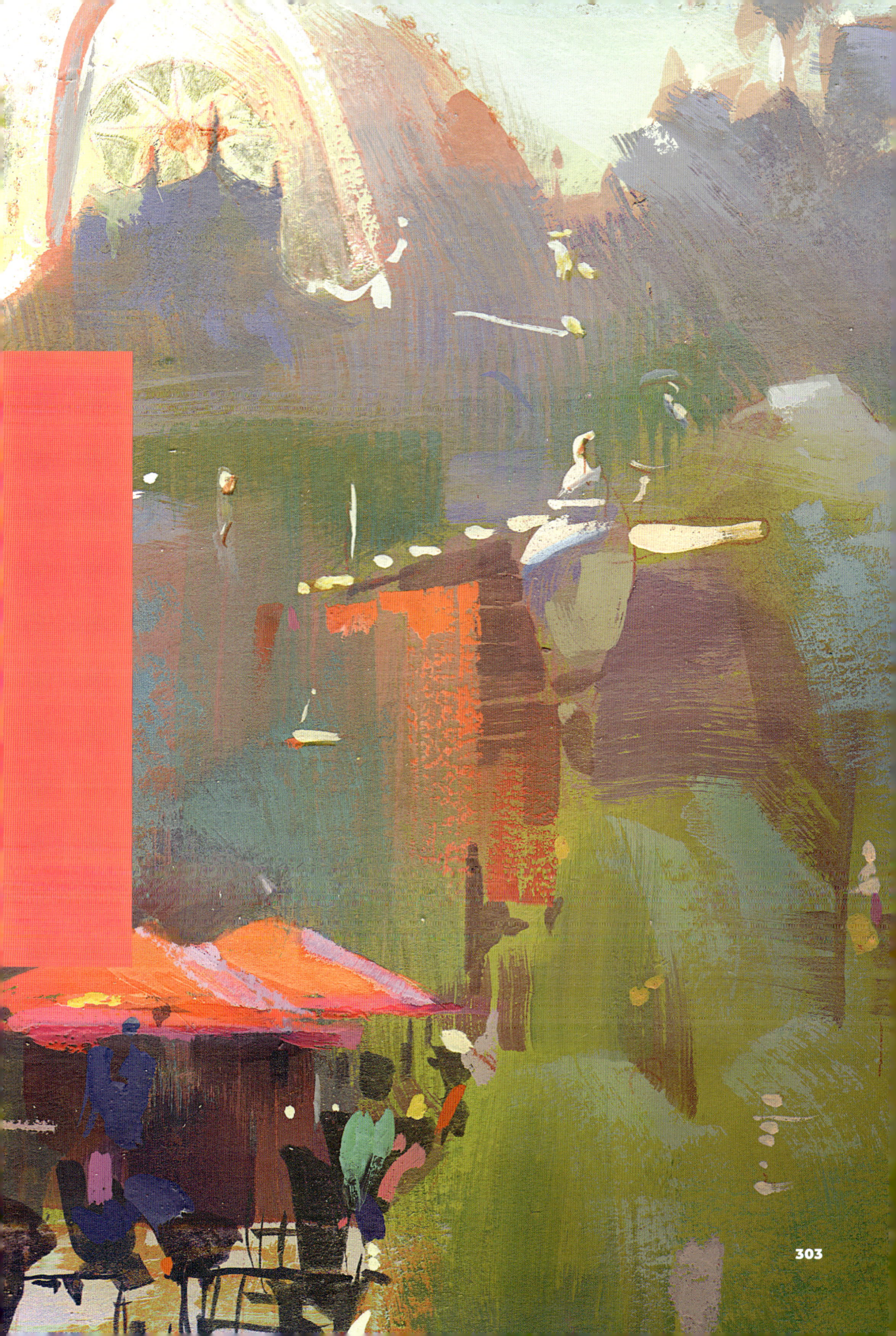

01 MATERIALS LIST

Before we begin, here's a list of my materials for the traditional painting side of this project. It is not essential to replicate these completely, but it will be helpful for you to see my general tools setup before we get into my process.

Brushes:

· Princeton flat #4350st, sizes 1" and 3/4"
· Robert Simmons white sable #721 flat, sizes 1/2" and 1/4"
· Da Vinci Maestro 35, sizes 4 and 6 (or any good round sable watercolor brush)

Paper:

· Strathmore toned gray mixed-media paper, 400 series

Additional materials:

· Red pencil (Prismacolor Verithin in Carmine Red)
· Artist's acid-free masking tape
· Spray bottle
· Water bin for cleaning brushes
· Alvin Heritage palette
· Blow dryer

02 A RANGE OF COLOR

These are the colors I use, so feel free to try them. They are by no means the "correct" colors – they simply contain the full range of possibilities that I find to be useful. You will notice in the photo that the yellows are used twice – this is because the pools of color get dirty quickly and the extras are a convenience. All are Winsor & Newton watercolors unless otherwise noted.

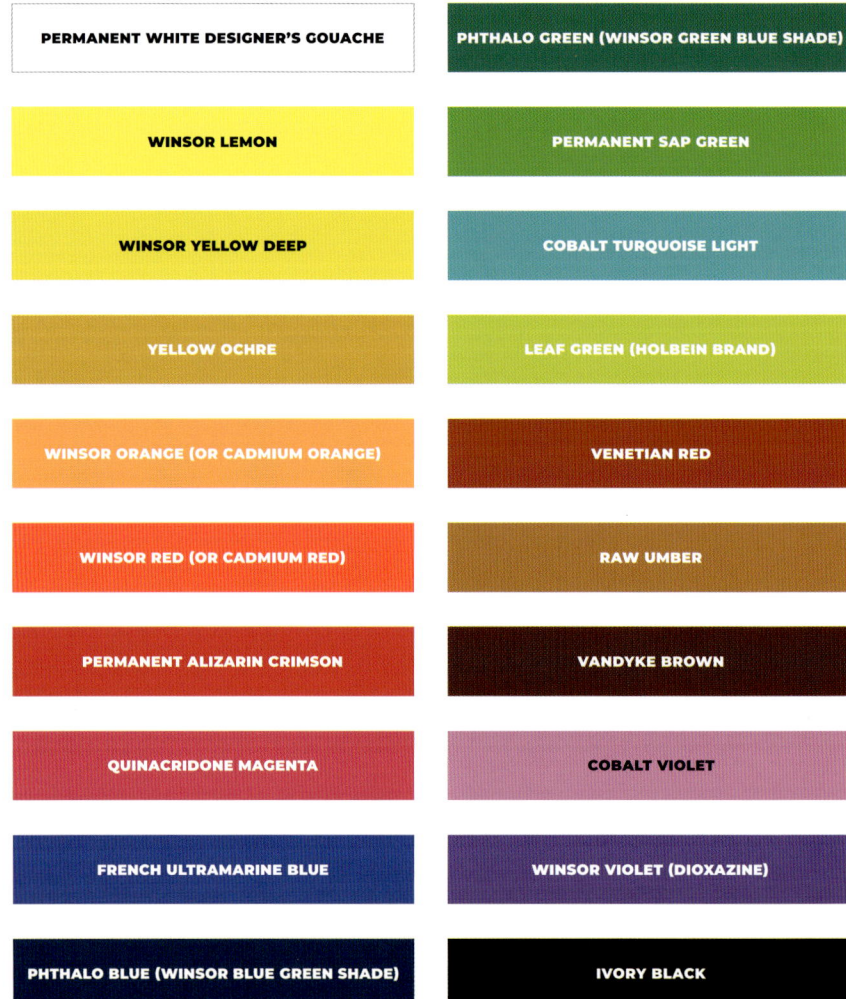

PERMANENT WHITE DESIGNER'S GOUACHE

WINSOR LEMON

WINSOR YELLOW DEEP

YELLOW OCHRE

WINSOR ORANGE (OR CADMIUM ORANGE)

WINSOR RED (OR CADMIUM RED)

PERMANENT ALIZARIN CRIMSON

QUINACRIDONE MAGENTA

FRENCH ULTRAMARINE BLUE

PHTHALO BLUE (WINSOR BLUE GREEN SHADE)

PHTHALO GREEN (WINSOR GREEN BLUE SHADE)

PERMANENT SAP GREEN

COBALT TURQUOISE LIGHT

LEAF GREEN (HOLBEIN BRAND)

VENETIAN RED

RAW UMBER

VANDYKE BROWN

COBALT VIOLET

WINSOR VIOLET (DIOXAZINE)

IVORY BLACK

WHY WATERCOLOR WITH GOUACHE?

The primary reason I use watercolors is their speed and versatility for painting outdoors. Other mediums like acrylics and gouache can dry out quickly on the palette and are difficult, if not impossible, to bring back to life. Oil paints are wonderful, but they are such a mess to travel with, at least for me!

My watercolor palette can dry up in the California sun, but a quick spritz of water brings it right back to life. I use white designer's gouache with my watercolors, and usually paint quite thickly, treating the pools of pigment as if they were oils. Working this way recreates the opacity of some other mediums, which I like.

I have come to love this outdoor approach so much that it has followed me into the studio and is now my primary way of painting, indoors and out.

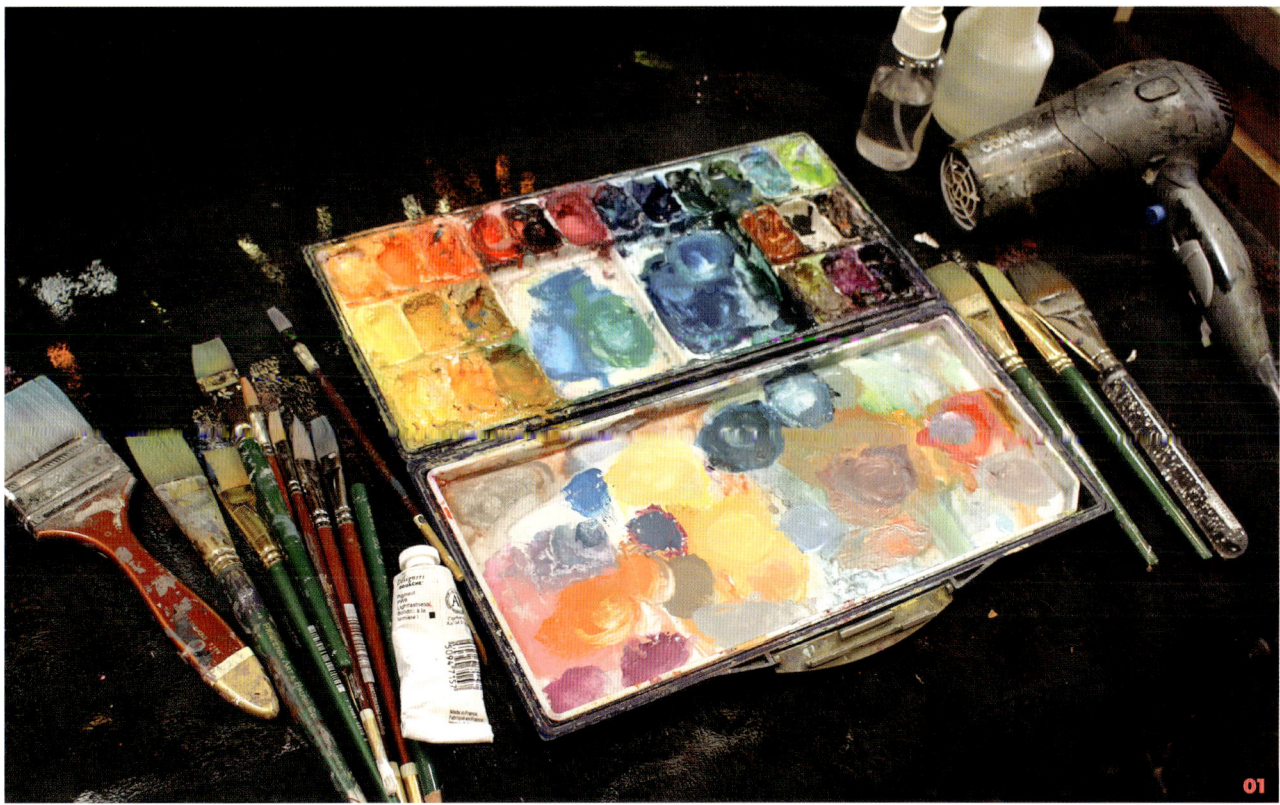

01 My painting materials include a palette, water for both rinsing and spraying, a blow dryer, and a range of brushes (mostly flat, but some smaller for details).

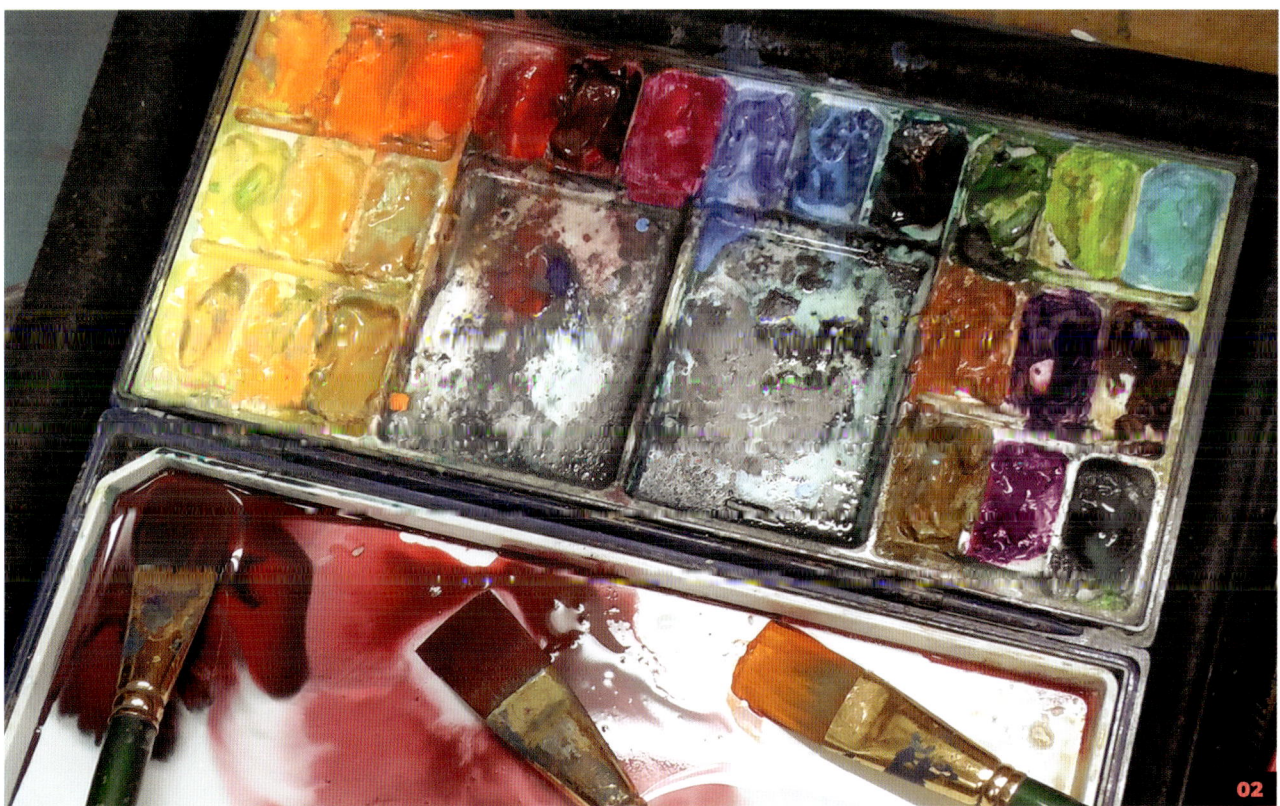

02 My watercolor pigments. I will also be using a tube of white gouache, as shown in the previous photo.

03 REFERENCE PHOTO

Here is the photo reference for my painting. I make no claim to be a great photographer, and this is very intentional! If I shoot a gorgeous photo, I feel like the job is done and there is no need for a painting. However, if I snap a quick shot on my phone, I get the gist of the scene, leaving the painting open for design and experimentation. I prefer to take notes and make sketches on location for my actual color reference, as you will see in a moment.

04 TAKING A CLOSER LOOK

Here is a crop of my photo reference, showing more detail of the area that will appear in the final painting. My idea is that the big, simple mass and grandeur of the building will give the painting a strong graphic against the glowing sky. At our eye level, you can see colorful umbrellas, tables, and badly dressed tourists. This will be a great area of primary visual interest against the simple, shadowy backdrop of the buildings. The sidelighting creates another sprinkle of visual interest that I can use to draw attention down to the focal area of the umbrellas.

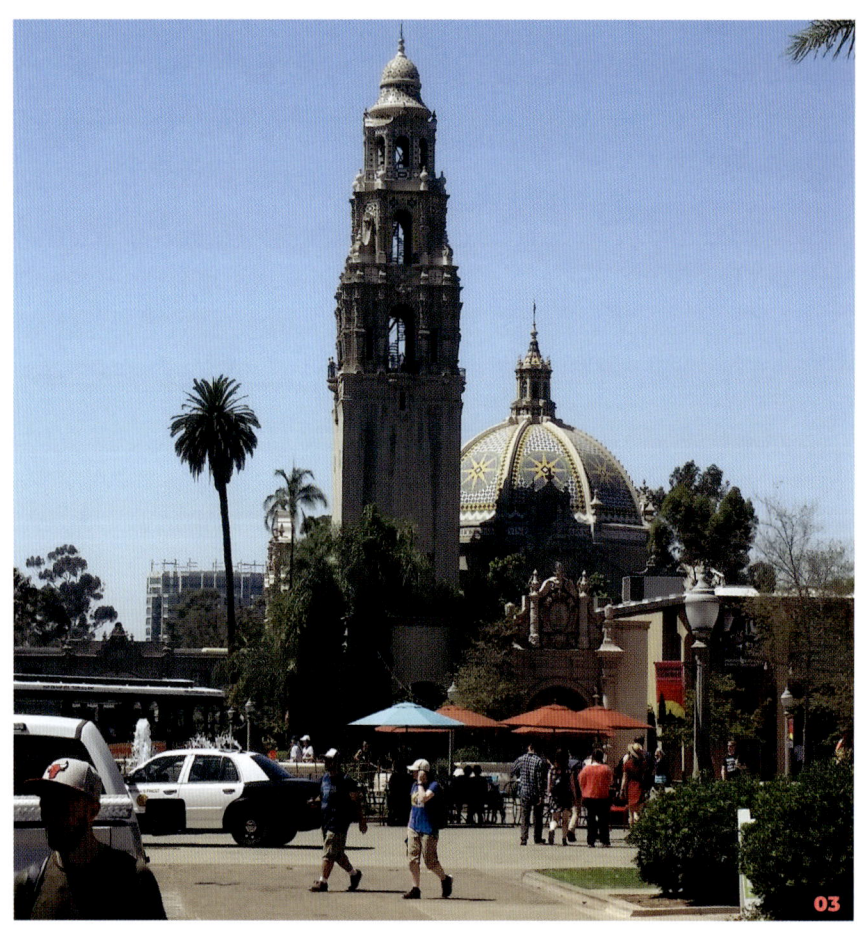

03 My location photo reference: Balboa Park, San Diego, California. It's just a quick picture, not a finished art piece in itself – the painting is where I will perfect my impression of the scene.

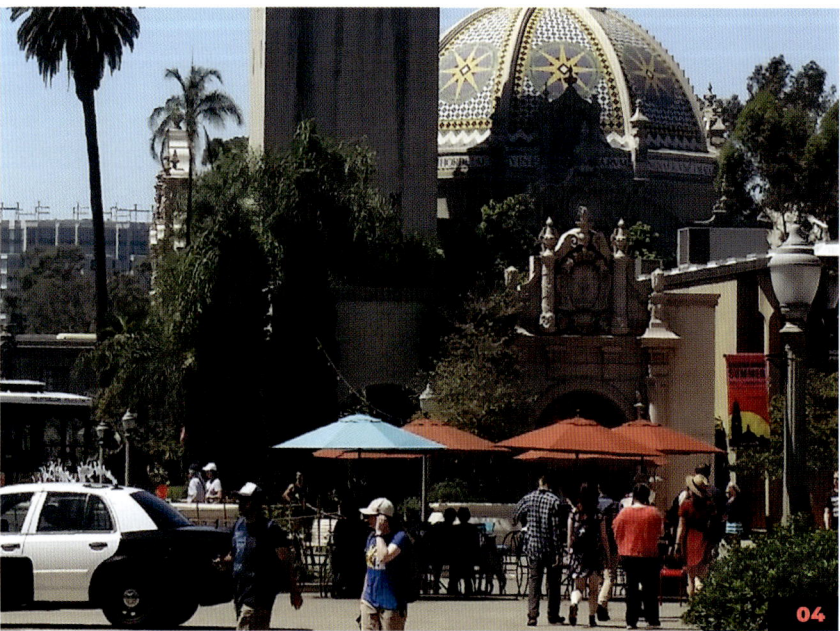

04 The location photo reference, close-up on the area I want the painting to focus on. The palm trees give a windblown "California coastal" flavor!

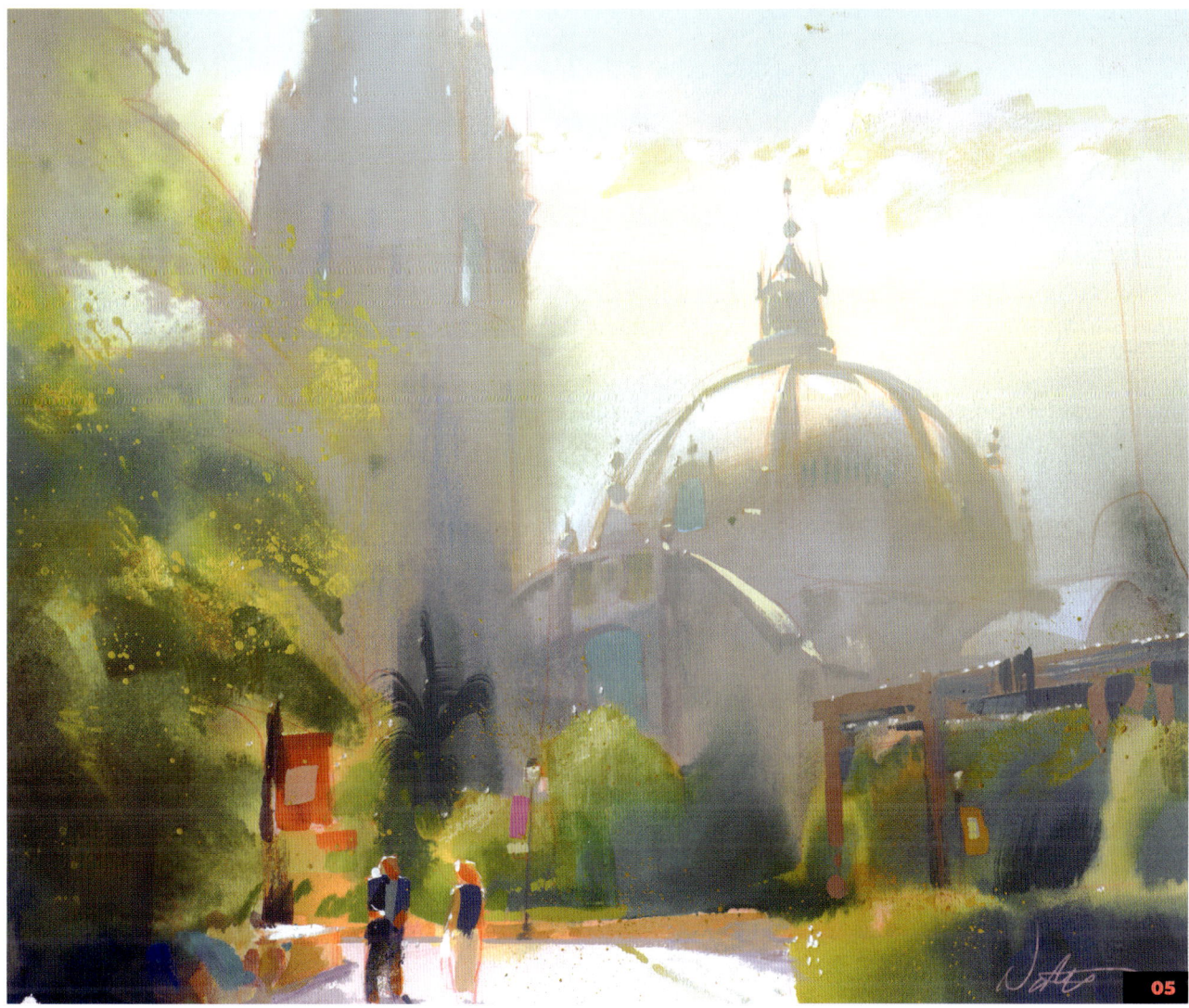

05 My on-location reference sketch, in watercolor, of Balboa Park. I will use this, combined with my photo references, as the basis of the final painting in the studio.

05 ON-LOCATION WATERCOLOR STUDY

This is a watercolor study that was done on location. I will use it to inform my palette of local colors, light, and quality of atmosphere. Comparing this image to the photograph, you will notice the strong difference in the atmospheric feeling. Even a beautifully shot photo doesn't capture the emotional experience of the ocean breeze, marine layer, and smell of salt in the air! That is why location studies are so important – they have an emotional component that is difficult to achieve in the studio.

I plan to keep an eye on the rich local colors in the foreground and contrast them with the neutrals of the buildings. The building shadows are also critically important. They are loaded with subtle warm and cool secondary lights; blue skylight from above, and warm bounce light that enters the shadows from the illuminated ground. These warms and cools will be the key to successful shadows in my painting, and they create the quality of Californian coastal atmosphere that I am after.

06 DIGITAL PAINTING PREP

After sketching on location and shooting my photo references, I come home enthusiastic to do more painting. With the location fresh in my memory, I create this digital painting in Adobe Photoshop. It is not the same architecture that I will be painting for you later, but it is the same location. Through this painting, I explore the backlit lighting palette of the scene that captures the atmospheric luminosity so well.

Of additional interest is the light falling across the foliage and the palm trees, and especially the sprinkle of local colors illuminated along the middle ground. Some of those colors are suggested by my photo reference, but some of them are invented to complement the greenery and create additional visual interest.

There is particular emphasis on the marine atmosphere here – you can see a transitional glow of sunlight from the sun outside the upper right of the frame. This glow is a key aspect of this painting's "flavor" and will be an influence on the step-by-step painting that follows.

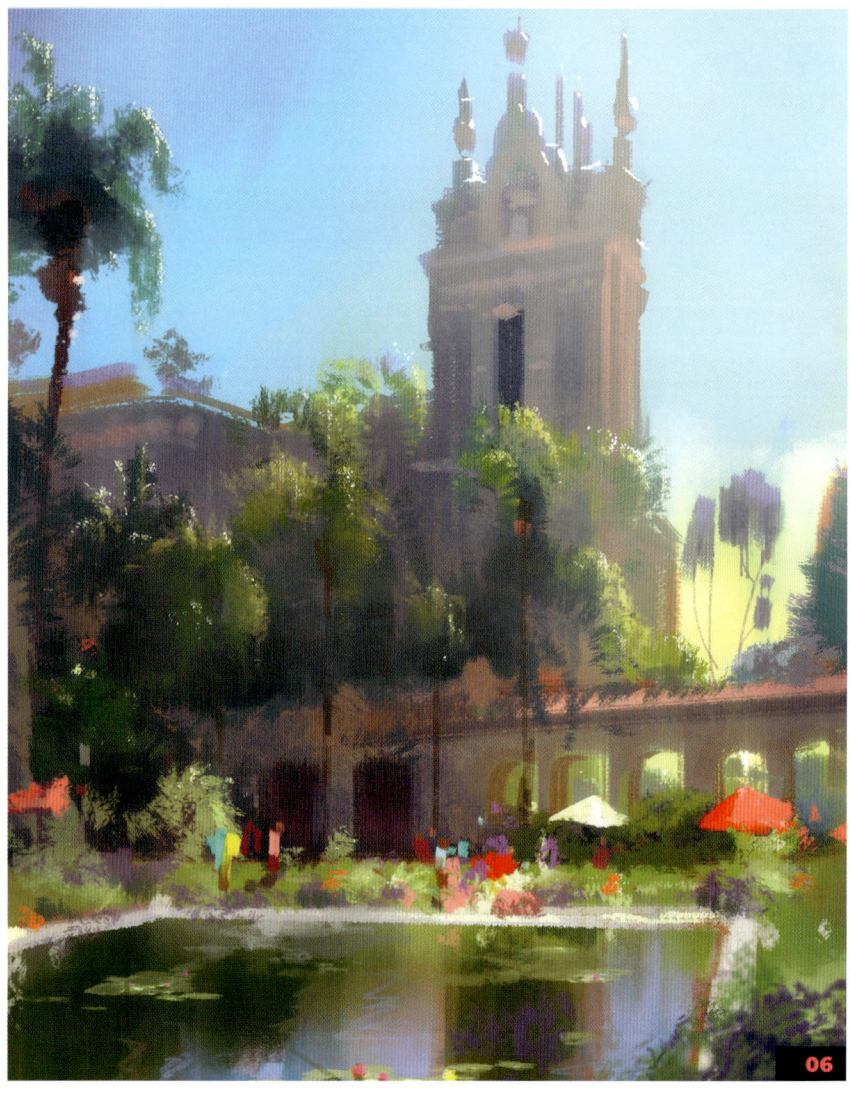

06 The digital reference study done in Photoshop upon returning to my studio. It's a very different view from the same location, but my focus is on color and mood rather than architecture.

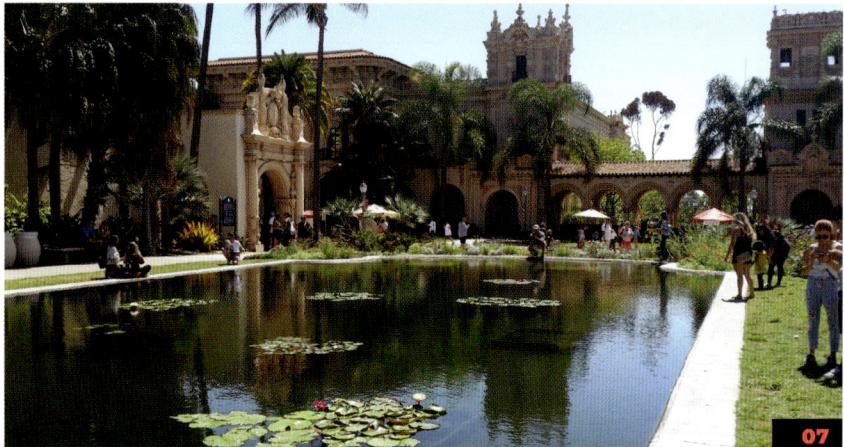

07 The photo reference for my digital practice study. You can see that I have taken artistic license with some hues to make my study more interesting and emotive than the photo.

07 SECOND PHOTOGRAPHIC REFERENCE

Below left, you can see the photo reference used for the digital study in step 06. As you can see, I am not at all interested in adhering exactly to reality. I see no need to, when my camera can do that faster and better than I can! Standing there in person, however, the architecture had a grandeur and presence that I was enthusiastic to emphasize. My painted image uses a vertical composition with stretched architecture, and I make some changes to the local colors as well.

In the previous step, I mentioned color adjustments to the outfits and umbrellas. Note how, in the photo reference, many of those elements are white or washed out – something I rectified in my painted version. For the final painting, I'll choose to emphasize the contrast in the hue of these elements instead of the light/dark value contrast. I will discuss the importance of hue contrast on page 316.

08 ROUGHING OUT A "COMP"

So, with our materials and references in place, we can officially begin. When working out ideas, I like the speed and versatility of digital painting. I am going to start by roughing out a "comp" in Adobe Photoshop – a "comprehensive layout" that maps out the direction of the final piece. My day job is designing for animated movies, and this is how I usually begin roughing out lighting and scenic ideas. Let me be clear that this is not a demonstration of digital techniques, but rather a demonstration of how to think about color and light.

I like to use basic organic and textured digital brushes that have an opacity based on stylus pen pressure. Below are the four digital brushes that I will use. The brush shown at the top is used for at least seventy percent of the painting, the middle two are used for foliage and texture, and the fourth is used when I need cleaner lines.

There is nothing particularly special about these digital brushes, and similar ones can be found online by the thousands – you can use any selection of large, textured brushes that you like.

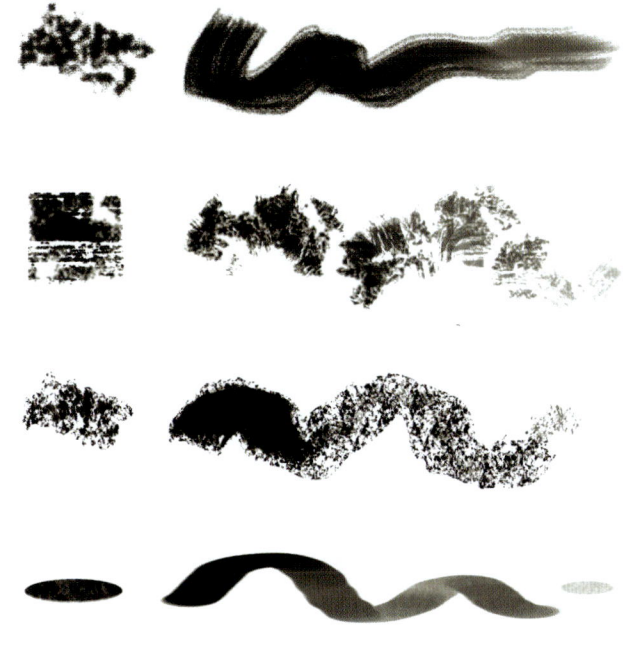

08 The textured brushes that I will use to create a digital "comp" in Adobe Photoshop.

PRACTICE, PRACTICE!

As you can see, I am constantly sketching and practicing my craft. Sometimes we artists worry about whether we have enough talent, but it's too late for that! We already are who we are, so worrying about talent is irrelevant. My experience is that the people who find success in this field are the ones who just can't let go of it. They make constant sacrifices to find time to sketch and practice. They are the ones who do the heavy lifting necessary to train their hand, eyes, and mind to make the marks that become meaningful art.

#FFFF8D

09

09 Laying a foundation by choosing a background color – in this case, lemon yellow – to begin establishing a warm, sunny atmosphere.

09 LAYING DOWN A LEMON YELLOW

I always begin a painting by working out in my mind exactly its purpose and emphasis. I want this image to express my delight at the quality of Mediterranean light and atmosphere in this setting. With this quality in mind, it is time to lay down a ground color that will be the foundation for these effects. My approach tends to be to put the very simplest ideas down first, and then slowly build in complexity. Since I want a warm, glowing, backlit, sunny feeling, I begin by laying down a lemon yellow in preparation for the sky and architecture.

10 AN AERIAL GRADIENT

If you look at my photo reference of this location, you will see a rather passive sky, but that is not the truth of really being there. My lived experience included a brisk, salty breeze that came up from the ocean and kept the location in motion. The sky is my opportunity to convey that effect to the viewer. It has a color transition that I want to start with – an ultramarine blue at the top that moves into a cyan, and finally gets warmer toward the horizon. I exaggerate

10

10 Bringing life to the sky by adding a gradient of blue toward the top. Visible brushstrokes give the gradient motion and texture.

this effect by leaving the yellow at the bottom and letting the top of the sky take on a violet hue. To portray a wind and sky that are in motion, I let my brushstrokes remain very active throughout the transition from cooler to warmer light.

11 BLOCKING IN THE ARCHITECTURE

Since I want my painting to have a strong graphic statement, I block in the architecture as simply as possible. I have mentioned that my process is to put the simplest idea down

first, and this is my opportunity to carry through on that idea. The buildings are made of a warm, light-gray stone that is mostly in shadow, so I use a warm gray midtone to block in their shape. In later steps I will be adding cool atmospheric tones and skylight into the shadow, and this warmth will keep the landscape from becoming too cold later.

11 Blocking in the landscape as simply as possible, using a midtone that will serve as a warm foundation for the rest of the landscape later.

12 Suggesting secondary lights and local colors in the landscape, such as warm and cool planes and greens for the foliage.

13 Adding direct sunlight, finalizing skylight in the shadows, and loosely suggesting architectural details on the main buildings.

12 SECONDARY LIGHTS AND LOCAL COLORS

Now it is time to create some color variation in the scene by suggesting secondary lights and local colors. By secondary lights, I am referring to the cooler light that comes down from the sky into the shadows, and warmer lights that bounce into the shadow from adjacent sunlight.

On the tall spire, the front is cooler because it is receiving more skylight, and the left-side plane is warmer since it receives more bounce light from adjacent illumination. These big plane changes are what I'm looking for when creating warm and cool variations in the shadow. The ground plane is painted with a lighter value, since it picks up a good deal of cool skylight. I also lay in an underpainting of green local color where the foliage will be located.

13 SUNLIGHT AND SHADOW

Most of the work so far has been underpainting and shadow, so it is now time to commit to the direct sunlight falling across the location. For the tall spire, I am careful to show that the left-side planes are illuminated, with some broken brushstrokes that suggest the ornamental variations.

I make sure that the sunlight wraps around the dome in a way that describes its form – even though this is a loose and suggestive approach, plane changes are still important to capture. The sunlight itself is a warm white, so I keep a hint of yellow in it, with a bit of pink here and there. I also add additional skylight to the front and top planes, in the shadow.

14 A COASTAL ATMOSPHERE

Palm trees are crucial to the mood of this location, so it is time to suggest those along the skyline. I begin with red to reinforce the backlit quality of the scene. Then I add some green for the local color of the trees, followed by blue atmospheric light. This is not the time for rendering, so I am careful to keep the trees as simple as possible.

Next, I add a sprinkle of direct sunlight at the center of the image to suggest detail. I am ignoring what is really happening in my photo reference, instead choosing to selectively use contrasts to draw the eye toward the lower-middle segment of the image, which will shortly become the scene's center of interest.

14 Suggesting palm trees and a sprinkle of detail with sunlight, taking some liberties with my reference to pick out details that are eye-catching.

15 HUE AND VALUE

Here is a close-up of the palm trees on the left-hand side. I have zoomed into this area to show how important it is to not overlabor at this stage, and instead to suggest shape and luminosity. I want to emphasize how, while my chosen color hues have significant contrast, the values are very similar. The only exception to this is the atmospheric blue, which needs to be a touch lighter than the green local color, as it is a product of illumination from the sky.

16 CLOSE-UP TEXTURES

I also want to show you this tight crop-in of the central area of the painting, to give you an idea of the quality of brushstrokes and layered textures. The segments of warm light on the middle-right are meant to represent top and side planes catching direct sunlight, though they remain simple and abstract. Texture is also important here: the warm surface and cool light at the bottom represent a gravelly ground plane, so a good amount of texture is appropriate to suggest the quality of the surface. There is also texture concentrated in the greens to the right, which helps to suggest the visual activity of foliage.

17 POPULATING THE SCENE

The top of the painting has come to life, so now is the time to move downward and create the primary area of interest. After all, everything so far has been building up to this moment. I want the umbrellas to really pop, so they need to have value, hue, and saturation contrast. I am using dark, loose strokes to suggest the people sitting beneath their umbrellas, and also the shadows that they cast along the ground. The people are wearing a variety of local colors, so I choose the ones that will enhance the visual interest of the area. I emphasize yellow and cyan, since they echo colors elsewhere in the study, and contrast with the warmth of the immediate background.

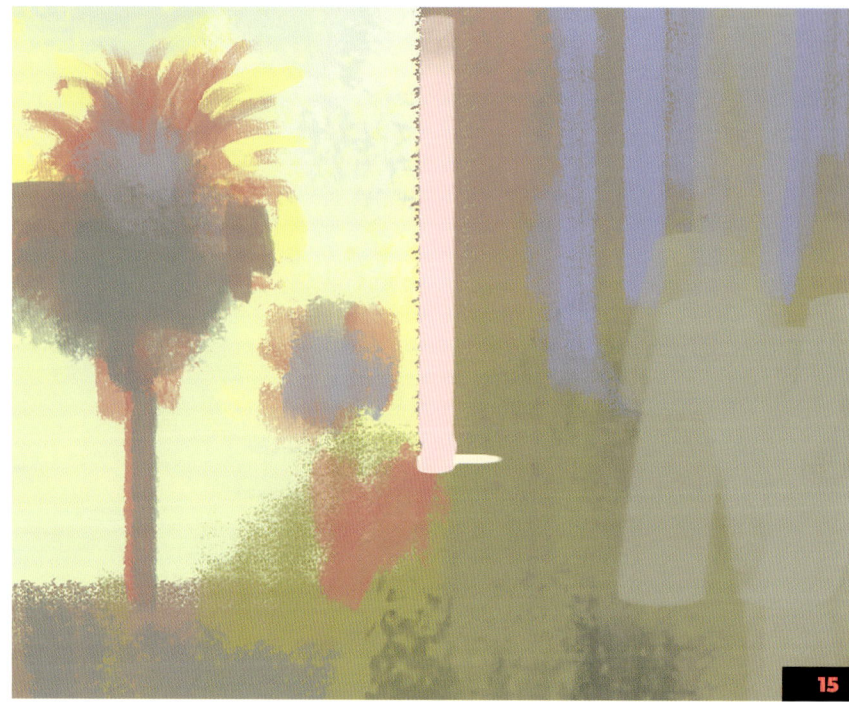

15 A palm tree close-up to show how little detail is actually used at this stage – the impression of the tree's sunlit leaves is created with color and texture.

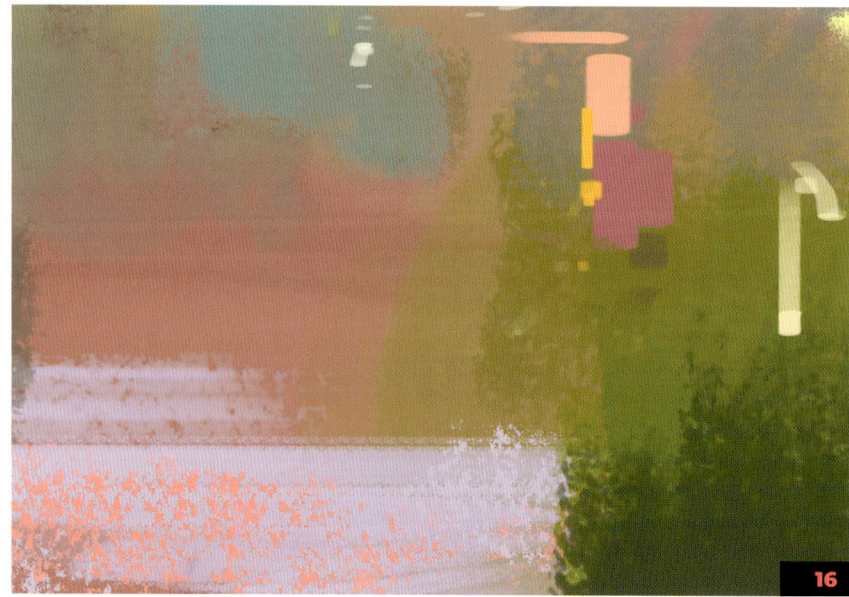

16 Close-up of the central area of the painting. Again, the specifics of the environment are heavily simplified and abstracted, but the impression of rough ground and green foliage is still there.

17 Creating the center of interest.

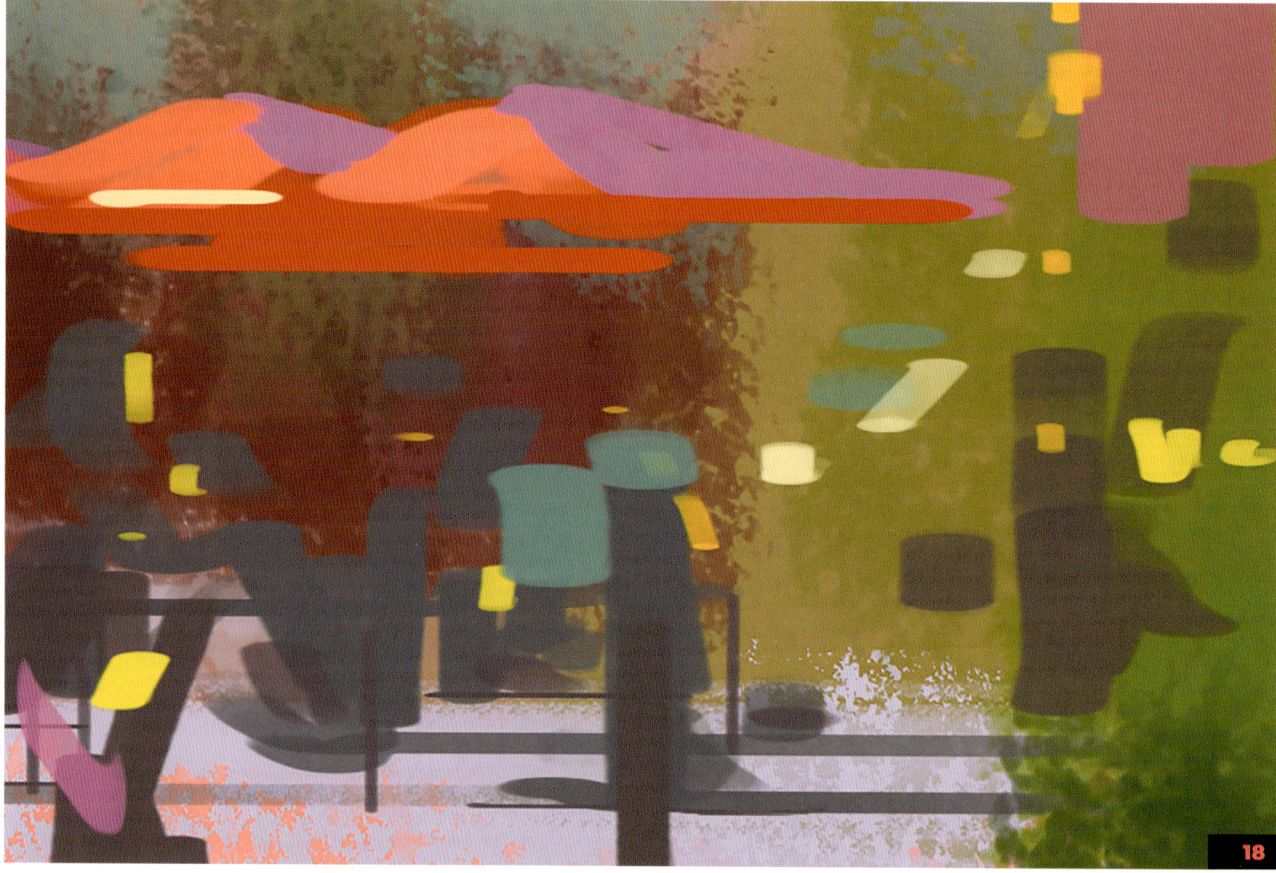

18 A close-up of the primary area of interest, showing the level of loose, energetic dynamism I'm aiming to capture in my brushstrokes.

18 ZOOMING IN

I want to be sure to show the quick and loose quality of the primary area of visual interest. Up close, the people and tables don't look like people and tables at all; they are a mere suggestion. A bit of rendering is needed in the umbrellas, however, as there is warm light coming from the left, cool skylight coming from the top right, and a darker red local color of the umbrellas underneath. Note the active, expressive quality of the brushstrokes – I want them to have a crackling electricity!

19 FINISHING TOUCHES

And here is the completed comp. At a glance it may look identical to the previous step, but there are some important subtleties here that are worthy of discussion. This is the stage where I look carefully at my design of contrast, and ask myself two questions:

- Are there any areas that are demanding too much attention?

- Are there any areas that need to command more attention?

One area that is creating a subtle but problematic distraction is where land meets sky at the middle-right and middle-left. To solve this, I create a hazy marine layer, which reduces the contrast by softening the edges and creating a value step between the land and sky. There is also too much contrast at the edges of the spire and dome, so I soften and reduce contrast there as well.

We have now wrangled all the competing elements into their proper places to emphasize the purpose of the image: a breezy, windswept, Mediterranean-feeling location that has a visual center of activity.

20 HARMONY AND CONTRAST

I have charted the major color notes from my painting onto a color wheel, shown right, to display an important quality of their relationships. Let's refer to these relationships as "harmony and contrast." The human eye tends to like harmony. If all the elements of an image feel like they belong together in some way, the painting will have a feeling of purpose.

Notice how the majority of colors create a clump in the center of the wheel. They are less saturated and so fall around the middle, with the center being a neutral gray. These colors have a relative "grayness" in common, and feel similar compared to the contrasting hues on the outskirts of the wheel – they have *harmony*. Color harmony is a great way to create a feeling of unity in a painting.

However, be aware that too much harmony is really, really boring – the eye also wants some excitement! This is why the saturated color in the umbrellas is so important. The red, magenta, and cyan are very different from one other, and high in saturation. They have lots of *contrast* from one other and from the rest of the painting. They are shown to fall near the outskirts of the color wheel. For me, *harmony with contrast* is one of the most useful ideas for designing the color relationships that the viewer will be captivated by.

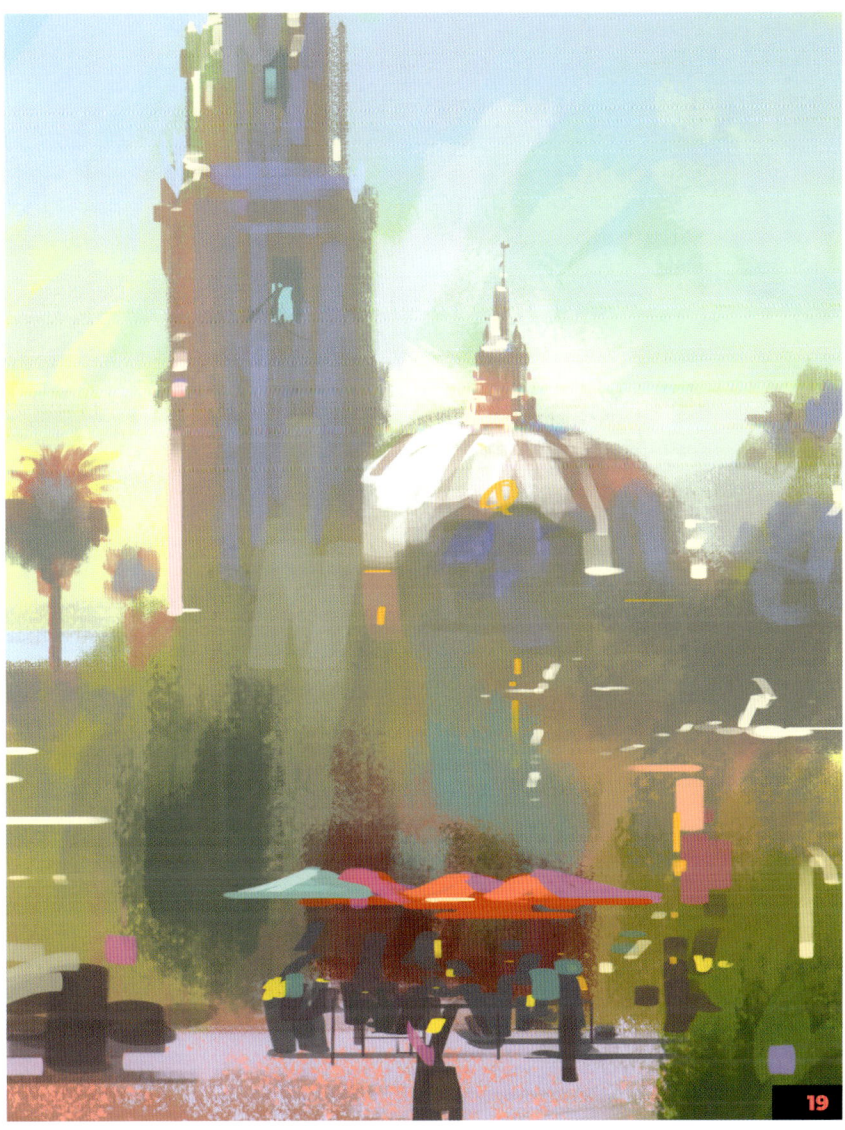

19 The completed comp. I softened some edges around the horizon and edges of the buildings to add more coastal haziness to the scene.

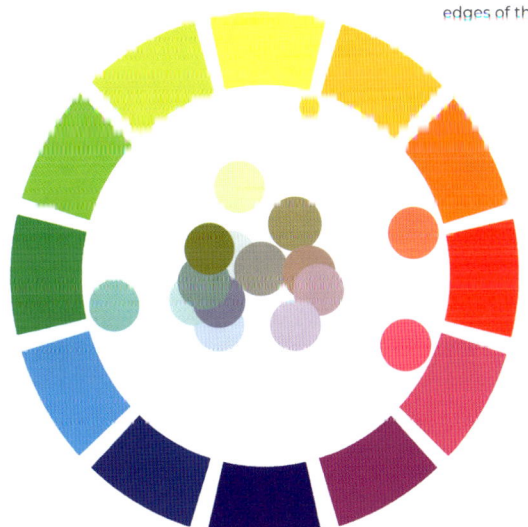

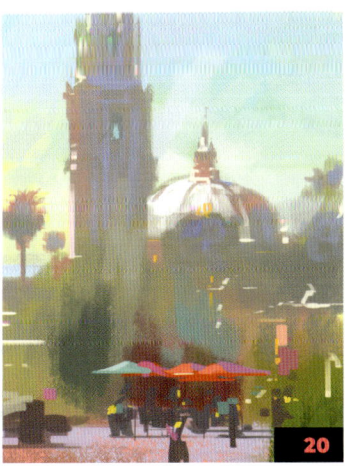

20 Diagram of the color theory and color relationships in the comp. Note how the saturated magenta, red, and cyan stand out vividly against the more muted colors of the scene.

21 PAINTING PREP

Now we are ready to begin the final painting. I use a wide range of papers depending on the needs of the subject; my favorites are Arches 140 lb cold-pressed watercolor paper blocks and Strathmore Series 400 Mixed Media toned paper. For this project, I will be using the latter and a red Prismacolor pencil. I have chosen the toned paper because it will do some of the work for me, as I do not want my underpainting to lift into my final strokes as I paint. The toned paper minimizes the amount of paint I need to initially put down, thus avoiding a great deal of pain and suffering later!

I prefer to tape the paper down to a drawing board with an acid-free artist's tape to minimize the paper buckling from the wet media. I prefer using a red Prismacolor pencil for sketching because the color tends to work with my painting – it does not lift off and smudge the way charcoal or graphite would. With these materials in place, I am ready to begin sketching out the final piece.

22 SIMPLE GUIDELINES

My drawing here is simple but important. The red lines will be my guide in the following steps, where I will block in an opaquely painted sky. I am happy with the composition of my initial study, so I am carefully placing the big shapes based on that, rather than following the literal photo reference. It is another case of doing what feels right, rather than following the exactness of the location. This is art – feeling and emotion is what matters!

23 A WASH OF YELLOW

Like in the digital comp, I begin by laying in an initial wash of color. The medium and materials are different now, so my technique and approach are different as well. My method here is to choose the overall average value of the landscape. Getting this right will save me a lot of time – by letting these tones work for me, it will be as if my shadows are

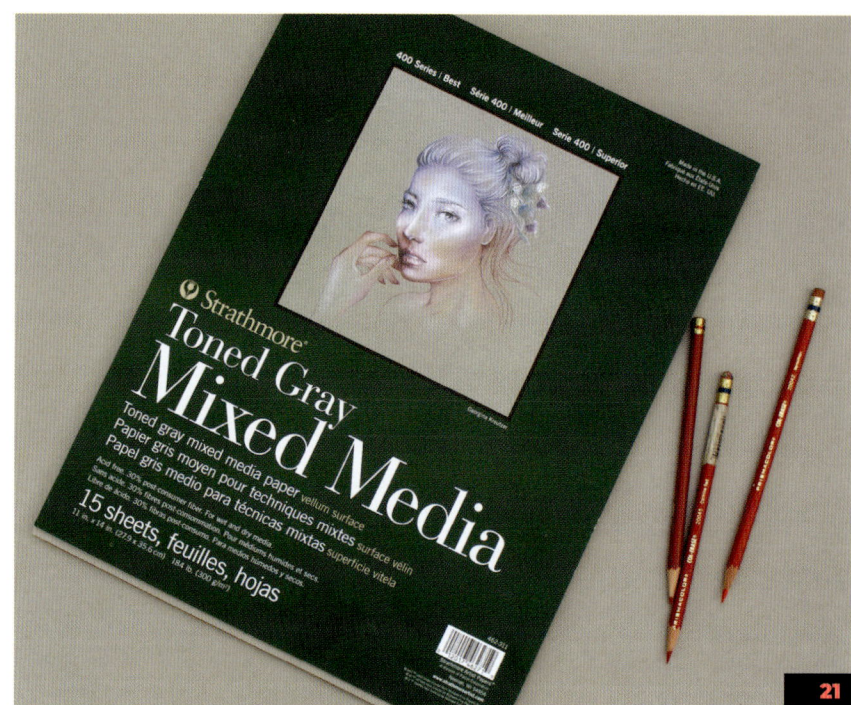

21 My paper and pencils for the final painting.

already blocked in. The watercolor I am using is yellow ochre, wetly scumbled (see the tip on page 321) across the surface. I want it to have some texture and brush movement, but not to the point of distraction. The warmth of the color serves the same purpose that it did in the comp – when I lay in the cooler atmospheric colors, this underlying warmth will contribute to the feeling of luminosity in the painting.

24 PALETTE AND MATERIALS

This is what my palette and materials look like at this point. Everything is wet and thick and ready to go! The brushes and the surrounding paint shown here should help give you a feel for the paint thickness. The brushes are filled with white gouache, a tiny bit of yellow, and very little water.

I also have a blow dryer handy. There's no reason to sit around and wait for paint to dry – I am constantly blow-drying the underpainting so that I can get to the next layer as I work.

22 My initial drawing lay-in using red pencil on toned paper. I am following the design established by my comp sketch rather than adhering closely to the original photo.

23 My foundational wash of color, scumbling yellow ochre onto the page for a warm, textured base.

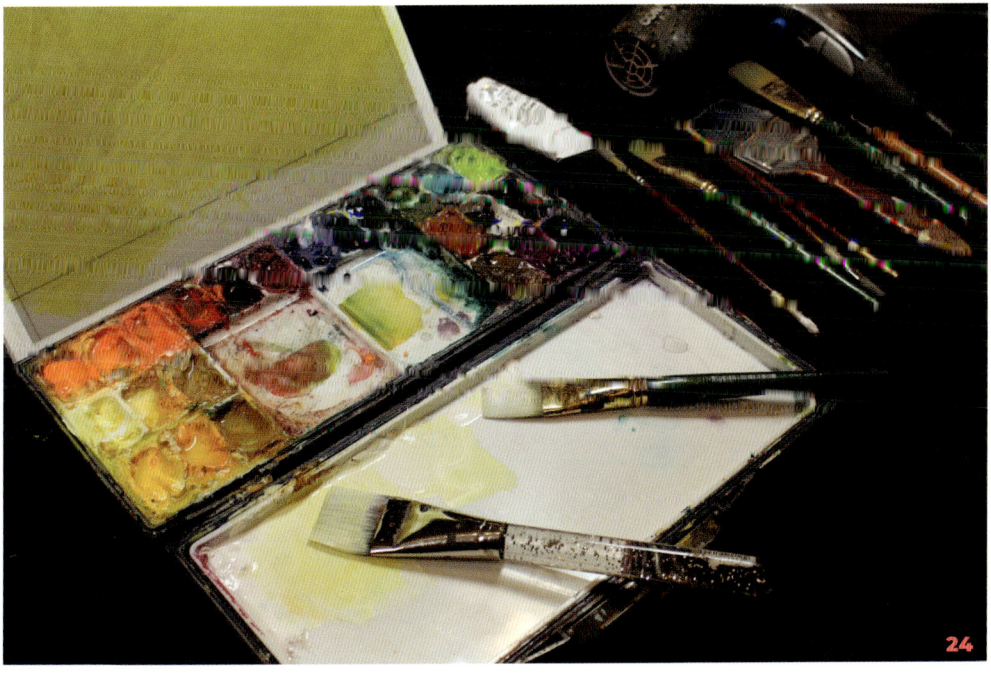

24 My initial palette and materials for the final piece. I think it was my daughter who nicked out the foreground brush with glitter in the handle!

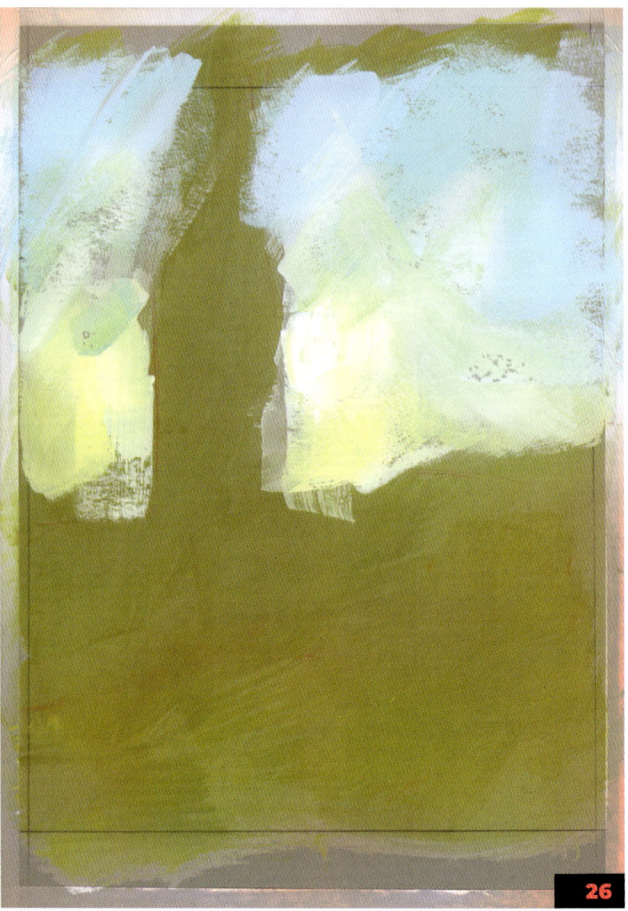

25 Beginning the sky with a layer of opaque pigment, using textured strokes of thick white gouache with a hint of yellow.

26 Painting transitional colors in the sky using blue, turquoise, and green hues, leaving the silhouette of the tall spire roughly intact for later.

25 AN OPAQUE SKY

For the initial sky color, I mix a little Winsor yellow with white designer's gouache, being careful to keep my paints as thick as possible. This layer will need to opaquely cover the underlying color, so I load up the brush with as much pigment as I can and drag the side of the brush along my surface to apply the pigment. Texture and brush movement are key here to create that dynamic sky with organic variation.

26 A GRADIENT SKY

To finish off the sky, I am using the same gradation of colors that I used in the comp, continuing to paint very thickly with a drybrush technique. I am using Ultramarine Blue, Phthalo Blue, and opaque white at the top, then adding Cobalt Turquoise and grading down to a green hue by adding yellow to my mix. The colors blend fairly smoothly into each other because I am working quickly before each application of paint dries, but a perfect blend of colors is not favorable here. I don't want to bore my audience with totally smooth blending!

I leave the underlying color for the architectural spire, since it will be needed shortly, but the benefit of working opaquely is that I don't have to be too mechanically careful at this point. I can mold the painting's design and shapes as I go.

THREE TECHNIQUES FOR PAINTING WITH WATERCOLOR AND GOUACHE

I typically use three techniques for laying down my colors when working with watercolor and opaque white gouache: washes, scumbling, and drybrushing. A wash is a very wet application that quickly fills an area with color. Scumbling uses less water for a drier, more active application of pigment. For this technique, I typically use large, flat brushes that are damp with pigment but not dripping wet, using the side of the brush to work the color into my surface. For drybrushing, I use very little water with the paint as thick as possible. I drag the pigment across the surface, creating a very textural application of paint, like the example shown below.

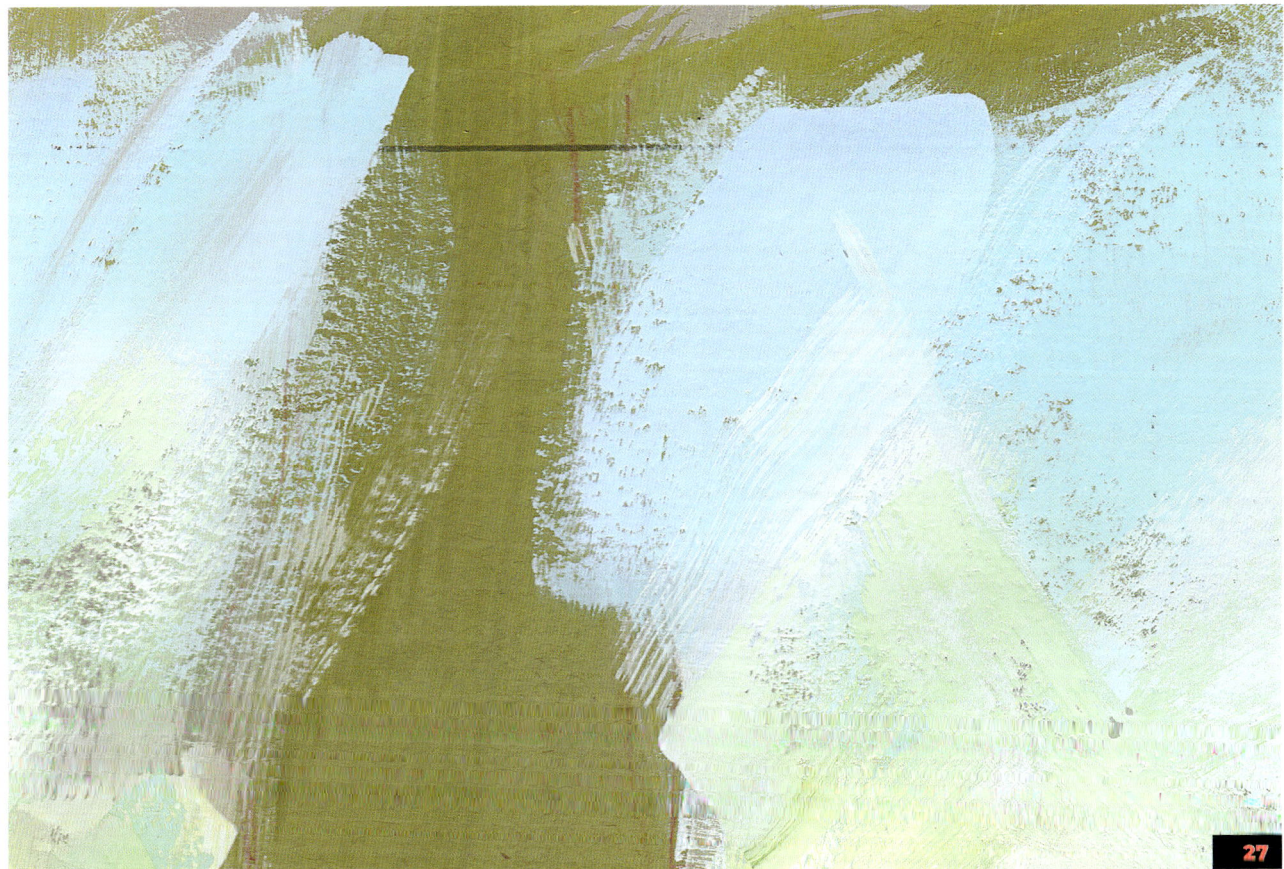

27 Close-up showing the sky painting technique – you can see how thick, opaque, and dry the paint application is in the sky colors.

27 DRYBRUSH TECHNIQUE

This close-up will help you understand how I apply my paint, since this technique is often central to my approach. The paint is applied thickly, and dry enough that the underlying color does not lift into it.

As we get into further discussions of color-mixing later in this project, you will see how this drybrush technique is used as part of my color design as well, with the color of the opaque paint and the color showing through beneath carefully chosen to achieve specific visual effects.

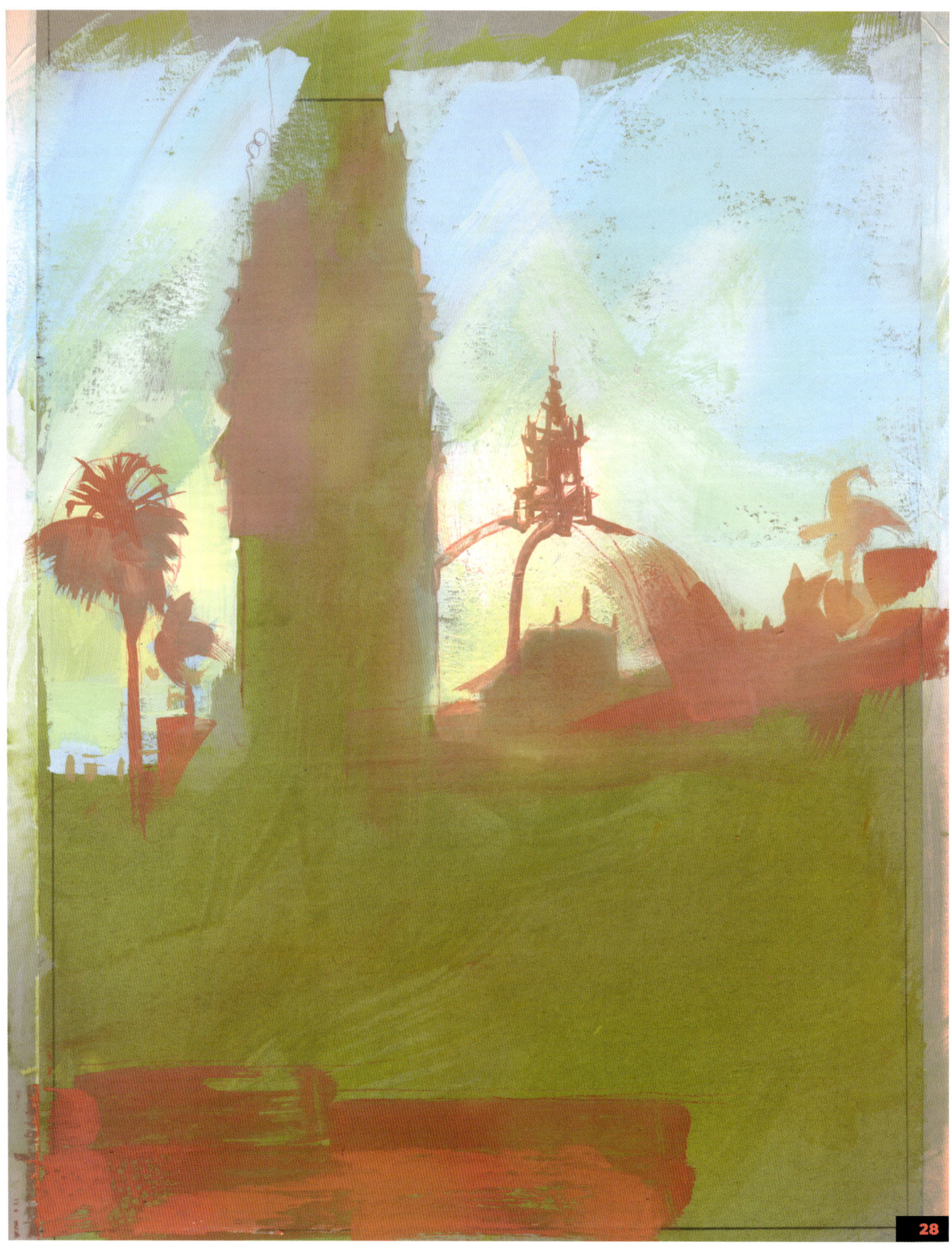

28 Refining shapes and adding warm underpainting. These washes are more translucent than the thick strokes used for the sky.

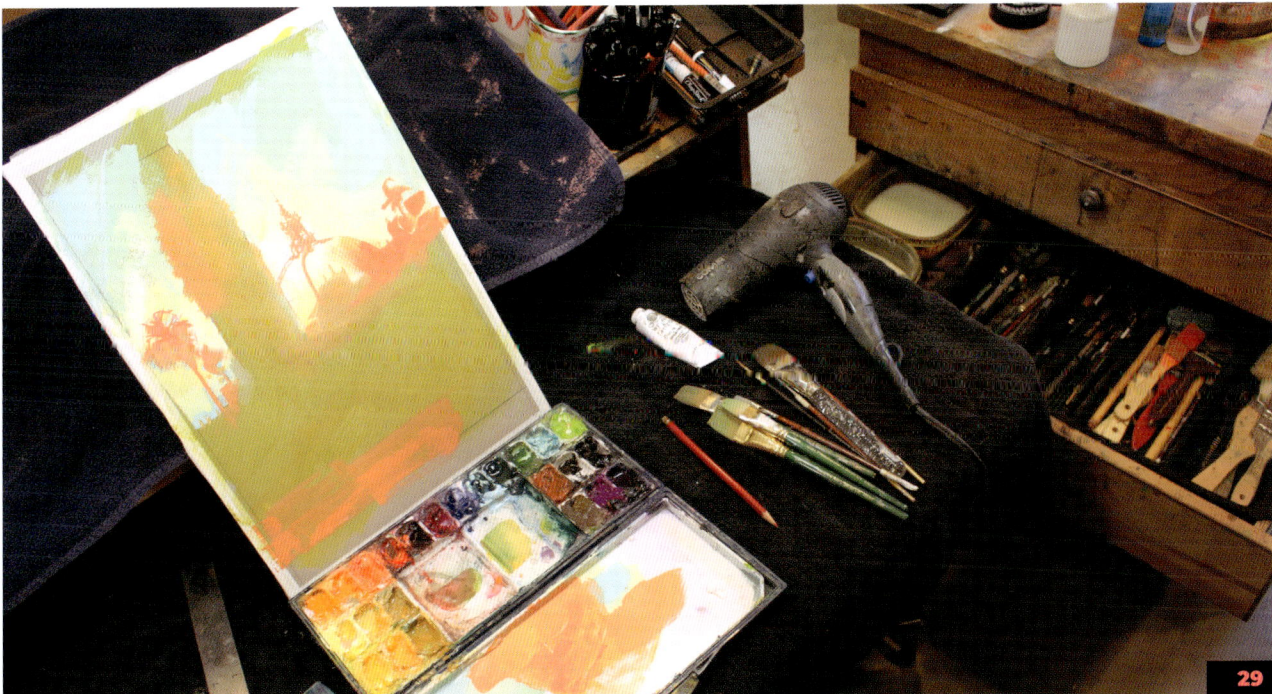

29 The painting setup in progress. I never use an easel, instead opting for the freer feeling of painting on a loose board.

28 REFINING THE SILHOUETTES

With the sky roughed in, I am ready to refine the shapes of the landscape and architecture, and apply warm notes to the underpainting. The trick here is to suggest the ornamental quality and complexity of the architecture without making the shapes too busy and confusing. I keep my eye on the overall silhouettes, making sure that the smaller shapes do not become overwhelming.

As in the digital comp, the warm tones are used to create the backlit quality of the scene and suggest warm bounce light in the shadows. I am applying the paint in translucent washes, and I only get one shot at these strokes – a second stroke over a wet area will lift up the underlying paint and make a mess. This might sound frustrating, but I love the "do or die" quality of committing to the correctness of each brushstroke. A painting filled with confident brushstrokes has a feeling of spontaneity and authority. At the same time, no one's perfect – if I mess up, some thicker, more opaque paint over the top can help correct errant brushstrokes.

29 CURRENT PAINTING SETUP

I thought you might like to see my painting setup at this point. I do my best to keep organized. There is no easel here; in fact, I never paint at an easel, not even outdoors. I am not at all against easels, but for me they just end up being a hassle. Instead I am sitting down in my studio, with my painting board loose so I can easily tip and move it around. This freedom of movement helps me avoid glare from the lighting and get just the right level of brush contact.

My water bins and extra brushes are in a taboret off to the side. I always use two water bins – the first gets the bulk of pigment off the brush and the second gives the final clean. This way I am not always fighting a single bucket of very dirty water. For me, convenience is important to painting both indoors and out. I simply do not have the time nor the energy to be fighting my tools!

THE IMPORTANCE OF MASSING

You will notice at this stage in the painting (and at a similar stage in the comp) that the landscape, trees, and architecture are massed against the sky very simply and with a clear commitment. By "massing," I mean that these objects are grouped into one simple, graphic silhouette. Every painting has its own considerations, but it is often true that a bold, graphic composition will grab viewers from across the room and give a purposeful quality to a painting. That is definitely my approach here.

THE VITALITY OF SKIES

I have touched on the topic of skies, and promised further discussion, which we'll get into now. I have experienced extraordinary frustration and gone to enormous lengths to bring life to paintings on my two-dimensional drawing board, and skies are a part of the solution. In real life, skies are an actual light source. They have a luminosity that goes beyond what we can achieve with pigment on a page, and this is why I feel that extraordinary lengths sometimes have to be taken.

As you can see in the comp sky below, I have taken warmer and cooler hues and exaggerated them to get a greater sense of luminosity. I often add activity to my brushstrokes that doesn't visually exist in real life, but that you feel in the wind. So, in the final painting, I very carefully move my brushstrokes in a consistent diagonal direction. These diagonals convey a sense of action and movement that flat, horizontal gradations can never achieve.

Finally, there is one quality of skies that has staggered me since the beginning. They look deeply blue on a clear sunny day, but, at the same time, the sky's hue somehow seems to have an underlying warmth. The technique that I have developed to suggest this effect is to put warm hues down first, then drybrush over them with blues so that some of the yellows and warms peek through and create that underlying luminosity. You can see some of that effect happening here, and I will discuss it further on page 330.

Initial comp sky

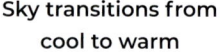

Sky transitions from cool to warm

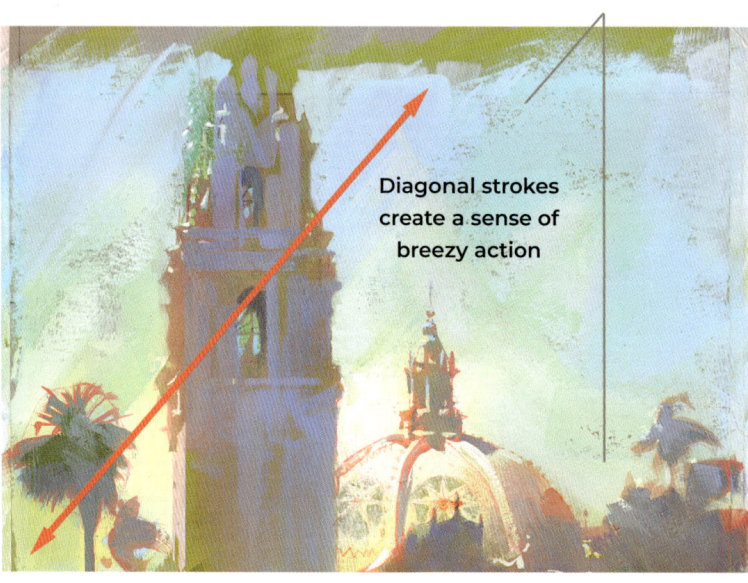

Diagonal strokes create a sense of breezy action

Dynamic skies. I add life to my skies by using warm underpaintings, temperature transitions, and dynamic brushstrokes.

30 PALE SHADOWS

Now it is time to really dig into the shadows. This primarily consists of laying down some dark tones for the deeper recesses, and then drybrushing cooler atmospheric light over the top. I also start thinking about the local colors of the foliage and pushing greens into those areas. I am careful to move my brush in the direction in which the foliage naturally grows, which tends to be vertical here, and I am mostly drybrushing to get some texture.

Next is the atmospheric light, working with very thick paint to avoid lifting up the underpainting. I know that I keep mentioning the paint thickness, but my experience in teaching this approach is that students tend to use *way* too much water at this stage. The paint is meant to be very thick and the brush quite dry – there should be no drippy wetness here!

The atmospheric light tends to fall across the top and left-side planes, so I am concentrating my efforts on those. Notice that my overall values are still fairly grouped in the shadows. Remember that all of this is still a backdrop – a setup for the primary visual interest that will be laid over top. If this area gets too busy and varied in value, it will compete with the visual interest that I need in later stages.

31 CAREFUL LAYERING

I have provided another close-up on the right to give you an idea of how the paint is layered. This overlapped approach is one of the primary reasons that I use my watercolors in a more opaque fashion. You will remember that the warms were applied first. This step shows how the cooler tones are scumbled and drybrushed over the top. This technique allows the underlying warmth to glow through, creating that Mediterranean luminosity that I have aimed for all along. Also note the consistent direction of the brushstrokes – this is very intentional to create the windblown effect of the location. As one last reminder about value, note how these overlapping tones are all very close in value. If the value is not controlled, that luminous quality will be lost.

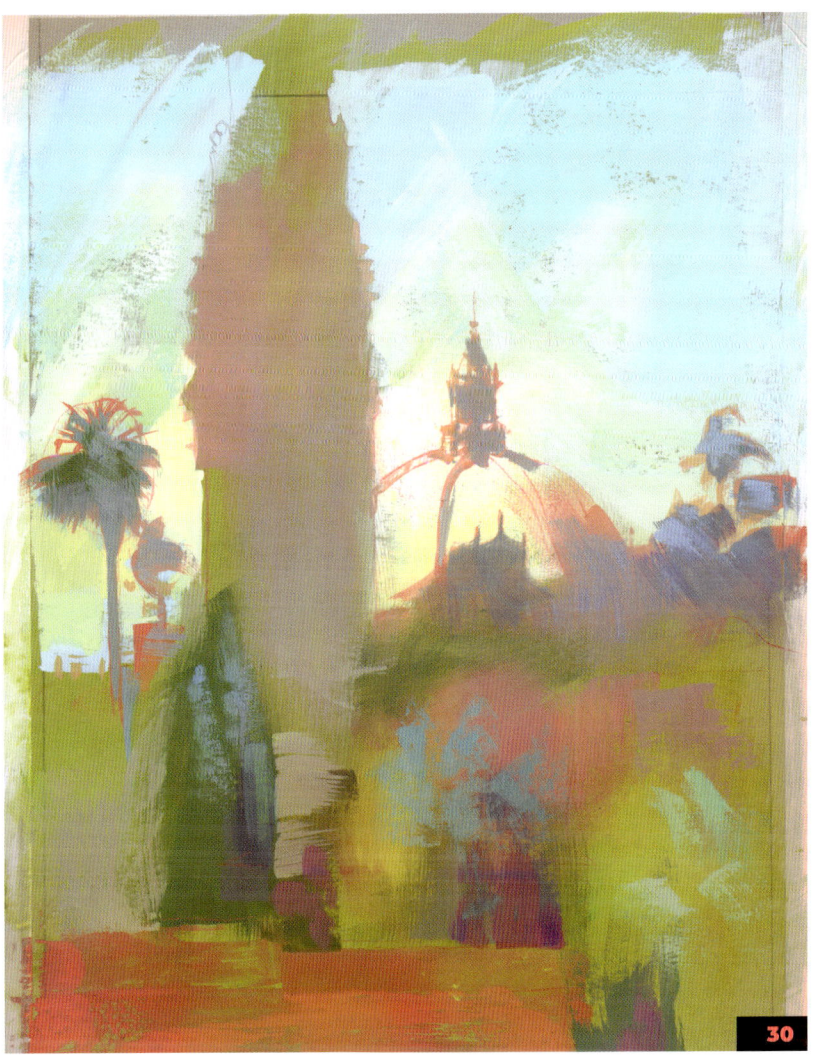

30 Working with skylight and local color in the shadows, keeping the values quite closely grouped together – this is still just a backdrop, where brighter values will be added later.

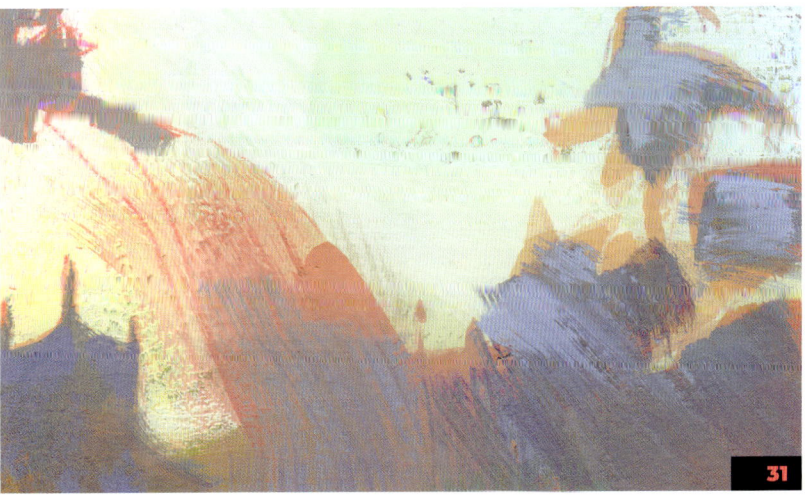

31 This close-up shows the layering technique of the paint. Keeping these overlapping strokes close in value creates the desired warm glow.

32 CREATING VISUAL INTEREST

The stage is set, and now I am ready to add the centerpiece. Before I paint the umbrellas, I add some warm darks behind them to create a strong contrast with the background. Then I can move on and begin the umbrellas themselves. Their color is highly saturated, just about as pure as my pigment will go, though I do indicate plane changes; they are darker underneath, and the top left of each umbrella is in shadow.

If my underpainting did not quite make sense to you previously, I hope it does now. All the carefully placed greens, cools, and darks were intentional, but they did not look quite right until the umbrellas were added. It takes experience to learn what is needed in an underpainting, but regular practice and study is well rewarded.

I also add more cool light to the top and front planes of the spire, as well as giving it windows. These accents are important to give that area a bit of finish and visual interest.

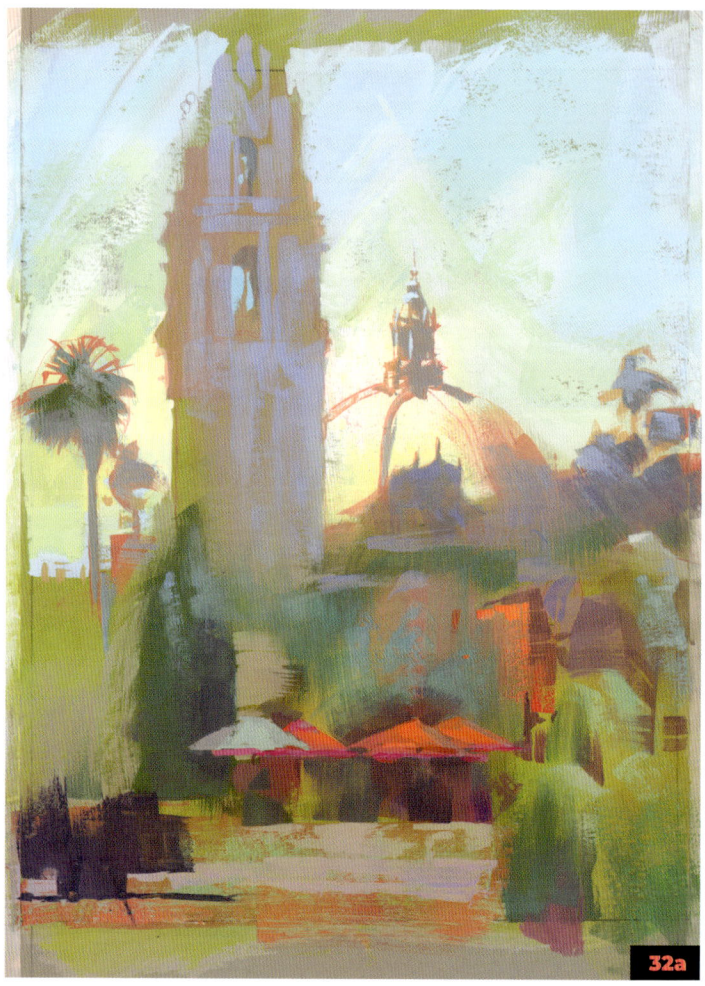

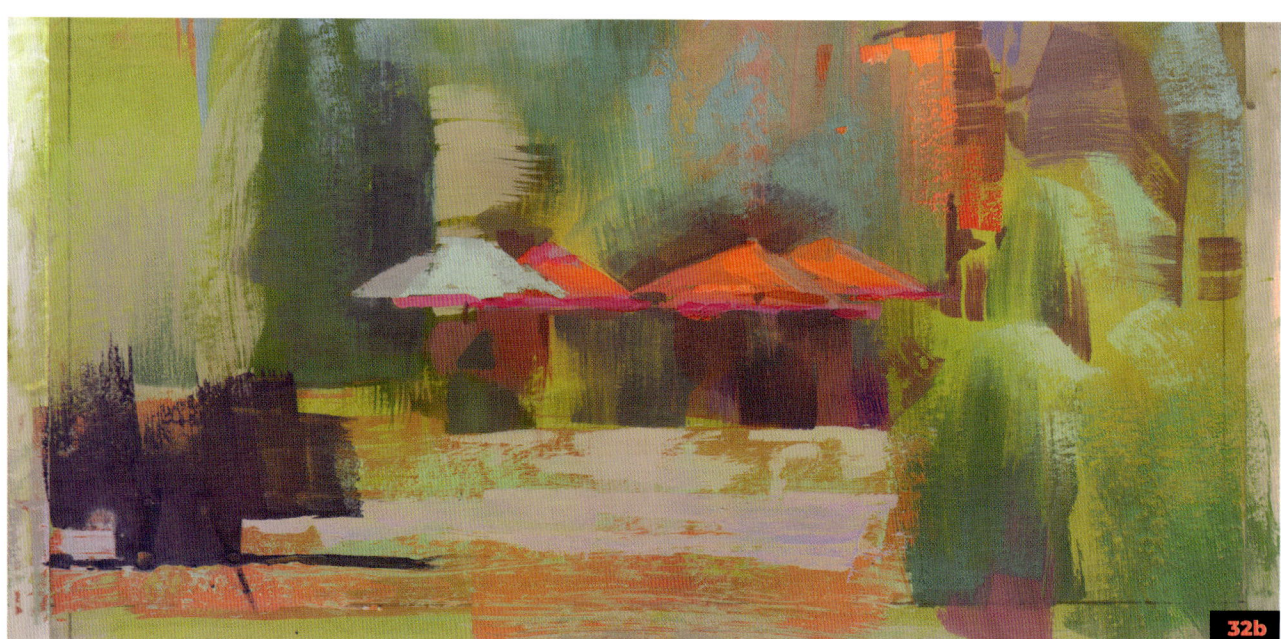

32a – 32b Adding the main focus of the image: the colorful, saturated umbrellas in the center of the environment. This is when all the careful underpainting finally pays off.

LUMINOUS ATMOSPHERE

I have been touching on the idea of luminous atmosphere throughout this demonstration, and it is now time to take it further. Our light sources consist of direct sunlight, warm light bouncing from illuminated areas into shadow, cool light from the sky, and subsurface scattering. Subsurface scattering is the light that is able to pass through translucent objects such as palm fronds. This light is usually apparent on the shadow side of an object, adjacent to where it is directly illuminated. In a backlit situation like ours, it can create a warm glow in an object (as you see in the palm tree here on the left). The local color of green is painted into the more recessed areas of the tree,

and then the cooler atmospheric tones are glazed into the area exposed to the sky. There is a lot happening here, and yet this cool-over-warm glowing effect has been fairly easy to achieve.

I want to also point you to the front plane of the spire as a prime example of cool skylight over a warm surface. The shadow itself is a warm, neutral color, and when I carefully scumble a lighter, bluer pigment over areas open to the sky, the contrasting warm and cool become brilliant together. I love this. By themselves, they are just a cool gray and a warm gray, but put them together and they spark!

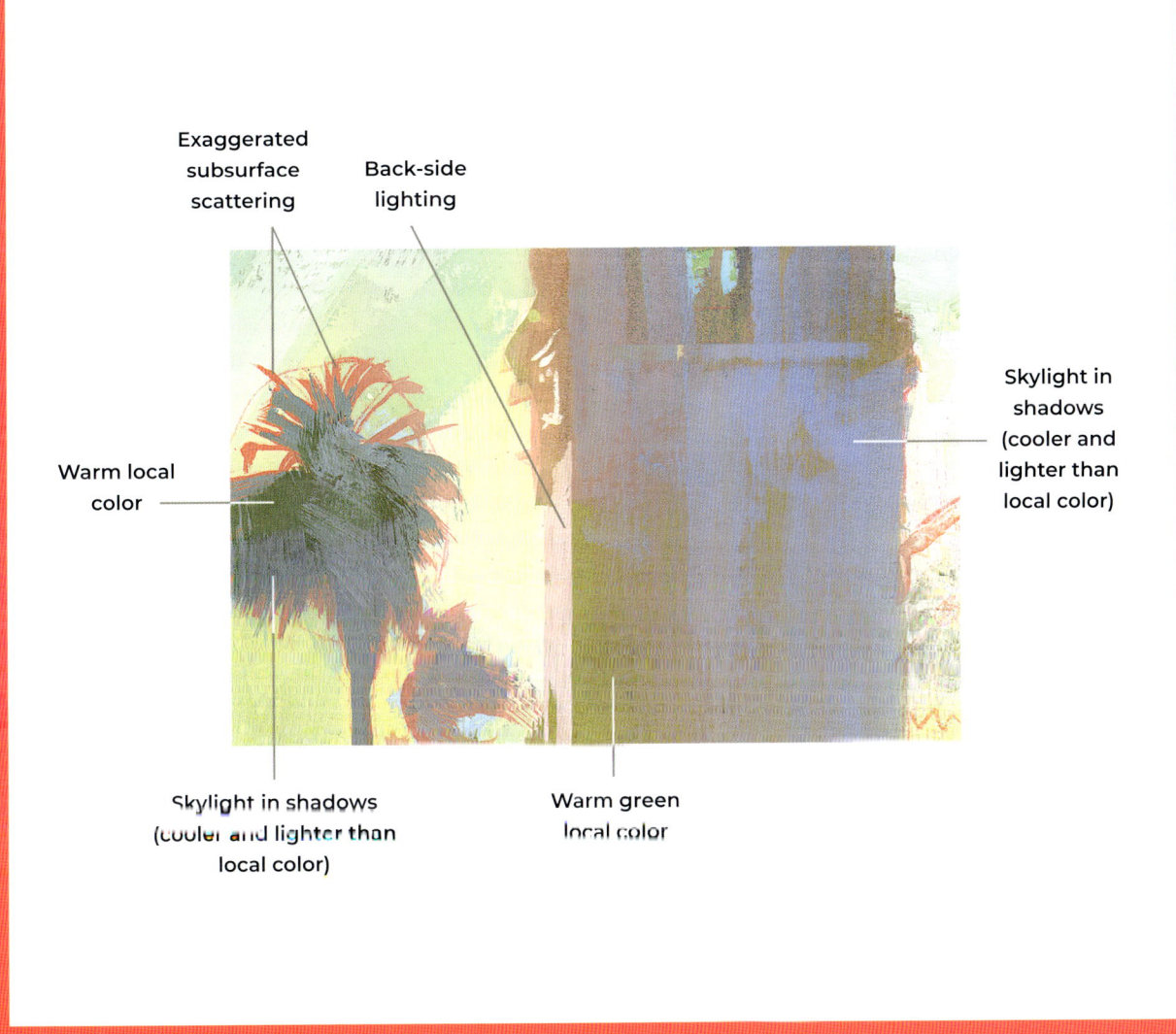

Exaggerated subsurface scattering

Back-side lighting

Warm local color

Skylight in shadows (cooler and lighter than local color)

Skylight in shadows (cooler and lighter than local color)

Warm green local color

Luminous layers. Painting with a "cool-over-warm" approach helps create the rich, sunlit luminosity that I want the whole scene to convey.

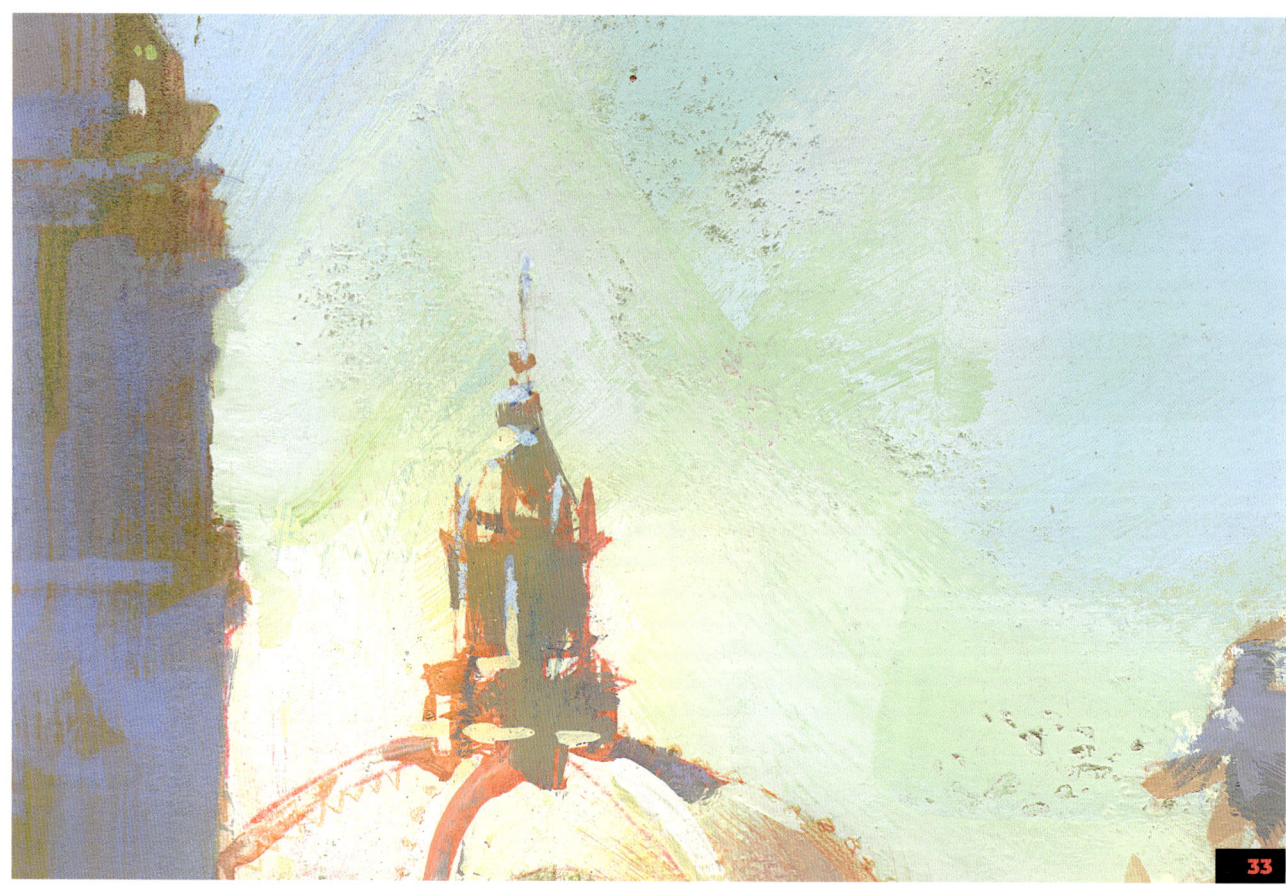

33 I am handling the architectural crest of the dome with a "less is more" approach, thinking in terms of simple light and shadow shapes.

33 SIMPLE ARCHITECTURAL DETAIL

Let's take a close-up look at the top of the dome, specifically the architectural detail at its crest. This is another example of handling complexity by keeping things as simple as possible. To start with, I ask myself: *"What is in the light and what is in the shadow?"* Then I block in the shadow shapes with warm middle-value tones, and add a cooler hue of about the same value to the front planes and deeper recesses. That's all it takes! Just get your drawing fairly accurate and add simple masses of light and shadow with simple relationships of warm and cool.

34 MY PALETTE IN PROGRESS

Here is what my palette looks like at this point in the process. I have already cleaned it off once to make way for new paint. I do not have any special methods for how to arrange my paint-mixing on the palette, since every painting has its own considerations, but my primary contrasts at this stage are reds and greens, so I have big groupings of those across from each other. As I prepare new color mixtures, I can judge how they will look on my painting by mixing them adjacent to colors already on the palette.

I also never put my white gouache into a single isolated pool, but rather place it in long stretches along the edge of the palette's mixing area. If I kept it in one confined pool, it would become dirty with the first few strokes and be impure from that point onward. By stretching it in a long line, I always have plenty of clean white paint that I can reach for.

35 FOCAL POINT CLOSE-UP

Here is a close-up of the lower area of the painting. At this stage it is important to take a look at the handling of the paint, since it utilizes the specific technique of layered, drybrushed color. We have discussed the technique for this on page 321, and next I will show you how this approach can be used to create a brilliance in your paintings that is difficult to achieve with any other technique.

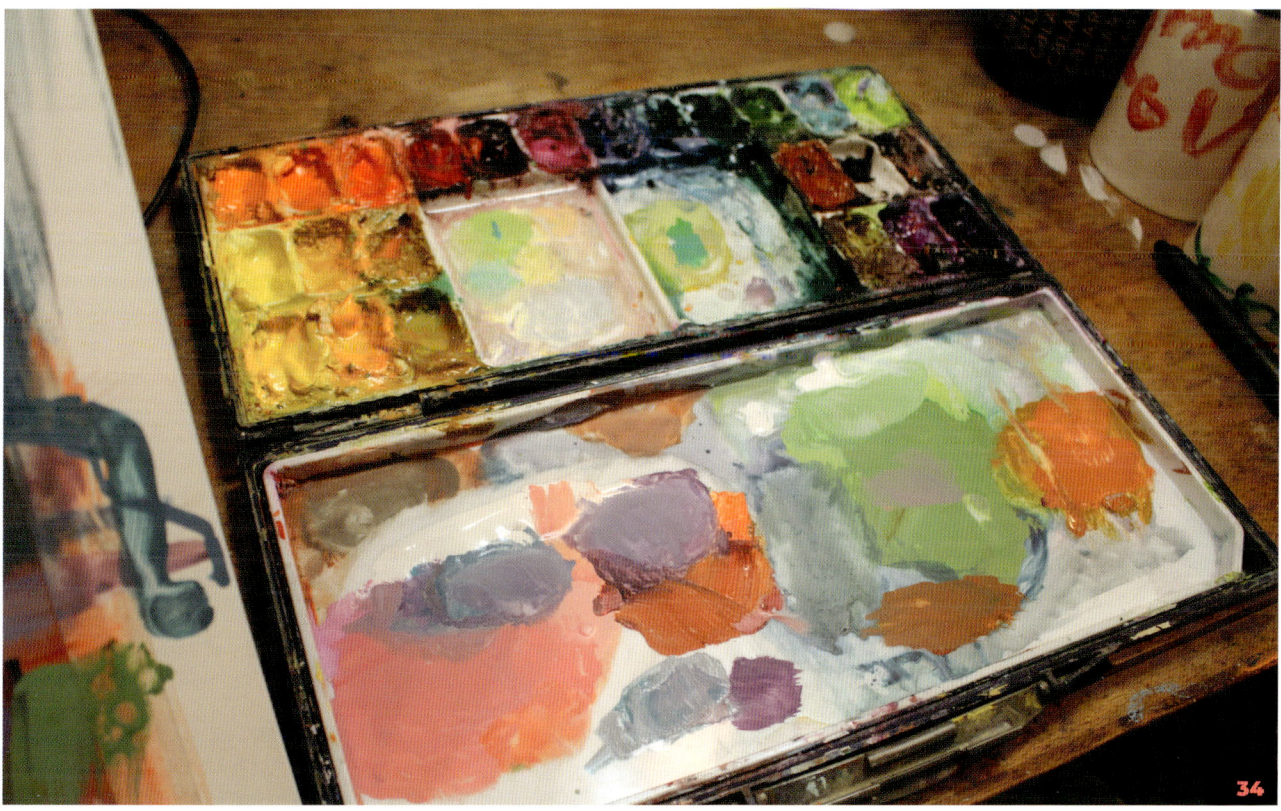

34 The palette in progress, with two large groupings of contrasting red and green hues, and white gouache in a long line to avoid dirtying it all at once.

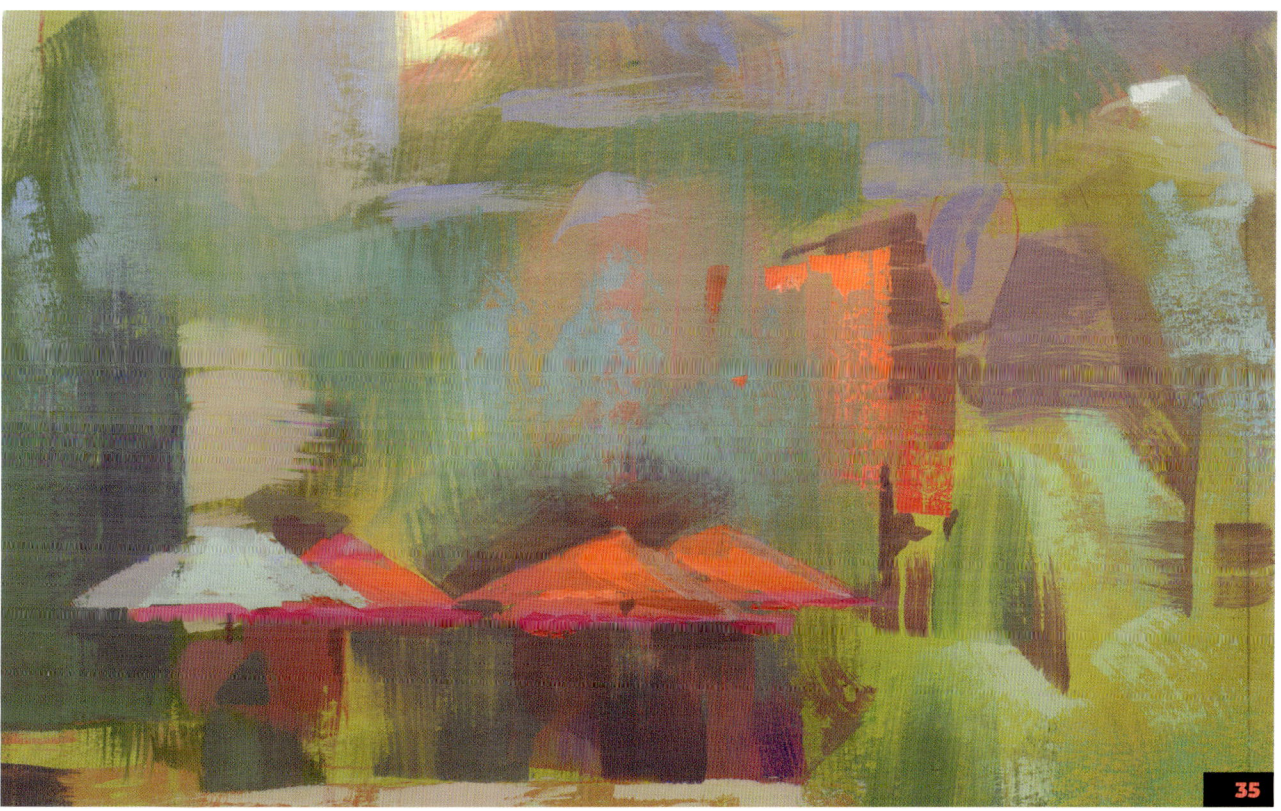

35 Close-up of the lower section of the painting in progress. Note how thick, textured, and opaque the colors are, especially for watercolor.

"POOR MAN'S IMPRESSIONISM"

At last, it's time to dive deeper into one of my favorite topics. Let's quickly jump back to the advent of Impressionism in the 1800s. The breakthrough at that time was the optical mixing of color, as mentioned on page 38. For example, an artist could simply mix a gray color, but that was it – it was just gray. The Impressionist approach was to lay down dots and dashes of different hues of the same value, which would *appear* to be gray when viewed at a distance. An optical color will tend to have a greater sense of luminosity and the color almost appears to vibrate. This effect is called "simultaneous contrast" and is at the heart of Impressionism. I have shown that effect below with a "gray" made of orange, green, and violet. Both versions appear gray at a distance, but the mixed color example has a greater visual interest and sense of luminosity.

I have referred to the importance of luminous atmosphere throughout this project, and the simultaneous contrast of color is my ticket to creating it. On the right are three examples

from my painting for you to take a look at. Each has layers of contrasting hues that are very close in value. You will notice that the majority of my painting is made up of neutral colors that are low in saturation, but the last thing I want is to bore you with a dead gray painting. I make sure that, wherever possible, a gray or neutral color is actually made up of two or more different colors that optically mix. This takes a little planning ahead, but the effect is worth it.

As you saw on page 321 earlier, one of my favored techniques is to drybrush contrasting hues on top of each other, and the textural gaps allow the underlying color to show through. This layered approach is much faster than the side-by-side Pointillist strokes that many Impressionists used. I refer to my approach as "poor man's Impressionism." It came about as I tried to capture the luminosity of the environments I painted, while I was limited to about an hour of painting time due to the rapidly changing sunlight.

Side-by-side color strokes in opaque
watercolor create an "optical" gray

The same opaque watercolor shown
in grayscale – an actual gray

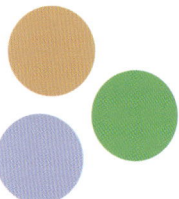

Three contrasting hues are used,
each with an identical value

The same colors shown
only in grayscale

"Gray" versus gray. Optical color mixing enables you to create "grays" that are more vibrant and luminous.

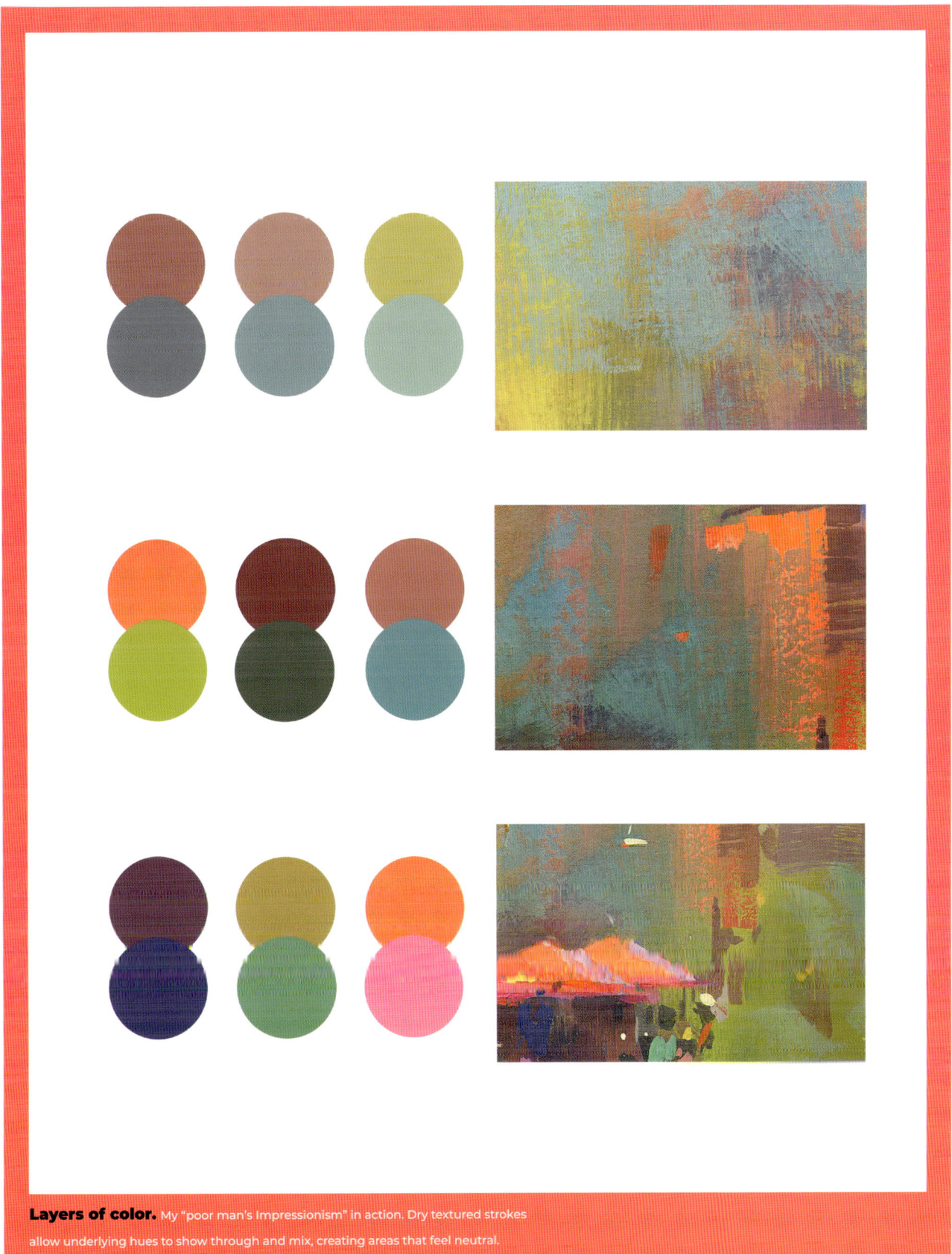

Layers of color. My "poor man's Impressionism" in action. Dry textured strokes allow underlying hues to show through and mix, creating areas that feel neutral.

36 TABLES AND PATRONS

We are almost there! Let's complete the focal area now by suggesting tables and patrons very simply, much like in the comp. I start out by suggesting horizontal and vertical lines that will feel like tables and chairs. Most important here are the cast shadows where they connect to the ground, as these will maintain the quality of direct sunlight.

The people are not much more than simple silhouettes: brushstrokes that have the proportions of people, but with no real detail. They are mostly in shadow, though sunshine remains very important to create contrast, so I sprinkle the suggestion of sunlight coming in from the left and hitting the figures here and there. The nice thing about painting crowds is that people can be wearing any color that I want them to, so I go with mostly warm accents and a few magentas and greens. Finally, sunlight glints off small surfaces, so I add a few dots and dashes of warm white to suggest this reflective quality.

37 FINAL ARCHITECTURAL DETAILS

This area is the final section that needs to be finished, and to me, it is the most difficult. The rendering itself is not difficult, but choosing *what kind* of rendering to use is. If the area is too active and hard-edged, it will demand too much attention up at the very top of the painting. If it is not active enough, it will feel like a missed opportunity to suggest the beautiful ornamentation of the architecture.

In my chosen approach, you will notice the very top edges of the silhouette become quite soft and atmospheric, even starting to disappear into the sky. At the same time, sprinkles of highlight glint off the architectural ornamentation and give the area all the visual interest it needs. What I have done here is very much a break from what is happening in the photo reference, but I believe that good paintings are highly selective – the artist chooses what is of greatest importance, then emphasizes those aspects.

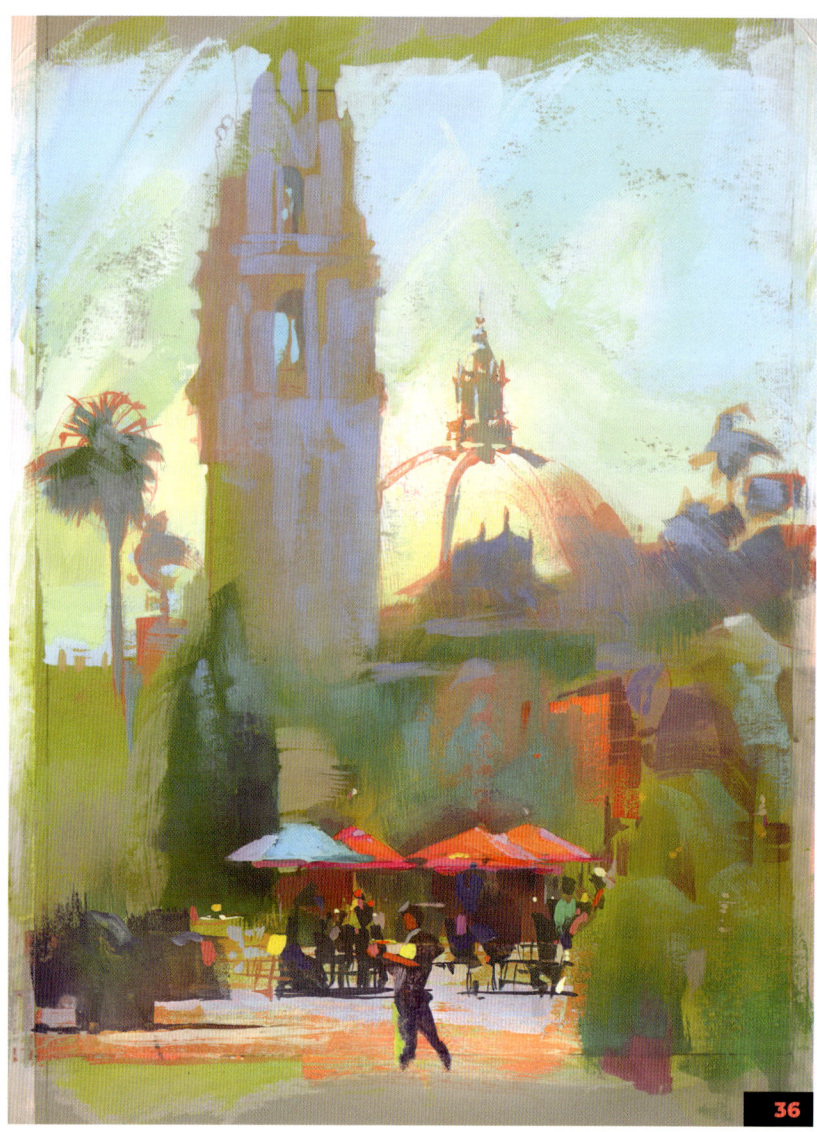

36 Completing the focal area with very simple suggestions of tourists, tables, and chairs – they are really just brushstrokes and lines.

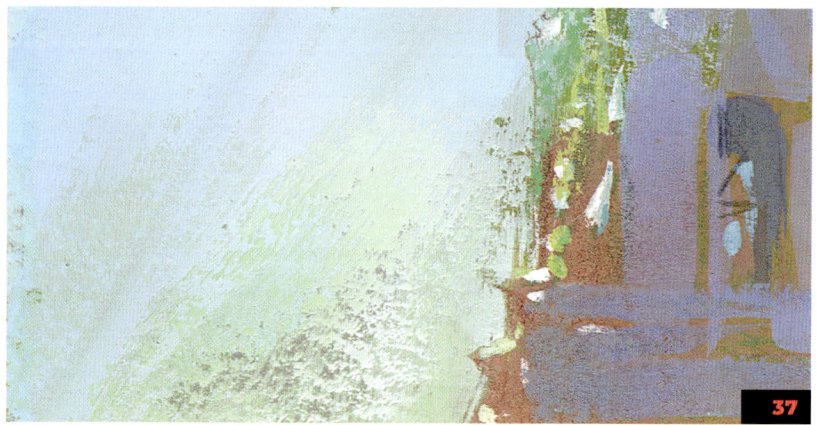

37 Suggesting detail on the spire, while simultaneously blending the upper edge into the sky by softening it with green.

THE DESIGN OF CONTRAST

Over the years, I've come to understand that much of what we do as artists is the design of contrast. People are hardwired to pay the most attention to areas of high contrast, and this makes sense. Contrast is where the most information is contained, and our eyes and brains want us to gather as much information as we can, as quickly as we can. A primary part of my approach to painting lies in designing where the contrast is placed and where it isn't.

There are many kinds of contrast, but I have what I call my "foundational five": contrast of value, shape, edge, hue, and saturation. I also consider texture to be a primary way to create contrast, but it tends to be created by some combination of these five. Often, students can very easily understand value contrast but are not used to thinking in terms of hue contrast. I have

highlighted some examples for you here. To me, hue contrast is wonderful. I often want to bring additional sophistication to a painting without weakening the simple graphic shapes of value, and hue contrast allows me to do that. A color hue can be the exact same value as its surroundings, but feel starkly different in contrast.

So, as I try to design a sense of purpose into my paintings, I do so by deciding not only where the contrast will be, but also where it *won't* be. It is surprising to realize that what we *don't* put into a painting is just as important as what we do. To me, this selectivity is the difference between making art and simply copying a reference.

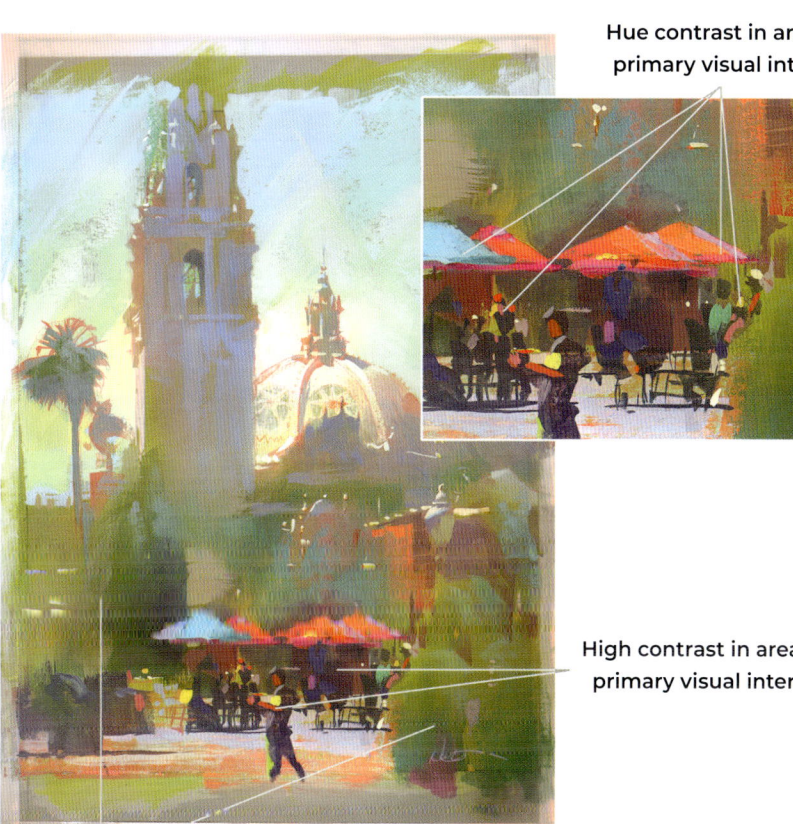

Hue contrast in areas of primary visual interest

High contrast in areas of primary visual interest

Grouped passive areas that contain less contrast

Creating contrast. Contrast equals visual interest – whether that is contrast in value, hue, shape, edge, or saturation.

THE FINISHED PAGE

One of the most common questions I am asked is how I know when a painting is finished. I usually ask myself two questions to wrap up a painting:

- Are there any areas calling too much attention to themselves?

- Are there any areas I consider to be of importance that are not yet demanding enough attention?

I carefully look the painting over and double-check my design with these questions in mind – then it's time to wipe the sweat off my brow and call the painting finished!

The very last step is to carefully peel the tape off the page and remove the painting in preparation for matting and framing. As you remove the tape, it is important to pull it outward from the painting. Should there happen to be a tear as you pull, it will move away from the painting and no visible damage will be seen once it is framed. If you ever have trouble with tearing as you lift the tape off the paper, try blow-drying the tape as you go. The heat will soften the glue and make the tape removal much smoother. Don't worry about this too much, though. I often joke with my students that I should tear my paintings intentionally – it gives a rugged, handmade quality that pays extra!

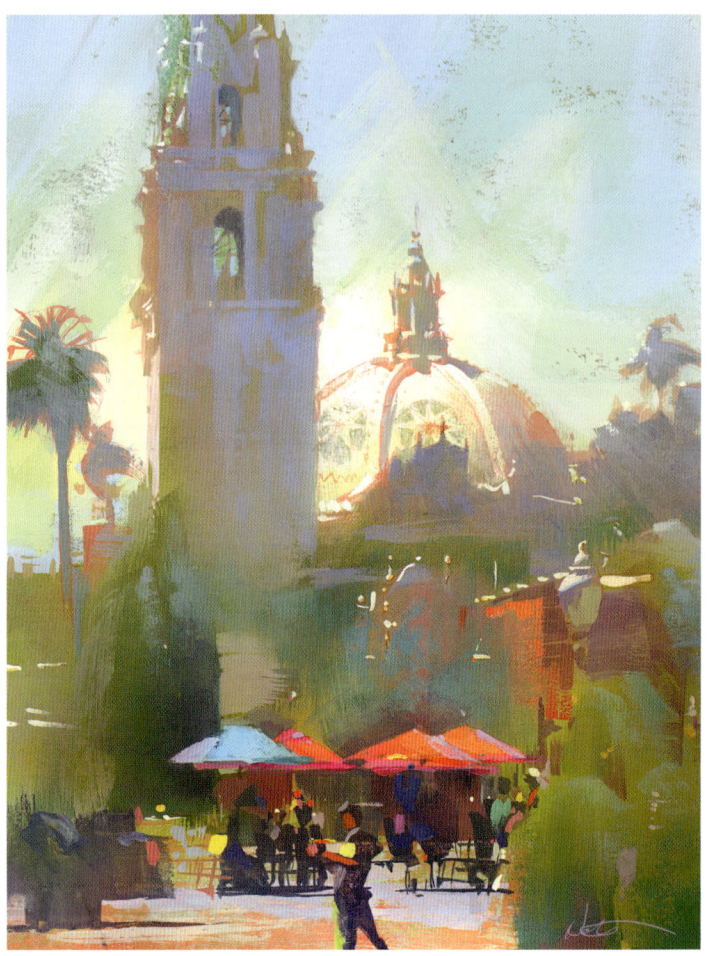

Balboa Spire. The final painting after any final tweaks have been made and the tape has been carefully removed.

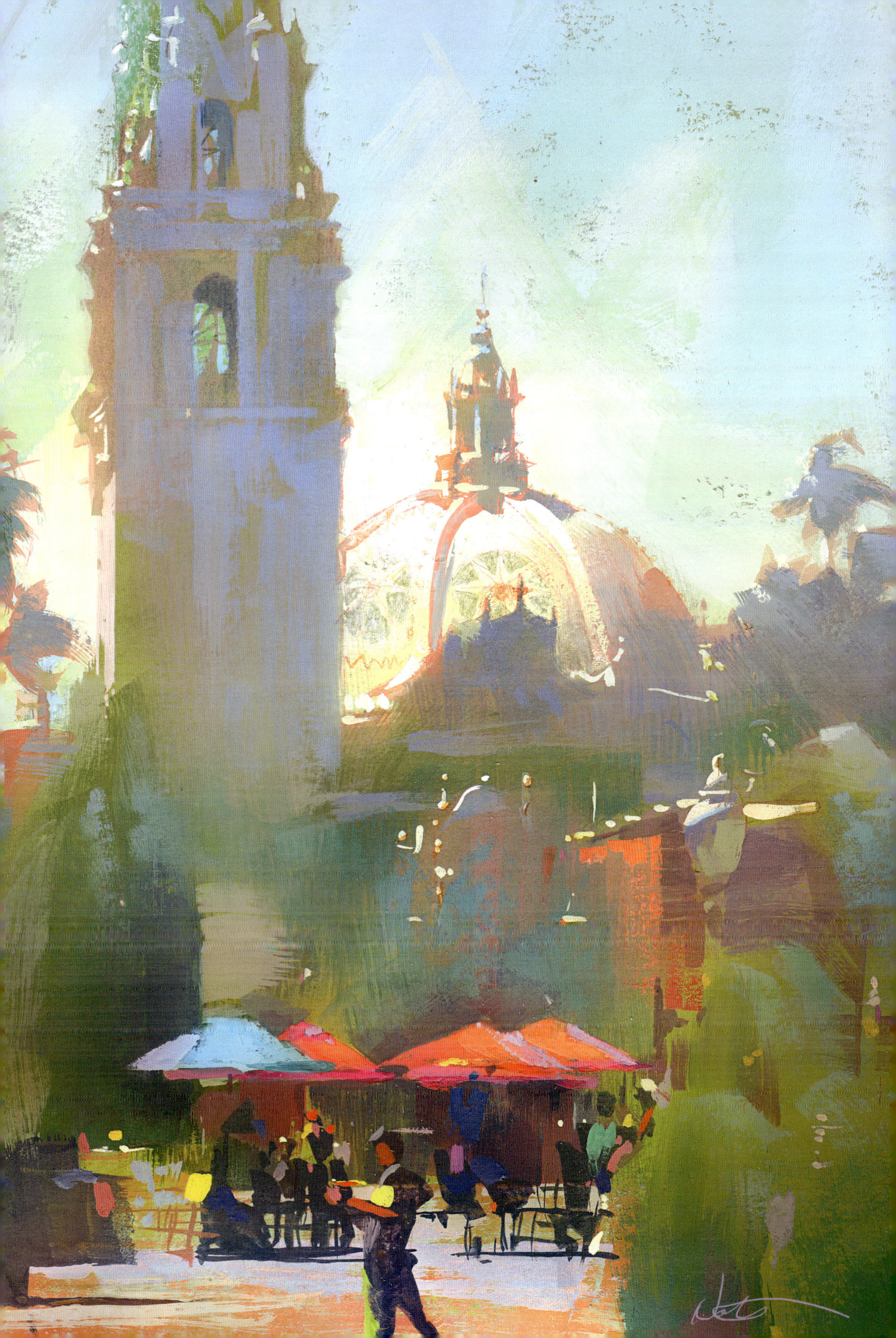

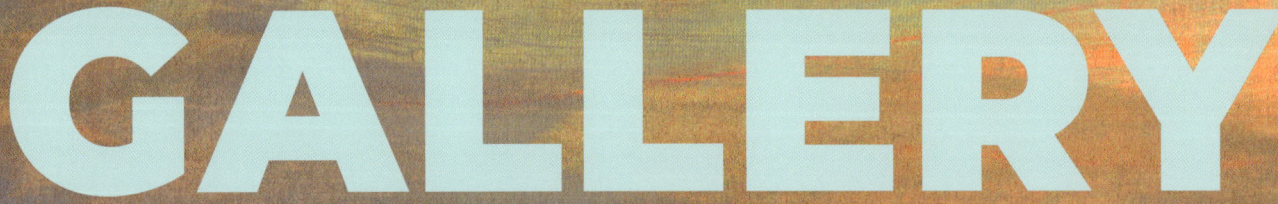

GALLERY

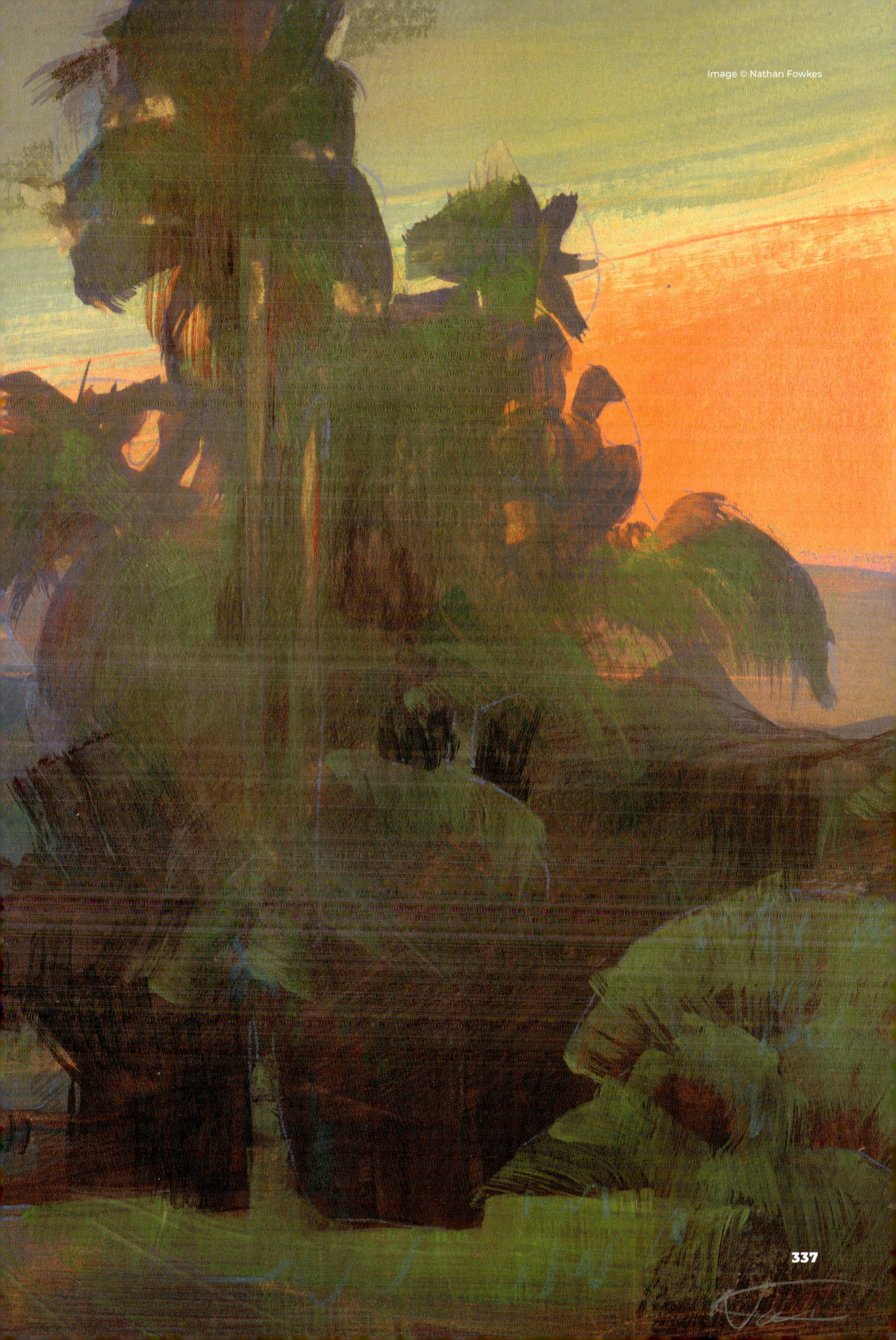

Image © Nathan Fowkes

337

DJAMILA KNOPF

I love playing with color and creating different palettes and atmospheres in my images. My philosophy when it comes to color – and art in general – is combining a basic understanding of theory with intuition and just "winging it." In my work, I put a special emphasis on storytelling, and color and light are great tools to evoke an emotional response in the viewer – my goal is to make images that look believable and appealing, not perfectly realistic. I prefer not to get too scientific and allow myself some creative freedom.

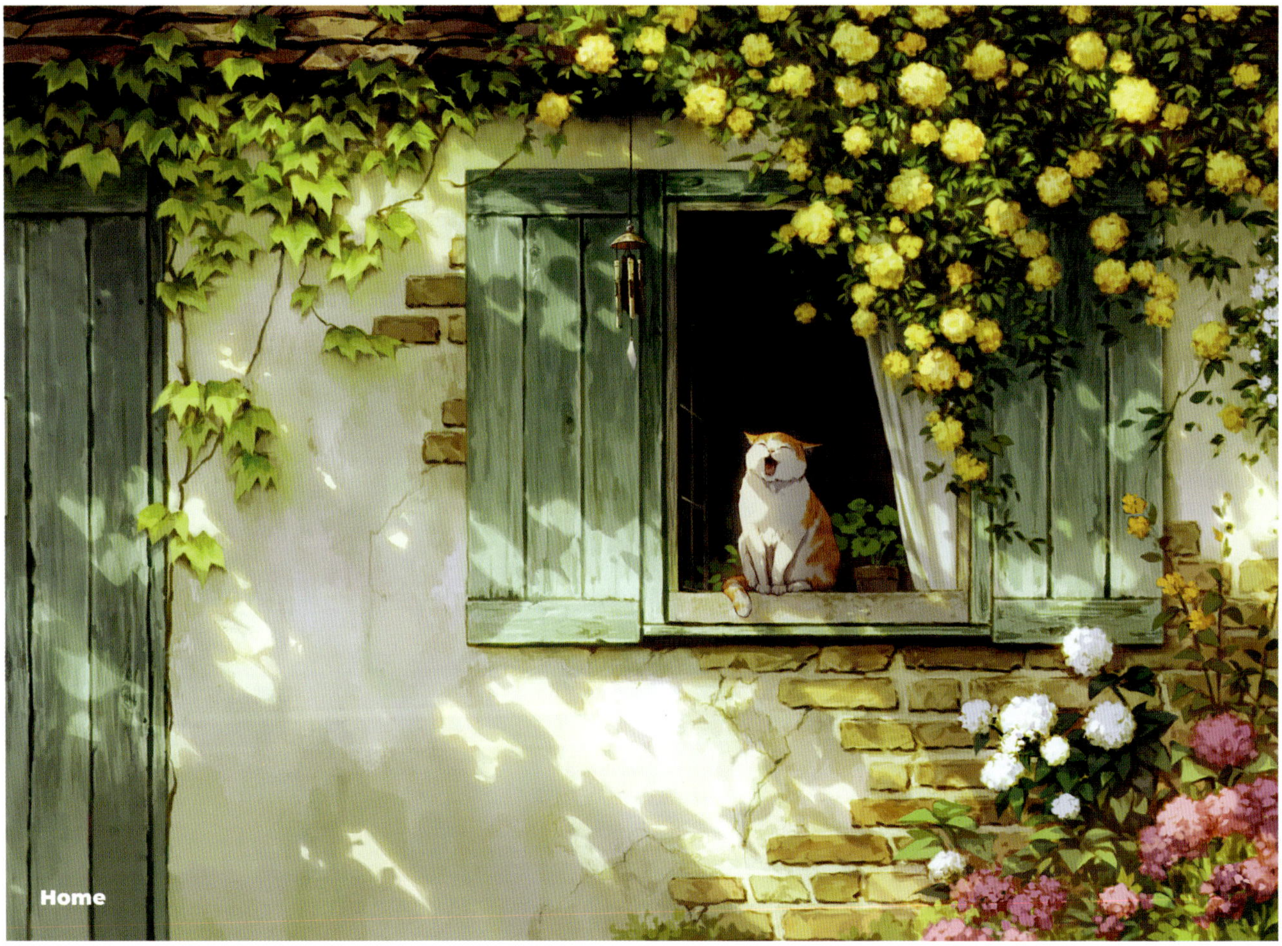

Home

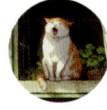

Home

I think yellow is an underappreciated color that adds positivity and cheerfulness to a scene, and I like to use it wherever I can. My goal here was to make the viewer feel comfortable and cozy. I created warm, dappled light to emphasize that feeling. The plants all around create a lot of visual noise that could potentially be distracting, so, to guide the viewer's attention, I placed the cat in front of the dark window.

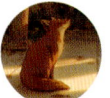

Fox shrine

Autumn leaves can bring such a beautiful glow to any scene. I used yellow and orange as the dominant colors here, combining them with the character's green jacket and the fox's brown fur. My favorite part of the painting is probably the light on the ground. I wanted to evoke the impression of a sunset, and the shadows became nice compositional elements. I wanted the whole scene to look inviting, but a bit mysterious.

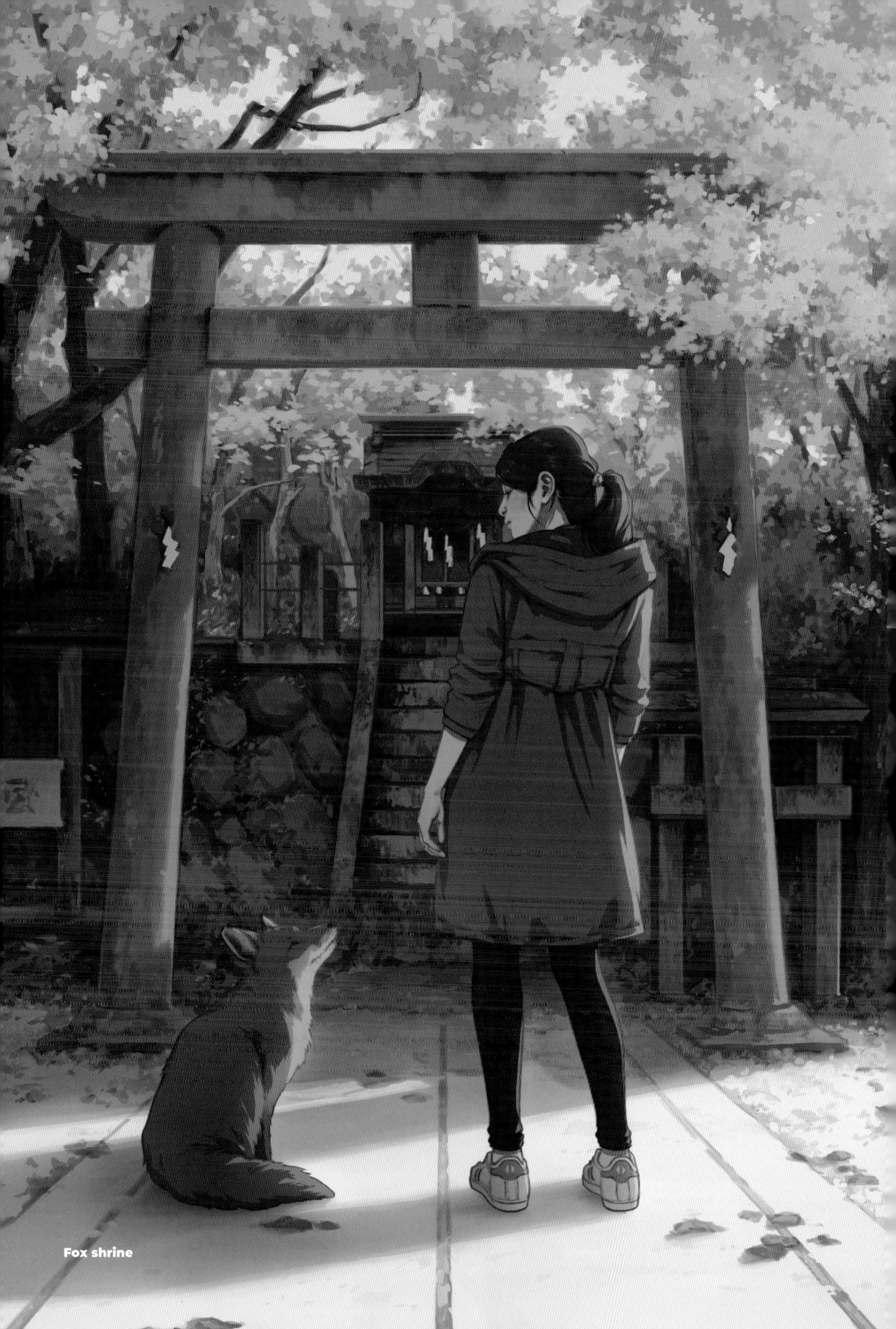

Fox shrine

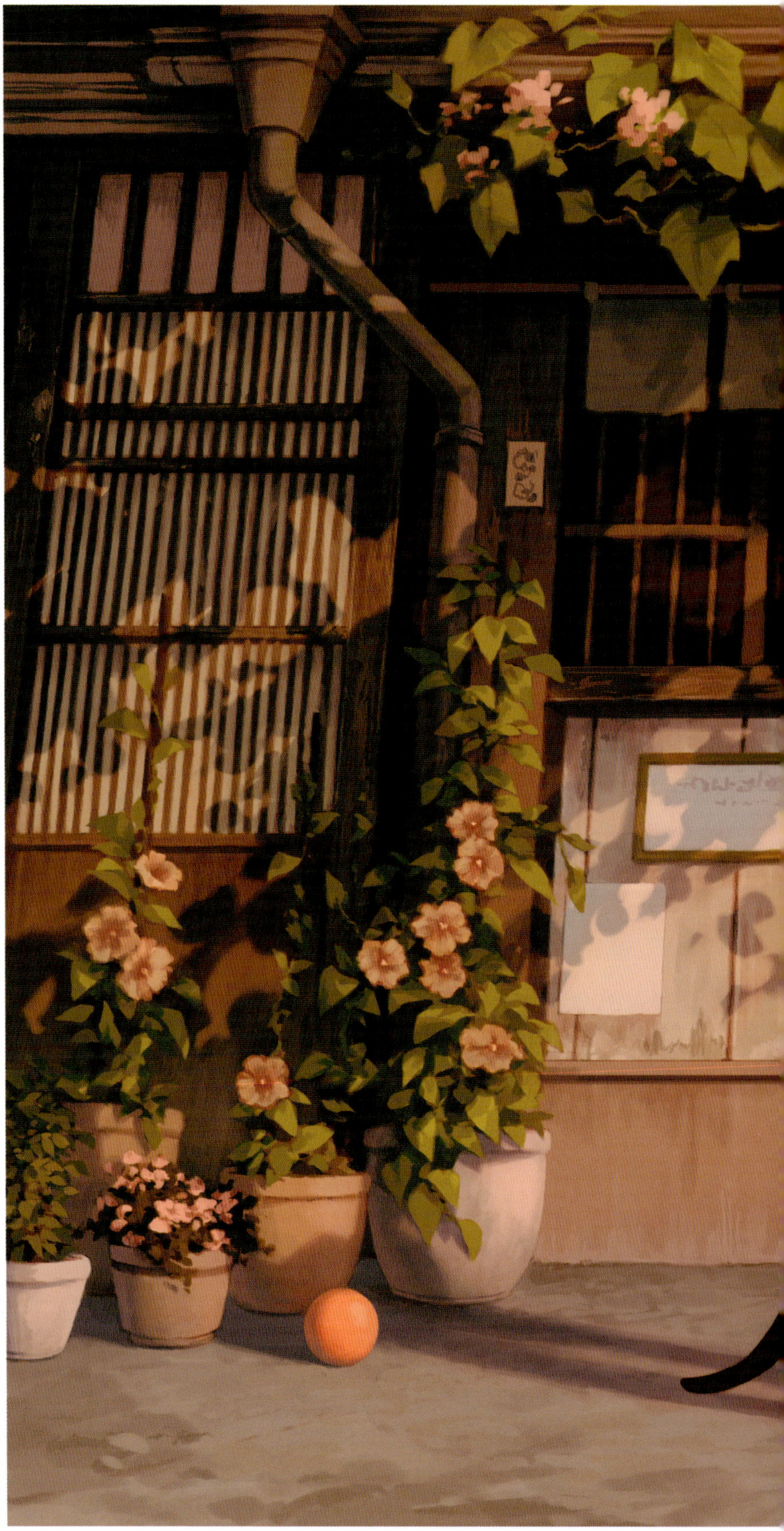

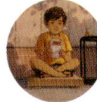

Game Boy

When I started this painting, I wasn't planning on using a warm color palette. But, as I progressed, I felt like it could use some warmth, and a bit of "romantic nostalgia." It tells the story of a kid playing with his Game Boy. Through this theme I am channeling my own fond childhood memories. Visually speaking, my favorite parts of the painting are the shadow patterns, the pink against the warm greens, and the character's yellow shirt.

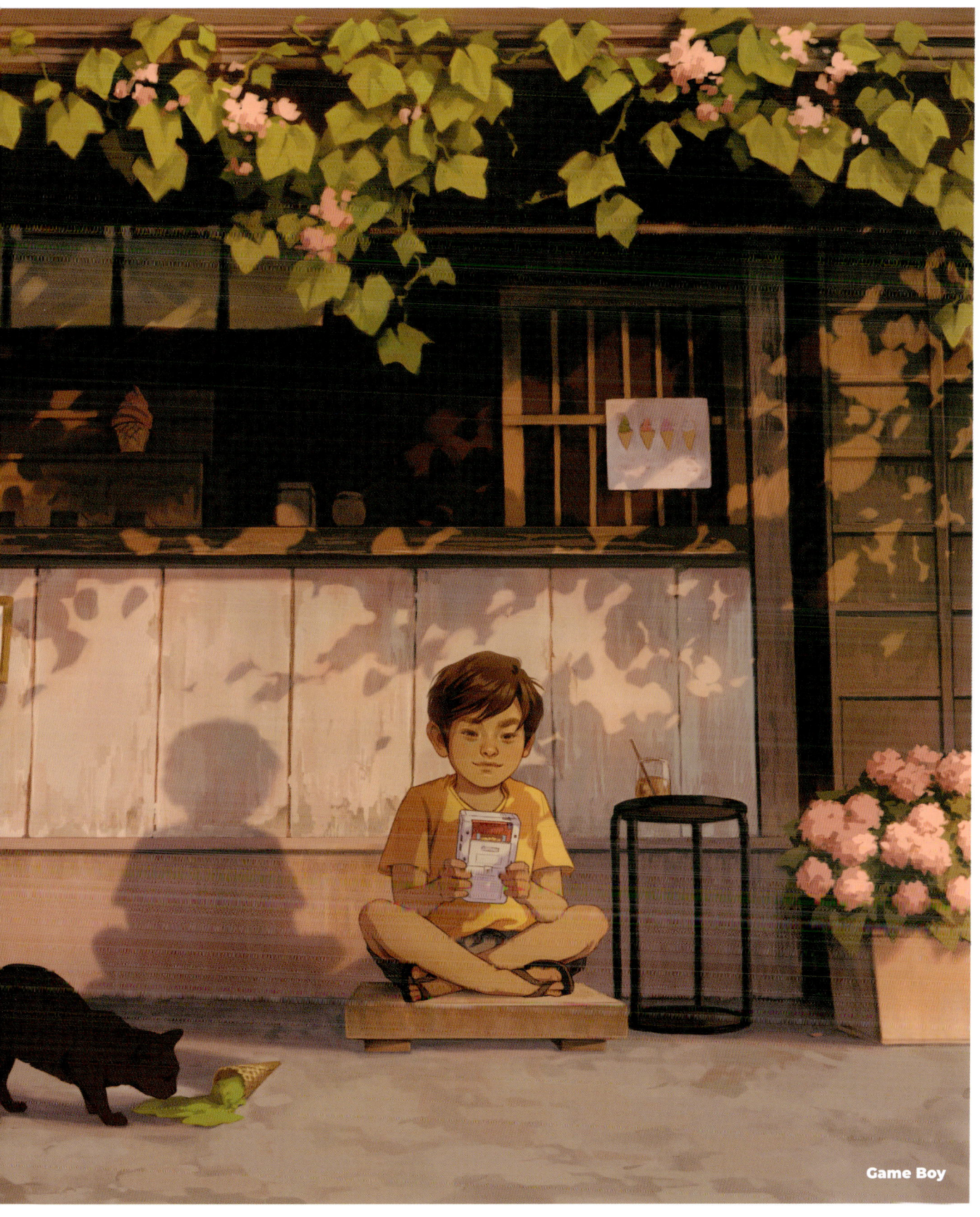

Game Boy

GUWEIZ

I enjoy drawing somewhat dark and moody scenes, partly because they allow me to spend more time on the details that matter while the rest gets obscured by shadow. Done right, they can also draw viewers in to investigate further beyond the cursory glance.

The right colors, lighting, and setting can prompt a direction and theme – and designing them is fun – but I do like to leave some leeway for the viewer's imagination as well. What do you think when you look at these?

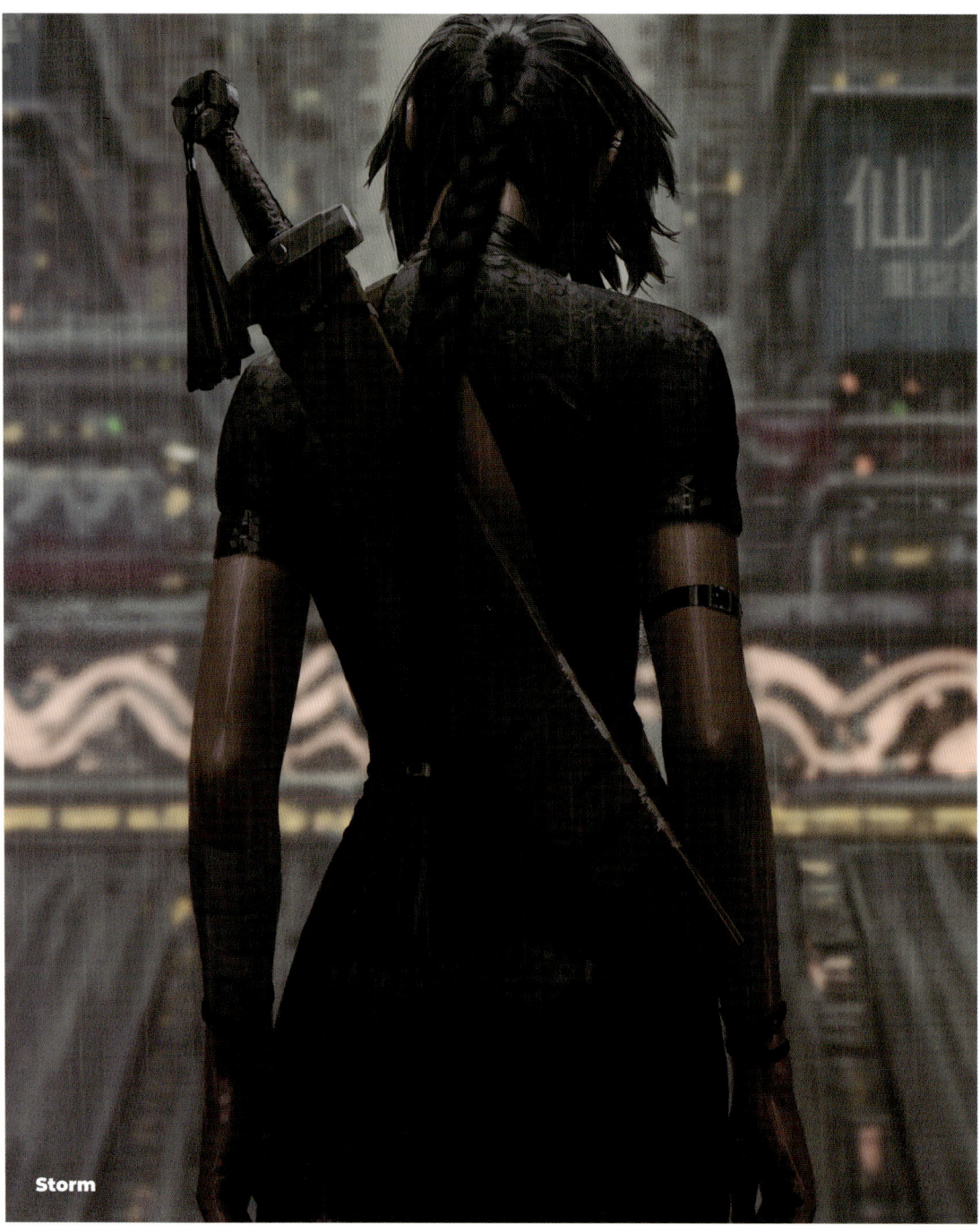

Storm

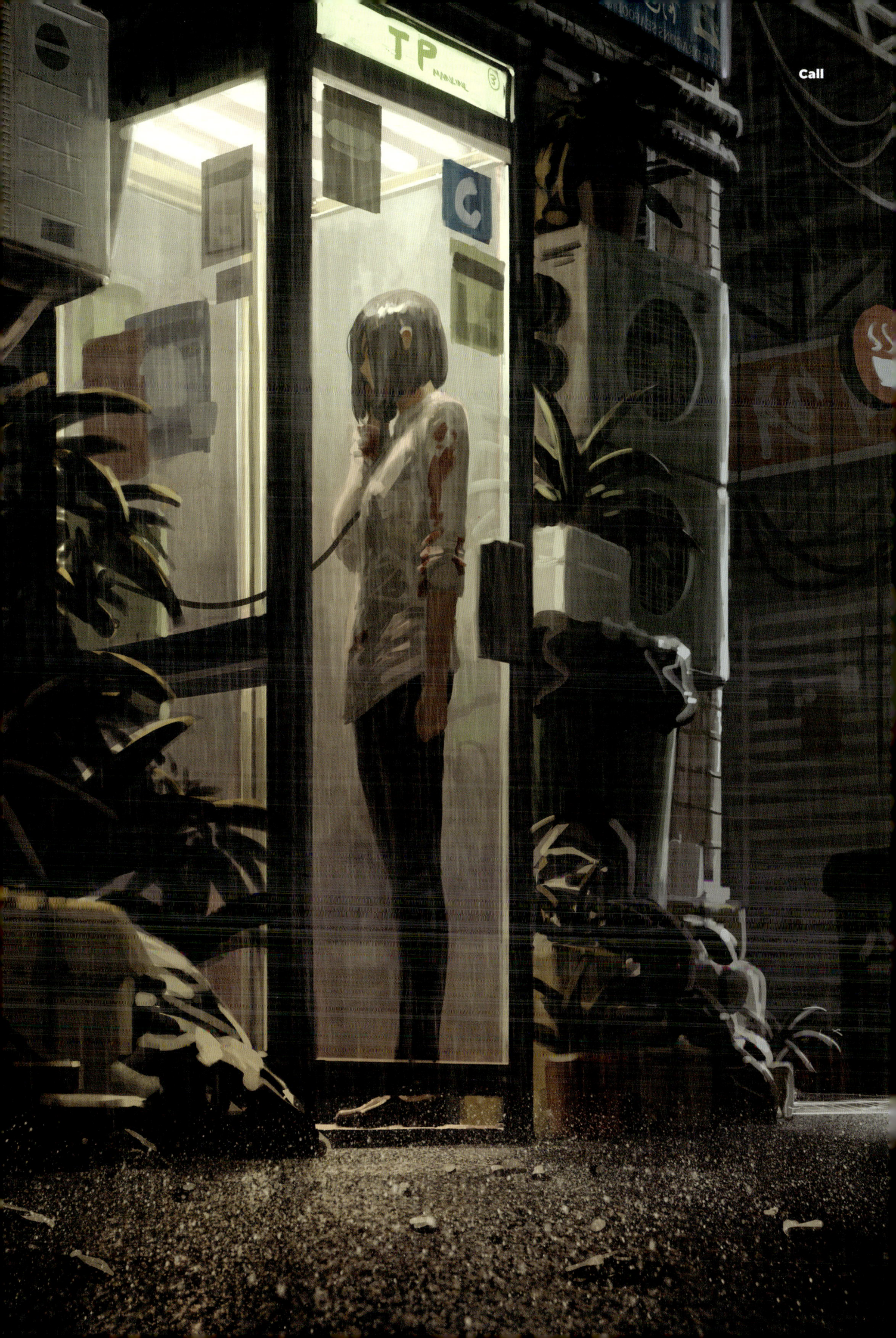

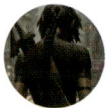

Storm

A mysterious character arrives in the dark underbelly of a strange town. The palette is fittingly grayish and overcast, while the pouring rain helps create wet highlights on the character's hair, skin, and accessories. The blurred background feels both cinematic and like it's obscured by the gray haze of rainfall.

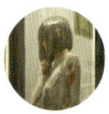

Call

A character making an important call in a downpour. Again, slick highlights help sell the feeling of heavy rain, with speckled textures creating the impression of water bouncing up off the ground and catching the light from the phone booth. The lighting of the booth itself makes it feel warm and sheltered.

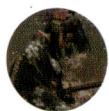

Blossoms

A character remembering a forgotten time. There are many local colors, patterns, and textures at play here, but the overall muted palette helps them work well together. I wrapped the drapery textures around the forms with the technique shown on page 296, which was helpful for shading and lighting the patterned fabric convincingly.

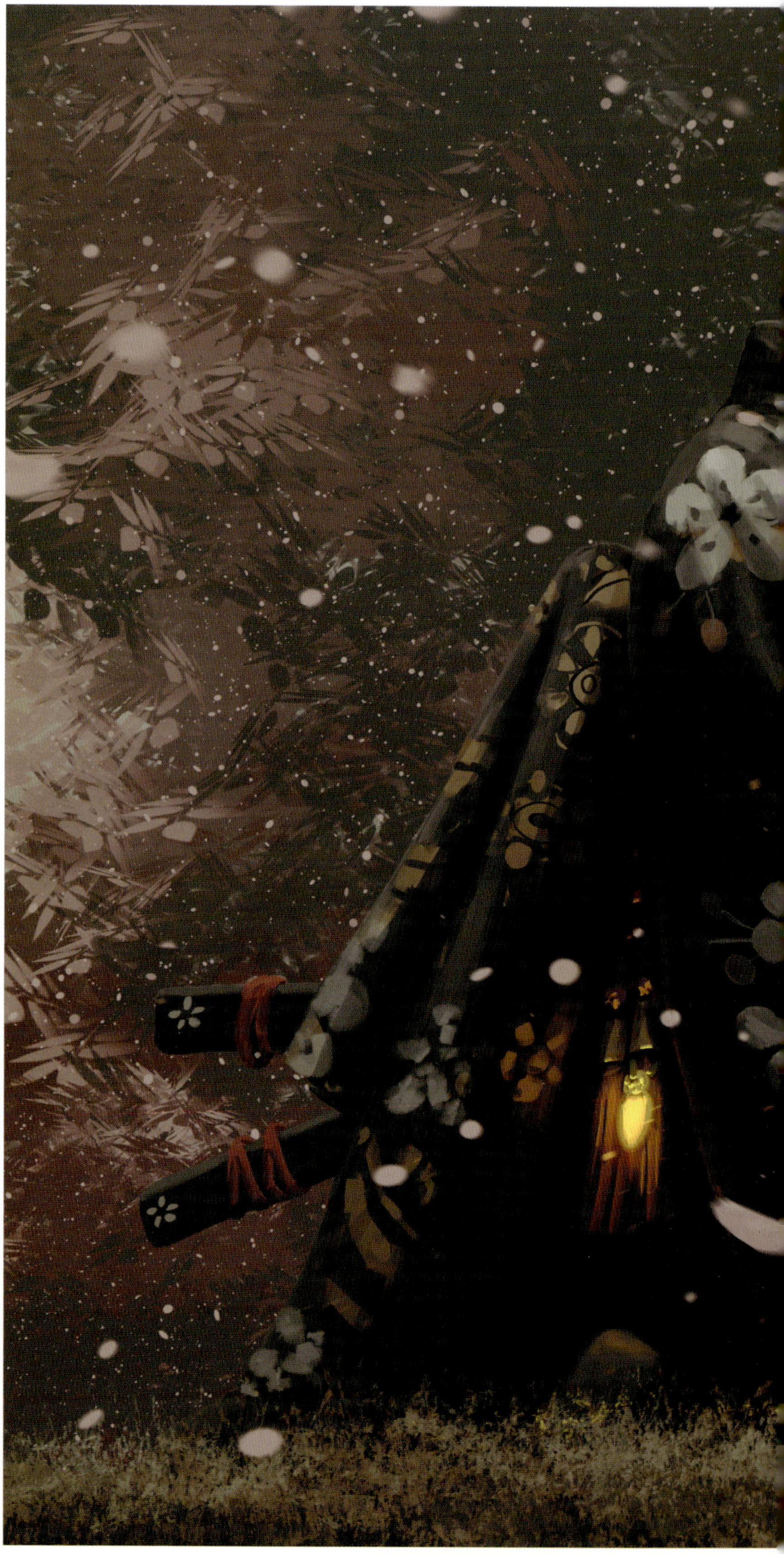

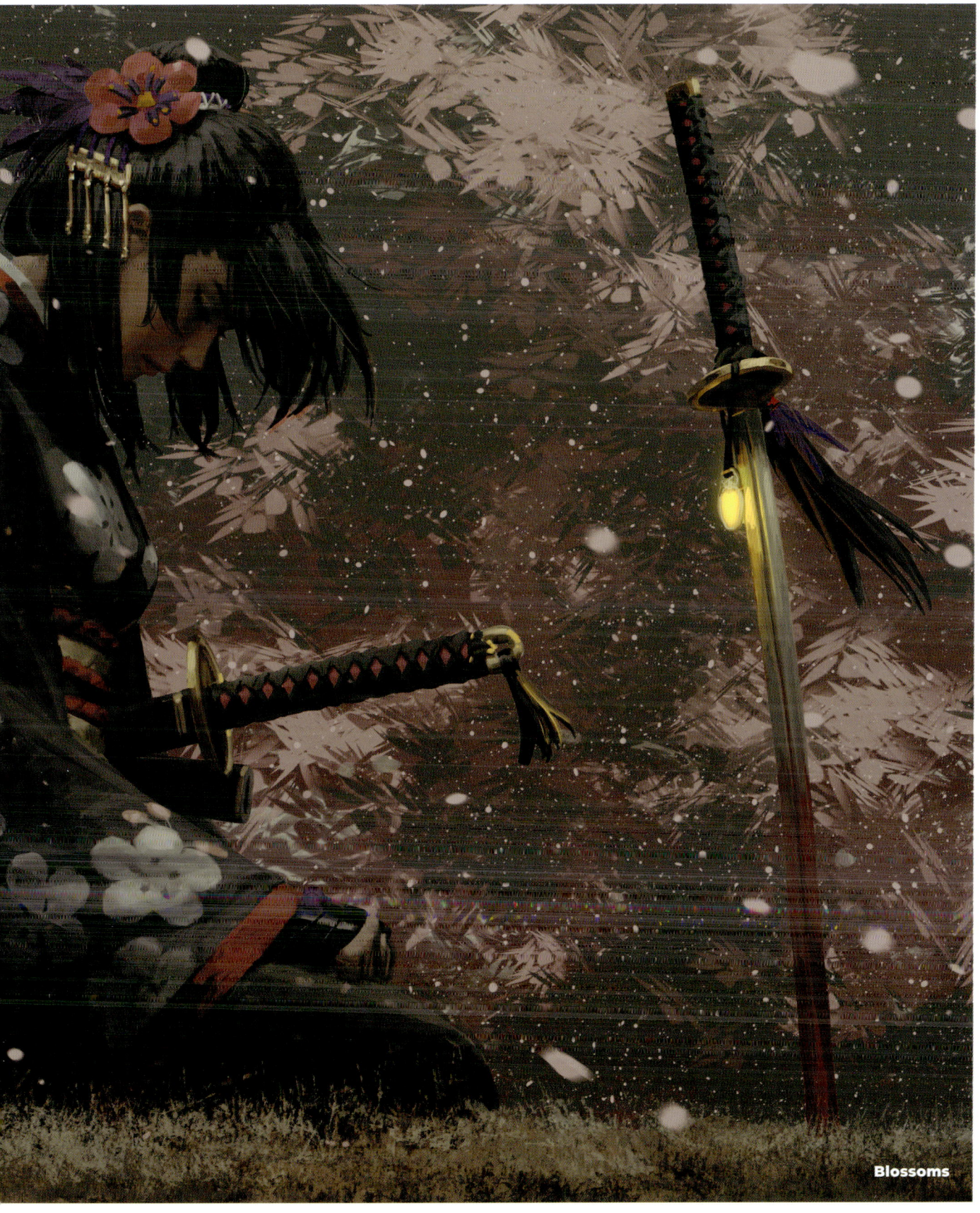

Blossoms

NATHAN FOWKES

My goal when creating a painting or illustration is to identify a sense of purpose and emotion, then attempt to design my color and light to serve that purpose. For instance, if I am painting a landscape, I'll identify what quality made me pick that particular spot, then emphasize that quality and edit out all other elements that might distract from it. Likewise, in a more imaginative illustration, I always try to identify the mood and emotion, then make sure the color and light serve them. I even have a final step that I call "search and destroy," where I go through the image and try to identify any potential distractions that weaken it! I am very much interested in the simple statement of the image. I believe that a painting is not just about what we choose to put in it but also what we choose to edit out.

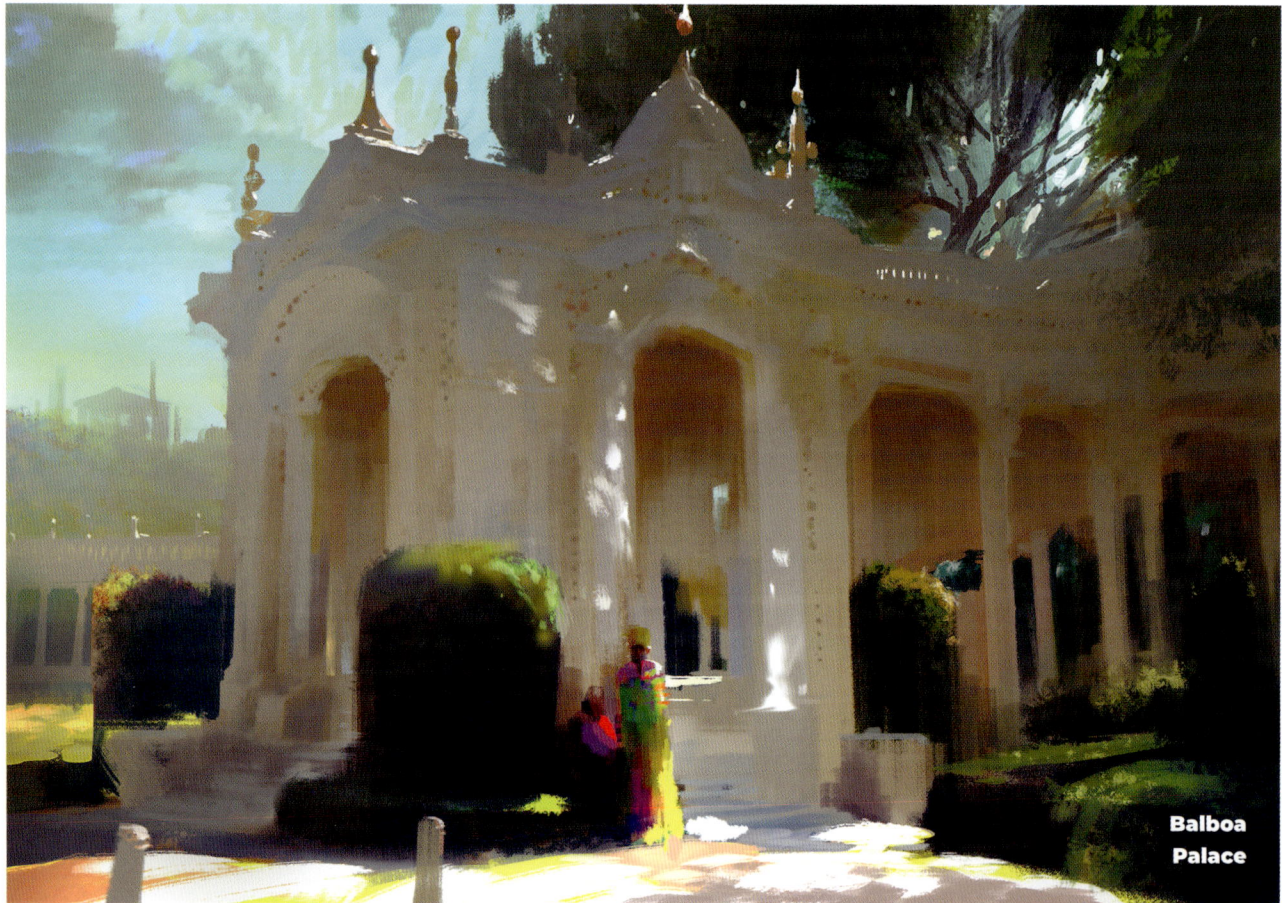

Balboa Palace

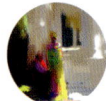

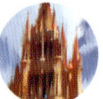

Balboa Palace

This is another painting inspired by Balboa Park in San Diego, California. It is very stylized for a storybook feel. The sky is pushed toward cyan and green for a slightly otherworldly, mythological quality. The browns and greens of the scene are accented by some colorfully costumed characters in the foreground.

Church cathedral in San Miguel de Allende, Mexico

Everyone can tell by now that I love the upward sweeping vertical quality of city monuments. San Miguel de Allende has a particularly good one. The cathedral here is surrounded by a vibrant marketplace and the orange granite of the building contrasts beautifully with the blue and cool gray of the sky.

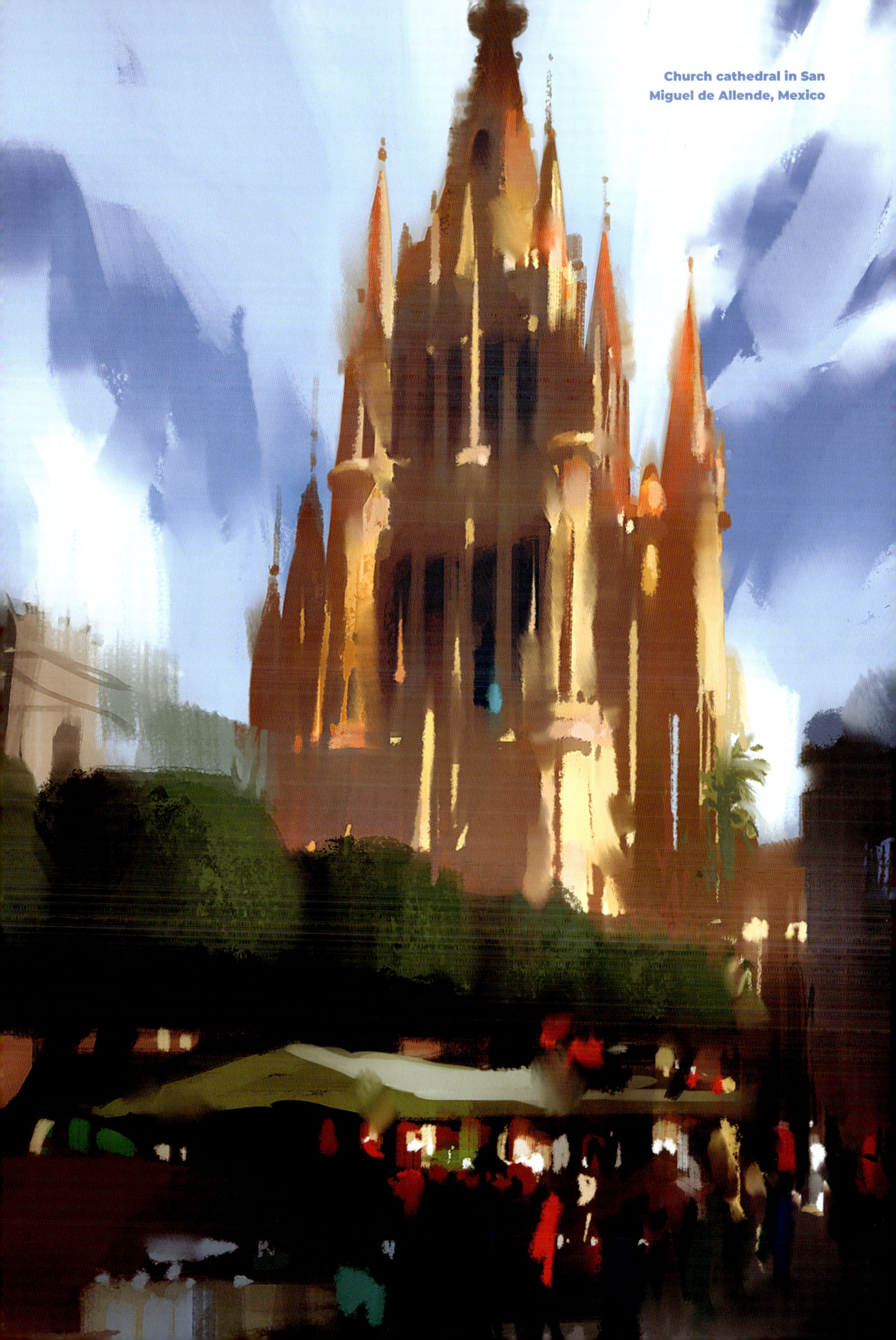

Church cathedral in San
Miguel de Allende, Mexico

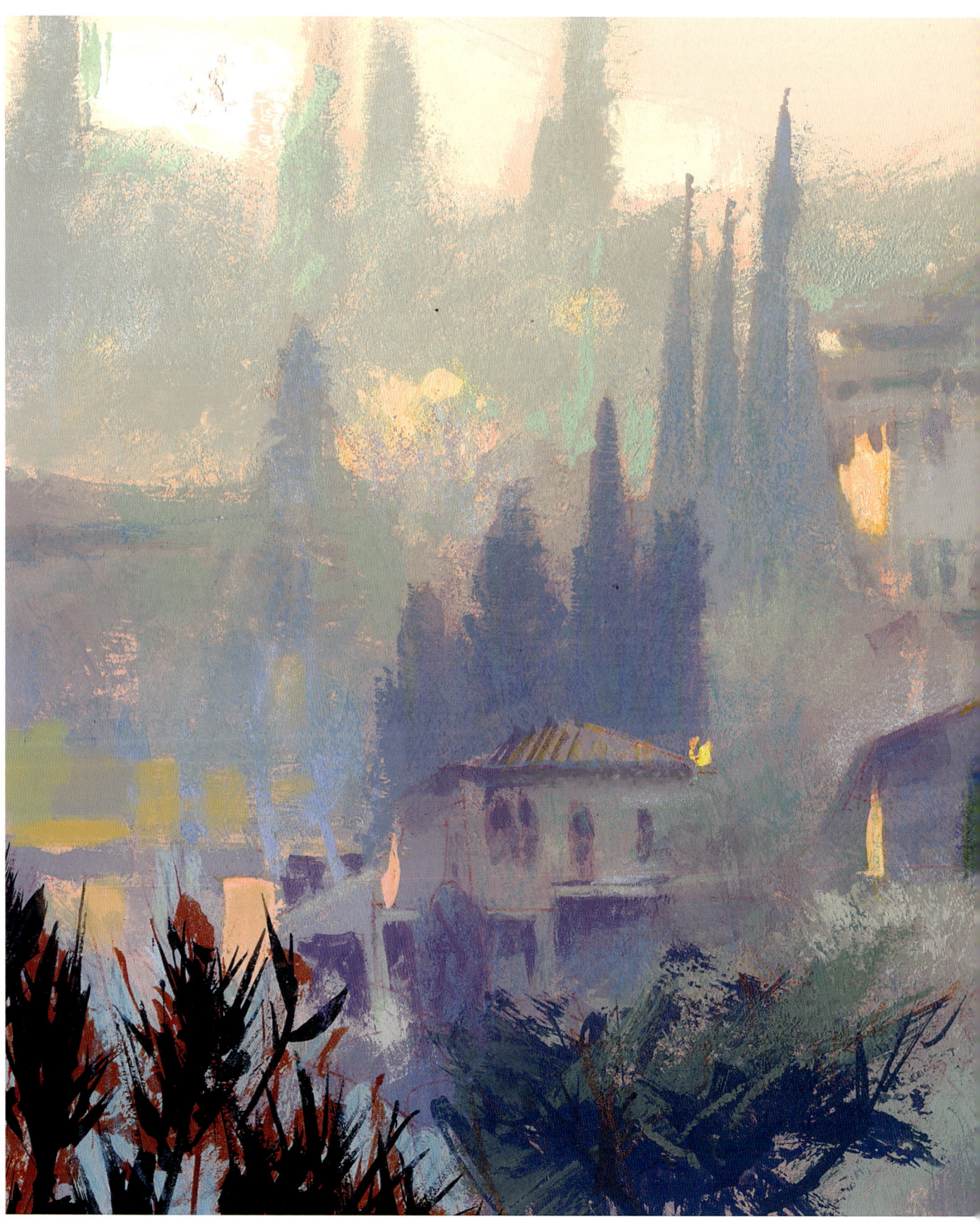

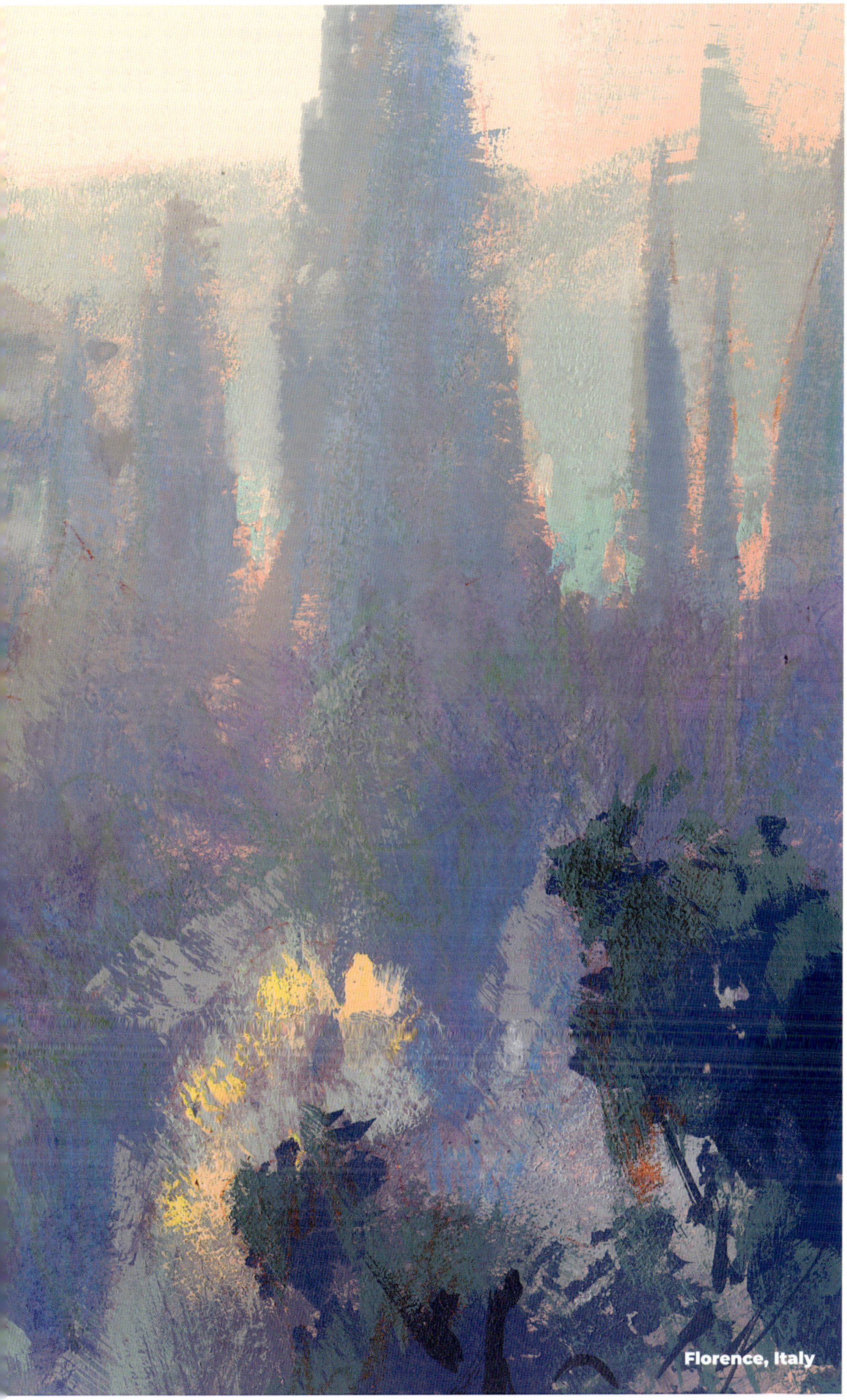

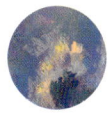

Florence, Italy

There was a great deal of subtlety and rich color at this location, so I layered my colors one over another with drybrushing. The entire painting is done with this technique. This is another example of cool over warm, creating the quality of atmosphere in a luminous, Mediterranean location. The warmth of the illuminated side planes contrasts strongly with the cyans and purples of the atmospheric shadows.

Florence, Italy

BEATRICE BLUE

Light and color are definitely some of my favorite aspects of visual storytelling. When I think about them, there's a list of things that I consider alongside them. Each image carries a mood, an emotional weight, and a story behind it, and I like to explore my options with color and light in order to convey all of those things in the best possible way. I always try to encapsulate the right mood and emotions for the story that I'm trying to tell, so my colors and palettes usually vary a lot.

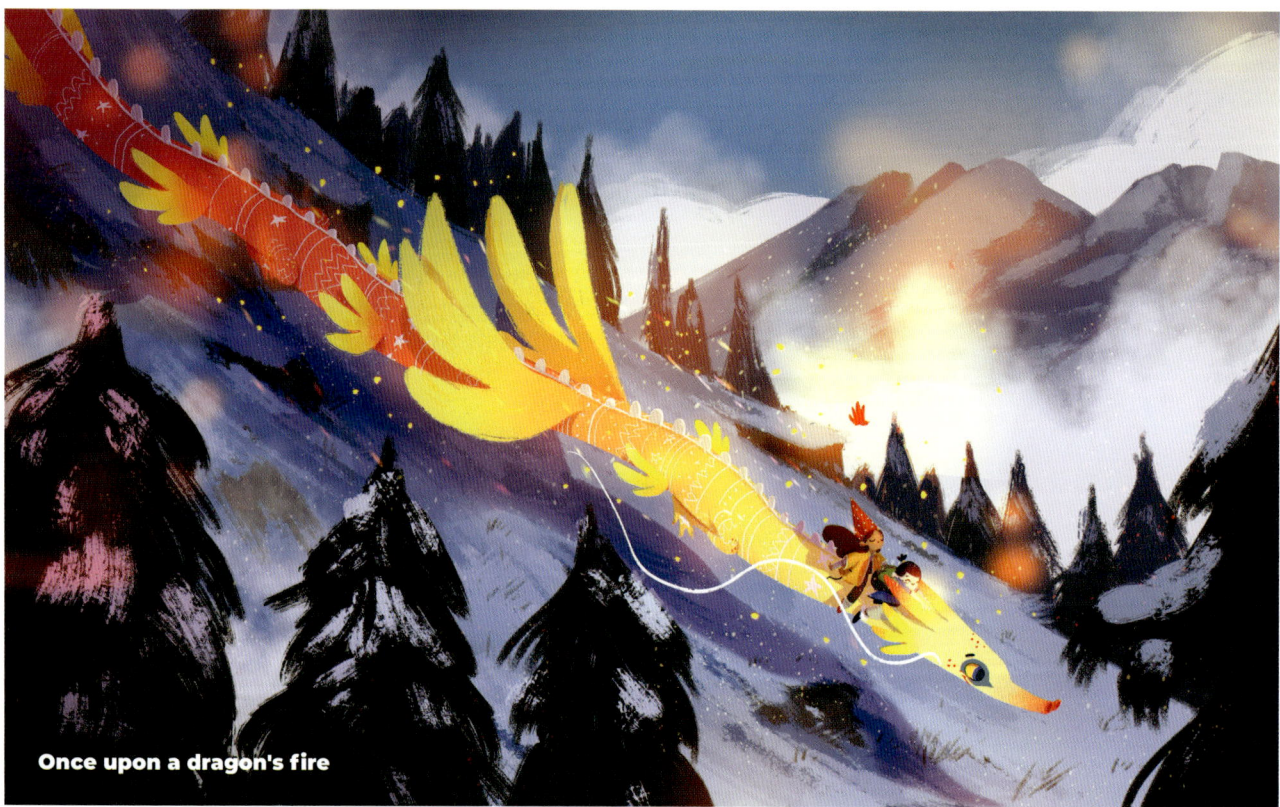

Once upon a dragon's fire

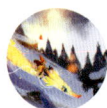

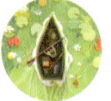

Once upon a dragon's fire

This image is from the second picture book I wrote and illustrated, *Once Upon a Dragon's Fire*. In the book, the characters meet a dragon who is feared by their townsfolk, and discover that he is not evil at all – just lonely. By the middle of the book, the dragon feels loved for the first time, and we see his colors (and the overcast setting) change into warmer tones. My intention here was to guide the reader through a set of emotions that would gradually transport them through the book as the story and moods changed. The warm/cool contrast between the local colors, chosen at the beginning of the process, was extremely important for conveying all of this.

Once upon a mermaid's tail

I wanted this image to capture the mood of a very special moment when a child discovers a little secret lagoon. I wanted it to look like a strange, new, incredible place that I'd like to go to, but also safe, like a secret paradise. The cast shadows on the sides and top of the image support this feeling of a private, quiet place, while the vibrancy of the water and swimming creatures make it burst with energy and adventure to come. Spots of warm tones break the monotony of the colder green scenery. I enjoy trying reduced palettes, then mixing up the colder and warmer tones in smaller percentages around the image. That way, the image stays balanced and keeps you looking.

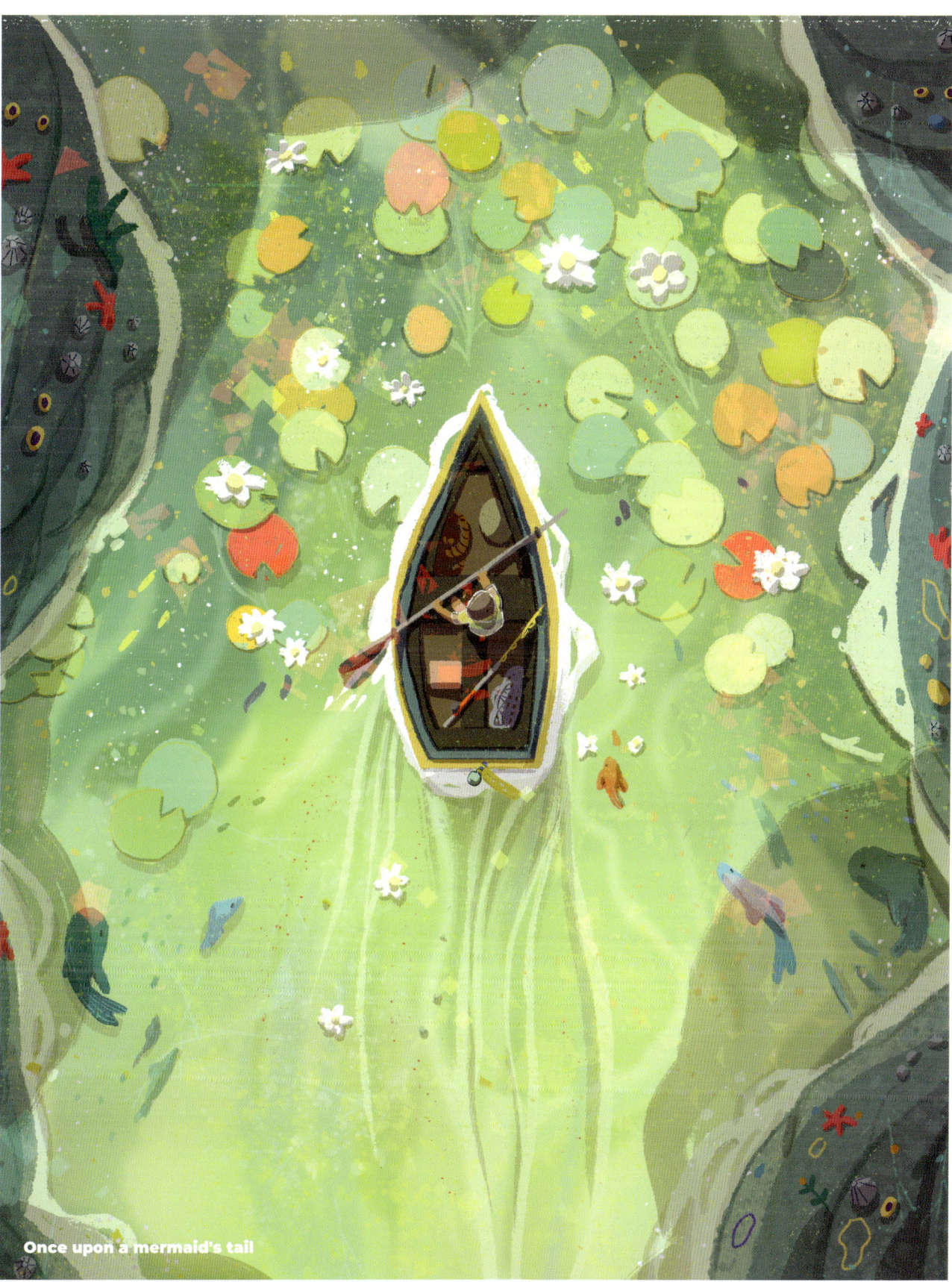

Once upon a mermaid's tail

Once Upon A Mermaid's Tail, written and illustrated by Beatrice Blue, published by Frances Lincoln Children's Books, an imprint of The Quarto Group, copyright © 2020. Reproduced by permission of Quarto Publishing Plc.

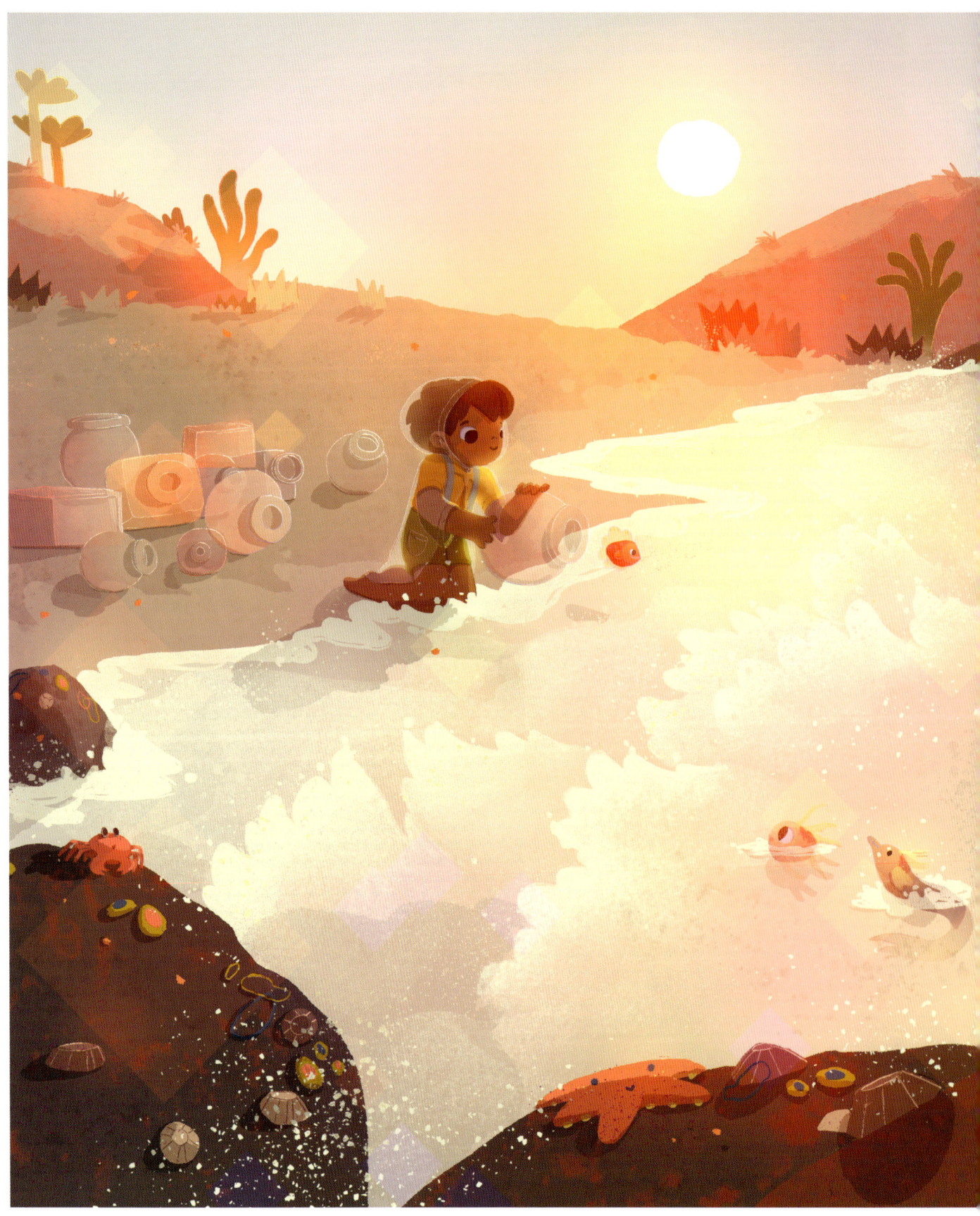

Once Upon A Mermaid's Tail, written and illustrated by Beatrice Blue, published by Frances Lincoln Children's Books, an imprint of The Quarto Group, copyright © 2020. Reproduced by permission of Quarto Publishing Plc.

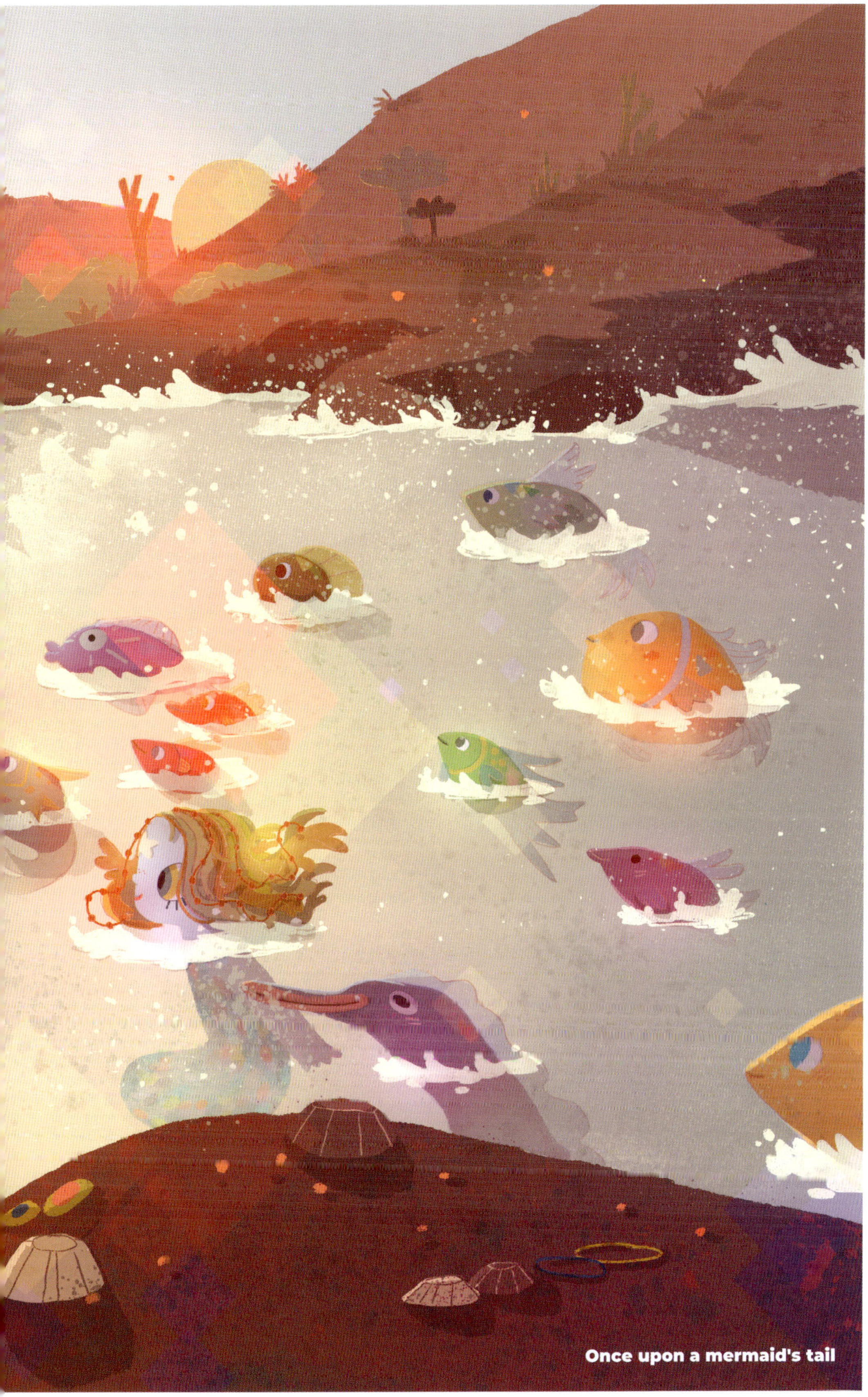

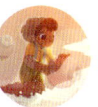

Once upon a mermaid's tail

This was fun to paint. It was slightly challenging because of all the colorful fish I wanted to include, as well as the complexity of capturing a very warm moment of the day. I wanted the result to feel calm but strong.

I do not often use red-pink tones for my backgrounds, so that was a particular challenge for me! But it was nice to explore some tones I am less comfortable with. I always try to challenge myself and push my boundaries a little bit, especially when it comes to color and light.

I always have such a clear idea of what I want in my head before I start to paint, and I want the viewer to get the same picture – or at least the closest one to mine as possible! Color and light are so subjective – there is always a challenge and an endless world of possibilities.

Once upon a mermaid's tail

DIBUJANTE NOCTURNO

Color is a fascinating and complex aspect of artmaking. I like working in black and white because of how perfectly it can distinguish values, but color has a magical quality that changes everything.

When I begin a sketch, I consider which areas of the artwork I want to illuminate, and which parts will remain in darkness. The most important thing for me is the strength my image transmits. Lighting is always the best resource for this.

I begin coloring my sketches with less-saturated shades that create an elegant, delicate base. I start from my sketchbook, and then go into Photoshop to add color. Working digitally means that I can take risks and conduct infinite experiments with color. This sense of freedom is the best thing about combining digital and traditional mediums.

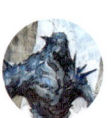 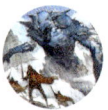

Ice giant

In these scenes, I tried to create a luminous atmosphere and a beautiful setting in which the viewer might imagine themselves.

Despite their small size, the characters have a sense of importance within the composition. This is due to a combination of the strong light coming from behind them, and the contrasting warm tones of their garments.

I make small color studies like these so that I can easily visualize finished illustrations. These two drawings measure only a few centimeters in reality.

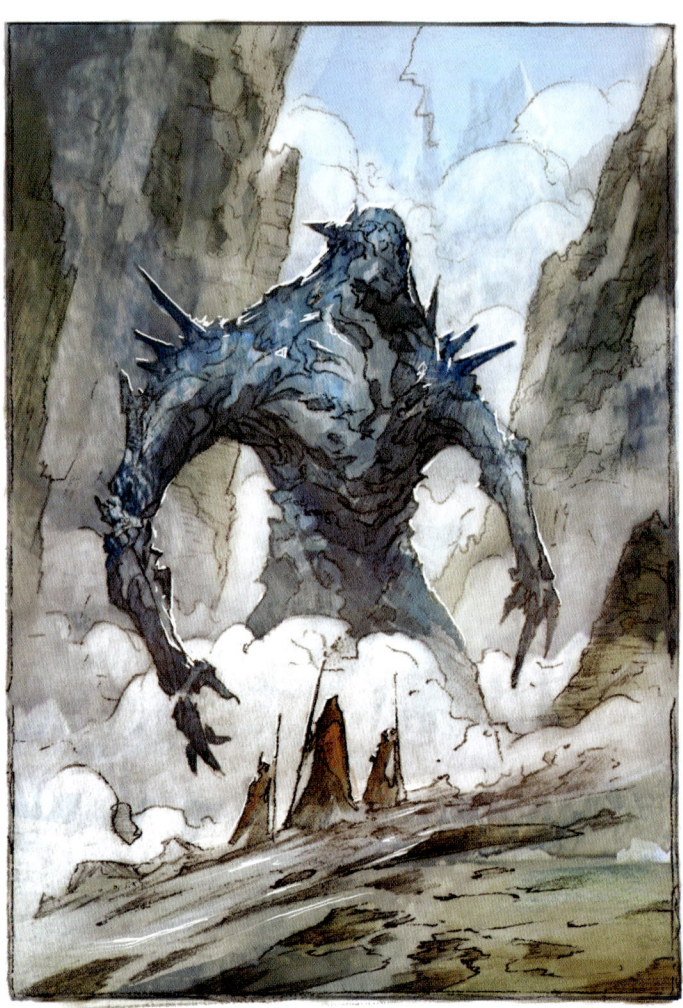

Ice giant

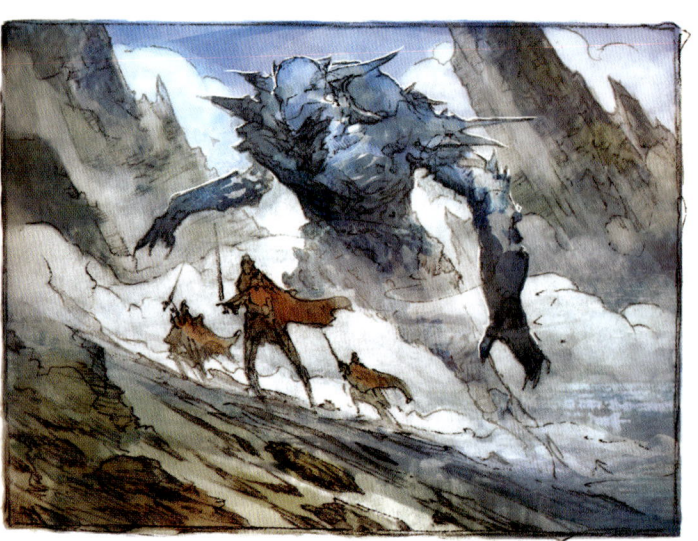

Images © Fran Garcés (Dibujante Nocturno/Night Sketcher)

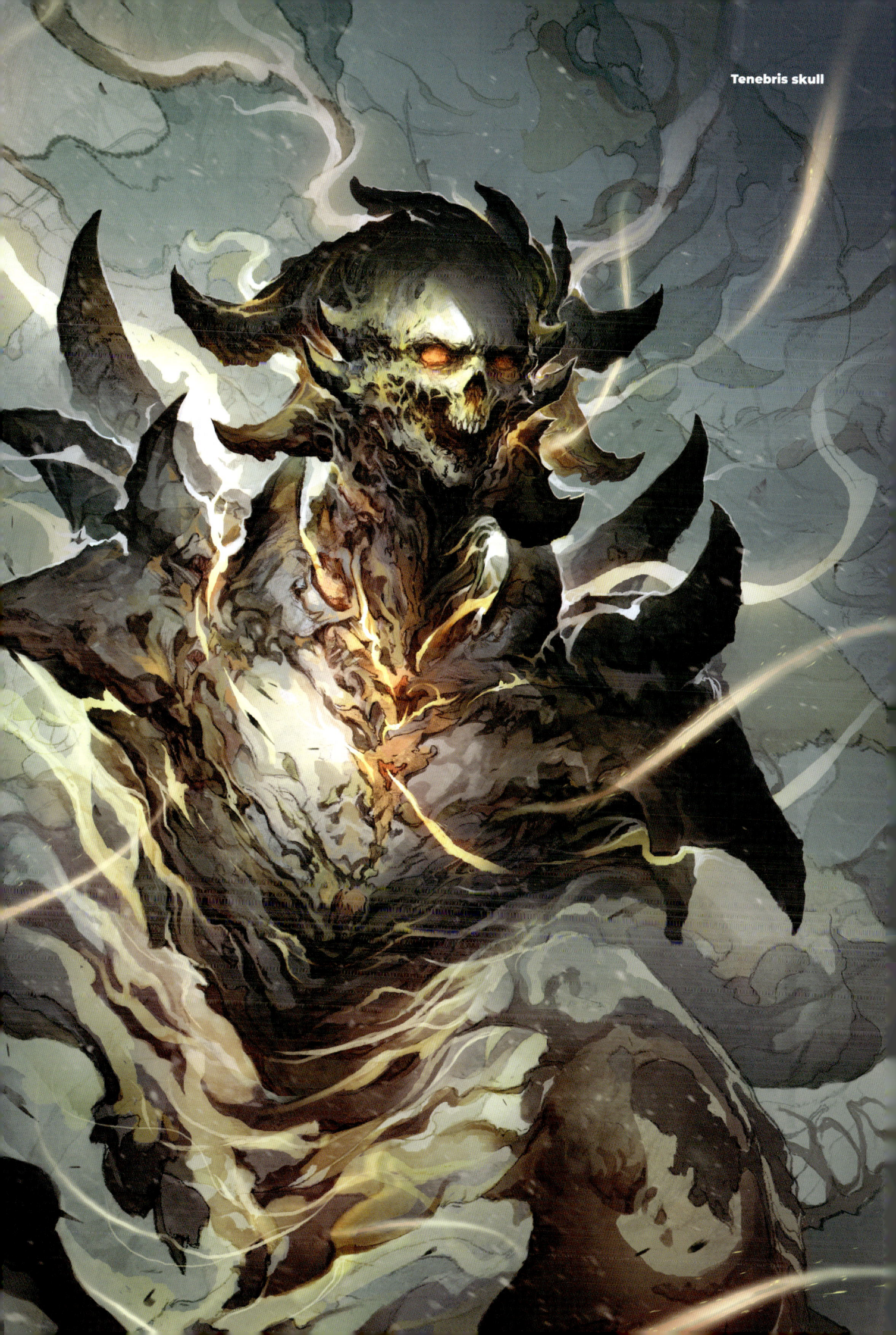

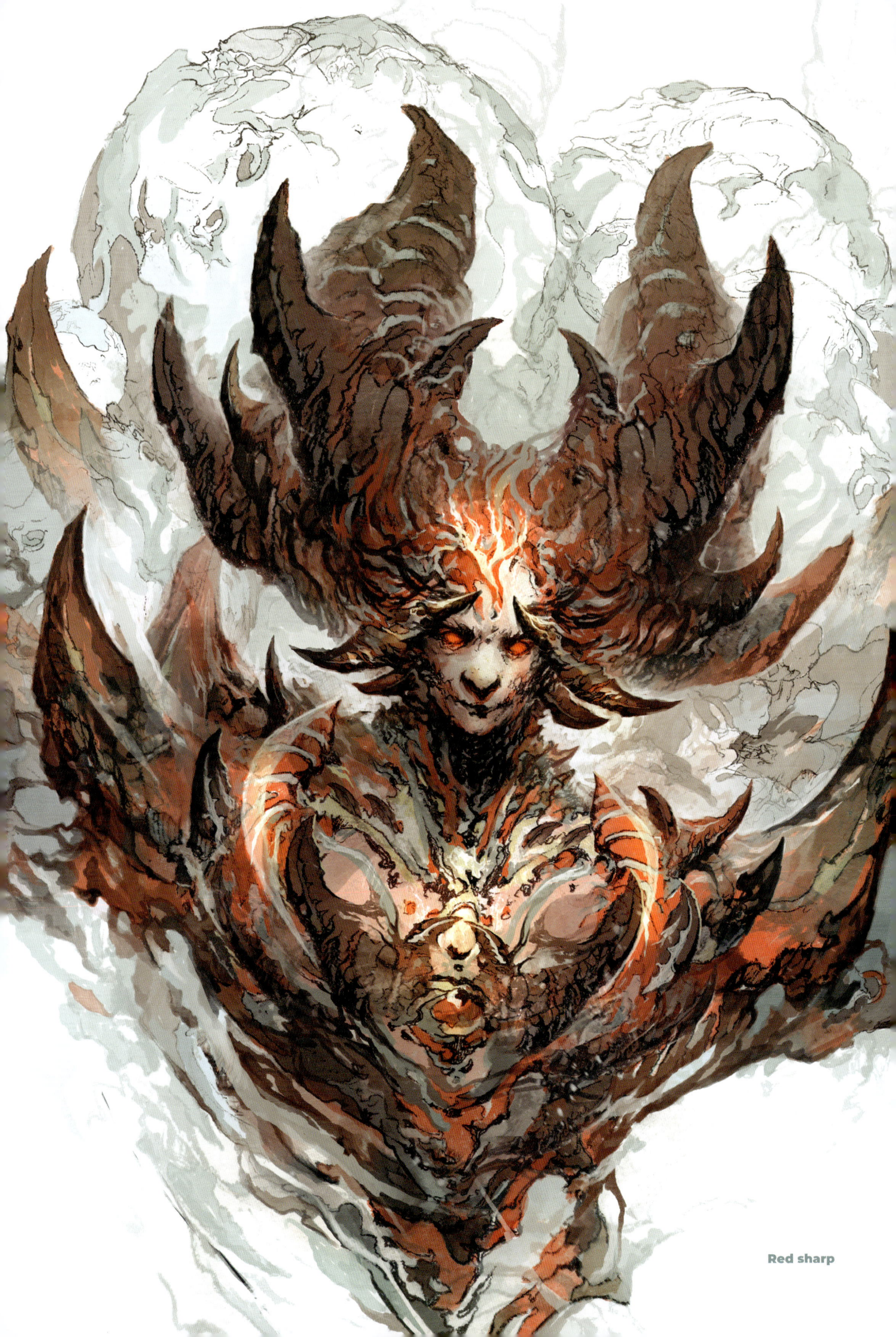

Red sharp

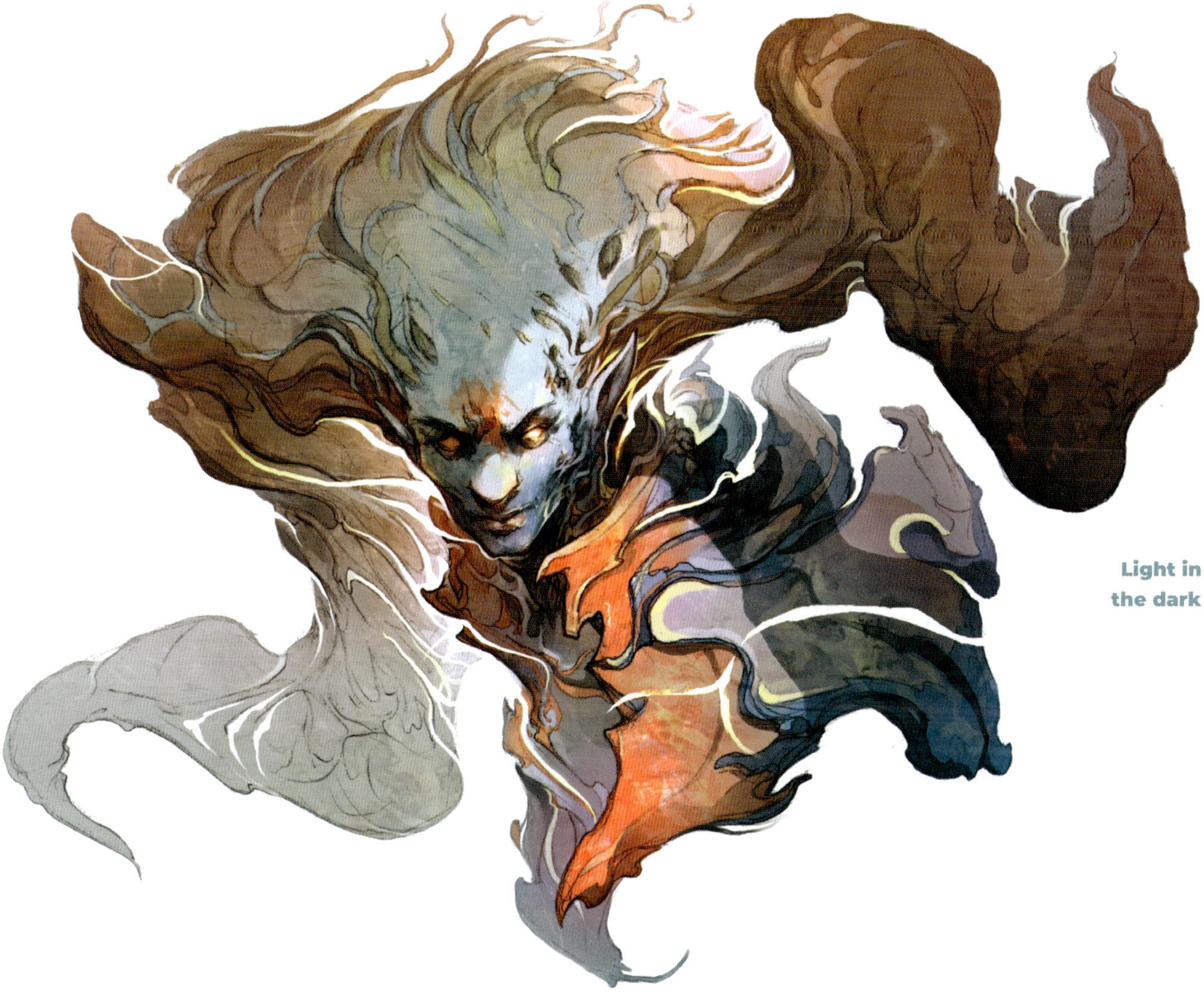

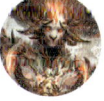

**Light in
the dark**

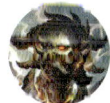

Tenebris skull

Here, I have created a dark atmosphere that still has threads of light. A magical effect envelops the character and creates a dynamic, interesting composition. The color saturation is concentrated on the character, while the rest of the image remains very soft in tone. It's an attractive contrast, where the color transforms the dark imagery into something very beautiful.

Red sharp

It's always exciting to watch as the layers of paint and color build up to transform a simple sketch into something alive! With his warm and dark colors, this character stands out intensely from the light, low-contrast grays of the background. A few spots of hot, vivid light frame the face area, implying a powerful character.

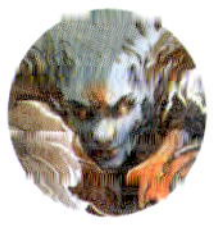

Light in the dark

I like to paint characters and creatures against a white background – even without detailed surroundings, you can achieve vibrant results. I often blend my characters into the background using white paint and light effects. This character is surrounded by a magical, dynamic, and intense light. The soft, textured tones give the sketch an elegant finish.

SIMONE GRÜNEWALD

For a long time, while painting, I felt intimidated by color and light. I would always try to work by feel, and there was an element of guesswork. Over the last few years, however, I have finally delved into this topic, and can still say that I have only scratched at its surface. I am so glad for all the light and beauty that the world has to offer, and I love to study it through my art. Whenever an image's lighting catches my eye, I feel the need to try and capture it. Sometimes I will stay close to reference, and other times I will make it completely my own, in an attempt to capture a particular lighting essence. I find myself drawn to scenes of untouched nature and love to go on adventures and explore beautiful landscapes.

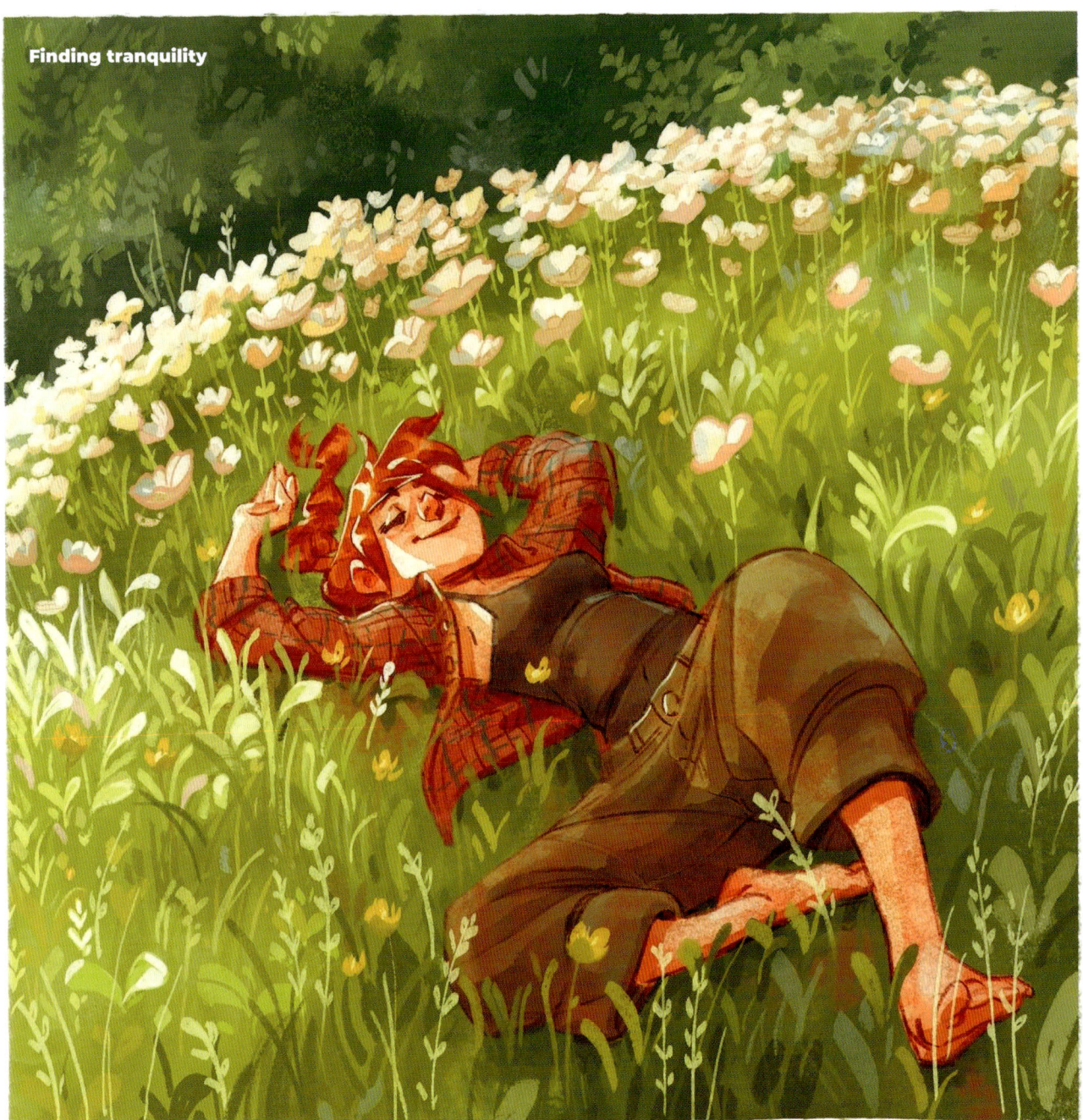

Finding tranquility

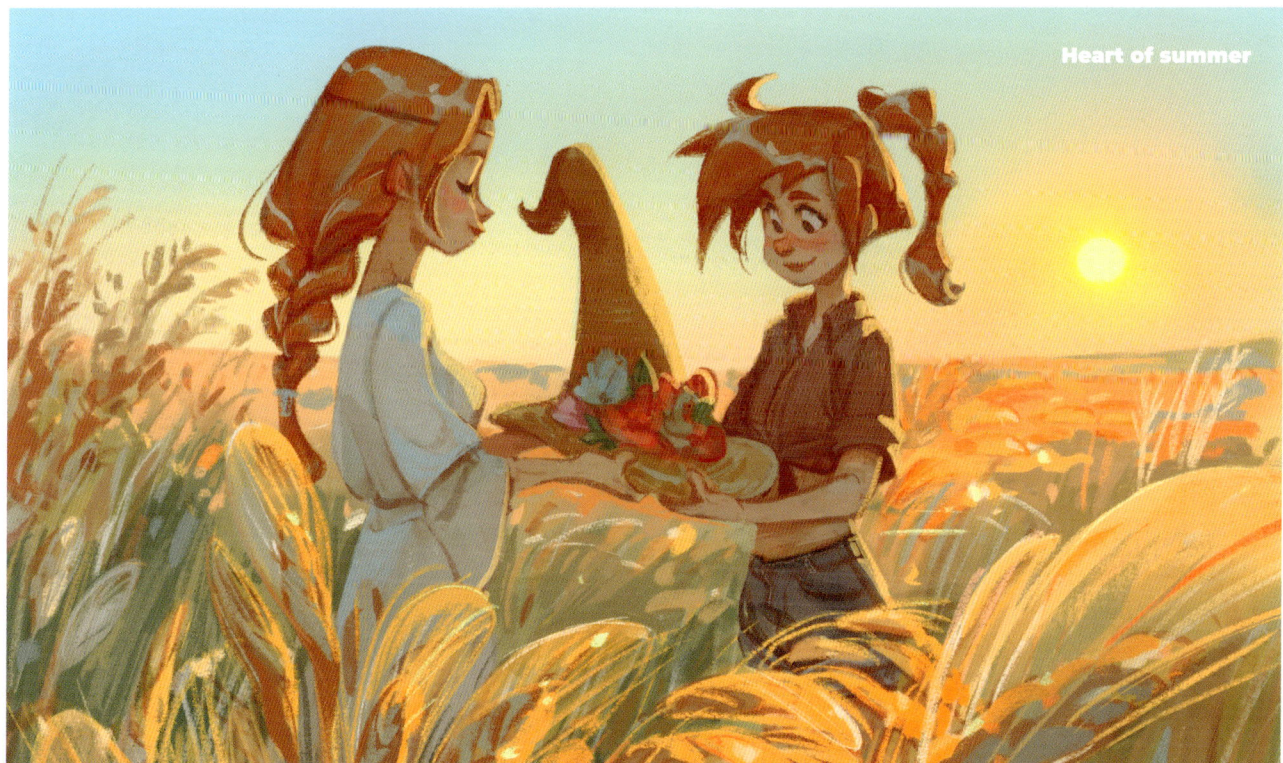

Heart of summer

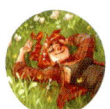

Finding tranquility

Flower fields have always fascinated me. I just want to soak up their color and light and feel close to nature. The visual busyness of all the elements fascinates me, and holds endless possibilities to stylize. Strong light coming from the left gives lovely definition to the flowers and the character.

The flowers appear white in the light, but clue you to their pinkness with their underbellies. The flowers may have rich colors, but they aren't noisy in their hue changes, which range subtly from blue to yellow. They contrast beautifully with the saturated, juicy grass. Against the greens, the character's complementary red pops out as an accent. It also gently reflects onto the surroundings, tying the character back in. I don't like to isolate colors completely, even if I want them to stand out, so this moment of reflection is important.

Strong light from one side creates most of the hard, stylized edges, bringing attention to the character's tranquil face. I also added some reflected sky blue to the areas not directly hit by hard light, creating variance from the main red/green contrast. I use bluer green for the bushes in the background, pushing them further away.

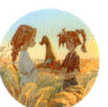

Heart of summer

This is one of my favorite illustrations. It gives me joy, and I am particularly proud of the balanced colors – it is very colorful, and yet nothing is jarring. Everything is harmonious. There's a good contrast and balance between warm and cool. The palette is mainly warm, but within the warmth, cool tones can always be found. I was inspired by the pockets of shade that you find underneath ears of wheat, and used cool, desaturated gray-greens, blues, and violets to depict this.

If everything were fully saturated, this image would be unbearable. Instead, the desaturated colors enable the saturated colors to shine even brighter. In the background, everything in the light is saturated, and everything in the shadows is desaturated. For the backlit characters, it is the opposite – they are mainly in desaturated shadow, but their deep, occluded shadows are rather saturated. Their darker, purplish hues make them pop out from the sunlit field.

Backlighting is my favorite way to create interesting lighting on characters, with the benefit of casting soft reflected light on them. This backlighting also added subsurface scattering to the ears of corn, brightening their edges and illuminating them beautifully.

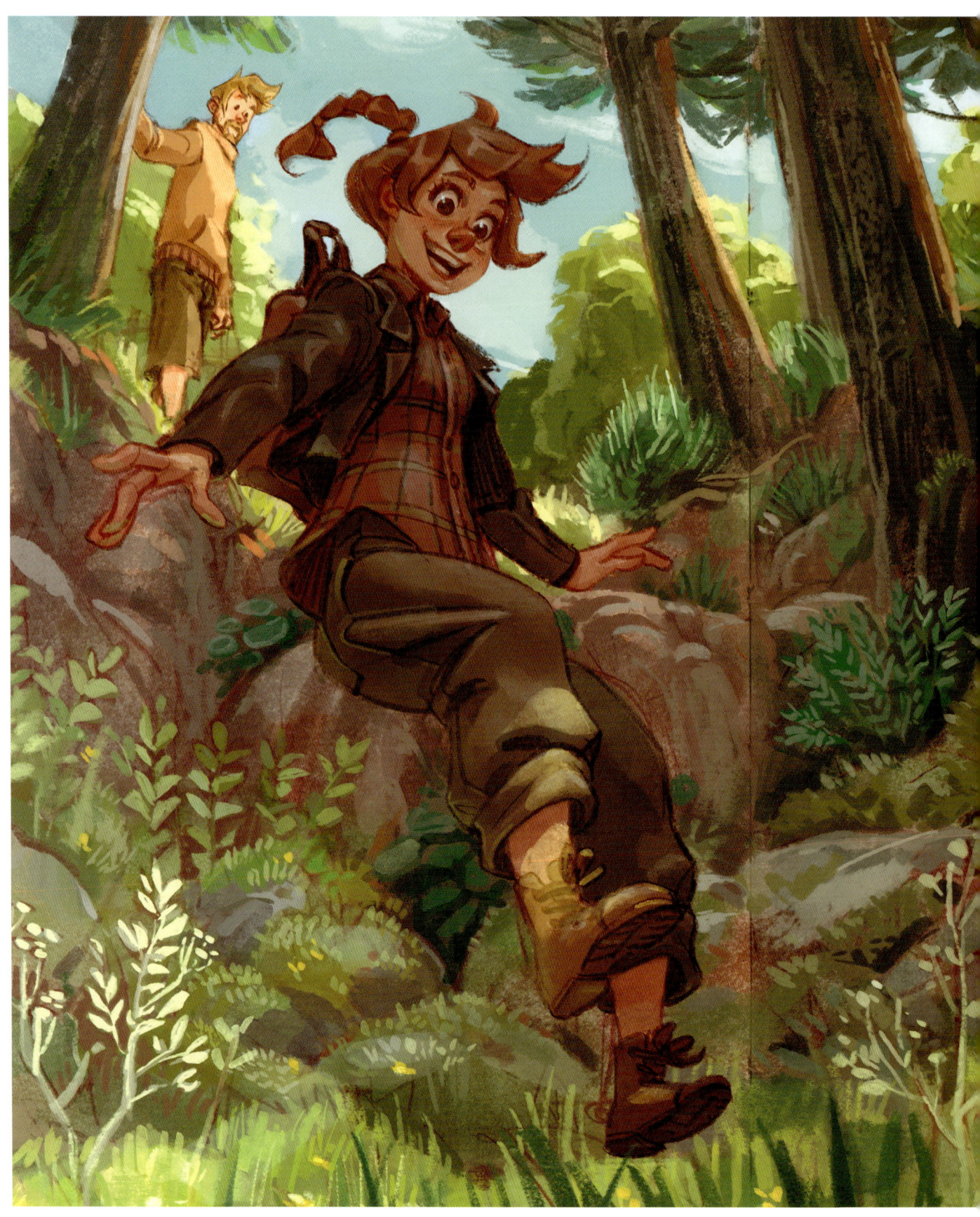

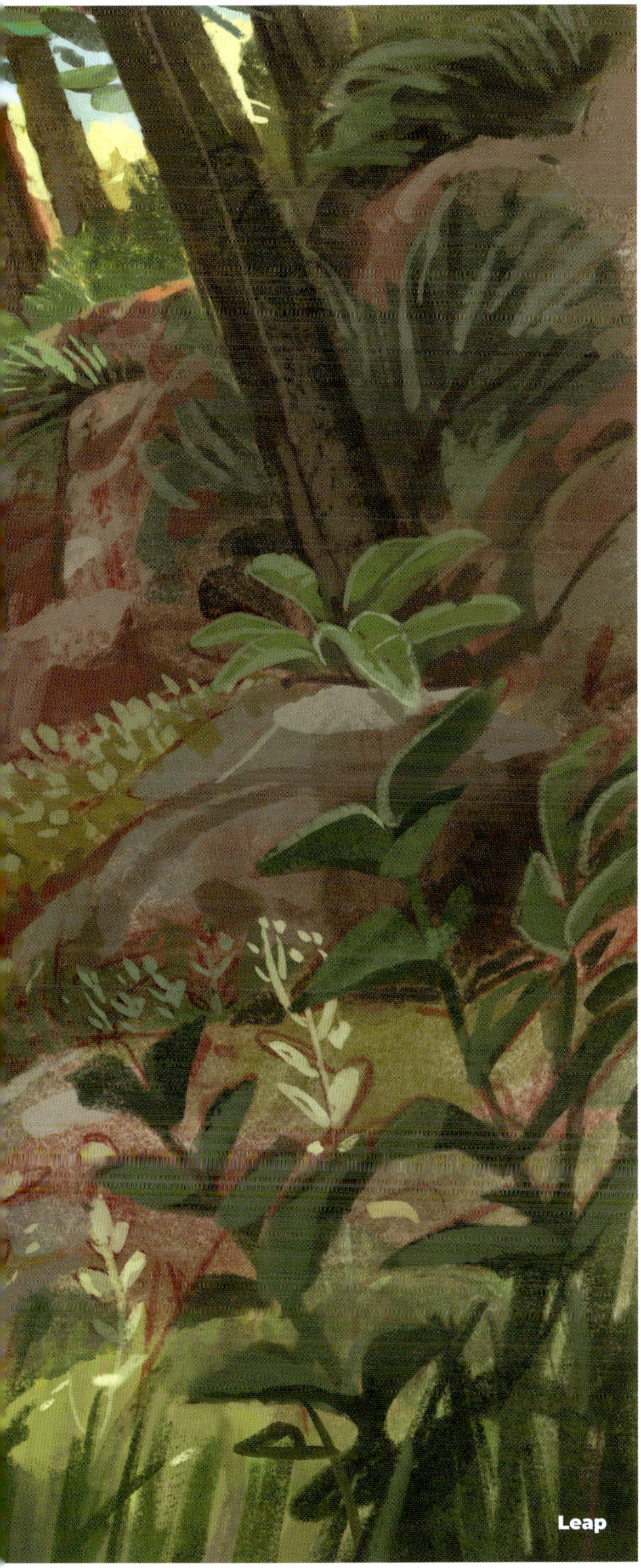

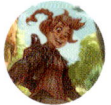

Leap

I love trying new approaches for my illustrations. As preliminary work for this piece, I painted a study of a nature scene, using a photo reference. I then imagined a completely new scene, adding characters and an altered background, but still containing fundamental aspects of that study. Moving forward, I could heavily lean on my first painting, and treat all elements in a similar manner.

I first established my color palette: various values and saturations of purple and green-gray go into the stones and tree trunks. A juicy saturated green depicts the grass in the light, and some more desaturated hues of green cast the shadow. Finally, I used a bright cyan for the sky.

I like to focus detail either in the shadow or light area, but not both. That adds to the story that you want to tell. So, if a part of an image isn't as important, keep it diffuse. It doesn't need to hold the viewer's attention. In this case, the largest portion of the illustration is in shadow, from which the main character jumps into the light. For the viewer, I wanted to emulate the feeling of looking up from the complex shade toward the bright and simple light.

I used digital watercolors, which are great at creating some traditional texture and variation in color and saturation, adding to the overall richness of the image. I sometimes find it hard to achieve this feeling when working with clean digital brushes.

Leap

IRAVILLE

When I paint with watercolors, my preferred medium, thinking about color and light is essential. It helps to know about physical and chemical aspects, asking questions such as: "Where does this particular pigment come from?" and "When you apply paint to paper, what happens to the wavelengths that are reflected into your eyes?"

Just as I paint "false" perspectives intentionally, I do not use color and light "correctly." My art does not intend to portray reality, and color and light are devices that serve the overall composition. It is all about the final image itself.

I rarely draw lines, so my forms are separated by contrasting colors, mostly complementary or almost complementary. I never use paints directly out of the tube or pan, but rather mix them on my palettes first. Additionally, I use many transparent layers of paint, so that the colors mix by overlaying each other, which leads to more depth in the final image.

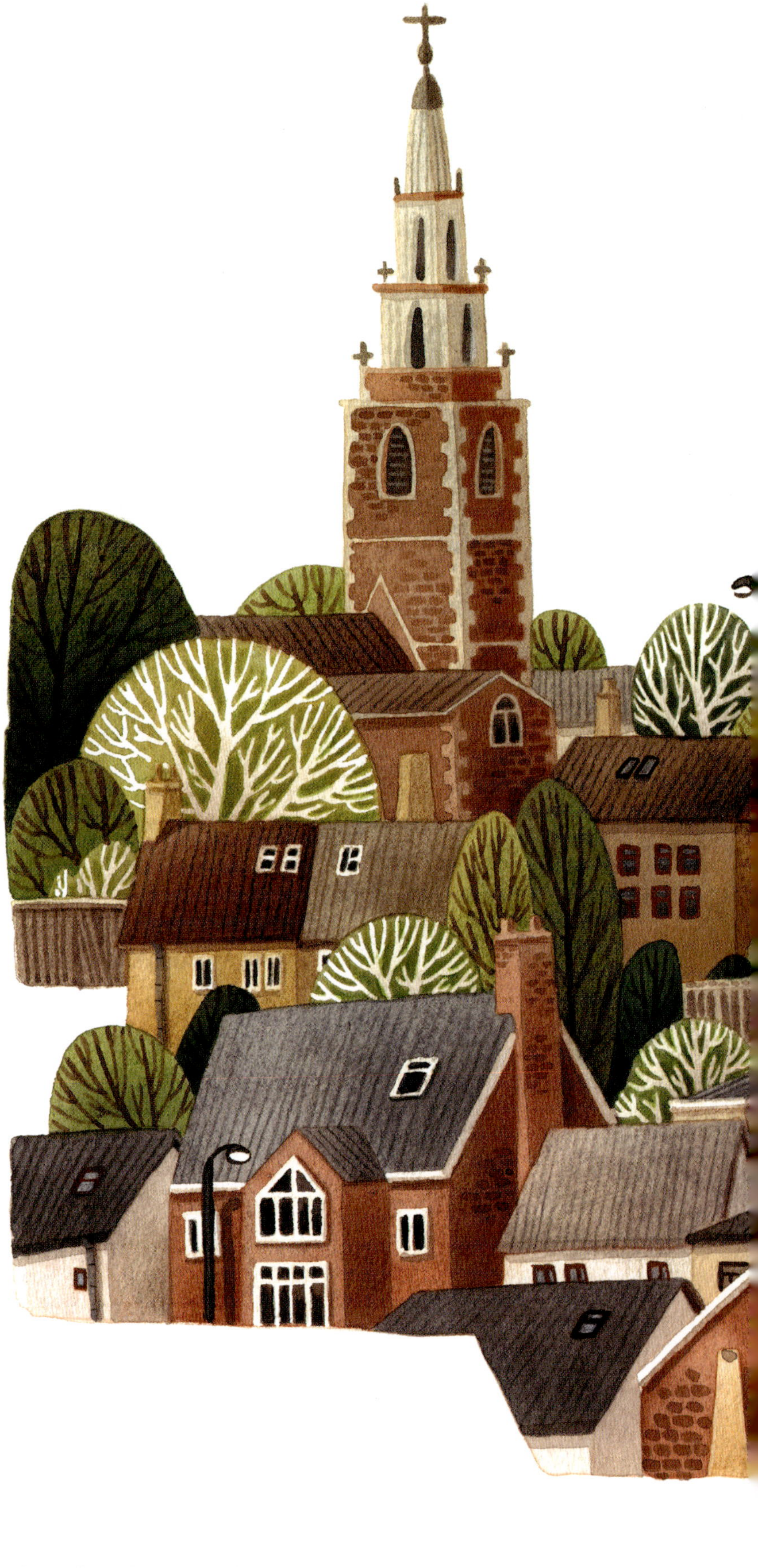

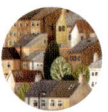

Irish town

When painting with watercolors, I mainly use a lot of layers and just a few very basic paints. I constantly, intuitively mix them before applying them with varying amounts of water. Here, this technique helped emphasize the variety of the townscape. No wall or roof has the same color! To prevent the image from getting too cluttered – as it already contained a lot of detail – I simplified the light and shadows without caring about physical correctness.

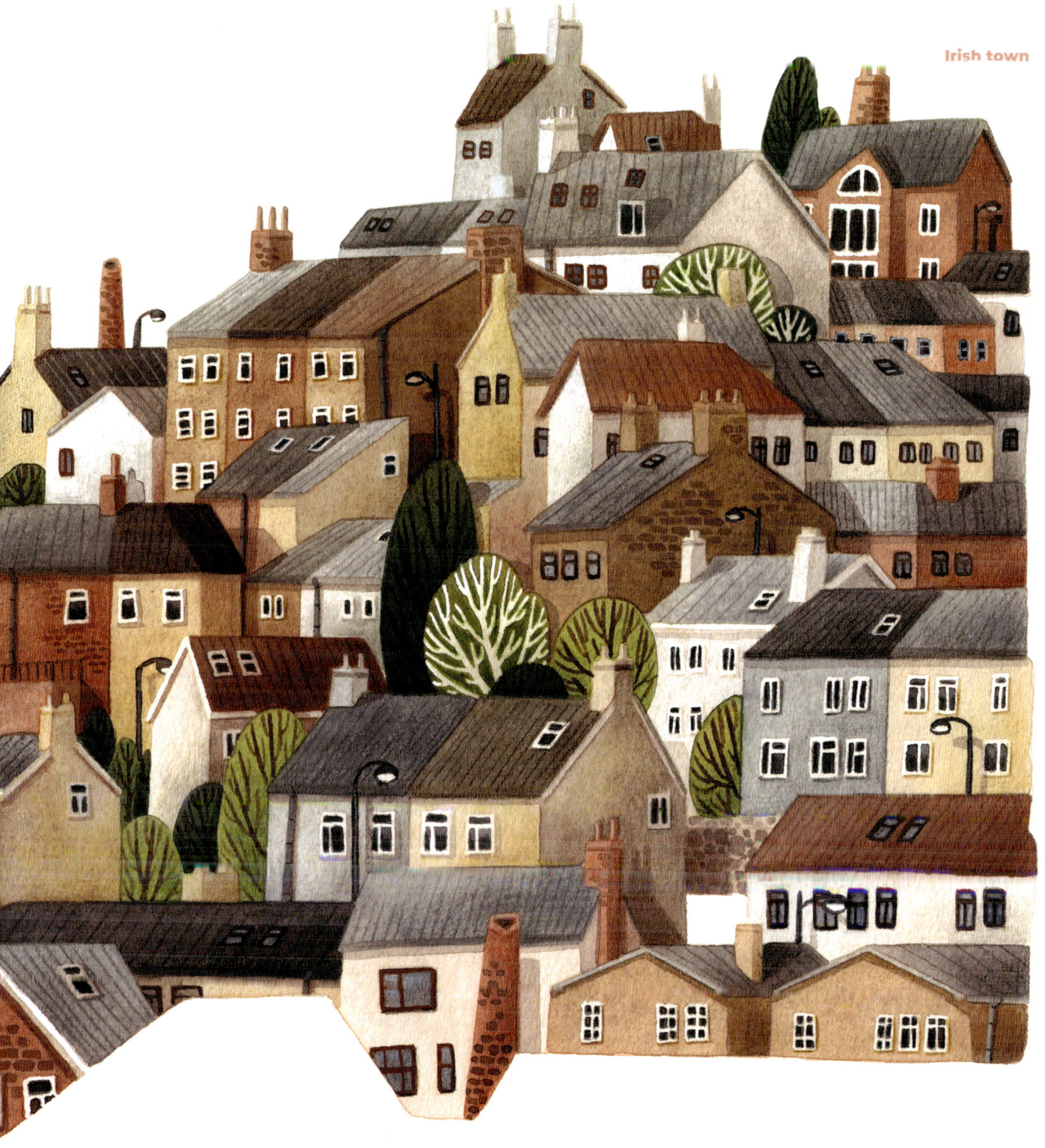

Irish town

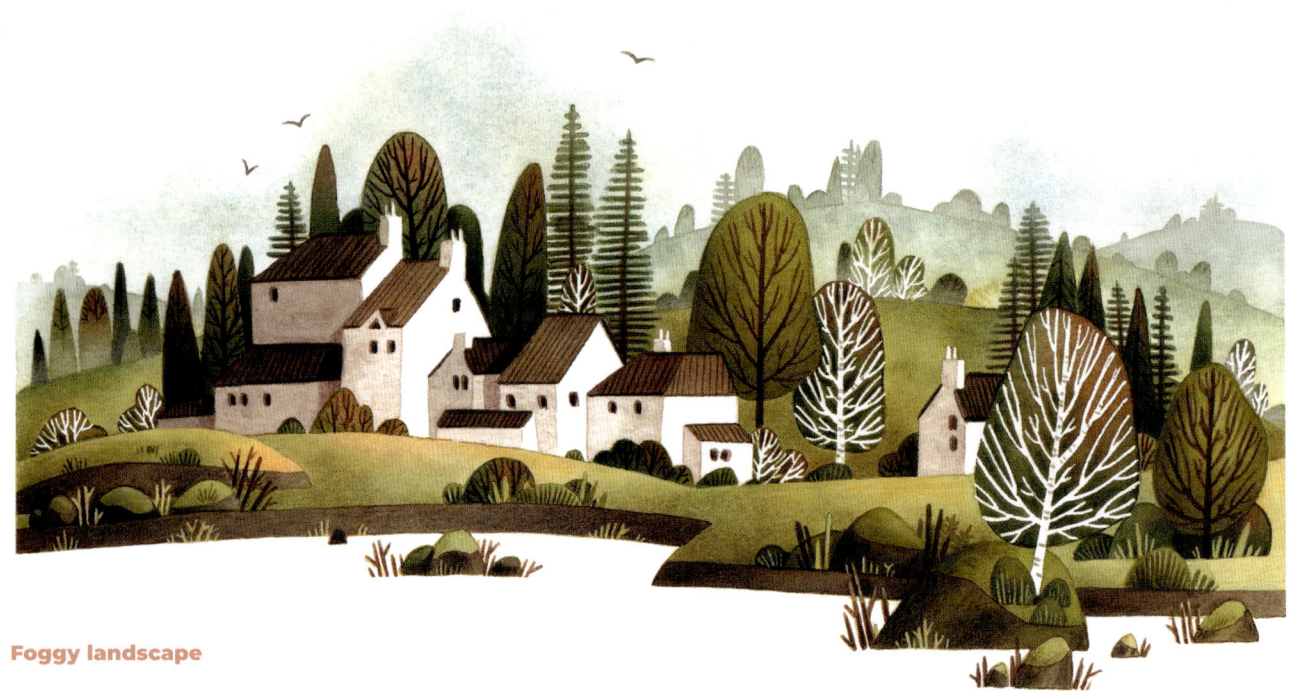

Foggy landscape

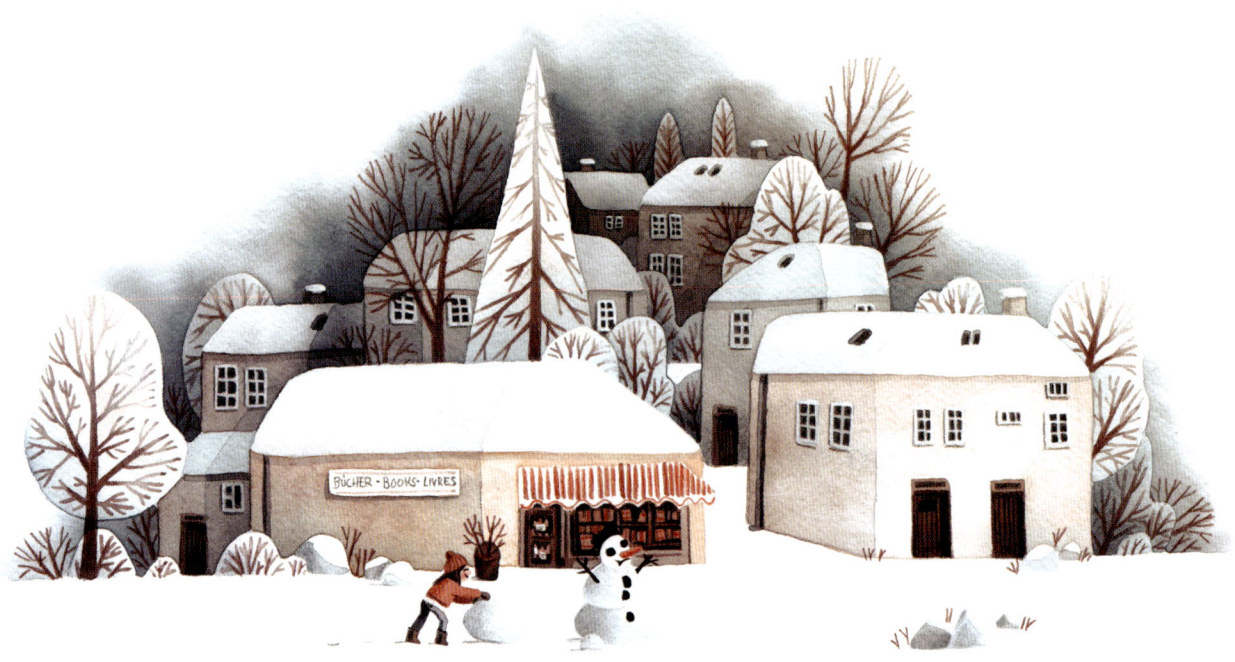

Snowman

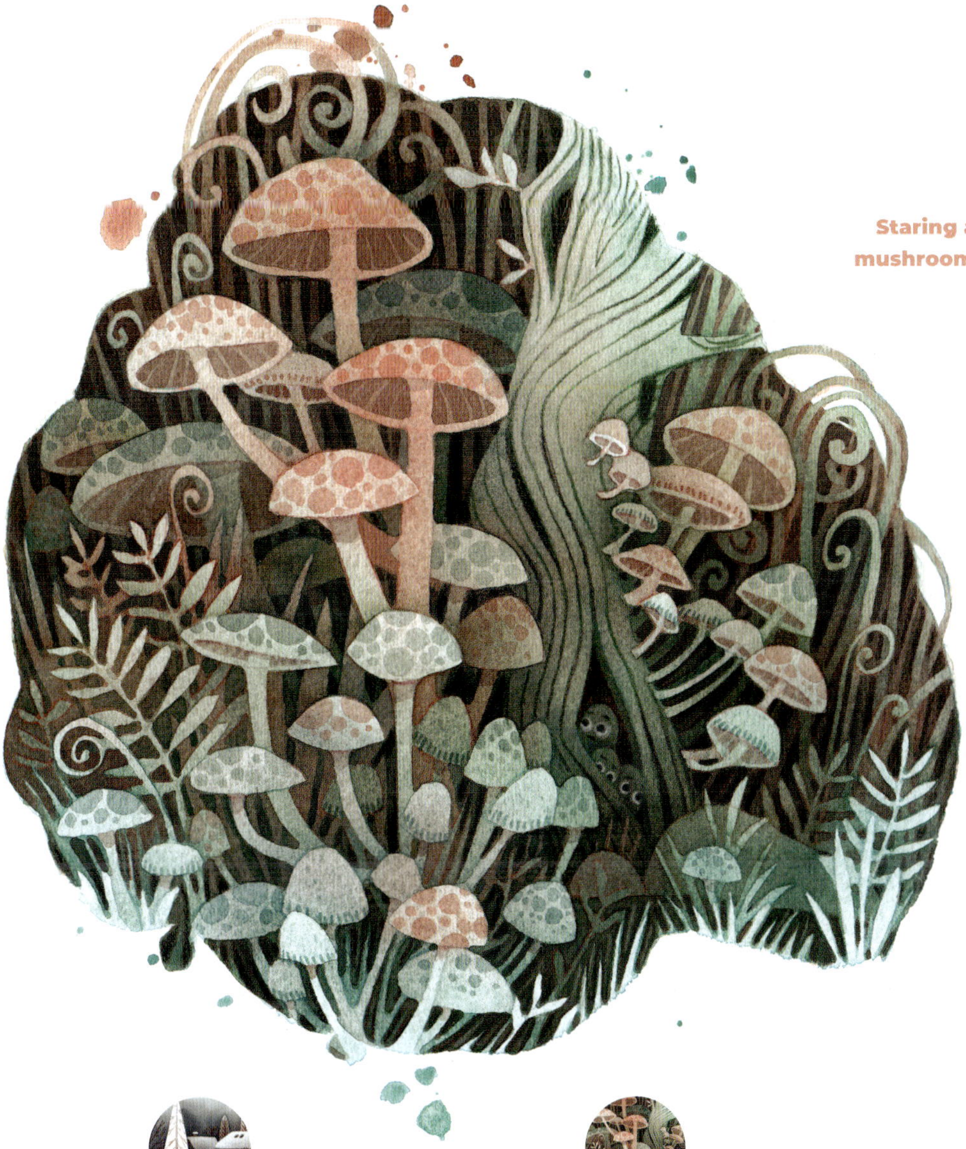

Staring at
mushrooms

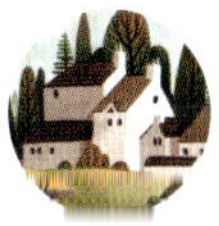

Foggy landscape

If you look out over a distant landscape, you will see that the colors of faraway objects become less saturated and seem to merge with the horizon. It is the same with contrasts: The difference between highlights and lowlights reduces with increasing distance from the viewer. The presence of fog heightens this effect even more. To visualize this, I painted the distant landscape with fewer layers, more water, and more blue tones, while using warmer yellow-orange and green tones in the foreground.

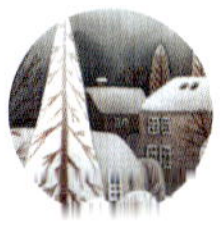

Snowman

For this image, I wanted some kind of spotlight effect to emphasize the action in the foreground. The buildings and trees appear darker, colder, and have less contrast the more they are placed in the background. The two houses in the foreground are warmer and brighter, but not as bright as the snow, which is formed by negative space.

Like in reality, the gray parts are never neutral, but a little bit brownish, bluish, or even violet sometimes.

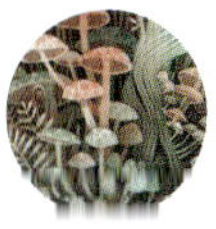

Staring at mushrooms

Here, the otherworldly luminance of the mushrooms is achieved with the help of two nearly complementary colors and many light gradations. The frontal light seems to come from the mushrooms themselves. Objects in the background are painted darker and are more toned down, with just small shadows directly under their heads. To further intensify the colors, cold blue-green forms are surrounded by warm reddish shadows behind them, and vice versa.

DEVIN ELLE KURTZ

Since I was very young, light has been one of my favorite subjects to paint. Just like a person, or a landscape, I have found it to have a character of its own. My work changed radically when I started considering light and shadow as compositional elements, rather than as an afterthought.

I tend to envision the light and color in a painting from the very beginning, as soon as I establish my concept. Will there be bounce light? A warm or cool palette? Subsurface scattering? Multiple light sources? These considerations always make me excited to work on a piece!

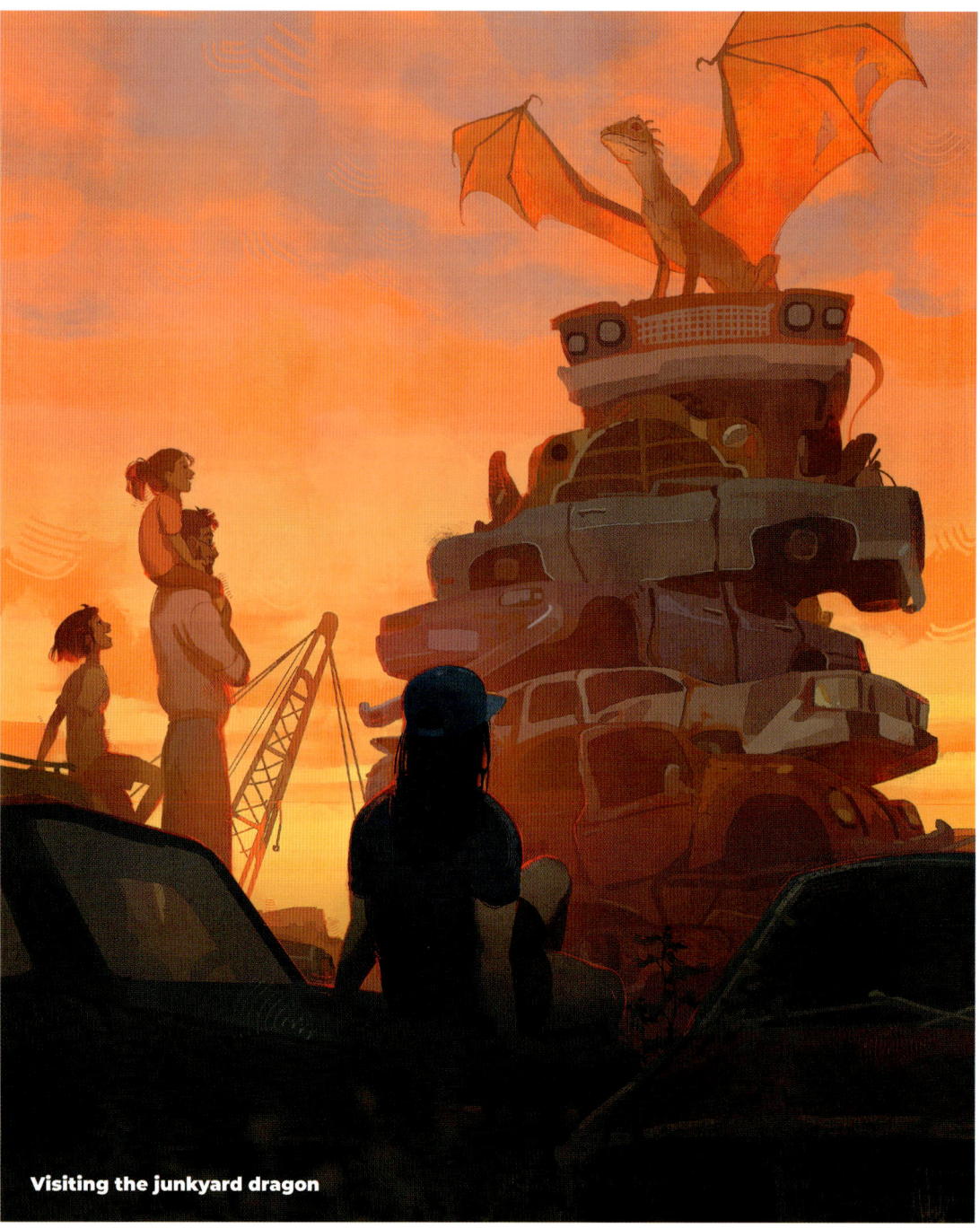

Visiting the junkyard dragon

Images © Devin Elle Kurtz

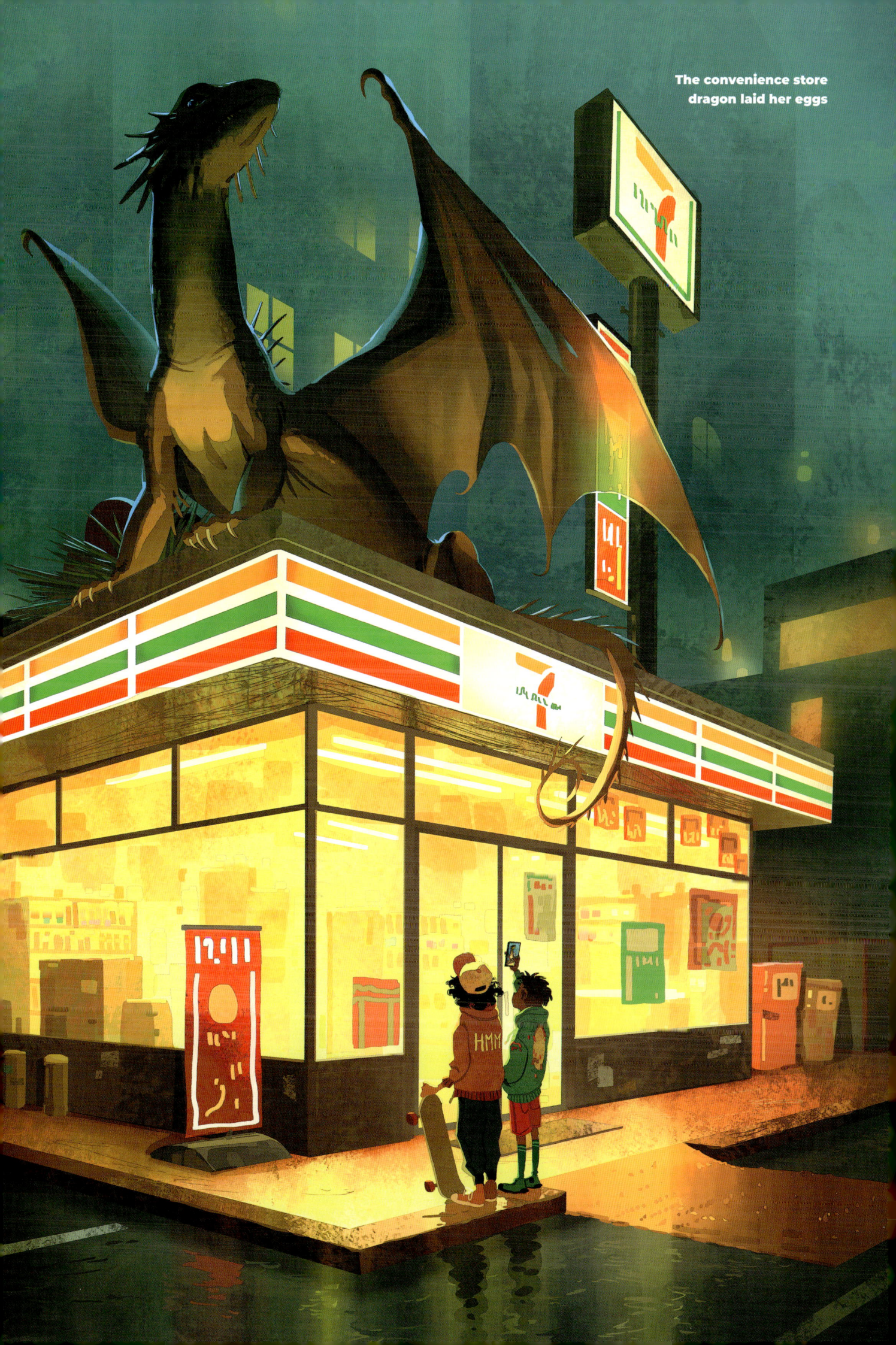

The convenience store dragon laid her eggs

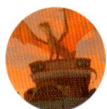

Visiting the junkyard dragon

For this piece, I wanted to create a warm and triumphant feeling. In this story, this junkyard-dwelling dragon was rescued as a baby with an injured wing, and here he is visited by his childhood saviors who are now grown up with children of their own. I chose a warm sunset palette that envelops the characters like a hug. The yellow toward the horizon glows brightest to draw our attention to the people, and their gazes point us back up to the dragon.

I kept all of the cool hues in the palette very muted, so they contrast softly with the warms. Each car in the stack has its own unique color, but, due to their overall similarity in hue and value, they group together visually as a single silhouette.

I used a saturated red rim light to define the characters' silhouettes and add a bright kick to draw the eye. This balances the bright red of the wings, allowing them to sit more naturally against such a saturated sky. This is one of my favorite little tricks to make my characters glow against a sunset.

I created a layer of fog between the middle ground and foreground by using a medium gray on a Luminosity layer. This unified the values toward the bottom of the middle ground, creating stronger silhouettes for the foreground cars and the woman. "Luminosity" and "Lighten" layers are great for setting areas of a painting back in space.

I added a few strokes of neutral pink to the very top of the sky to create more cohesion in the palette and tie it into the neutrals in the car stack. Digital art can sometimes look disjointed, so I like to create some repetition in my color and compositions to tie my illustrations together.

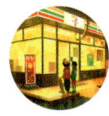

The convenience store dragon laid her eggs

There are two light sources in this piece: the bright, warmly lit convenience store and the cool, cyan night sky. I knew from the beginning that I would use these two sources together to sculpt the three-dimensionality of the dragon. The convenience store serves as the primary light source and defines the dragon's body, while the blue rim light brings interest to her silhouette.

The color palette in this image relies on a cool-warm contrast, based loosely around the classic colors of the convenience store. I decided to skew the foggy blue night slightly toward green, which created a pleasing overall palette that is repeated within the sign and the store.

I kept the interior of the store within a similar value and hue range so that it could glow warmly while feeling unified. I also kept the contrast fairly low within the windows, and used similar colors and values to add little details. The store's interior feels full without demanding focus in the composition.

I brought attention to the boys by adding the whole range of the palette's hues to their outfits in a very condensed area. That, combined with their detailed and dark silhouettes, draws the eye and creates a focal point. We then follow their gazes right back up to the dragon!

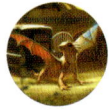

Releasing the baby dragon

The light source here is a lot warmer and more neutral, which allows me to sneak in bright pops of color without it feeling overwhelming or oversaturated. I love adding colorful accents to a piece with bright, hard light, because that color tends to bleed out as light bloom and bounce light.

I separate the main middle-ground stage from the foreground and background by way of color temperature. The stack of cars at the back collapses into a neutral, cool range, as do the foreground pipes and tires. The middle ground stands apart by expanding into a fuller value range, with a color palette that skews dusty and yellow.

I use light to show depth by having the background trees fall in and out of the shadows. This creates a sense of dimension. The leaves in the sunlight seem to come toward us in space, while the leaves in the shadows fall back and group with the cars behind them. The contrasting use of blue emphasizes the narrative element of the baby dragon's repaired wing.

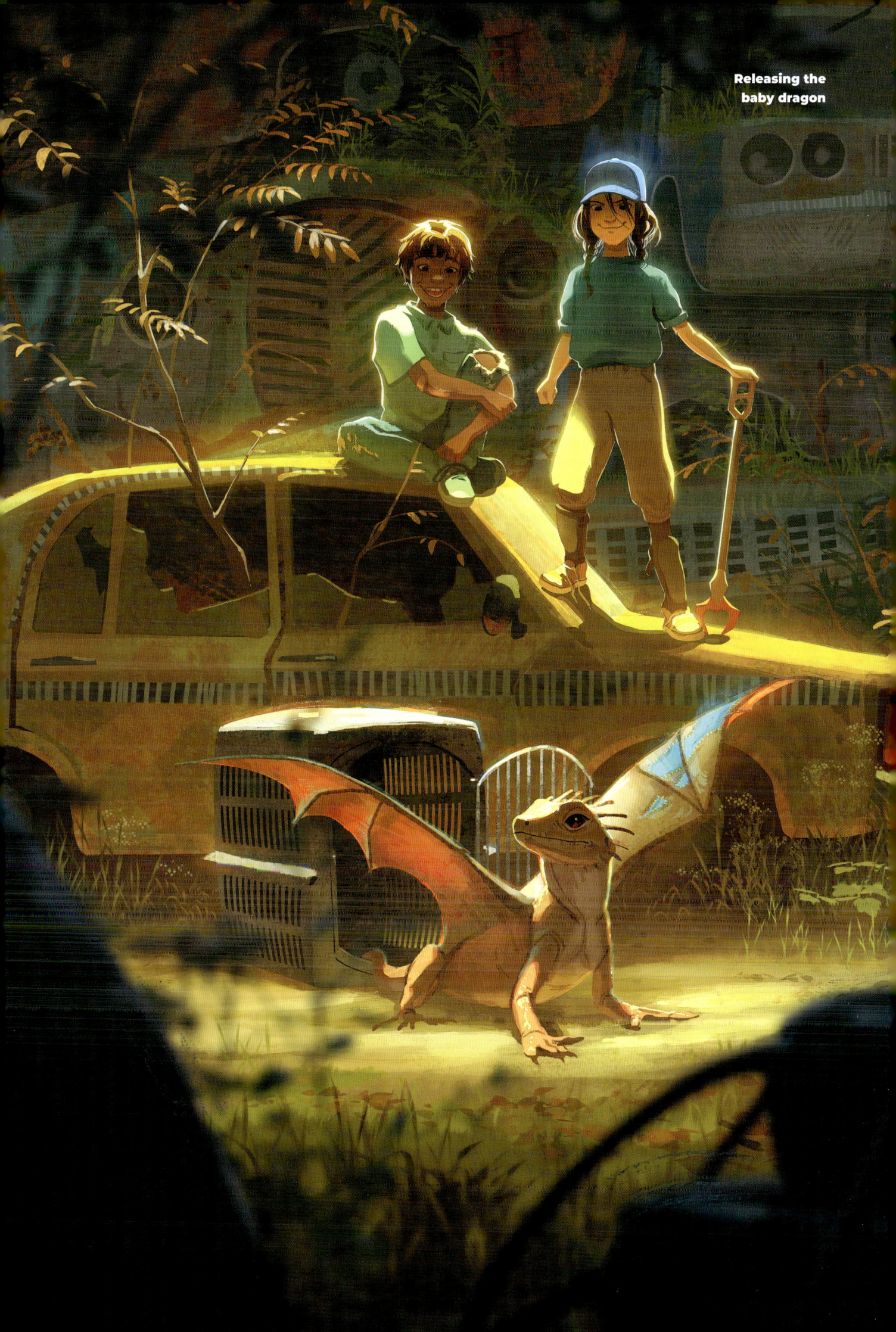

Releasing the baby dragon

ASIA LADOWSKA

When creating illustrations, I work mainly based on intuition, using colors that I think look good together and that make me happy when I look at them. As an artist that works in a style inspired by manga and anime, I like to create colorful and vibrant illustrations – so paintings with a lot of light and color in them!

I like to make my illustrations look like they glow instead of focusing on more traditional light sources. You will often see me use butterflies or glowing flowers as light sources! I think it is really important and helpful to learn fundamentals and apply them in your art, but don't forget that art is a journey and it is meant to be a fun one. Here I am sharing with you my colorful and glowing pictures, but who knows – tomorrow I might get back to studying and change my style and approach completely!

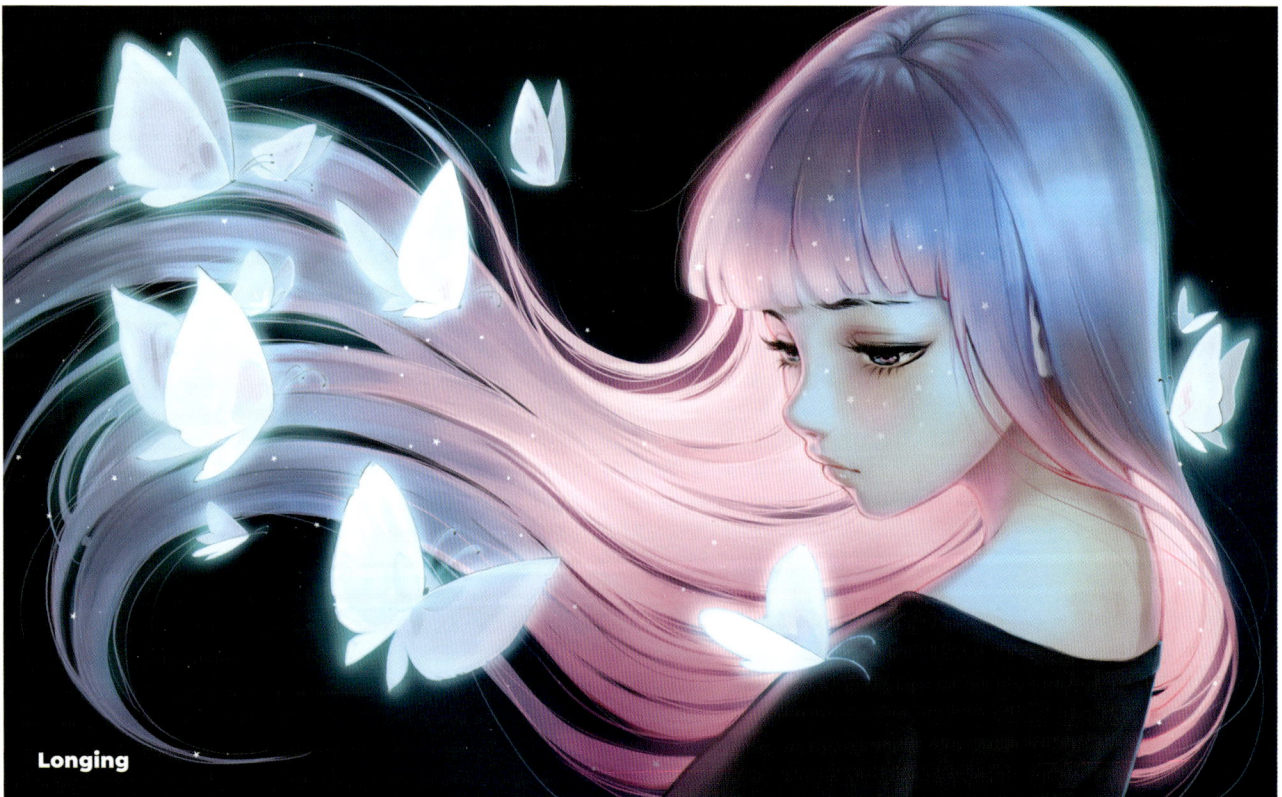

Longing

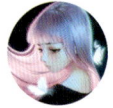

Longing

One of my favorite illustrations is this one that I created for the cover of my first book, *Sketch with Asia*. It has everything I love the most about art and painting: glowing elements, butterflies, stars, weightlessness, a lot of pink, and a lot of blue.

Glow is rather tricky to work with, which is why I chose a dark background to create more contrast and make the elements stand out more. The image would not have made the same impact if the surroundings were light. To emphasize the strength of the pink light coming from the glowing hair, I reflected the color in my character's face and neck. For the glow effect around the butterflies I added a layer in Screen mode and painted the glow with a vibrant blue.

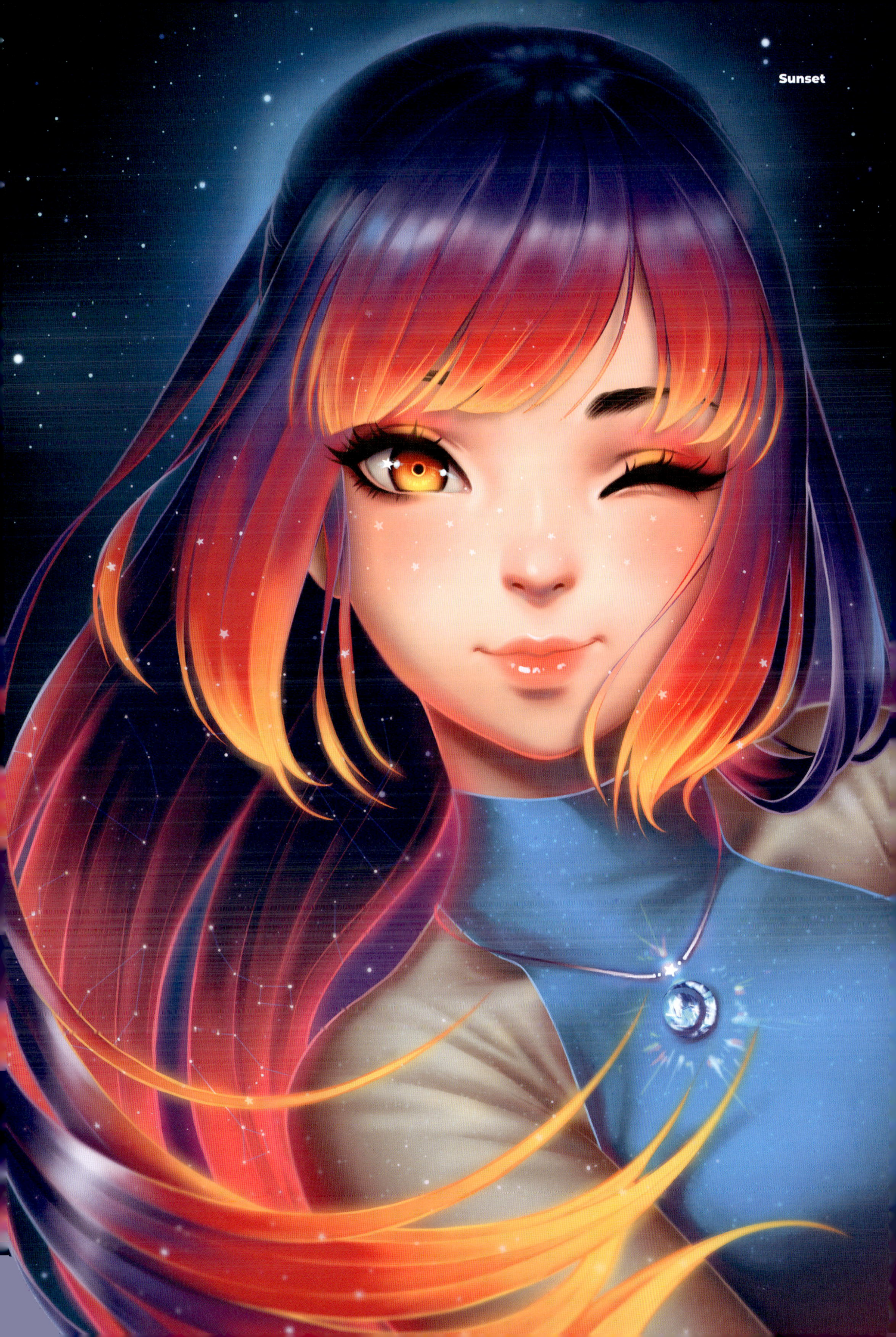

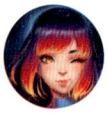

Sunset

Meet Sunset, a magazine-cover space model! I played a lot with colors and light while painting her portrait, making sure I included stars and a lot of glowing elements as well as bringing the focus to her face – hence the light in that area is the strongest. To emphasize the glowing elements, once again I painted the non-glowing surfaces, like skin and fabric, with some of the glow color – you can see this most strongly with the pink and orange light from her hair. When painting the necklace that represents the Sun and Moon, I added a colorful shimmer around it to show the light shining through the crystal.

With so many glowing and shimmering elements, I had to be careful not to overdo all the light effects. For example, even though there are a lot of tiny stars all around the image, I chose not to add a glow to those. That would have been too much!

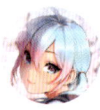 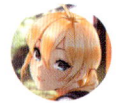

Mai

I made this portrait to explore how different colors and lighting can change one illustration. I intuitively gravitated toward using pink and blue hues in the first version, but, being aware of my tendencies, I purposely tried out something different in the second illustration.

I created interesting light effects in both images by painting bokeh, dust, and sparkles. If you look closely, you can see the bright circles in various places around the character, creating a dreamy, sunlit effect.

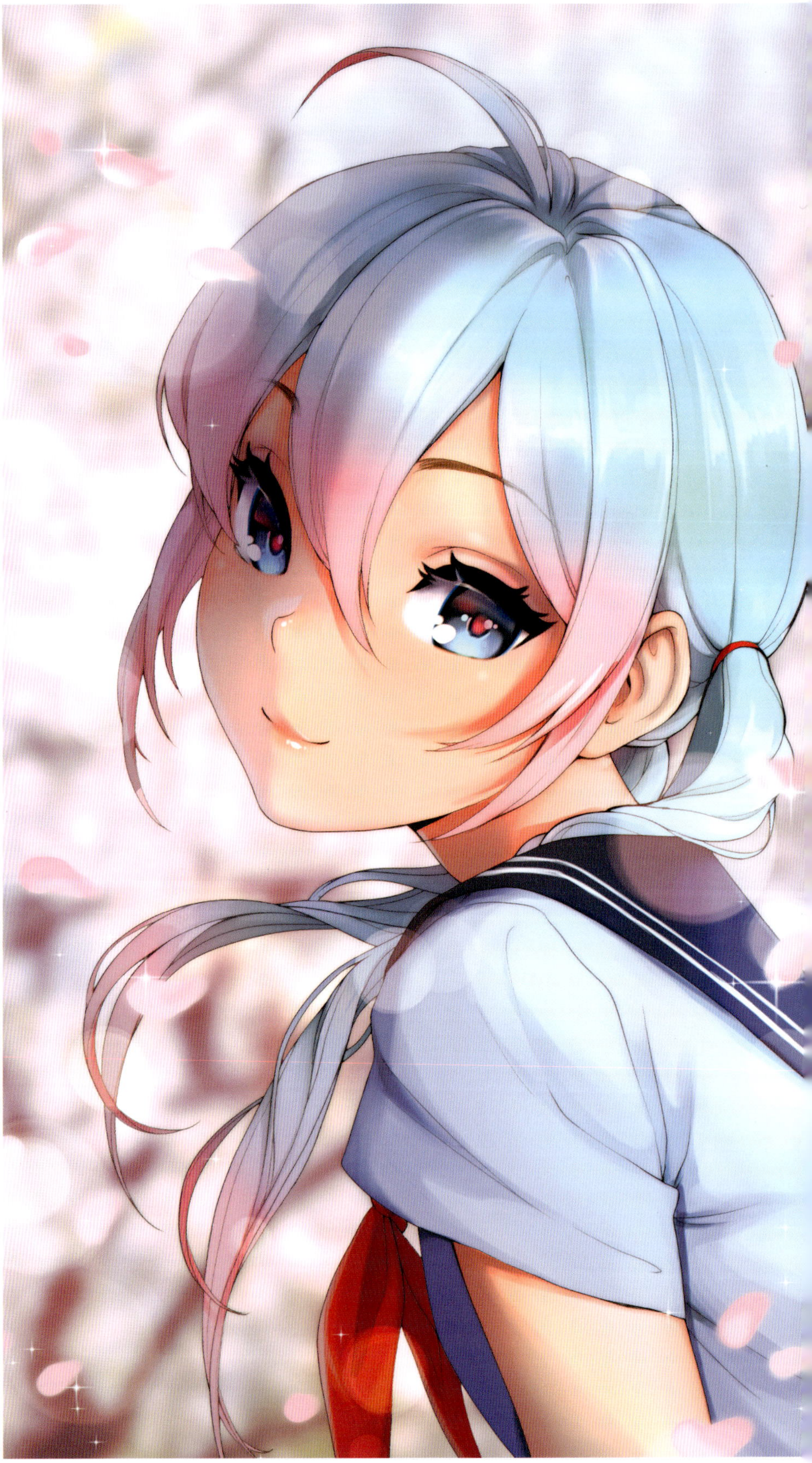

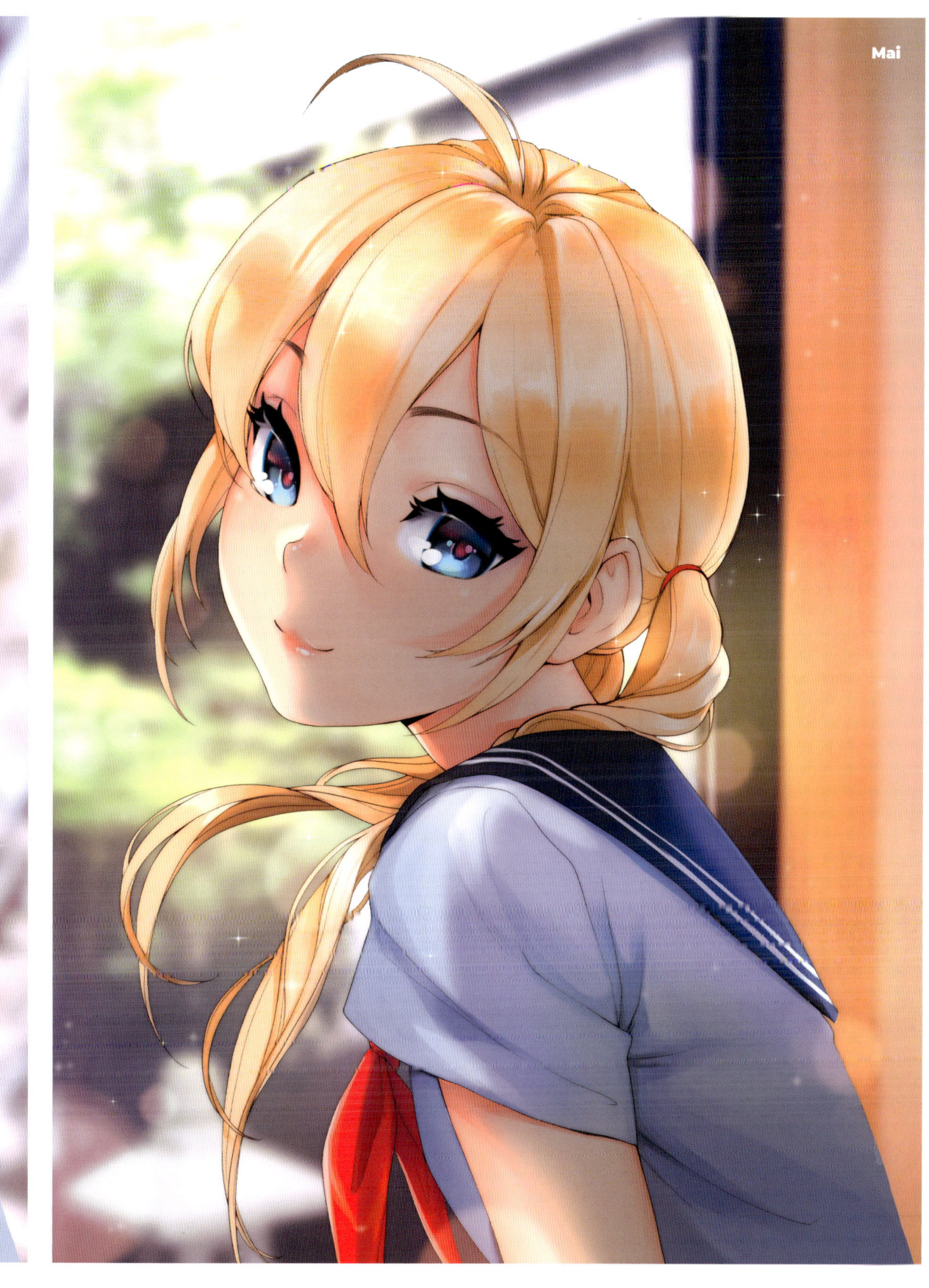

Mai

PERNILLE ØRUM

Color is the most expressive and interesting part of illustration for me. I get most of my inspiration from color. I always "collect" colors when I'm out and about, and get inspired by combining them and finding new ways of working with them. Having the light contrast or complement my selected color is a way to make an image come alive and to add more interest. Knowing and understanding how light and color interact is a lifelong journey to master, which is also why it stays so interesting to work with and study. If you, like me, find it inspiring, don't hesitate to jump in and start playing around and pushing the boundaries.

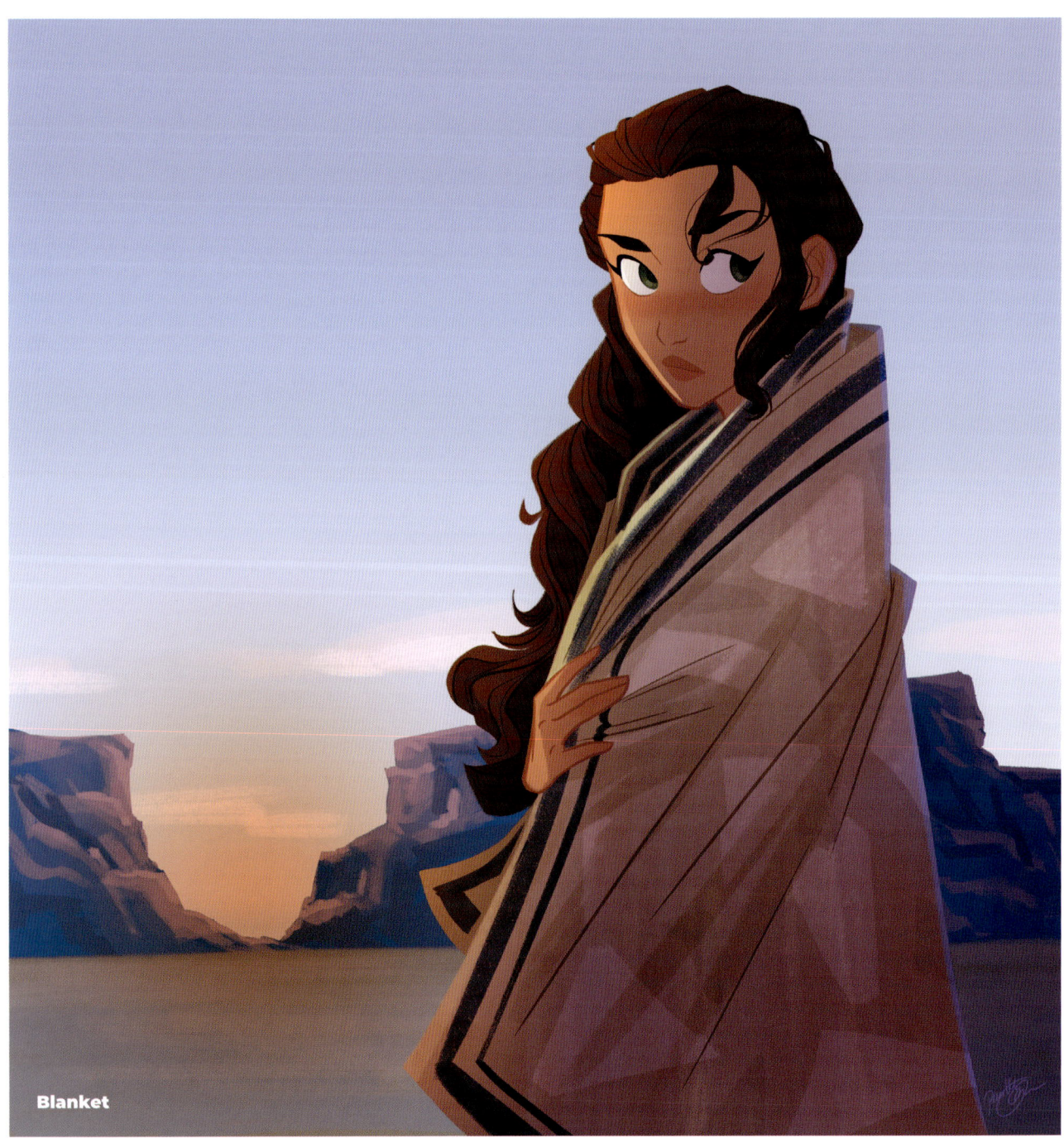

Blanket

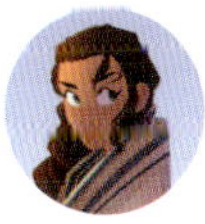

Blanket

I seldom do backgrounds with my characters, but in this one I wanted to capture the beautiful light of the desert. Most of my color inspirations come from traveling – I love how I am reminded of a trip just by the colors. The orange of the setting sun creates a beautiful dynamic with the purplish light.

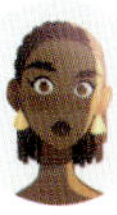

Beauty

In this image, I tried to capture the beautiful morning light in Kenya, where I live, but only on a character. The purplish tones of her skin are a great contrast to the warm tones of the sunlight. I added a hard-edged light with a whiteish gradient to achieve a dewy glow

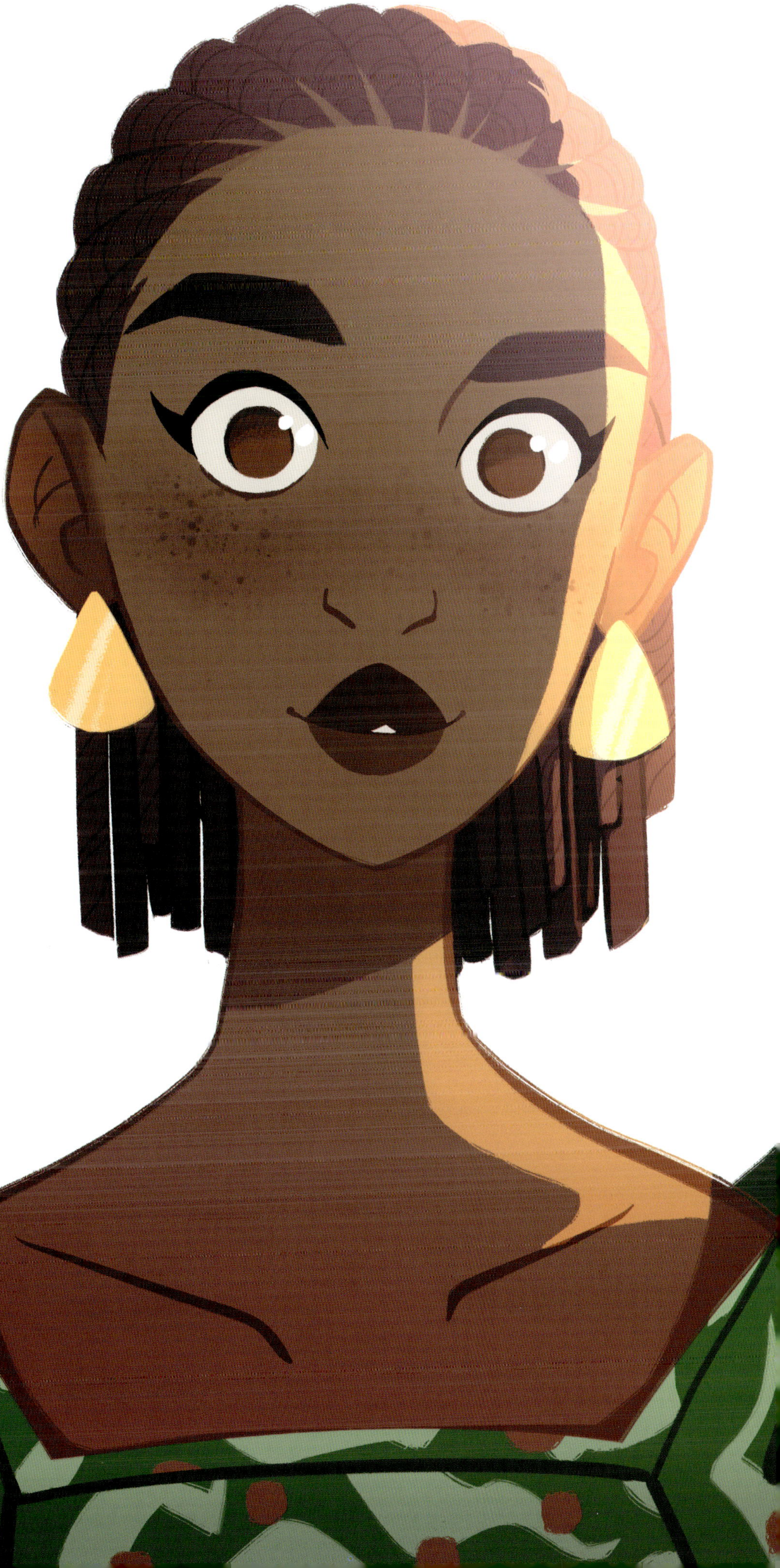

Ostera

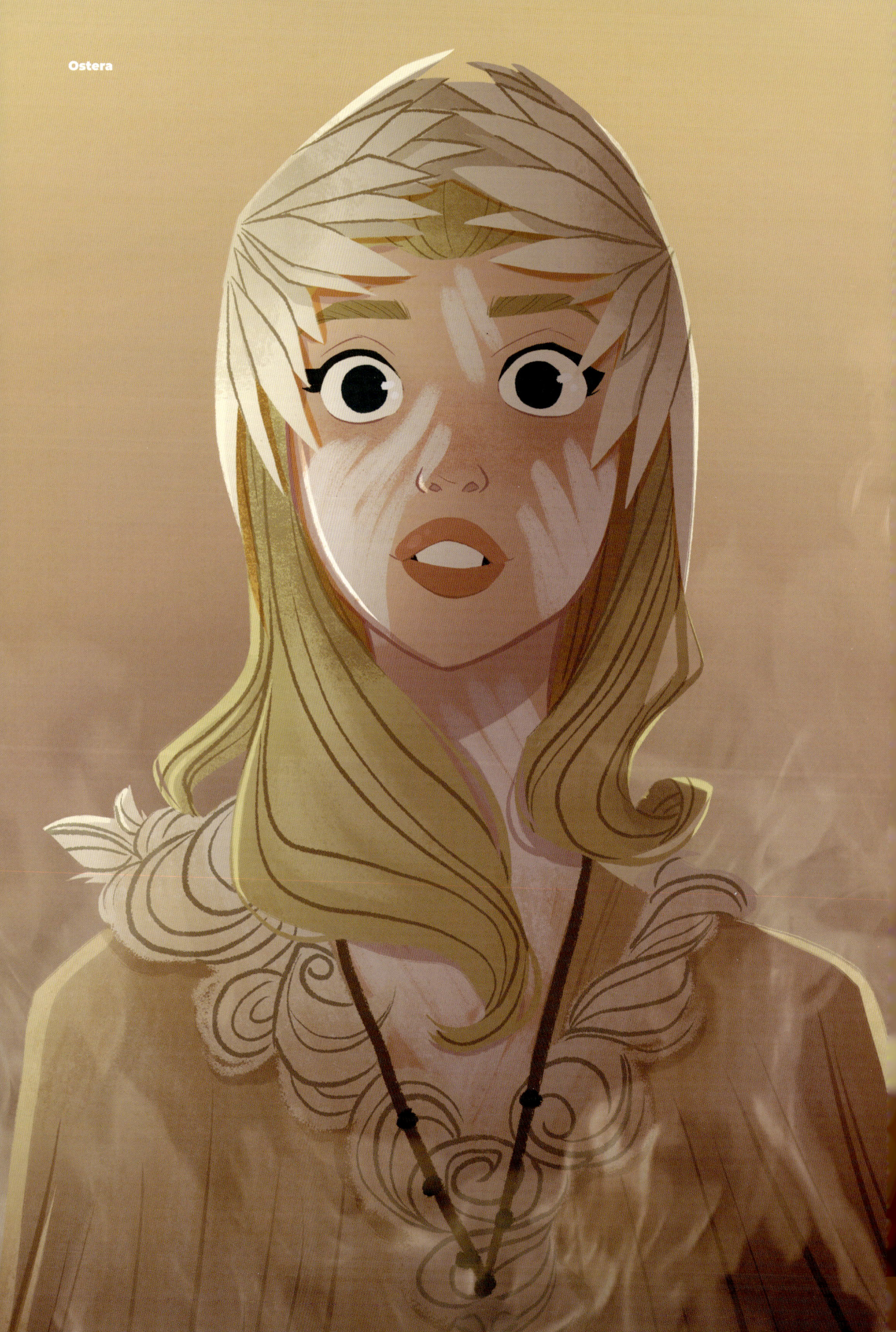

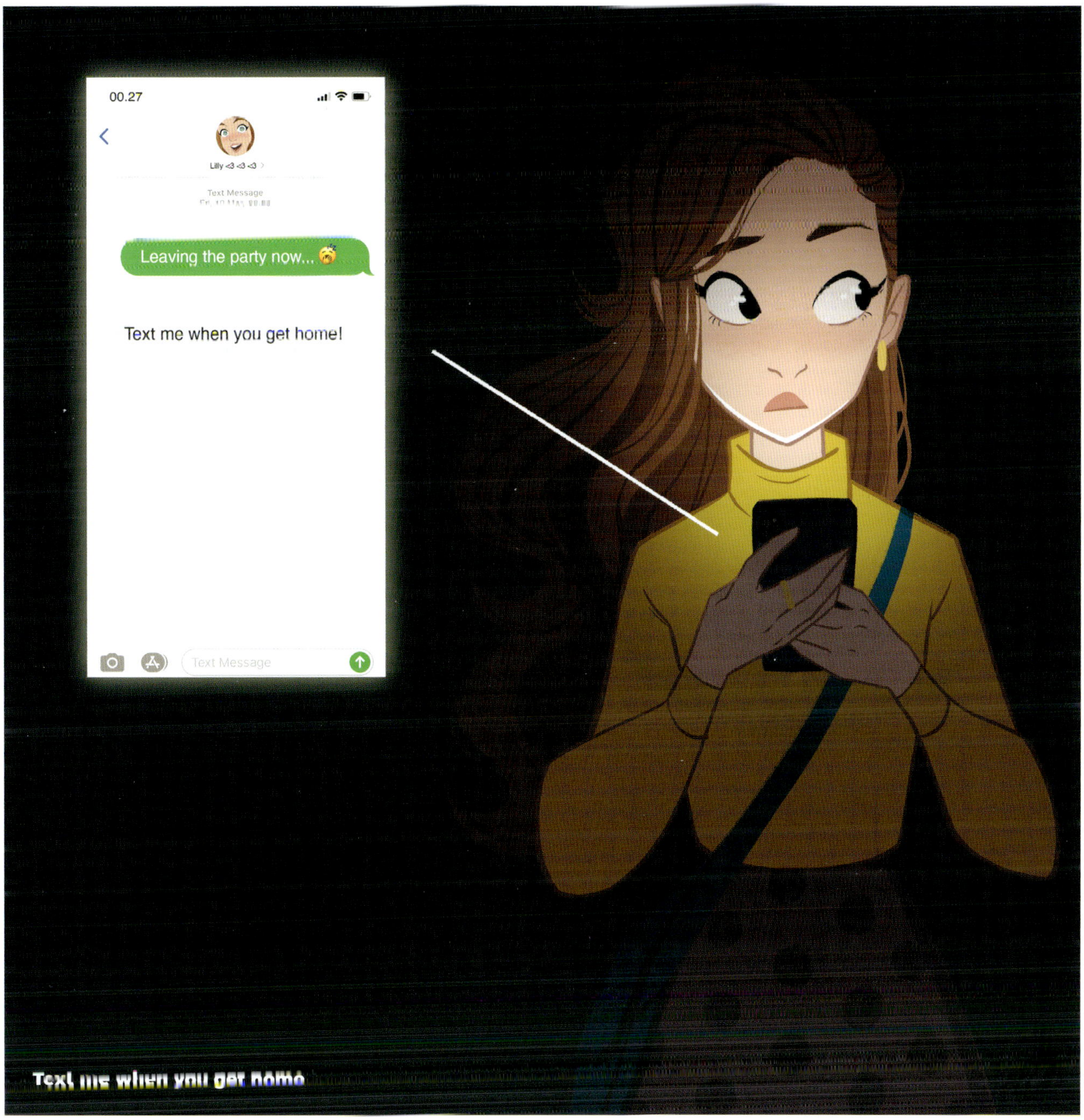

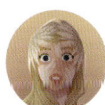

Ostera

I wanted this image to feel mysterious and dark while still remaining warm and naturally lit. The main colors are yellowish and brown, so I used shaded purple (adding black) in Multiply mode to create a shadowy feel all over the character. By removing the purple on the edges of the character, I could easily create yellow highlights.

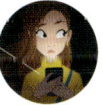

Text me when you get home

Light is the whole impetus behind this image. Everything is in darkness with only a small light source illuminating the character and making her visible to the viewer. The result achieves the lonesome, closed-in feeling of walking home alone at night and not feeling safe.

CONTRIBUTORS

 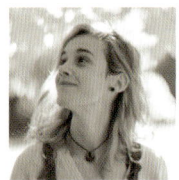

BEATRICE BLUE

beatriceblue.net

Beatrice Blue is an author and art director currently working in publishing and animation. She loves to travel and learn about different cultures and landscapes, always carrying a camera and sketchbook with her. She also loves music and playing guitar, drums, and synths. Profile photo © Florian Aupetit.

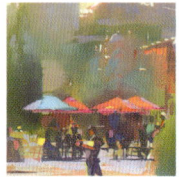 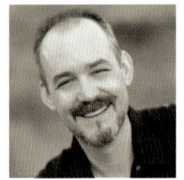

NATHAN FOWKES

nathanfowkes.com

Nathan Fowkes is a Los Angeles–based artist and teacher with a specialty in color scripting for feature animated films. His clients include DreamWorks and Disney, with film credits including *The Prince of Egypt*, *Spirit: Stallion of the Cimarron*, *Shrek*, *How to Train Your Dragon*, and *Raya and the Last Dragon*.

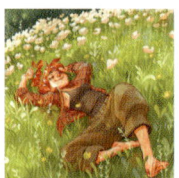 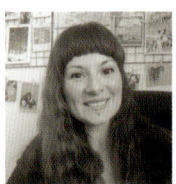

SIMONE GRÜNEWALD

instagram.com/schmoedraws

Simone Grünewald, also known as Schmoedraws, is a visual development artist from Germany. She has worked in the game industry for over ten years and is now happily freelancing and creating tutorials on her Patreon.

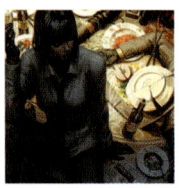 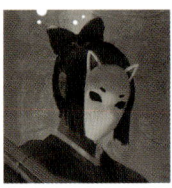

GUWEIZ

artstation.com/guweiz

Gu Zheng Wei, also known as Guweiz, is a digital illustrator based in Singapore, freelancing while sharing tutorials and process videos on Patreon.

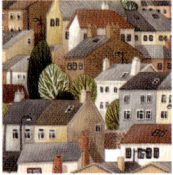 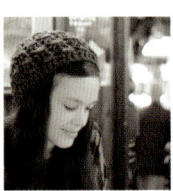

IRAVILLE

iraville.de

Ira Sluyterman van Langeweyde, also known as Iraville, is a Munich–based illustrator and character designer with a passion for watercolors, fall, nature, birds, and cozy things.

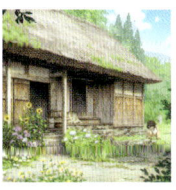 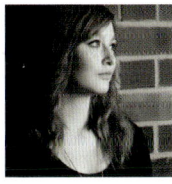

DJAMILA KNOPF

djamilaknopf.com

Djamila Knopf is an independent artist and Schoolism Instructor based in Leipzig, Germany, creating illustrations that evoke wonder and nostalgia. In her work, you can catch glimpses of summers spent strolling through the woods and fields near her grandparents' garden, and her love for Japanese animation.

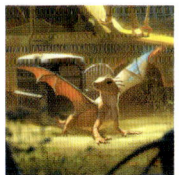 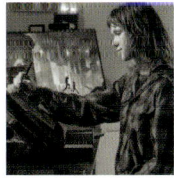

DEVIN ELLE KURTZ

devinellekurtz.com

Devin Elle Kurtz is an illustrator and visual development artist from Santa Cruz, California. She moved to Los Angeles in her teens to work in the animation industry, and most recently worked on Netflix's *Disenchantment*. In her free time, she loves to paint colorful, magical images.

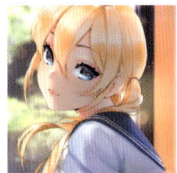 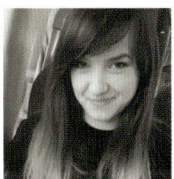

ASIA LADOWSKA

ladowska.com

Asia Ladowska was born in Poland. She creates both traditional and digital illustrations that mostly depict female characters inspired by Japanese manga and anime.

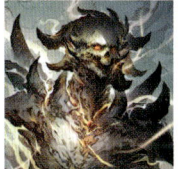 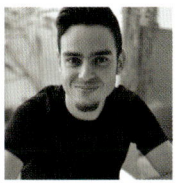

DIBUJANTE NOCTURNO

www.dibujantenocturno.com

Fran Garcés, also known as Dibujante Nocturno, is an illustrator and creator of fantastic creatures. A lover of ink drawing, he works creating illustrations for games like *Magic: The Gathering*, and recently published his own art book.

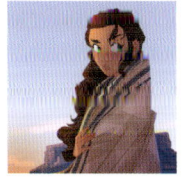 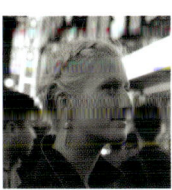

PERNILLE ØRUM

pernilleoe.com

Pernille Ørum is a Danish illustrator and character designer living as a freelancer in Nairobi, Kenya. She graduated from The Animation Workshop in 2011 with a bachelor's degree in character animation.

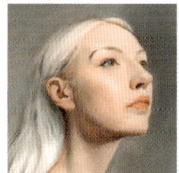 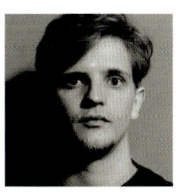

CHARLIE PICKARD

charliepickardart.com

Charlie Pickard is a figurative oil painter living and working in London. His work is primarily exhibited in London but can be found in collections worldwide.

INDEX

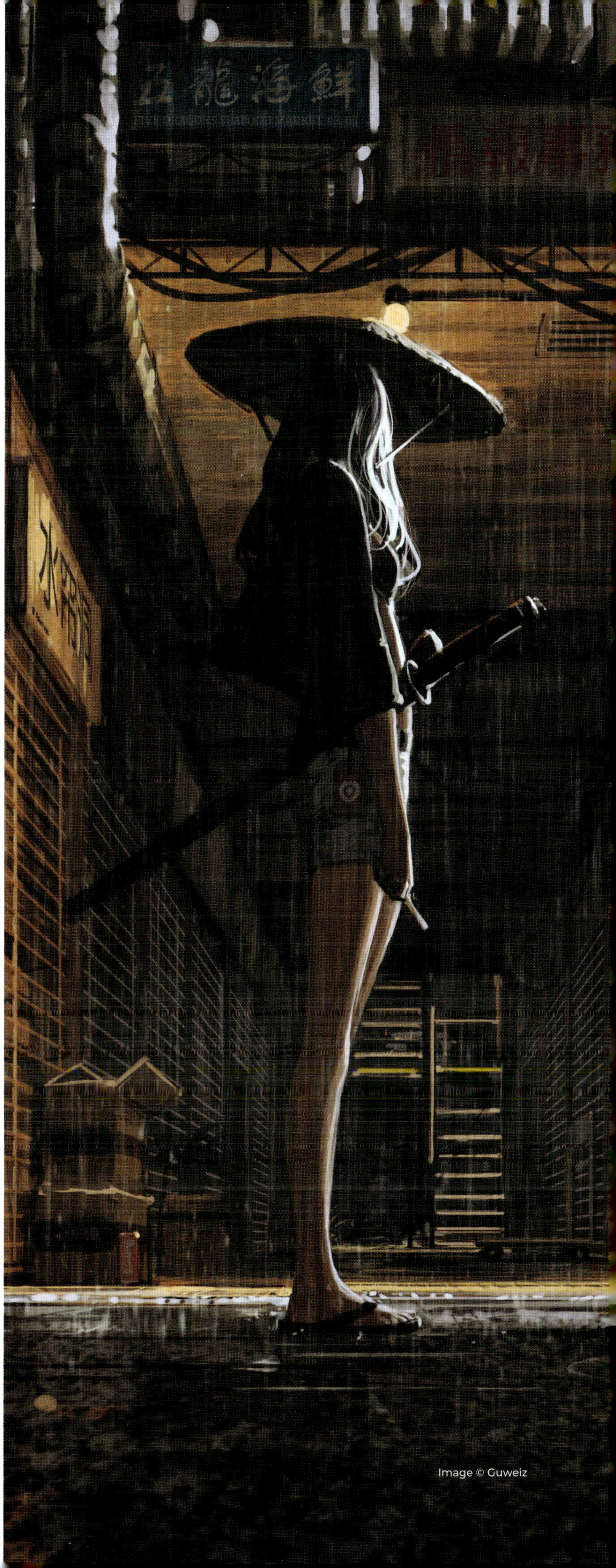

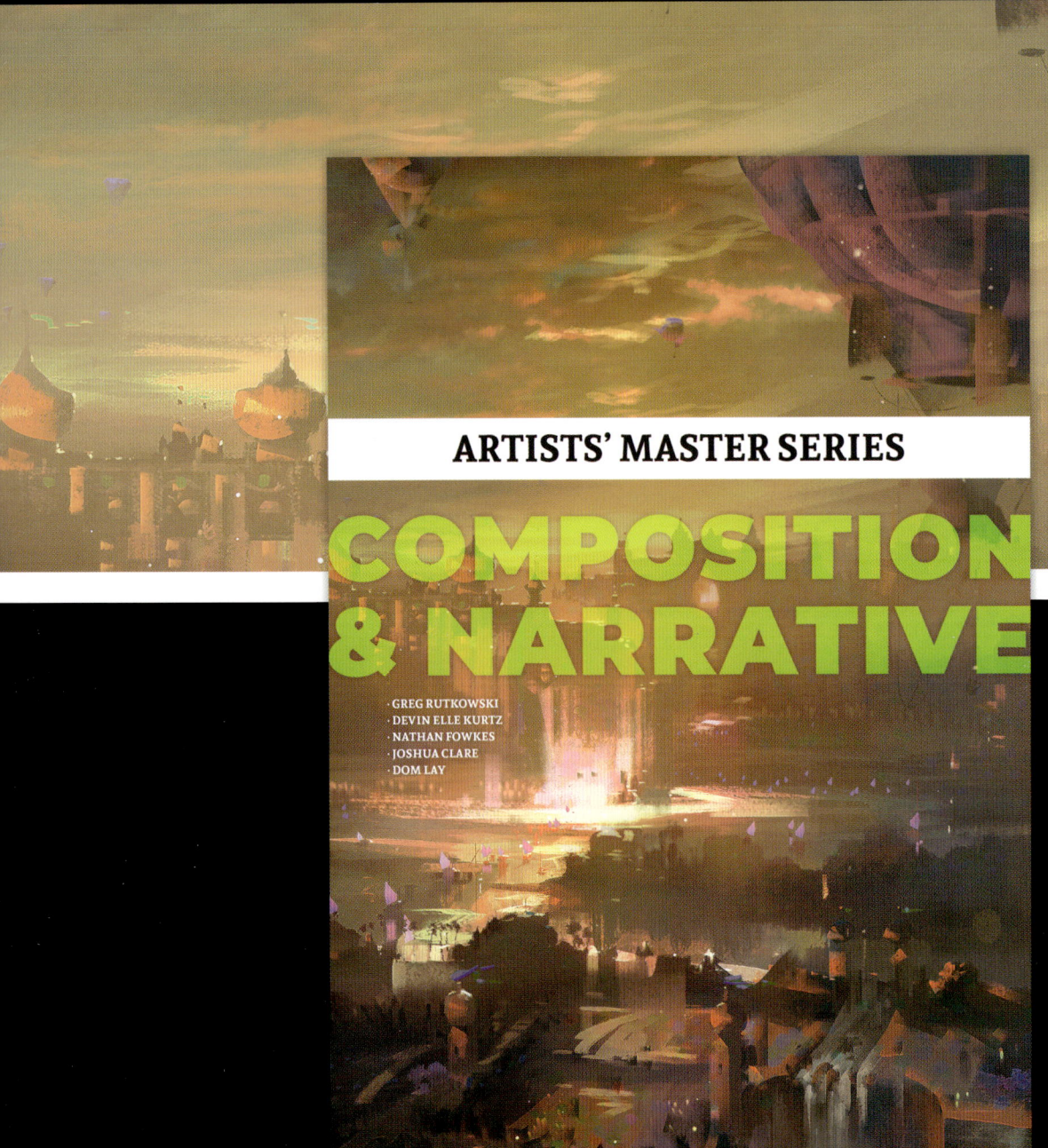

ARTISTS' MASTER SERIES

COMPOSITION & NARRATIVE

- GREG RUTKOWSKI
- DEVIN ELLE KURTZ
- NATHAN FOWKES
- JOSHUA CLARE
- DOM LAY

Drawing from a wealth of experience, experts including Greg Rutkowski, Devin Elle Kurtz, Nathan Fowkes, Joshua Clare, and Dom Lay fully dissect the theory and practice of using composition and narrative to advance your art.

Master artist Greg Rutkowski explores composition in great detail with stunning visual examples, showing the methods used throughout history to achieve good composition, from mathematical rules to intuitive ones. Next, dive into the art fundamental that ties everything together: narrative. Learn how storytelling has always been a principal focus for artists around the world, and explore diverse approaches such as humor, ambiguity, foreshadowing, symbolism, and exaggeration. This unique in-depth study of composition and narrative offers a single, comprehensive reference at your fingertips.

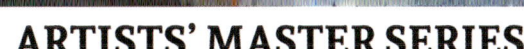

ARTISTS' MASTER SERIES

PERSPECTIVE & DEPTH

- MIKE HERNANDEZ
- DEVIN ELLE KURTZ
- NATHAN FOWKES
- GUWEIZ
- ORENJIKUN

This third title in the highly popular *Artists' Master Series* offers a comprehensive guide to using perspective and depth in your art, with direction from world-class artists such as Mike Hernandez, Devin Elle Kurtz, Nathan Fowkes, Orenji, and Guweiz.

As an established authority on art and design with a growing stable of high-calibre artist-authors, 3dtotal Publishing is uniquely placed to produce *Artists' Master Series*. Launched in 2021 with *Artists' Master Series: Color & Light*, and followed up by *Artists' Master Series: Composition & Narrative*, the series reaches its third volume with an engaging analysis of the theories of perspective and depth in art. No matter your medium, this combination can be the driving force that elevates your art from 'good' to 'world-class'.

3dtotal Publishing

3dtotal Publishing is a trailblazing, creative publisher specializing in inspirational and educational resources for artists.

Our titles feature top industry professionals from around the globe who share their experience in skillfully written step-by-step tutorials and fascinating, detailed guides. Illustrated throughout with stunning artwork, these best-selling publications offer creative insight, expert advice, and essential motivation. Fans of digital art will enjoy our comprehensive volumes covering Adobe Photoshop, Procreate, and Blender, as well as our superb titles based around character design, including *Fundamentals of Character Design* and *Creating Characters for the Entertainment Industry*. The dedicated, high-quality blend of instruction and inspiration also extends to traditional art. Titles covering a range of techniques, genres, and abilities allow your creativity to flourish while building essential skills.

Well-established within the industry, we now offer over 100 titles and counting, many of which have been translated into multiple languages around the world. With something for every artist, we are proud to say that our books offer the 3dtotal package:

LEARN · CREATE · SHARE

Visit us at store.3dtotal.com

3dtotal Publishing is part of 3dtotal.com, a leading website for CG artists founded by Tom Greenway in 1999.

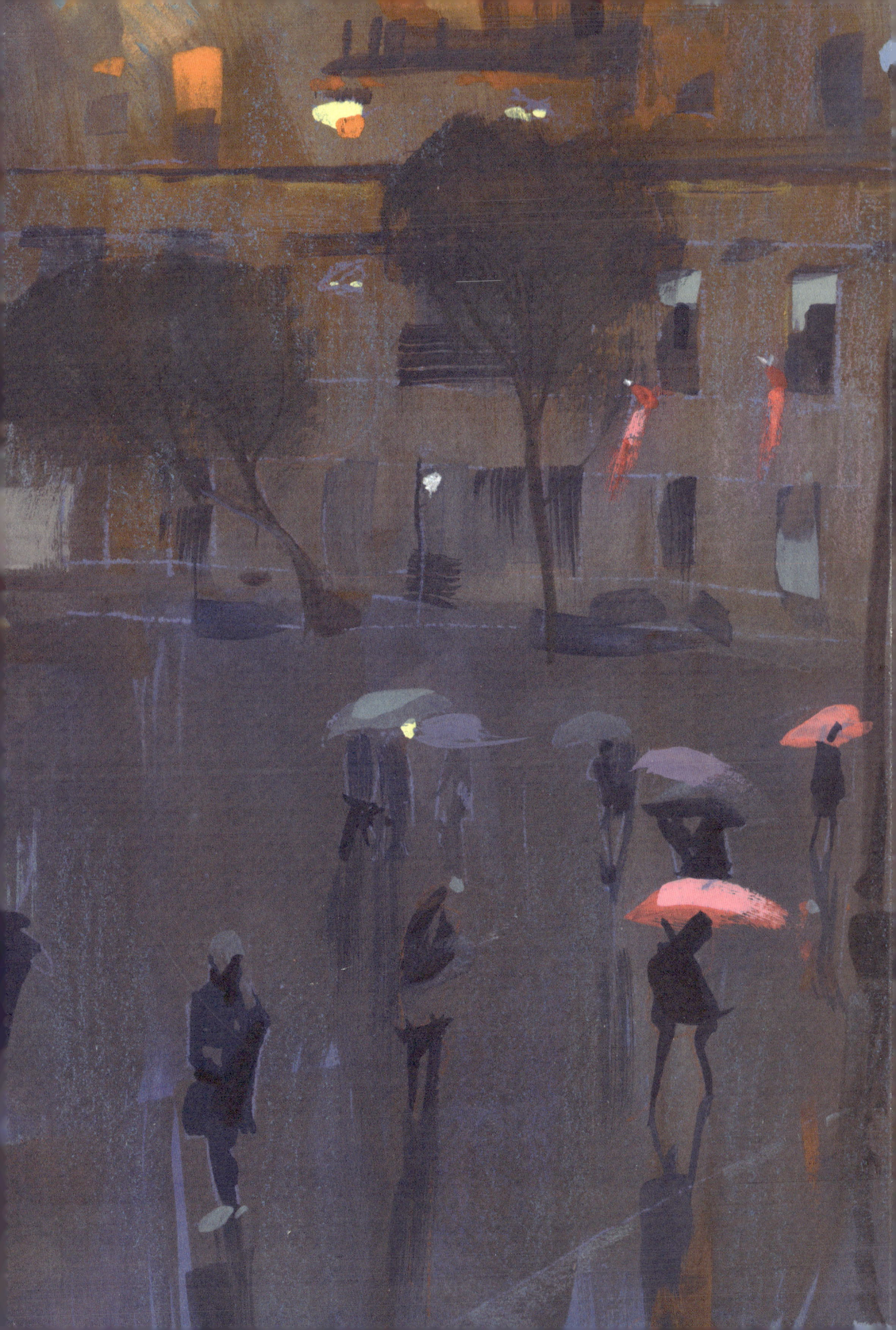